Free World

TIMOTHY GARTON ASH

Free World

Why a crisis of the West reveals the
opportunity of our time

ALLEN LANE
an imprint of
PENGUIN BOOKS

ALLEN LANE

Published by the Penguin Group

Penguin Books Ltd, 80 Strand, London WC2R ORL, England

Penguin Group (USA) Inc., 375 Hudson Street, New York, New York 10014, USA

Penguin Books Australia Ltd, 250 Camberwell Road, Camberwell, Victoria 3124, Australia

Penguin Books Canada Ltd, 10 Alcorn Avenue, Toronto, Ontario, Canada M4V 3B2

Penguin Books India (P) Ltd, 11 Community Centre, Panchsheel Park, New Delhi – 110 017, India

Penguin Group (NZ), cnr Airborne and Rosedale Roads, Albany, Auckland 1310, New Zealand

Penguin Books (South Africa) (Pty) Ltd, 24 Sturdee Avenue, Rosebank 2196, South Africa

Penguin Books Ltd, Registered Offices: 80 Strand, London WC2R ORL, England

www.penguin.com

First published 2004

2

Set in Sabon by Palimpsest Book Production Limited, Polmont, Stirlingshire
Printed in England by Clays Ltd, St Ives plc

A CIP catalogue record for this book is available from the British Library

ISBN 0–713–99764–8

For
Thomas and Alexander

For Freedom's battle once begun,
Bequeathed by bleeding Sire to Son,
Though baffled oft is ever won.

These lines from Byron's 'The Giaour' were written on a scrap of paper by an unknown hand, using a translation by Adam Mickiewicz, the Polish Byron, and pinned up outside the gates of the Lenin Shipyard in Gdańsk in August 1980, to support the nationwide strike that gave birth to the free trade union Solidarity. The unknown copyist omitted the word 'bleeding'. This ruined the metre but improved the sense.

Contents

To the Reader

If we are free, we can work with other free people towards a free world. Nothing can stop us, except the walls of ignorance, selfishness and prejudice that divide free men and women from each other, and the free from the unfree. These walls are not outside and beyond us, like the Alps or the Rocky Mountains. Minds build them; minds can knock them down.

The mind-walls have grown higher and more forbidding since 11 September 2001, the '9/11' of fear that was the true beginning of the twenty-first century. But we can take heart from another 9/11, written European-style, with the day before the month. On the evening of 9 November 1989, citizens began to hack away at the roughcast concrete of the Berlin Wall with whatever they could lay their hands on – and the wall came down. That marked the effective end of the short twentieth century. It was our 9/11 of hope.

In Part One of this book, I examine the crisis that has engulfed Europeans and Americans at the start of a new century. I try to establish what has really happened and why. I weigh many sorts of evidence, to confront myths with facts. It turns out that much of today's disarray can be traced back to the impact of those two very different 9/11s, the fall of the wall in Berlin and the fall of the twin towers in New York. Now it seems we will have to add a third date, 11 March 2004, when the terrorist bombing of Madrid, exactly two and a half years after the 11 September attacks on the United States, gave Europe its own epiphany of fear.

Anyone who writes 'history of the present' knows that it will have to be revised in the light of such events. Because things keep changing, the experience of reading this kind of book can be less satisfying than, say, settling down with some annals of ancient Rome, but it can also be more exciting – because things may still be changed. As you read, you will know more about parts of this story than I do today, either because you have special knowledge of one of the many areas of world politics that I discuss or simply because you will know what has happened since. And, vitally, your own political voice will itself be a part of the unfolding story. You will affect the outcome, and therefore the way future historians write about our time. When you peruse those annals of ancient Rome, you are reading history; here, you're also writing it.

So please treat this as a joint work in progress. If we can agree to attack the mind-walls, then, like the Berliners during that unforgettable night of 9 November 1989, we shall have the encouragement of hearing others zestfully hammering away to left and right of us. As the walls come down, we shall discover a surprising prospect. For this crisis actually reveals a great opportunity. Today, more people in the world are more free than ever before. Despite all the frightening problems of our time, we have unprecedented chances to achieve a further enlargement of human freedom. In Part Two, I go beyond a history of the present to suggest some ways in which we can seize those chances over the next twenty years, leaving behind us the rubble of demolished walls. Even if you can't agree with all these suggestions, I hope we can share this starting-point: it's up to us.

TGA
Oxford
25 March 2004

PART ONE

Crisis

A Crisis of the West

When you say 'we', who do you mean?

Many of us would start the answer with our family and our friends. Widening the circle, we might think of our town or region, supporters of the same football team, our nation or state, a sexual orientation, a political affiliation ('we on the Left', 'we Conservatives'), or those who profess the same religion – world-straddling fraternities these, with more than 1,000 million Muslims and nearly 2,000 million Christians, though fraternities scarred by deep internal divisions. Beyond this, most of us have a strong sense of 'we' meaning all our fellow human beings. Some would add other living creatures.

Yet these largest senses of 'we' are seldom what people really have in mind when they say 'we must do this' or 'we cannot allow that'. The moral 'we' of all humankind is today more important than ever, but it's not the same as our operational 'we'. So let us pose the question more precisely: 'What's the widest political community of which you spontaneously say "we" or "us"?' In our answer to that question lies the key to our future.

For me, an Englishman born into the Cold War, that widest political community used to be something called 'the West'. My friends and I didn't spend much time worrying about its boundaries. If you had asked us, we could not have said exactly where it ended. Was Turkey part of the West? Japan? Mexico? But we had no doubt that it existed, as Europe existed, or communism. At its core, we felt, were the free countries on both sides of the Atlantic ocean, in Western Europe and North America. This Cold War West faced a hostile power that we called 'the East'. The East meant, in the first place, the

Soviet Union, its Red Army, its nuclear missiles and its satellite states in what was then labelled Eastern Europe.

Occasionally, Western politicians or propagandists tried to persuade us that non-communist countries everywhere should be described as 'the free world' – even if their governments were torturing critics at home, gagging the press and rigging elections. My friends and I never accepted that claim. We did not think Chile under General Pinochet was a free country. Altogether, this tag 'the free world', with its strident definite article, implying that all inside are free, all outside unfree, has seldom been used in public without pathos or in private without irony. 'We're the most hated cops in the whole of the free world,' boasts a Los Angeles Police Department officer in the Jackie Chan film *Rush Hour*.

But the West – yes, that was real. Anyone who travelled regularly behind the Iron Curtain, to countries like Poland, was confirmed in this belief. My friends there talked all the time about the West. They believed more passionately than most West Europeans did in its fundamental unity and its shared values; they feared it might be weak and decadent. 'We', they said, 'are the West trapped in the East.' At the time, I felt these Polish, Czech and Hungarian friends were, so to speak, individual members of the West far more than I felt Turkey or Japan were collectively part of it. Others, with different personal experiences, saw things differently. Where you stand depends on where you sit. Everyone had his or her own West, just as everyone today has his or her own America,* France or Islam. There are as many Italys as there are Italians. None the less, Italy exists.

This political community of the West was, like all political communities, both real and imagined. At its military front line, it was as real as real can be. On a cold winter morning, Dutch, Belgian, British, German, Canadian and American soldiers stood shivering all the way down the frontier between West and East Germany, ready to die together – 'all for one and one for all' – in the event of an armed attack from the East. The community was imagined in the sense that behind these men and women prepared to die together in battle there

---

* I hope other inhabitants of the Americas will forgive me for using 'America' throughout this book as shorthand for the United States of America. It's what we usually say in Europe, and it is shorter.

stood another army of assumptions made by the people who put the soldiers there, but perhaps also by the soldiers themselves; assumptions about what united 'us' and what made 'us' different from the people on the other side of the barbed wire. A mental army of the West.

Many believed, for example, in what they called 'Western values'. The West stood for freedom, human rights, democracy, the rule of law. These good things, they thought, had grown mainly in the West and distinguished us from others. The (hi)stories we tell ourselves are also the history of our own times – and a sometimes unintentional account of our intentions. During the Cold War, generations of American school and university students were taught an inspiring story of Western Civilization, marching onwards and generally upwards from ancient Greece and Rome, through the spread of Christianity in Europe, the Renaissance, the Reformation, the Enlightenment, the English, American and French Revolutions, the development of capitalism, the bourgeoisie and universal suffrage, two World Wars and the Cold War, to the sunlit uplands of an American-led 'Atlantic Community'. In the grand narrative of 'Western Civ', the West began in Europe and ended in the hands of America. It went from Plato to Nato.

On a dusty bottom shelf in the library of Stanford University in California I once found an example of this story told at its most confident and simplistic. *Life's Picture History of Western Man*, published in 1951, began by asking 'Western Man – who is he and where did he come from?'[1] The identity of this 'most wonderfully dynamic creature ever to walk the earth' apparently became clear in Europe 'about 800 AD (earlier in some places, later in others) and he was ready to set out on his bright-starred mission of creating a new civilization for the world'. In those good old days, Western Man – always capitalized – was 'fair of skin, hardy of limb, brave of heart, and he believed in the eternal salvation of his soul'. Darker-skinned persons, not to mention women, hardly got a look in. Western Man 'worked towards freedom, first for his own person, then for his own mind and spirit, and finally for others in equal measure'. *Life's* handsomely illustrated picture history followed Western Man's progress 'from his first emergence in the Middle Ages to his contemporary position of world leadership in the United States of America'. 'A new vehicle called the Atlantic Community', it concluded, 'now carries Western Man on his way.'

At once fed by and feeding these assumptions about a shared future written in the past, there developed in the second half of the twentieth century an immense, intricate, close-knit web of special relationships between government and government, military and military, company and company, university and university, intelligence service and intelligence service, city and city, bank and bank, newspaper and newspaper, and above all, between millions of individual men and women, aided by the rapid growth in the speed and volume of air travel and telecommunications. On this teeming worldwide web, each kind of thread had a hundred bi- and multilateral variants, French-American, French-German, British-American, American-Polish, Portuguese-Spanish, Slovenian-Italian, New Zealand-Europe, Australia-America, the European Community, the North Atlantic Treaty Organization and so on and on. Ever more people met, telephoned, wrote or faxed each other ever more often for ever more purposes. And that was before e-mail. Start drawing these links in different colours on a map and the map would soon disappear entirely beneath the inky tangle. There was a proliferation of such ties all around the world – people had begun to speak of 'globalization' – but no strands were thicker than those between Western Europe and North America.

If I close my eyes and try to conjure a visual image of this West, I come up with something so mind-numbingly conventional that I immediately open them again. What I see are those endlessly familiar newspaper photographs of our leaders meeting each other, which they now do constantly, unlike leaders in most of recorded history, who met only on very rare occasions, if at all. Turning the pages of this mental album, I come first to the group portrait of a dozen or more heads of government on the steps of some palace or grand hotel, almost all of them middle-aged white men in dark suits. (Western Man in his Native Dress.) Next come those demonstratively bonhomous, back-patting, elbow-clutching bonding displays between French president and German chancellor. Here's a grainy old snapshot of four men in tropical wear sitting under a beach umbrella in Guadeloupe, talking nuclear missiles; then a newer, digital image of an open-shirt and jeans encounter at some country retreat, with the American president and British prime minister serving as unpaid fashion models for Levi's, GAP or Banana Republic. And finally there's the perennial buggy scene – in which, somewhere in America, two middle-aged men, grinning boyishly, snuggle close together in the front seat of a golf buggy. The closeness is the message.

'Friendship' is the name diplomatically given to these relations between statesmen or stateswomen and, by two-way symbolic extension, to relations between the states they represent. If the states are friends, their leaders had better be; if the leaders become friends, that helps relations between their states. These instant, speed-glued political 'friendships' are interesting to observe. You wonder how genuine they can possibly be. When Winston Churchill and Franklin Roosevelt met aboard a battleship off the coast of Newfoundland in August 1941, singing 'Onward Christian Soldiers' with their massed British and American crews, they made one of the great symbolic bondings of the twentieth-century West. In what sense were Churchill and Roosevelt ever really friends?

Yet in the modern world we're not condemned to stand around like peasants at the Field of the Cloth of Gold, wondering how the Great Ones are getting on inside the marquee. We're not swineherds nervously contemplating the quarrels of the gods on Mount Olympus. We make our own history. Whatever the truth about the 'friendship' between, say, Margaret Thatcher and Ronald Reagan, or Helmut Kohl and François Mitterrand, I know that, for me, Pierre in Paris, Helena in Warsaw, John in Washington and Michael in Bonn were, and remain, friends. These friendships were born in the particular circumstances of a time and place. What friendship is not? We stood for the same things and against the same things: not all the same things, all the time, but quite enough to make common cause. We wanted to preserve freedom in the West and win it for people in the East. We had that essential fellow feeling. We felt that we were 'we'. And so we were.

To be sure, I also had quite a few good acquaintances who thought of the West as 'them'. The bloody Americans, the fucking Tories, the *Scheissliberalen* – imperialist, oppressive, exploitative, corrupt, responsible for toppling Salvador Allende in Chile and napalming children in Vietnam. Yet these critics were often measuring the Cold War West against its own proclaimed moral standards. Even as they savaged the hollow, hypocritical rhetoric of 'the free world', they were confirming the West's existence. Unless you are Don Quixote, you don't attack a chimera. So the Cold War West was a reality. If enough people think a political community is real, it's real.

With the disappearance of the communist East at the end of the Cold War, this West slowly descended into crisis. There were omens of discord throughout the 1990s, like a gathering storm, as well as endless speculation about what the new world order, or disorder, might be. At the beginning of the twenty-first century, the storm broke. When a group of Islamist terrorists flew two aeroplanes into the twin towers of the World Trade Center in New York on 11 September 2001, it seemed that the most influential prediction for the shape of the post-Cold War world was coming true. Here, surely, was Samuel Huntington's 'clash of civilizations'. For those planes seemed to be aimed at the heart of the West, one of Huntington's 'civilizations', in the name of another, Islam.

At first, the rest of the West rallied to America's side, under a heroic motto proclaimed by the editor of *Le Monde*, 'We Are All Americans'.[2] But within a year this crisis *for* the West had become a crisis *of* the West. Faced with the problem of how to fight an abstract noun – 'Terror' – the nations of the West did not pull together as they had in the late 1940s against Stalin's Red Army; they fell apart in bitter disagreement. The administration of President George W. Bush decided that the 'war on terror' required a war against Iraq; most Europeans disagreed. By the spring of 2003 we had the unprecedented spectacle of France actively canvassing for votes against the United States in the Security Council of the United Nations, on a question of war or peace that the United States considered vital to its own national security.

The American neoconservative Richard Perle concluded that France was 'no longer the ally it once was' and therefore Nato 'must develop a strategy to contain our erstwhile ally'.[3] Many Europeans thought the United States was threatening world peace. 'Is this a free world or Bush's world?' demanded a banner at a million-strong demonstration against the Iraq War in London on 15 February 2003. This was just one of several massive demonstrations in European capitals that day. They seemed, for a moment, to unite the continent in a single European 'no' to America's proposed war.

So the West was divided between Europe and America. Or was it? Certainly, most Europeans opposed the war and most Americans supported it. Political writers on both sides of the Atlantic saw in this an expression of deep underlying differences. One liberal American writer averred that the coming 'clash of civilizations' could be not the West versus the Rest, but Europe* versus America.[4] 'Americans are from Mars and Europeans are from Venus' wrote the conservative American Robert Kagan in an influential one-liner, suggesting that Americans are at once Martian, martial and the real men.[5] The original book title to which his quip alluded was *Men are from Mars, Women are from Venus*. Many on the European left hastened to agree: yes, Europeans and Americans are from different planets; yes, Europe, scarred by so many wars – lovely Europa, remembering her bad experience with bulls – proudly represents the female virtues of peace.

On closer examination, things were not so fabulously simple. The West did not split neatly into a European and an American half, like a well-cracked walnut. A large minority of Americans opposed the war and a large minority of Europeans supported it. At least eighteen European governments gave some endorsement to the American-led action. Crucially, the four countries at the heart of any history of the modern West – Britain, France, America and Germany – were divided two against two. To put it another way, the states with the first and seventh largest economies in the world (America and Britain) lined up against the fifth and sixth (Germany and France).[6]

I was reminded of George Orwell's competing blocs in *1984*, 'Oceania' and 'Eurasia'. This Oceania of 2003 aligned the two major European countries that face the Atlantic ocean, Britain and Spain,

---

* In this book, I have reluctantly followed our confusing practice of using a single word, 'Europe', to mean at least five different things: a historical concept, a continent with unclear frontiers, a number of European states acting through their national institutions, the European Union, and a vision of what that Union should be. Wherever possible, I have tried to make it clear which is meant.

with the great power across that ocean. As they went to war against Iraq, their leaders met literally in mid-Atlantic, on the Azores islands, with Portugal as proud host. Eurasia comprised France, Germany and Russia, in what the French newspaper *Libération* called 'The Anti-War Axis'.[7] Yet this nice dichotomy of Oceania and Eurasia also breaks down, since most of the states in the central zone of Europe between Germany and Russia supported the American-led war.

Like the earlier 'friendships', these enmities were represented to us, almost in pantomime, by the symbolic acts and body language of our rulers. Word came down from Olympus that for months President Bush had not even spoken on the telephone to Chancellor Schröder of Germany. Senior officials fluttered about, giving a passable imitation of courtiers in the time of Louis XIV, telling you *'das Verhältnis ist sehr schlecht'* (the relationship is very bad) and 'Schröder's screwed it completely'. When the heads of the opposed groupings had to meet, at a long-scheduled multilateral summit, newspaper photographs showed Presidents Bush and Chirac looking tensely in opposite directions – for all the world like Prince Charles and Princess Diana as their marriage broke up.

Behind the pantomime, there was real emotion. What European leaders said about each other in private was poisonous. At No. 10 Downing Street, they called Dominique de Villepin, the French foreign minister, 'Vile Pin'. The prime minister of another major European state (not Britain) privately described Chirac and Schröder as 'a dangerous couple'. Nor were these emotions confined to politicians. A student at Yale University confided in his professor, 'I wake up every morning feeling furious at the French.' I met a man in California who told me he had cancelled his order for two of the latest Mercedes cars in protest at German opposition to the war. (He was not, you will gather, a poor man.) I went to my doctor in Oxford and he said 'that Bush is such a cowboy, isn't he?' At every level, from the president to the postman, there was this confusion, or elision, between a particular government or leader and the whole nation or group. Was it Bush you were angry with or 'the Americans'? Chirac or 'the French'? Romano Prodi or 'the Europeans'?

This confusion, or elision, is typical of nationalism. In the Iraq crisis of 2002/3 we again saw nationalism in the familiar form of the people of one nation getting angry with those of another. Many English people, for example, egged on by some of their newspapers and politicians, got angry with the French – something they had been doing, on and off, for more than 600 years. But we also saw nationalism in the larger, transferred sense identified by George Orwell in his 'Notes on Nationalism'. Orwell says that other 'isms' – his own idiosyncratic list includes communism, pacifism, Catholicism and anti-Semitism – share a common mental structure with nationalism. It is, he says, 'the habit of assuming that human beings can be classified like insects and that whole blocks of millions or tens of millions of people can be confidently labelled "good" or "bad"'.[8]

The broader nationalisms that found expression in this crisis of the West can be called, in crude shorthand, anti-Americanism and anti-Europeanism. How can we know when we are in the presence of these broader nationalisms? How can we distinguish them from the positive patriotisms of both Americans and Europeans? Well, it's never easy, but here's a rough and ready test. If we hear a voice generalizing angrily about '*the* Americans' or '*the* Europeans', the disease is close. And if that voice turns out to be our own? Then we should stop, and examine our assumptions.

I am writing soon after these events, when tempers have barely cooled. We don't yet know if the war of words over the war on Iraq was just another of those family quarrels that have regularly punctuated the life of the West, or something far deeper. Is this the last or merely the latest crisis of the West?

After all, many historians insist that what characterizes 'Western Civ' is its divisions: between Rome and Byzantium, between church and state, between monarchs and feudal lords, between self-governing town and surrounding country, between Protestants and Catholics, between each and every nation-state (the nation-state being one of modern Europe's most enduring and double-edged contributions to the world), between executive, legislature and judiciary, between the old world and the new. It is precisely these divisions, this diversity, that has made the history of Europe and America different from that of China. Inasmuch as there is a historic unity of the West, this is the shared fruit of its own incessant internal partings. Disunity may be the West's deepest unity.

As for the closer political unity of the Cold War West: that was only forged in the late 1940s after fierce disagreements about how to confront the new threat from 'the East'. Transatlantic solidarity was then shaken again and again by rows that have long faded into the history books – disengagement, Suez, de Gaulle's military withdrawal from Nato, the neutron bomb, Solidarity in Poland, the deployment of Cruise and Pershing missiles – crisis upon crisis, their very names now remembered only by old men and historians. Sleeping-pills for schoolchildren. I have in front of me as I write a yellowing pile of weighty articles, dating back more than fifty years, each averring that the latest crisis is unprecedented, worse than any before, insoluble, et cetera. If you look inside even the closest political partnerships of the West, such as the British-American 'special relationship', you find, documented in the diaries and secret papers, nasty purple rashes of mutual mistrust, resentment and contempt. Yet the Cold War West survived.

A few important things are, none the less, different at the beginning of the twenty-first century. The states of the post-1945 West are no longer held together by a single common enemy, with a massive Red Army deployed in the heart of Europe. The threats we now face are more diffuse, hidden, ill-defined. There is far more room for disagreement about who or what they are, let alone how best to deal with them. Following the collapse of the Soviet Union, America has become the world's sole superpower. It is much less clear to Americans that they require the partnership of Europe to secure their own freedoms.

For its part, Western Europe no longer needs the United States to defend it against the Red Army. Instead, most of the countries that used to be occupied by the Red Army are now members of the European Union. Europeans are struggling to find an emotional glue to hold together this extraordinary project of voluntarily associating twenty-five very diverse European countries in a single political community. Such emotional glue has traditionally been found, or manufactured, by identifying an alien and threatening 'them' – an 'Other', in the dread jargon of identity studies, or, in plain English, just a good old enemy – against which 'we' can warmly bond. With the fading of Europe's other Others, of which more below, Europeans are tempted to find that Other in the United States. We are to define ourselves by what we are not: America! And the wretched of the earth are to be saved not by the hard grind of Americanization but by the soft charm of Europeanization.

Like an electric storm, this crisis of the West has harshly illuminated a jagged landscape – with a question mark on every peak. Is the world now divided between the West and the Rest? Is the West now divided between Europe and America? Can the West be put together again and, even if it can be, should it be? What is the right 'we' for our time?

I begin my exploration of this jagged landscape at home, in Britain, which of all the heartlands of the West is the one most painfully torn between Europe and America. From this divided country, our journey will proceed outwards, first to Europe, then to America, and finally to the world beyond the West.

I

Janus Britain

PUTNEY

If you take the Number 74 red double-decker bus from Baker Street you will eventually cross the River Thames at Putney. On the south bank of the river, immediately to your left as you come across Putney Bridge, you will spy a church, half-hidden behind trees. Most of your fellow passengers – their faces set in the tired, closed mask of the London commuter – will not spare it a glance. Yet in this Church of St Mary the Virgin, on 29 October 1647, one Thomas Rainsborough spoke words that have resounded through the modern history of the West.

At the height of the English Civil War, England's revolutionary army was debating who should have the vote in elections to the Westminster parliament. Radical 'Levellers' among the officers and regimental delegates were locked in fierce dispute with Oliver Cromwell. According to notes made at the time, Colonel Rainsborough said:

For really I think that the poorest he that is in England hath a life to live, as the greatest he; and therefore truly, sir, I think it's clear, that every man that is to live under a government ought first by his own consent to put himself under that government; and I do think that the poorest man in England is not at all bound in a strict sense to that government that he hath not had a voice to put himself under.[1]

The poorest she still did not get a look in, but this was nevertheless a revolutionary statement of the claim for government by consent and equal political rights for all citizens. Here in Putney, in 1647, a plain-spoken English gentleman described and demanded the essence of what we mean today when we say 'democracy'. His claim echoed around the old world – and into the new. Thomas Rainsborough's sister married John Winthrop, the Puritan governor of the Massachusetts Bay Colony who declared that New England should be 'as a City upon a Hill'.[2] His younger brother settled in Boston.[3] There are six towns called Putney in the United States.[4]

If you step inside St Mary's, you will find that only the original tower survives of the church where Rainsborough spoke. Yet in the nave, with its 'theatre in the round' seating, the radical democratic spirit of the Levellers is still carried forward by the vicar, the very unreverential Reverend Giles Fraser – stocky, bald-headed, pugnacious, dressed in T-shirt, jeans and trainers.[5] Leaving the church and turning left up Putney High Street, this is what you will see: Hot Wok Express, Il Peperone pizzeria, Enoteca (an Italian restaurant), the Odeon cinema (probably showing an American movie), Sydney (an Australian bar-restaurant), La Mancha (a Spanish tapas bar and restaurant), Pizza Hut, Blockbuster video, La Noche (another Spanish tapas bar and restaurant), Superdrug, McDonald's and right next to it the coffee place Costa, Caffé Nero (the Reverend Fraser's favourite observation post), Starbucks, United Colors of Benetton, Pret à Manger, Burger King, Rogerio's café, the Piccolo bar – and that's only up to the railway station.

In between are the old, sturdy British familiars: Thomas Cook's travel agency, Millets, British Home Stores, the Abbey National building society turned bank, Boots the chemist, Thornton's chocolate shop, the Halifax, W. H. Smith's. Halfway down the high street there is a pub called Ye Olde Spotted Horse, which features, amidst its faux-Elizabethan white-and-black half-timbering, a large and rather handsome nineteenth-century model of a black-and-white spotted dray horse. But the British horse, unlike the leopard, can change his spots. For inside this Victorian pub, blackboards above the bar now offer 'Wines of the Day: Merlot – Chile, Pinot Noir – NZ, Rioja – Spain, Shiraz Cabernet – Australia, Cotes du Rhône – France'. The menu promises 'Linguine with Ham and Goat's Cheese Sauce' and 'Crème de Menthe Ice Cream Bombes'. A Young's Brewery poster on the wall promotes not beer but wine, with this incentive: 'Win a Trip to Spain!'

You may say this is just the superficial, brand-and-chain Americanization and Europeanization that we now encounter everywhere in the developed world; what has been called the Euro-American shopping mall. But the internationalism of Putney goes a little deeper. Quite a few of the apartments in the riverside block that looms behind the church are rented by city firms for their foreign staff: 'A lot of Yanks,' says Reverend Fraser. The French community can be met in St Simon's Church in Hazlewell Road, and there was until recently a French bookshop in Lower Richmond Road. Nearby, there's the headquarters of Voluntary Service Overseas, which in 2002 sent some 1,600 British volunteers to work in forty three developing countries.[6] In Upper Richmond Road you can call on Longview Solutions, a software company promising to provide you with 'a single source of financial truth'.[7] Its other offices are in Toronto, Philadelphia, Chicago, Dallas, San Jose, Atlanta and Madrid.

Everywhere there are what a local estate agent snootily calls 'the Antipodeans'. Australians and New Zealanders – 'thousands of them' cries the estate agent, with a mixture of personal disgust and professional delight – pack into rented accommodation and cram the Sydney bar. No worries. The district of Southfields, a maze of small streets, is now a little South Africa. The local MP quotes an estimate that as many as 20,000 South Africans live there. People from the rest of the Commonwealth – that noble republican moniker of the Cromwellian revolution, now incongruously applied to Her Britannic Majesty's former Empire – from Pakistan, India, Africa and the Caribbean, are not yet so numerous as in neighbouring parts of London. Putney can nevertheless already boast a Sikh temple, an African Families Association, and, in Gressenhall Road, the world headquarters of the Ahmadis, a dissident Muslim sect originating in the Punjab and claiming millions of adherents in seventy countries. Finally, and resented by many local people, who believe they are taking scarce council housing, jobs and benefits, there are the asylum-seekers from every unhappy corner of the world.

What you glimpse here, in Putney, are the many faces of Britain at the beginning of the twenty-first century. Janus, the Roman god of doorways, passages and bridges, had two faces, usually depicted on the front and back of his head, pointing in opposite directions. Janus

Britain has four. The back and front faces can be labelled 'Island' and 'World'; the face on the left says 'Europe' and that on the right 'America'. No wonder Britain's head aches.

At the end of this chapter I shall examine the latest attempt to cure that national headache – the Blair bridge project – and ask what it tells us about the wider relationship between Europe and America. But it's a great mistake to divorce foreign policy from domestic reality. The high street is the place to start. So let's look first at the four faces of Britain's everyday life, and the competing narratives that go with them.

ISLAND WORLD, WORLD ISLAND

'Island' is a face that the whole world knows: 'this scepter'd isle / This earth of majesty, this seat of Mars'.[8] Or, as a German newspaper once less flatteringly put it, 'the largest holiday island in the world'.[9] 'Messieurs,' the French historian Jules Michelet used to begin his lectures on British history, 'l'Angleterre est une île.'[10] He thus perpetuated in four words two hardy continental myths – that Britain is the same as England and that it is just one island. In fact, the history of Europe's largest group of offshore islands has been shaped by the workings of four nations, the English, the Scottish, the Welsh and the Irish. But 'Island' will serve as fitting shorthand for a face that looks back with pride at a version of the British past which, like all national(ist) (hi)stories, blends fact and myth, memory and forgetting, true continuity and invented tradition.

'Island' is the Britain, but more especially the England, of the parish church, the pub, the club, the college; of the retired colonel (no Rainsborough he) reading the *Daily Telegraph* and the gardener reading the *Daily Mail*; of country lanes, cricket, warm beer and shepherd's pie. Here is an England that sees itself still in the mirror of Orwell's often quoted and imitated sketch *The Lion and the Unicorn*, and reassures itself with that gruff celebration. In 1993, the Conservative prime minister, John Major, declared that 'fifty years from now Britain will still be the country of long shadows on country grounds, warm beer, invincible green suburbs, dog lovers and pool fillers and – as George Orwell said – "old maids cycling to Holy Communion through the morning mist"'.[11]

This Britain, understood largely as an extension of England, prides itself on an exceptional history of continuous freedom, self-government and the rule of law. The British, another historian remarks, 'have a genius for the appearance of continuity'.[12] Yet, stripped of all sentimental mythology and invented tradition, the facts are still remarkable. There has been an England, and a people who have called themselves the English, continuously since at least 937, when King Alfred's grandsons defeated a Northumbrian coalition, including Danes and Scots, in the battle of Brunanburh.[13] The county or shire – a term now made familiar to hundreds of millions of cinema-goers as the bucolic homeland of the hobbits – is one of the oldest continuous units of territorial self-government in the world.

What people call 'the law of the land', that is, English common law, was there already when the Normans came, and still survives. From Magna Carta in 1215 to the English revolutions of the seventeenth century, the human and civil rights – including individual property rights – that would come to be seen as characteristic of 'Western Civ' advanced furthest and fastest in England. The English parliament *was* the mother of parliaments. These things are true. They distinguish Britain, and especially England, from continental countries shaped by the legacy of Napoleonic administration, devastating wars on their own territory, and successive occupations. It is not a mere chimera that generations of continental Europeans, from Montesquieu to Jean Monnet, and generations of Americans have admired. The legacies of these things live on, in what British people say and do every day.

'World' seems, at first glance, the opposite of 'Island'. Certainly a Rastafarian evening in Neasden or an Eid-ul-Fitr among the converted cotton mills and new-built mosques of Bradford is a very long way from the rural England of weekend cricket, church and pub. But the historical connection between 'World' and 'Island' is direct and simple. The world has now come to the island because the island first went to the world. England expanded, initially absorbing all the other parts of these offshore islands in an internal empire, then scattering across the high seas, to every corner of the earth, its own language, goods, customs and people – now including the Scots, Welsh and Irish as well as the English. In the process, Britain became already by the nineteenth century a 'world island'. While remaining an 'island world' it was also an island engaged throughout the world, at once stubbornly insular and relentlessly international.

In the second half of the twentieth century, as Empire folded into that ever vaguer Commonwealth, the peoples of the former Empire came, in growing numbers, to live on the island. Roughly one out of every twelve people now living in Britain belongs to what are awkwardly classified as 'minority ethnic groups'.[14] There are well over two million 'Asian or Asian British', mainly from India and Pakistan, more than one million 'Black or Black British' and a quarter of a million Chinese.[15] They have brought their own languages, religions and customs to the British, as the British once exported theirs to them. They strengthen old ties and create new ones, with India, Pakistan and the rest of Asia, with the Caribbean and Africa, with the Middle East, with every corner of the world.

I am writing this page in Oxford, less than a mile from where J. R. R. Tolkien penned his romantic agrarian fantasy of the shire. Our local newsagent is Mr Mansha, who was born in Pakistan, our pharmacist is Mr Ahmed, who was born in Pakistan and worked for years in Saudi Arabia, our grocer is Mr Ayyub, who was born in India, married a Czech and has a flat in Prague, and our dentist, Mr Sapsford, is a cheery New Zealander. Were you to retrace Orwell's road to Wigan Pier, nearly seventy years on, you would find yourself staying often in Asian neighbourhoods. When the Indian state of Gujarat was hit by an earthquake in 2001, thousands of families among Britain's estimated 650,000 people of Gujarati descent were directly affected.[16] At the same time, there were some 75,000 Iraqis living in London.[17] A careful study has found that more than 300 languages are spoken in the capital.[18] Only New York can seriously compete with London for the title of most cosmopolitan city in the world.

These back and front faces of Janus Britain, 'Island' and 'World', make a strong contrast: between past and future, and, to some extent, between country and city. There's also an uncomfortable tension between the two. 'We Can't Keep Them Out' shrieks a headline in the conservative *Daily Express*, over a photograph of asylum-seekers running for a Britain-bound train in northern France.[19] Many Islanders do not want more World. Not in their 'neck of the woods' anyway.

JANUS BETWEEN EUROPE AND AMERICA

The contrast between Britain's left and right faces, 'Europe' and 'America', is less extreme; both are, after all, faces of Western modernity. Yet politically it's the conflict between these two that has been tearing Janus Britain apart.

If a Londoner went to sleep in 1939 and woke up today, what would strike him most forcefully is the degree to which the old island has become both Europeanized and Americanized. The first shock would await him already on Putney High Street, with Starbucks to his right and Caffé Nero to his left. Our once famously awful British food has been transformed: pizza and panini are on sale at every corner, while you must hunt to find a suet pudding or a Spotted Dick. In Ye Olde Spotted Horse, and 60,000 pubs across the land, the British now drink twice as much continental lager as they do traditional British beers.[20] The once distinctive British crowd is hard to distinguish in dress and physical appearance from the everyday shopping crowd on a high street in Germany or a mall in Wisconsin. People from Seattle to Sheffield to Sarajevo wear the same brands of T-shirt, jeans and trainers. To judge merely from outward appearance, the Reverend Fraser could as well be a Canadian software specialist or a Slovenian journalist.

As soon as our visitor from 1939 works out how to turn on the television, he will find himself transported to America. One teenager of my aquaintance concludes that *all* the entertainment programmes he and his friends have watched regularly, as they grow up, are American imports. *Friends, West Wing, Frasier, Star Trek, The Simpsons, Buffy the Vampire Slayer, Fresh Prince of Bel Air, ER*: they permeate British popular culture. The head of one television channel explains that he and his fellow executives make an annual journey to

Los Angeles to purchase these programmes. Their trip to LA is, he says, 'like the *haj*'.

Together with the prevalence of American films and music, this has led to the Americanization of British English. British teenagers use 'like' as a verbal link in the same way as their American counterparts: 'he was, like, "shall we go to Caffé Nero?" and I was, like, "oh no . . ."'. (Their parents would have said 'um' or 'er', or nothing at all.) Another teenager tries to convince me that the American 'butt', as in 'kick butt', is an English word for bottom, bum or arse, which of course it was – in the seventeenth century. In 2002, John Major was asked on the radio about the first Gulf War. It was, said Mr Major, all too easy for 'Monday morning quarterbacks' to be wise after the event.[21] He obviously assumed that his invincibly British old maids, preparing to cycle to Holy Communion through the morning mist, would at once understand the meaning of a phrase from American football.

Faced with this tsunami of Americanization, our visitor from 1939 might turn with an expectation of relief to proper football – association football or soccer – the game England gave to the world. Then he would be startled again to find that leading British clubs routinely field teams composed largely of foreign players.* For an early twenty-first-century Englishman, the heroic names 'familiar in his mouth as household words',[22] to quote the most famous of all Shakespeare's patriotic speeches, are no longer 'Harry the King, Bedford and Exeter'; they are Arsène Wenger (the French manager of Arsenal football club), Ruud van Nistelrooy (the Dutch striker for Manchester United), and Sven-Göran Eriksson (the Swedish manager of the England team). At a pub in Aldershot, I talk to English private soldiers – 'squaddies' – who are ferocious English nationalists. They are just back from holidays in Spain and drinking many litres of Stella Artois, the Belgian beer. As we speak, Eriksson's face

---

* At a match against Southampton in December 1999, Chelsea played the following team: Ed De Goey (Holland), Albert Ferrer (Spain), Celestine Babayaro (Nigeria), Emerson Thome (Brazil), Frank Leboeuf (France), Dan Petrescu (Romania), Gustavo Poyet (Uruguay), Didier Deschamps (France), Roberto Di Matteo (Italy), Tore Andre Flo (Norway) and Gabriele Ambrosetti (Italy). So far as I can establish, this was the first time a British team took the field without a single British-born player.

comes up on a large television screen in the corner. 'That man,' roars a half-drunk squaddie, 'that man has done more for England than Tony Blair!'

Yes, there is still the very English football star David Beckham, but he has moved to Spain, to play for Real Madrid. Beckham is not alone. At least 100,000 British people live in Spain. Some stand for office in local elections. In the popular British gangster film *Sexy Beast*, Spain is portrayed as a land of found content, replete with sun, wine, sex and emotional ease; Britain, by contrast, is all rain, discomfort and repressed anger. In total, some half a million British people live or work in the European Union, while perhaps three quarters of a million continental Europeans live or work in Britain.[23] At Boots the chemist one morning, I hear a German student asking nervously for a 'recipe' for her inflamed eye. 'You mean a *prescription*,' the pharmacist patiently explains. The pharmacist is Spanish. It could equally well have been a Ugandan Asian pharmacist correcting the English of a Polish building worker. At the same time, perhaps one million British people live in the United States, and more than a quarter of a million Americans live in Britain.[24]

The famously insular British took more than 56 million trips abroad in the year 2000, when the total population was just under 60 million. Spain was the top holiday destination, receiving 28 per cent of all British visits, then France, with 18 per cent, then the United States, with 7 per cent.[25] Some 4 million British people go to the US each year.[26] If you are clever in booking your flight with Ryanair or Easyjet, you can fly to Rome for £4.99. On the front page of the *Daily Telegraph* you find a horror story about the European Union right next to an advertisement for these cheap flights to European destinations. Inside there will probably be a feature about some middle-class English couple who are making a wonderful new life restoring a farmhouse in Provence. But this is not just a cosmopolitanism of the prosperous middle class. One melancholy autumn day, a London taxi driver is complaining, as usual, about the weather and the traffic. He now plans, he says, to spend half of each year abroad. Where? He answers without a moment's hesitation: 'Florida or Spain.' Spain is close, sunny and he has a brother-in-law running a bar in Alicante. Equally sunny Florida is not so close but 'they speak the language'.

'Florida or Spain' – there, in a single throwaway line, you have Janus Britain.

Britain's everyday intimacy with continental Europe is nourished by physical proximity; that with America – and with the other 'English-speaking peoples', especially in Canada, Australia, New Zealand and South Africa – flourishes in spite of distance. In business, the media and academe, the transatlantic interchange is incessant. British and American professors rotate in and out of jobs in their respective universities. British magazines, such as *Granta* and *Encounter*, have been edited by Americans; American magazines, such as the *New Yorker* and *Vanity Fair*, by British journalists. The *New York Review of Books* sometimes seems to have more British contributors than the *London Review of Books*. *Newsweek* has identified a new city called NY-LON, inhabited by a privileged transatlantic elite who live and work in *both* New York and London.[27] The sixty-seven British dead in the 9/11 attacks on the World Trade Center bore solemn witness to that intimacy. Then the altar in St Paul's Cathedral was draped with the Stars and Stripes, Her Majesty the Queen sang 'The Battle Hymn of the Republic', and, emerging, was seen to wipe away a tear.

Three thousand miles are reduced to thirty yards in the phrase British people often use to locate America: 'across the pond'. At one semantic stroke, the Atlantic becomes narrower than the Channel. In 2003, the proposition 'that the Channel is wider than the Atlantic' was put to a well-heeled, somewhat conservative London audience in a public debate. A majority voted in favour, although a large minority disagreed.[28] On the European side, there is geography; on the American, language. With America, there is shared culture, history, economics and politics. With Europe . . . shared culture, history, economics and politics.

The British, writes a former American ambassador in London, 'seem to know mainly what they used to be'.[29] But even that history keeps changing. Until well into the 1970s, most English schoolchildren were told a charming story about what the bestselling popular historian G. M. Trevelyan memorably called 'a strange island anchored off the Continent', and how that Island became a great Empire.[30] This Island-to-Empire story was transmuted by Winston

Churchill into a grand narrative of what he christened 'the English-speaking peoples', with the United States as part of the same political community as the United Kingdom, together with its Commonwealth and Empire. By the end of the twentieth century, you could fill a small library with books chronicling, dissecting and often celebrating the shared history of what was now called 'the Anglosphere' – with, at its heart, Britain, America, and their common 'language of liberty'.[31]

Then, in the 1990s, a new wave of historians came with an alternative story: that of Britain's long, shared history with continental Europe. We were now reminded that Britain has only been physically separated from the continent for a mere seven to eight thousand years, and is already joined to it again, by a tunnel under what is no longer called the English Channel, just the Channel or *la manche*.[32] For a millennium, the people of these islands were Catholic Christians, like most other Europeans; when we became Protestant, we were far from being the only Protestants in Europe. Many of our kings and queens were by origin French, Dutch or German. Britain was for centuries part of a single 'trans-channel polity'.[33] In short, we British are not half so unique as we think we are.

This alternative story is not arbitrary or invented; the facts it assembles are generally true. It would not be equally possible to write the history of Britain as, say, an Asian country. You cannot make bricks without straw. But how historians combine the straws and arrange the bricks reflects their personal preferences, and the circumstances of their own time. Clearly, this rewriting of the history of Britain as a European country has something to do with the fact that Britain is now more closely involved with its continental neighbours than at any time since the English lost possession of Calais in 1558. To say 'we have always been a European country' is not just to explain a new present, it's also to point to – or at the very least, to hint at – a likely future. So the battle over Britain's unpredictable past is also about Britain's future.

Economically, more than half Britain's trade is with the European Union and slightly less than one sixth with the United States. Roughly half its foreign investment is in or from Europe, but another third is in or from the United States.[34] Some three million British jobs depend on trade with Europe; more than a million depend on American-owned companies.[35] Britain's version of capitalism is somewhere in between those of continental Western Europe and the United States. The way British industry relies on the stock market to raise capital, with an increasingly frenetic emphasis on 'shareholder value', is more like America, but the way the government redistributes national income through the welfare state is more like France or Germany. Britain has created more new jobs than France, but less than America; those jobs are often worse paid and less secure than in France, but there is still not the large underclass of 'working poor' that you find in America.

Politically, Britain shares great chunks of its formal sovereignty and effective power with the European Union. In many fields, EU legislation takes precedence over English or Scottish law. British citizens routinely appeal from the highest British courts to both the European Court of Justice and the separate European Court of Human Rights. This makes truly 'history' – in the dismissive American usage of the word – Henry VIII's Act in Restraint of Appeals of 1533, with its seminal statement 'this realm of England is an empire'. Empire, that is, in the sense of sovereign authority from which there is no appeal. If you have to put a new level of fire insulation in your office door, or modify the way you package your apples or computer parts, this is probably as a result of a British regulation implementing some EU directive. Britain, one of the great trading nations of the modern world, no longer negotiates its own trade agreements. That is done by the responsible European Commissioner, most recently a Frenchman. Senior British officials spend much of their time in Brussels, trying to shape decisions that will directly affect British citizens and consumers.

Britain is also formally committed by Article 5 of Nato's North Atlantic Treaty to go to the assistance of any one of twenty-five other countries, most of them in Europe, if they are attacked. For sixty years, this country has had troops continuously stationed on the continent of Europe. In theory, the United Kingdom still retains its unlimited sovereign right to make war or peace. In practice, it could not have won the last war it fought on its own, the Falklands War of 1982, without the overt and covert assistance of the United States.

Scattered across East Anglia are bases with signs outside saying RAF Lakenheath, RAF Alconbury or RAF Mildenhall; these are, for all practical purposes, US Air Force bases, from which planes are despatched to foreign military engagements on orders from American commanders. An American military website for RAF Lakenheath describes it as 'England's largest US Air Force-operated fighter base'.[36]

Britain prides itself on possessing an independent nuclear deterrent, but its nuclear missiles cannot function properly without American support.[37] In 2002, £1.5 billion worth of Apache attack helicopters were reportedly sitting useless in sheds in Shropshire, because the US Congress had held up the transfer of software for a pilot-training simulator.[38] As the British public discovered during the Iraq War of 2003, the British and American intelligence services are virtually married to each other, exchanging operational intelligence at all levels almost every day. A former head of the CIA has said he thinks the CIA is much closer to Britain's Secret Intelligence Service (MI6) than it is to the FBI; and American naval intelligence, he went on mischievously, is probably closer to British naval intelligence than it is to American army intelligence.[39]

In government, different jobs bring different tilts. If you are a civil servant dealing with the environment, trade or immigration, you spend much of your life working with other European officials, and trying to implement EU decisions. If you sit in the Ministry of Defence, you spend your life trying to keep up with the Americans, as they leap financially and technologically ahead of all other military powers. If you are prime minister, you keep turning from one side to the other, like a man who can't get to sleep in an uncomfortable bed. So the duality of Europe–America is replicated at every level of British life, from the taxi driver to the prime minister.

FOUR STRATEGIES AND A PELTING FARM

Does any of this matter to anyone except the British? If the Janus dilemma were unique to Britain, it would still matter a little to the rest of the world because Britain – with the world's seventh largest economy,[40] a permanent seat on the UN Security Council, a big member state's influence on any EU decision and a tradition of worldwide military and diplomatic engagement – still matters a little in the world. But Britain's dilemma is not unique; or rather, unique only in its intensity, and in the banal sense that each national case is always unique.

Every other European country has its own version, though usually less extreme, of Island vs. World, if one takes 'Island' to mean not the mere condition of being land surrounded by water (a physical fact of ever diminishing importance) but the nurtured peculiarities of a real or claimed exceptionalism. France, with its 'cultural exception', Germany, with its historical 'special path' (the *Sonderweg*), Spain, Italy, Poland – all have their own version of Island. And all have a growing portion of World, whether Muslim Turks in Germany, Muslim Algerians in France or Muslim Moroccans in Spain. All will therefore be directly affected by any 'clash of civilizations', such as some have seen looming between the West and the Islamic world since 11 September 2001. All are torn between Europe and America. Most European countries have more Europe in their hearts than Britain; none has as much America. But they are all getting more of America, whether they like it or not, and they are all, in some measure, facing both ways.

The writer Robert Musil said wonderfully of his native Austria after 1918 that it was 'an especially clear case of the modern world'.[41] Today, Britain is an especially clear case of the modern world. It is a place where the impact of one great potential conflict of the early twenty-first century – the West versus the Rest – is clearly visible, and another – Europe versus America – is most sharply felt.

Throughout the Cold War, Germany was the world's central divided country. Germany, and especially divided Berlin, was a thermometer of the worldwide struggle between the two blocs known as 'East' and 'West'. Limited though Germany's sovereignty was, everyone looked with interest (and some nervousness) to see what new ways, if any, the Germans themselves might find to lower the Berlin Wall. Now Britain is the divided country – divided not by a concrete wall, of course, but by what Germans call the *Mauer im*

Kopf, the wall in our heads. Britain is a thermometer – or is it a seismograph? – on whose trembling needle you can measure the improvement or deterioration of relations between Europe and America. Limited though Britain's effective sovereignty is, everyone looks with interest (though also with much weariness) to see if the British may yet develop new ways to resolve a dilemma with which we have wrestled so ineffectually for more than fifty years.

First impressions are not encouraging. The British have no less than four different answers to their Janus dilemma – and therefore none. 'The trouble with this country', says a Canadian friend who lived in Britain for many years, 'is that it doesn't know what story it wants to tell.' Exactly so. These competing answers are at once attempts to formulate a national strategy, projected forward from a version of the national story, and stories projected backwards from a chosen strategy. The four competitors are: 1. regain independence; 2. choose America; 3. choose Europe; and 4. try to make the best of our intimate relations with both America and Europe.

The strategy of regaining independence builds on the old island story. It says: we have an exceptional history; we have been a free and independent country longer than anyone; personal freedom and national independence go hand in hand; our freedoms and independence are now under threat, mainly from Europe; as so often in the past, we must fight to defend them. This narrative draws on an immensely powerful self-image: that of Britain fighting heroically on, led by Winston Churchill, after France had fallen to Hitler's armies in the summer of 1940. 'Very well, alone' – as the cartoonist David Low captioned that famous picture of a British soldier defiantly shaking his fist at bomber-filled skies, from the cliffs of an island almost engulfed by storm waves.[42]

This story speaks with great emotional force to many British people, and by no means only to the dwindling number of those old enough to remember 1940. It is also shamelessly exploited by Britain's tabloid newspapers. When the European Union was to be presented with a new constitution, in the summer of 2003, the country's most popular newspaper, *The Sun*, produced an unforgettable front page. Under the slogan 'Save our country', with a Union Jack waving behind, it said: '1588 – WE SAW OFF THE SPANISH [photograph of Queen Elizabeth I], 1805 – WE SAW OFF THE FRENCH [photograph of Nelson], 1940 – WE SAW OFF THE GERMANS [photograph of Churchill], 2003 – BLAIR SUR-RENDERS BRITAIN TO EUROPE [unflattering photograph of Blair].'[43] 'Tony Blair', began the story inside, 'is about to sign away 1,000 years of British sovereignty . . .' Papers like *The Sun* and the *Daily Mail* feed upon the simplistic version of 'Our Island Story' that many British people have grown up with, and daily reinforce and coarsen it. 'We appear', an agonized reader wrote to the *Daily Mail* in 1997, 'to be one tick of the clock away from losing our sovereignty, our independence and not just 1,000 years of history but history from when the first man fought to protect this country from an invader.'[44]

Logically, the advocates of 'independence regained' should be as much opposed to sharing Britain's sovereignty with the United States as they are to sharing it with the European Union. But only a very few still uphold that consistent defence of sovereignty – 'Come the three corners of the world in arms, / And we shall shock them'[45] – which was enunciated with classical lucidity by earlier politicians such as Enoch Powell, on the old British right, and Peter Shore, on the old British left. Instead, most now make a sharp distinction between bonding with the US (good) and with the EU (bad).

The story-strategy of 'independence regained' therefore shades into the second one: choose America. Britain, says this school, cannot go on doing the splits between an emerging federal superstate, a United States of Europe run from Brussels, and the only remaining superpower, the United States of America. It has to choose; it should choose America. 'Britain's final choice: Europe or America?' was the title of a lecture given in 1998 by Conrad Black, then the proprietor of the country's bestselling conservative broadsheet, the *Daily Telegraph*.[46] Britain, argued Black, should loosen its bonds with the EU and instead join the North Atlantic Free Trade Area with the United States. Britain must plump for its 'common Atlantic home'.[47] This was emphatically the view of the country's most influential prime minister since Churchill, Margaret Thatcher. In her lifetime, she said – and if she said it once, she said it a thousand times – all the problems had come from across the Channel and all the solutions from across the Atlantic. For this school, as for the first, the prime witness, role model and adopted patron saint is Winston Churchill.

Language, they say, trumps geography. The Anglospherist poet and historian Robert Conquest imagines an 'English-Speaking Union' as an alternative to the abhorrent European one.[48] The American option is extended to embrace the whole of the Anglosphere, identified as 'the set of English-Speaking Common Law nations',[49] including Canada, Australia and New Zealand as well as Britain and America. These five countries also happen to be partners in a worldwide electronic intelligence-gathering operation known as Echelon. Yet it's Anglo-America that remains at the heart of Echelonia. As the old Anglo-American military alliance of 1941 was self-consciously reforged in the Iraq War of 2003, one usually sober British commentator described America and Britain as 'the most reliable axis of good in the world for many years'.[50]

It's a political fact of the first importance that some combination of these two positions, which are together known in British political shorthand as 'Eurosceptic', is emphatically supported by the country's most widely read newspapers. Every day, more than 22 million people – nearly three out of every four readers of a national daily – pick up a dose of Euroscepticism.[51] Papers like *The Sun*, the *Daily Mail* and the *Daily Telegraph* advance these positions not only in their editorial and comment pages but, more importantly, on their news pages. The iron distinction, still upheld by some of the quality press in continental Europe and North America, between news reporting and commentary – 'fact is sacred, opinion is free' – has long since disappeared. Their daily news stories are linked across the weeks and years in a kind of meta-story, an implicit grand narrative in which plucky Churchillian Britain, small yet Great, ably assisted by our English-speaking cousins across the seas, holds out once more against a threatening, invasive, bad old Europe.

This is partly because two major clusters of these papers have for years been the personal property of two of Britain's Anglosphere cousins – testimony, in itself, to the openness of the world island. The Australian-American Rupert Murdoch owns, among many other media, *The Sun*, *The Times* and the *Sunday Times*. Until his spectacular fall from grace in 2004, the Canadian-British Conrad Black owned the *Daily Telegraph*, the *Sunday Telegraph* and *The Spectator*, an important gadfly weekly. Eurosceptics both, Murdoch and Black have chosen their editors to suit. However, there is also a distinct, domestic history of two generations of conservative journalists who, deeply influenced by Margaret Thatcher, and traumatized by the pound sterling's bad experience with the European Exchange Rate Mechanism, found in opposition to the EU their new great fight after the end of the Cold War. For them, Brussels was, and perhaps still is, the new Moscow. Then there's the intense commercial competition between British newspapers. Good 'knocking copy' sells well, and knocking the French is the oldest British pastime of all.

Whatever the precise mixture of causes, the result is plain to see on any news-stand almost any day of the year. It's strictly impossible to prove how much these 'Eurosceptic' papers shape popular views, and how much they merely echo and reinforce them, but it seems reasonable to assume that what some 22 million people read every day in their newspapers does influence their politics.[52] In any case, one essential point is clear: British governments have, for more than a decade, ceased to believe that they can safely defy these papers on the issue of Europe.

The third story-strategy – choose Europe – is the exact mirror-image of the second. Starting from the same premiss, that Britain faces a fundamental choice between Europe and America, it comes to the opposite conclusion: Britain must plump for Europe. The key political question of our time, wrote the *Guardian* columnist Hugo Young, one of the most eloquent advocates of this view, was 'could Britain . . . truly accept that her modern destiny was to be a European country?'[53] While 'Eurosceptics' lament that Britain is in thrall to the European Union, 'Europhiles' lament that Britain is in thrall to the United States. In the last column Hugo Young wrote before his untimely death in 2003, he despairingly reflected on the way in which Tony Blair's attachment to the 'special relationship' with the United States had led his country into the Iraq War. 'What does this mean?' he asked, and answered himself: 'That we have ceased to be a sovereign nation.'[54] Which is exactly what Eurosceptics say about Britain's relations with the EU.

So all of the first three schools – 1. regain independence, 2. choose

America, 3. choose Europe – echo, in their different ways, the words that Shakespeare put into the mouth of the dying John of Gaunt. For that famous speech about 'the scepter'd isle' descends to these despairing lines:

> This land of such dear souls, this dear, dear land,
> Dear for her reputation through the world,
> Is now leased out – I die pronouncing it –
> Like to a tenement or pelting farm.[55]

The three schools just cannot agree who owns the pelting farm.

In British parlance, the competing tendencies are sometimes called (by Anglospherists) 'anti-Americans' and 'pro-Americans', or (by Eurospherists) 'pro-Europeans' and 'anti-Europeans'. Both sets of terms are inherently prejudicial. The first implies that those who are against the current trajectory of the European Union must be against Europe; the second, that those who oppose the policies of a particular US administration must be against America. Of course there are people in Britain who are genuinely anti-European and genuinely anti-American. You don't have to go far to meet them, in pub or club, disco or demo. (To find both in one person – to find, that is, a consistent British or English nationalist – is now a rarity.) Yet to use these terms implies that the person thus tagged is guilty of nationalist prejudice until proven innocent. Intellectual justice, like the old English common law, requires us to make the opposite assumption.

Anglospherists say Britain should loosen its ties with Brussels and tighten those with Washington; Eurospherists say Britain should loosen its ties with Washington and tighten those with Brussels. Eurospherists say it should join the single European currency, the Euro; Anglospherists say 'never'. If you press both sides to explain what exactly the 'final choice' means, answers became fuzzy, even evasive. Does the Anglospherist consider that Britain should leave the European Union? Well, not yet, not necessarily; but it must change it. Does the Eurospherist think Britain should leave Nato? Well, not exactly; but it must change it.

Both sides agree, however, that this choice is not just about foreign policy. It's also about domestic policy, about values, about what kind of country we want Britain to be. 'Choose America' mingles with 'regain independence' as the mantra of Britain's majority right-wing newspapers; 'choose Europe' is most often heard from those of the left, especially *The Guardian* and *The Observer*. The *Observer* columnist Will Hutton, a passionate spokesman for the 'choose Europe' school, claims that Britain shares far more features of its social and economic life with Europe than with the United States. Britain, he maintains, is 'unambiguously European'.[56] It merely needs to 'rediscover and reassert the European value system at its core'.[57] To choose Europe is to place a premium on social justice, solidarity, the environment, the welfare state and the quality of the public sphere. Many on the right agree: to choose America means, for them, to prefer the free market, an enterprise culture, the American business model, low taxes and the minimal state.

Others on the left argue that to choose Europe means to 'modernize' Britain's constitutional arrangements: to introduce a written constitution and specified, appealable rights, such as most continental European countries enjoy, to devolve power from Westminster to Scotland, Wales and Northern Ireland, and perhaps even to abolish the monarchy. Roll on the Federal Republic of Britain. During the Iraq crisis, another sense came to the fore: to choose Europe is to favour peaceful solutions to international disputes, multilateralism, respect for international law and aid to the developing world.

So the geopolitical options are also ideological ones. Nothing in Britain is ever quite simple. It's a columnist of the left, Jonathan Freedland, who wrote a sparkling book arguing that Britain should 'bring home the [American] revolution' and become more like the United States.[58] The Labour Chancellor of the Exchequer, Gordon Brown, is fascinated by American solutions. None the less, as a general rule, 'choose Europe' is now a story-strategy of the left and 'choose America' is a story-strategy of the right.

Finally, there is the fourth option: to try to preserve what can still be preserved of British independence in an increasingly interdependent world, maintain close ties with America *and* be fully in Europe. Here is an attempt to reconcile all the four faces of Janus Britain, both Island and World and, more especially, Europe and America. I might be tempted to call this the fourth way, were it not for the fact that the idea of a 'third way', as revived by ideologists of the post-Cold War liberal left, and popularized by Tony Blair, has met such widespread scepticism, mounting to derision. Unlike the 'third way' this fourth option is not some vague ideological construct. It is what most British governments have in practice more or less consciously attempted to do ever since, in 1961, Harold Macmillan made what he called the 'grim choice'[59] to apply to join the European Economic Community.

Some prime ministers have leaned more to the European side, like Edward Heath, others more to the American, like Margaret Thatcher, but all have attempted to do both. This is what the Blair government has tried programmatically to do; what most senior officials pronounce 'sensible'; what representatives of many larger businesses, with interests across the Atlantic and the Channel, urge upon them. It is what a great many British people, perhaps even a silent majority, will privately agree that Britain should do, if they are pressed beyond their first reactions. Its advocates can call in aid the holiest of all British household gods: Common Sense.

The combination option has eloquent apostles in journals such as the *Financial Times* and *The Economist*, but it is less prominently represented than any of the others in the newspapers that most British people read. In a fiercely competitive press, strong, dramatic, simple views trump mild, complicated ones. 'EU to hijack our economy' (*The Sun*), 'A vote to save our country!' (*Daily Mail*), 'Queen: Is Blair Out To Axe Me?' (by accepting a European constitution, that is, according to the *Sunday Express*) and 'Blair losing battle over United States of Europe' (*Daily Telegraph*) are all more exciting than 'US and EU agree a moderately useful initiative'.[60] The British, famous around the world for understatement, have always had an appetite for overstatement. To be sure, centrist, pragmatic conclusions can be heard on the BBC. But even the BBC, facing constant accusations of 'bias' from the Anglospherist right, and concerned to retain listeners and viewers by livening up its programmes, will generally prefer – in the name of 'balance' and the cause of entertainment – a lively, polarized debate betwen a militant 'Eurosceptic' and a passionate 'Europhile'.

The result is curious. A strategy that is the official policy of the government is the one least represented in the British media. This is obviously better than the position in totalitarian states, where nothing but the government's policy is represented in the media; it's still a little odd.

Moreover, the strategy that the government has actually tried to implement is the only one without an emotive story to support it. Tony Blair has endeavoured to tell such a story in successive speeches and interviews since he came to power in 1997. His is a story about how the world island has become a 'bridge' between Europe and America; a rather active bridge, since it also tries to pull Europe and America closer together. But this story, unlike the other three, is not underpinned by history, myth, literature or popular imagination. Unlike Churchill, with his *History of the English-Speaking Peoples*, Blair has not penned a magnificent, widely read, four-volume 'History of the Bridge'. Nor has anyone else. The imaginative fire-power of historians, writers and journalists has fusilladed in other directions. There are no poems to the bridge. There are no songs about the bridge. As Europe and America clashed over Iraq, commentators of both Anglospherist right and Eurospherist left gleefully agreed that Blair's bridge had collapsed. Yet in the minds of most British people, the bridge has probably never existed in the first place. They have no idea they are supposed to be in, of, over or under a bridge. It is, in this very important sense, the bridge that never was; or at least, never yet has been.

Before we examine Blair's bridge, however, we must reflect for a moment on the legacy of the giant who looms above all these competing story-strategies.

CHURCHILL AND CHURCHILLISMS

All British foreign policy since 1940 has been footnotes to Churchill. The British are still living with the consequences of his strategic choices between America and Europe. Most of their ongoing dilemmas are anticipated in his speeches. His black-and-white photograph on the wall as you ascend the staircase at No. 10 Downing Street is no bigger than that of Neville Chamberlain or Clement Attlee, but he is the only former prime minister to have another, large portrait photo (the famous one by the Canadian photographer Karsh) prominently displayed on the ground floor. In a moment of national extremity, every prime minister asks, 'what would Churchill have done?' Tony Blair, in the Iraq crisis, was measuring himself against the defining hero as much as Churchill's immediate successor, Anthony Eden, had done in the Suez Crisis of 1956. Churchill was still around to say, privately, that Eden had got it wrong over Suez. He is no longer around now, so everyone can answer 'what would Churchill have done over Iraq?' in their own way.

After Churchill came not just Churchillism but Churchillisms. Every side in the national argument makes its Churchillian case. His own inspirational, protean, often deliberately vague and sometimes self-contradictory words furnish a memorable quotation for every school: Churchillism against Churchillism. No one can conclusively adjudicate these rival claims. We can never know what Churchill himself would have done. What Churchill actually did – the subject already of more than 3,000 published works[61] – can only be understood in its full, dense historical context. None the less, there are a few things that need to be said here about the real Churchill and the competing Churchillisms.

'We shall defend our Island, whatever the cost may be, we shall fight on the beaches, we shall fight on the landing grounds, we shall fight in the fields and in the streets, we shall fight in the hills; we shall never surrender . . .'[62] Churchill's most famous words defined the British to themselves in the summer of 1940; turned their worst into their finest hour. This was his greatest moment, but it was not the state he wished the British to be in. That is so obvious in the historical context that it would hardly need pointing out, were it not for the fact that a Churchillian stance of solitary defiance is endlessly replayed on the front pages of *The Sun* and the *Daily Mail*, as if every new directive from Brussels were one of Hitler's Messerschmitts. An island standing alone was the last thing Churchill wanted Britain to be. No one could have been less of a Little Englander.

What Churchill most wanted was for Britain to remain the centre of a glorious, world-straddling Empire and Commonwealth, if possible 'for a thousand years'.[63] Even after the Second World War he still pictured world politics as three intersecting circles: the United States, an emerging United Europe and the British Commonwealth.

Again, it is so obvious, yet so widely overlooked, that the vision dearest to Churchill himself is the only one that features not at all in early twenty-first-century Churchillisms. No one in their right mind now thinks Britain should centre its national strategy on the Commonwealth.

In fact, Churchill's hope was doomed as soon as Hitler's own perverted version of 'thousand-year empire' brought Britain to war with Nazi Germany. Faced with that challenge, Britain had to look for help, either to Europe or to the United States, or to both. Europe meant, above all, France. Although he always bore America firmly in mind, and heart, Churchill looked first to France, a country he loved and admired. He was, noted the diarist Henry 'Chips' Channon, 'a fanatical Francophile'.[64] When he spoke in April 1939 of 'a solid identity of interest between the Western democracies,' he meant Britain and France.[65] 'The French', he said a month later, 'have the finest, though not the largest, army in existence at the present time.'[66] Only when that army was so shockingly defeated in June 1940, only when his last, extraordinary offer of a complete political union between France and Britain failed to forestall Pétain's capitulation to Hitler, did he turn all his efforts to the United States.

The way he then conjured the British Empire's tenuous, tense pre-war relationship with America into an enduring Special Relationship (with, for the British if not for Americans, a capital S and R) was to prove the most enduring Churchillism. If you want a glimpse of the great conjuror at work, read the eyewitness account by H. V. Morton of Churchill's August 1941 meeting with Roosevelt in Canada's Placentia Bay. Morton shows him rehearsing, like a film director, the joint church service at which the assembled British and American crews would sing 'Onward Christian Soldiers' and 'O God, our Help in Ages Past' on the deck of the battleship HMS *Prince of Wales*: 'Mr Churchill walked about inspecting every detail, often taking a hand by moving a chair an inch one way or another and by pulling out the folds of the Union Jack.'[67]

Then, in a radio broadcast, he interpreted his own theatrical production to the world, evoking 'that densely packed congregation of fighting men of the same language, of the same faith, of the same fundamental laws, of the same ideals, and now to a large extent of the same interests, and certainly in different degrees facing the same dangers'. They represented 'two major groupings of the human family, the British Empire and the United States, who, fortunately for the progress of mankind, happen to speak the same language and very largely think the same thoughts, or anyhow think a lot of the same thoughts'.[68] Notice how the essential qualifications, 'very largely', 'a lot of', 'certainly in different degrees', are scattered like foam in the wake of a battleship advancing at full speed. In fact, America was not at war with Hitler in August 1941 and, to the disappointment of the British, did not come in as a result of that Atlantic meeting. 'Why not now?' Morton asked.

After the fall of France, the political marriage with the United States always came first for Churchill. He had grown to adulthood at a time when Britain and America were first cautiously contemplating a shared 'Anglo-Saxon' supremacy to supplant their long nineteenth-century rivalry. (On the British side, this impulse already reflected a sense of declining relative power.[69]) Inspired by the Anglo-American comradeship in arms at the end of the First World War, he had spent part of the inter-war years working on his *History of the English-Speaking Peoples*, discovering a common future in the shared past. Everything had prepared him to be the Shakespeare of Anglo-Americanism. If he were born again, he told a companion on his way to deliver his 'iron curtain' speech at Fulton, Missouri, in 1946, he would like to be born an American.[70]

Yet he never forgot Europe, and especially France. The maxim of British policy expounded by a conservative commentator in 2002 – 'Love America, Hate France'[71] – would have been abhorrent to him. He loved both. He admired Charles de Gaulle as much as he was exasperated by him. He fought fiercely for the restoration of France as a great power after the war. Behind Churchill's back, his 'friend' Roosevelt made fun of this to Stalin, in a private meeting at the Yalta summit in February 1945. According to the official American record, Roosevelt confided to Stalin that 'the British were a peculiar people and wished to have their cake and eat it too'.[72] But Churchill persisted and won, for de Gaulle, France's seat at the top table.

Voted out of office by the British people in 1945, he devoted much time in opposition to advancing the cause of a United Europe. 'The first step in the re-creation of the European family must be a partnership between France and Germany,' he declared at Zurich in 1946.[73] As 'ten ancient capitals of Europe' disappeared behind the Iron Curtain, those European peoples who could still unite in freedom should do so.[74] He was feted like Charlemagne at the Hague Congress of Europe in 1948. He was a founding father of the Council of Europe, the original pan-European organization of democracies, and spent weeks actively involved in its debates. During its meeting at Strasbourg in 1949, he addressed – *'Prenez garde! Je vais parler en français'* – the largest, most enthusiastic outdoor rally that city had ever seen in the cause of European union.[75]

He was, however, grandly ambiguous and inconsistent about Britain's role. Would the British Empire be a benign external 'friend and sponsor', like the United States, as he explained at Zurich, or was it for 'France and Britain to take the lead', as he declared in the Albert Hall in 1947?[76] Generally, he stuck with the less committed stance, frustrating practical enthusiasts of European integration such as Jean Monnet. When France and Germany went ahead, without Britain, to develop the Schuman Plan for the European Coal and Steel Community, he moved a motion in the House of Commons criticizing the Labour government for not joining in. But when he became prime minister again, in 1951, he did nothing to reverse that decision. He poured scorn on the planned European Defence Community, calling the proposed multinational army 'a sludgy amalgam'.[77] 'We shall', he said, reaching new heights of inspirational vagueness, 'work in true comradeship for and with United Europe.'[78] The German Chancellor Konrad Adenauer came to No. 10 Downing Street to discover what on earth this meant. Churchill sketched on a card his map of three circles, marked 'United Europe', 'USA' and 'Br Com' (British Commonwealth), with fairly small areas of intersection. A decade later, Adenauer reproduced the map in his memoirs, commenting drily 'nothing has changed in this posture of Great Britain's'.[79] It was the self-styled 'good European' Churchill who declined for Britain the role of leading a European union.[80]

Instead, he went with America. The 'Special Relationship' shaped by Churchill's two premierships was, as one of its best historians writes, a British diplomatic strategy.[81] Its goals were, first, to save

Britain from defeat; then to preserve as much as possible of Britain's fast failing power, by sticking close to its hegemonic successor; and to keep America engaged in Europe in ways that Britain thought best, for Britain of course, but also for Europe and the world. In January 1953 President Eisenhower noted irritably in his diary that his old wartime comrade 'had developed an almost childlike faith that all the answers are to be found merely in British–American partnership'.[82] As Churchill completed his great memoir-history of the Second World War, he worried about offending the Americans: 'If I am going to die, then I can say what I like . . . but if I live and am still Prime Minister, then I must not say things which will anger Ike.'[83] So in the very writing of the book that indelibly lodged in British minds a horror of appeasement (appeasement of Hitler, that is, or Nasser, or Saddam Hussein), Churchill was himself practising a kind of literary appeasement – of the American president. For self-censorship is the political writer's appeasement.

Here, then, was the Churchillian legacy: unambiguous commitment to the United States, ambiguous commitment to Europe. Joint action sustained by a shared language on the one side; fine words often unmatched by deeds on the other. For all that had changed over the intervening fifty years, many on the continent of Europe, contemplating the stance taken by Tony Blair in the war to depose Saddam Hussein, would mutter: *plus ça change, plus c'est la même chose.*

THE BLAIR BRIDGE PROJECT

At the turn of this century, between 1997 and 2003, Tony Blair became the most prominent and articulate spokesman, among serving politicians, of the proposition that Europe and America must work together, for their own advantage and for that of the wider world. An acute Bulgarian observer wrote that in the conflict over Iraq, central and east Europeans 'supported Tony Blair rather than George W. Bush'.[84] In Washington, American Democrats had tears in their eyes when Tony Blair unfolded this vision before a joint meeting of both houses of Congress in July 2003. If Europe and America work together as partners, he said, 'then the other great nations of our world, and the small, will gather around in one place, not many'.[85] No one else made this argument with the same clarity, authority and evangelical certainty; not his counterparts in any of the capitals of Europe, not the president in the White House. Atlanticists everywhere looked to Blair, just as opponents of American hegemony and supporters of a rival European superpower looked to the French president Jacques Chirac, with his doctrine of 'multipolarity'.

Yet by the end of Blair's first six years in office many, even among the supporters of his vision, felt that he had failed. Blair's bridge, they said, was buried somewhere in mid ocean: an Atlanticist Atlantis. That harsh judgement might still prove premature, but self-evidently he had not succeeded in preventing a crisis of the West, the most profound since the end of the Cold War, which left France and the United States facing each other more like enemies than friends. To ask 'why did Blair's bridge fall down in 2003?' is thus a way of asking 'how, if at all, could those who share his strategic vision of partnership between Europe and America do better in future?'.

You might think we do not yet have enough evidence to answer the first, historical question, let alone the second, speculative one. On the contrary. Even as the story unfolded, participants spoke with remarkable if partisan frankness about what was going on behind supposedly closed doors. Within weeks, we had eyewitness accounts of what was said in the Oval Office in Washington and across the Cabinet table in London. Within months, we were reading the internal e-mails of the most senior officials in British government, including their debates about the public presentation of secret intelligence. This new openness of Western government is only partly intended. It's a kind of market-led glasnost. It horrifies officials and places strains on the smooth workings of government, since nobody can be sure that anything they say will remain confidential for long. Yet that's a price worth paying for the democratization of political knowledge; and only with this democratization of political knowledge can we begin to build a free world.

Doubtless there are still a few secrets left, but the historian's problem – as so often with very recent history – is not a drought but a flood of evidence. A rich alluvial crop of 'instant histories' has already told, with ever more first-hand detail, a story whose stages were soon familiar: Blair's first summit with George W. Bush in February 2001 (known as the 'Colgate summit' because, asked what he and Blair had in common, President Bush said, 'well, we both use Colgate toothpaste'[86]); the emotional response to the 9/11 attacks ('thank you for comin', friend'[87] declared Bush to the pale-faced British leader standing tall in the gallery of the US Congress); a crucial discussion on Iraq at the president's ranch in Crawford, Texas, in April 2002; an angry face-off with Jacques Chirac at an EU summit in October 2002, dubbed by the British '*le row*'; what British and American diplomats called the 'de Villepin ambush' at the UN on 20 January 2003; Donald Rumsfeld's dismissal of France and Germany as 'old Europe' two days later, soon followed by the 'Letter of Eight' pro-Atlanticist European leaders; Chirac's neo-Gaullist '*non*' to a second UN resolution on 10 March, answered by Blair's neo-Churchillian speech to the House of Commons on 18 March, and so on.

What conclusions can be drawn from this already familiar story? Unsurprisingly, many have blamed the collapse of Blair's bridge on Blair himself. They have charged him with 'amateurism' in foreign policy, with 'hubris' and with becoming 'Bush's poodle' – that is, preferring a subordinate relationship with a right-wing administration in the United States to a partnership of Social or Christian Democratic equals in Europe. Carefully examined, the grain of truth in each of these charges soon opens out into a larger truth about something more than just the character of a singular politician.

Take 'amateurism', for a start. When Tony Blair came to power in May 1997, he had no experience of foreign policy. Shortly before his election, he invited a small group of academics to tell him about Europe over a mug of tea in the garden of his Islington home. He introduced the discussion by saying frankly that he did not know so much about the subject; he had spent his whole political career trying to make the Labour party electable; he had not had time to travel around the continent like Denis Healey (a veteran Labour politician), getting to know the people and the politics there. He therefore had to learn on the job. This was difficult, even when you had first-rate diplomatic advisers sitting just down the corridor in No. 10 Downing Street. So he made mistakes. For example, it was a mistake to publish, in a 'dossier', British intelligence guesswork about weapons of mass destruction in Iraq, as the justification for a war towards which the Bush administration was advancing for diverse reasons of its own.

Yet he was not alone in this occasional callowness. The democratic politics of our time are full of career politicians in early middle age, who come to office as accomplished experts in all the techniques of winning power at home – but complete amateurs in the exercise of power abroad. George W. Bush and Gerhard Schröder were two others. They all learned on the job; they were all unduly influenced by their personal relations with each other; they all made mistakes. The diplomacy of the Iraq crisis of 2002/3 was a case study, on all sides, in how not to run a world. In its blunderings – though not, fortunately, in its results – it was justly compared with the months leading up to the outbreak of the First World War in 1914.

Then take 'hubris'. Tony Blair, like most people who get to the top, had an extraordinary drive and self-belief. This helped him to do bold and admirable things. Without it, for example, he would not have held out in 1999 – ahead of and angering the then American president – for the deployment of ground troops to halt an ongoing genocide in Kosovo. By the autumn of 2002, however, a touch of hubris, the occupational disease of all human beings in power, was detectable. In one conversation with a group of journalists he uttered these unforgettable words: 'I've fought two wars – or three, if you count Sierra Leone.' 'I've fought' – as if he personally had marched through the mud of Kosovo and the rocky mountains of Afghanistan. He seemed to believe at this time that his personal charm and leadership could keep Europeans and Americans together, as the Bush administration advanced towards a war to depose Saddam Hussein. He did not anticipate that France and Germany would combine to plot a very different course.

Yet this hubris was not just a personal trait, nor simply a *déformation professionelle* of all powerholders. It was a recurrent characteristic of a certain British approach to the world. Even before he became prime minister, Blair's speeches were full of the need for Britain to play a leading 'role', to have 'influence', to 'lead' in Europe. Under the slogan 'We will give Britain leadership in Europe', the New Labour election manifesto in 1997 showed Jacques Chirac looking wonderingly at a youthful, well-thatched Blair. A caption read 'Tony

Blair takes the lead in talks with President Jacques Chirac of France.'[88] When he came to power, he began by lecturing other centre-left leaders about how they must 'reform' the EU. This pre-occupation with 'leadership', with your country's role and status in the world, was shared, in this acute form, by only one other European country: France.

The leitmotif of the bridge appeared early in his premiership. It is intrinsically hubristic. Why should a German chancellor go via Britain if he wants to talk to Washington? Why should an American president, if he wishes to reach Madrid, Rome or Warsaw? It mixes a general proposition – that Europe and America should stick together – with a particular claim for Britain's special role, which Blair else-where described as 'pivotal'.[89]

That claim is part of a long-running attempt, from Churchill on, to maximize the declining influence of a former world power. France has been doing exactly the same since 1945, although by a different route. Blair, the neo-Churchillian, and Chirac, the neo-Gaullist, are brothers under the skin. Both countries share this obsession with what de Gaulle called 'rank', as if nations were ambitious army officers or rival football teams. So France will certainly never walk over a British bridge to Washington. But the hubristic metaphor irritates others in Europe too. Chancellor Schröder once sarcastically remarked that the traffic over the bridge seemed to be all in one direction.[90]

What, then, of the charge that Blair became 'Bush's poodle'? In his attitudes to Europe and America, Blair is a child of Janus Britain. He likes both. He speaks passable French and once spent a summer working as a barman in Paris. 'The first time I voted',[91] he recalled in 1999, was to vote 'yes' in the 1975 referendum. This asked 'Do you think that the United Kingdom should stay in the European Community (Common Market)?' While seeking election to parliament in the early 1980s he trimmed to the Labour party's line, which then called for Britain to leave the European Community. But he stood for the party leadership in 1994 on a moderately 'pro-European' platform. *The Guardian*'s Hugo Young, who talked to him often at this time, concluded that Blair had become 'a proper European'.[92]

'A *proper* European' – but what did that very English phrase, at once lofty and prim, really mean? It meant, to be sure, that the new prime minister liked the continent of sunshine, French wine, *polenta* and wonderfully chic women. It meant that he had none of the hang-ups about Europe of an older generation of politicians, both Labour and Conservative. It meant he was convinced that Britain must be fully involved in the European Union – 'at the heart of Europe', in the plangent phrase of his predecessor John Major – for at least four reasons: to secure trade, investment and jobs for Britain, to 'lead' Europe to internal economic and political reform, to maintain Britain's influence in the world, and to secure the eastern plinth of his transatlantic bridge between the United States and Europe. It meant he wanted to overcome, once and for all, a half century of British ambivalence about the European project. It meant all these things. But did it mean he liked the European Parliament or Commission? Did it mean that he was steeped in European history, as Churchill was, and heard the subterranean melodies that moved Germans or Italians or Spaniards to act as they did? Did it mean that he could, in this deeper sense, 'speak European'? It did not.

Like many British 'Europeans' before and alongside him, like Roy Jenkins, Edward Heath and Kenneth Clarke, Blair was a very British pro-European. He genuinely wanted to be in there. His government joined the 'social' chapters of the Maastricht Treaty, which the Major government had rejected. He tirelessly sought ways to strengthen Britain's connections with her major partners: a joint 'third way' paper with Chancellor Schröder of Germany, the St Malo initiative on European defence with President Chirac of France. When it became clear that the single currency was going ahead, he privately resolved to take Britain into the Eurozone if he possibly could, for political reasons. But in private he could be distinctly sceptical about the actual mechanisms and institutions of European integration. His main idea, he told one small meeting of advisers around the Cabinet table, was 'a Europe of nation-states'. Mandarin knights coughed discreetly and explained that this would have a disastrous impact in Europe, since it would make him sound like Margaret Thatcher. 'So why is it,' he asked, 'that Chirac can say that and I can't?'

His keynote European speeches, even when they were delivered on the continent, tended to turn into speeches about why Britain had to be in Europe rather than about Europe as Europe. The 'island story' myths of a conservative British household in the 1950s, and the history lessons of an English public schoolboy in the 1960s, kept breaking through. In a speech in Warsaw in 2000, he described Britain as 'the victor in World War II, the main ally of the United States, *a proud and independent-minded island race (though with much European blood flowing in our veins)*' (my italics).[93] Island race! After a subsequent Blair speech in Warsaw, I asked the first prime minister of independent Poland, Tadeusz Mazowiecki, a Catholic baptized in the deepest waters of European history, how he liked it. 'It was good,' he said, 'but I don't know, there was something missing . . .' And when Blair explained his European commitment to a joint session of Congress in Washington in July 2003, it came out like this:

You know, people ask me after the past months, when, let's say, things were a trifle strained in Europe: 'Why do you persist in wanting Britain at the centre of Europe?' and I say 'Well, maybe if the UK were a group of islands 20 miles off Manhattan, I might feel differently. But actually, we're 20 miles off Calais and joined by a tunnel.[94]

Although he immediately went on to say 'we are part of Europe, and we want to be', it rather sounded as if he wished Britain were twenty miles off Manhattan.

This was more than just a politician trimming to his audience of the day. In America, unlike in Europe, Blair had perfect pitch. Standing where Churchill and Margaret Thatcher had stood before him, he played all the right Anglo-American chords: a hint of the King James Bible, a touch of the Shakespearean ('11 September was not an isolated event / but a tragic prologue, Iraq another act / and many further struggles will be set / upon this stage before it's over'), a dash of *Friends* ('I know this is kind of late, but sorry,' he said, apologizing for the British having burned the Congressional library in 1814 in colloquial language that one star of the American sitcom *Friends* might use to another), and whole buckets of the Churchillian. From start to finish, the speech was soaked in that 'language of liberty' which had made a common Anglo-American political discourse for almost four centuries. The words 'freedom', 'free' or 'liberty' appeared twenty-seven times. The speech climaxed in this astonishing hymn to America:

Tell the world why you're proud of America. Tell them when the Star-Spangled Banner starts, Americans get to their feet, Hispanics, Irish, Italians, Central Europeans, East Europeans, Jews, Muslims, white, Asian, black, those who go back to the early settlers and those whose English is the same as some New York cab drivers I've dealt with, but whose sons and daughters could run for this Congress. Tell them why Americans one and all, [sic] stand upright and respectful. Not because some state official told them to, but because whatever race, colour, class or creed they are, being American means being free.

Small wonder a group of Americans launched a 'Blair for President' campaign. It's hard to imagine him ever finding such words for a hymn to Europe.

Blair's eloquent pro-Americanism, his emotional Anglospherism, was heartfelt and culturally deep-rooted. It was also the expression of a strategic choice. In the Clinton years, things had been easy. Blair and his colleagues had made pilgrimages to Washington to learn from the 'New Democrats' how 'New Labour' (as it then became) might win an election. He and Clinton were ideological soulmates. Once elected, he could repair the damage done to Britain's relations with Washington by the Major government's feebleness over Bosnia, while also repairing its frayed ties with Europe. The 'third way', that capacious, woolly poncho, would envelop them both.

Suddenly he was faced with a very different president, George W. Bush. Blair and his advisers made a most deliberate choice: to get close to him and stay close to him. Their first grappling hook was Churchill. Having learned that Bush was a fan of Churchill, the British ambassador to Washington chose as Blair's present for the 'Colgate summit' a facsimile of the Atlantic Charter, agreed by Churchill and Roosevelt in Placentia Bay in August 1941, including Churchill's handwritten corrections. Shortly before the meeting, Bush's political adviser Karl Rove rang up to say that the president was looking for a bust of Churchill. The Blair team flew over with a bust of Churchill by a contemporary British artist in their plane, but decided it wasn't good enough. A few months later, the British ambassador proudly presented the president with a handsome Jacob Epstein head of Churchill, taken from the British government art collections. On loan, to be sure. Churchill would surely have approved this use of his graven image, in the kind of minutely choreographed political wooing that he himself began on the deck of the HMS *Prince of Wales*. His bust now stood in the Oval Office. President Bush said Churchill seemed to him 'like a Texan'. 'Sometimes', he reported, 'Churchill will talk back, sometimes he won't, depending upon the stress of the moment, but he is a constant reminder of what a great leader is like.'[95]

Blair then immediately grasped how the 9/11 attacks changed everything for America. All the Churchillian bells rang. He went to Ground Zero, where Mayor Giuliani was himself drawing inspiration from Churchill's conduct during the Blitz; he received his first standing ovation in Congress ('thank you for comin', friend'); he dashed around the world, covering more than 40,000 air miles, having fifty-four meetings with other leaders in the course of eight weeks, trying to help the US to respond wisely to the challenge.[96] Britain had once again appointed itself Athens to America's Rome.

As the Bush administration's agenda moved from destroying al-Qaeda in Afghanistan to regime change in Iraq, Blair stuck to his strategic choice. He seemed genuinely to believe that the combination of terrorism, rogue or failed states, and weapons of mass destruction was the great new challenge of our time – comparable, in scale if not in kind, to fascism in the 1930s or Soviet communism in the 1950s. But he also argued that Britain must 'remain the closest ally of the United States'[97] to try to prevent Washington from overreacting, to bring it back to multilateralism, and to 'broaden its agenda' to include, for example, a peace process between Israel and Palestine. 'I tell you that we must steer close to America,'[98] he admonished the British Cabinet in March 2002, according to the diaries of a former foreign secretary, Robin Cook, who was at the Cabinet table. By the autumn of 2002, Blair had almost become an internal player in the factional infighting of the Bush administration. There was, one experienced Washington observer told me at the time, a 'Cheney–

Rumsfeld faction' facing a 'Powell–Blair faction'.[99] Journalists joked that the British government was 'the provisional wing of the State Department' (by sarcastic analogy with the provisional wing of the IRA).[100] When Blair was wondering how to begin his broadcast on the outbreak of hostilities in Iraq, one of his closest aides suggested 'My fellow Americans'.[101]

This was the personal choice of a particular Englishman in his late forties; it was also the characteristic choice of a British prime minister. 'Tony's default position is to go with the Americans,'[102] concluded one of his senior advisers. That could have been said of every British prime minister since Churchill, except for Edward Heath. It came at a price. A letter drafted for Churchill to send to Roosevelt in 1940, asking urgently for support, said that the partnership between Britain and America could not flourish after the war if either country 'should be placed in the position of being the suppliant client' of the other.[103] Churchill deleted the phrase 'suppliant client', yet found himself in that position. 'What do you want me do?' he once angrily asked, when discussing a loan arrangement with Roosevelt. 'Get on my hind legs and beg like Fala?'[104] Fala was Roosevelt's dog.

Now that America was the world's only superpower, and Britain an empireless medium-sized European power, Blair accepted a subordinate role. 'Newest US Ambassador', said a headline in the *Wall Street Journal Europe*, 'is Prime Minister of the United Kingdom'.[105] A former foreign secretary, Douglas Hurd, commented that the Special Relationship was like a pennyfarthing bicycle in which Britain was the farthing – the tiny wheel at the back. It was all very well 'standing shoulder to shoulder' with Washington, but what if your shoulder only came up to the other man's knee?[106] 'I know that we used to be a colony of Britain,' a student at a small liberal college in Kansas said to me at this time, 'but what I want to know is: when did Britain become a colony of the United States?'

That was only half the price; the other half was paid in Europe. In 1963, an agreement between Harold Macmillan and President Kennedy to give Britain an American nuclear missile system had been taken by de Gaulle as the pretext for rejecting Britain's application to join the European Community.[107] Instead, de Gaulle signed the Elysée Treaty with Konrad Adenauer – the founding charter of France's special relationship with Germany. (Their Placentia Bay had been a dramatic *tableau vivant* of reconciliation in the Cathedral of Reims, with de Gaulle taking the Churchillian role as stage manager.) Forty years later, as Britain again went with America, Germany again lined up with France. And the coordinated Franco-German '*non/nein*' to the Anglo-American war on Iraq coincided, not accidentally, with the solemn reaffirmation of the Franco-German political marriage in celebrations to mark the fortieth anniversary of the 1963 Elysée Treaty, in January 2003. This was a piece of political theatre every bit as emotional, and as calculated, as the Anglo-American replays of Placentia Bay.

So the two key political couples of the Cold War West faced each other across a Channel that seemed wider than the Atlantic. Except that more than a million British people marched through London one bright winter Saturday – 15 February, a date to remember – to show that on this issue, at least, they felt more like their fellow Europeans across the Channel. This, in turn, increased Blair's suppliant dependency on Washington. It was precisely because much of British public opinion, and his own party, was in this sense 'European' that Blair had to go cap in hand to Washington, begging the president to support British efforts to achieve a second UN resolution sanctioning military action against Iraq. One of Blair's closest advisers told me he felt like a man hanging on by his fingertips to one side of a crevasse and his toes to the other. When that last diplomatic attempt failed, they fell into the crevasse.

It is often overlooked that the attempt and then failure to win a second UN resolution sanctioning war on Iraq resulted from an unbridgeable difference between the old European rivals Britain and France, not between the United States and France. And it was, characteristically, at the European end that Blair's bridge fell down. Whether by more skilful European diplomacy his government could have prevented Germany and France from lining up together so forcefully against the American–British position is an interesting speculation. Blair's own conclusion was that it would only have been possible if the Bush administration had itself been prepared to woo at least one of these two countries to its cause, which it was not.[108] Yet certainly the Blair government did not devote anything like the same political and diplomatic effort to the European side that it did to the American one.

At this point, however, we have to broaden the picture to include the whole of Janus Britain. For had Blair been able to do what he wanted over the previous six years, Britain might have drawn, in this crisis, on deeper wells of solidarity with and from Germany and France. It would, for example, have been close to sharing a single currency with them. But he had been frustrated in this by his own Chancellor of the Exchequer, Gordon Brown, who preferred American ways and the security of his own domestic political position to a European economic gamble, whose political justification was more clearly seen from No. 10 than from No. 11 Downing Street. Blair now had a foreign secretary who was lukewarm about Europe and a Cabinet from which many of the enthusiasts for the European cause had departed.

Beyond that friendly front bench he faced a Conservative opposition and a coven of newspapers stoking all the popular doubts and prejudices about Europe that I have already described. Blair had come to power by wooing these newspapers and he was frightened of taking them on. At the very moment of his first election, in 1997, he had made a Faustian bargain with Rupert Murdoch's *The Sun*, coveting its matchless access to millions of potential swing voters.[109] His political adviser Philip Gould records that, worried about Conservative attacks on Blair's openness to Europe, 'we got *The Sun* to run an article by Blair the next day, promising that he would "Slay the Euro-dragon".'[110] Those that live by *The Sun* will die by *The Sun* – or at least, must always fear that they will. In the autumn of 2003, Murdoch made no secret of the fact that he disliked the European constitution as much as the Euro, and indicated that *The Sun* could again give its support to the Conservatives.[111]

SO NOW?

The Blair bridge project has been based, instinctively but also rationally, on the very nature of Janus Britain. It is, so to speak, Putney made policy. Britain's connections with both Europe and America are so thick and vital that to 'choose Europe' or 'choose America' would be to cut off the country's left or right leg. So it must keep trying to pull America and Europe together. This would be a complex and ambitious strategy even if the country were united behind its prime minister. But the country has not been united behind its prime minister; instead, it has been torn apart in a bitter, unending argument between four competing national strategies, of which Blair's bridge is the one least vividly represented in the media and least effectively underpinned in the popular imagination by a story blended from history and myth.

There is a real question whether even a master statesman – a Palmerston, Bismarck or Churchill – could successfully implement such a complex game-plan with such a divided country behind him – and especially under the intensely volatile conditions of television democracy, twenty-four hours a day, seven days a week. All democracies have arguments about foreign policy, otherwise they are not democracies. But if a country is successfully to follow any sort of national strategy then it does require a minimal consensus about what it is and where it would like to be. It needs to have some idea 'what story it wants to tell'. Many European countries have such a minimal consensus at the beginning of the twenty-first century; Britain does not.

So a second possible conclusion from this story has to do with Britain, and its need for such a minimal consensus, rather than with Tony Blair and the failings of his own highly personal diplomacy. However, we also have to consider a third hypothesis: that the forces pushing Europe and America apart are so powerful that any attempt to hold the two together, by however skilful a British prime minister, however strongly supported by a nation however united, would still be doomed to certain failure. In that case, the whole project is futile. Whatever the cost, Britain will have to choose. A man standing astride two oil tankers that are moving apart, and trying to hold them together with just the strength in his legs, is not a statesman – he's an idiot.

Yet the things we call 'Europe' and 'America' are not oil tankers. They are political assemblages of millions of individual human beings. It's time to look at them more closely.

2

Europe as Not-America

A NATION IS PROCLAIMED

'On Saturday, 15 February, a new nation was born on the street. This new nation is the European nation.'[1] Such was the conclusion drawn by Dominique Strauss-Kahn, a former French finance minister, from the simultaneous demonstrations across Europe on 15 February 2003, protesting against the Bush administration's advance to war with Iraq. Europeans already knew, wrote Strauss-Kahn, when they strolled down the high street of a European town or watched a European film, that they were in Europe. Anyone who was ill, old or unemployed appreciated the value of that social security which characterized the European model, and distinguished it from the prevailing models in the United States, Japan, India and China. But this was something more: 'the birth of a European nation. On one and the same continent, on one and the same day, and for one and the same cause, the peoples rose up. And suddenly we realize that these peoples are one.' 'We' – but who exactly were 'we'? – realized too that 'the Europeans have a common view of the organization of the world: far removed from solitary decisions in an Oval Office, instead preferring collective decisions in the framework of international institutions'. At the invitation of the President of the European Commission, Dominique Strauss-Kahn was at this time chairing a round table of eminent Europeans searching for a new project or, as he put it, 'myth' for tomorrow's Europe.[2]

That summer there appeared in many European newspapers an appeal for 'the rebirth of Europe', co-signed by Jacques Derrida and Jürgen Habermas, two of the continent's most famous living

54

philosophers. In an introductory note, Derrida said they felt it to be both 'necessary and urgent' for 'German and French philosophers to raise their voice together'.[3] The text, written by Habermas, began by rhetorically contrasting two recent moments. First, there was the publication in various newspapers of the 'Letter of Eight' pro-Atlanticist European leaders, described by Habermas as a 'declaration of loyalty to Bush', which, he claimed, the Spanish prime minister had invited 'those European governments bent on war' to sign 'behind the backs of their EU colleagues'. Then there was 15 February 2003, 'when the demonstrating masses in London and Rome, Madrid and Barcelona, Berlin and Paris, reacted to this surprise attack'. While acknowledging the divisions within Europe, and the existence of a larger West as a 'spiritual contour', Habermas, like Strauss-Kahn, argued that what happened on 15 February can help to catalyse the formation of a European identity – if we Europeans want it to. We can forge this identity by consciously 'making our own' some parts of our historical heritage, while rejecting others.

He went on to list what he called six 'candidates' for building a European identity. First, there is the European separation of religion from politics: 'in our latitudes it's hard to imagine a president who begins his daily business with public prayer and relates his momentous political decisions to a divine mission'. Then there's the European belief in the 'formative power of the state' to correct the failures of the market. Thirdly, since the French Revolution Europe has developed a political party system – composed of conservatives, liberals and socialists – which continually confronts the 'sociopathological consequences of capitalist modernization'. The legacy of Europe's labour movements and its Christian-social tradition, meanwhile, is an ethos of solidarity, an insistent demand for 'more social justice' against 'an individualist performance ethos which accepts crass social inequalities'. A moral sensibility, informed by the memory of the totalitarian regimes of the twentieth century and the Holocaust, is reflected 'among other things in the fact that the Council of Europe and the EU have made the renunciation of the death penalty a condition of entry'. Finally, the way Europe has overcome its warlike past in forms of supranational cooperation has strengthened Europeans' conviction that 'globally, too', the domestication of the state's use of force requires a mutual limitation of sovereignty. Having lived through the rise and fall of empires, Europeans can now carry 'the Kantian hope of a world domestic policy'.

What Habermas argues with philosophical density, and Strauss-Kahn with eloquent political hyperbole, is that Europe is *different* from the United States, that in these differences Europe is, on the whole, *better* than the United States, and that a European *identity* can and should be built upon these differences – or superiorities. Europe, in short, is the Not-America. This triple claim is quite popular in Europe today. You hear and see it made repeatedly, often in cruder forms, but always with some of the same themes: solidarity and social justice, the welfare state, secularism, no death penalty, the environment and international law, peaceful solutions and multilateralism, transcending sovereignty, counterbalancing the US. Moving the motion 'This House would rather be European than American' at the Oxford Union, a university debating society, one student charmingly summed up the advantages of being European thus: 'You're less likely to get shot. This is a good thing. And if you are going to get shot, you're going to have social provision in hospital.'[4]

The arguments for Europe as Not-America can be heard at every turn in Paris, but they are also the stuff of pleas by British authors such as Will Hutton for Janus Britain to 'choose Europe'. Even before George W. Bush came to power, a senior and respected German journalist, Claus Koch, was admonishing Europe to face up to the fact that 'the American empire must be declared the enemy'.[5] More sophisticated protagonists of the Not-America school, like Habermas, do not deny the existence of an overarching West. But, says the most agile dialectician of German foreign policy, Egon Bahr, there are two Wests: a European West and an American West.[6] Responding to the US Defense Secretary Donald Rumsfeld's famous dismissal of France and Germany as 'old Europe',[7] the German philosopher Peter Sloterdijk wrote: 'Old Europe, honourably represented by France and Germany, is the advanced faction of the West, which, learning the lessons of the twentieth century, has turned to a post-heroic cultural style, and a corresponding policy; the United States, by contrast, is stuck in the conventions of heroism.'[8]

This emerging European self-image was dramatically reinforced from America itself. According to the American writer Robert Kagan, Americans still operate in 'an anarchic Hobbesian world' where individual nations have to use military might, while Europeans are moving on to a world 'of laws and rules and transnational negotiation . . . a post-historical paradise of peace and relative prosperity, the realization of Immanuel Kant's "perpetual peace"'.[9] What came to be known as 'the Kagan thesis' appeared, with perfect timing, just as America was gearing up to go to war on Iraq, and made a large impact in Europe. 'Yes,' excited Europeans exclaimed, 'that's who we are: systematic peace-loving Kantians!' (Derrida and Habermas also invoked Kant.) The fact that this confirmation came from a rightwing American – indeed, one of the fabled, demonized cabal of 'neoconservatives' – doubled the impact. It was as if the devil had just certified the status of the angels.

Europeans had already derived their two biggest political ideas of the post-Cold War era from the United States: Francis Fukuyama's 'End of History' and Samuel Huntington's 'Clash of Civilizations'. Like Kagan's *boutade*, both had started as journal articles with a striking, deliberately overstated thesis. The authors' subsequent caveats and qualifications in the longer, book versions passed largely unnoticed. But this was something more. For here, Europeans were getting their own idea of themselves played back to them by an American, in an exaggerated form. We come from different planets! Americans are from Mars! And it must be true, because an *American* tells us so . . .

But which Europeans are we talking about? To leap from a scrapbook of quotations to a sweeping generalization about 'Europeans' or, worse still, '*the* Europeans', is to make precisely the mistake I've already criticized. In fact, it would take a whole essay to do justice to the views of a single European intellectual such as Jürgen Habermas.*

---

* The evolution of that profound thinker is curious: here is the intellectual high priest of German post-nationalism and 'constitutional patriotism' now pleading for an emotional identification with Europe, presented as distinct from and superior to America, in a fashion strongly reminiscent of the old-fashioned identity nationalism of European nation-states. So is it a case of German nationalism – bad, European nationalism – good?

It would call for a whole book to describe the variety of German approaches to this problem, another for France, yet another for Poland – and in geographical Europe there are at least forty countries, so we would need as many books. If you were serious, you would have to consider the governments, which change, the intellectuals, who write and talk so much, and the peoples, whose views may (we fondly imagine) be tracked in opinion polls and referendums. Combine those three levels, over time, in more than forty countries, and you have a moving matrix impossible to draw.

On both sides of the Atlantic there is plainly a felt need for simplifying generalization. To analyse is always to simplify, but here, the unavoidable simplifications of analysis are mixed up with other kinds of simplification: those of distance, ignorance and caricature, those for political and commercial effect, and those of an attempt to construct identity. In this chapter, I will look briefly at the European quest for identity, and some of the specific, national reasons for the 'Euro-Gaullist' stance taken by France and Germany in this crisis of the West. After stepping back to explore the reality of the alleged civilizational differences between Europe and America, I will examine what I call Euroatlanticism, the countervailing tendency to Euro-Gaullism. I make no apology for the fact that this part of our journey is like a winding path through a tangled wood. Europe *is* a tangled wood, and any cruder simplification does unacceptable violence to the reality. My conclusion, none the less, is simple: the whole of the new, enlarged Europe is engaged in a great argument between the forces of Euro-Gaullism and Euroatlanticism. This is the argument of the decade. On its outcome will depend the future of the West.

FIVE HUNDRED MILLION CHARACTERS IN SEARCH OF AN OTHER

Two alternative explanations were widely offered for the vehemence of European criticism of the United States in the early twenty-first-century crisis of the West. Some said it was caused by the provocative, high-handed, unilateralist behaviour of the Bush administration;

others, that it was an expression of deep-seated, almost genetic European 'anti-Americanism', a phenomenon comparable to (and, some suggested, in part motivated by) anti-Semitism. If it were the former, it could be burned away like morning mist by the sun of a different administration; if the latter, it would not disappear so easily.

The truth is, of course, that it depends which Europeans you are talking about. There are Europeans without a scintilla of anti-Americanism in their being, who were deeply worried by what they saw as the arrogant, clumsy, militaristic unilateralism of the Bush administration, and especially that part of it represented by Defense Secretary Donald Rumsfeld and Vice President Dick Cheney. So were many Americans. Were they anti-American Americans? However, it's also true that prejudicial stereotypes of America, which can be traced back in European political culture through most of the twentieth century, were given new vigour by a president who seemed to fit an old stereotype so well: the brash, philistine Texan cowboy. Behind my Oxford doctor's throwaway remark – 'that Bush is such a cowboy, isn't he?' – there lay a world of cultural assumptions, reinforced by images that America had projected of itself, on the big and small screen, in a thousand Westerns. Some of the matching assumptions about Europe's embattled moral and cultural superiority are also very old. A French school textbook, published in 1904, lamented that 'America is becoming the material pole of the world' and asked wistfully 'for how long will Europe remain its intellectual and moral pole?'[10]

Both these explanations, the short-term, contingent (anti-Bushism) and the long-term, endemic (anti-Americanism), contain elements of truth. But the most important part of the explanation lies in the historical shift following the end of the Cold War. Europe and America are no longer held together by a single, clear common enemy. The United States is now both absolutely and relatively more powerful, and needs Europe less than it did when the old continent was the central theatre of its confrontation with the Soviet Union. But the shift is even more profound and unsettling for Europe. For the United States, it poses the question 'what should the United States' role now be in the world?' It does not compel Americans to ask 'What is America?', let alone 'Where is America?' or 'Why do we have

America at all?' Yet it forces Europeans to ask precisely those fundamental questions: 'What is Europe?', 'Where does Europe end?' and 'Why Europe?' – meaning, what is the project of European Union ultimately for?

In the Cold War, the case for the European project was easy; or at least, so it appears with hindsight. A relatively small number of West European countries, which already had a great deal in common, were brought together by two overwhelming imperatives. First, never again should the nationalistic competition between nation-states reduce the continent to the horrors of total war and Holocaust, to that bestiality, humiliation, penury and rubble which everyone in the 1950s and 1960s still remembered. And second, a European community must be built as a bulwark against the threat of Soviet communism. So what was this Europe for? To save us Europeans from ourselves, who had made that bloody past, and from the Red Army; from the barbarians at the gate and the barbarian within us. These two themes sounded, like Wagnerian leitmotifs, through all the early debates about European integration. They grew fainter, more confused, in the music of the 1970s and 1980s, when enlargement from six to twelve member states made the European orchestra more polyphonous, and détente softened the conflict between communist East and anti-communist West; but they were still there in the minds of the men and women who shaped the European project.

Then came Europe's 9/11 of hope,* the fall of the Berlin Wall and that year of wonders, 1989, which saw the threat of Soviet communism softly and suddenly vanish away. What an opportunity – and what a crisis! Fifteen years later, the European Union comprises twenty-five enormously diverse European states, including, incredibly, three Baltic republics which in 1989 were still part of the Soviet Union. It stretches from the Atlantic to the River Bug, from the North Cape to Cyprus. The continent has never been so close to a dream of unity in freedom. These countries share a common market, a common legal framework,

---

* '9/11 of hope' may be easier to say on this side of the Atlantic because we don't instantly associate 9/11 with the telephone number for emergencies, which is 911 in the United States but 999 in Britain, and a bewildering assortment of different numbers in other European countries, as well as the standardized but little-known 112 across the European Union.

common political institutions; twelve of them have a single currency. The political project called 'Europe' goes both wider and deeper than it ever has before. But where on earth will it end, both geographically and politically? What is it ultimately *for*?

Not, obviously, to defend us against Soviet communism. That old, simplifying, uniting enemy has gone, and with it much of the enthusiasm of the United States for supporting European integration. Is it still to defend us against ourselves, against the European barbarian within? After all, European barbarism has just shown itself again, for a whole decade in the Balkans, with neighbour butchering neighbour, in fratricidal wars that cost more than 200,000 lives, and with the attempted ethnic cleansing of several million human beings, mainly Muslim Bosnians and Kosovars but also Christian Serbs and Croats. Once again, the West's 'intellectual and moral pole' has needed American help to stop Europeans murdering each other. So this is still a very good reason for 'making Europe'. However, it does not seem to be a compelling one for the majority of Europeans today. Most Europeans under the age of fifty now take peace and relative prosperity for granted. In this sense, Europe is a victim of its own success. And the fool's paradise is not just inhabited by West Europeans: in the 1990s, most Czechs were as indifferent to the plight of besieged Sarajevo as most Germans had been to the sufferings of Prague a decade before.

One much older account of Europe's purpose has been given a new lease of life since the 11 September 2001 terrorist attacks, and through the debate about Turkey's possible membership of the European Union. Shortly after the 9/11 attacks, the Italian prime minister Silvio Berlusconi made some typically crass remarks about the West's mission to civilize backward Islamic peoples.[11] The veteran Italian journalist Oriana Fallaci fulminated wildly against 'our Muslim invaders', engaged in a 'Reverse Crusade' to conquer and profane Europe.[12] In such remarks we see a garish resurrection of the original, medieval definition of 'Europe' as Christendom defending itself against militant Islam. The first known mention of 'Europeans' comes in a chronicle describing an eighth-century battle against the Arab heirs of Muhammed, who were by then advancing across the Pyrenees from what is now Spain into what is now France.[13]

'Europe' first became established as an alternative term for Christendom in the writing and preaching that the great Renaissance Pope Pius II directed against the encroaching Muslim Turks.[14] Habermas and other writers of the European left may trumpet secularism as a defining feature of contemporary Europe, but you have only to hear European Christian Democrats talking about Turkey and Islam to understand that the equation of Europe with Christendom is still far from dead.

Yet this old equation cannot be the basis of a viable political identity for Europe in the early twenty-first century. For a start, Europeans are now among the most secular people on earth. Many of those most directly engaged in the European project see it as a secular, humanist application of the Enlightenment. They ensured that Christianity did not even receive explicit mention as part of Europe's heritage in the preamble to the draft European constitution.[15] Moreover, those Europeans who are religious are increasingly likely to be Muslim rather than Christian. While no one knows exactly how many Muslims live in the European Union, legally or illegally, a minimum realistic estimate is 12 to 13 million.[16] There are perhaps another 7 million in Balkan countries such as Albania and Bosnia, which will sooner or later join the European Union. The EU has in principle accepted Turkey as a candidate for membership. Although Turkey is a secular state, its rapidly growing population of around 70 million people is largely Muslim. And this is not to count Russia, with perhaps as many as 20 million Muslims. The populations of Europe are ageing fast, so more immigrants will be needed to support the pensioners, and these will largely be Muslim immigrants. For this increasingly Muslim Europe to define itself against Islam would be ridiculous and suicidal.

The lifting of the Iron Curtain has therefore revealed a stage on which Europe must confront its own radical indeterminacy. In a sense, Europeans are now face-to-face with Eratosthenes, the Greek geographer who in about 220 BCE drew 'Europe' on a map, covering roughly the area we still know as Europe today.[17] This purely geographical delineation, though arbitrary, has at least the sanction of great antiquity. Yet according to Eratosthenes, Europe stopped at the Bosporus. In the Roman and Byzantine periods, what is now western Turkey was part of a single Mediterranean world; but when Europeans started to draw proper maps again, in the fifteenth century, they followed Eratosthenes and drew the frontier on the Bosporus. Now, partly as a result of promises made during the Cold War, the European Union has crossed even that ancient line, explicitly recognizing Turkey as a European country. So what on earth is to bind this far-flung group of twenty-five going on forty enormously disparate countries together? As the French historian Jacques le Goff once remarked: 'Europe has had a name for twenty-five centuries, but it is still in the design stage.'[18]

Sophisticated answers can, of course, be found about the need for larger units than the nation-state to meet 'the challenges of globalization'. These will not provide what I have called the emotional glue to keep this sprawling Union together. Traditionally, in all human communities, that glue has been found in the celebration of difference from (and usually superiority to) some other human community. Often, this 'Other' was an enemy fought in wars. These differences are both real and 'constructed' – evoked, imagined, dramatized by politicians, playwrights, poets, historians and songwriters. Britain, for example, a peculiar nation composed of four nations, was forged in real wars against France; but Britain also, to sharpen its own sense of what it was, 'created in France its opposite'.[19] Such identities are usually 'forged' in both senses of the word: beaten into shape while heated, and falsified.[20]

Europe, the German historian Rudolf von Thadden has argued, will not be made without an Other.[21] But what Other remains? America is one thing all Europeans – now so broadly defined – have in common. Since the United States is the most powerful country in the world, most Europeans share that mixture of fascination and resentment which dominant powers have always attracted. 'Anti-Americanism' is in this sense less like anti-Semitism than it is like anti-Britishism in the nineteenth century, anti-Frenchism in the eighteenth, anti-Romanism throughout the Roman empire, and, no doubt, anti-Mesopotamianism in the third millennium BCE. Henry Kissinger has interestingly compared attitudes in the EU to those in other contemporary regional groupings, such as the Association of Southeast Asian Nations (ASEAN) and Mercosur in South America. He argues that each grouping defines itself 'sometimes subconsciously, often deliberately . . . in distinction to the dominant powers in its region. For ASEAN, the foils are China and Japan (and, in time, probably India); for the European Union and Mercosur, the foil is the United States, *creating new rivalries even as they overcome traditional ones*'[22] (my italics).

This is not to say that the differences discovered by Habermas, Strauss-Kahn and other European writers don't exist. That remains to be examined. It is to say that there's a powerful temptation for anyone who believes in the project of European union to highlight and accentuate such differences: to define Europe by contrast with, if not outright opposition to, America. And the line between Europe as Not-America and Europe as Anti-America is not clearly marked on any map.

GAULLISM VERSUS CHURCHILLISM

'Euro-Gaullism' is a convenient label for this view of European identity. French intellectuals and politicians are its most frequent proponents. Yes, a French Gaullist parliamentarian agreed with me during a discussion in Paris, 'the West' certainly exists, but there is also, he insisted, something specific to Europe, 'and if I had to sum it up, I would say *l'intelligence européenne*'. The French Gaullists Jacques Chirac and Dominique de Villepin led the opposition to America's war on Iraq, in the name of 'old Europe' and a 'multipolar world'. However, it was Blair's Britain, not Bush's America, which insisted on the second UN resolution that Chirac's France then successfully blocked. At the finishing line, the diplomacy of the Iraq crisis came down to a clash of two old-European strategies, Gaullism and Churchillism. In the French case, as in the British, an overall approach to international relations was inextricably bound up with a national diplomatic strategy to preserve as much as possible of a former world power's dwindling status and influence.

The relation of Gaullisms to the historical Charles de Gaulle is as complex as that of Churchillisms to the real Churchill. We need to distinguish sharply between Gaullism at home and abroad. The former is a domestic political tendency of the centre-right, the latter an approach that can count on much wider support. Nor can we ever know what de Gaulle himself would have done. For all his pursuit of independence from the Americans, de Gaulle showed unstinting solidarity with the administration of John F. Kennedy during the Cuban missile crisis. Perhaps, contemplating Chirac's defiance of the United States over another matter that Washington considered vital to its national security, de Gaulle might have muttered *'surtout, je ne suis pas Gaulliste'*. In two separate imaginary conversations with the General in 2003, de Gaulle's French biographer and a distinguished British historian of France both came to the conclusion that he would have acted differently.[23]

Yet certainly the origins of these divergent strategies can be traced back to those two grand old sparring partners, Churchill and de Gaulle, and to one year: 1940. Nineteen-forty was, as David Reynolds has written, the fulcrum of the twentieth century.[24] For Churchill, that great Francophile, the traumatic fall of France meant launching Britain on the only path that remained available to preserve its greatness: conjuring a special relationship with the United States, however subordinate Britain's role might at times become. For de Gaulle, it meant launching a crusade to restore the greatness of France from the ashes of total defeat. In the first place this involved convincing the French that their true national spirit lay in the anti-Nazi Resistance, and in securing recognition for France as a great power during and immediately after the war.

When he returned to office in 1958, de Gaulle was smarting from another blow to French pride, this time delivered by the United States over Suez. Again, Britain and France drew very different conclusions. Britain would stick closer than ever to Washington while de Gaulle set out to bolster French greatness through what he called a 'European Europe'. This meant a warm embrace of Germany, cultivating relations with Russia and China, demonstrating independence from the United States by withdrawing from the military structures of Nato, and his famous *'non'* to British membership in the European Community. When Paul Reynaud, the prime minister of 1940 whom both de Gaulle and Churchill had urged to go on resisting Hitler's advancing armies, dared criticize de Gaulle's *'non'* to Britain in 1963, de Gaulle sent him a letter. Or rather, an empty envelope – but on the back was written, in a familiar hand, 'if absent, forward to Agincourt or Waterloo'.[25] The ancient rivalry with England is as much a constituent part of Gaullism as the modern differences with the United States.

Unlike the British, the French are generally quite happy to speak for Europe and to adjudicate which Europe is or is not truly 'European'. This comes the more easily because there is an old French tradition, dating back at least to the eighteenth century, of regarding Europe as an extension of France. In 1777 an Italo-French man of letters, Louis-Antoine Carracioli, even published a book entitled *Paris le modèle des nations étrangères ou l'Europe française* (Paris, the Model for Foreign Nations, or French Europe).[26] 'He talks of Europe, and means France,' Macmillan commented on de Gaulle.[27] With just a little exaggeration we might say that the British are incapable of identifying themselves with Europe and the French are incapable of distinguishing themselves from it.

Having suffered that shattering defeat in 1940, and German occupation, and many changes of constitution (the country is now on its *Fifth* Republic), the French are also less inclined than the British – more particularly, the English – to fetishize formal sovereignty. Even French conservatives have usually concluded that national power and influence may be maximized through the institutions of European integration. De Gaulle himself was more reserved than many of his compatriots in this regard. He was reluctant to share more sovereignty than was strictly necessary in the European Community, and provoked its first great internal crisis by his attitude. His Europe was to be, so far as possible, intergovernmental rather than supranational. He wanted to make Europe *à l'Anglaise*, but without the English. None the less, France's 'rank' was to be secured through the institutions of Europe, with French political leadership supported by Germany's economic weight. It's no accident that at the beginning of the twenty-first century, de Gaulle's grandson, Pierre de Boissieu, sat in Brussels, pulling the strings at the intergovernmental heart of the European Union.[28]

Other French politicians – not domestically Gaullists, indeed anti-Gaullists – have been prepared to go much further towards a supranational or 'federal' Europe. But for them, too, the specifically French motivation is almost invariably present – just as the specifically British motivation is rarely absent among British advocates of Atlanticism. A classic example is Jacques Delors, the French socialist who, as head of the European Commission, presided over dramatic advances in European integration, from the completion of the single market to the Maastricht Treaty, which paved the way for European monetary union. In 1988 Delors published a book entitled *La France par l'Europe* – the very title is eloquent. It contained this sentence: 'Creating Europe is a way of regaining the degree of liberty necessary for a "certain idea of France".'[29] A 'certain idea of France' was, of course, de Gaulle's signature phrase.

The fall of the Berlin Wall plunged this strategy into crisis. With the enlargement of the European Union to include the new democracies of central and eastern Europe, Germany, not France, would be at its centre. Germany, soon united and fully sovereign, would no longer be prepared to play the horse to France's rider – a simile that de Gaulle himself is alleged to have used. However skilful its diplomacy, France would not be able to shape European policy in a Europe of twenty-five member states as it had in a Europe of twelve, or, better still, the original six.

The French language, too, would be further marginalized. Once the universal language of European civilization and international diplomacy, French is now used less and less: vanquished by American English and even overtaken by Spanish. In vain do French politicians attempt to restrict the amount of American music on the radio, American films on television, and Franglais everywhere. When the European Court of Justice ruled that EU governments could not require all foodstuffs on sale in their countries to be labelled in the national language, a furious article in *Le Monde* denounced this treacherous manoeuvre of the 'Anglophone party in Europe', and 'the programmed hegemony of Anglo-American'. However, the author concluded, the French with their 'cultural exception', now rebaptized as 'diversity', will fight back. Adapting Marx, he proclaimed a fighting slogan: 'Cultural and linguistic minorities of all countries, unite!'[30] Here was a fine example of the universalization of a national dilemma. The French have become an endangered minority – therefore they will be the spokesman of all endangered minorities.

You can't begin to understand the emotions behind the French position in the early twenty-first-century crisis of the West unless you appreciate the full trauma of this loss of political and cultural centrality – in the world, in Europe, and now even in the European Union. The French Gaullist foreign minister, Dominique de Villepin, personified the Euro-Gaullist resistance to American policy when he spoke 'in this temple of the united nations' (that is, the UN Security Council chamber in New York) on 14 February 2003. Making an obvious allusion to Donald Rumsfeld's dismissal of 'old Europe', he concluded 'this message comes to you today from an old country, France, from a continent like mine, Europe, which has known wars, occupation and barbarity'.[31] In a rare gesture, the multinational audience in the UN chamber applauded.

It must have been an intoxicating moment for de Villepin, a forty-nine-year-old professional diplomat and man of letters who had recently published an 823-page book entitled *Éloge des voleurs de feu* (Hymn to the Thieves of Fire), evoking the glorious if fated role of the French poet in a nasty world. A year earlier he had produced *Le cri de la Gargouille* (The Cry of the Gargoyle), a plangent appeal to France to rouse itself 'from the temptation of resignation [that] threatens a nation as it feels torpor overcoming it'. 'For many abroad,' he wrote, 'the French funeral has already been held!'[32] And before that, he published *Les Cent-Jours ou l'esprit de sacrifice* (The Hundred Days or the Spirit of Sacrifice), which celebrated, in equally purple prose, Napoleon's last, heroic, doomed attempt to regain power – ending at the battle of Waterloo.

It would be absurd to suggest that all his compatriots embraced this particular political aesthetic of glorious if doomed resistance, let alone that all Euro-Gaullists share the French national complexes. But Euro-Gaullism is unimaginable without the contribution of French Gaullists, and Americans have not been wrong to see in France the political leader of Europe as Not-America.

GERMAN EMOTIONS

France is the leader, but it was Germany that made the difference over Iraq. Without German involvement there would have been no Paris–Berlin–Moscow axis in 2003. The West would not have split down the middle. In defying America, France was continuing the foreign policy tradition of its Fifth Republic; Germany was abruptly departing from the foreign policy tradition of its Federal Republic. Since the 1960s there had always been German Gaullists, but the golden rule of (West) German foreign policy was always to stay as close as possible to both Paris and Washington. This meant that the German position was usually somewhere between the French and the British ones. Knowing that American support was vital to the Federal Republic and West Berlin in the Cold War, Konrad Adenauer had never gone with de Gaulle against the US. Every federal chancellor since Adenauer had maintained this line. Grateful to America for its wholehearted pursuit of German unification – by contrast with the hesitations of Britain and France – Helmut Kohl and, in his early years as chancellor, Gerhard Schröder, continued the tradition. It was also well accepted at home. In a 1995 poll, 50 per cent of those asked said the United States was Germany's best friend.[33]

When he came to power in 1998, Chancellor Schröder was concerned that unified Germany should behave, and be treated, as a 'normal' grown-up European nation-state, not a hunchback of history.[34] This 'new normality' meant that he would send German troops to help bring peace and freedom to Kosovo, and take a leading role in the reconstruction of post-Taliban Afghanistan. But for him, it also meant that he would on occasion say 'no' to the United States. His 'no' over Iraq came in a very messy way. In the spring and early summer of 2002 he gave Bush to understand that Germany would not publicly oppose an action to 'do' Iraq. Then, faced with the prospect of losing an election, he suddenly came out on the hustings against any war on Iraq. He would not, he said, 'click his heels' and say 'yes' to whatever America decided.[35] President Bush felt personally betrayed. Germany was then cold-shouldered by Washington in a way unimaginable during the Cold War, thus in turn deeply offending the German chancellor. Umbrage was given, taken, and given again.

There are a couple of general lessons to be learned here. One is about the danger of political opportunism, such as Schröder's, which allows even basic tenets of a nation's foreign policy to be abandoned in the cause of re-election. Another is about the folly of making the relations between major states dependent on the personal relations between stubborn middle-aged men.

It is, however, as important to understand the specific German emotions to which Schröder appealed and by which, at least to some extent, he and his colleagues were also swayed. American observers were quick to spy 'anti-Americanism'. Of course there was a seam of anti-Americanism in Germany, as there was in every European country. 'What we hold against the American nation', said a German government press statement in 1942, 'is in the first place [its] complete lack of culture.'[36] The signatory was Adolf Hitler. In revulsion against that perverted notion of German 'culture', and as a result of American occupation and support, West Germany after 1945 became one of the most Americanized and pro-American societies in Europe. 'Germans may make bad Germans,' America's viceroy in Germany, General Lucius D. Clay, is supposed to have said, 'but they make damn good Americans.'[37]

At West Berlin's Tegel airport they erected a solitary signpost: 'Los Angeles 9684 km'. An arrow helpfully points in the right direction. In the mental geography of the West Germans, it often seemed that Los Angeles was closer than Leipzig, the Atlantic narrower than the River Oder. However, the protest generation of 1968 was, to say the least, highly critical of 'American' imperialism – partly in reaction to what they saw as the excessive and even slavish pro-Americanism of their parents, whom they also charged with complicity in Nazism. Gerhard Schröder and his foreign minister, Joschka Fischer, both belonged to Germany's class of '68. That matters. But two other sources of emotion matter at least as much.

First, the Germans, much more than the British or the French, have a deep and vivid revulsion from all and any war. In 2002/3, the country was going through an intensive phase of collective 'recovered memory', relating particularly to the horrors of the wartime bombing of German cities, which had recently been evoked in television

programmes and bestselling books.* We must do everything to avoid
a war over Iraq, said Germany's defence minister during a television
discussion in February 2003, 'because millions of innocent people
will die in it'.[38] Millions? French opposition to 'America's war' was
mainly about America; German opposition was about both war and
America, in roughly equal parts.

For a second source of deep frustration was that Germans very
much wanted their country to be treated by America as a grown-up.
France had been trying to restore its 'rank' as a great power since
1945, but it had at least been a fully sovereign country – or if it surrendered sovereignty, it did so voluntarily, trading *de jure* sovereignty
for *de facto* power. Germany, by contrast, had until 1990 been a
divided country, its sovereignty involuntarily limited by treaty, its
once and future capital city divided by a concrete wall and cut into
sectors still humiliatingly controlled by Soviet, American, British and
French military administrations. Its 'normality' as a sovereign nation-
state was brand new and precious. Germans wanted to be wooed
with the promise of being 'partners in leadership', as President
George H. W. Bush had done in 1989.[39] They hated the way they
were being treated by his son. Phrases like 'not a colony', 'not to be
treated as a vassal' and 'the need for emancipation' surfaced again
and again in the German debates.[40]

Beyond political opportunism, this was, I believe, the dominant
emotion in Schröder's case. Nor was it absent in the German foreign
minister, Joschka Fischer. I had a memorable conversation with Fischer
in the summer of 2003. We met on a Sunday afternoon at a café in central (formerly East) Berlin. He was dressed not in one of his formal
three-piece suits but in T-shirt, jeans and trainers: American uniform.
He said wise and mature things about mending the rifts in the West. He
illustrated with two glasses and a sugar bowl on the café table how
Germany was almost invariably somewhere between France and
Britain: closer to London on some issues, closer to Paris on others.

* I say 'recovered memory' because no one under the age of fifty-seven could possibly
have remembered the wartime bombing, since they would not have been born in
1945. Still, they sometimes talked as if they did: 'we remember', 'we, who suffered'.
Another interesting example of the uses of 'we'.

For the foreseeable future, he observed, Europe would oscillate between the Gaullism of Paris and the Atlanticism of London. The arguments with the United States were 'all in the family'. But then, as I pressed him on the detail of his government's troubled relations with the Bush administration in Washington, he leaned forward conspiratorially and muttered 'don't we want to make a Boston tea party?'[41] It was a joke, of course. Perhaps it was meant to tease an Englishman about Blair's too servile proximity to Bush. The Boston tea party, he added, had done both Britain and America good. None the less, this was an astonishing thing for a German foreign minister to say. The clear implication was that Europe (or who else were 'we'?) was in some sense a colony of the United States. When he got up to leave, he completed his all-American uniform by putting on a black baseball cap inscribed 'American Eagle'. 'Yes,' he smiled, 'I bought it in Boston.'

The leader of the opposition Christian Democrats, Angela Merkel, used a motherly metaphor to describe these German emotions. With its constant talk of 'emancipation', Schröder's Germany was, she said, like a thirteen-year-old child going through puberty – and revolting against the American dad.[42] These emotions were strong and widely shared. Combined with revulsion against war as such, hostility to Bush as the stereotypical Texan cowboy, and an eminently reasonable scepticism about the actual case for military action to depose Saddam Hussein, they produced a dramatic swing in German public opinion – from America to Europe. The proportion of people who thought America was Germany's best friend fell from that 50 per cent in 1995 to just 11 per cent in March 2003.[43] Those who thought France was Germany's most reliable partner rose from 23 per cent in 1996 to 56 per cent in 2003.[44] In another poll, people were asked whether the European Union or the United States was more important to the vital interests of their country. In summer 2002, 20 per cent of Germans said the US and 55 per cent said the EU; a year later, just 6 per cent said the US and 81 per cent said the EU.[45]

It would be very premature to deduce from these startling results a permanent shift from German Atlanticism to German Gaullism. What they do show is the extreme volatility of opinion in Europe's central power. For though Tony Blair might like to describe Britain's role as 'pivotal', Europe's real pivot is Germany.

IS EUROPE BETTER THAN AMERICA?

We could go on exploring the different mix of motives in, say, Italy, Spain, Greece or the Netherlands, and every case would be interestingly different. But I've probably said enough to indicate why a view of Europe as Not-America has been so vigorously propagated by political intellectuals and intellectual politicians in Europe at the turn of this century. We now have to step back and ask: is the claim of Europe's civilizational difference from America true? And is it believed by enough Europeans to forge a sustainable political identity? The answers to these two questions are quite distinct. Something can be true but not believed, or believed but not true. Most national identities have a large dose of the latter. A nation, it has been said, is a group of people united by a common dislike of their neighbours and a shared misunderstanding of their own past.

Let's start with the question 'is it true?' The claim is that Europe is a) different from and b) better than the United States. The claim of difference has to mean, if it's serious, that European countries have important things in common that also distinguish them – each and all – from the United States. Or, to rephrase it as another question: do all Europeans have more in common with each other than they do with Americans? How, beyond personal impressions, can we measure significant difference between such vast assemblages of individual human beings? The best that scholars can come up with is to look, over time, at the policies of states and groups of states, at economic and social statistics, and at opinion polls that try, with some sophistication, to get at attitudes and underlying values.

The most salient European–American differences seem to cluster around six things: religion, the role of the state, inequality, the environment, national sovereignty, and, last but not least, the ownership of guns and capital punishment for using them. Americans are, in aggregate, much more religious than Europeans. A few striking results from recent opinion polls illustrate this clearly: 83 per cent of

Americans say they regard God as important or very important, compared with 49 per cent of Europeans; 47 per cent of Americans say they attend church at least once a week, as against less than 20 per cent of Europeans;[46] 58 per cent of Americans say you have to believe in God in order to be moral.[47] Four out of every five Americans believe in life after death, and one in three thinks the Bible is 'God's word, literally true'.[48] In its religiosity, America is the great exception: the one country in the world to be both rich and religious.

Americans, in aggregate, also think it more important that government should leave them free to pursue their own goals, whereas Europeans think it more important that governments should guarantee that no one is in need.[49] Correspondingly, Americans feel that success or failure depends more on the individual's own efforts.[50] Europe consequently has more of the 'welfare state' than the United States. The federal tax burden in the United States is under 30 per cent, whereas the average tax burden for the fifteen member states of the European Union in 2003 was just over 40 per cent.[51]

In the distribution of wealth, America is more unequal than most European countries. The richest tenth of the population earns nearly six times more than the poorest tenth; in Germany and France, the ratio is just over three to one. The United States also has the largest proportion of its people in long-term poverty.[52] Meanwhile, it boasts some three million millionaires. The richest 1 per cent of the population hold nearly two fifths of the country's wealth.[53] So middle-class America is sandwiched between a chronically poor underclass and a super-rich overclass. As we shall see in a later chapter, America also stands out from other developed countries in its gas-guzzling environmental profligacy, a product of the distinctive 'American way of life'.

Most Americans are more patriotic than most Europeans. Even before the surge of emotion prompted by the 9/11 attacks, 72 per cent of Americans said they were 'very proud' of their country, compared with just 49 per cent of the British and 40 per cent of Germans.[54] Americans, unlike most Europeans, also own guns; lots of them. There are some nine guns in private hands for every ten Americans, compared with less than three for every ten Europeans.[55] The homicide rate in the United States is more than quadruple those in Britain,

France and Germany, despite what many Europeans regard as the barbaric deterrent of capital punishment.[56]

So Habermas's catalogue of European–American difference is not based on nothing. From the other side of the Atlantic, the American social scientist Seymour Martin Lipset has summarized these differences as 'American Exceptionalism'.[57] Yet such aggregate figures only tell part of the story. For a start, which Europe are we talking about? Habermas's European vision immediately struck another leading German political thinker, Ralf Dahrendorf, as an evocation of the old West Germany before unification.[58] Habermas's generalizations may hold to some extent for the original six member states of the European Community, but even in the European Union of fifteen member states, at the time Habermas was writing, and certainly in today's European Union of twenty-five, let alone in the geographical Europe of forty-plus, the divergences between European countries are immense.

For example, it is not empirically serious to talk of a single 'European model' of democratic capitalism. A major academic study comparing 'Varieties of Capitalism' identifies two major types of capitalist economy: the liberal market economy and the coordinated market economy.[59] It classifies Britain and Ireland, along with America, as liberal market economies; Germany, Belgium, the Netherlands and the Scandinavian countries are placed among the coordinated market economies. The authors find that France, Italy, Spain, Portugal and Greece occupy 'more ambiguous positions', possibly constituting 'another type of capitalism, sometimes described as "Mediterranean", marked by a large agrarian sector and recent histories of extensive state intervention'.[60] All vary in their labour markets and social policies. The tax burden in Sweden is more than 50 per cent of its gross domestic product, whereas in Britain the figure is less than 38 per cent.[61]

So that is three sorts of capitalism among just fifteen EU states. This picture does not begin to consider the new capitalist economies of central and eastern Europe, very different again, that are now inside the EU; let alone those European countries, such as Ukraine, which are not yet capitalist democracies heading towards EU membership. Does the life of a lawyer in Hamburg more closely resemble that of a lawyer in Kiev or in Boston? The answer must surely be Boston. The same would be true of a teacher, a plumber or a bus driver. Like nation-builders of old, Habermas and others are *attributing* to a very diverse human community commonalities that do not yet exist, in the hope that this will help those commonalities to emerge. The 'European model' is a prescription presented as a description.

Even on the indicators that seem most clearly to reveal a transatlantic gulf, the differences across the wider Europe can be very large. Take patriotism, for example. Three out of every four people in Ireland say they are 'very proud' of their country – more than in the United States – and the Poles are nearly as proud, while only one in five of the Dutch confess to such an old-fashioned sentiment.[62] Or take religion: more Ukrainians than Americans say it is necessary to believe in God to be moral, and a staggering 84 per cent of Turks agree – though most of them would know that God as Allah. Even between France and Germany there is a large gap on that question: 33 per cent of Germans agree, against only 13 per cent of the French.[63] Habermas says it is unimaginable that in Europe a president would begin his daily business with public prayer, but this is exactly what the British parliament does. The United States has never had an established church; Britain still has one, and progressive, welfarist Sweden only disestablished its Lutheran Church in 2000. It's undoubtedly true that European societies are generally more secular, and the gap between religion and politics is becoming wider in Europe even as it narrows in America. Yet, as we've seen, the afterlife of Christendom still has a powerful influence on the self-definition of Europe.

The generalizations about America may seem more securely founded. But here, too, we face a puzzle. There's an old joke from the time when European dictatorships, of left and right, were in the habit of declaring 99 per cent 'yes' votes on a 99 per cent turnout: 'Why is it that I only meet the 1 per cent?' Quite a few Europeans feel this way when they try to compare their own, personal American encounters with the poll results. Why? Perhaps because they spend their time on the more liberal East and West coasts rather than in the conservative Midwest and South.

In fact, polling analysis shows consistent, deep differences between these two Americas – tagged, rather confusingly to a European ear, 'blue America' (for the more liberal states, especially those on the two coasts) and 'red America' (for the big L of the conservative heartlands and the South). If one disaggregates 'blue' and 'red' America, then 'blue' America often turns out to be a quite European shade of pink. On several of the key social issues claimed as defining Europe, American Democrats turn out to be closer to Europeans than they are to Republicans. And this 'blue' America is not a small, embattled minority. If you add up the votes cast in the 2000 presidential election for the Democrat Al Gore and the left-wing maverick Ralph Nader, they outnumber by more than three million those cast for the conservative Republican George W. Bush.

The profusion of guns is a real difference between America and Europe – except for parts of Europe's 'Wild East', in the Balkans and today's eastern Europe (Ukraine, Belarus, Moldova), where handguns are still freely toted. It's tempting to extrapolate from this American domestic phenomenon to foreign policy: cowboys at home, cowboys abroad. The American satirist Michael Moore does this vividly in his film *Bowling for Columbine*, drawing an imaginative connection between the shootings at Columbine High School in Colorado and the Clinton administration's bombing of Serbia. A slightly more serious version of this argument is advanced by Robert Kagan: Americans retain a readiness to use military force in a dangerous 'Hobbesian' world.

Except that, from the end of the Vietnam War to the 11 September 2001 terrorist attacks, France and Britain were generally more willing to send their soldiers into dangerous action than the United States. It was Tony Blair who urged the American president to deploy ground troops in Kosovo, while French troops repeatedly intervened in Africa. It was American governments that were petrified of their boys coming home in the notorious bodybags. On this record, the two most important military powers in Europe, the British and the French, are at least as much 'from Mars' as the Americans. After 9/11, many Americans felt their country was under attack, so a majority supported the wars in both Afghanistan and Iraq. Only time will tell how lasting this shift in attitudes will be. On 15 February

2003 – that birthday of the 'European nation' – an estimated 200,000 people in San Francisco and 100,000 people in New York protested against President Bush's proposed war on Iraq.[64] Presumably that made them Europeans too?

Some 200,000 people also demonstrated in Sydney, Australia, which brings us to a further problem with the stylization of difference between Europe and America. What about the other capitalist democracies of the developed world? Are they not wrestling with the same problems of balancing wealth-creation and distribution, individual enterprise and social cohesion? Are they not confronting the same difficult dilemmas of war and peace? The Australian government, for example, sent troops to participate in the Iraq War, but only half the population supported it.[65] If you add Australia, Canada, Japan and the other developed countries in the Organization for Economic Cooperation and Development (OECD) to the scatter charts, America and Europe look less than ever like two distinct and discrete blocks.[66]

Thus, in the considered view of the comparative political economists, Canada, Australia and New Zealand join America, Britain and Ireland as liberal market economies. In economics, the Anglosphere is an empirical reality. Meanwhile, Japan joins Germany as a coordinated market economy, and Turkey sits somewhere with France and Spain as a Mediterranean one.[67] In respect of the welfare state, Canada and Australia are somewhere in between America and continental Europe – along with Britain. America is, in Seymour Martin Lipset's phrase, the 'welfare laggard' of the developed world.[68] But even that contrast is not as stark as many Europeans believe.

Take healthcare, for example. America actually spends a larger proportion of its gross domestic product on health than any European country – 13.9 per cent in 2001. The nearest European country was Switzerland, with 10.9 per cent, while Britain spent just 7.6 per cent.[69] Yes, the larger part of this was private healthcare, for those Americans who could afford it. But remarkably, the figure for *public* expenditure on health was exactly the same in Britain and the United States: 6.2 per cent of GDP. America's Medicaid programme alone spends more on caring for 40 million poor Americans than Britain's cherished National Health Service does on looking after all the country's 60 million people.[70] Spends it badly, to be sure: if I were old, poor and sick, I'd rather be in Britain. None the less, except for its worst inner-city slums, America is not the primitive capitalist jungle of European imagination, where human beings slink away like wounded animals to die in bloodstained holes.

Altogether, America's public spending priorities are less different from those of European welfare states than you might think. The US budget distinguishes between National Defense and Human Resources, in which it includes education, training, employment, social services, social security and healthcare – in short, the 'social' functions of the state, broadly conceived. It is interesting to track the ratio between them over the last sixty years. In 1945, the ratio was 89 per cent on defence to 2 per cent on social spending (the balance is accounted for by other budget categories). As late as 1970, America spent more on national defence than on social welfare. By the end of the Cold War, however, the ratio was roughly 24: 49 (defence: social), and in the last year of the Clinton administration it had fallen to 16: 62. All the huge hikes in military spending under George W. Bush only pushed that up to an estimated 20:65 in 2004.[71] As the country's ageing and often overweight baby-boomers move into retirement, either that ratio will increase still more to the advantage of domestic social spending or the system will go bust. Just like Europe.

Ah, you may say, but what about the underlying *values* that inform the whole European approach? Surely these are different? Values are tricky things to measure, but there's a group of professional pollsters and analysts who have spent more than twenty years trying to do exactly that. Consolidating and cross-checking the responses of more than 120,000 people in 81 countries, in the latest round of the World Values Survey, Ronald Inglehart has drawn a 'cultural map' of the world along what seem to be two key axes.[72] The result is printed on page 257 below. As you will see, there is no single, solid bloc of Europe versus America. Instead, Inglehart identifies distinctive though adjacent groupings of Catholic Europe, Protestant Europe, English-speaking, and ex-Communist countries. On the Inglehart values map, France is closer to Australia than it is to Sweden, let alone to Bulgaria. Of course, the methodology and choice of criteria can be disputed. But if we were trying to build a European identity around, say, hair colour or vegetables, and the experts in hair colour or vegetables told us there is no distinctive European hair colour or vegetable, we would surely take notice. Why not with values?

The Euro-Gaullist claim is not just that Europe is different; it's that Europe is better. (Hard to build a European patriotism around the idea that Europe is worse.) In what sense is this true? The economic historians find no clear evidence that one variant of capitalism has produced a better long-term economic performance than another. Different models have different advantages – and disadvantages. For example, a liberal market economy gets more people into paid employment, while a coordinated market economy has lower income differentials and makes more welfare provision for those out of work.[73] But is it better for someone to have badly paid work, as in America, or, as in Germany, slightly better-paid long-term unemployment? It's a matter of opinion which of the two is more debilitating for the human spirit. After all, the European Union's own charter of rights includes the 'right to engage in work'.[74]

You can be fired more brutally in the US; you can also be hired more easily. Americans work more and more; most West Europeans work less and less. In 1999, the Germans worked on average just over 1,500 hours per year against the Americans' nearly 2,000.[75] Almost three quarters of the population of working age in the United States was employed, compared with less than two thirds of the Germans and French.[76] (The British were once again in between, with just over 1,700 hours worked on average per year and more than 70 per cent of the working-age population in employment.) However, those Europeans lucky enough to have a job are generally guaranteed a higher minimum wage and more job security. This is what we call 'social' Europe – and it's a choice. Especially in the 'Mediterranean' societies, it leaves more time for the other good things of life: family, friends, food, recreation, *la dolce vita*. However, that comes at a price; one that is paid most painfully by the long-term unemployed, including a disproportionately large number of young people from Europe's Muslim immigrant communities.

America spends far more money on research and development than Europe: not just military but also medical. So Americans work out the newest, most original ways to take human lives but also to save them, to kill and to cure. Primary education is excellent in Scandinavia; higher education is better in America – unsurprisingly, since the US spends 2.7 per cent of its gross domestic product on it, compared to 1.0 per cent in Britain and Germany.[77] Europe might still like to think of itself as 'the intellectual and moral pole' but the top American universities are the best in the world. Europeans redistribute more money to the poor via the state, but Americans give far more in private philanthropy.[78]

Many European societies, especially Britain and France, still suffer the curse of class, but American society still has the curse of race – the legacy of slavery. On the other hand, America is better than Europe at making new immigrants feel at home. The German government famously offered long-term residence to 20,000 Indian IT specialists, but the Indians preferred Silicon Valley.[79] Comparative polling shows Americans taking a far more positive view of their ethnic minorities than Europeans do.[80] How, then, will Europe cope with the massive inflow of Muslim immigrants? Might it, perhaps, learn from America?

Inevitably, all that I can offer here is a small scattershot of examples, to chip away at the mind-walls of prejudice and constructed difference between Europe and America. Yet most of us can add to these more or less scientific findings our own personal impressions of Europe and America, Europeans and Americans. Taking all in all, we may emerge from this tangled jungle of claims and data with two alternative conclusions:

a) 'America and Europe are two different, strongly contrasting civilizations, and one is better.' (For 'one' insert Europe or America according to taste.)

b) 'America and most of the diverse countries of Europe belong to a wider family of developed, liberal democracies. America is better in some ways, Europe in others.'

Statement b) is less interesting, less galvanizing, but it has the boring old merit of being true.

EUROATLANTICISM

To be sure, Europeans can believe the claim of civilizational differ-ence and moral superiority even if it is not true. In a poll conducted in the summer of 2003, 79 per cent of Europeans said they thought Europeans and Americans have different 'social and cultural values'.[81] Whether or not the facts bear out that belief, the belief is itself an important fact. Yet overall, the polls present a more contra-dictory and volatile picture than this one spectacular finding would suggest; and polls, like X-rays, only capture one black-and-white slice of an intricate reality. The reality is that Europeans are deeply divided about the United States and Europe's relationship to it. The divisions run through political parties, social classes and intellectual milieux; they also run through individual hearts and minds. Many a European can exclaim, like Goethe's Faust, that two souls contend in his troubled breast.

In fact, Europeans spend far more time talking about America than they do talking about Europe. The Convention on the Future of Europe, which met throughout the period of the Iraq crisis to produce a draft European constitution, was supposed to generate a Europe-wide political debate. Jürgen Habermas hoped that intensive com-munication between Europeans about the constitution would help create a European public sphere.[82] Perhaps this would even be the embryo of a European *demos*. Instead, most Europeans spent the year of the Convention debating American policy and the Iraq War. The president they argued about was not the proposed president of Europe but the president of the United States. As we've seen, Habermas himself ended up seeking Europe's intercommunicative identity not in the constitutional debate but in opposition to Bush's war and the American 'Other'. It's not just in Britain that your atti-tude to the United States is a defining feature of your political iden-tity. Of all Europeans, we can say: tell me your America and I will tell you who you are.

Typically, even Europeans' characterization of their own divisions is borrowed from America. On 22 January 2003, as the entire parlia-ments of France and Germany were meeting in Versailles to reaffirm their countries' special relationship, the American Defense Secretary

Donald Rumsfeld was asked at a press conference about European reluctance to join his war against Iraq. 'You're thinking of Europe as Germany and France,' he replied. 'I don't. I think that's old Europe.'[83] The centre of gravity of 'Nato Europe' was shifting to the east, he said, and there were lots of other countries in Europe who were 'with the United States' and not with France and Germany. Eight days later, an article appeared in the *Wall Street Journal Europe*, and a number of European newspapers, which seemed to bear out this contention. Signed by the leaders of eight European states – Spain, Britain, Italy, Denmark, Portugal, Poland, Hungary and the Czech Republic – what became known as the 'Letter of Eight' was not, as Habermas claimed, a 'declaration of loyalty to Bush', but more a general reaffirmation of a Western community of values and transatlantic solidarity in the war against terrorism.[84] Shortly thereafter, following some behind-the-scenes drafting by a forceful American advocate of Nato enlargement, the leaders of ten central and east European countries that were applying to join Nato (the 'Vilnius Ten') signed an open letter with even more explicit support for the United States.[85]

Europeans, having obsessively discussed two American big ideas, the 'end of history' and the 'clash of civilizations', and then seized on the American Robert Kagan's essay to characterize their own elusive identity, now went around clucking about 'old Europe' and 'new Europe' in a thousand conferences, speeches and commentaries, as if Donald Rumsfeld were some Michelet, Gibbon or Ranke, speaking with profound authority on the deep divisions of European history. (Couldn't Europeans have a big idea of their own for a change? Or did intellectual hegemony inevitably go with political hegemony?) This fascination with Rumsfeld's crude distinction was justified only in so far as his comment reflected an attempt by part of the Bush administration to 'divide and rule' in Europe.

As analysis, the dichotomy between 'old Europe' and 'new Europe' has somewhat less value than a cartoon-strip. Poland, Spain and Britain are hardly 'new'. When Dominique de Villepin criticized American policy at the UN Security Council on behalf of his 'old country' and continent, the British foreign secretary Jack Straw replied that he also came from a very old country, 'founded in 1066 by the French'.[86] The implication of Rumsfeld's distinction was that there was a group of European countries who were solidly pro-American and another group who were solidly anti-American. This was completely wrong. In all these countries, the majority in public opinion polls was consistently against Rumsfeld's war. Political and intellectual opinion was also divided, and even the governments had many doubts. Tony Blair and José Maria Aznar may have been convinced of the case for war against Iraq, but many of their ministerial colleagues were not. Silvio Berlusconi of Italy told Bush he thought the war was ill-advised, but said he would support it out of solidarity with the United States. A change of government in Italy or Spain could rapidly have produced a different stance; as it might have done in Germany, but in the other direction.

Against the motley array of constituencies and individuals that I've called 'Euro-Gaullist' there's another motley array that can be labelled 'Euroatlanticist'. Britain is a traditional bulwark of Atlanticism, but divided, as we have seen, between those who reject the European side of the Blair bridge project, those who reject the American side, and a few who still reject both. Spain and Portugal are also torn. Both countries have their own historic Atlanticisms. These connect them more directly with Spanish- and Portuguese-speaking Latin America, although North America too is becoming increasingly Spanish-speaking. However, the Spanish right, with a long memory, still recalls how the Americans robbed Spain of the remains of its transatlantic empire at the end of the nineteenth century; the Spanish left has not forgotten how the US supported General Franco. Ireland – to stay with the countries of Europe's Atlantic rim – is deeply conscious of its ties to 34 million Irish-Americans,[87] but it is also a traditionally neutral state that strongly identifies with Roman Catholic Europe, and with the European Union in which it has so visibly prospered.

The most unambiguous voices of Euroatlanticism come from the new democracies of central and eastern Europe, and especially from the largest of them, Poland. Poland, like Ireland, is tied to the United States by a history of immigration. There are some 10 million Americans of Polish origin and, unlike Americans of German origin, many of them keep lively connections with the motherland. A Woodrow Wilson Square in Warsaw reminds Poles of America's part in resurrecting independent Poland after the First World War. Despite Polish resentment of the American (and British) 'betrayal' at Yalta in 1945, most Poles feel a debt of gratitude to the United States for helping them win their own liberation from communism during the Cold War. In France and Germany, the student protest of 1968 was directed against the authorities at home and the United States; in Poland, the student protest of 1968 was directed against the authorities at home and the Soviet Union. The Polish '68ers, who went on to participate in their country's liberation movement, Solidarity, discovered how much Americans cared for the cause of freedom in their country through first-hand, direct experience – visits by American human rights activists, US diplomats exceeding their brief, writers' declarations of solidarity and smuggled dollars for underground printing presses.

From the grey, costive reality of a battered concrete apartment block under martial law, the American dream, as seen in a hundred Westerns, seemed even more fascinating than it was to Italians or Spaniards (and they were fascinated too). Sometimes, Polish Americanophilia took rather extreme forms. At a time when millions were protesting against the deployment of American Cruise and Pershing missiles in Western Europe, a graffito appeared in Warsaw. It read: 'I kiss your Pershings.' The Polish romance with an American dream of freedom and courage was perfectly captured by the placard with which Solidarity campaigned for support in the country's first semi-free election for more than forty years. It showed Gary Cooper wearing a Solidarity badge, and it said 'Solidarity – at High Noon, 4 June 1989'. The designer of this famous poster obviously assumed that a reference to the American Western *High Noon* did not have to be explained to an ordinary Polish voter.

After the end of communism, Poland set out on its 'return to Europe', but some of its key economic advisers and strongest supporters came from the United States. Thanks to American policy, it was Nato, not the European Union, that first welcomed Poland into membership – along with the Czech Republic and Hungary. Most of the new democracies of central and eastern Europe, and the Baltic states above all, continue to feel threatened by an unstable, resentful Russia. Understandably, they believe that the US is the most effective guarantor of their security. Poland bought American F-16 fighters to strengthen its own defences, sided with the Bush administration in the controversy over the Iraq War, and even agreed to head an occupation zone in Iraq.

For some in France, this is the final proof that Poland – for so long France's soulmate in the other Europe, and the only European country that still praises Napoleon in its national anthem – has become a fifth column for America. This is another complete misunderstanding. Most educated Poles, like their counterparts in other central and east European countries, believe passionately in Europe; more passionately than most west Europeans. The Czech dissident and post-liberation foreign minister of Czechoslovakia, Jiří Dienstbier, entitled a book he wrote while he was compelled for political reasons to work as a stoker, *Dreams of Europe*.[88] When I was travelling through the Iron Curtain in the 1980s, to and fro between what were then called Western and Eastern Europe, I concluded that Cold War Europe was indeed divided into two halves: the West, which had Europe, and the East, which believed in it. These true believers have, to be sure, been disillusioned by the grudging welcome given them by the European Union over the long fifteen years it has taken to get from liberation to membership. They thought they would be welcomed like long-lost cousins into the bosom of a family; they found themselves treated as provincial applicants to an exclusive metropolitan club. Dienstbier's sequel, a decade later, was entitled *From Dreams to Reality*.[89]

Still, they have no doubt that their future lies in Europe. So they believe in both Europe and America. In other words, they believe in the West – the more so, because for nearly a century they have felt themselves to be not fully part of it. Oswald Spengler, when he published his *Decline of the West* in 1918, defined the 'culture' whose demise he portentously prophesied as 'the *west*european-american' (my italics).[90] In the Cold War these countries were cut off from the West by the Iron Curtain. Rather as German or Hungarian nationalism was most pronounced among the minorities outside the frontiers of the nation-state, so Westernism was most emphatic along the West's excluded periphery, in what the Czech writer Milan Kundera memorably called 'the kidnapped West'.[91] 'When we said West,' recalls the Romanian philosopher and politician Andrei Pleşu, 'it never crossed our minds that . . . Western Europe and Northern America were divergent entities.'[92]

Yet this was not a blind passion. In the writings of Václav Havel, both as dissident essayist and after he became president, you can find the most considered reflection on the values that Europe and America have in common. It was Havel, and other leaders of post-communist central and eastern Europe, who introduced into the post-Cold War debate the word 'Euroatlantic', often in the slightly clumsy form 'Euroatlantic structures'.[93] So far as I can establish, this term had not been used before. People in the West had talked about 'the Atlantic alliance', 'transatlantic relations' (a notion that itself did not exist before 1945), and 'the Atlantic community', but the prefix 'Euro' is significant. The point was precisely to combine, in equal measure, the European and the American. No one talked more eloquently of the deeper meaning of the *European* project than Václav Havel did. A new balance was implicit in the new word.

These central and east European leaders were, in this sense, Blairite long before Blair. When, in the crisis of the West, Europe seemed to come into conflict with America, they were as torn as the British were. Poland's negotiator with the European Union, Jan Kułakowski, described their feelings: 'We're asked, "Are you for America or Europe?" It's like choosing your mother or your father.'[94] But this very Blairite refusal to choose was, in the eyes of at least some Gaullists, tantamount to a choice: the wrong one. After the 'Letter of Eight' and that of the 'Vilnius Ten', President Chirac angrily commented that these countries were proving themselves to be '*pas très bien élevés*' (not very well brought up) and that they had 'lost a good chance to remain silent'.[95] Far from being grateful for this lesson in European etiquette, from a past master of *politesse*, central and east Europeans were furious. Was it only the French who were allowed to speak for Europe? For them, Chirac's rebuke seemed to be a new version of a famous slogan from Orwell's *Animal Farm*, which they had read with fascination in smudgy samizdat editions. Someone had again repainted the motto on the end of the farm barn, at the behest of a pig called Napoleon. It now read: All Europeans are equal, but some Europeans are more equal than others.

None the less, we must beware of oversimplifying. Havel, for

example, was not typical of his compatriots. The Czech prime minister did not sign the 'Letter of Eight' and Czech public opinion was
strongly opposed to the war on Iraq. Young Polish students happily
joined with their Italian peers in anti-globalization protests. There is
a strong chance that, as these countries become more closely integrated into the European Union, so their peoples will identify more
with Europe than with America.

Meanwhile, Chirac did not go uncriticized in his own country. He
reached intoxicating heights of personal popularity during his
Napoleonic hundred days of glorious if doomed opposition to Bush's
war. Yet even some Parisian intellectuals – traditionally among the
most anti-American people on earth – were quick to criticize his arrogant assumption that he could speak for Europe. 'With the European
community divided and Nato splintering,' commented the philosopher André Glucksmann, 'the Franco-German duo calls itself
"Europe" and says it speaks for 25 nations, but represents only three
(thanks to Belgium). The "old Europe" couple criticizes American
"arrogance" and "unilateralism", compliments that can easily be
turned back on them. Is there a more insane way to saw off the
branch you're sitting on? Is there a less productive path to European
unity?'[96] Glucksmann went on to write a sharp, short book entitled
West Against West, in which he also pilloried French and German
appeasement of Putin's Russia.[97] Instant books with titles like France
Falls, French Disarray and French Arrogance excoriated the hubris of
the Chirac regime.[98]

Bernard-Henri Lévy, perhaps the most famous living Parisian intellectual, came to speak at a debate in London on the motion that 'the
American empire is a force for good'. He spoke for the motion. While
he had opposed the war on Iraq, he said, he was fed up with the US
being blamed for all the misery of the world and he was fed up with
anti-Americanism – which, he added, he knew well as a Frenchman,
'because we invented it'.[99] Two distinguished French academics published books analysing and criticizing French anti-Americanism.[100]
This French anti-anti-Americanism is not the same as Euroatlanticism, but it does mean that Euro-Gaullism is eloquently challenged in its very capital. Long-time Euroatlanticist political writers
such as Pierre Hassner, who for years have ploughed a somewhat

lonely furrow in the footsteps of Raymond Aron, now enjoy belated recognition. A Paris-based 'republic of ideas', both a network and a journal, is devoted, among other things, to narrowing the intellectual Atlantic. To be sure, this is still an intellectual minority, in quantity if not in quality.

If French intellectuals are divided about Euro-Gaullism, the French business community is more Euroatlanticist. A former American ambassador to France, Felix Rohatyn, says he finds business people to be America's best friends in France.[101] That is even more true in Germany, although in both countries you have to distinguish between more cosmopolitan big business and more defensive smaller companies. Even the more outward-looking French and German business leaders don't necessarily favour the 'American business model' and the kind of deregulation pioneered by Ronald Reagan and Margaret Thatcher. Some do; others think their own varieties of capitalism can compete quite well.

What all European business leaders see, however, is the huge and growing interdependence between the American and European economies, and the damage that can be done to their businesses by political disputes. This is not just a matter of the rich Californian cancelling his order for two Mercedes. The much-publicized trade disputes between the US and the EU over steel tariffs, genetically modified foods or corporate tax breaks are more important. Yet according to an incisive study by Joseph Quinlan, transatlantic trade comprises just 20 per cent of all transatlantic commerce, and trade disputes have affected less than 1 per cent.[102] What has really transformed the transatlantic economic relationship is investment, meaning that American companies own European ones and vice versa, selling goods and services through their respective foreign affiliates. American firms invested more capital overseas in the 1990s than in all the previous four decades combined – and half of it went to Europe. Accordingly, in 2001 half the total foreign earnings of US companies came from Europe. The United States had more assets in Germany than in the whole of Latin America; in the year 2000, its foreign affiliate sales in Germany were ten times those in China.

Europe has an even larger stake in the United States. European firms hold roughly two thirds of all foreign-owned assets in the US, and sales by European-owned companies in the US were worth $1.4 trillion in 2000 – four times the value of European exports to the United States. To illustrate these figures with a few familiar brand names: American Chrysler is owned by German Daimler, American AirTouch by British Vodafone, American Arco and Amoco by BP. The American publisher of this book, Random House, is owned by the German company Bertelsmann.

This also means jobs. If you add together direct and indirect employment, then by Quinlan's reckoning nearly 6 million Europeans owe their livelihoods to American investors and some 7 million American workers depend on European investors – who, he adds, 'on average pay higher wages and provide greater benefits than domestic US employers'.[103] So the 'European social model' is right there, in America, and the 'American business model' is right here, in Europe. In the business world, Euroatlanticism already exists, without a hyphen.

Transatlantic economic interdependence grew spectacularly after the end of the Cold War, in precisely the period when the transatlantic political community was heading for crisis. Economics and politics moved in opposite directions. The political West is no longer cemented together by the threat of Soviet communism, but a surviving Soviet Marxist would predict a political solidarity of bourgeois states arising from these huge shared material interests of capitalists on both sides of the Atlantic. However, a Soviet Marxist might yet again be wrong. The very high degree of economic interdependence in Europe before 1914 did not stop the old continent tearing itself apart.

Last but not least, there is the Americanization of everyday European consumer life. Even on Jean Monnet Square, named after the founding father of the European Union, in the heart of the smartest quarter of Paris, the 16th arrondissement, there is a McDonald's – although it's the most elegant McDonald's in the world, with cream and crimson painted woodwork, *fin-de-siècle*-style lamps, and a glass cabinet displaying works by Victor Hugo. Around the corner, a bust of Voltaire looks down from the wall of the Lycée Janson on to a shop called USA Concept Sport. A little further up the Rue de la Pompe, Racine and Molière gaze stony-eyed at another sportswear shop, Compagnie de Californie. The *lycée* students wear trainers, baseball caps and T-shirts proclaiming I ♥ NY.

Europeans across the continent enjoy American movies and music.[104] If you ring the office of Jacques Delors's think tank, Notre Europe, and they put you on hold, the canned music down the line is 'All that Jazz', sung in American English. What the French called '*l'Amérique dans les têtes*', the America-in-the-head, is everywhere. Of course it's entirely possible to love *Ally McBeal* and hate George W. Bush, to enjoy a Big Mac before going out to demonstrate against American foreign policy. That's what a great many young Europeans do. If they are anti-American, they are deeply Americanized anti-Americans. But most Europeans are well able to make the distinction between an administration and a nation. Asked in summer 2003 'what's the problem with the US?', nearly three quarters of those in France and Germany registering a negative view of America said 'mostly Bush', against less than a quarter saying 'America in general'.[105] Even when they are critical of the United States, Europeans retain a favourable view of Americans as people.[106]

A POWER FOR WHAT?

Euroatlanticists and Euro-Gaullists generally agree on one thing: Europe should play a bigger role in the world. So, apparently, do most Europeans. More than two thirds of those asked in a poll in the summer of 2003 said the European Union should become a superpower.[107] After all, this enlarged EU of twenty-five states has far more inhabitants than the United States, and a combined economy of comparable size. The draft European constitution envisages a European foreign minister, and a common foreign and security policy, 'including the progressive framing of a common defence policy'.[108] But a power for what?

At one end of the spectrum, there are those who want the European Union to become a second 'world nation', in the words of the former French foreign minister, Hubert Védrine.[109] Very few of these European nationalists (that is, protagonists of a European nation) say outright that they want it to be a rival to the United States.

The senior German journalist who wrote 'the American empire must be declared the enemy' is an exception.[110] This is not considered politic – or polite. After all, did not the French intellectual Jacques Attali observe, in a defence of 'old Europe', that politeness is a European invention?[111] (The Chinese of Confucius' time might have been surprised.) So the Gaullist president of the Convention on the Future of Europe, Valéry Giscard d'Estaing, pleaded for Europe to acquire 'the power to take on the giants of this world'.[112] Euro-Gaullists talk of *l'Europe puissance* and, at their most explicit, of the EU as a counterweight to the US. Americans are not wrong to suspect in this more than meets the eye.

However, the European nationalist or Euro-Gaullist aspiration is not simply directed against the United States. There are also Euro-Gaullists, especially among the elites of the former European great powers, for whom aspiring to be a world power is an end in itself. De Gaulle expressed this almost as a syllogism when he said that France 'because she can, because everything invites her to do so, *because she is France*, must carry out in the world policies that are on a world scale' (my italics).[113] Churchill would have said much the same for Britain. And I will never forget hearing the passion with which a distinguished, white-haired former president of Germany spoke of how Europe might one day become a *Weltmacht* (a pre-1945 German term for world power). In this view, France, Britain and Germany can no longer be world powers on their own – but together, as Europe, perhaps they might. An aspiration that is both unrealistic and discredited for individual European nation-states is somehow considered realistic and respectable for Europe as a whole.

Then there are Europeans who want Europe to play a larger role in the world for almost the opposite reason. Europe, they feel, has learned from its terrible history of competing nation-states, each aspiring to mastery. After giving the world the curse of the nation-state, Europe should now offer the global antidote. The European Union is a model of how nation-states can overcome their differences, in a law-based transnational community of peaceful cooperation. That model is now ripe for export. It's already embracing many post-communist democracies of Europe. It exercises a benign magnetism in the Balkans and in Turkey. In this spirit, one senior and liberal German diplomat confesses that his ultimate ideal would be 'the Europeanization of the world'. If America has a universalist aspiration, born of the Enlightenment, so do France and Germany.

In the same spirit, such patriots of transnational Europeanism emphasize Europe's contribution to promoting 'global public goods'. Europe gives nearly three times as much as the United States in foreign development aid.[114] Europeans are involved in peacekeeping operations and reconstruction after conflict around the world. They support the International Criminal Court. They wish to implement the Kyoto Protocol on climate change, and are altogether more solicitous of the environment. Here the claim of difference from, and even superiority to, the United States does not amount to hostility; it is, so to speak, friendly rivalry in a good cause.

Finally, there are those who believe, like Tony Blair, that in shaping its own foreign and security policy Europe must always stay close to the United States. Its goal should be to try and broaden Washington's agenda by neo-Churchillian engagement. Those global public goods can only be achieved by Europe and America working together.

You will typically hear more French and German voices at one end of this spectrum, and more British and Polish ones at the other. When the French commentator Bernard Guetta challenged the Polish writer Adam Michnik to agree that Europe should become a world power as a counterweight to the United States, Michnik crisply replied: 'Power, Yes. Counterweight, No.'[115] But the division is not simply along national lines. If Americans are confused about Europe's intentions, they have every reason to be, because Europe is itself confused. Millions of Europeans are swinging between the two poles of Euro-Gaullism and Euroatlanticism, in the argument of the decade.

Which of the two positions is more realistic, in the sense of 'capable of being realized'? The crisis of 2002/3 showed that the Chiracian version of Euro-Gaullism is a hiding to nowhere. An attempt to unite Europe around a rival policy to the United States ended up splitting Europe down the middle. France and Germany, it emerged, could no longer plot a course for the whole of the European Union, as they had before 1989. They still aspired to be the 'magnetic core' of the EU but had the reverse effect: magnetically repelling rather than attracting other European states. The neo-Gaullist vision of a unipolar Europe in a multipolar world ended with a multipolar Europe in a still unipolar world. Europe – to be more accurate, the part of Europe France and Germany could rally – was not powerful enough to stop the United States doing what it wanted. America can win the hot wars on its own. This does not mean it can win the subsequent peace, as it has discovered in Iraq. For that, it will always need the help of others, but whether those others have to include the reluctant powers of 'old Europe' is an open question. One of the secondary political resources available to Washington is its ability to play European countries off against each other, as offshore imperial Britain did in the nineteenth century.

This critical verdict on the failure of the Chiracian version of Euro-Gaullism does not mean that the Blairite version of Euroatlanticism was a success, or any more likely to succeed in future. Blair failed quite as much as Chirac to rally Europe around his position. A policy aimed at uniting the West ended up helping to split it more sharply. This in turn strengthened the popular support for Euro-Gaullism in much of Europe, including Britain, thus making the prospect of Europe-wide consensus on a Euroatlanticist position more remote than before. A Euroatlanticist strategy is necessarily based on the hope that Washington will want the European Union to be a single coherent partner for the United States. But why should Washington want that, when it can choose its partners, mission by mission, from among the disunited states of Europe? Perhaps American leaders will be quite content, now the Soviet Union no longer threatens us all, to see Europe carry on in mild disarray? Why take the risk of the old world uniting against the new, as a rival superpower? If European nationalists can think more than they say in public, so can American nationalists. They can be 'polite' too.

Any serious judgement on the right way forward for Europe therefore depends on an assessment of the trajectory, motives and interests of the United States of America. To this I now turn.

3

America, the Powerful

INSIDE THE GIANT

Sometimes one remark says it all. President George W. Bush is talking to a small group of visitors in the oval drawing room on the first floor of the White House. From its windows, they have a fine view of planes taking off from Ronald Reagan National Airport. This is one of the last months of the innocent time when planes in the skies over Washington are just that – planes – and not potential weapons of mass destruction. The meeting is to prepare the president, still new in office, for his first official trip to Europe, but just now he's recalling, in his clipped, tautly smiling way, a Summit of the Americas the previous month. At one point during the summit, feeling that he had already talked too much, he had indicated to the chairman that he would 'pass' on this topic. 'But Mr President,' the chairman expostulated, 'you are the most powerful man on earth.' As President Bush reflects on this, he comments wryly, 'It takes a little time to grow into this job.'[1]

That could also be said of the whole country, in its new job. After the fall of the Berlin Wall on 9 November 1989 (9/11, European-style), America gradually woke up to the realization that it was no longer just one of two competing superpowers. 'Hyperpower', 'superduperpower', 'American empire', 'new Rome', 'unipolar world' – all these terms attempt to capture the new reality of a global predominance that arguably has no precedent in the history of the world. After the fall of the twin towers on 11 September 2001 (9/11, American-style), the United States has been wrestling with the revelation that all this plenitude of power could not protect its own innocent civilians from foreign attack in the heart of the American homeland, a trauma Americans had not experienced since British troops sacked the White House in 1814. Incomparable power, unprecedented vulnerability.

Something else is new too: the world can not merely observe the actions but actually sees inside the brain of this giant called America, as it wrestles with its paradoxical pre-eminence. Like a bank of electronic monitors on a hospital ward, CNN, the BBC and the World Wide Web register every heart-beat, every spasm. Like anxious relatives, hundreds of millions of people, from London to Sydney, watch through the glass. Washington 'players', known across the globe simply as 'Bush', 'Condi' and 'Kerry' become characters in a worldwide soap opera, a kind of political *ER*. On Thursday, you watch the fictionalized *West Wing*; the rest of the week, you have the real thing. Europeans, like Latin Americans, Asians and Africans, often know better what is going on in Washington than they do what is happening in other capital cities on their own continent.

Monitoring America seems so much easier than monitoring Europe. Europe is more than forty countries, governments and national foreign policies; the United States is just one of each – or so, at least, it claims. Beside the plethora of information about the inner workings of American domestic and foreign policy there is a wealth of analysis. The European stereotype used to be – and for some still is – that experienced old Europeans have the sophisticated, detailed understanding of the world ('*l'intelligence européenne*') while Americans are like the hapless Pyle in Graham Greene's *The Quiet American*, well meaning but brash and ignorant, blundering into complex foreign crises without knowing a *stupa* from a beehive. The truth is that Washington has at its fingertips a range and depth of foreign policy analysis, in government, think tanks, universities and the media, which London has not matched for fifty years and no other European capital, least of all the EU 'capital' of Brussels, can begin to approach. This analysis probes every corner of the world; even more, it probes Washington's own policies.

The commendation of that large advantage must be hedged about with a few warning notes. This sophisticated self-analysis of the Washington body politic has two characteristic shortcomings which are the products, respectively, of the commercial and the political marketplace. As analysts jostle for attention in the crowded market of ideas they have to shout loudly, like traders on the floor of a stock exchange. Shouting loudly, to clinch an intellectual 'trade', requires overstatement. It means taking a grand, simplifying idea and, egged on by your magazine editor or book publisher, hyping it still further: The End of History! The Clash of Civilizations! Europeans are from Venus! The Coming Anarchy! The End of the American Era! Here are the *terribles simplificateurs* of whom the great nineteenth-century Swiss historian Jacob Burckhardt once warned, but now they are driven less by ideological fervour or philosophical hubris than by the commercial pressures of, so to speak, intellectual capitalism.

Then there's the political marketplace. In Washington, some three to five thousand jobs in government are filled by political appointees every time a new administration comes to power. Many people, in think tanks, academe and journalism, covet these jobs. You, too, could be a Kissinger, a Brzezinski, an Albright or a Rice! So they cast and trim their analyses to increase their chances of getting the job – or, at least, of continued access to and influence upon those who hold the top jobs. 'Thanks for e-mailing me your entry in the Kennan stakes; here's mine,' wrote one such aspirant to another, at a time when American journals were full of attempts to do for post-9/11 American foreign policy what George Kennan's 'Mr X' article in *Foreign Affairs* did for its Cold War policy. The waters of American self-analysis are therefore deep but far from pure. Description and prescription, the personal and the political, are always mixed. In each case you have to ask 'where's he or she coming from?', which often means 'to what office would he or she like to go?' Many's the book or article whose unwritten sub-title is 'A Job Application'.

I just suggested that, unlike Europe, America is one country with one government and one foreign policy, but anyone who knows Washington will tell you that this is a most dangerous oversimplification. Not only does American foreign policy change rapidly over time, in the course of as well as between administrations, but on any given day there are usually two or three American foreign policies: one from the State Department, another from the Pentagon, perhaps a third from the National Security Adviser. And a fourth will be inserted, episodically, by Congress, which plays a role as part of 'the government' unlike that of any parliament in any major European state. As for 'one country', that is, in some obvious sense, true – the United States is a single federal nation-state. But in another sense it is less true, since the country has become increasingly divided and polarized on cultural-political lines, so the voters of 'red' (Republican) and 'blue' (Democrat) America disagree sharply on fundamental issues. Controversies about foreign policy, especially on national security policy, are less clearly polarized on party lines, but they are still quite sharp. At any given moment, you therefore have to ask 'which foreign policy?', 'which government?' and 'which America?'. 'The US', writes the British Euro-Gaullist Will Hutton, 'is hostile to all forms of international cooperation and multilateralist endeavour.'[2] *The* US? Which US?

One illuminating analysis, by Walter Russell Mead, identifies four American ways of looking at foreign policy which, he argues, have competed and coexisted through two centuries. 'Hamiltonians', he suggests, look to increase domestic prosperity by securing a favourable external environment for trade and business; 'Wilsonians' believe in spreading democracy, self-government and the rule of law; 'Jeffersonians' think it matters more to safeguard democracy at home, leading the world mainly by example; 'Jacksonians' make fierce, warlike defence of the physical security and economic well-being of the American people.[3] In practice, these approaches ebb and flow between and within groups, and even within individuals. For example, someone might be more 'Jacksonian' after the 9/11 attacks than he or she was before.

Others emphasize the importance of 'where you're coming from' being understood quite literally. A background on the East or West coast, in the Midwest, the deep South or, not least, in the great state of Texas, shapes how a particular policymaker views the world. 'I sit before you an unvarnished Texan,' said President George W. Bush, introducing that White House discussion of Europe with polished, not to say varnished self-deprecation. Yet for all his Yaley varnish, George W. Bush was the first Southern conservative to occupy the White House since before the American Civil War.[4] At critical moments the decision would come down, as it always does, to a set of individual biographies interacting with a set of unforeseen events.

My purpose in this chapter is obviously not to treat the whole of American foreign policy. It's to seek an answer to this question: how likely is it that we will (again) see a United States that treats Europeans, and other free people, as full and serious partners in a common enterprise? For one major cause of this crisis of the West is that many Europeans, and other free people, have not felt they are being so treated.

A TALE OF TWO NEW EUROPES

In the beginning, the United States was the new Europe. It defined itself against what Alexander Hamilton called 'the pernicious labyrinths of European politics'.[5] Bad old Europe was, in this sense, America's founding 'Other'. The temporal adjective – old – was as important as the spatial noun – Europe. European nations might forge their identities from an imagined past, American identity would flow from an imagined future. The nineteenth-century novelist Herman Melville summed up this quintessentially American belief. 'The Past', he wrote, 'is the Textbook of Tyrants; the Future the Bible of the Free.'[6] In a New England, free men and women would build a new Jerusalem, Governor John Winthrop's 'City upon a Hill', and in a New Orleans they would make a better France. In the New Amsterdam that became the multinational city of New York, generations of European immigrants to the United States relived this history in their own personal biographies. Summarizing the background of a Californian billionaire of Hungarian origin, the money magazine *Forbes* said simply: 'family fled Europe'.[7] Europe was the place you fled.

But America was not simply the Not-Europe; it was the Would-Be-Better-Europe. 'America,' wrote Irving Howe, 'began as an idea of Europe. Whatever may be reformative in European culture, and a modest part of whatever is revolutionary, finds a locus of desire in the idea of America.'[8] Many of the Founding Fathers were Englishmen with a deep admiration for France. Thomas Jefferson wrote that if he could not live in America, he would choose to live in France.[9] Alexis de Tocqueville repaid the compliment, with his admiring account of

Democracy in America. In the nineteenth century, the English in Massachusetts and Virginia, the French in Louisiana, the Spanish in California, the Poles in Chicago, the Germans in Wisconsin and the Scandinavians in Minnesota created what Jacob Burckhardt called 'a large-scale laboratory experiment of Europe's future'.[10] America was the first European Union.*

This ambivalence about Europe, this mixture of fascination and repulsion, runs through American history. In every period, one can find examples of anti-Europeanism and Europhilia, just as in every period of European history one can find anti-Americanism and Americanophilia (*'Amerika, Du hast es besser!'* wrote Goethe. 'America, you're better off!'[11]). What matters, on both sides, is the way the mixture changes and how it translates into policy. At the turn of the nineteenth to the twentieth century, there was a clear rapprochement between the United States and the two European nations which had done most to define it at birth: England and France. Winston Churchill, with his British father and American mother, was quite literally the child of this coming-closer. The Statue of Liberty, a present to the United States from the people of France, was its enduring monument.[12] Henry James's *The Europeans* portrays the intricate dance of attraction and repulsion between the transatlantic cousins at this quivering moment.

In the First World War, a sense of cultural and political solidarity with the Anglo-French West became military commitment. One of the leading American historians of 'Western Civ', William H. McNeill, tells us that the first course in Western Civilization at Columbia University in New York was 'designed to teach soldiers what it was they would be fighting for in Flanders Fields'.[13] While America soon withdrew militarily from Europe, the teaching of Western Civilization continued at Columbia, Chicago and other American universities. It was, as McNeill recalled from his own student days, a 'liberating message . . . it conveyed membership in the great cultivated, sophisticated world of "us" . . .'[14]

---

* Of course this first European Union was also built on the labour of slaves, thus storing up generations of shame and trouble for itself; but then, today's European Union has been partly built on the labour of darker-skinned immigrant workers – poorly treated by the higher standards of our time – thus storing up future trouble for itself.

That American self-image of a common transatlantic 'us' was re-inforced by the experience of fighting together in the Second World War and then standing together in the Cold War. The author of *Life's Picture History of Western Man* expressed this naively but also quite eloquently in 1951:

On his lonely pinnacle, the American can survey more history than he has seen before. During the past generation, he rediscovered his personal links with Western Man and his membership in Western civilization. Somewhere in these turbulent years America's acceptance of responsibility for its parents' lands, for the mother and father of its own past, quietly placed itself beyond question. When Franklin Roosevelt in 1939 said, 'Our American frontier is on the Rhine,' he felt obliged to deny that he had said it. That frontier has subsequently been placed on the Elbe without objection.[15]

Well, almost without objection. Actually, a proposal for American 'Disengagement' from Europe emerged soon thereafter from one of the leading architects of America's Cold War policy, George Kennan, and the temptation of disengagement recurred throughout the Cold War. Indeed, the temptation of disengagement – sometimes more pejoratively called 'isolationism' – must be considered an enduring feature of such a vast, self-defining and in many ways still inward-looking country. We are told that roughly four out of every five Americans don't even have a passport.

While working on this book, I travelled to the heartland Bible-belt states of Kansas and Missouri. Wherever I went, I asked the people I met – farmers, shop assistants, high school students – a simple ques-tion: 'If I say "Europe", what do you think of?' Many reacted with a long, baffled silence, sometimes punctuated by giggles. They really, visibly, could not think of anything. Vernon Masqua, a carpenter in McLouth, said: 'Well, I guess they don't have much huntin' down there.' Richard Souza, whose parents came from France and Por-tugal, reflected: 'Well, it's a long way from home.' And after a very long pause for thought, Jack Weishaar, an elderly farmer of German descent, weightily concluded: 'Well, it's quite a ways across the pond.' If you said 'America' to a farmer or carpenter in Europe, even in the remotest mountain village of transcarpathian Ruthenia, he would, you may be sure, have a whole lot more to say on the subject. And many of those I talked to in Kansas and Missouri thought America should concentrate on putting its own house in order. James Kimmel, a farmer on the road to McLouth, told me: 'I think we're trying to run the business of the world too much . . . like the Romans used to . . .'[16]

However, I also met, in chance encounters, local people who had served in the American armed forces in Europe or had otherwise lived, worked or travelled there. The human bonds developed over more than sixty years of large-scale American presence in Europe, from the 1940s to the 1990s, are not just confined to some 'East coast elite'. The 'us' of the West is much wider than that. Many millions of former US service people, and their families, have vivid memories of life in Europe. Folk memories also live on among those who have never been to Europe. Jack Weishaar, the Kansas farmer, had never travelled to the East or West coasts of the US, let alone abroad, but when I asked him for his view of the Germans he said, 'Well, I'd better not have anything against them because that's where my ancestors came from.' Even historical ignorance can foster transatlantic warmth. More than half of those asked in a national test of high school seniors were unable say who the US fought against in the Second World War. Nearly one in five believed that the Germans had been America's allies.[17]

The United States, that first European Union across the sea, also encouraged on the old continent the creation of a new European Union. The US supported early European federalist movements, both overtly and covertly. It made Marshall Aid conditional on closer economic cooperation between European states. Praising the project of European union in 1962, President John F. Kennedy said: 'The United States looks on this valiant enterprise with hope and admiration. We don't regard a strong, united Europe as a rival but as a partner. To aid its progress has been the basic objective of our foreign policy for the past seventeen years.'[18] Making generous allowance for the gilded hyperbole of Camelot ('*the* basic objective'?) that was a fair statement of the broad strategic direction of American policy. Speaking in Philadelphia on America's Independence Day, Kennedy went on to call for a 'Declaration of Interdependence' between the 'new union now emerging in Europe and the old American Union founded here 175 years ago'.

With many hesitations, and perhaps growing ambivalence, the United States continued to encourage the 'valiant enterprise' of European integration for another thirty years, until that enterprise formally became, shortly after the end of the Cold War, the European Union. This support was partly the product of sympathy and idealism: after all, one of the first proposals for a 'United Europe' was made in 1693 by William Penn, the founder of Pennsylvania.[19] However, post-1945 American policy was far more the product of enlightened self-interest. By increasing the attraction of the free western half of Europe to the unfree eastern half, European integration strengthened America's hand in a global duel with the Soviet Union whose main geopolitical arena was Europe and whose centre was Berlin. The magnetic dynamism of the European Community in the 1970s and 1980s, with its visionary goal of a single market to be 'completed' in 1992, did then contribute directly to the end of communism in the Soviet bloc. Western Europe's '1992' was a cause of Eastern Europe's 1989.

The fall of the Berlin Wall signalled that the Soviet Union had lost this Cold War with the United States. The administration of President George H. W. Bush sealed the victory, using quiet, skilful multilateral diplomacy to help the Germans – America's new 'partners in leadership' – to win Gorbachev's assent to their unification. President Bush (Senior) also summarized Europe's own larger purpose better than any European in a single phrase: 'Europe whole and free'. On Christmas Day 1991, Mikhail Gorbachev gave the West his final gift, sealing the end of the Soviet Union by his resignation.* Just a fortnight earlier, the leaders of the European Community had resolved at the Dutch town of Maastricht to make an economic and monetary union. This was designed to ensure, among other things, that the new, united, sovereign Germany would be firmly held within a warm European embrace. In anticipation, the Community renamed itself the European Union. Then the two halves of the old Cold War West had to consider what the relationship between the new EU and the new US would be.

---

* Perhaps fittingly, this was Christmas Day in the Western Christian but not the Eastern (Orthodox) Calendar.

As I have stressed already, this geopolitical shift on the continent of Europe was fundamental, but there were also two longer-term cultural-historical shifts on the American continent. First, the ethnic character and cultural self-identification of the United States changed as a result of the long-overdue recognition of the equal civil rights of African-Americans in the 1960s and the growth of immigration from countries outside Europe following the 1965 Immigration and Nationality Act. In the next quarter-century, more than fifteen million people entered the United States legally under the provisions of that Act.[20] The Asian-American population rose from 1.5 million in 1970 to nearly 12 million in 2000.[21] More than 20 million Mexicans have come across the Rio Grande. Together with another 15 million people from other parts of Latin America, they constitute a large and growing group of Hispanic-Americans.

Generally, these non-European Americans have a higher birth rate than European Americans.[22] The population has also grown more on the Pacific coast, looking to Asia, and in the South, looking to Latin America, than on the Atlantic seaboard of the country, looking to Europe. The proportion of US citizens who are of European origin is projected to decline from 80 per cent in 1980 to 64 per cent in 2020, while that of Hispanic-Americans is expected to rise from 6 to 15 per cent and of Asian-Americans from 2 to 7 per cent.[23] Even on these projections, European Americans will remain a clear majority. Hispanic-Americans come from Latin America but they speak a European language, Spanish – a fact which Spain very reasonably hopes to capitalize on, strengthening its own special relationship across the Atlantic. Most Hispanic-Americans are also members of a Christian church that still has its headquarters in Rome, Europe.[24] Nevertheless, the change is fraught with consequence.

African-Americans, Hispanic-Americans and Asian-Americans can hardly think of Europe as 'parents' lands' or 'mother and father', to recall the language of *Life*'s 1951 picture history, in the way that Jack Weishaar somehow still does. Nor can they readily identify with Western Man ('fair of skin, hardy of limb'). Instead, their cultural representatives have recalled the 'Black Atlantic' of the slave trade, demanded that less attention be paid to authors who are Dead White European Males, and chanted 'Heigh ho, heigh ho, Western Civ has got to go!' Which it has, in most American universities, at least in name. A country that is increasingly multi-ethnic in practice has become self-consciously multicultural in theory. At the beginning of the twentieth century, few Americans doubted that America was in some sense a child of Europe – a better version of an older self. At the beginning of the twenty-first, many no longer think of it as umbilically linked to Europe.

A second underlying change has occurred among European Americans, especially those of a younger generation. Crudely put, this is the fading of the Henry Jamesian cultural fascination with Europe and the disappearance of any lingering sense of cultural inferiority. No longer does the celebration of a shared Western Civilization give American students the thrill of belonging, in William McNeill's perhaps unintentionally revealing words, to a 'great, *cultivated, sophisticated* world of "us"' (my italics). Gone are the days when a young American would sit star-struck in a corner of the Deux Magots café in Paris, while intellectual demi-gods called Sartre or Merleau-Ponty swanned by, and remain long in awe of Oxford's honey-stoned medieval quadrangles. A retired American diplomat of long European experience expressed this subtle change vividly in an e-mail to me. 'When I first went to Europe in the 1940s and 1950s,' he wrote, 'Europe was superior to us. The superiority was not personal – I never felt demeaned even by condescending people – but civilizational.' Not any more. America, he concluded, 'is no longer abashed'.[25]

Europeans, especially British Europeans, sometimes still like to think they can be, as Harold Macmillan put it, Greeks to America's Rome.[26] But the new Rome has absorbed what the Greeks have to offer. Its best universities, journals and think tanks are, on the whole, better than Europe's. The traffic in ideas now generally flows from New York to Paris and Harvard to Oxford, not the other way round. And if there are still a few clever Greeks left, well, they can usually be hired to augment those American universities, journals and think tanks.

The end of the Cold War made a difference in this respect, too. During the Cold War, Americans might not have liked the ideas coming out of Paris or Rome or Berlin, but they clearly mattered since the

United States was engaged in a political conflict, centred on Europe, that was also an ideological one – a battle of ideas. Today, who cares what Paris is thinking? Yet five minutes in any Parisian bookshop shows you how passionately Paris still cares what Washington is thinking. The connection between the balance of power and what we might call the balance of fascination is complex and two-sided. Power is fascinating. (Americans were a lot more interested in what Russian novelists wrote when Russia was a superpower.) But being fascinating is also power. The charms of both 'high' and popular culture are part of what Joseph Nye has called 'soft power',[27] the power to attract, and this is by no means simply a by-product of military or economic power. Like the balance of hard power, the balance of fascination has shifted from Europe to America.

The gradual metamorphosis in European–American relations can be illuminated by pursuing the family metaphors so often invoked to characterize those relations. For the growing number of non-European Americans, Europe never was 'mother' or 'father'. For many European Americans, *Life*'s 'mother and father' have become somewhat troublesome adolescent children. This is an image I heard repeatedly in the 1990s, not least from members of the Clinton administration. But for many Europeans the 'daughter of Europe' – as de Gaulle called the United States – has turned into a large and bossy uncle. Europeans don't like to think of themselves as America's nephew, let alone its son – are they not, after all, its parents? – but some such dependent relationship is implicit when they talk of 'emancipation'. Parents do not usually seek 'emancipation' from their children. Putting this all together, we find that Europe is an adolescent son rebelling against an American uncle who was himself originally Europe's daughter. These hopelessly mixed metaphors of age, sex and family relationship are not simply the product of confusion. Rather, they perfectly reflect the tangled historical and emotional crossovers between the old new Europe on the western side of the Atlantic and the new old Europe on its eastern side.

Let's stay for a moment with the American picture of Europe as 'petulant sixteen-year-old'.[28] Anyone who has had teenage sons knows how uneven they can be: very mature in one way, still childish in another. Today's EU is a clear case of uneven development: already middle-aged as an economic power; a young adult in civilian aspects of foreign policy; pre-pubescent in its (in)capacity for coordinated military action. Yet the US also exhibits symptoms of parental ambivalence. Its usual complaint is that 'the Europeans' cannot 'get their act together', but it's equally worried when they do – in trade disputes, for example, or on environmental policy. It was easy for John F. Kennedy to say in 1962 that the United States did not regard a strong, united Europe as a rival, since the then European Economic Community of just six countries, with Germany divided and wholly dependent on American protection, could not possibly be a rival to the United States. Viewing the European Union of 1992 and after, that is less immediately clear – to Europeans, especially Euro-Gaullists, but also to Americans. So America's problem with Europe is partly that it will not 'grow up' and partly that it has.

EUROPEAN AMERICANS AT WORK

Iraq was not the first post-Cold War crisis of the West. Bosnia was. When Yugoslavia began to be torn apart by post-communist nationalists in 1991, the administration of President George H. W. Bush decided to leave this one to 'the Europeans', as the United States' European allies are habitually known in Washington. 'We have no dog in that fight,' Secretary of State James Baker is often quoted as saying.[29] Some European leaders, levitating with the euphoria of the time, were delighted to take up the challenge. The Luxembourgeois foreign minister Jacques Poos, on a mission to disintegrating Yugoslavia, declared that the hour of Europe had come.[30] 'If one problem can be solved by the Europeans,' said the ineffable Poos, 'it is the Yugoslav problem. It is not up to the Americans or anyone else.'[31]

A year later James Baker seriously considered military intervention against the Bosnian Serbs, but his right-hand man and successor Lawrence Eagleburger was adamant: the US should not intervene. This would be a test for the Europeans. If they managed to pass it, that would lighten an American foreign policy agenda already heavy with the disintegration of the Soviet Union and the Gulf War against the occupier of Kuwait, Saddam Hussein. If they failed, as Eagle-burger suspected they would, that could usefully curb their Euro-Gaullist pride. 'They will screw it up,' Eagleburger said, according to a note-taker present at one State Department meeting, 'and this will teach them a lesson.'[32]

Europe 'screwed it up' all right. While EU representatives made endless diplomatic efforts to halt the bloodshed, and while EU national governments argued among themselves, more than 200,000 Europeans, among them many unarmed civilians, women and children, were brutally murdered by other Europeans. At least 3 million people were driven out of their homes. This was bad old Europe, as it had not been seen since 1945. If Milošević was the new Hitler, then for some politically engaged Americans the British prime minister, John Major, was the new Neville Chamberlain, closely followed by the perfidious French. The point here is not to argue the justice or injustice of these American charges.* The point is about the impact on American attitudes to Europe.

Bosnia made many in Washington feel – or feel once more – that you could not trust 'the Europeans'. The Europeans were appeasers: weak, divided, duplicitous and even downright treacherous. (Three French officers were found to have been spying for the Serbs.) The sentiment could be heard not just among right-wing Republicans traditionally suspicious of Europe but among lifelong liberal Euro-peanists, in the State Department and elsewhere. On this occasion, the British were definitely among 'the Europeans'. In stark contrast to the Iraq crisis, Britain stood shoulder-to-shoulder with France in blocking American policy over Bosnia. Indeed, for some Americans involved, John Major and his foreign secretary, Douglas Hurd, represented the worst of cynical old European *Realpolitik*. By the autumn of 1994, when transatlantic tensions came to a head over the issue of whether to launch air strikes to save the so-called 'safe area' of Bihać, sober observers suggested that relations between Washington and London were as bad as they had been during the Suez Crisis of 1956 – when Britain had also stood with France.

* In truth, every major Western state, including the United States, deserved a share of the blame, but it would require another book – an important book, and one that still needs to be written – to establish in what proportions.

Yet what was most instructive was the outcome of this first post-Cold War crisis of the West. The Clinton administration, which had agonized and vacillated about Bosnia ever since it had come to power in January 1993, decided that mending the rifts in the transatlantic alliance took priority over air strikes to drive back the Serbs around Bihać. As one senior official explained at the time, American leaders 'agreed that Nato is more important than Bosnia . . .'[33]

By 1995, the Clinton administration had finally resolved to end the Bosnian war, an engagement personified by the rumbunctious figure of Richard Holbrooke. However, it would do so multilaterally, not unilaterally. It would work with its traditional European allies, forcefully, even overbearingly in private, but still work with them and not around them. If military force was needed to stop the Bosnian Serbs, and Slobodan Milošević, it would wherever possible apply that force through its long-established transatlantic alliance. What's more, the Clinton administration would make the renewal and enlargement of Nato, to include the new democracies of post-communist Europe, the strategic centrepiece of its European policy. Beside the new EU there should be a new Nato. Together, these should constitute the 'Euro-atlantic structures' to sustain a Europe whole and free, as Václav Havel and other central European leaders put it repeatedly, to some effect in Washington. The West could be reborn, even without a Soviet devil to fight.

This was the strategy the Clinton administration pursued for the next six years. Its climax came in the spring of 1999 when Nato was enlarged to include Poland, the Czech Republic and Hungary, and then, within a fortnight, went to war for the first time in its history to prevent Milošević perpetrating 'another Bosnia' in Kosovo. Americans were also influential behind the scenes in supporting the Serbs who finally overthrew Milošević in a largely peaceful revolution in the autumn of 2000. The European Union carried the main burden of civil reconstruction after conflict, in Bosnia and elsewhere, but wherever I went in the Balkans at this time, people said 'the international community . . . I mean, the Americans'. Poles, Czechs and Hungarians felt that, of the two great Brussels-based institutions of the Cold War West, the American-led Nato had embraced them sooner and more warmly than the European Union. They had thought the EU was their family but found it behaved towards them like a rich man's club; they had thought Nato was an exclusive Western club, but received a family welcome.

There were good as well as bad reasons for this asymmetry. The EU was a qualitatively different and far more complicated organization than Nato. It asked more of new members but would also, in time, give them more. None the less, the contrast reinforced an already very positive image of America in most of central and eastern Europe. When Donald Rumsfeld noted with satisfaction the positive stance taken by 'new Europe' towards America's policy of toppling Saddam Hussein, he was benefiting from the aversion to dictators of people who had until recently lived under dictators; he was also bringing in Clinton's harvest.

This policy reflected a rational calculation of enlightened self-interest by the United States. It was the work of European Americans and American Europeanists, moved by memories and sentiments as well as calculations. Clinton's second Secretary of State, Madeleine Albright, was Czech. She had been born in Prague and her family driven into exile by the communist takeover in 1948. She was steeped in the lessons of European history. At one fractious meeting about Kosovo in London, she dismissed a compromise proposal with the words 'do you think we're in Munich?'.[34] You had only to see Madeleine Albright in the company of Václav Havel and other Czech friends to understand how much it meant to her that her native land should join Nato. Richard Holbrooke had worked in the trans-atlantic foreign policy community for years, and been ambassador to Germany. A concluding section of his book on Bosnia was entitled 'America, Still a European Power'.[35] Another of Clinton's key foreign policy advisers, Strobe Talbott, was a leading specialist on Russia. He had started translating Khrushchev's memoirs while at Oxford University, and much of his life had been spent charting Soviet–American relations. Clinton himself had studied at Oxford. He had written essays on European politics, demonstrated in London against the Vietnam War and travelled to Scandinavia, the Soviet Union, Czechoslovakia and Spain.

These biographies matter. Clinton's elective affinities with Europe were also ideological. In what he called a 'floating opera'[36] of meetings to discuss a political 'third way' he sought broad, internationalist left-liberal answers to the common problems facing developed capitalist democracies in an age of globalization. This dialogue was wider than just Europe and America – it included Australia, Canada and Latin American countries such as Brazil – but at its heart was a transatlantic conversation with fellow left-liberal politicians of the same generation, especially Tony Blair and Gerhard Schröder. Instead of confronting a common military enemy, the Soviet Union, they would now tackle common economic and social challenges. For example, Clinton argued that a free market society like the United States had a regrettably high level of income inequality but 'in countries that have chosen to make sure that did not happen, very often there have been quite high levels of unemployment . . . which is another form of social inequality'. However, he went on, 'I think virtually every European country has done a better job than the United States in providing adequate family leave policies, adequate child care policies, adequate supports.'[37]

Unsurprisingly, this kind of discourse went down well in Europe. When Clinton then talked of 'shared values' between Europe and America, Europeans were more likely to believe him. Except for his Baptist religiosity, the internationalist, welfare-oriented, socially and sexually liberal old '68er Bill Clinton spoke like a European – which is precisely what the Republican right hated about him. America's cultural revolution of the 1960s had provoked a cultural counter-revolution. During the 1990s, the divide between these two Americas widened. In her book *One Nation, Two Cultures*, the conservative historian Gertrude Himmelfarb wrote 'Europeans used to complain of the Americanization (the "coca-colaization") of European culture. They may be getting their revenge by witnessing the Europeanization (or de-moralization) of American culture.'[38] So for Himmelfarb, Europeanization meant de-moralization.

Polemicists of the right attacked both Clintonites and liberal Europeans with equal acerbity. One of the most outspoken of them, Jonah Goldberg, popularized the label 'cheese-eating surrender monkeys', originally drawn from an episode of *The Simpsons*, to describe the French, and charged Europeans with 'thinking they achieved lasting peace through endless conversations in Swiss hotels with bottles of bubbly water and plates of runny cheese scattered around the table'.[39] In attacking 'Europeans', Goldberg explained to me in a conversation in Washington, he and his fellow conservatives were also attacking self-hating American liberals who assumed that abroad, especially Europe, must be better. Conversely, 'Europeans' were also stalking-horses for American liberals. So, in effect, Clinton was a European? 'Yes,' said Goldberg, 'or at least, he *thinks* like a European.'[40]

This was not intended as a compliment. But it could be taken as such, especially if the president happened to be in Europe. At the end of his second term, Clinton was awarded the Charlemagne Prize in Aachen – the first American president ever to receive this most prestigious European political honour. In his acceptance speech, a summing-up of his European policy, he said '[the] shining light of European Union is a matter of the utmost importance, not just to Europeans, but to everyone on this planet'.[41] The EU could be a model for other parts of the earth. Europe was 'a unifying idea as much as a particular place'. Europe and the United States had repeated differences, but 'the simple fact is that, since Europe is an idea as much as a place, America also is a part of Europe, bound by ties of family, history and values'. Emphasizing the scale of transatlantic economic interdependence, he concluded: 'Lord Palmerston's rule that countries have no permanent alliances, only permanent interests, simply does not apply to our relationship. For America has a permanent interest in a permanent alliance with Europe.' You must, of course, discount for the speaker's desire to please his European audience of the day, but this still remains an amazing statement of commitment. Ten years after the end of the Cold War, and 224 years after the Declaration of Independence, an American president said: 'America also is a part of Europe.'

As Clinton's presidency came to an end, the transatlantic alliance had therefore in some respects been renewed. Conducting a bombing campaign with eighteen allies – some of them demanding a veto on individual targets – had not endeared the idea of coalition warfare to the Pentagon. The failure to reach a peace settlement between Israel and the Palestinians, despite all Clinton's strenuous efforts, left a time-bomb still ticking for transatlantic relations. There were nagging concerns about differing responses to international terrorism, Iran and Saddam Hussein's Iraq. But the Democrats' candidate to succeed Clinton, Al Gore, could look forward to addressing these problems with, for the most part, like-minded Europeans, and Europeans could look forward to working with a man they already knew quite well.

In the presidential election of 2000, Al Gore won roughly half a million more votes than George W. Bush. It is, of course, impossible to know what would have happened if the American electoral system had translated those votes into victory or if the Supreme Court had not stopped the Florida recount. It would be absurd to imagine that any president could simply have continued with 'business as usual' after the 9/11 attacks, but Gore's track record as vice president in the Clinton administration would suggest an approach to the world in general, and Europe in particular, very different from that of George W. Bush.

If so, a President Gore would have had some support from his voters. In December 2002, the Ipsos-Reid polling group included in their regular survey of American public opinion a few questions formulated for the purposes of this book.[42] Asked to choose one of four statements about American versus European approaches to diplomacy and war, 30 per cent of Democratic voters but only 6 per cent of Republican voters chose 'The Europeans seem to prefer diplomatic solutions over war and that is a positive value Americans could learn from.' By contrast, only 13 per cent of Democrats but 35 per cent of Republicans chose 'The Europeans are too willing to seek compromise rather than to stand up for freedom even if it means war, and that is a negative thing.' The divide was even clearer when respondents were asked to pick between two statements about 'the way in which the war on Iraq should be conducted'. Fifty-nine per cent of Republicans as opposed to just 33 per cent of Democrats chose 'The US must remain in control of all operations and prevent its European allies from limiting the States' room to maneuver.' By contrast, 55 per cent of Democrats and just 34 per cent of Republicans chose 'It is imperative that the United States allies itself with European countries, even if it limits its ability to make its own decisions.'

So was it, as Robert Kagan would argue, that Europeans were

from Mars and Americans were from Venus? Or was it simply that Republicans were from Mars and Democrats from Venus?

UNILATERALISM

'Do we want the European Union to succeed?' asked President Bush, at the White House meeting to prepare him for his first official visit to Europe in the summer of 2001.[43] When two British visitors insisted that they certainly did, and the United States should too, the president quickly said, with a tight smile, 'that was a provocation!'. But he was not alone in posing this question. Many American policymakers, especially but not exclusively Republicans, were asking whether it was in the American national interest to have a strong, united Europe. The answer was less evident to them than it had been to American presidents from Truman to Clinton.

At the same time, Europe was simply less important to them than it had been to Americans for at least sixty years, since the United States entered the Second World War in 1941. From the lofty vantage point of Washington's new global pre-eminence, politicians who had no special ties to Europe could view the old continent as just one among many. Europe was no longer the central theatre of world politics. With Milošević gone, it was not the source of any urgent foreign policy problem for the United States. Given the European Union's underdeveloped foreign policy coordination and military capability, it was a complicated, troublesome, endlessly time-consuming partner – and one that seemed inclined to define itself, in Gaullist fashion, against the United States. Perhaps, in the new strategic situation of the United States, it might be simpler and more rewarding to build alliances with a few major individual European powers?

We should always beware the danger of attributing to an American administration a coherence that it does not possess. The Bush administration was torn between strong personalities in key departments with differing approaches: Colin Powell at the State Department, Donald Rumsfeld at the Pentagon, Dick Cheney as vice president. Each can only be properly understood through an individual biography. But in this administration there were at least three distinct strands. One was a traditional moderate Republicanism, pursuing American national goals through what Colin Powell called 'a strategy of partnerships'.[44] Another, endlessly discussed by Europeans, was the 'neoconservatives': highly focused, ideological, committed to building up American military strength but also to a policy of actively transforming the Middle East around Israel, in the name of American values as well as interests. The third strand was an American nationalism which looked to make the United States a dominant, even invulnerable power, both militarily and economically, but did not have an ideological agenda for the domestic transformation of other parts of the world. Although this strand was often hard to separate from the 'neoconservative' one, and practically allied to it in many cases, the starting-point was different. Cheney, Rumsfeld and probably Bush himself started closer to this position.

Nationalism is such a chameleon word, and nowadays usually a pejorative one, that I should say briefly what I mean here. European nationalists, in the particular sense in which I have used the term, aspire to make Europe a nation, and preferably a second 'world nation' to rival the United States. Like nineteenth-century German, Italian or Polish nationalists, their aim is to create a political entity that does not yet exist. American nationalists, in the sense in which I'm using the term here, are different. Their sovereign nation-state already exists. But for them, the pursuit of its military, economic and political interests, including its thirst for oil, will almost always override those of other nations or a wider international community, let alone the long-term future of humankind on this planet. Where exactly someone crosses the line between patriotism, in the sober defence of your country's legitimate interests, and this kind of nationalism is often hard to say. It would be foolish to pretend this is a sharp, clear-cut distinction. But I have no hesitation in asserting that this administration contained American nationalists. The one thing they had in common with European nationalists was the mental habit, so sharply identified by George Orwell, of assuming that whole blocks of tens of millions of human beings can be lumped together and confidently labelled 'good' or 'bad'.

In the end, the president's voice would be decisive, but in the summer of 2001 the president was still finding his way. He started, as he told his European visitors, with 'a certain feeling' that 'our great country' was too much tied into multilateral alliances and international organizations. He also felt that the Clinton administration had intervened too indiscriminately in countries around the world, using soldiers for inappropriate humanitarian tasks, such as escorting children to school – 'cross-walk soldiers', as he put it – and for so-called nation-building.

With little personal knowledge of Europe, he set a lot of store by his personal impressions of individual European leaders. He liked Blair and, funnily enough in the light of subsequent developments, he liked Jacques Chirac. He 'had some problems' with Gerhard Schröder and Joschka Fischer. Part of his problem, I suspect, was that both were '68ers, of the kind he thoroughly distrusted. He was himself the flip side of that '68er generation: the conservative un-Clinton. Schröder was a German Clinton and Joschka Fischer, worse still, was a Green. If there was one thing Bush definitely did not like, it was Greens. (A former speechwriter, David Frum, reports that he privately referred to them as 'green-green-lima-beans'.[45]) So he had no regrets about withdrawing from the Kyoto Treaty on global warming. 'Kyoto is mush,' he said. It would have been bad for the US and, frankly, he thought that in the Kyoto negotiation the Europeans 'were trying to screw us'. The US needed more energy, not less. Other, technologically smart ways should be found to conserve energy and save the environment – and he had some people looking into them.[46]

The environment was one of two foreign policy areas on which the new president had firm, well-developed views. The other was defence. He made a sharp and passionate case for a space-based national missile defence. In his inaugural address, he had said plainly: 'we will build our defenses beyond challenge'.[47] A detailed report from an important conservative pressure group, the Project for a New American Century, had already spelled out in September 2000 how this should be done and what extra defence spending would be needed. Several of its signatories – including Paul Wolfowitz, I. Lewis ('Scooter') Libby and Dov Zakheim – were now on the job, in the Pentagon and the vice president's office. In the summer of 2001, they had already requested a $32 billion increase in defence spending.[48]

This administration's neo-Reaganite determination to seize a historic opportunity to make the United States militarily invincible predated the 9/11 attacks.

In these two areas, to the horror of most Europeans, the Bush administration started life by walking away from a whole series of proposed or existing international agreements, not only the Kyoto accord but a treaty to control the worldwide traffic in small arms, a treaty to eliminate landmines, and the Biological and Toxic Weapons Convention. It clearly signalled its intention to terminate the Anti-Ballistic Missile (ABM) Treaty with Russia and to oppose the creation of an International Criminal Court. This approach was celebrated by one of its most vigorous journalistic supporters, Charles Krauthammer, as 'the new unilateralism'. 'After a decade of Prometheus playing pygmy,' he wrote, here at last was 'an administration willing to assert American freedom of action and the primacy of American national interests'.[49] Prometheus unbound.

Assertive unilateralism was thus a hallmark of the second Bush presidency from the outset. But in many areas of policy its position was still unclear – and internally disputed. The first presidential trip to Europe, in June 2001, was conciliatory in tone. It included a strong endorsement for the further eastward enlargement of America's favourite multilateral organization, Nato, a more perfunctory expression of support for the EU, and a clear statement that there was no conflict between the two. His choice of destinations was interesting: not France or Germany, not even Britain, but, apart from Brussels for a Nato summit, Sweden, Spain and Poland. Was this already Rumsfeld's 'new Europe' in the making? Or was it the crablike beginning of a return to a more multilateral approach? What would have happened if Osama bin Laden had not attacked the United States? We will never know. George W. Bush himself cannot know what George W. Bush would have done in less traumatic circumstances.

WAR

'The Pearl Harbor of the 21st century took place today,' Bush dictated into his diary on the night of 11 September 2001.[50] That comparison with Pearl Harbor was repeatedly made by Condoleeza Rice, his National Security Adviser. The media agreed with the president that America was now 'at war'. The country was bedecked with flags and joined in a great outpouring of patriotic solidarity, from sea to shining sea. Only the most hard-bitten European anti-American could remain unmoved by the suffering of the victims' relatives and the spontaneous singing of 'America, the Beautiful'. There was also a harsher tune, which sounded through already in the rescue workers' persistent chants of 'USA! USA!' as President Bush visited Ground Zero for the first time – a note of belligerent defiance, hissing, like the rattlesnake on the old Revolutionary flag, 'Don't Tread on Me'. Bush would catch that Jacksonian note very clearly.

In Washington, more clearly than anywhere else, you saw the clash of power and vulnerability; and the closer you were to the centre of power, the stronger your sense of both. The 'most powerful man on earth' was told after the 9/11 attacks that any one of those planes he could watch through the windows of the oval drawing room, taking off from Ronald Reagan National Airport and flying up the River Potomac, could alter course and hit the White House in about forty seconds.[51] A senior military aide to the vice president told me that the more they learned about possible ways for terrorists to use atomic, biological or chemical weapons, the more alarming it became. However, the people at the top also knew better than anyone what extraordinary, no longer just metaphorically 'space-age', military power lay at their disposal. The so-called 'revolution in military affairs' had already taken them another technological generation beyond the satellite-controlled precision bombing of Kosovo. Like the Martians in H. G. Wells's *War of the Worlds*, they possessed the technology to find and destroy almost anything or anyone, anywhere in the world, with the target never knowing what had hit him.[52] Yet it was they, the Martians, who had been hit. They must fight back, and win. But how, and against whom?

If Americans outside Washington gradually lost this sense of being actively 'at war', most Europeans never had it. Tony Blair, who flew to New York and Washington immediately after the attacks, was an exception to prove the rule. During the Cold War, Atlanticists had constantly worried whether America would really put its life on the line against a threat which only directly affected Europe. Few had anticipated that it would happen the other way round: an attack on America which did not directly threaten Europe. Yet initially, Europeans rallied to America as if the Red Army had just attacked Berlin. A black drape on the Brandenburg Gate declared 'we mourn with you'. For the first time in its history, Nato invoked Article 5 of the 1949 North Atlantic Treaty, declaring this attack on one Nato member to be an attack on them all, and offering every possible assistance.

The offer was politely acknowledged, but not taken up. A revealing account of a meeting between Bush's top officials on 30 September 2001, based on official records, notes 'after a brief discussion of the Nato resolution invoking Article 5 . . . Rumsfeld turned to the idea of a white paper'.[53] Pressed by Condoleeza Rice to say what the French, Germans, Canadians or 'Aussies' could do to help, Rumsfeld stalled. As the veteran reporter Bob Woodward summarizes Rumsfeld's argument: 'The coalition had to fit the conflict and not the other way round . . . Maybe they didn't need a French frigate.'[54]

It's interesting to speculate what would have happened if the Bush administration had taken a conscious political decision to make the war of self-defence against al-Qaeda in Afghanistan a Nato war, however little that helped – indeed, however much that complicated – the actual military operation. That was what the more instinctively multilateralist administration of George H. W. Bush probably would have done, but the ways of the son were not those of the father. Nato might still be the centrepiece of America's political strategy for Europe; it would be marginal to America's military strategy for a global 'war on terror'.

Over the next eighteen months, America acted and Europe reacted. Although the bombing of civilians in Afghanistan was fiercely criticized by anti-war protesters in Europe, the Afghan war against al-Qaeda generally carried mainstream European opinion with it. However, a first wave of wider criticism followed the detention without trial or customary rights of suspected terrorists at Guantanamo Bay, including some who were citizens of European states. Bush's State of the Union address in January 2002 then identified an 'axis of evil' linking Iraq, Iran and North Korea. Europeans were unsettled by the religious moralism of the word 'evil', but even more by the word 'axis'. For unlike the Second World War 'Axis' of Nazi Germany, fascist Italy and imperial Japan, Iraq, Iran and North Korea were not allied in any way. European policymakers saw their policy of constructive engagement with 'reformers' inside the Iranian regime threatened by this rhetoric, rather as they had seen their policy of détente with Eastern Europe in the 1980s imperilled by Ronald Reagan's description of the Soviet Union as an 'evil empire'.

In early 2002, the conflict between a renewed Palestinian intifada and the militant, right-wing Sharon government in Israel reached new heights of brutality, with Palestinian suicide bombers killing Israeli civilians and Sharon's forces killing Palestinian civilians and besieging Yasser Arafat in his headquarters. That time-bomb for transatlantic relations, which Clinton had tried so hard to defuse, now exploded. Few Europeans noticed that Clinton himself had blamed Arafat for failing to accept the best offer of a Palestinian state that Israel had ever been persuaded to make. (When Arafat congratulated Clinton on being 'a great man', the outgoing president reportedly replied: 'The hell I am. I'm a colossal failure, and you made me one.'[55]) But for months the Bush administration's policy was one-sided: effectively demanding that the Palestinians replace Arafat with another leader while endorsing Sharon's brutal campaign as part of the global 'war on terror'. It was no accident that the largest banner at an anti-Bush demonstration in Trafalgar Square, on the president's visit to London in 2003, read simply 'Free Palestine'.

However, European support for the Palestinian cause was often as one-eyed as the Bush administration's endorsement of the Sharon government. European pro-Palestinianism, in turn, fed accusations on the Republican right that the old vampire of anti-Semitism was again abroad in Europe. 'In Europe, it is not very safe to be a Jew,' wrote Charles Krauthammer in the Washington Post. 'What we are seeing is pent-up anti-Semitism, the release – with Israel as the trigger – of a millennium-old urge that powerfully infected and shaped European history.'[56] In making these sweeping charges, American commentators conflated three different things: European sympathy with the Palestinians and criticism of Washington's one-sided support of Sharon's Israel; residual or revived anti-Semitism among Europe's native populist right; and violent attacks on Jews by Muslims living in Europe. The first was disqualified by conflating it with the second and third. Such swingeing accusations, in turn, encouraged some Europeans to mutter about the influence of a 'Jewish lobby' or 'Zionist neoconservatives' in the US, which, in turn, spawned more accusations of European anti-Semitism, and so on and down.

Innocuous by comparison, but none the less contributing to the deterioration, was President Bush's imposition in March 2002 of tariffs on imports of European steel. This undermined the Hamiltonian high ground he had consistently taken on free trade. It was seen for what it was: a piece of political opportunism, wooing steel-producing swing states before the mid-term Congressional elections. Above all, it reinforced his pre-9/11 reputation for unilateralism.

In September, the president unveiled his new national security strategy.[57] Europeans fastened, with alarm, on two points: his aspiration to put American military power 'beyond challenge' and his endorsement of 'pre-emptive actions' against threats from terrorists and rogue states, such as had materialized on 9/11 a year before. In fact, the aspiration to make America militarily invincible had been expressed in identical words in his inaugural address, well before 9/11. The doctrine of pre-emption, however, was new. To be sure, President Clinton had already ordered, in a 1995 directive on US counter-terrorism policy, that the US should 'deter *and pre-empt*, apprehend and prosecute . . . individuals who perpetrate *or plan to perpetrate* [terrorist] attacks' (my italics).[58] There was 'no higher priority', Clinton's directive concluded, than preventing terrorist groups acquiring weapons of mass destruction. But it took the combination of the 9/11 shock and this particular administration to make pre-emption a central plank of national security strategy.

Europeans rightly argued – as did many Americans – that this doctrine could set a dangerous precedent. Any state could strike at any other, claiming that it was thereby 'pre-empting' a potential terrorist threat. (When Israel had bombed an Iraqi nuclear reactor in 1981, the United States had condemned the attack.) Moreover, any state might claim that, in order to protect its sources of secret intelligence, it could not even fully divulge the nature of the threat. You'd just have to take it on trust. On the other hand, Europeans, not feeling themselves to be at war, were slow to acknowledge that the combination of secret terrorist cells, rogue or failed states and weapons of mass destruction posed a qualitatively new kind of threat. Did Europeans have any security strategy of their own to meet this challenge? They did not. The EU's High Representative for Foreign and Security Policy, Javier Solana, only produced a draft European security strategy nine months later, trailing behind the American one.

Europeans also fixed on a blank restatement, in the national security strategy, of America's refusal to submit its citizens, and especially its soldiers, to the International Criminal Court. Yet they often ignored the rest of the document, which emphasized the need for international cooperation, the importance of free markets and free trade (give or take the odd steel tariff), the imperative of development aid for the half of humankind living on less than $2 a day, and, above all, the need to spread human rights, the rule of law and democracy. 'Banalities', you might say, 'like motherhood and apple pie.' But you would be wrong. This was seriously meant, and it was a significant departure for a president who had started with an instinctive preference for preserving America as a Jeffersonian beacon rather than making it a Wilsonian crusader for democracy. 'Wilsonianism' is not a quality I'm arbitrarily attributing to this document. Lamenting European reaction to the national security strategy, one senior administration official told me 'the Wilsonian is getting buried'. What they aimed to do, said this very senior official, was 'to merge Wilsonianism with power'.[59]

The test case, both for pre-emption and for offensive Wilsonianism, was to be Iraq. Pre-emptive actions, said the national security strategy, would always be 'to eliminate a specific threat to the United States or our allies and friends. The reasons for our action will be clear, the force measured, and the cause just.' What was the 'specific threat' in Iraq? What were 'the reasons for our action'? Plainly, no one believed that Saddam was behind al-Qaeda. Did American leaders really conclude from their own intelligence sources that there was a clear and present danger from Saddam's weapons of mass destruction? Tony Blair convinced himself of that, but did George W. Bush?

Iraq had been unfinished business for some Republicans ever since President George H. W. Bush had refrained from going all the way to Baghdad at the end of the first Gulf War. When Saddam Hussein expelled UN weapon inspectors in 1998, the Project for a New American Century had written to President Clinton urging that American policy should now aim 'at the removal of Saddam Hussein's regime from power'.[60] An impressive number of signatories to that letter were now in key positions in the second Bush administration. They included Donald Rumsfeld, Paul Wolfowitz and Richard Perle, all now at the Pentagon; John Bolton and Richard Armitage, both now at the State Department; and Robert F. Zoellick, the country's main trade negotiator.

At the very first meeting of the new National Security Council, in January 2001, Bush asked of his National Security Adviser, Condoleeza Rice, 'what's on the agenda?' and she replied 'How Iraq is destabilizing the region, Mr President'. They then pored over a 'tablecloth-size' grainy photograph of what the director of the CIA, George Tenet, said might be a factory producing materials for chemical or biological weapons.[61] We also know that Rumsfeld and Wolfowitz forcefully raised the possibility of going after Iraq at top-level meetings with the president immediately following the 9/11 attacks. But a decision was taken: not now, not yet.[62]

Seen from the Oval Office, the escalation to war with Iraq was therefore slow and measured. It had been on the conservative agenda long before George W. Bush came to power. It had been considered and put aside, for the time being, in September 2001. Washington was at war, and this 'war on terror' was not going to stop with Afghanistan – especially as the United States had been denied the crowning symbolic victory of capturing Osama bin Laden, dead or alive. Militarily, Iraq was a conventional war which the United States' armed forces could undoubtedly win, unlike the shadowy war against al-Qaeda. It was the obvious next step. Should the United States do it unilaterally? The president's position was much as it had been over Afghanistan: 'if we have to go it alone, we'll go it alone; but I'd rather not'.[63] Blair's was only one voice among many that took him down 'the UN route'. Bush gave the UN route six months and Colin Powell's best shot, but he would not wait any longer for two second-rank old European powers, France and Britain, to sort out their obstinate diplomatic differences. So far as he was concerned, it was not for the US to prove its case to the UN; it was for the UN to prove its relevance in a global war against evil.

Our subject here is not America's long and winding road to war with Iraq; it's what that road revealed about America's changing attitude to multilateralism, to working with 'the Europeans' and other free people around the world, including Canadians, 'Aussies' and many more. As regards Europe specifically, three elements were both highlighted and exacerbated. First, there was Europe's lost centrality. In the index to Bob Woodward's blow-by-blow account of Washington's policy from 9/11 to the end of the war in Afghanistan, the names Chirac and Schröder do not appear at all, and Nato only gets six mentions.[64] If President Bush did not phone Chancellor Schröder for months at the height of the Iraq crisis, thus encouraging Schröder to line up with Chirac against Blair, this was partly because Bush felt he had been double-crossed by that German Clinton. But it was also because an American president no longer felt he needed to phone the German chancellor on the central issue of the day.

Second, there was an undercurrent of anti-Europeanism. The Bush administration had European Americans and American Europeanists of its own. Donald Rumsfeld himself was of German ancestry and had served as ambassador to Nato in Brussels. Richard Perle and Paul Wolfowitz knew Europe well. But precisely those who knew Europe best were most suspicious of it. 'The Europeans', in their view, had been weak, divided, duplicitous appeasers of Hitler in the 1930s, of Moscow in the Reaganite 1980s, of Milošević over Bosnia in the early 1990s; now they would again be weak, divided, duplicitous appeasers of Saddam. In the tradition of cynical European *Realpolitik*, 'the Europeans' cared in each case more for 'stability' than for human rights and democracy. Europe, said Richard Perle in November 2002, had lost its 'moral compass' and France its 'moral fibre'.[65] To the extent that Britain was an exception, it was not European.

In addition, Europeans were smothered by outsize welfare states, rampant relativism, and lifestyle liberalism: they were, so to speak, congenitally Clintonian. Also, the old European demon of anti-Semitism was raising its head again over the issue of Israel and

Palestine, while European countries with large Muslim populations (such as France) were appeasing their own minorities. Taken all in all, this amounted to a settled, negative view of 'the Europeans' which can fairly be described as anti-Europeanism, although anti-Europeans would naturally deny that charge, just as anti-Americans usually deny being anti-American. Anti-Europeanism and anti-Americanism are, however, deeply asymmetrical. The emotional leitmotif of European anti-Americanism is resentment mingled with envy; that of American anti-Europeanism is irritation mixed with contempt.[66]

Finally, there was the temptation to divide and rule. During the Bush administration, the United States' growing ambivalence about the European Union for the first time resulted in the formulation of an American policy of 'disaggregation'.[67] That term came from Richard Haass, a moderate Republican Europeanist at the State Department. Haass himself explained this as a pragmatic reaction to the difficulty of getting a coherent position out of a divided and enlarging Europe. He would subsequently praise Europe as America's 'best pool of partners' in the world.[68] But the image of a 'pool of partners' itself implies something very different from the old Nato alliance. If all the little and medium-sized European fish want to swim along with the big American carp, as one European shoal, that's fine; if not, America will find enough individual fish for any given purpose.

One conservative commentator went further, arguing that the United States should have a conscious strategy of 'cherry-picking' its allies in Europe.[69] Given the presence of pro-American governments in Britain, Spain and Italy, and what the Bush administration tended to see as a solidly pro-American bloc in central and eastern Europe, why not call upon this 'new Europe' to redress the balance of the old? In summer 2003, the *Wall Street Journal Europe* spelled out the logical conclusion. If French hostility to the US persisted, it threatened, 'the US will have no choice but to treat the Atlantic alliance itself as a coalition of the willing'.[70]

This notion of 'coalitions of the willing' did not apply only to Europe. As early as 1992, a draft Defense Planning Guidance prepared by Paul Wolfowitz in the Pentagon had observed 'we should expect future coalitions to be ad hoc assemblies, often not lasting beyond the crisis being confronted, and in many cases carrying only general agreement over the objectives to be accomplished'.[71] Donald Rumsfeld repeated almost as a mantra the view that he had articulated soon after 9/11, responding to the Nato offer of support: 'the mission determines the coalition; the coalition must not determine the mission'.[72] When Britain's participation in the war looked politically uncertain, he said that America didn't even need the help of British forces to defeat Saddam Hussein.

At the height of the Iraq crisis I talked to another very senior administration official. In the course of our conversation, he several times referred to 'the Europeans' as 'a pain in the butt'. When I asked him 'Do you need the Europeans?' his answer was, 'no, militarily not at all'. What if Europe continued to be weak, self-obsessed and carping, as he had characterized it? 'Well,' he said, 'the first question is: does it matter?' To some modest extent yes, he answered himself, mainly because America needed the cooperation of European intelligence agencies and police forces to track down the Islamist terrorists, many of whom came through Europe.

And how would this 'war on terror' end? 'With the elimination of the terrorists.'[73] Although he did go on to say that the United States would have to do 'nation-building' after occupying Iraq – and he acknowledged that the administration had changed its mind on nation-building since 9/11 – the implication was that the United States could unilaterally, or with some limited help from a 'coalition of the willing', win the 'war on terror' by military and police means. Power seemed to be equated in his mind almost exclusively with military power. Savour his phrase: 'The *elimination* of the terrorists.' The ancient Greeks had a word for such an attitude. They called it hubris. This was the hubris of men and women who knew, like no one else, the full extent of America's military power, but who had also felt the shock of America's vulnerability after 9/11. It was the hubris of the wounded.

RETURN TO A NEW STARTING-POINT

After the predictable military victory and the symbolic toppling of the statue of Saddam in Baghdad on 9 April 2003, two things changed.

First, the chorus of American and European voices calling for the transatlantic relationship to be 'repaired', 'renewed' or 'reborn' rose to the fortissimi of the last movement of Beethoven's Ninth Symphony. Not a day passed without at least one op-ed commentary, open letter, speech, conference, workshop, think tank meeting, high-level group or task force devoted to putting the West together again. Often these meetings or initiatives were financed by a German-owned American company, or an American-owned British company, or one of the hundreds of other businesses with a direct stake in the transatlantic economy. The Atlantic community which had grown over sixty years – and, in a larger but weaker sense, over four hundred years – defended itself like a human body fighting off a virus.

Secondly, hubris was punished, as it always is. In this case, it was punished on the streets of Iraq, where the American military found themselves experiencing the very same mixture of power and vulnerability that Washington had felt after 9/11. The euphoric flowering of Iraqi democracy, promised by Iraqi exiles to Pentagon civilians such as Paul Wolfowitz and Richard Perle, and by them to the president and the American people, was, to say the least, slow to materialize. Against the advice of its professional military commanders, the United States did not have enough troops on the ground to cope with initial anarchy and then guerrilla war. In the six months after President Bush announced the end of 'major combat operations', on 1 May 2003, more American soldiers were killed in Iraq than during the war itself.[74] Most of these killings were calculated for maximum media effect, and the American media were happy to oblige: 'if it bleeds, it leads'.

Had the United States been the oil-thirsty bully of anti-American caricature, none of this would have mattered so much. After 'pre-emptively' removing the alleged Saddamite threat, it could have handed over to some new but friendly despot, brought most of its troops home, and let the oil flow to the United States under the protection of an autocratic local regime, as it had for decades in Saudi Arabia. Now no one could accuse this administration, headed by a former oilman, of being indifferent to the interests of the oil industry. As early as February 2001, the Defense Intelligence Agency had prepared a document on 'Foreign Suitors for Iraqi Oilfield Contracts'.[75]

But the United States was not that simple caricature. Nor were the dreaded neoconservatives. They might be the people most ready to use America's military power unilaterally for the advancement of American interests, but they were also those most committed to an ambitious plan to spread democracy in the Middle East, starting with a beacon of post-Saddamite democracy in Iraq.

It was precisely through democratic modernization that they hoped to 'drain the swamp' in which the terrorists that threatened the US multiplied like mosquitoes, and, at the same time, to produce a more favourable neighbourhood for embattled Israel. In fact, their Iraq policy started from a critique of old-fashioned conservative 'realism', such as had characterized the first Bush administration, with its readiness to prefer 'stability' in places like Saudi Arabia to the spread of democracy and human rights in the Middle East. So they were fiercely Jacksonian but also boldly Wilsonian. They plotted nothing less than a revolution from above. Trotsky, an inspiration to some of them in their youth, would have applauded the means though not the end. Recalling a famous description of Napoleon as 'the French Revolution in boots', Pierre Hassner described this approach as 'Wilsonianism in boots'.[76]

Faced with the chorus for transatlantic renewal, and the quagmire in Iraq, the Bush administration moved – somewhat. In Afghanistan, it had long since accepted a European lead in the post-war occupation and, in the summer of 2003, handed overall control to Nato. Now it started looking beyond its 'coalition of the willing' for assistance in policing post-war Iraq, and sought a role for Nato there, as well as proposing a faster handover of power to Iraqis. America had spurned Nato in winning those wars; now it was calling on Nato to help it not lose the peace.

In November 2003, President Bush gave a speech in London strikingly different in tone and content from those of two or three years before. The peace and security of 'free nations', he argued, rested on three pillars.[77] First, 'international organizations must be equal to the challenges facing our world'. 'Like eleven Presidents before me,' he said, 'I believe in the international institutions and alliances that America helped to form and helps to lead.' In case you're wondering, 'eleven Presidents' takes you back to Franklin Delano Roosevelt. He even uttered the M-word, with a brief, tight-lipped prayer for 'the success of multilateralism'. His second pillar was the readiness of free nations 'when the last resort arrives, to restrain aggression and evil by force'.*

The third pillar was 'the global expansion of democracy'. The cause of freedom required more development aid, the fight against AIDS and 'working for justice' in Burma, the Sudan and Zimbabwe. But central to it now was the hope of 'the greater Middle East' joining 'the democratic revolution'. 'In an arc of reform from Morocco to Jordan to Qatar, we are seeing elections and new protections for women and the stirring of political pluralism.' Islam was entirely compatible with democracy. And then he made a remarkable confession: 'We must shake off decades of failed policy in the Middle East. Your nation and mine, in the past, have been willing to make a bargain, to tolerate oppression for the sake of stability. Longstanding ties often led us to overlook the faults of local elites.' Listen and tremble, the house of Saud. 'Yet this bargain did not bring stability or make us safe. It merely bought time, while problems festered and ideologies of violence took hold.' Instead, his administration was now 'pursuing a different course, a forward strategy of freedom in the Middle East'.

Obviously Bush was seeking to please a particular audience, and these fine words might not be matched by deeds. In the Middle East, unlike in central Europe, the United States had given repeated cause to doubt its staying power. But they still marked an extraordinary change from the offensive unilateralism of Bush's early months and the hubris of the wounded at the height of Washington's war of 9/11. The president who had started out so sceptical about foreign entanglements, 'cross-walk soldiers' and nation-building now publicly endorsed both Wilsonianism and multilateralism. This was in some sense a return to the great continuity of those eleven Presidents since Roosevelt, but it was a return to a new starting-point.

---

* What he actually said was '*retain* aggression and evil' but a footnote to the transcript on the White House website reassuringly indicates that 'restrain' is what he was meant to say.

PARTNER?

What, then, can Europeans and other free people expect from this new old United States in the first decades of the twenty-first century? When Harold Macmillan was asked to identify his biggest problem as prime minister he is said to have replied 'events, dear boy, events'.[78] So also for the political writer. If the event is a big one, the outdating effect is more extreme. A political book finished on 10 September 2001 would have been seriously outdated on 11 September 2001. But that's a risk you always have to take, if you want to draw lessons for the future from the recent past. Accepting that we will always be surprised by what Donald Rumsfeld once called, in an unfairly derided distinction, 'the unknown unknowns', we can still say something about what he called the 'known knowns' and the 'known unknowns'.[79] The word 'probably' is to be understood next to most of the statements that follow.

First among the 'known knowns' is American hyperpower. This is three-dimensional. In 2002 the United States spent more on defence than did the next eighteen military powers combined.[80] The imbalance can be seen clearly on the proportional map on page 255. For 2004, its defence spending was lifted yet again, to around $400 billion. Its cumulative military advantage is multiplied by its space-age technological edge. In large-scale wars, the American military can defeat anyone anywhere. Its regional commands cover the whole of the earth's surface and their commanders-in-chief are, as one of them himself observes, the new proconsuls.[81] America has no military rival in sight.

Another proportional map of the world, on page 254, gives a vivid impression of America's economic strength. If you replace the names of the federal states on a more conventional map of the US with those of national economies of equal size, Texas is Canada, California is France and the whole of Russia fits into New Jersey. This is, to be sure, the dimension of American power over which there hangs the largest question mark. How long can a country with, as I write, a $500 billion budget deficit, and a trade deficit of about the same size, sustain a $400 billion annual defence budget, and still meet a growing demand for social spending? The historian Paul Kennedy has suggested that the United States, like most previous great powers, may eventually succumb to the tension between military superstructure and economic base.

None the less, according to current projections the United States is still set fair to remain the world's largest economy for three decades to come.[82] The European Union can grow larger geographically, in a way the United States would find difficult. (Canada and Mexico are not applying for US membership.) However, America will, on current trends, grow faster demographically. That demographic growth, in which successfully absorbed immigration plays a large part, will probably help increase the gross domestic product of the United States beyond that of even a further enlarged European Union.[83] Last but not least, America's soft power, its worldwide power to attract, through everything from Hollywood, McDonald's and Levi's to Stanford, Toni Morrison and the Metropolitan Opera, will remain intensely fascinating for as far ahead as the eye can see.

This power, especially the military power, will continue to bring with it the temptation of unilateralism: go it alone, just because you can. The argument made by many mainstream American policymakers, including John Kerry, that patient multilateralism is in the United States' long-term self-interest, will constantly rub up against this short-term temptation. Moreover, America will continue to defend an unbridled national sovereignty which most European states have long since abandoned. Thomas Jefferson wrote in 1791: 'No court can have jurisdiction over a sovereign nation.'[84] That remains his country's position. The United States is now, in effect, the last truly sovereign European nation-state. This respect for sovereignty does not, however, apply equally to foreign states, especially those from which the United States sees threats to its own security. The asymmetry between America's calculus of sovereignty for itself and that for other states will not always be as extreme as it was during the post-9/11 wars of Afghanistan and Iraq, but it will still be there. We can expect it to be sustained by a fierce and sometimes bellicose patriotism, spilling over into nationalism, of a kind rarely to be found in contemporary Europe.

Uniquely, America will continue to define its national purpose in idealistic terms originally drafted by a group of often Francophile

Englishmen more than two centuries ago. Of course the content of this 'American creed' has developed with time, but its central commandments remain remarkably constant. Contemporary Europe has nothing to compare.[85] The American creed has two gods: one is called Freedom, the other is called God. In the scattersheet of early twenty-first-century capitalist democracies, religion is more than ever at the heart of American exceptionalism. America's muscular Christianity feeds into a moralistic rhetoric of freedom which many Europeans dismiss as humbug.

'They say Christ and mean Cotton,' the great nineteenth-century German novelist Theodor Fontane has one of his characters say of the imperial Englishmen of his time.[86] 'They say Democracy and mean Oil,' is the modern German version, applied to today's imperial Americans. As with the rhetoric of all great powers in history, there is certainly some humbug, although the boundaries between outright lies, semi-conscious hypocrisy and genuine belief are always unclear. The late nineteenth-century President McKinley gave a wonderful account of pacing the floor of the White House night after night, praying to 'Almighty God' for guidance, until his divine national security adviser persuaded him that he had no alternative but to occupy the Philippines 'and educate the Filipinos, and uplift and civilize and Christianize them, and by God's grace do the very best we could by them as our fellow-men for whom Christ also died'.[87] One day we may read an account of the advice that the Almighty gave George W. Bush. Bush clearly saw the war on terror as part of a Christian's 'good fight' against evil. 'I think,' a friend told a *New York Times* reporter, 'in his frame, this is what God has asked him to do.'[88]

It's a great mistake, made by many Europeans, to assume that America's moralistic rhetoric of freedom is merely a cloak for self-interest. Rather, belief in the twin gods of the American creed is a genuine, autonomous motivating force. Americans were Wilsonian long before Woodrow Wilson, and it seems a safe guess that some version of 'Wilsonianism in boots' or the 'marriage of Wilsonianism with power' will remain a recurring feature of American policy for years to come. The fact that American foreign policy perennially defines itself by values as well as interests is a challenge that Europeans will, if they are wise, prepare to take up. The core of American foreign

policy, writes the neoconservative Richard Perle, is 'the universalization of American principles'.[89] But most of these 'American principles' are actually new versions of old European ones, or, in some
cases, old American versions of principles now being newly defined in
the European Union.

America, at the beginning of the twenty-first century, is deeply
engaged in the world, and most Americans support this in principle.
Seventy-seven per cent of those asked in one poll in summer 2003 said
it was best for the future of the US to take an active part in world
affairs, the highest figure since 1947.[90] Another polling organization
found that 50 per cent completely and 40 per cent mostly agreed with
an almost identical proposition. What is more, the combined figure
for those who agreed had remained around 90 per cent since the late
1980s.[91] However, they also found 76 per cent agreeing with the suggestion that less attention should be paid to problems overseas and
more to those at home.

The temptation of disengagement will remain for a country which,
unlike imperial Britain, is itself a huge continental empire – Jefferson's
'empire for liberty'. There will always be an inclination, when the
going gets rough abroad or when times get hard at home, for America
to withdraw into its own 'vast carelessness' – to adapt a telling phrase
from Scott Fitzgerald's *Great Gatsby* – leaving the job half done in
Somalia, or Bosnia, or Kosovo, or Afghanistan, or Iraq, or wherever.
This will be exacerbated by the media's short attention span, the
seemingly congenital difficulty of getting Washington to concentrate
on more than one major foreign policy issue at a time, and the
pressure of the electoral cycle.

So far as American policy towards Europe is concerned, first
among the 'known knowns' is the old continent's loss of centrality in
world affairs. This was bound to happen sooner or later. Europe
hastened its own toppling, with a sustained period of European barbarism and self-destruction in what has been called the 'European
civil war' or 'second Thirty Years War' from 1914 to 1945. However,
the Cold War then artificially restored Europe's centrality, since the
western end of Eurasia became the main theatre of confrontation
between two half-European superpowers. With the benefit of hindsight, the Clinton administration looks like a long afterglow of

habitual American Europeanism. If the West is now to be renewed, it will be in a different shape and on different terms.

As Europe has lost its geopolitical centrality to the United States, it has also lost much of its centuries-old Jamesian cultural fascination. The balance of fascination has shifted, like the balance of hard power. And militarily, Europe is a dwarf beside the American giant. In 2003, the non-American members of Nato (including that almost-European country, Canada) had some 1.25 million men and women under arms, and a further 1 million in reserve, but only 55,000 troops that could be deployed at any one time.[92] These troops would usually be airlifted in somebody else's transport planes and guided by American satellites. Even if Europe's national armed forces are prepared to combine (which they will do only very slowly and reluctantly), even if they can agree on standardized equipment (ditto), even if they buy their own transport planes and send up their own satellites (ditto), even if Americans share some of their secret space-age weapons technology (ditto), even if European publics are ready to pay to make Europe a military superpower (which all polls suggest they are not), even then, Europe will still only be a sluggish five footer to America's six foot six inch military Michael Jordan. A European rapid reaction capability will make Europe militarily more relevant to the US, but still very far from an equal. Seen from the Pentagon, it will have roughly the importance of the reformed alcoholic deputy sheriff in the film *Rio Bravo*.

Economics is a different matter. Even if the American economy will again pull ahead of the combined European economy in absolute size, while China and India are rising fast, Europe will still be the United States' nearest competitor for the foreseeable future. And the two are now so deeply intertwined. In case we get numbed by shorthand billions and trillions, it's worth spelling out the zeros in full: in 2000 American firms had some $3,000,000,000,000 worth of assets in Europe, and European firms had some $3,300,000,000,000 worth of assets in America.[93] There is more European investment in Texas than there is American investment in all of Japan. The US also partly depends on Europeans continuing to buy American bonds, to sustain those huge deficits. In trade negotiations, the EU talks to the US as giant to giant. The Euro has the potential to became a rival reserve currency to the dollar, especially if oil sales begin to be denominated in Euros. American notions of unbridled sovereignty will be qualified by these economic realities. Yet the fact that America has to take Europe seriously economically does not mean it will do so politically. As in pre-1914 Europe, there is no automatic 'read-across' from economics to politics. All that European investment in Texas did not stop George W. Bush behaving as he did.

As Bill Clinton might have said: 'It's the politics, stupid.' The politics of the American approach to Europe is the most difficult part to guess. So much will depend on the 'known unknowns'. European policy is unpredictable because it is made by twenty-five going on forty different nations; American policy, because of the competition between different institutional parts of the government. Washington's motto comes from Walt Whitman:

> Do I contradict myself?
> Very well then I contradict myself,
> (I am large, I contain multitudes.)[94]

While foreign policy approaches do not correlate neatly with party affiliation, Democrats tend to be more like Europeans in cultural attitudes and somewhat more pro-European, whereas Republicans are more susceptible to anti-Europeanism. These differences have deepened with the growing divide between the 'two nations', or at least, two cultures, in America. For Europe, the oscillation between Democrat and Republican administrations may therefore be even more unsettling than it was during the Cold War.

In a system where the making of foreign policy depends so much on the decisions of a few men and women at the apex of a highly politicized upper bureaucracy, personalities and biographies will continue to matter enormously. If Europeans are canny, they will redouble their efforts to seduce young, bright, politically minded Americans with the fading charms of the old continent. (Reversing the Greek myth, Europa starts nuzzling the bull.) It will make a difference if a future American president has known, as a young man or woman, the glories of Rome and the beauties of Kraków.

American policy will continue to be its own prime mover. We will be sure to see again that familiar pattern: America acts, Europe reacts.

None the less, the transatlantic interaction is an important input to this policy. American anti-Europeanism, for example, is much stirred by European anti-Americanism, and real or imputed European anti-Semitism. Anti-Europeanism in turn stokes that anti-Americanism. The crucial interaction, however, will be between two strategic arguments, one on each side of the Atlantic. The European argument, as we saw in the last chapter, is about America: Euro-Gaullism versus Euroatlanticism. The American argument is about America's own role in the world. To simplify, it is the debate between unilateralism and multilateralism.

How might these two great debates influence each other? Let's play through the transatlantic variations. A solidly Gaullist Europe will certainly encourage American unilateralism. (You cooperate with a would-be partner but try to beat a would-be rival.) Equally, a unilateralist America will strengthen Euro-Gaullism, as we saw plainly during the Iraq crisis. A solidly Atlanticist European Union will encourage a multilateralist United States; indeed, it will have the economic and soft power to exert some pressure on the United States to be more multilateralist. Equally, a multilateralist US will encourage European Atlanticism. But none of these pure variants is likely. So far as we can foresee, Europe will continue to be torn between powerful constituencies for Euro-Gaullism and Euroatlanticism, while America will continue to be torn between the temptations of unilateralism and the sober councils of multilateralism.

So the question then becomes: what effect might a divided Europe have on a divided America, and vice versa? A Europe divided between Gaullist and Atlanticist national governments will, as we saw during the Iraq War, encourage the United States to steer a course somewhere in between unilateralism and multilateralism. This is the politics of à la carte multilateralism and 'coalitions of the willing', also known as 'cherry-picking', 'disaggregation' or divide-and-rule. Conversely, an America oscillating between unilateralism and multilateralism will encourage European mood-swings between Euro-Gaullism and Euroatlanticism.

Will the United States want a more united Europe? As we emerge from the most acute period of this crisis of the West, we find a strategic stand-off. In effect, America says to Europe: 'we'll again support

European unity if you assure us it won't be directed against us'. Europe says to America: 'our efforts to unite won't be directed against you, so long as you can assure us that you'll take more notice of what we say'. The main heirs of the old West are like the two proverbial Polish noblemen standing in the pouring rain outside a restaurant door, saying 'after you!', 'no, after you!', 'but I insist, after you!', 'but no, it's *I* who insist', and so on for half an hour, while both get soaked. In this joke, told by Poles at their own expense, one of the noblemen does finally go first and the other says, 'shameful – he argues with me for half an hour and then he goes first anyway!' Can Europe and America be more sensible?

Before turning to that question, we need to spend a little time looking at the rain in which both are standing. What are the new threats and global challenges of the early twenty-first century that will shape the future of both Europe and America? Will they impact differently on the two continents, creating a further divergence of attitudes? Or do Europe and America really have a common interest in confronting these problems and, so to speak, getting out of the rain?

4

The New Red Armies

TERROR AGAINST HOPE

History books record that from 1939 to 1945 the world was engaged in the Second World War and, from about 1946 to 1989, in the Cold War. What will historians call the chapter of world history that began on 11 September 2001? 'The War on Terror' suggested the Bush administration. But what does that mean? Nazi Germany and the Soviet Union were states; terror is a state of mind. Even if we understand 'terror' to be just a snappier word for terrorism, it's still quite unclear what the aims of this war are and in what circumstances it can reasonably be said to be won.

A senior State Department official responsible for counter-terrorism has described the goal of American policy as being 'to assure final victory in the global war against terrorism'.[1] Terrorism is defined by the US government as 'premeditated, politically motivated violence perpetrated against noncombatant targets by subnational groups or clandestine agents, usually intended to influence an audience'.[2] The State Department's annual reports on *Patterns of Global Terrorism* judge that what they call 'domestic' terrorism is probably more widespread than 'international' terrorism, but concentrate on the latter because it has a 'direct impact on US interests'. People getting killed in Chechnya, Rwanda or Sri Lanka are, by this criterion, of less concern. Defining international terrorism as 'involving citizens or the territory of more than one country', these reports chart a history of international terrorist attacks which reached a numerical high point in the late 1980s but then generally declined.[3] Because of the scale of the 11 September atrocity, 2001 bucked the trend, but the report for 2002 noted a 45 per cent drop on the previous year, with 196 attacks by 'international terrorists' rather than the previous year's 355, and 717 people killed.[4]

These 'frozen tears',[5] as one statistician called such cold numbers, only tell a small part of the story, but they do raise some interesting questions. Will the agenda of world politics really continue to be dominated for decades to come by a few hundred international terrorist attacks, especially if their number is generally diminishing? Each individual attack, with its televised horror and unquantifiable human tragedy, can be linked, by politicians and the media, in a meta-story of 'War on Terror' – especially if the victims are Westerners. But how long will such television images retain the interest and maintain the political support of an already horror-jaded public? If there is no second major attack on the American homeland, might not the day come when an American president will be tempted to declare the end of, so to speak, 'major combat operations' in the War on Terror? To say, as I did at the beginning of this book, that America's 9/11 of fear began the twenty-first century does not mean that the United States will spend the next hundred years fighting a few thousand terrorists. Even a big war need not be a long one: the Second World War lasted less than six years. And in international relations, as in life, problems are often not solved, just overtaken by other problems. The world has plenty of those to offer.

If, however, we consider these 'frozen tears' to be just the tip of an iceberg; if, to change the metaphor, international terrorist attacks are like boils on the skin of the body politic, merely the symptoms of more serious diseases below; then the agenda is a huge one, stretching decades ahead. It will involve tackling not just the terrorist groups but the rogue or failed states which support or shelter them and the proliferation of weapons of mass destruction. In the wrong hands, these weapons can be instruments of terror a thousand times worse than a hijacked airliner flown into a tower block.

The War on Terror will end, that senior Bush administration official told me, 'with the elimination of the terrorists'. But there is no finite stock of terrorists to be 'eliminated'. People are not born terrorists, as they are born English, Chinese or Creek Indians. They become terrorists in specific political and personal circumstances, and might cease to be terrorists when those circumstances change. At one point in his career, Nelson Mandela was arguably, by the State Department's definition, a terrorist. If you kill ten terrorists, without changing the political circumstances, and they become martyrs for their own community, you can give birth to a hundred more. Terror is a means not an end – except for a few psychopaths. To be sure, even for non-psychopaths, terrorism can, with time, become a way of life, and of supposedly honourable death. It is often deeply entangled with organized crime and profiteering. None the less, for most terrorist leaders, most of the time, terror is like war in Clausewitz's famous definition: the continuation of politics by other means.

If you look more closely at the politics of early twenty-first-century terrorism, the distinction between 'domestic' and 'international' soon becomes blurred. 'Domestic' in this context means 'inside one country'. But what most terrorists in the world want is precisely that one country should become two, or that two parts of different countries should become one new country, or, in any case, that a state should be fundamentally re-made. The point about those 'subnational groups' is usually that they wish not to be *sub*national any more. This is true, for example, of the Irish Republican Army, the Basque ETA, Kurdish terrrorist organizations, the Kosovo Liberation Army (which the United States first characterized as terrorists and then worked closely with), the Tamil Tigers, the Palestine Liberation Organization and Hamas. As the last two cases indicate, a national grievance – that of the Palestinians – can also be a cause of international terrorism. On one interpretation, Osama bin Laden's first concern was the Islamic 'purification' of the politics of his own country, Saudi Arabia. So to eliminate the causes that might turn people into 'international terrorists' the West (in so far as it still exists) will have to address a baffling range of national political grievances across the globe.

And not just national grievances. The suicide terrorists of 11 September 2001 were not poor, but surroundings of poverty and hopelessness can feed the desperation that leads men and women to kill civilians, and themselves, for a cause. The suicide bombers who claimed the life of the British consul in Istanbul in November 2003 came from one of the poorest Kurdish areas of Turkey. In any case, President Bush made this connection. Announcing a 50 per cent increase in the United States' official development aid, previously the lowest of any country in the developed world, he said: 'We fight against poverty because hope is an answer to terror.'[6]

The section of America's 2002 national security strategy devoted to combating 'Global Terrorism' made another very large connection, between the lack of political freedom and terrorism. 'Freedom and fear', it said, 'are at war.'[7] The epigraph to that section quoted President Bush's still more ambitious claim, in his address in Washington's National Cathedral three days after the 9/11 attacks, that America's 'responsibility to history' was 'to answer these attacks and *rid the world of evil*' (my italics). Following more conventional Christian theology, the only way to rid the world of evil would be to rid the world of human beings, but even if one takes a secular, Enlightenment view of human nature this would be no small task.

I don't mean to be snide at the expense of political and moral hyperbole in a moment of national extremity. I merely want to show how the agenda of an American-led 'War on Terror' could begin as a focused military, intelligence and police operation, to prevent a few thousand existing terrorists from taking another American life, and end up as a plan to change the whole world by lifting more than two billion people out of poverty and unfreedom in a way not attempted by any power in history. For against their own narrative of fear, starting from the trauma of 9/11, Americans have unrolled an even more dramatic narrative of hope. This is the story, told by both Republicans and Democrats, of the global spread of freedom and democracy. In telling it, they reach back to the Founding Fathers and the Wilsonian tradition. They also stand in a great continuity of American policy, from Roosevelt's 1941 proclamation of the 'four freedoms'[8] – of speech and of religion, from want and from fear – through the whole of the Cold War and the generous American response to Europe's 9/11 of hope in 1989.

'The human race has witnessed,' writes Condoleeza Rice, 'in little more than a generation, the swiftest advance of freedom in the 2,500-year story of democracy.'[9] American scholars, of both left and right, have gathered evidence to support this bold claim. At the turn of the nineteenth to the twentieth century, there were some ten to twenty countries in the world which could make some plausible claim to having their governments changed by popular vote, although none of them met today's requirements for being full liberal democracies.[10] Five, including the largest, were the children of England: the United States, Britain, Canada, Australia and New Zealand. The second largest group comprised continental European countries, of which the most important was France. Ancient European republics like Switzerland were joined by constitutional monarchies with varying degrees of limited parliamentary democracy, including Denmark, Holland, Belgium, Portugal, Sweden, Norway, Greece and, to some extent, Italy and Germany. They all had their own native traditions of freedom, but were also influenced by the signal examples of France and England. A third group was in Latin America. A half-century later, in 1950, some 22 of the then 80 sovereign states in the world were democracies, by a much more exacting standard.[11] Most of these democracies were in what was then called the West. By 1973, there were 39, but since the number of sovereign states had grown as a result of decolonization, the proportion was still about the same – just over a quarter.

In the spring of 1974, with the 'revolution of the carnations' in Portugal, there began what can be seen, with hindsight, as an extra-ordinary rolling wave of democratization around the world. Greece followed, and Spain, and much of Latin America, and the Philippines, and then, after the velvet revolutions of 1989, most of the post-communist world. It didn't stop there. Thirty years on, Freedom House counts 117 democracies out of 192 sovereign states in the world – that is, nearly two thirds of them.[12] One can argue about the inclusion of this or that state as a democracy. There is also a very important distinction, made by these scholars themselves, between 'electoral democracies' and full 'liberal democracies'. Beside regular elections, liberal democracies have an effective rule of law, an in-dependent judiciary, well-protected individual freedoms, human rights and minority rights, free, pluralist media, civilian control of the military and a strong civil society.[13] Only these countries truly enjoy the liberty which, as John Locke insisted, is inseparable from law.

Freedom House has developed a rough and ready way of measur-ing political rights and civil liberties. It finds that only 88 of those 117 electoral democracies are, by these criteria, 'free'.[14] Another 55 states are, it finds, 'partly free'. (Note that a country can be 'partly free' even if it is not a democracy, as was the case of many European countries with constitutionally limited government in the nineteenth century.) Only 49 countries are simply 'unfree'. By this reckoning, some 2.8 billion people, nearly half the world's population, live in countries that are free, some 1.3 billion in those classified as partly free, and some 2.2 billion are unfree. Of the unfree, more than half are accounted for by just one state – China. So in these thirty years, the realm of freedom has extended far beyond the West, by all but the most generous definition of that term.

This is, obviously, to paint with a very broad brush. There is a real question how many of those 2.8 billion men, women and children living in states classed as free are in any meaningful sense themselves, individually, free. The great twentieth-century liberal philosopher Isaiah Berlin always insisted, against the Marxists of his time, that we keep two things distinct: freedom is freedom, poverty is poverty. Everything is what it is and not another thing. But plainly the unemployed Moroccan illegal immigrant I met one sultry evening in the Lavapies neighbourhood of Madrid – 'I live', he told me, 'like a wolf' – is not free in the sense that I and you, if you have the money, education and leisure to read this book, are free. 'Are the poor free?' is one of the most pressing questions facing us, the free, at the beginning of the twenty-first century.

It applies most painfully to the nearly half of humankind living on less than $2 a day.[15] The economist Amartya Sen argues compellingly that freedom and development are inextricable.[16] Only above a certain level of development can we seriously talk of people being free, but equally, a certain level of political freedom, good government and the rule of law is indispensable for development. You have to be free to develop and develop to be free. Sen famously observes that no democracy has ever known a famine. Other writers spell out the connection between democracy and development. It is plainly wrong to maintain that no poor country can be a democracy: Sen's own mother country, India, is a billion-strong counter-example. And it is wrong to suggest that people in poor countries, whether Islamic, Confucian or African, do not want freedom and democracy: opinion surveys consistently show that they do. But it does seem to be empirically, historically true that the higher a country's per capita GDP, the better its chance of becoming and *remaining* a democracy. Above about $6,500 dollars a head, it is rare for a country not to be a democracy – although there are, as always, exceptions, notably the oil-rich Arab states. Below $2,000 dollars a head, it is rare for a country to remain a democracy for long.[17] The tasks of freedom and development are therefore inseparable.

Now Americans, with their characteristic historical optimism, have laid out a breathtaking proposition to the world: that we – we, the free – can, by our own endeavours, so foster this unprecedented advance of freedom that it will, in time, embrace the whole of humankind. Then there will be no cause for terror. Underlying the starkest version of this vision is an equally breathtaking analytical premiss: that there is now 'a single sustainable model for national success: freedom, democracy and free enterprise'.[18] This recalls Francis Fukuyama's argument for a 'worldwide liberal revolution' in his hugely influential article of 1989 and subsequent book on *The End of History*,[19] and the so-called 'Washington Consensus' of the IMF and World Bank in the 1990s.

The bald simplicity of this claim for a 'single sustainable model', with its implicit image of America as a model for the future of all humankind, has offended many Europeans, Africans, Asians and others who have themselves long been committed to such a post-Enlightenment, global meliorist aspiration. Kofi Annan, for example, in accepting the 2000 Nobel Peace Prize for his work as secretary-general of the United Nations, quietly observed: 'The idea that there is one people in possession of the truth, one answer to the world's ills, or one solution to humanity's needs, has done untold harm through-out history – especially in the last century.'[20]

The claim is also contested inside America. Samuel Huntington's *Clash of Civilizations*, a political essay even more influential than Fukuyama's, is underpinned by profound, almost old-European intel-lectual pessimism. Huntington argues, like Oswald Spengler, that the West is in decline.[21] The decline of the West, he suggests, might take as long as the rise of the West – about four hundred years – which may be some consolation. Yet the West is already being challenged by two competing 'civilizations' in particular, those of Islam and China.

These civilizations are incompatible with the West, and its model of democracy, and likely to clash with it. 'Some Westerners,' Huntington wrote in 1997, 'including President Bill Clinton, have argued that the West does not have problems with Islam but only with violent Islamist extremists. Fourteen hundred years of history demonstrate otherwise.'[22] And he concluded by imagining a war between the United States and China in 2010. The United States should leave other 'core states' to look after their cultural neighbourhoods, and defend its own – the declining West.

Of course these are not the only narratives or paradigms by which political writers are attempting at once to interpret and to change the world at the century's beginning. Another popular paradigm is 'globalization', carefully defined by Joseph Stiglitz as 'the closer integration of the countries and peoples of the world which has been brought about by the enormous reduction of costs of transportation and communication, and the breaking down of artificial barriers to the flows of goods, services, capital, knowledge, and (to a lesser extent) people across borders'.[23] People 'living on opposite sides of the world [are now] linked in ways previously unimaginable', writes Peter Singer, in his marvellous book on the ethics of globalization, *One World*.[24] Sitting at home in Paris, you can play chess on the internet with someone in China. When you go to a remote African village, you find the locals watching *Basic Instinct* on video.[25]

The rapid, worldwide spread of this notion of 'globalization' is both a product and a catalyst of the process it describes. To some extent, it's a self-fulfilling prophecy. The more reports we have on World Population, World Development, World Trade, World Drugs, World Crime, World Cinema, Global Public Goods, World Sport, World Health, Global Civil Society, and the more international organizations, both official and non-govermental, monitor violations of human rights and minority rights, elections, war, genocide or AIDS worldwide, the more we think of it as one world. The more we think of it as one world, the more it is one world. For many free people under the age of thirty, the nation is no longer the main political locus of 'imagined community'. At one level, globalization is a hard, economic and technical process, driven by satellites, microchips and the latest technologies of information, transport and communications. At another, it's what the poet W. H. Auden called a 'mind-event'.

Globalization, this Microsoft among concepts, none the less faces major competitors. One is the revival of the term 'empire' – now used to describe not the old colonial powers, such as Britain or France, but the former champion of anti-colonialism, America. The United States' role in the world is today almost routinely characterized as that of an empire. The European Union is also described by some analysts as an empire, although they add the tags 'post-modern' or 'neo-medieval' – the two apparently meaning very similar things.[26] Then there's the stark thesis of the *New York Times'* foreign affairs columnist Thomas Friedman that 9/11 began 'World War III' between the 'World of Order' (built on 'five pillars', the US, the EU, Russia, India and China) and the 'World of Disorder' (comprised of rogue states, failed states, messy states, terrorists and organized crime).[27] Or Philip Bobbitt's argument that nation-states are increasingly becoming 'market states'.[28]

Any serious attempt to analyse – that is, to simplify the better to understand – this new world is welcome. Such ideas matter, not least because they sometimes influence, directly or indirectly, what our leaders do. For example, the mistaken idea that the wars of the Yugoslav succession were the inevitable product of centuries-old 'ancestral hatreds' reinforced the reluctance of Western governments to become involved there. That meant people got killed who might otherwise still be alive.

In this chapter, I will look briefly at four important global challenges to the West as it begins to emerge from its turn-of-the-century crisis. I will ask: What is the basic character of each challenge? How big an issue is it, compared with those that preoccupy Americans and Europeans elsewhere in their mutual relations? Do Americans, Europeans and other free people have convergent or divergent interests in this field? What potential is there for them to disagree even if their interests largely coincide? What difference can it make if Europeans, Americans and other free people cooperate rather than compete in their response?

NEAR EAST

In the beginning, none of the places we call the East thought of themselves as the East. All versions of the East – whether European, Communist, Near, Middle or Far – were originally coined by people living in the West. The label was sometimes then accepted by some of the people living in these places, but often not. From the late 1940s until 1989, we talked of 'Eastern Europe', 'the East bloc' and 'East–West relations'. At the beginning of the twenty-first century, that East has gone; older ones have re-emerged. Young men and women who in the 1950s would have learned Russian now queue up to study Arabic, in courses still quaintly called Oriental Studies. But what is the unity or bloc they should study?

One popular answer is 'Islam'. This term is confusing, since it refers both to a religion and to the history and culture of the peoples who profess that religion – as if we had only one word for both 'Christianity' and 'Christendom'. Yet the claim of the Huntingtonian 'clash of civilizations' school is precisely that political effects can be predicted from the fact that a group of people, whether in a state, a nation or a 'subnational group', profess the Islamic faith. In fact, Huntington took the very phrase 'clash of civilizations' from a discussion of 'Muslim Rage' by one of the West's most influential orientalists, Bernard Lewis.[29]

Two contrasting interpretations have received wide currency since the 9/11 attacks. One, favoured by secular Europeans as well as Huntingtonians, sees the heart of the problem in the Islamic religion itself. Islam, it is said, needs to have 'its Reformation', by which secular Europeans often really mean its Enlightenment – and preferably its outright European-style secularization. The other interpretation is that these attacks are the result of a specific history of particular people, many of whom had been radicalized and battle-hardened while fighting against the Russians in Afghanistan, with American support. The holy men of Islam should no more be held responsible for the fact that Osama bin Laden attacked the twin towers in the name of Allah than the Pope or the Archbishop of Canterbury should be blamed if a madman murders in the name of Christ.

For obvious reasons, Western leaders like Tony Blair and, after one unfortunate early use of the word 'crusade', George W. Bush have publicly given Islam the benefit of the doubt. Both Western and Islamic analysts support this in two ways. First, they show how the Koran, and its acknowledged interpreters, condemn the killing of innocent civilians and, in important passages, call for tolerance, pluralism, justice and good government. To be sure, these passages and interpretations are contradicted by others; like all religions, Islam is 'multi-vocal'. Second, they point out that roughly half the world's Muslims live in electoral democracies. However, many of them do so as minorities in states of another majority culture. The second largest Muslim population in the world is in India.

Among countries with a Muslim majority, the record of democracy is thinner. None the less, at this writing, Turkey is an electoral democracy, with an Islamist government behaving moderately in power; the world's largest Muslim country, Indonesia, is trying to be a democracy, though with very serious flaws, as is Bangladesh; small, impoverished Mali and Senegal are not just electoral democracies but ranked by Freedom House as free countries; and Europeans should not forget their own chaotic, semi-democratic Albania, and the EU protectorate of Bosnia, with its culturally Muslim plurality. Anyway, perhaps Muslim majority countries have a thinner record of democracy because they are poor rather than because they are Muslim? Two scholars have shown that, in sustaining electoral democracies, *non-Arab* states with a Muslim majority have done as well as, if not better than, countries of comparable poverty.[30]

So perhaps the real problem is not 'Islam' but the particular history of the Arabs? Here, the record is most depressing. Of the twenty-two members of the Arab League – twenty-one sovereign states and the Palestinian Authority – none is a democracy, unless you are now prepared to count Iraq. The landmark *Arab Human Development Report* of 2002, compiled by Arab scholars, dwelt at length on the region's 'freedom deficit'.[31] It produced a chart of 'freedom scores', aggregating civil and political liberties, on which Arab countries emerged as by far the worst in the world, achieving less than half the 'freedom score' of the next-worst region – Sub-Saharan Africa.

Having advanced this tough self-criticism, the authors nevertheless argued that the problem of Israel and Palestine – what they called

'Israel's illegal occupation of Arab lands'[32] – was one of the largest obstacles to progress across the Arab world. The Palestinian issue, they said, was used by Arab rulers as an 'excuse' for 'retarding political development'.[33] The successor report, in 2003, began with a wail of pain about the suffering of the Palestinians under Israeli occupation, with more than 2,400 dead and more than 40,000 wounded in twenty months after September 2001. They also made a more cautious complaint about how the American occupation of Iraq had inflamed Arab opinion and delayed reform in other Arab countries.[34]

Without minimizing the threats of non-Arab Islamist terrorism, as seen also in Indonesia and Afghanistan, it therefore seems clear that the major challenge to the West lies in the region that is now usually called, in English, the Middle East. I prefer the older English term 'near East', which is still used in many other European languages. If we say 'the Middle East', people generally think of Israel and Palestine, and the Arab countries around them, whereas in fact we need to look at the whole arc of Arab countries from Morocco to Iraq, as well as Iran and Turkey. Moreover, the term 'near East' usefully reminds us Europeans just how near this region is: nine miles at its closest point to Spain. You can cross the Straits of Gibraltar in a small boat, and many thousands of Moroccans already have.

This very near East presents three main challenges: the economic, political and social development of the Arab countries and the Islamic Republic of Iran; the creation of a viable state for the Palestinians in a peace settlement that should also enhance the future security of Israel; and the possible future of a Turkish liberal democracy in a further enlarged European Union, with knock-on effects for its neighbours on all sides, from the Balkans to the Caucasus to Iraq. Each challenge is daunting in a different way.

Despite the immense oil revenues of some Arab states, the combined gross domestic product of the 280 million citizens of the Arab League is less than that of Spain.[35] Of twenty-two countries across the world identified by the World Bank as being below the 'water poverty line' of a thousand cubic metres of water per person per year, fifteen are Arab.[36] Illiteracy rates are the highest of any region in the world.[37] Less than half the women in the Arab countries can read or write. Women are routinely deprived of what in the West are considered basic, universal human rights. The media are largely unfree. Education is often heavily influenced by Islamist sects, such as the Wahhabis in Saudi Arabia. Under the guise of semi-Western constitutional forms, distended 'royal families', clans and tribes rule through the old virtue of *'asabiyya*, defined by a great historian of the Arab peoples, Albert Hourani, as 'solidarity directed towards acquiring and keeping power'.[38]

They have been encouraged or at least tolerated in these ways by the West for much of the twentieth century. European colonial powers originally drew the arbitrary frontiers of their states, installed some of their ancestors as rulers, and sought to preserve cosy 'client' relationships even after decolonization: the British with the King of Jordan, the French with the King of Morocco, and so on. The anticolonial United States has for decades been prepared to treat the oil-producing Arab countries as 'a big dumb gas station', in Thomas Friedman's striking phrase.[39] If an Arab country does hold an election there is now always a danger that a radical Islamist party will come to power – and then it might be 'one man, one vote, once'. Where there has been a revolution, in Iran, it was an Islamic revolution. The Iranian experience suggests there might be no better cure for radical Islamism than a good long dose of Islamist rule, but such countries may be even more uncomfortable company for the West during the years or decades that the patient is taking that cure.

If dealing with the communist East kept the Cold War West together, dealing with this near East has been the source of some of the most bitter arguments between Europe and America. Even during the Second World War, Britain and America quarrelled over Arabia. The Suez Crisis was all about differing approaches to the near East, and the 'oil price shock' of the early 1970s also generated transatlantic tensions. The early twenty-first-century crisis of the West began in the near East (the leaders of al-Qaeda were a Saudi and an Egyptian), was exacerbated by events in the near East (the alienating impact on European opinion of America's support for the military and police campaign against the Palestinians by Israeli Prime Minister Ariel Sharon – a 'man of peace', according to George W. Bush), and culminated in the near East (the storm over Iraq). As we have seen, it has revived the worst mutual stereotypes. Conservative American polemicists denounce

Europeans as anti-Semites and appeasers. Appeasers, that is, of both near Eastern dictators and their own growing Muslim populations. Liberal Europeans mutter about the influence of 'the Jewish lobby' in the United States, and complain that America is behaving like a cowboy in a mosque. They insist that the negative consequences will be felt in Europe, not across the Atlantic. Contemplating the large Muslim minority in France, one senior French official said: 'US policy in the Middle East could be seen as a security risk by my government.'[40]

Of all the difficult regions in the world, the near East seems the one most likely to keep dividing the West. Yet transatlantic arguments are more about means than about ends. To be sure, the European Union's 2003 strategy paper on relations with 'the Arab world' is less explicit and missionary about the goal of spreading Freedom and Democracy, with a capital F and D. It prefers more cautious, eirenic formulations such as 'prosperity, peace and stability', with 'political pluralism and democracy' consigned to a second paragraph.[41] But the main transatlantic differences are those about means that we've already rehearsed, with Europeans preferring quiet diplomacy, 'constructive engagement' and UN-led multilateralism to an American policy of kick-starting regional democratization through the unilateral invasion of Iraq, accompanied by a megaphone diplomacy of eradicating 'evil'.

The fundamental interests of Europe and America in the near East are, if anything, more convergent in the early twenty-first century than before. For a start, both Europe and America are painfully dependent on imported energy. America is the great gas-guzzler, the SUV among nations, but the EU's security strategy soberly notes that Europe is the world's largest importer of oil and gas. These energy imports account for 50 per cent of Europe's energy consumption, projected to rise to 70 per cent by 2030, and most of it comes from the Gulf, North Africa and Russia.[42] We can imagine competition between Europe and America for scarce energy, and there are active rivalries between oil companies and governments for particular souces of supply. However, oil companies like the merged BP-Arco-Amoco are themselves part of an increasingly integrated transatlantic economy. The national or corporate special interest in a particular deal is dwarfed by the common interest of these two vast, interdependent economies in securing their overall sources of supply.

Politically, the 9/11 attacks have revealed a deeper common interest in a new way. The near East is near to Europe but far from America. In classic geopolitics, such a geographical difference would suggest a political difference. But Osama bin Laden and his associates have shown that the Atlantic can be narrower than the Mediterranean. In an age of 'globalization', terrorism, too, is global. Several of the 9/11 terrorists came through Europe. The United States, the 'Great Satan', will probably continue to be their first target, but, as the Madrid bombings of 11 March 2004 showed, European countries come a close second in what al-Qaeda calls 'the Crusader-Zionist alliance'.

If the fabric of American democracy is threatened by terrorist attacks, and by the curtailment of civil liberties in response to those attacks, that of European democracy is threatened by the difficulties most European countries experience in making millions of mainly Muslim immigrants from the near East feel at home. 'Our suburbs, after all, pray to Allah,' writes the French socialist Régis Debray.[43] Not just our suburbs and not just in France. I shall never forget standing in Trafalgar Square one cold November afternoon in 2003. Just down the road, Tony Blair and George W. Bush were discussing the future of Iraq. As darkness fell, I stood amidst a large protesting crowd ('Stop Bush!') and listened to a voice from loudspeakers at the foot of Nelson's column booming out across the square: '*Allahu akbar*! Allah is great!' (What would Nelson have made of it?)

The alienation and radicalization of the second generation of often unemployed Arab and Turkish youth in Spain, France, Italy and Germany is already far advanced. Meanwhile, nativist resentment of immigration has spawned a poisonous populist politics, from Jean-Marie Le Pen in France, through Pim Fortuyn in the Netherlands, to Jörg Haider in Austria. These populists have come close to destabilizing the traditional party system in long-established European democracies.* What these quite disparate populist parties have in common is one theme: hostility to immigration. Anti-Muslimism is now more widespread among post-Christian Europeans than anti-Semitism,

---

* Jacques Chirac owed his re-election in 2002 only to the fact that his opponent in the second round run-off was Le Pen. 'Better a crook than a fascist,' said French leftists, voting unhappily for Chirac.

while the worst anti-Semitic outrages are sometimes the work of Muslims rather than post-Christian Europeans.

Coping with this immigration from the near East, and the ugly native European reactions to it, is the biggest single challenge for European domestic politics at the century's beginning. But the once-sharp distinction between domestic and foreign policy is impossible to maintain. With Europe's population of working age in sharp decline, Europeans will have to accept many more of these immigrants, in their own interest. Yet Europe must simultaneously address the reasons why these people flee the near East, concealed in packing cases, hidden under lorries, risking their lives in tiny, leaking boats, to make a new life here.

The population of the Arab countries is expected to rise from 280 million to somewhere between 410 and 460 million in 2020 – roughly equal to the projected population of the EU of twenty-five member states in the same year.[44] The majority of this population will be under thirty years of age. Roughly half the teenage Arabs interviewed in a recent survey conducted by Arab scholars say they wish to emigrate from their own countries.[45] Of those who wish to emigrate, somewhere between a third and a half say they would like to come to Europe.* You don't have to be Albert Einstein to do the resulting equation. If nothing changes in their Arab homelands, tens of millions of young people will want to leave the near East for the near West. If Europe does not bring more prosperity and freedom to these young Arabs, these young Arabs will come to Europe. So the peaceful economic and political transformation of the near East is an even more vital interest for Europe than it is for America.

Moreover, it's impossible to see how Europe can achieve that transformation without America, or America without Europe. Their strengths lie in different departments, but the instruments at their disposal are complementary. For example, it is now more than ever a distinct American interest that Turkey should remain a Western-oriented democracy, especially if it has an Islamist party in power. But the key to that lies in Turkey's relations with the EU. When the US Deputy Defense Secretary Paul Wolfowitz was trying to secure Turkish

* Another third to a half say they would like to go to America or Canada, but it's harder to take a small boat from Morocco to New York.

support for the invasion of Iraq, he came to Europe and told the EU it must accept Turkey as a member. This was not tactful or clever.* However, it did illustrate the point. The United States has a vital interest in something only Europe can do.

In the case of Israel and Palestine, America will remain the principal outside voice. None the less, Europeans have developed a close working relationship with the Palestinians, funded many of their civil projects and perhaps won their trust. It is naive to imagine that Europe can 'deliver' the Palestinians to a peace settlement while America 'delivers' Israel; but it can certainly help. And the diplomacy of the so-called Middle East Peace Process is carried forward by a 'Quartet' consisting of the US, the EU, Russia and the UN.

There is no way that America can achieve on its own the peaceful transformation of what Americans have taken to calling 'the wider Middle East'. The real question is whether America and Europe, acting together, have the means, commitment and tact to enable the Arabs to do it for themselves. In the aftermath of the Iraq War, we saw how Arab countries might sometimes prefer to be seen to make concessions to European diplomacy rather than to American force. In a rare piece of high-profile coordinated action between Europe's 'big three', the French, German and British foreign ministers jointly visited Teheran, and secured some assurances from the Iranian regime on subjecting its nuclear programme to international supervision. Colonel Gaddafi of Libya went via the British to negotiate secretly with America the dismantling of his weapons of mass destruction. In both cases, it seems reasonable to assume that the threat of American force helped persuade these near Eastern regimes to shift their position, but it certainly did no harm to have the softballing Europeans on hand for the talking. As during the Cold War, the division of labour between a European 'soft cop' and an American 'hard cop' can be effective, even though – or perhaps especially because – it is less a calculated double-act than two cops genuinely disagreeing about the best way to handle a suspect.

In the longer term, the countries of the near East can only be stable

* Imagine a European politician travelling to Washington to tell the United States it must accept Mexico as the fifty-first state, so that Mexico would support a European invasion of Guatemala.

and free if they develop. So long as they only export oil, or other raw materials, they are likely to remain *rentier* states, not democracies. Development means enabling people to make goods or deliver services which others want to buy. Who will buy these goods or services? Next door, in Europe, is one of the largest markets in the world. Inside its borders, millions of people from the near East already live and work. Europe therefore stands to the near East as the United States does to Mexico. Either you allow in more of your poor neighbour's goods or you take more of their people. Without a Mediterranean Free Trade Area, which only the EU can create, an American development strategy for the 'wider Middle East' is unsustainable. It is also mainly up to Europeans to demonstrate that Muslims have a lasting and secure place, as Muslims, in Western societies that once defined themselves against Islam.

Now many Europeans rightly argue that invading and occupying Iraq was not the best way to initiate this peaceful transformation of the Arab world. Quietly supporting the forces for change inside countries such as Iran, Egypt and Saudi Arabia, while advancing a peace settlement between Israel and Palestine, would have been a better way to start. But the occupation of Iraq has happened, for reasons we have explored. Europeans may wish to say, like the man asked for directions at a fork in the road, 'If I were you, I wouldn't start from here', but here is where we are. Now it is in the long-term interest of Europeans even more than Americans that Iraq should become a stable, prosperous, free country. Worse will not be better for anyone except the Islamist enemies of the West.

Even if the West unites to pursue a sustained strategic project for the near East, this will be a very tall order. Yet such a project has one priceless ally: people in the near East themselves. The *New York Times* columnist Thomas Friedman reports that wherever he travels in the region, strangers sidle up to him to express quiet support for his advocacy of democratic change.[46] For the most part, this support can only be articulated in private, since media are under state control and dissidents thrown into prison, but the websites, satellite television and newspapers based in less oppressive places give it public voice. One talkshow on the satellite television channel al-Jazeera debated the question, 'Have the existing Arab regimes become worse than colonialism?' Seventy-six per cent of those who phoned in said 'yes'.[47] A brave Egyptian dissident, Saad Eddine Ibrahim, who was imprisoned for nearly three years by America's protégé, President Hosni Mubarak, finds in the seventh-century Charter of Medina, 'some five to six hundred years before Magna Carta . . . all the elements of pluralism, which is the prerequisite of democracy'.[48] If this is not so much accurate history as the 'invention of tradition', who is the West to complain? We've been at it ourselves for centuries.

Comparative opinion polls show a high level of support for democracy even in Arab and Muslim countries where hostility to the United States is most acute, especially in the wake of the Iraq War.[49] A commentator in the Arabic international newspaper *Al-Hayat* captures this ambivalence in a single sentence: 'We need to reform our educational systems even though the Americans tell us to.'[50] Most remarkably, data from the World Values Survey shows that rejection of authoritarian rule and belief that 'democracy is the best form of government' are higher in the Arab countries than in any other region of the world, including Western Europe, the United States and other English-speaking democracies.[51] Those that have freedom least want it most.

FAR EAST

Among the heterogeneous half of humankind that Europeans and Americans, following the lead of the ancient Greeks, have arbitrarily lumped together as 'Asia', there is almost every kind of state – except the integrated, 'post-modern' European variety. These 'Asian' states offer almost every kind of difficulty known to international relations. In what Westerners call the far East, North Korea poses the urgent problem of a totalitarian regime acquiring nuclear weapons while starving its own people; Burma that of an Orwellian dictatorship oppressing its own people while some of them grow opium for the world; Indonesia and Malaysia those of possible Yugoslav-style fragmentation in the always explosive transition from multi-ethnic dictatorship to multi-ethnic democracy.

Yet the main challenge that the far East poses to the West is very different from that in the near East. It's not these failed, rogue or messy states, troublesome though they are. It's not even economic backwardness, although more than half the world's poorest people are still to be found in Asia.[52] On a stage many times larger than the near East by any measure – geographic, demographic, economic or military – what the West faces here is the challenge not of failing but of rising powers. As you can see from the proportional map on page 257, China and India have more people in one country than the whole of Europe and America combined. Each of those countries is not just a nation but a whole civilization concentrated in a single state. Both are getting stronger. These huge rising powers have the potential, over the next two to five decades, to shift the global balance of power from the Atlantic to the Pacific.

In the longer perspective of centuries, the shift would be from one end of the Eurasian landmass to the other – or rather, back to the other. For in what Western history books called the Dark and Middle Ages, the places Europeans saw as the East had civilizations that were, by many of the criteria traditionally used to measure civilization, more advanced than those of the West. This was true of the world of Islam in Europe's Dark and early Middle Ages, and of China until what Europeans themselves called Europe's 'rebirth', its 'Renaissance', in the fourteenth and fifteenth centuries according to the Christian calendar – that is, until the middle of the fourth millennium of Chinese civilization. As late as 1800, China alone still had a larger share of world manufacturing output than the whole of the West.[53] The West achieved its unprecedented, capitalist industrial 'take-off' partly by borrowing skills and technologies from the East. China, for example, led the way in developing gunpowder, printing, the compass and a meritocratic state bureaucracy. (The British still call their senior civil servants 'mandarins'.)

Now the East has borrowed back. In what Alice Amsden has called 'The Rise of the Rest', most of the non-Western countries that have achieved economic take-off since 1945 lie in Asia.[54] They have launched into rapid, sustained economic growth not by making their own inventions but by borrowing Western ones and improving on them, or simply by manufacturing them cheaper, witness the Japanese cars on our roads and the Chinese radios, saucepans and tools in our

homes. China has become, in the words of one specialist, 'a manufacturing hub for the rest of the world in low-end labour-intensive
goods'.[55] Meanwhile, India shows that services as well as manufacturing can be lifted from the West. When you ring your building
society in Edinburgh or your bank in Boston, you can easily find
yourself talking to someone sitting in a call-centre in Bangalore. The
oldest symbolic meanings of West and East are now revived to serve
in a thousand business-page headlines: the West as the evening country, the *Abendland*, where the setting sun goes in search of Elysium,
the East as the realm of the rising sun.

Just how quickly that sun will rise is disputed. Japan was already
held to be the world's second largest national economy in the 1990s,
but how big are the economies of China and India, how fast are they
growing and how fast are they likely to grow? Depending on your
level of distrust in official statistics, and whether or not you use 'purchasing power parities', you can put China as the sixth or the second
largest economy in the world today, India as the eleventh or the
fourth.[56] You can have the Chinese economy growing at an average
of 9.5 per cent between 1979 and 2001, or much less than that.[57]
These varying assessments imply important differences in time-scales;
none casts doubt on the basic direction.

Whether fast or slowly, the eastern economic sun is rising. What
does this mean for politics? Henry Kissinger has made the interesting
suggestion that 'the international order of Asia . . . resembles that of
nineteenth-century Europe more than that of the twenty-first-century
North Atlantic'.[58] These states use their new wealth to build up
armies. Their forces are still no match for American military hyperpower, to be sure, but they are gradually modernizing their armaments and, in the case of China, India and Pakistan, they possess the
trump card of nuclear weapons. As in nineteenth-century Europe,
these states also have disputed borders and contested territories.
China and India fought a minor border war in 1962. India and
Pakistan have clashed in Kashmir, the Alsace-Lorraine of South Asia.

Meanwhile, China claims Taiwan, in the name of 'the reunification
of the motherland'.[59] European visitors to the region find a kind of
nationalism that has largely died out in twenty-first-century Europe.
These nationalisms are fed by memories of past victories, defeats and

occupations – as, for example, between China and Japan. India aspires to a kind of hegemony in the subcontinent, following, in this respect, the strategy of the British Raj. China seemed to be patiently edging towards something similar in East Asia. A Western analyst describes China's diplomatic strategy as 'neo-Bismarckian'.[60] Chinese commentators themselves recommend that their country should move from a 'victim mentality' to a 'great power mentality'.[61] Here, then, are rising great powers jockeying for position in all too familiar fashion. When the historian A. J. P. Taylor wrote a book about nineteenth-century European diplomacy, he called it *The Struggle for Mastery in Europe*. Perhaps one day another historian will write *The Struggle for Mastery in Asia*? Wars between these Asian 'strategic rivals' are not likely, writes Kissinger, 'but neither are they excluded'.[62]

Against this sombre interpretation, several counter-arguments are advanced. First, these Asian states may look like the European nation-states that emerged after the seventeenth-century Peace of Westphalia, but they are informed by different spirits, whether Confucian, Buddhist, Muslim or Hindu. The region is 'dressed in Westphalian clothes but . . . not performing according to a Westphalian script'.[63] Second, their overwhelming imperative is domestic economic modernization. In a globalized economy, dependent on volatile capital markets, this requires states to behave differently from nineteenth-century Germany, Austria or France. In any case, Japan has, under American tutelage, long practised pacific multilateral cooperation, though combined with statist protectionism at home. India has, in the tradition of Gandhi and Nehru, been a pillar of the United Nations and all its works. China is increasingly engaged in all sorts of international institutions, notably the World Trade Organization, and multilateral ties. Having got over Nato's accidental bombing of its embassy in Belgrade, it even approached Nato for a series of 'conversations'. In a unipolar world, Chinese leaders also see 'multipolarity' as a way of constraining a unilateralist hyperpower America.

In their international relations, there is therefore some chance that these rising powers of Asia can, as it were, skip the European twentieth century, jumping from nineteenth-century, European-style great-power rivalry to twenty-first-century, Euroatlantic-style strategic cooperation. (After all, Asia has already had a terrible twentieth century of its own.) Certainly, it is the overwhelming common interest of America, Europe and free people everywhere to encourage that outcome. Few things are more important for the future of the free.

Do American and European interests in the region otherwise diverge? Take two definitions of the American national interest in Asia. According to the conservative realist Henry Kissinger, 'America's national interest in Asia is to prevent domination of the continent by any single power, especially an adversarial one; to enlist the contribution of Asian nations to overall global prosperity; and to mitigate intra-Asian conflicts.'[64] The liberal internationalist Bill Clinton identifies no less than six American national interests in relations with China: global order, with China 'not only playing by the rules of international behaviour but helping to write and enforce them'; 'peace and stability in Asia', including the restraint of North Korea; 'keeping weapons of mass destruction . . . out of unstable regions and away from rogue states and terrorists' (this, *nota bene*, in a speech delivered in 1997); 'fighting drug trafficking and international organized crime', which is often based in China and neighbouring areas; 'making global trade and investment as free, fair and open as possible', especially for American exports to China; and, finally, China will soon overtake the United States as the world's largest emitter of greenhouse gases which, this American president stated categorically, 'lead to climate change'.[65]

Is there a single one of these interests, whether on Kissinger's list or Clinton's, that Europe does not wholly share? Roughly two thirds of America's foreign trade is with Asia. In 2002, China overtook Japan to become the EU's second largest trading partner outside Europe.[66] Both America and Europe run monster trade deficits with China, $105 billion for the US and €47 billion for the EU in 2002.[67] Both are anxious to sell more of their goods in a market potentially bigger than the whole European Union and North American Free Trade Area combined. Both have large and growing stocks of direct investment in Asia.

Not just the economic but the military and diplomatic behaviour of these rising powers will be shaped by the evolution of their domestic politics. Japan is a secure democracy, though of a slightly peculiar kind. India shows that you can already have a democracy in a vast, linguistically diverse and still poor country, but its tolerant pluralism is threatened by drastic inequality, Hindu nationalism and answering fanaticisms. Pakistan is a deeply unstable regime, hovering between flawed democracy, military dictatorship and Islamist extremism.

In China, nobody can predict how the politics of combining a still ostensibly communist regime with a vibrant, corrupt, drastically unequal capitalist economy will work out. 'Leninist capitalism' does not seem a stable condition. If the correlation that we explored earlier between per capita GDP and democracy holds good, then China should be a democracy some time in the 2020s.[68] But nobody knows if the correlation will hold for a vast country with such old and different political traditions. To give just one example: the bedrock of a secure liberal capitalist democracy is what the early nineteenth-century American president John Adams called 'the government of laws, and not of men'. But the Sinologist Simon Leys notes that in the Confucian understanding, 'the government is of men, not of laws'. This, he adds, 'remains one of the most dangerous flaws in the Chinese political tradition'.[69] Yet optimists see the rule of law already beginning to take hold, in response to the requirements of a market economy.[70]

So the long-term interests of America and Europe in the far East largely coincide. This does not, however, result in Americans and Europeans being equally interested, let alone in coordinated long-term policies. Anyone who spends time on both continents can see that America is, as a matter of observable everyday fact, much more interested in the far East than Europe is. For example, you cannot keep reliably informed about the politics of the region from the newspapers and journals of any European country, including Britain.[71] On the West coast of America, by contrast, it is sometimes difficult to keep informed about anywhere but Asia.

The United States entered the Second World War not following Roosevelt's meeting with Churchill in Placentia Bay – despite the Atlantic Charter – but when the Japanese bombed the American fleet at Pearl Harbor, on an island in the Pacific. For many Americans, the war in the Pacific was *the* war. As Kissinger points out, the US then fought two more major foreign wars, in Korea and Vietnam, to prevent a single, hostile power becoming predominant in Asia. The US military's Pacific Command has some 300,000 serving men and women deployed in some forty-three countries and ten US territories across the whole region. It has 37,000 troops stationed in South Korea alone. If mainland China threatens Taiwan, the US has said it will go to Taiwan's aid. (President George W. Bush ended the earlier policy of 'strategic ambiguity'.) This interest in the region is now stoked by 12 million Asian-Americans, whose votes every national politician has to weigh and woo. If anything, Washington's problem has been a surfeit rather than a dearth of Asian policies.

None of this applies to Europe. Following the handover to China of Hong Kong and Macao, no European power has any significant territory or military presence in the region. European investors and businesspeople are deeply engaged in Asia, but political and public interest in the far East is sporadic at best. Britain is the only European country to have a significant Asian population, but even in Britain the level of ignorance is impressive. In one session of the British television quiz show *University Challenge*, eight of the country's brightest, best-informed students were shown a map of India, with the position of several main cities marked by anonymous blobs. No one could name a single one. (Churchill must be harrumphing in his grave.)

Europe as a whole has nothing that can seriously be described as a far Eastern strategy. Instead, individual European countries conduct policies towards individual Asian countries, or groups of them, based on historic ties, national perceptions and commercial self-interest. For China, as for America, this brings the irresistible temptation to divide and rule. In the late 1990s, for example, China consummately picked away country after country from public condemnation of its abysmal human rights record. It punished those European states, such as Denmark, that supported the regular condemnatory motion at the UN Human Rights Commission in Geneva, while rewarding those, such as France and Germany, which refrained. So much for European solidarity.[72] Mindful of this experience, which he had watched at first hand from Hong Kong, the EU's External Relations Commissioner, Chris Patten, subsequently pulled together, on paper at least, an EU policy towards China.[73] But European solidarity is still in short supply, particularly when national economic advantage is involved.

The far East seems less likely than the near East to divide Europe from America, simply because Europe is so relatively uninterested, with no alternative strategy of its own. There will continue to be fierce competition for commercial advantage, although this will be as much between multinational companies as between nations. There will surely be differences of diplomatic emphasis, often along familiar lines, with continental Europeans tending to prefer dialogue and 'quiet diplomacy' to America's more public denunciations of human rights abuses, and Britain, together with Anglosphere countries such as Canada and Australia, standing somewhere in between. If tensions in the far East lead to a military confrontation involving the United States – over North Korea, for example, or over Taiwan – there is the potential for another crisis of the West, with Europeans shying away even from the threat of warlike action, especially in the defence of faraway countries of which they know little.

Yet there is also a real opportunity for a coordinated strategy, involving not just Europe and America but also the free countries in the region itself, including the old-established Anglosphere democracies of Australia and New Zealand. Such a strategy must be based on a sober assessment of the limits of Western power. The truth is that even the most powerful country in the history of the earth, the early twenty-first-century United States, can have only a secondary impact on the internal evolution of a huge, proud and self-referential country like China. If most of the free countries of the world, which for the time being still control most of the world's wealth, adopt a similar basic approach, coordinated in all the international fora where China wishes to be accepted and respected, the positive impact could be slightly greater.

Even if the odds against success are long, the prize is enormous. To have China eventually join Japan and India as a cooperative liberal democracy would be the biggest payout in the history of freedom. Then the great and once great powers of the West might look forward, not with complete equanimity, but certainly with less alarm, to history's slow, glacial shift in the balance of power, from West back to East.

RICH NORTH, POOR SOUTH

If you think of the world as a city, then the early twenty-first-century West is a gated community of the rich, surrounded by poorer neighbourhoods and terrible slums. In round figures, roughly one billion of the world's six billion inhabitants are rich. They have an average income of approximately $70 a day – which means, of course, that many have less but some have much more.[74] They live mainly in Europe, North America, Japan, and a few other prosperous countries. In the mental geography of development rather than geopolitics, the West of the free is the 'North' of the rich. (Thus Australia, though in the southern hemisphere, is part of the 'North'.) At the other end, in the poor 'South', more than one billion men, women and children live on less than $1 a day. Only slightly better off are another one to two billion people living on less than $2 a day. According to UN figures, between 1999 and 2001, some 840 million people went hungry; one in every seven people in the world.[75] At the same time, nearly one third of Americans suffer from the serious health problem of obesity. Who needs a parable? In the South, men, women and children are dying because they don't have enough to eat; in the North, they are dying because they eat too much.

It has been estimated that in 1999 the assets of the world's three richest people, Bill Gates, Warren Buffett and Paul Allen, exceeded the total annual gross national product of all the world's least developed countries, with a combined population of some 600 million.[76] At the World Economic Forum in Davos in 2001, where companies with combined annual sales of around $5 trillion were represented, the immensely decent-seeming John Thornton, then president of Goldman Sachs, said that when he contemplated the way in which some parts of the world were so much focused on accumulating ever more private wealth he felt 'almost a kind of embarrassment'.[77] Almost a kind of . . .

On 11 September 2001, the day that just over 3,000 people were killed in the al-Qaeda attacks on New York and Washington, some 30,000 children died around the world from preventable disease.[78] And the next day. And the day after that. And every day of the year. Altogether, an estimated 22 million people died from preventable disease in 2001, of whom more than 10 million were children.[79] Ten million is the population of Greater London and its suburbs inside the M25 motorway; of Michigan; of Hungary. Please take a moment to picture to yourself a London peopled entirely with dying children. And the next year, a Michigan of dying children. And the year after that, a Hungary.

A cool head and cold heart might retort: "twas ever thus'. So far back as historians can discern, a large part of humankind has always lived on the edge of extreme poverty, with the accompanying plagues of hunger, disease, unfreedom, illiteracy, violence and early death. But some things have changed. In the past, the world's rich were not able to watch, on their television screens, as the world's poor died. A growing number of the world's poor can also glimpse, on video, film or television, how the other half live. Never before has the world had the resources, derived from economic growth, to tackle worldwide deprivation. And never in recorded history have the world's rich been so much richer than the world's poor. In 1820, the income gap between the five richest and the five poorest countries in the world is estimated to have been about 3 to 1; in 1913, it was 11 to 1; in 1992, 72 to 1.[80] The main reason for this soaring global inequality is the unprecedented economic development that began in the West with the industrial revolution. This is what has made the rich so much richer. Has it also made the poor poorer?

Here is the charge made against 'globalization' by the so-called 'anti-globalizers'. Yet the more thoughtful of them acknowledge that globalization is too complex a phenomenon to be summarily condemned. Some aspects of economic globalization have been good for some of the world's poor, others bad. The biggest reductions in poverty have come in those Asian countries which have begun to 'take off' economically. Economic growth has enabled them to reduce the number of their people living in absolute poverty, even though their populations have also grown. These countries have 'taken off' precisely because they have managed to plug in to the world economy, selling their goods and services abroad. A team of World Bank economists concludes that poor countries with some 3 billion people are among these 'new globalizers', but around 2 billion people are in danger of falling by the wayside, as their countries fail to break into world markets.[81] So the question at century's beginning is not 'whether globalization?' but 'what kind of globalization?'. Even the 'anti-globalizers' have restyled themselves *altermondialistes* or 'alternative globalizers'. Can we achieve globalization with a human face?

To .contribute to this end, the governments of the world held a United Nations 'millennium summit' in 2000. They agreed an unprecedented set of Millennium Development Goals for all humankind. The clearest targets are these: to halve, between 1990 and 2015, the proportion of the human race living on less than $1 a day and the proportion suffering from hunger; to ensure that, by 2015, all the world's children can complete a full course of primary schooling; to reduce by two thirds, between 1990 and 2015, the mortality rate among children under five, and, by three quarters, the mortality rate among mothers giving birth; to have begun to reverse, by 2015, the spread of HIV/AIDS, malaria and other major diseases; and to halve, by 2015, the proportion of people without sustainable access to safe drinking water.[82] These audacious goals will be especially difficult to achieve because the world's population is expected to increase to some 7 billion by 2015, while its natural resources will be diminished.

Most of those professionally involved in fostering development agree that the first responsibility lies with the governments of the developing countries themselves. If a government is corrupt, inefficient and exploitative, as so many of them have been, then all the aid in the world will just be good money thrown after bad. As Amartya Sen argues, the causal connections between freedom and development go both ways. Increasingly, development specialists concentrate on what they call 'good governance' in the countries concerned. This is the key to ensuring that aid and the profits from trade do not go straight into the pockets of the local rulers, their families and their cronies; that budget cuts, where they are demanded by the International Monetary Fund, the World Bank or the European Union, fall on wasteful ostentation, bureaucracy and the military, rather than – as happened too often in the 1990s – further penalizing the poor by cutting expenditure on health systems, education and minimal social security for the unemployed and destitute. None the less, the best imaginable government in the whole poor South cannot achieve balanced, sustainable development for its people without help from the rich North – meaning, mainly, the West.

Beside good advice, the two most important things the poorest countries of the world need from the rich North/West are aid, including debt relief, and trade. How are the main pillars of the North/West doing in these respects? In 2002, the United States spent a little over $13 billion on official development assistance. That was just 0.13 per cent of its GDP – or 13 cents out of every $100. This was the lowest proportion of GDP spent by any of the twenty-three rich donor countries in the Development Assistance Committee of the Organization for Economic Cooperation and Development. So the richest country gave least. By comparison, America's defence expenditure in that year, including the costs of the Iraq War and the early months of the occupation, was in the order of $430 billion.[83] Its total expenditure on Iraq alone was roughly eight times what it spent on overseas aid. Moreover, the largest part of this official aid budget is devoted, for political reasons, to a number of countries, including Egypt, Russia, Israel and Serbia, which are by no means among the poorest of the poor.

The official US Agency for International Development argues that 'American aid' overall is much larger than this, claiming a further $12 billion for assistance given by other government agencies, although this very questionably includes items such as Pentagon 'foreign military loans', and a sweeping $33.6 billion for 'private assistance', which even more questionably includes $18 billion for 'individual remittances'.[84] There is just half a point here. As we have seen, Americans tend to do less through the state and more through private giving. At the front line, in countries in distress, you will often find charities like George Soros's Open Society Foundation, Human Rights Watch or the Ford Foundation, working closely with European charities such as the Oxford-based Oxfam, the London-based Amnesty International and the French-founded *Médecins sans frontières*. These voices of the other America are clear and strong in the chorus of what has been called 'global civil society'.[85] But such private generosity does not begin to excuse the American government for a miserliness that truly beggars belief. In the spring of 2002, President George W. Bush announced a headline 'fifty per cent' increase in American development aid, channelled through a Millennium Challenge Account.[86] Welcome though this was, the $13 billion that the richest country in the world condescended to spend on the world's poor would only rise to around $15 billion in 2006.[87] Meanwhile, for the years 2002 to 2004, the United States was already committed to spending more than $165 billion on the occupation of Iraq and Afghanistan.[88]

Europeans pride themselves on doing better. And so they do – relative to the United States. In fact, if one adds together the aid given by individual EU member states and that given collectively by the EU, Europe gives nearly three times more than the United States in foreign aid, despite having a slightly smaller total economy.[89] But in absolute terms, and relative to our overall wealth, the aid record of Europeans is merely bad rather than abysmal. In 1969, the Canadian prime minister, Lester Pearson, proposed that the rich countries of the world should aim to give 0.7 per cent of their GDP in foreign aid.* This target was endorsed by the UN General Assembly in 1970.[90] Thirty years later, the rich countries of the world gave, on average, just 0.22 per cent of their GDP. Shockingly, this figure has actually fallen since 1990. The West has taken its 'peace dividend' after the end of the Cold War by cutting aid.

Yet to achieve the Millennium Development Goals in 2015, the UN Development Programme reckons that rich countries will have to spend a total of at least $100 billion a year, or roughly double what they give at present. Lester Pearson's 0.7 per cent would make it $165 billion. Here is just one indication of what this increased aid could mean: a group of economists and health specialists working for the World Health Organization calculate that $25 billion would provide basic life-saving health services (immunizations against killer diseases, and so forth) for at least two thirds of the population of the poorest countries. Epidemiologists at the London School of Hygiene and Tropical Medicine estimate that this would save eight million lives per year.[91] Do we think these eight million mainly African lives worth an extra $25 from each of us, the rich billion? Apparently not.

* *The New Republic*, a leading Washington weekly, once held a competition to find a headline even more *boring* than 'Worthwhile Canadian Initiative'. But let them jeer down in Washington, this really was a worthwhile Canadian initiative.

The misery of the world's poor is exacerbated by the fact that many of the poorest countries, especially those in Sub-Saharan Africa, are heavily in debt to Western banks, governments, and international financial institutions such as the World Bank and the IMF. In the past, these loans were often irresponsibly thrust upon them by petrodollar-rich Western banks and misused by corrupt, undemocratic rulers. Some of these tyrants simply siphoned the money back into other Western banks as their private wealth. The interest that their subjects now have to pay back is often more than all the aid their countries receive. Spurred on by an international civil society campaign for debt relief called Jubilee 2000, Western/Northern governments have launched an imaginative if complex initiative for heavily indebted poor countries, but the linkage it makes to IMF programmes is controversial and its progress painfully slow. Even in countries that are doing everything the North/West asked, and have been relieved of much of their debt, the remaining burden of interest payments can still overwhelm their meagre earnings from exports.

The biggest single thing the rich North can do for the poor South is not aid or debt relief, but simply to allow those exports in. Yet this is what rich countries have most spectacularly failed to do. They preach free trade to the world, and even impose it to open up the markets of poorer countries to their goods. But they surround their own markets with high protective walls: permanent, overt ones, called tariffs; temporary, semi-overt ones, called 'anti-dumping' measures; and covert ones, through a tangled skein of special regulations. The World Bank calculates that these trade barriers cost developing countries at least $100 billion a year in lost exports – much more than the rich currently give them in aid.[92]

That's not all. What the poorest of the poor are most likely to be able to export to the rich are the basic products of the earth, grown cheaply on their farms and tended with their hands. Yet rich countries pay huge subsidies to their own agricultural producers. As a result of these subsidies, their exports undercut those of farmers in poor countries. In 2001, the rich countries paid $311 billion in domestic agricultural subsidies: approximately six times what they gave in aid, and more than the total combined GDP of Sub-Saharan Africa.[93]

Many Europeans like to think of themselves as morally superior to

Americans in their concern for the 'Third World' – as some still call it, although the Second has disappeared in the meantime. When it comes to giving aid, they generally are; but not in openness for trade. In a darkly amusing parody of the 'indices' now produced for almost every aspect of global development, Oxfam has compiled a Double Standards Index to show the level of protectionist trade policies against exports from developing countries deployed by the richest and most powerful trading nations. The European Union comes a clear first – that is, worst.[94] In 2000, the annual dairy subsidy paid by the European Union was $913 per cow. This was nearly double the average annual income of someone living in Sub-Saharan Africa. In aid, the EU gave $8 per head to Sub-Saharan Africa. So, that is $913 for a European cow and $8 for an African person.[95] European agricultural exports, subsidized by the EU's Common Agricultural Policy (CAP), drive farmers in poor countries out of business – and into destitution.[96] But where are the crowds on the streets of European capitals protesting against the CAP?

European policymakers are aware of the injustice and have tried to address it. In 2001, the EU took an imaginative initiative to remove tariffs on 'Everything But Arms' imported from the poorest countries in the world.[97] They have also made endless, contorted efforts to reform the CAP. But one of the formative moments of the 'old Europe' alliance in the crisis over Iraq was a deal cut between Schröder and Chirac in the autumn of 2002 which effectively saw off radical reform of the CAP. Defenders of the Common Agricultural Policy say it is needed to preserve the rich, variegated European countryside, yet most of the CAP money goes not to the beautiful, traditional small farms of Provence or Tuscany but to those agricultural industrialists who are defacing the European countryside with endless, hedgeless fields of sugar beet or yellow rape.[98] These agricultural subsidies are still much the largest single item of EU expenditure: 46 per cent of its budget in 2003, and seven times what it spent on foreign aid. So at the heart of what the EU actually does, there is a policy irrefutably causing avoidable harm to the poorest of the world's poor. So much for Europe's moral superiority. America is, in aid policy, the world's leading miser, but Europe is, in trade, the world's leading hypocrite.

To be sure, the United States comes not far behind in the Double Standards Index, followed by Canada and Japan. In 2002, President Bush signed into law a farm bill promising another $180 billion in subsidies to American farmers.[99] Many of these are as indefensible as the European ones. For example, the US gives more than $2 billion in annual subsidies to just 25,000 American cotton farmers.[100] These subsidies depress the world cotton price, costing Third World producers an estimated $350 million a year.[101] Consider the impact on Benin, one of the world's poorest countries, but nevertheless a fragile democracy, classified by Freedom House as 'free'.[102] For years, Benin has been struggling to pay off its inherited debts, with its debt service payments exceeding its spending on basic social services.[103] The key to its development is earnings from exports. Three quarters of its exports are in one crop: cotton. It has seen the world price for cotton fall by more than 40 per cent in the five years from 1997 to 2002.[104] American subsidies are punishing poor cotton farmers in Benin as surely as European subsidies are punishing poor tomato farmers in Ghana.[105]

In yet another index, the Center for Global Development in Washington and *Foreign Policy* magazine rank the rich countries by their 'commitment to development'.[106] They use six measures, starting with aid and trade, but going on to look at foreign investment, migration (letting people into rich countries can help their poor relatives back home), contributions to peacekeeping, and environmental policies (on the grounds that poor countries suffer worse from the effects of climate change, such as drought or flooding, and the spread of infectious diseases). In 2003, the Netherlands did best, closely followed by Denmark and New Zealand. Japan just pipped the United States for bottom place.

Everywhere in the West/North, in America as in Europe, there are committed people using such indices, advertising campaigns, the internet and other new forms of political activism to draw our attention to the selfishness and hypocrisy of all the rich countries. However, twenty-first-century democracies give ever more effective power to another group of highly skilled and motivated people: lobbyists. The two world capitals of lobbying are Washington and Brussels. In Washington, at least 20,000 registered lobbyists represent myriad special interests and fifty federal states.[107] In Brussels, at least 10,000 lobbyists represent special interests, twenty-five nation-states, and powerful regions (Bavaria, Galicia, Tuscany etc).

In many areas of trade and development policy progress depends on a structured, multilateral negotiation in which countries say to each other 'if you do this, I'll do that'. The most important of these is the so-called 'Doha round' of trade talks, led by the World Trade Organization. In recognition of a global priority for development, this has been dubbed the 'development round'. It was meant to be completed by the end of 2004, but at Cancún in Mexico in September 2003, the rich countries dismally failed to do enough to satisfy the increasingly demanding poor. Their hands tied by a thousand lobbies and special interests, the American miser and the European hypocrite competed in selfishness.

In making their argument for generosity, the Western/Northern advocates for the poor often appeal to self-interest. If the West/North does not do more for the world's poor, so the argument goes, we must face the consequences in instability, organized crime, drugs, illegal migration, terrorism and even threats of military action with small, easily portable weapons of mass destruction. This is true. But it is also true that women and children dying in Sub-Saharan Africa do not pose a major security threat to rich people living in the gated community of the West. We can, if we want, afford to let Africans go on dying miserably in large numbers, as we have for most of recorded history. There are risks, but they are, on a pure calculus of interest, manageably small. To be sure, where the poor South actually touches the rich North/West, as in north Africa, Turkey or central America, poverty is an immediate political problem, which threatens to destabilize the domestic politics as well as the foreign policies of both Europe and America. But in regions such as Sub-Saharan Africa, poverty is essentially a moral challenge to the conscience of the West/North.

Some would make this moral case by arguing from historic, collective responsibility: it was the bourgeois capitalist industrial development of the West which produced this soaring global inequality, and Western colonialism that created the states these people are now in. But that kind of argument is not necessary, nor especially wise, since the moral balance sheet of both industrialization and colonization is disputed within the West. All that is needed is to refer to the ethical first principles of the West. The most basic shared moral claim of Europeans, Americans and free people everywhere is that every human being has an inalienable right to a life of minimal human dignity. That right is being denied every day to hundreds of millions of men, women and children in the poor South. Their miserable lot, even if it was not originally caused by the West/North, is being demonstrably and substantially exacerbated by policies of the North/West. Here is today's moral crisis of the West.

HUMANS THREATEN EARTH

How long can the planet Earth sustain ever more human beings consuming ever more food, water and energy? That is the largest challenge facing us all at the beginning of the twenty-first century. It is also the most difficult to write about, since our assessment depends on fiercely disputed scientific predictions.

With consciously spurious precision, the United Nations declared 12 October 1999 as the day on which the world's population passed 6 billion. They even designated Adnan Mević, born in the Kosevo Hospital in Sarajevo at one minute past midnight, the 6-billionth baby.[108] World population growth has been accelerating. We needed millions of years to reach our first billion, in about 1804. According to UN estimates, it took 123 years to add the next billion by 1927, 33 years to reach 3 billion in 1960, then 14 years to 4 billion, 13 years to 5 billion and just 12 years to 6 billion.[109] On a United Nations website, there's a mesmerizing counter showing the estimated world population today. At exactly 1 p.m. on Thursday 25 March, just before I sent this book to the typesetters, the figure was 6,353,098,684, but there's one born every two fifths of a second.[110]

Were the world's population to carry on growing at this rate, it would be close to 13 billion in 2050.[111] But the experts don't think it will. They think the world is experiencing an outsize version of the 'demographic transition' that many individual countries have gone through as they developed. First, food supplies, living conditions and healthcare improve; as a result, life expectancy goes up while birth rates remain high, so population increases rapidly. Then, as people become more affluent, women more emancipated, and parents more confident that their children will survive, the curve flattens off – until eventually we start worrying about having too few children rather than too many. None the less, the UN's median prediction puts the likely world population at nearly 8 billion by 2025 and just under 9 billion by 2050.[112]

Surprisingly, the experts think that, for the foreseeable future, there will be enough food to go round. In 1798, when the world had barely one billion people, Thomas Malthus foresaw terrible disasters flowing from the imbalance in 'the proportion between the natural increase of population and food'.[113] But in a global perspective of two centuries, Malthus has been proved wrong. Thanks largely to the so-called 'Green revolution', food production per head has increased in every region of the world except Africa since the late 1970s, despite the spectacular growth in the number of mouths to feed. In China, it has nearly doubled.[114] The trouble with the world today is not that we can't grow enough food; it's that too much of the food is in the wrong stomachs. As we have seen, hundreds of millions of people in rich countries eat too much, and suffer ill-health as a result, while more than 700 million still go hungry in Africa and the poorer parts of Asia. Obviously, there are still countries with painful shortfalls in domestic food production, but the main problem is one of distribution – or, if you will, redistribution.

In principle that's also true of the other basic necessity of human existence: water. After all, most of the surface of our 'blue planet' is covered by water, in the oceans and ice caps. In practice we mainly depend on the tiny proportion of the world's water that falls or flows on land, or rests under it. Here there is a gathering crisis. As we've seen, one of the Millennium Development Goals is to halve by 2015 the proportion of people without sustainable access to safe drinking water. At the moment, roughly one in three people in rural areas of the developing world does not have such access.[115] The total number is over 1 billion. As population grows, and water usage increases with economic development, that number may actually get larger. Already, some 1.7 billion people live in countries facing 'water stress'.[116] In

Europe, there are four countries which are considered to be water-stressed – Italy, Spain, Cyprus and Malta. But the shortage is most dramatic in the Middle East and parts of Africa. Competition for scarce water has sharpened conflicts between states; not least between Israel and its Arab neighbours. Water supplies will probably be further disrupted by the effects of global warming. In the future, we may see 'water wars'.[117]

Then there's energy. We humans, like other animals, derive our basic daily energy from the food we eat. Since the discovery of fire, we have augmented our own body-power by burning wood, dung or other natural products. Astonishingly, some 2.4 billion people still depend entirely on these primitive sources of energy for their cooking and heating.[118] The rest of us can barely imagine living without electricity, gas and oil to heat and light our homes and offices, pump our drinking water, power our cars and buses, and manufacture the objects we use every day. When we have a small taste of life without artificial power, as Bosnians did during the siege of Sarajevo, we talk of a return to barbarism. Most of this external energy is derived from burning the decomposed remains of plants and plankton that have accumulated over 400 million years. These so-called fossil fuels – oil, gas and coal – account for more than three quarters of all the energy we use. As countries develop economically, so their demand for such energy soars.

Looking a quarter-century ahead, the experts predict a future in which total world energy consumption will have grown by nearly two thirds, with the increased demand coming mainly from the developing countries of Asia, and especially China.[119] They seem to agree that most of the extra energy will continue to be derived from burning oil, gas and coal, rather than from nuclear power, or so-called 'renewable' sources such as the natural forces of wind, waves and rivers, the heat of the sun and that of the Earth's own core. They also think that in twenty-five years' time there will still be enough conventional energy sources to meet these increased needs, although, like the food, much of it will not be in the places where it is most needed. The developed countries of Europe and North America will produce less oil and gas of their own, and therefore be more dependent than ever on imports from the OPEC oil- and gas-producing states, especially those in the near East, and from Russia and other countries around the Caspian Sea. These experts may be wrong; but if they are right, important consequences follow.

A better distribution of food is primarily a moral challenge to the West/North. It is part of the agenda of development that I discussed in the last section. So is access to safe drinking water, although the politics of water also have the potential to catalyse conflict in unstable regions of the world, such as the near East. The politics of oil and gas have a more direct impact on Western policies. They heavily influence, some would say dictate, the priority given to some regions and countries rather than others. They generate a constant temptation to tolerate or even prop up undemocratic regimes, as Americans and Europeans have long done in the near East, and are now inclining to do in Russia, central Asia and the Caucasus. Since the vital material interests of states and politically influential corporations are involved, there's also the potential for conflict between free countries. It's unlikely that the dividing line will fall sharply between Europe and America, but this will remain a challenge of the first order for Western policymakers.

Yet securing enough fossil fuel to burn, without coming to blows or utterly compromising our own principles, is only half this challenge. The other half is the long-term threat to human life on Earth that will result from burning too much of it. There are, of course, many other global environmental concerns, most of which flow ultimately from the exponential growth in human exploitation of the physical world since a young Scotsman called James Watt harnessed the power of heated water to turn the first modern steam engine in 1769.[120] Development economists talk of 'global commons': things like the extent of the world's forests or the condition of the oceans. They identify an intrinsic difficulty: individual countries rarely have sufficient incentives to act to preserve these 'global commons', since they can themselves only capture a small part of the rewards for doing so and those rewards will only accrue if others do the same.[121] Indeed, the short-term interests of a single nation and the long-term interests of the wider world will often conflict. Brazilians have short-term economic gains from cutting down their rain-forest, while that reduces for all of us the capacity of the Earth to reabsorb carbon dioxide and other greenhouse gases. Japanese whalers have short-term profits from overfishing the high seas, while the depletion of oceanic fish stocks is a long-term worry for us all.

Of the many such threats to 'global commons', including the degradation of land and sea, persistent pollutants and the dwindling number of plant and animal species, I will concentrate on two: depletion of the ozone layer and global warming. Now you may object that depletion of the ozone layer is yesterday's story. But that's exactly the point. It is yesterday's story because a real danger was met, probably just in time, by coordinated multilateral action to reduce worldwide output of ozone-depleting chlorofluorocarbons, or CFCs. The United States was among the leaders here, banning all non-essential CFC aerosol sprays in 1978 and then signing the multilateral Montreal Treaty in 1987. As a result, the atmospheric concentration of ozone-depleting substances began to fall within a decade.[122]

Nothing of the kind has yet happened with global warming. The main generic reasons are that the problem is bigger and more complex, the human causes of global warming still contested and the financial costs of addressing them much larger. However, a very important specific reason is that the United States, instead of being among the leaders, as it was in saving the ozone layer, has dodged and ducked to evade its unique responsibility.

The facts of global warming are disputed, but there seems to be a consensus of mainstream scientific opinion on the following. Over the past million years, the surface of the Earth has gone through an alternating series of glacial periods, when the ice comes down and the weather is distinctly chilly even for an Inuit, and 'interglacial' periods, when it's warmer. The last of these interglacial periods, the Holocene, began some 10,000 years ago and we're still in it. According to evidence from ice cores, this appears to be the longest stable warm stretch for as far back as we can see.[123] The Holocene is the precondition for all known human civilization. The average surface temperature of the Earth has oscillated throughout these millennia, but not, on the available evidence, by very much in the thousand years from 900 to 1900 CE. We can say with more confidence that it rose sharply from 1910 to 1945, declined somewhat for the next quarter-century, and then started skyrocketing again after 1976.[124] The summer of 2003 was the hottest on record for 500 years.[125]

This rise in global temperature has consequences: melting ice, rising sea levels, more unpredictable storms and floods. According to one of the world's leading reinsurance firms, Munich Re, natural disasters, mostly caused by extreme weather, cost some $60 billion in 2003.[126] As Europeans debated the Iraq War in the summer of 2003, they experienced a heatwave which caused some 20,000 deaths and $10 billion in agricultural losses. We cannot say with absolute certainty that this heatwave was a result of long-term global warming, but the hot air generated by debate about Iraq does not seem a sufficient explanation. On the whole, though, the specialists conclude that the poorer countries will be worst affected by the consequences of climate change. Poorer countries don't have the money or technology to deal with natural disasters. If the Indian ocean rises just one metre, Bangladesh will lose half its current rice production.[127] But will the ocean rise? That depends on the global temperature.

The findings of the Intergovernmental Panel on Climate Change – described by Margaret Thatcher as 'an authoritative early-warning system'[128] – are worth quoting in all their scientific caution. 'There is new and stronger evidence', the panel concludes in its latest report, 'that most of the warming observed over the last 50 years is attributable to human activities.'[129] The main human activities responsible are our increased emissions of greenhouse gases, and, to a lesser degree, our cutting down the forests that reabsorb some of these gases. The panel looks at various scenarios for future emissions, and predicts 'an increase in globally averaged surface temperature of 1.4 to 5.8 degrees Centigrade over the period 1990 to 2100. This is about two to ten times larger than the central value of observed warming over the twentieth century and the projected rate of warming is very likely to be without precedent during at least the last 10,000 years.'[130] Within this range of scenarios, average worldwide sea level could rise between 0.09 and 0.88 metres by 2100, but more in some places and less in others.[131]

The scientific evidence seems beyond reasonable doubt: the world is rapidly getting warmer and the main reason is the heat-retaining greenhouse gases we are pumping into the sky. More than half these harmful emissions are accounted for by one gas, carbon dioxide, which is produced mainly by burning oil, gas and coal. The panel points out that the warming effect will continue long after we've reduced our emissions, since the gases will already be up there. So common sense would suggest that we'll soon be reducing carbon dioxide emissions, as we did those ozone-depleting chlorofluorocarbons. But if we turn back to the authoritative study of world energy use, we read that, on current trends, global energy-related emissions of carbon dioxide will increase by 1.8 per cent per year, reaching 38 billion tonnes in 2030 – 70 per cent more than today.[132] Two thirds of the increase is expected to come in developing countries, especially China, but the largest single emitter will still be the United States.

Here we must confront what I've called the *unique* responsibility of the United States. This responsibility does not derive merely from its position of world leadership, as the sole hyperpower. I have thus far explored many fields in which the differences between Europe and America are smaller than most people think and it is unclear which side of the Atlantic is doing better or worse. Not so with carbon dioxide. Having less than 5 per cent of the world's population, America belches out nearly 25 per cent of humankind's annual production of greenhouse gases.[133] The EU, an economy of roughly equal size to the US, emits much less. Every year, the skies must absorb a staggering twenty metric tons of carbon dioxide for every American, compared with less than nine metric tons for every European.[134] And it has been getting worse. In 2000, America's carbon dioxide emissions were 14 per cent higher than in 1990.[135]

In their profligate burning of fossil fuels, Americans really are living as if there's no tomorrow. Some have suggested that this careless attitude to natural resources lies deep in the psyche of a people who settled such a vast, richly endowed country. The great American novelist John Steinbeck observed that the early settlers 'burned the forests and changed the rainfall; they swept the buffalo from the plains, blasted the streams, set fire to the grass, and ran a reckless scythe through the virgin and noble timber. Perhaps they felt it was limitless and could never be exhausted . . .' Writing in the early 1960s, Steinbeck bitterly concluded: 'We would not think of doing to the moon what we do every day to our own dear country.'[136] Well, Americans are not doing it to the moon, but they are now doing it to the Earth.

When asked by representatives of developing countries to put on the agenda of the 1992 Rio Earth Summit the over-consumption of resources by developed countries, and especially the United States, the administration of President George H. W. Bush replied: 'the American lifestyle is not up for negotiation'.[137] Now that expansive lifestyle is actually one of the aspects of America that most appeals to many Europeans: those outsize cars and fridges, open roads, endless shining lights and, for a European, unbelievably cheap petrol. What is it over-excited English visitors always say about New York? 'I love the *energy*.' Yes, exactly. But an American defence of unbridled national sovereignty in this domain is different from that in any other, since what the United States pumps into the skies from inside its own borders threatens the well-being of everyone outside them. In this context, it is worth reflecting for a moment on the comment of an eminent British climate scientist: 'I have no hesitation in describing [climate change] as a weapon of mass destruction.'[138]

When President George W. Bush decided at the beginning of his administration that he would not pursue ratification of the Kyoto Protocol, under which the Clinton administration had committed itself to a 7 per cent reduction in its greenhouse gas emissions by 2012, he cited, among other objections, the fact that no emission limits were specified for developing countries. After all, most of the global growth in emissions is expected to come from them. Moreover, a country like China emits more carbon dioxide per dollar of GDP than the US – in other words, Chinese industry and domestic heating are a bit 'dirtier' than America's.[139] So instead, President Bush introduced his own Global Climate Change Initiative, trumpeting a commitment by the United States to reduce its 'greenhouse gas intensity' – that is, the amount of greenhouse gas per dollar of GDP – by 18 per cent by 2012.[140] However, his government's own International Energy Administration quietly pointed out that, since current trends of 'business as usual' growth would anyway result in a 14 per cent fall, what the president was promising effectively amounted to a 4 per cent cut against 2002 levels, rather than the Clinton administration's post-Kyoto commitment to 7 per cent on 1990 levels – a huge difference.[141] It was said of ancient Rome that the emperor Nero fiddled while the city burned. In the new Rome, the president fiddled while the Earth burned.

The contrast with Bush's closest European ally, Tony Blair, is instructive. As he was preparing to wage war on Iraq, shoulder-to-shoulder with Bush, Blair delivered a speech in which he reaffirmed Britain's Kyoto commitment to a 12.5 per cent cut in its 1990 greenhouse gas emission levels, which were already much lower than those of the US. He went on to say that even if everyone adhered to Kyoto, it would only produce a global reduction of 2 per cent in emissions, whereas the science suggested that what we need is a 60 per cent reduction by 2050. A team of scientists had reported to him that this could be done, by creative investment in renewable sources of energy (sun, wind, waves) and alternative fuels, such as hydrogen. So he and the Swedish prime minister had written a letter to the EU presidency, proposing that the whole EU should sign up to the target of a 60 per cent reduction by 2050.[142] On global warming, this other weapon of mass destruction, Blair has been every centimetre the European.

Any informed citizen, drawing on reliable science, can see what is now needed. There has to be a multilateral agreement which assigns to all relevant countries, including developing ones like China, a timetabled 'quota' for greenhouse gas emissions. There then has to be provision for 'emissions trading' between countries, which is the most cost-effective way of achieving the desired result. For this to happen, America is, in Madeleine Albright's phrase, the indispensable nation. We cannot possibly expect a booming China to sign on to such an agreement if the largest and richest gas-emitter, the United States, does not. Even with America, Europe and free countries such as Canada and Australia working closely together, it will be difficult enough to persuade newly industrializing states to exercise a restraint that we have ourselves so obviously lacked.

Will America step up to this challenge? Perhaps an alarming consultants' report to the Pentagon, envisaging wars sparked by the effects of climate change, might help to change even right-wing Republicans' minds.[143] But once again, it is a great mistake to confuse America with George W. Bush. The man who got more votes than him in 2000, Al Gore, was on to the issue of climate change sooner than most Europeans. As Clinton's vice president, he flew to Kyoto in 1997 to salvage a last-minute compromise on the Protocol, although he was not able to stop it subsequently being voted down in the US

Senate. The conservative Republican senator John McCain, not an obvious 'green-green-lima-bean' (to recall President Bush's tag for environmentalists), reported that when he went on the campaign trail, 'in town-hall meeting after town-hall meeting, young people would stand up and say: "What is your position on global warming?"'[144] American scientists have been in the forefront of raising international consiousness on the issue.

A great deal can be done by the kind of technological innovation at which America excels, moving rapidly to renewable and low-carbon sources of energy. None the less, this is a major test for American democracy. To give a lead, America will have to change its cherished lifestyle more than any other nation. There are few votes in this for any candidate and immensely powerful lobbies against it. It calls for two of the most difficult things in politics: putting the wider international interest before the narrowly conceived national one; and the long term before the short term. On any sober reading of the past record and current state of American politics, such an outcome looks woefully unlikely. What arguments can America's friends, in Europe and elsewhere, offer to encourage it? Only that on America's choice will depend the fate of the Earth.

TOGETHER?

We have seen, in previous chapters, that a simple dichotomy between a European model and an American model, European values and American values, is impossible to sustain, even if you look only inside the extended family of the West. There are almost as many contrasts within an ever more diverse Europe, and within an increasingly polarized America, as there are between Europe and America. Important Western countries such as Canada and Australia further complicate the picture, turning a dichotomy into a continuum. In this chapter, we have stepped outside the West into what Westerners call, with a mental geography at once arbitrary and loaded, the East and the South.

If you travel just nine miles south from Spain, across the Mediterranean to the nearest East, all the differences within the West fade into insignificance by comparison with those between the conditions of the Arab and the Western worlds. That is equally true of the contrast with the far East. When you look at the miserable condition of more than a third of humankind, in the poor South, the hyperbolic claims of civilizational difference between 'old Europe' and the United States do not merely seem artificial; they seem criminally self-indulgent. From the viewpoint of someone struggling to survive in Sub-Saharan Africa on less than $1 a day, these internal quarrels of the West can only be characterized by a withering phrase of Sigmund Freud's: the 'narcissism of minor differences'.[145] Finally, the challenge of sustaining dignified human life on the Earth over the next decades, with perhaps 8 or 9 billion human beings demanding more and more of its natural resources, makes these transatlantic squabbles look like the dance of lemmings on a clifftop.

The British diplomat-intellectual Robert Cooper suggests as a maxim of twenty-first-century diplomacy a remark that he attributes to Jean Monnet: if you have a problem you cannot solve, enlarge the context.[146] But this wider, global context of the divisions within the West does not have to be artificially enlarged. It merely has to be seen for what it is. Here are huge common challenges for the West, which, indeed, can no longer be clearly distinguished from the Rest, just as foreign policy can no longer be neatly separated from domestic policy. Tens of millions of people from the Rest already live in the West, shaping its politics. Economically dynamic and increasingly free countries among the Rest are beating the West at its own games. For the poor among the Rest, the rich West is setting the terms of life and death.

To be sure, some areas of the Rest have the potential to divide Europe and America – especially the near East, that most persistent source of crises of the West. But this is not because the interests of Europe and America in these regions fundamentally diverge. Everywhere, there will continue to be competition within the West for commercial advantage and scarce sources of energy. Both of these competitions, however, will as likely be between European states or transatlantic multinational corporations as between one trading bloc and the other. Apart from this, it is impossible, on a sober analysis, to discern any major differences of long-term *interest* between Europe,

America and the other rich and free countries of the West, in any of the fields we have discussed, including the near East. The differences are of historic ties, identities, perceptions and approaches.

Altogether, the argument between Europe and America is most often about means rather than ends. Questions about means can still be first-order questions. Much of the sharpest transatlantic conversation at the beginning of the twenty-first century has been focused on the issue of intervention: when, how, under what conditions and with what authority should one state be allowed to intervene in another? 'Intervention' is generally taken to mean military intervention, although Western states actually intervene in the affairs of other states all the time by economic, diplomatic and cultural means, often quite 'forcefully'. But military intervention is the hardest case, as we saw over Iraq, and before that over Afghanistan, East Timor, Kosovo, Rwanda, Bosnia and Somalia.

There is an extreme 'new American' position: that the United States is entitled to intervene unilaterally anywhere, anytime, to pre-empt a potential threat to its national security which only its secret intelligence can detect, and because the president feels this is theologically right. That is unacceptable to most other free countries in the world. There is an extreme 'old-European' position: that nations can only use force in 'self-defence' against an actual 'armed attack', according to a strict interpretation of Article 51 of the 1945 United Nations Charter, or with explicit authorization from the UN Security Council. This is equally untenable. It is inadequate for the new security risks of the early twenty-first century, in which convergences of international terrorism, rogue or failed states and weapons of mass destruction create threats quite unlike those of a conventional *Wehrmacht* massing at the frontiers of the Third Reich or nuclear missiles in Red Army silos. Al-Qaeda, based in the failed state of Afghanistan, demonstrated that.

It is also, so to speak, morally outdated in the face of an emerging Western consensus on the need to prevent regimes or dominant ethnic groups from committing genocide against people living inside the frontiers of the same state. European states intervened in Kosovo, together with the United States, to stop Slobodan Milošević perpetrating 'another Bosnia' against the mainly Muslim Albanian

Kosovars, although they had no explicit authorization from the UN Security Council to do so. They did, however, have the support of most of the democracies in the world, and most of Serbia's neighbours. A great deal will depend on whether Europe and America, working with other free countries in the United Nations, can now agree some broad 'rules of the road' for future interventions. Each new case will be unique and difficult, with even the facts being disputed, especially if those 'facts' are based on secret intelligence, but it will help to start with some agreed principles. An Italian policy intellectual called Thomas Aquinas prepared an excellent first draft in the thirteenth century, but the 'just war' principles of his *Summa Theologiae* are in need of some revision.[147]

At the beginning of the twenty-first century, a pessimistic 'realist' would judge that the combined power of Europeans, Americans and other free people, working all together, is probably insufficient to meet even the smallest of the global challenges that I have identified: the near East. In any case, this pessimistic 'realist' might add, these Western consumer-oriented teledemocracies do not have the capacity for sustained political engagement abroad and they will not agree among themselves. He, or she, might well prove to be right. Certainly, none of these challenges can be met if Europeans, Americans and other free people work against each other. In each case, progress will only be possible if Europeans and Americans seek to win as allies the free countries that now extend far beyond the boundaries of the old, Cold War West. Vital allies are also to be found among those working for freedom in states that are still unfree. Europe alone is not enough. America alone is not enough. The West alone is not enough.

Crisis as Opportunity

We have now completed our tour around the jagged landscape illuminated by the early twenty-first-century crisis of the West. A red, double-decker mind-bus has taken us from Baker Street to the ozone layer. You might say that was the wrong way around; logically we should start with the biggest problems and work downwards. But in real life, most of us do think outwards from home. The familiar slogan of alternative globalization, 'think global, act local', makes equally good sense when reversed: 'think local, act global'. A shot fired in Kashmir can hit Putney, through the Ahmadi community in Gressenhall Road. Global warming affects Putney High Street too: when did Ye Olde Spotted Horse last see a white Christmas?* Distant events change our everyday lives, so foreign policy is no longer foreign.

What we have discovered, by the light of this electric storm, is an earthscape very different from the one many people imagined at the height of controversy between the Washington of Bush and the Paris of Chirac. Here is no inexorable drifting apart of two solid continental plates, Europe and America. Quite a lot of people believe this, on both sides of the Atlantic, and we have found clever human beings encouraging this belief, with partial reports, aggregate statistics and terrible simplifications. But looking closely and carefully, what we find are overlapping continental shelves and floating islands. There are not two separate sets of values, 'European' and 'American', but

* But it may again. In a fine example of Murphy's Law, the longer term effect of global warming is predicted to be that Britain will get *colder*. An alarmist consultants' report to the Pentagon has even suggested that, by 2020, Britain's weather might begin to resemble Siberia's.[1]

several intersecting sets of values, with the largest area being the intersection. And we find that the personalities and biographies of individual politicians, domestic political imperatives and historical contingencies are often as important as larger forces. In politics, as Machiavelli once observed, chance and luck are usually the half of it.[2]

There are also deeper trends, resulting both from changes in the international system following the end of the Cold War and from longer-term shifts in the balances of power, wealth and fascination between Europe, America and Asia. These have contributed to two great debates. America is divided by a great argument about itself. Europe is divided by a great argument about America, which is, however, also a symptom of Europe trying to make sense of its own transformation. Both meet in Janus Britain, an 'especially clear case of the modern world'.[3]

We find some real, hard conflicts of political and economic interest, but these are multiple and cross-hatched, running not just between but also within continents and countries. Faced with daunting global challenges – the new Red Armies – Europeans, Americans and free people everywhere have an overwhelming common interest. But will they grasp this? The key to progress lies in how we see and what we think, not in any extra-human reality. Transatlantic continental drift is four parts pyschology to one part geology.

Our lightning tour therefore reveals a possibility: that things may be changed for the better because minds are changed for the clearer. The word 'crisis' is so over-used these days that most have forgotten its original meaning. In sixteenth-century English, 'crisis' meant the decisive moment in a sickness, when you started either to get better or to die. So it is with this crisis of the West. The medicine is in our own hands.

If we choose to start recovering, then we face a great opportunity. Over the sixty years since the 1940s, both wealth and freedom have spread further, faster, than in any earlier period. There is still a vast distance to travel, and many a cold mountain to climb, but it's no longer utopian fantasy to set our sights on the goal of a free world.

PART TWO

Opportunity

Twenty Years and a Thousand Million Citizens

We don't know what will happen tomorrow, let alone in twenty years' time, so why try to write about the future? Because if we don't know where we want to go, all paths are equally good. Let us therefore work out together the direction in which we should head, knowing full well that we'll be knocked off course by unexpected events. I propose that we should set a course from '*the* free world' of the Cold War, which no longer exists, towards *a* free world. Never in the history of grammar has a shift from the definite to the indefinite article been more important.

We won't arrive in twenty years, but I nevertheless suggest aiming twenty years ahead. First of all, this lifts our eyes beyond the four or five years of any particular presidency, chancellorship or premiership. Our leaders come and go, but the problems remain. All the global challenges that I've identified require a longer timescale than the one on which our politicians operate, especially in early twenty-first-century teledemocracies, with their chronic short-termism. The Millennium Development Goals are set for 2015, and that's still ambitious. If democracies start to emerge in the near East, some of them are likely to elect Islamist governments and pass through rocky years of transition. A time-frame of twenty years also reminds us that any larger foreign policy strategy, like that of the Cold War West, must be sustained by a minimal consensus between the main political parties competing for power – Republican and Democrat, Conservative and Labour, Gaullist and Socialist, Christian Democrat and Social Democrat – and between the main countries involved, especially those of Europe and America.

More than twenty years is too long. By sketching possible futures, we aim to change them. Orwell wrote *1984* so that it wouldn't happen. Yet there comes a point when the accumulation of the unpredicted, and perhaps even the corrective impact of our own sketches of the future, makes it essential to revise those sketches. Who could have guessed in 1984 what the world would look like in 2004? And with the accelerating speed of technological change, the half-life of sensible prognosis has probably shortened.

Another reason for not going beyond twenty years concerns the likely rise of the far East. Unless China's economic growth falters dramatically, perhaps due to political turmoil, China in 2025 will be such a major power – with Japan still formidable, and India coming up as well – that there will be no point in conceiving a political strategy for Europe and America separately from the intentions and dynamics of Asia. So the old Atlantic-centred West, which has been shaping the world since about 1500, probably has no more than twenty years left in which it will still be the main world-shaper. That's another reason why it's so stupid for Europeans and Americans to waste any more time squabbling with each other. In a longer historical perspective, this may be our last chance to set the agenda of world politics.

But who do I mean when I say 'our'? If you look at the map on page 258, you will see that freedom has already spread far beyond the bounds of the West, by any traditional definition, whether cultural, historical or geopolitical. In a stimulating account of what they call 'Occidentalism', Ian Buruma and Avishai Margalit write: 'the question, then, is how to protect the legitimate idea of the West, that is to say, the world's liberal democracies, against its enemies. And the West, in this sense, includes such fragile Asian democracies as Indonesia and the Philippines.'[1] But can the term really be thus infinitely extended, with every state that becomes a liberal democracy, whatever its geography or history, immediately adopted as part of the West? Precisely if we do believe that the possibility and value of liberal democracy are not confined to one culture or region, isn't it better to accept that the West, in going so far beyond its historic self, also ceases in some important sense to be the West?

Seeing the collapse of the Cold War West, on the one side, and the spread of liberal democracy on the other, it seems wiser to agree that the thing we are trying to reconstruct should have a different name.

To speak already of a worldwide community of democracies, or a global coalition of the free, is to describe an aspiration rather than a reality. So perhaps, for this transitional period, we should talk of the post-West. Today's post-West still has at its core the free countries on both sides of the Atlantic, but it is already very far from being confined to them. Its future evolution is open-ended. The post-West is a pre-something else. Our goal should be to make that 'something else' a free world.

So, to return to the question posed at the very beginning of this book: who, now, are 'we'? Morally, the answer must be all humankind. 'Moral globalization' is not just a pious dream but a spreading reality. More and more individual men and women, especially in the post-West, really do think of themselves as citizens of the world. One reason younger Europeans don't believe as strongly in Europe as their parents did is that they feel Europe is not enough. They are habitual internationalists and, so to speak, one-worlders. Their race is the human race. This is a great step forward in political consciousness. All it needs now is for passive oneworlders to become active freeworlders.

Morally we should regard the poorest Burmese slave labourer in the jade mines of Hpakant as the equal of a Rockefeller. Yet it is clear that he does not have the same opportunities for influencing the world. He can't even secure freedom for himself, let alone help people in other countries to be free. A Rockefeller can. Fortunately, these days you don't need to be a Rockefeller. Any free person in a rich and free country has some such opportunities.

How big is this operational 'we'? Plainly the number is not as large as the 2.8 billion living in countries classified by Freedom House as 'free'. A beggar in Calcutta may live in a free country, but he is not himself free in the sense that an affluent person in Europe or America is free. By voting in an election, he can theoretically influence the policy of the Indian government towards other countries, but in practice his impact will be negligible. In countries like America or France, by contrast, only a small minority, composed of the truly destitute, incarcerated or otherwise incapacitated, do not belong to the operational 'we'.

If we tot up the free Europeans and Americans who have some real possibilities for affecting the world outside the frontiers of their own state, we may arrive at a figure somewhere between 700 million and 800 million. To them, we must add citizens of other developed, free countries, such as Japan and Australia. We should also include a smaller tally of the well-to-do residing in partly free or unfree countries. Russia's super-rich oligarchs, for example, can affect the balance of freedom, for good or ill, more directly than most middle-class Americans or Europeans. So can the rich of Latin America or the near East. And we should not forget those who, while often in prison and certainly not rich, are working for freedom in the most unfree places in the world. They are free in spirit if not in body:

> Stone walls do not a prison make
> Nor iron bars a cage.[2]

Like the dissidents in communist-ruled Eastern Europe, human rights activists in the military dictatorships of Latin America, and freedom fighters in South Africa under apartheid, they can have an influence way beyond their numbers.

Taking all in all, shall we cautiously estimate our operational 'we' at around a thousand million citizens? That's a lot of people with a lot of money, a lot of votes, a lot of voices. There's a poem by G. K. Chesterton called 'The Secret People', which memorably concludes: 'For we are the people of England, that never have spoken yet.' Well, we are the thousand million, that never have spoken yet.

The trouble is that so many citizens of the post-West are now utterly fed up with politics. It's often those who care most about the state of the world, about poverty in Africa, the environment, Burma and Palestine, who are most likely to say that 'They' – our political leaders – are all in the pockets of big corporations like Shell, Bechtel or Halliburton. Many don't even bother to vote: 'If voting changed anything, they'd abolish it.'[3] Apathy is too weak a word for this attitude; it is active, angry disillusionment. At the same time, since we in the post-West live in quite peaceful, prosperous societies, with no Hitler or Stalin massing troops just down the road or across the water, most people feel there's no great urgency about getting involved in debates about foreign policy. Except when there's a dramatic issue, like Bosnia or the Iraq War, the effect is to leave the conduct of foreign policy to a small group of politicians and officials, influenced by lobbyists, journalists and pollsters.

This is dangerous. Men and women who have reached the top in politics often possess an impressive combination of qualities, amongst which being lucky is merely the most important one. But having a well-informed, enlightened, strategic approach to the rest of the world is not necessarily among those qualities. When you get a few glimpses into the way major foreign policy decisions are made, you are left with a sense of mild incredulity that this is how the world is run. It is vital that we all appreciate this simple truth about our rulers: half the time they really don't know what they're doing.

Foreign policy is too important to be left to the politicians. We need to mix in and shape it ourselves. But how? In the second part of this book, I offer a few personal answers to Vladimir Ilyich Lenin's still pertinent question 'What is to be done?' As in the first part, I proceed in an outward spiral – Britain, Europe, America, world – before ending with a couple of thoughts about direct action by citizens of the world. These personal answers are based on the 'history of the present' analysis contained in the first part, but they don't aspire to be comprehensive in any way. They are simply one citizen's suggestions – to advance a conversation among us, and to lift our leaders' sights.

This means finding the right mix of realism and idealism. There's no point in offering a prescription which is so 'realistic' that it's like a diplomat's internal brief to his or her government – trimmed already to all the existing constraints. There's equally little point in writing a Sermon on the Mount. But when the politicians look only one or two weeks ahead, we, the citizens, should compel them to look one or two years ahead. When they raise their sights to one or two years, we should insist on ten to twenty. We should not demand the impossible of them; just the nearly impossible. Demand it of them, and of ourselves. For we are the thousand million, that never have spoken yet.

5

Britain Finds its Role

'Britain Finds its Role.' What a headline that would be. Dean
Acheson's famous jibe that 'Great Britain has lost an empire and not
yet found a role' is as apt today as it was when he made it in 1962.[1]
Forty years on – older but no wiser. Those to the left say 'choose
Europe', those to the right say 'choose America', those behind say
'remain a right little, tight little England', and those in front have no
one to support them.

Yet the role for Britain is staring us in the face. Or rather, in the
four faces of Janus Britain: Island and World, Europe and America. A
country's role must reflect its nature. Historically, Britain is a child of
Europe and a parent of America. Those ties were attenuated, but
never broken, by the experience of Island-Empire. Since 1940, the fulcrum of the twentieth century, they have grown closer than ever
before. Economically, politically, culturally, militarily, intellectually,
socially, gastronomically, we are now inextricably intertwined with
both Europe and America. To choose one or the other would require
a major amputation.

It follows that our vital national interest is to bring Europe and
America as close together as possible. I have argued that this is in the
interest of the world as well; the human race has no chance of making a free world without the combined efforts of its two largest
conglomerates of the rich and free. That argument stands or falls
irrespective of the special British interest. It is neither true nor false
because someone who is British advances it. None the less, the British
have no reason to hide this special national interest. In fact, we had
better not.

There's an old, bad tradition of states advancing their special interests under the flag of a larger community or common good. 'Europe' is the classic example. 'I have always found the word "Europe"', said Bismarck, 'in the mouths of politicians who wanted from other powers something they did not dare to demand in their own name.'[2] France and Germany have both habitually advanced their national interest in Europe's name. This should not be the British way. We should say frankly: 'Here we stand. Britain is Janus. We have this special motive for wishing to shrink the Atlantic. Now listen to our arguments.'

At the height of the fighting between Serbs and Albanians in Kosovo, I met a woman called Violetta. She was against the fighting. I soon understood why: her mother was Serb, her father Albanian. She, like Britain, had a special motive. But she also happened to be right. Violetta's voice could not stop her mother's people and her father's people killing each other. Britain's voice, alone, cannot bring America and Europe together again, although it counts for a lot more, relatively speaking, than Violetta's did. Fortunately, Britain's voice is not alone. I have quoted in the first part of this book just a few of the many voices urging the same strategic imperative, from both sides of the Atlantic. There is nothing ineluctable about America and Europe drifting apart.

Take continental Europe, for a start. Scepticism is one of the greatest intellectual virtues. Scepticism about the integrity, efficiency and accountability of the organs of the European Union is entirely justified and needed at all times. But this thing we in Britain call Euroscepticism is something else. Euroscepticism is, at bottom, defeatism. It takes Churchill as its mascot, but ducks the good fight. It waves the Union Jack, but its real flag is white. For the basic premiss of Euroscepticism is that the continental Europeans are advancing inexorably towards a federal superstate, like a Napoleonic army. Eurosceptics argue that this Bonapartist superstate, shaped by the French and Germans, will inevitably define itself in a Gaullist way, as a rival to the United States. We can't stop them. The only choice we have is whether to fight or flee back to England. And the plain conclusion of the Eurosceptic argument is that, unlike the Duke of Wellington, we should flee.

Yet across the whole continent there is this massive debate going on about what Europe should be and how it should relate to the United States. Euro-Gaullists and Euroatlanticists are quite evenly balanced, especially in the European Union of twenty-five and more. The British could make a real difference to the outcome. But Eurosceptics would have us linger at the edge of the field. Crying 'no surrender!', they propose that we should surrender. As a historian, I must again give the cautionary warning that we can never know what Churchill would have done, had he been alive today. As a citizen, I say Churchill would have been out there in the heart of the battle, fighting to win the day for the Euroatlanticist cause – and using all his execrably pronounced French to urge our valiant French neighbours to join us.

There is an equal and opposite mistake, which we might call Americascepticism. Americasceptics are not necessarily anti-American, just as Eurosceptics are not necessarily anti-European. However, they assume that the United States is advancing inexorably, like a tank, towards a settled, conservative, rich man's, muscular Christian, imperialist, unilateralist posture in the world: the rogue hyperpower. This assumption is also wrong. America, like Europe, is split down the middle, with a national debate raging around exactly such issues. The most withering critiques of American conservative unilateralism have come from Americans themselves. In fact, British Americasceptics subsist on a healthy American diet of Michael Moore, Paul Krugman, Noam Chomsky, Bill Clinton, Al Franken, Peter Singer and Joseph Stiglitz. Americans, not Europeans, will decide this intra-American argument, but of all Europeans, the British have the best chance to influence it at the margins.

So the role that stares us in the face is to be the most vigorous advocate and creative practitioner of the most intensive cooperation between Europe and America, together with other free countries, especially those of the Anglosphere. To be friend and interpreter in both directions. To take the spirit of a twentieth-century West, created, in no small part, by Winston Churchill, and carry it forward into the twenty-first-century post-West: a West that goes far beyond the boundaries of the historic West, and therefore, in an important sense, ceases to be the West, as it works towards a free world.

Tony Blair has grasped and articulated this British national interest, role and chance better than any of his predecessors. In setting the basic strategic direction for Britain in the world, he has been bold, consistent and sometimes politically brave. But his central image of 'the bridge' is not a good one. Bridges are narrow, rigid structures. To say *the* bridge implies that Britain is the only, or at least the main bridge between America and Europe – which also suggests that Britain is not part of Europe. It confuses the broader purpose with the narrower national one of preserving status and 'rank' for this diminished former world power. To mix Blair's favourite image with another stale metaphor of British diplomacy, 'the bridge' is a way of keeping our 'place at the top table'. Or of kidding ourselves that we do.

Why should a German or Polish or Spanish leader walk over London Bridge to reach Washington? Or an American president to talk to Paris or Rome? In practice, European leaders do sometimes privately turn to London to explain something to Washington, and vice versa. This illustrates the part Britain can play, but the goal of our national strategy must be that other European leaders talk as easily and directly to America as British leaders do. Far from nursing the treasured exclusivity of our Special Relationship – so special, the former German chancellor Helmut Schmidt once remarked, that only one side knows it exists – we should want every country in Europe to have a relationship with the United States as close as ours. In fact, politicians and writers in many other European countries have also suggested that their countries are or could be bridges across the Atlantic. I've heard this said in Poland, Italy and Spain. In Germany, there is even an organization called 'Atlantic Bridge'. This is just as it should be. The bridge we need is one between the *whole* of Europe and America. It should be the biggest bridge in the world: 3,000 miles long and as many lanes wide.

In the new, enlarged European Union, Britain, like America, faces a choice. We can cultivate alliances of the willing, as during the Iraq War, or we can seek to win the whole of Europe to what seems to us the right course. The latter approach is more difficult, but offers a much bigger pay-off at the end. It is on the European side that Blair's bridge strategy has fallen down. Partly because he has felt his hands to be tied by Eurosceptic opinion at home, he has not transformed our relationship with our main continental partners as he had hoped. They still view us as semi-detached.

This is where we have to do more. Ultimately, what we need is nothing less than a historic compromise with our ancient enemy, France. For in respect of relations with America, France and Britain are the two magnetic poles of a divided Europe, tearing it apart between a neo-Gaullist and a neo-Churchillian strategy. The competition between England and France is probably the oldest continuous national rivalry in the world. It dates back at least six centuries, to the Hundred Years War. Britain, as it became Britain rather than England, defined itself as the Not-France. Being rude about the French is still a British national sport. A senior backbench Conservative MP, a 'knight of the shires', was once complaining that Margaret Thatcher was very anti-German. I pointed out that she was also very anti-French. 'Oh, *that's* all right!' said the jovial knight, as if this was self-evident to any right-thinking Englishman.

France and Britain are like Walter Matthau and Jack Lemmon in the film *Grumpy Old Men*, two old-timers who have known each other since they were babies and have so much in common, yet go on hurling childish insults and playing silly tricks. In the footsteps of Churchill and de Gaulle, each country still comports itself as a world power, though privately both must acknowledge that their relative power in the world has diminished, is diminishing, and will continue to diminish. Oddly, Britain is more often defensive and resentful in the relationship than France. Yet, calmly considered, Britain has the stronger position. Because of the hegemonic succession from the British Empire to the United States, the world is speaking English, not French, and more often adopting Anglo-Saxon than Gallic ways. The British are winners acting like losers. We should have the confidence to be more generous.

This historic compromise with France would, by definition, be somewhere between the neo-Churchillian and the neo-Gaullist positions. That is also substantively the best position. Britain alone is too small and weak to be a major partner for the United States, especially since American leaders generally feel they can take the British for granted. If even Churchill, with the whole might of the British Empire behind him, found himself compelled to 'beg, like Fala' (Roosevelt's dog), how much more must that be true of a medium-sized European state in relation to the world's only hyperpower. Blair discovered this over Iraq. Speaking to Washington on behalf of 60 million British is one thing; speaking on behalf of 460 million Europeans would be quite another. By contrast, trying to rally 460 million Europeans around a neo-Gaullist alternative 'pole' to the US is a hopeless cause. Half of them won't follow; the American hyperpower will ignore Paris and go it alone, or divide and rule in Europe.

Trying to gather most Europeans around a common position as a consistently Euroatlanticist partner of the United States is the best course for both Britain and France. It is an honourable compromise between the ghosts of Winston Churchill and Charles de Gaulle – who are, I imagine, still quarrelling in heaven. De Gaulle would wholeheartedly approve the achievement of a common European position, Churchill the spirit of transatlantic partnership.

Crucial to this new understanding will be the voice of Germany, the biggest of Europe's 'big three'. In its own enlightened self-interest, Germany should play the role of 'honest broker' between France and Britain. This alone will allow it to continue its own balancing act between Paris and Washington, which has served the Federal Republic so well. The other nations of Europe, small and large, should also gather round, like weary cousins and exasperated sisters, to urge this reconciliation on the two grumpy old men. America, too, should support this in its own enlightened self-interest. It will not be easy and it will take time, but history is full of surprises, and we are thinking in a time-frame of twenty years. If not with Chirac, then with his successor, if not with Blair, then with his successor, this is the way forward.

At some point down this road, Britain will have to decide whether to join the Eurozone. If the economic case for or against joining becomes distinctly stronger, that may be decisive. Assuming that the economic arguments for and against joining remain as uncomfortably balanced as they are at the moment, this will be a political decision. If we are consciously embarked on such a long-term national strategy, it will probably make political sense to go in, since the fuller our engagement in all the counsels of Europe, the greater the chance of steering them in the right direction. If we are not thus embarked, it may not make sense.

In order to implement this national strategy, however, Britain needs a minimal domestic political consensus on foreign policy. A house divided against itself cannot stand; a country divided against itself will never find its role in the world. Britain is a country divided against itself. We therefore need an internal historic compromise to complement, and in fact permit, the external one with France. The essence of this internal compromise is simple: the British right must accept Europe and the British left must accept America. This certainly doesn't mean to accept every stupid directive that comes out of Brussels or every stupid policy that comes out of Washington. It means accepting the basic reality of Janus Britain: that our future depends on attempting to influence the policies of Europe and America so they are compatible with each other and, so far as possible, with our own particular needs. To achieve this requires patient application, over twenty years. We've now seen a pro-American (as well as pro-European) Labour prime minister; then we need a pro-European (as well as pro-American) Conservative or Liberal prime minister; then another pro-American (as well as pro-European) Labour prime minister, and so on.

Looking at current British politics, this may sound fanciful in the extreme. There is, however, one interesting precedent. I earlier compared Britain, the most painfully torn country in today's divided West, to Germany, the central divided country of the Cold War. After 1949, West German politicians argued for two decades about how best to reunite their country. Then Willy Brandt's Ostpolitik proposed that the only way to put Germany together again was to put Europe together again. While making its own 'small steps' across the Berlin Wall, the Federal Republic would do everything in its power to draw the Soviet-led East and the American-led West closer to each other. This policy was bitterly contested by the conservative opposition, but then gradually accepted and largely continued by them while they were in government, under Helmut Kohl. So for two decades the leaders of the Federal Republic pursued a national strategy based on an attempt to bring together two geopolitical blocs even larger than today's Europe and America.[3]

In the end, just when they had almost given up hope, the Germans succeeded in achieving their original goal, although by a different route from the one they had anticipated and thanks to forces beyond their control. But still: they had a national strategy; they knew where they wanted to go; they plugged away at it for twenty years; they got there in the end. Never mind the different route; as Machiavelli said, success is usually half down to luck. Is it quite unthinkable that the British will one day have the common sense to do the same?

Such a strategic foreign policy consensus between the political parties could not exist in a vacuum. It would have to be sustained by published opinion and accepted by public opinion. The very last thing I want to propose is that the old semi-mythical national narrative of 'Our Island Story', from Alfred the Great to India, should be replaced by a new semi-mythical national narrative: 'Our Continental Story', from Hengist and Horsa to the Eurozone. The historian's job is to dismantle myths, not create new ones. History as teleology is always bunk. But at the moment, because of the way history is taught in British schools, few children can locate themselves in any national story at all.

How about every schoolchild learning the story of Britain in terms of the interaction between those four faces, Island and World, Europe and America? There would obviously be more of one face apparent in some periods of British history than in others. Along the way, schoolbooks and teachers would offer alternative interpretations, so children could get used to making their own judgements. None the less, the schoolbooks would show, in a coherent narrative, how Britain came to be this four-faced Janus. That would involve teaching more American as well as more European history. British children get the American version of the English language from television and films, but if you say 'Thomas Jefferson' they'll probably ask which film he was in.

It would also help if British children knew another European language, which less and less of them do. Just one in three British teenagers speaks any foreign language. The government has recognized that language-learning needs to start in primary school, as in Germany and France.[4] Only when we know the language can we really get inside the skin of France or Spain or Italy, places from which our great British football heroes come and to which we regularly travel in large numbers. All British children should also have the chance to spend some time in the country of their choice, if they want to. A different country, with a different culture and spirit embodied in a different language, yet part of the same extended family: that's Europe, not Brussels bureaucracy and asinine EU regulations. It's also the best way to understand this country better: 'What should they know of England who only England know?'[5]

Finally, there's politics. How many people in Britain grasp the relationship between the US Congress, Supreme Court and President? How many know the difference between the president of the European Commission and the presidency of the European Council? A world island needs a 'civics' to match. Most British school-leavers don't even possess the basic facts. 'European studies' or 'American studies' at British universities are, at the moment, the second storey of a house built on sand.

After education, there's information for adults. Britain is remarkably well informed in some respects. BBC Radio 3 and 4, and the BBC's superb website, are alone worth all the support the BBC receives from the public purse. Our biggest weakness is our newspapers. These serve well as entertainment, and offer a wide range of vigorous, interesting commentary. What they don't give us is enough news, especially foreign news. The term *news*paper is by now a misnomer. If we imagine we can be seriously, accurately informed about what is happening in Europe or Asia by reading a British daily paper, we are suffering a dangerous delusion.[6] (British papers are generally better on America.) Most British papers no longer distinguish between fact, which should be sacred, and opinion, which is free. The distinction between broadsheets and tabloids has increasingly broken down: *The Times* is a broadloid, the *Daily Mail*, a tabsheet. On policy towards Europe, the Eurosceptic papers have tied the hands of governments since about 1990.

What we need is two revolts. We need a revolt of the politicians, who should finally summon the courage to face down the media barons. Politicians, not newspaper proprietors, are the elected representatives of the British people. The press tycoons now more than ever enjoy what an earlier British prime minister called 'power without responsibility, the prerogative of the harlot through the ages'.[7] But we also need a revolt of the journalists. After all, journalists, not proprietors, actually write and edit these papers. Some of the cleverest, best educated, most enterprising people in Britain go into journalism.

In weekly journals, books and American magazines they write accurately, seriously, brilliantly. George Orwell, the patron saint of English journalism, would be proud of them there. Why can't we restore our great tradition of accurate, vivid, fair news reporting to British daily newspapers? We might be surprised how many readers such a newspaper could win.

A Britain thus politically focused, educated and informed will have notable strengths. Being so intimate with Europe and America means we have the chance to take the best of both. In many ways, this is what the New Labour government has tried to do. Gordon Brown puts it pithily: the US has enterprise but not fairness, Europe has fairness but not enterprise.[8] So, he argues, we should aim to combine American-style enterprise and European-style fairness, taking examples of innovation, tax credits and 'welfare to work' from America, but best practice in public healthcare or public transport from Europe. Of course, you can't always mix and match, and you have to make sure that you copy the best and not the worst of each. For instance, we're in danger of getting American prisons and German universities rather than American universities and German prisons. But the chance is there.

Then there's language. In the first part of this book I quoted the proposal of Robert Conquest, the Anglo-American poet and scholar, that Britain should join an English-speaking Union rather than the European Union. America, Canada, Australia – you get the idea. But what would an English-speaking Union really mean today? According to one study, there are now about 340 million native speakers of English, but a further 1,350 million who can use the language with 'reasonable competence'.[9] They speak what has been called English as an International Language or EIL. 'There are', the Czech writer and statesman Václav Havel once quipped, 'three kinds of English. There's the English that Czechs talk to Spaniards and Brazilians talk to Hungarians. Of that, you understand 100 per cent. There's American English – you understand 50 per cent. Then there's English English – and you understand nothing.'[10] Still and all, we invented it. Even if English English has become a strange dialect of itself, there are not many medium-sized nations who have this chance of speaking directly to the world.

All these variants of English can be heard on the streets of London. This world island has a world capital. The manner in which people of different nationalities and ethnicities coexist in London, and to a lesser degree in other British cities and regions, is unmatched in Europe. Here is a peculiarly British way of tolerance. It starts, perhaps, with the habits of privacy and mutual indifference ('live and let live', 'an Englishman's home is his castle'). It continues with the baggy, undemanding nature of 'Britishness', a woolly duffle-coat of an identity that from the start had to embrace four national identities, English, Scottish, Welsh and Irish. Only in pragmatic, illogical Britain could a rugby match between England and Scotland be called a 'home international'. But as the world has come back to the post-imperial island, so the duffle-coat of Britishness has stretched to accommodate many other identities.

In future censuses, we are told, we shall be able to categorize ourselves as 'Afro-Caribbean English', 'Chinese Welsh', or 'Asian Scottish'. Gisela Stuart, herself a German-British MP, describes a neighbourhood in her Birmingham constituency that has a large Asian population. Since Asian parents want the best education for their children, and the best school in the neighbourhood is a convent school, they send their daughters there. Never mind the Catholicism; that can be expunged by Islamic instruction after school hours, at the local *madrasah*. So there they sit, row upon row of girls in their Islamic headscarves, being taught maths, British history and, incidentally, the story of baby Jesus, by nuns in their Christian headscarves.[11] A complete muddle, of course, but Europe will need more such muddling through if it is to make its tens of millions of Muslims feel at home. And not just Muslims. Take Neena Gill, for example, a Sikh-British Member of the European Parliament, married to someone who is half Italian, one quarter English and one quarter Scottish. Her son is therefore Indian-Italian-English-Scottish-European. Welcome to the Europe of tomorrow. The British way of pragmatic, muddled tolerance cannot simply be imitated elsewhere in Europe, but it is a real asset both for ourselves and for a continent struggling with the challenge of inevitable, indispensable immigration.

Among the more traditional national constituencies of Britishness, the Welsh and the Scots seem to have less trouble accepting Europe than the English do. Scots, after all, drive around Britain with the name of their nation written on bumper stickers in French: *Écosse*. The Northern Irish are a small, difficult special case. The big problem is the English, and especially the English middle class. It is they – us – who can't work out what they – we – want Britain to be. Conservative, Eurosceptic English friends say: 'All your talk about "role" – that's Foreign Office talk. A country doesn't need to have a "role". All it needs is to be free, rich and at peace.' This, they suggest, can be achieved by a kind of geopolitical neutrality, semi-detaching ourselves from both Europe and America. Britain should be an off-shore Greater Switzerland.

I respect the clarity of this position, but question its feasibility. Would continental Europeans really give us all the benefits of free trade if we were not in the EU? Would Americans and Asians continue to invest so heavily here? Could we stand aside as an anti-American Europe clashed with an anti-European America? If Britain was unable to remain indifferent to the balance of power on the European continent in the nineteenth century, or to the continental clashes of fascism and communism in the twentieth, how could it in the twenty-first? And the illegal immigrants, terrorists and economic shocks coming from an unreformed near East will not stop at the white cliffs of Dover.

Yet even if this strategy for an offshore Greater Switzerland were sustainable, a further question would remain: is this who we want to be? It's one thing – and a fine thing – for the Swiss to be Swiss. It's quite another for the English to try to be Swiss. The last Archbishop of Canterbury once remarked that Britain is now quite an ordinary little island. Of all the silly remarks made by Archbishops of Canterbury, in the long history of that see, this is one of the silliest. These islands are anything but ordinary: for five centuries, until the American and French Revolutions, we were pioneers of freedom in the West; the British Empire meant oppression, exploitation and racism, but at the end of the day, the great democracies of the twenty-first-century world do include America, Canada, Australia, India and South Africa. Today there is a handful of Western nationalities that you meet around the world, trying to change things for the better, whether in national diplomacy, international organizations, charities, the media or culture. The British are always to be found among these world-shapers.

Of course it is always possible for someone who has the talent and track-record of a great violinist to make his living as a barman. Perhaps he could even be happy as a barman, though you would always doubt his professions of contentment. Yet even if he was happy, you would still feel it was a dreadful waste of his abilities. So also with Britain. This is not just a matter of

> We must be free or die, who speak the tongue
> That Shakespeare spake.[12]

It's a question of whether we could and should be indifferent to the unfreedom of others. I think we probably could not and certainly should not. If so, then we must have a national strategy that engages fully, on all fronts, with the world. The task is daunting but, given luck and the right allies, not impossible – like Churchill's promise of eventual victory in 1940. Writing that same year, Orwell concluded *The Lion and the Unicorn* with these words: 'I believe in England, and I believe that we shall go forward.'[13] We still can. The only obstacle is ourselves.

6

What Europe Can Be

If I go to Warsaw, Berlin, Paris or Madrid I am abroad. If I go to Warsaw, Berlin, Paris or Madrid I am at home. This 'being at home abroad' is the essence and wonder of Europe.[1] So much that makes life rich – the beauty of women and the styles of men, the theatre of politics, language, architecture, newspapers, cuisine – is intriguingly, gloriously different from country to country. Yet still, you are a European at home in Europe, and there's a special thrill that comes from thinking how odd and bold it is that the inhabitants of this tower of Babel have somehow got together in a single commune or condominium.

Some people don't like it. There's an amusing essay by the American comic writer P. J. O'Rourke entitled 'Among the Euro-Weenies'. A founding charter of American satirical anti-Europeanism, this describes a gloomy month he spent in Europe. 'I've had it with these dopey little countries and all their pokey borders,' he writes. 'Even the languages are itty-bitty. Sometimes you need two or three just to get you through till lunch.'[2] But that's exactly the delight. Each of the two or three languages you can talk before lunch reveals a subtly different way of life and thought, accreted over centuries. '*Awantura*' in Polish means a big, loud, yet secretly rather enjoyable row. '*Bella figura*' in Italian is an untranslatable notion of how a woman or man should really wish to be in the company of other men and women. The British say 'what on earth does that mean?' The Germans say 'what in heaven should that mean?' ('*was im Himmel soll das bedeuten?*'). A canyon of profound philosophical difference – empiricist against idealist – is revealed through that tiny semantic crack. As we say in English: *Vive la différence*. Europe is an intricate, multicoloured patchwork, unmatched anywhere else on the globe.

This Europe has an extraordinary story to tell. It's a story of the enlargement of freedom. At the height of the Second World War, in 1942, there were just four perilously free countries in Europe: Britain, Switzerland, Sweden and Ireland. By 1962, most of Western Europe was free, except for Spain and Portugal. By 1982, the Iberian peninsular had joined the free, and Greece had rejoined after an interval of dictatorship, but the whole of what we called Eastern Europe was still unfree. By 2002, there was only one country in Europe that Freedom House classified as 'not free' – Belarus – and just a handful, in the new eastern and south-eastern Europe, that it judged 'partly' rather than wholly free. With the enlargement of the European Union to twenty-five members, and of Nato to twenty-six, most of the countries of Europe belong to the same political, economic and security communities, with equal rights and obligations. That has never been true before. Never in its history has Europe come this close to being 'whole and free'. If that's not a story to be proud of, what is?

Being free is not a direct result of belonging to the European Union; in fact, you have to be free before you can join the EU. But the European Union certainly helps. It helps through the politics of induction.[3] First, there's magnetic induction. The magnetic attractions of West European freedom and prosperity induced in Spaniards, Poles, Czechs and Portuguese a desire to emulate and come closer to them. Then there's formal induction – into membership of the club. Because Europeans not in the club have been so strongly attracted to joining it, they have been prepared to accept its quite intrusive demands as they strive for membership. Those demands, now formalized in the EU's 'Copenhagen Criteria', include the refined essentials of freedom, from free elections, the rule of law and free markets to respect for individual and minority rights. For Poles, as for Spaniards, the return to freedom and the return to Europe have gone hand in hand. These politics of induction are unique to Europe. Southern neighbours of the United States don't imagine they will become states of the Union.

This enlargement of freedom is the great success story of Europe over the sixty years since the Second World War. It also provides a central purpose for the next twenty years. Enlargement is not complete when countries like Slovakia and Estonia are formally members of an EU of twenty-five. It has merely begun. To make the European Union work with so many member states, most of which are much poorer than the average of the EU of fifteen, is already a huge task – and yet it is only half the task. Who seriously imagines that the European Union can stop there for the next twenty years? Firm promises have already been made to Romania and Bulgaria. What earthly justification would there be for refusing the progressive rites of induction to the other hard-tried peoples of the Balkans, as and when they meet the Copenhagen Criteria, especially since the EU is massively present already in Bosnia and Kosovo, as part of an international occupying power? Depending how many new states we end up with in the Balkans – and we should reckon with the emergence of an independent Montenegro and an independent Kosovo – this brings you to an EU of between thirty-two and thirty-four. Then, who could turn away Norway, Switzerland or Iceland if they decided to apply? That makes thirty-seven. And this is on the risky assumption that we have no constitutional dissolution of existing member states: an independent Scotland, for example, or Basque Country, or Flanders and Wallonia.

The time has come for us to say clearly which countries we hold eligible for full membership of the European Union over the next twenty years. This doesn't mean they are any better or worse than others; just that these are the historically European or partly European countries which we believe the European Union can absorb over twenty years without ceasing to be a functioning political community. It is less a value judgement on them than a political judgement on ourselves. Such clarity can be helpful not only to those for whom the answer is 'yes' but also to those for whom the answer is 'no'. In fact, this clarity is a precondition for working out what we can do for the others, short of full membership.

In addition to all the Balkan states mentioned above, we should offer this twenty-year 'yes' to Turkey but not to the rest of the near East, including even very close countries of north Africa such as Morocco. We should offer it to Ukraine, Belarus and Moldova but not to Russia, nor to the states of the Caucasus. This painful choice is justified by current politics and recent history, not by older history, culture or religion. Thus far, Morocco is the only country to have been refused permission even to apply to join the EU, on the grounds that it is not a European country. But with what historical justification? I would hate to plead the case in any historians' court that Morocco is not a European country but Turkey is; even less, that Turkey is a European country but Russia is not. No, for all the historical claims of pre-1453 Constantinople and Byzantium, the plain fact is that by taking in Turkey, the European Union would be crossing one of the oldest borderlines of Europe, first drawn by the geographers of antiquity and central to Europe's self-definition from the fifteenth to the seventeenth centuries.

If we were starting from scratch, we would probably build special partnerships, not based on induction to full membership, with both Russia and Turkey. In these two countries, Europe does not exactly end but, so to speak, fades away into what Europeans have named Asia. However, we are not starting from scratch. We have promises to keep; promises that go back forty years, into the Cold War, and were made explicit at the Nice summit of the EU in 2000. If we break them, this will send a disastrous message to Muslims everywhere that they are not welcome in Europe, however secular their state and moderate their government. Europe will still appear to be what it was for Pope Pius II, a Christian club. If we keep our promises to Turkey, while insisting on the full rigour of the Copenhagen Criteria of freedom, then we may demonstrate that a largely Muslim country can take an honoured place as perhaps the most populous state in the European Union. That political prize is worth the historical inconsistency.

In 2025, the next most populous EU member state might be Ukraine. By bringing in Ukraine and Belarus, after Greece, Bulgaria, Romania and Serbia, the European Union would have crossed another Huntingtonian fault-line between 'civilizations'. For according to Huntington, the Orthodox Christian world is another separate 'civilization', like Islam. So one small thing Europe can do over the next twenty years is to prove Samuel Huntington wrong. By inducting Ukraine, the European Union would enhance the political stability of its own eastern borderlands and influence, for the better, the political formation of a genuinely post-imperial Russia.

The reason Russia itself should not be offered the hope of membership in these two decades has to do not with any civilizational fault-line (truly hard to discern between eastern Ukraine and western Russia) but with its sheer size – a land area larger than the rest of Europe put together and more than 140 million people. Russia's elites are themselves ambivalent about whether they want to be a 'merely' European or a world-straddling Eurasian power. Although formally an electoral democracy, the Russian Federation currently has strong authoritarian tendencies, and is attempting to recreate a sphere of influence in eastern Europe and the Caucasus. The European Union has been feeble in relations with Russia, both because major European states want to deal directly, on their own terms, with the energy-rich former superpower, and because the EU's politics of induction depend on offering a credible prospect of membership. In this case, Europe's other security community can help. Even a fully democratic and committed Russia would be too big for the European Union. It would not be too big for Nato, which already contains one outsize, half-European military power, the United States, and which is fast becoming a transcontinental security and peacekeeping organization. If the European Union should embrace a democratic Turkey, Nato should embrace a democratic Russia.

I've dwelt on these boundaries of enlargement to bring home the scale of the European project over the next two decades. It's daunting enough to make workable arrangements for a European Union of twenty-five states and twenty languages in 2005, but we should already be thinking ahead to an EU of some forty states and at least thirty-three languages in 2025. In the Council of Ministers building, on the Rue de la Loi in Brussels, there's a smart new conference table for fifty people – two representatives from each of the twenty-five states – and no one knows quite how decisions will be reached around it. Imagine the table of eighty.

Constitutionally, the EU is like no other polity. As Jacques Delors once put it, this is an Unidentified Flying Object. Trying to characterize its existing political system, political scientists have come up with neologisms like 'intensive transgovernmentalism'.[4] Trying to improve it, the Constitutional Convention produced a draft constitutional treaty which somewhat strengthened the parts controlled by member states, through the Council of Ministers, rather than the supposedly supranational parts, especially the European Commission and

Parliament. At the moment, that seems to be the institutional trend of enlargement.

If in ten years' time there is more of a European 'public sphere', if there are more genuinely pan-European political parties, newspapers, television channels, debates and personalities, there might be a renewed strengthening of the supranational. This is unlikely, because of the glorious diversity of Europe's languages and cultures, but if it emerges by mutual consent then it will help the Union to keep going.* Similarly, it would help if we had more effective means of emotional identification with European institutions – flags, symbols, a European anthem we can sing – to counter the centrifugal effects of enlargement. Ultimately, what matters is not the exact constitutional form, which will inevitably be hybrid. What matters is that the Unidentified Object continues to fly, with a reasonable air cushion of support from a majority of its people.

For this to happen, political pilots in a sufficient number of member states need to agree on a strategic direction for the Union, suggest the way forward to their colleagues in the EU, and secure the assent of their own peoples. But what is a sufficient number? From the early 1950s until the early 1990s, leadership was given by France and Germany. Many episodes in the years since the end of the Cold War, culminating in the Iraq crisis, have shown that a leadership group comprising just France and Germany is no longer sufficient, especially in an enlarged EU. Unless they extend the couple to make a three-some, Britain will form alternative ad hoc alliances, together with states such as Spain, Poland or Italy. Europe will then be torn between two magnetic poles, rather than gathering around one magnetic core. If France and Germany were to go ahead unilaterally in a 'pioneer group' as some, especially in France, like to envisage, they would look behind them and find half their fellow Europeans marching in a different direction. This is a sure formula for the continuation of a multi-polar Europe in a unipolar world.

* At the moment, Europe cannot even have its own '9/11', in the sense of a symbolic date associated with an emergency telephone number, because we all think of different national emergency numbers. How many Europeans would know what you meant if you said '112', the standardized, EU-wide emergency number? So instead, Europeans have started referring to the 11 March 2004 Madrid bombings as '3/11', taking an American-style date to make an American allusion.

No, the political question for the European Union at the beginning of the twenty-first century is not 'should France and Germany open their marriage to Britain?'. Obviously they should. It is not even 'can a *ménage à trois* work?' – although most human experience would counsel caution on that score. It is: 'will even those "big three" be enough to provide the strategic leadership and "critical mass" in a European Union of twenty-five, going on forty?'. The answer seems to me self-evidently 'no'. They will need to be joined by at least two or three other medium-weight states, such as Spain, Italy, Poland or the Netherlands. Yet even that constellation would sharpen the divide between so-called 'big' and 'small' countries in the Union, which emerged so clearly in the debates of the Constitutional Convention. It will therefore be essential for some smaller states also to be involved in giving a lead within the existing institutions of the EU.

Such a strategic coalition is very difficult to achieve, given that European politics are still mainly national, and national priorities and governments keep changing. We are more likely to end up with different groups of states working more closely together in different areas of policy. That will not be enough to provide an overall sense of where Europe is heading. We need to keep reminding ourselves that this attempt to bring together the states and peoples of Europe can also fail, as all previous attempts have done. A spectacular crash seems unlikely, but there is a real danger that the institutions of the European Union could gradually weaken into irrelevance, like the Holy Roman Empire, while real politics take place elsewhere.

Over the sixty years since the end of the Second World War, many of the existing member states of the European Union have achieved an enviable combination of economic growth and social solidarity. There is no single 'European model' but a diverse family of socio-economic models. One thing, however, all these diverse European models now have in common: they are all under threat. The EU has solemnly declared its intention to make the European economy the most competitive in the world by 2010. If it succeeds, I will eat my hat – and my shoes for dessert. As more of our manufacturing industries go to China, our service industries to India and our scientists to America, the question for the welfare capitalisms of Europe will be: how much are we prepared to fall behind the growth rates of other economies in order to preserve our social models? Or, how much are we prepared to trim down our social models for economic growth? There is a choice.

Even Jürgen Habermas, in making his case for social Europe as Not-America, would claim only that 'European welfare states were for a long time exemplary'.[5] Note the past tense. There is, to be sure, no reason at all why everyone should adopt the so-called American business model. Sweden has done as well as America. But it will require singular ingenuity for Europeans to continue to work shorter hours, take longer holidays, have a smaller proportion of our population in employment, and still produce as much. Over-regulation and high social costs for employers also lead to more unemployment, which is, as Bill Clinton sharply observed, 'another form of social inequality'.[6]

This challenge to the post-1945 West European way of life comes at a time when our populations are ageing fast. If we carry on as we are at the moment, then in 2025 our welfare states won't be able to pay our retired people a life-supporting pension. If we think that's unacceptable in 'social' Europe, then we need to reform our pension systems, have more children ourselves, and allow in more young and child-bearing immigrants to help fund those pensions. The trouble is that Europe has not been good at making large numbers of immigrants, especially Muslim immigrants, feel at home. Anglophone immigrant countries such as Canada, Australia and America are much better at it – with Britain, as usual, somewhere in between. For a fifteenth-century European, to say 'a Muslim European' or 'a European Muslim' would have been a contradiction in terms, like saying 'a she-man' or 'a he-woman'. In the twenty-first century, it's simply vital that this is possible to say. So far, we're not doing very well. It's quite an achievement for the main political organization of the most secular continent on earth to have come so close to convincing the Muslim world that it's a Christian club.

Being 'European' should be the overarching, multi-ethnic and non-religious identity that enables the Muslim immigrant to feel himself or herself to be a citizen and not a mere denizen – rather as being 'Canadian', 'American' or even 'British' is for citizens of those multi-ethnic polities. Unfortunately, Europeanness doesn't yet work this way. So the test will be whether second-generation immigrants can find secure, civic identities as Asian-British, Moroccan-Spanish, Turkish-German, Tunisian-French and so on. Each national path will be different, but we can learn from each other. As so often, the two extremes will probably be the Cartesian, republican secularism of France (school classes with no Muslim headscarves or yarmulkes) and the pragmatic, muddle-headed pluralism of Britain (schoolgirls in Muslim headscarves being taught by nuns in wimples).

If some or all of us fail, then we face a downward spiral which will be the curse of the national politics of Europe for years ahead. Populist, anti-immigrant parties will regularly break through the 15 per cent mark in regional and national elections, winning the votes of less affluent native-born voters who resent rapid change in their traditional ways of life, and blame immigrants for rising crime and job losses – even if those jobs actually went to Asia. Disaffected immigrant youths, themselves often among the long-term unemployed, will in fact be heavily involved in crime, while a minority will turn to Islamist extremism, anti-Semitic acts and terrorism. That in turn will feed the fires of anti-immigrant populism. To halt this downward spiral is the single most urgent task of European domestic politics in the next decade. We may already be too late.

This domestic imperative also dictates the top foreign policy priority for Europe: supporting change for the better in our 'near abroad'. I have argued in the first part of this book that unless we bring more prosperity and freedom to young Arabs, even more young Arabs will come to us. This formula applies also to Turkey, the Balkans, the new eastern Europe (Ukraine, Belarus and Moldova), the Caucasus and Russia, all of them being, in different degrees, sources of legal and illegal immigration, political radicalism and organized crime. I've suggested that we should pursue the EU's classic 'politics of induction' towards Turkey, the Balkans and the new eastern Europe, in a time-frame of twenty years. For the rest of our 'near abroad', stretching 10,000 kilometres along our southern and eastern borders, we need to craft a new kind of partnership which does not involve the promise – or even the flirted ankle – of full membership.

To create this arc of partnership, we have to combine all the various kinds of instruments that are at present wielded by many different hands, both in the institutions of the EU itself and in national governments. Europe has a hundred left hands and none of them know what the right hand is doing. Trade, development aid, immigration policy, education, cultural exchanges, classic diplomacy, arms sales and anti-proliferation measures, counter-terrorism, the fight against drugs and organized crime: each European policy has an impact, but the effects are fragmented and often self-contradictory. One left hand sells chemical or nuclear technology to a country in our near abroad, a right hand tries to prevent it developing weapons of mass destruction. Another right hand offers generous development aid, a left hand subverts this by trade protectionism.

Trade is our most effective single instrument. Our strategic objective must be to create an open trade area that includes the whole of our near abroad. Either we take more of their goods or we take more of their people. Opening up our markets is also much the biggest thing we can do for the poorest of the world's poor, especially those in Sub-Saharan Africa. Without it, we are giving with one hand and taking with the other. Trade is also Europe's strongest lever for affecting, at the margins, developments in Asia.

Our least effective instrument is military force. Europe can easily afford a well-armed and well-trained rapid reaction force, 60,000 to 100,000 strong. This can and should be used to prevent another Bosnia, whether in our own backyard or further afield. Where rulers or dominant ethnic groups are attempting to commit genocide, Europeans should always be ready to intervene. That is what our own history of European barbarism in the twentieth century cries out for us to do. Europe should also anticipate a lesson of the twenty-first century: that tyrants and terrorists must be prevented from gaining possession of weapons of mass destruction before it's too late. If we don't like the Bush Doctrine of unilateral pre-emption we had better develop a new practice of multilateral prevention. But in the larger scheme of what Europe does in the world beyond its borders, military force almost certainly will, and probably should, take a subordinate place.

At the Congress of Europe in The Hague in May 1948, one of the earliest and most passionate twentieth-century advocates of European union, Count Coudenhove-Kalergi, delivered a memorable warning. 'Let us never forget, my friends,' cried the old count, 'that European Union is a means and no end.'[7] I have now suggested a few answers to the question that a young European might very reasonably pose at the beginning of the twenty-first century: Why Europe? Why, that is, do we need a European Union at all? What is Europe for? The answers are not simple, but they are, I believe, compelling.

We need this Europe to prevent us falling back into the bad old ways of war and European barbarism, which stalked the Balkans into the very last year of the last century. As Bertolt Brecht wrote after 1945, 'The womb is fertile still, from which that crawled.'[8] However, the womb in question is not capitalism, as Brecht claimed to believe, but rather human nature, additionally misshaped by some distinctively European forms of stupidity. To be sure, we can never prove that a continent-wide collection of independent, fully sovereign European democracies would not behave in the same broadly pacific way, without the existence of any European Union. Maybe they would. But would you care to risk it? It makes sense to suppose that an organization, one of whose main original purposes was to prevent the recurrence of war, whose perennial occupation is endless rounds of negotiation to resolve conflicts of national and special interests, whose default setting is compromise and whose biggest product is fudge, should have contributed something to the fact that conflicts between its member states never result in the use of force. To adapt Churchill's famous remark about democracy: this is the worst possible Europe, apart from all the other Europes that have been tried from time to time.

We need this Europe to help us preserve the unprecedented prosperity and social security that West Europeans have acquired over the last sixty years, as we try to share them with the rest of the continent while being challenged by economic competition from Asia and America. If, in some ways, the present, over-regulated EU hinders us in that double task, we should change those ways, not discard the Union. We also need this Europe as a building block for a free world. It's an interesting question whether the European model is ripe and right for emulation. In our policy towards the near East, for example, should we perhaps be encouraging the formation of an Arab Union, as the Americans encouraged the formation of a European Union after 1945?

Whatever we think should happen, I tend to agree with Eric Hobsbawm's historically informed guess as to what will happen. At the end of the short twentieth century, Hobsbawm writes, 'the European Union stood alone and, being the child of a specific and probably unrepeatable historical conjuncture, was likely to remain alone'.[9] Yet even if it remains unique, an enlarged European Union can, constructed with the right mixture of pragmatism and vision, be a formidable component of a free world. Let's imagine, for a moment, Europe in 2025 at its possible best. A political, economic and security community of some forty free countries and 650 million people, embracing all the lands in which two world wars began, and producing, still, a large part of the wealth of the world. A further 650 million people, born in the most explosive parts of the early twenty-first-century globe, but now living in a great arc of partnership with this European Union, from Marrakesh, via Cairo, Jerusalem, Baghdad and Tbilisi, all the way to Vladivostok. That would not be nothing.

Please note that these prescriptions, this vision, this case for a sober European patriotism, are all derived entirely from an examination of Europe's own history, geography, nations and interests. Some comparison with America is inevitable, but it's a disease of current European debate that discussion of what Europe should be always starts, explicitly or implicitly, with America. Thinking about Europe should start with Europe; we must 'think Europe' from Europe outwards. To strive to create a European political identity by making America into Europe's Other, as Britain invented itself by making France its Other, is not European patriotism. It is European nationalism.

It's also bound to fail. I hope the first part of this book has given enough evidence to convince you of that, if nothing else. Of course there are some notable differences between the United States and Europe: about religion, for example, or the welfare state. We can't credibly say that either Europe or America is morally superior. Europe is better in some respects, America in others. Anyway, there are large and growing value divides within both Europe and the US, countries like Canada are somewhere in between, and most of our values are shared. The new old Europe on this side of the Atlantic and the old new Europe on the other are two parts of one extended family. On our landing walls, there hang portraits of the same great-great-grandparents. (My favourite is a beautiful old lady they nicknamed the Enlightenment, but there are other, grimmer-looking ancestors as well.) To try to build a European identity around transatlantic value differences, as Habermas and Derrida have proposed, will split the enlarged European Union, not unite it.

There are also some significant differences between European and American interests; how could there not be? These should be plainly stated. But most of our long-term interests are common, coincident or, at the very least, compatible. Economically, we are more interdependent than ever before. From the need to prevent terrorism, genocide and nuclear, biological or chemical war, through the betterment of the near East, influencing the rise of the far East and helping the poor South, right up to sustaining human life on earth, the global challenges that will determine the well-being of our children are unlikely to be mastered even by America and Europe working together. They surely won't be if we don't work together. Only America, Europe and the other free countries of the post-West, holding between them most of the world's economic and military power, have the resources to try.

Our starting-point should be what John F. Kennedy proposed more than forty years ago: a Declaration of Interdependence. In a constant dialogue, we should look to remove the remaining barriers to free commerce across the Atlantic; to ensure that Nato and the emerging military capacity of the EU don't work against each other; to develop common approaches to aid, debt relief, reducing agricultural subsidies, climate change. Together with other democracies and the UN, we should agree some modernized 'just war' criteria for when it is whose right and duty to intervene in the internal affairs of other states.[10] Institutionally, we need a more permanently structured relationship between the EU, as such, and the US. On difficult issues, however, which may be either themes or countries (eg. Iran), we will also need the well-tried model of 'contact groups' gathering representatives of the states most directly involved. If the political will is there, the institutional forms will be found.

Europe and America bring different strengths and weaknesses to the table. That's because they are themselves ineradicably different. A continent-wide community of more than forty different nation-states, speaking almost as many languages, will never be the same as a single nation of fifty federated states. It is folly for Europe to aspire to be a superpower taking on the American giant. Even in today's world, the most important single dimension of a superpower is military. The Soviet Union demonstrated that a one-dimensional purely military superpower will not endure, but no one has yet seen a superpower that is not militarily strong. The United States would be – and, in recent years, has been – stupid to believe that it can simply ignore Europe because of American military supremacy. Europe, with its economic, diplomatic and cultural power, can practise what has been called 'soft balancing'. In post-war Iraq, America has discovered again the truth of Talleyrand's remark that you can do everything with bayonets except sit on them. But without military power, Europe will not be a superpower in any meaningful sense of the word.

Most Europeans say they want Europe to be a superpower, but when pollsters then ask if they are prepared to increase military spending to make Europe a superpower, half of them say no.[11] As either our economic growth rates or our social welfare provisions, or both, are further reduced, will Europeans spend more on their armies? If you believe that, you'll believe anything. European nations differ considerably in their attitudes to the use of force, but there's a widespread reluctance that flows from Europe's own bitter experience of war. War is one of the things that the whole European project has always defined itself against. We have made a European Union to prevent war, not to wage it. Anyway, a multinational European community is most unlikely to achieve the unity of command, purpose and popular support needed to fight big wars.

To be sure, it would not be healthy for either side if America were to do all the war-fighting on its own, even in a cause that Europe accepted as just, and then expect Europe to do all the peacekeeping and reconstruction afterwards: 'America does the cooking, Europe does the washing-up.' In a just cause, Europe should be ready to do a bit more cooking, America a bit more washing-up. None the less, as in any good partnership, each side has different assets and qualities; not more or less valuable, just different.

Behind Euro-Gaullist fantasies of Europe as a rival to the United States there smoulder the old dreams of former European world powers and empires. But 'world power' is no more morally admirable a goal if pursued by a collectivity called Europe than it is if pursued by a single nation-state. European nationalism is no better than French, German, British or American nationalism; nationalism, in each case, being firmly distinguished from patriotism. With the idealism of the high Enlightenment, Goethe and Schiller once addressed this appeal to their compatriots:

> To become a *nation*, you hope, Germans, in vain;
> Make yourselves rather – you can do it – more freely into
>   human beings.*

We hope to become a *superpower*, fellow Europeans, in vain. Let us make ourselves, rather, comrades in a community of free people, working to build a free world.

---

* *Zur* Nation *euch zu bilden, ihr hoffet es, Deutsche, vergebens;*
  Bildet, ihr könnt es, dafür freier zu Menschen euch aus. (Xenien, 96)

7

Uncle Sam

What America will do is up to the Americans. If I were them, I'd be getting rather tired of worldly-wise lectures from Europeans in general and the British in particular. These lectures have a characteristic tone of mildly exasperated condescension. 'Now look here, you fellows,' they seem to say, 'we've been playing this game for centuries. We had empires when you were still in short trousers. Just sit quietly and we'll tell you how it's done.' If I were American, I'd reply, 'Thanks, but no thanks.'

Still, it may be helpful to say briefly what I, as an English European, would like America to do. And, in particular, what kind of America would encourage the Europe I've just envisioned. For a start, let's abandon the contested parenthood suit. Historically, America was the daughter of Europe, as de Gaulle said, but the daughter has become an uncle. If I had to summarize my message in a bottle, it would be this: 'So go on then, behave like an uncle. Be Uncle Sam.'

What does that mean? As I write, there's this absurd stand-off between Europe and America. America says: 'We'll support a united Europe so long as it's not anti-American.' Europe says: 'We won't be anti-American so long as you take seriously our uniting Europe.' I would urge America to go first and break the deadlock, both because it is the stronger of the two and because, being a single nation-state, it's easier for America to take clear, decisive action.

Americans should be bold, make a leap of faith, and say: 'We unequivocally, wholeheartedly support a uniting Europe (*sotto voce*: even if some Gaullist French are up there making trouble on the bridge). We've supported it since 1945, and we don't propose to change now. Europe's the first partner we need in building a free world. We wish there really was one telephone number we could call. Let's sign that Declaration of Interdependence. Let's make a transatlantic free trade area. Let's talk about better ways of coordinating the policies of the EU as a whole – not just individual European powers – with those of the US. Let's develop that common project for the near East.'

America should do this with a splash, keep repeating it, and really mean it. This would have a major effect during what is plainly a formative period in Europe's development. Combined with a deeper British involvement in Europe, and the impact of other new and old Euroatlanticist members of the EU, it could swing the great intra-European argument between Euro-Gaullists and Euroatlanticists.

This is a gamble, to be sure. The effects won't be immediately apparent, and there'll be flak along the way. The message would be more easily received if it came from a Democratic president. In recent years, as we've seen, Democrats have been closer to Europeans in their world-view. Yet a moderate Republican, such as the elder President Bush, could be very well respected in Europe, and deservedly so, since his statesmanship was critical to Europe's peaceful emergence from the Cold War. Europeans can hardly expect to tell Americans who to elect. At the moment, America is deeply divided between the 'blue' and the 'red' country. Power will continue to alternate between the two. That's democracy. From time to time, Europeans will therefore have to work with conservative, religious Republican administrations, speaking a political language very different from their own. If we can't manage this, we need to find ourselves another world. But Americans must also see that, after the unilateralism of the younger President Bush's first years in office, after what I've called the 'hubris of the wounded' following 9/11, and after the bruising experience of Washington's 'divide and rule' in Europe, some mistrust is understandable.

In these circumstances, a little more strategic breadth and consistency in American foreign policy would also help. In the first part of this book, I've mentioned some inherent problems of the American system: the country's peculiar habit of changing most of its top civil servants every four years, inter-agency battles that seem to be pre-programmed, the role of Congress, the dictates of the election cycle, a television news agenda that allows only one big story at a time. None the less, the United States managed a higher degree of strategic consistency during the Cold War. Consider, for example, the betterment of the near East. This will not happen in a year or two. In fact, things will probably get worse before they get better, especially if a free or semi-free election in an Arab country brings a radical Islamist party to power. Durable improvement will take at least a decade, probably two. If we Europeans are to sign up to this as one of the big transatlantic projects of the new century, we have to be sure that Americans will also stick with it. Since other problems will inevitably come along, that means Washington being able to sustain several major foreign policy projects at one time, and not giving way to attention deficit disorder.

We fear that America will retreat when the going gets rough, become wholly distracted by another foreign policy crisis, or retreat into America's own 'vast carelessness', absorbed by the domestic economic and social concerns of those heartland Americans for whom almost anywhere else in the world is 'quite a ways across the pond'. Trying to sum up for me his disillusionment with 'the Europeans' over a stately breakfast at a Washington hotel, one senior conservative American commentator said 'they are not serious'.[1] Consciously or unconsciously, this was an exact reprise of what de Gaulle used to say about the Americans: *'ils ne sont pas sérieux'.*[2] But Europeans still have some cause for doubting that the United States is, in this sense, serious.

There's also a difficulty that derives simply from the United States' unique plenitude of power. The British satirical magazine *Private Eye* has an occasional series of front covers on which the Queen is portrayed asking of prominent visitors the standard question that she puts to the people she meets while opening a new hospital, school or factory: 'And what do you do?' When President George W. Bush came on an official visit to Britain in 2003, *Private Eye* showed him standing next to the Queen, in white tie and tails, and answering: 'Whatever I goddam like!'[3] In many respects, the hyperpower can do whatever it goddam likes. And during the early twenty-first-century crisis of the West, Washington seemed to many people around the world set on doing exactly that.

Sitting in the library of Ditchley Park, an English country-house conference centre which is a kind of temple of transatlantic relations, I heard a veteran British historian, much of whose life has been devoted to cultivating those relations, sadly observe that the Bush administration was merely reminding us of the truth of the 'Melian dialogue' in Thucydides' *History of the Peloponnesian War*. Here are the once famous words that the fifth-century BCE Athenian pioneer of contemporary history put into the mouth of his fellow Athenians, as they addressed the much weaker Melians:

We will not make a long and unconvincing speech, full of fine phrases, to prove that our victory over Persia justifies our empire, or that we are now attacking you because you have wronged us, and we ask you not to expect to convince us by saying that you have not injured us, or that, though a colony of Lacedaemon, you did not join her. Let each of us say what we really think and reach a practical agreement. You know and we know, as practical men, that the question of justice arises only between parties equal in strength, and the strong do what they can, and the weak submit.[4]

Is that how Americans would like to be remembered?

Most states aim to maximize and leverage their power. They try, in a phrase which British diplomats use much too often, to 'punch above their weight'. I won't say that the challenge now for America is to punch below its weight – that would be silly, especially when the punch is landed in a good cause. But the challenge for America is to exercise a degree of voluntary self-restraint unusual among states. It would be foolish for the United States to pretend that it does not have the pre-eminent power that it has. It would not be foolish to *act as if* it had somewhat less power. The Romans found a good phrase for this: *primus inter pares*, first among equals. That's strictly a contradiction in terms: if you're first, you're not equal. However, it expresses an attitude of mind, an aspiration to treat other members of the society of states as if they were equals. This is also the advice of the song that Americans sang so movingly after the 11 September 2001 attacks. 'America, the Beautiful' counsels:

> Confirm thy soul in self-control,
> Thy liberty in law.[5]

Self-restraint can be exercised without reference to international organizations and international law. None the less, respect for international organizations and international law, which the United States itself did so much to create and spread after 1945, is an important sign of it. Chief among those organizations is Roosevelt's baby, the UN, with its charter and conventions. I can well understand why American leaders are frustrated with an organization in whose supreme body the world's largest authoritarian regime, China, and a cussed, very partial democracy, Russia, have a permanent veto. I can see why they think that a charter written in 1945 is not adequate to address the new security challenges of sixty years later.

So we need to change them, by consent. That, however, is very difficult. How would we arrive at a better UN Security Council? If we were reshuffling the pack of great powers, Britain and France should give up their permanent seats in favour of a single European Union seat. This would impose the necessity of reaching a common EU position on key foreign policy issues, and encourage France and Britain to make their historic compromise. (Regrettably, it would also increase the already high fudge content in Security Council decisions.) India and Japan would deserve places, on the grounds, respectively, of their demographic and economic weight, but how would you choose the 'great powers' from Africa, Latin America or the Middle East? A Security Council with no permanent members at all would be more universally acceptable – and even less effective. Updating the UN charter for the twenty-first century is equally difficult. Still, we should try.

In the meantime, America can look for sources of international legitimacy short of the full, explicit sanction of a UN Security Council resolution. Nato's military intervention to prevent genocide in Kosovo had less sanction from the UN Security Council than the war in Iraq. However, it had the support of a clear majority of the democracies in the world and a clear majority of Serbia's neighbours. It was illegal but legitimate.[6] The fact that more than half the states in the world are democracies creates a large opportunity. In 2000, US Secretary of State Madeleine Albright and the Polish foreign minister, Bronisław Geremek, convened a founding meeting in Warsaw of a worldwide Community of Democracies, assembling representatives of more than a hundred states. Not much has become of it since, but shouldn't we think of building a caucus of democracies at the UN? It could be the mother of all caucuses.

Ultimately, helping to make international rules and then playing by them will be in America's own interest. This is what the Melians replied to the Athenians:

> As you ignore justice and have made self-interest the basis of discussion, we must take the same ground, and we say that in our opinion it is in your interest to maintain a principle which is for the good of all – that anyone in danger should have just and equitable treatment and any advantage, even if not strictly his due, which he can secure by persuasion.[7]

The fact that the weak have an obvious motive for making this argument to the strong does not invalidate the argument. The case has been made by many Americans themselves, arguing that a unilateral use of America's military power, with neither international legality nor international legitimacy, will soon enough diminish America's other two dimensions of power: economic and 'soft'.

The vocal presence of these other American voices suggests that a vigorous, pluralist democracy like the United States is, to some extent, self-righting. And so it is, but only up to a point. The problem with American power is not, as some Europeans believe, that it's American. The problem is simply the power. It would be dangerous even for an archangel to have so much power. 'The strongest poison ever known / Came from Caesar's laurel crown' wrote the poet William Blake.[8] The authors of the US Constitution wisely determined that no single locus of power, however benign, should predominate. Even the best could be led into temptation. The President, the Congress and the Supreme Court must be presumed to share the same basic values, goals and interests, but better let them check and balance each other. Shouldn't the same principle apply in world politics?[9]

If Europe understands that it shares the same basic values, goals and long-term interests as America, then America should want Europe to be a benign check and balance on its own solitary hyperpower. For the reasons I've explored, Europe will always be a very different kind of power from the US. This makes it not more difficult but easier to structure the partnership. Admittedly, to want someone else to balance as well as complement your own power is a very unusual thing for any state to do, but the United States is a very unusual state, the European Union is not a state at all, and both are historic variations of one and the same dream.

Americans might also be in a little less of a hurry to jump up and down crying 'anti-Americanism!' every time someone criticizes what Washington does. That carpet bag of a word obscures more than it reveals. As we've seen, if you press most critical Europeans beyond their first derogatory remark about 'the Americans', they immediately distinguish between a particular administration and the country as a whole. There's a vital difference between disliking what America says or does and hating what America is. Even the most virulent European anti-Americanism is very rarely comparable with anti-Semitism. It is seldom directed against individual, ordinary Americans just because they are Americans; let alone calling for physical acts of discrimination, expulsion or extermination. (I accept that there are a few shocking exceptions, especially among Arabs living in Europe.) Much of what is called 'anti-Americanism' is criticism that comes with the turf of predominant power. The British, the French, the Spanish, the Romans all encountered it in their time. Often it's very unfair: 'The blame of those ye better, / The hate of those ye guard', as Kipling warned in a poem addressed specifically to Americans.[10] Wise uncles react calmly.

Unlike many Europeans, I like the high moral content of American political rhetoric and admire the strain of Wilsonian idealism in American foreign policy. But sometimes the assumption that America is God's own country, equipped by Moses (played by Charlton Heston) with all the answers, can get up even the most sympathetic European nose. At such moments, American presidents sound like a cross between the Puritan governor John Winthrop and a Coca-Cola advertisement. Of course we know where this comes from. I have before me as I write a seventeenth-century English bestseller, William Camden's *Remaines, concerning Britaine: But especially England, and the Inhabitants thereof.* 'The Kingdome of England', writes Camden, 'is God's own Kingdome, and for it God himself will provide.'[11] But we're in the twenty-first century now. In return,

Europeans – and Canadians – should drop their own forms of self-righteousness: the holier-than-thou assumptions of moral superiority in their attachment to international law or social justice, and the unbearable arrogance of Europe's claimed humility.

After Iraq, America should also go to war again. The enemy to be defeated in this war is not a state, a dictator, a terrorist group or an ideology, but extreme poverty and its accompanying plagues of disease, hunger and early death. There is a shocking disparity between what the United States has spent on the war in Iraq, and the subsequent occupation, and what it spends on development aid to the rest of the world. In round figures, at the time of writing, the US is spending some $80 billion a year on the occupation of Iraq and $13 billion a year on development aid to all other countries. Even if one includes a generous estimate for other forms of American government assistance, and allows for the increase which is to come into effect by 2006, the United States is still spending at least five times as much money on one potentially oil-rich country of 25 million people as it is on lifting more than 1 billion people out of an existence that scarcely deserves the name of life.

Let America's next war be the war on want. A country so large in spirit, so religious and so rich can surely be won for such a war. Let a campaign of well-administered aid, medicine, debt relief and trade liberalization be carried to the poorest of the world's poor. Let the world see again, as it saw once after 1945, just how generous America can be – with a great big Stars and Stripes on every packet. Let Europe be challenged to keep pace, matching packet for packet, this time with our own yellow-and-blue star-spangled banner stuck on the side. Why not? Because there are no votes in it? But that's up to us, the thousand million.

A special American responsibility is to reduce its excessive emissions of carbon dioxide. This requires Americans to change their 'way of life' somewhat more than Europeans, putting the long-term interests of the Earth before their own short-term interests. Without American commitment, we shall never reach international agreements that bind emerging industrial giants such as China. And then we'll all be cooked.

I believe that America is capable of taking these steps. If I'd been born in the Middle East, Latin America or South East Asia, I might be less inclined to believe this. As a historian, I know that, in the global competition of the Cold War and in its pursuit of oil and economic advantage, the United States has supported undemocratic regimes and licensed oppression. This was made worse by the hypocrisy of fostering unfreedom in the name of 'the free world'. But as an Englishman who has seen at first hand what the United States has done for Europe, I still believe it. And when I go to California, as I do every year, I wonder again at the way in which the sons and daughters of immigrants from utterly different cultures, from China, Indonesia, Somalia or Nicaragua, will embrace an ideal that was once proclaimed in a small church in Putney.

Perhaps this trust comes most naturally to an English European. Yet I encounter very similar feelings among the young Germans, Spaniards, Poles and Swedes I deal with almost every day in Europe. Even Europeans whom many Americans would call 'anti-American' are often disappointed lovers, measuring America against its own high ideal of itself. A Europe that likes the idea of America is a better Europe. Indeed, if we confront America with its own better self, we are confronting it, historically speaking, with a vision of a better Europe. And an America that likes the idea of the new Europe is, in turn, supporting another version of itself. The *New York Times* columnist Thomas Friedman puts it punchily: 'I support united Europe because I think two United States are better than one.'[12]

I believe that Americans can do these good things in the world, but they also need to remember that they don't have unlimited time. A point the Melians made in reply to the Athenians was that one day the Athenians might be down and out themselves, and then they'd want a system of international rules and justice to protect them. In Thucydides' account, the Athenians contemptuously dismissed this possibility, and it must seem very remote to today's Americans. But all powers decline in the end. In 1941, Henry Luce proclaimed in *Life* magazine the coming of 'the American century'.[13] We can argue about when the American century began, and how long it might last. Some would say the 'British century' that preceded the American one did last exactly a hundred years, from 1814 to 1914, although with a long epilogue. A humorous parody of British school history, *1066 and All That*, famously concluded that after 1918, 'America was thus clearly top nation, and History came to a.'[14] However, it's probably more realistic to date 'the American century' from 1945. This means, if it's to be a full century, that the United States has got about forty years to go; but history is accelerating, and the powers of the far East are coming up fast.

As time goes by – to recall the song from *Casablanca*, a great movie about relations between Americans and Europeans – the power of the United States will fade. As time goes by, Americans will be less and less able to shape the world around them. We cannot know how long this time will be, but it may be no more than twenty years. In those twenty years, however, Americans have a historic chance, working with Europeans, to go beyond 'the free world' of the old West and lay the foundations of a free world. There's a tune there waiting to be played; quite a complicated tune, to be sure, but America has practised it many times before and knows it by heart. Go on, Sam, play it.

8

Towards a Free World

We, the free, face a daunting opportunity. Previous generations, even if they lived in what was called 'the free world', could only dream of a free world. Now we can begin to make it. More people are more free than ever before. Our possibilities of helping the others out of unfreedom are also larger than ever. If Europeans, Americans and free people everywhere don't work together towards this goal, instead remaining sunk in a narcissism of minor differences, it will be impossible to achieve. If we do work together, the task remains daunting, perhaps nearly impossible – but the nearly impossible is what we should demand of our leaders and of ourselves.

I've indicated four key areas in which we are challenged to make a difference: the near East, the far East, the poor South and planet Earth. It would be absurd to sketch any sort of 'action plan' for these vast and complex challenges, each of which requires a fat report written by expert hands. Instead, I want to share a few tentative thoughts about the overall terms on which we in the post-West engage in this larger project, if that's what we agree to do.

In this book, I've talked cautiously about 'a' not 'the' crisis of the West, let alone the 'final crisis' or the 'end' of the West. It is still possible that a new common enemy will sharply revive the geopolitical unity of a slightly enlarged West. Neither rogue states, nor a portmanteau 'Islam', nor even a major terrorist attack on European soil, such as the 11 March 2004 bombings in Madrid, are currently having that effect; but perhaps something will. Yet that's not what we should hope for. What we should hope for is, in a longer perspective, already happening: that the West goes beyond the West, and in so doing, calls itself into question.

For the deepest crisis of the West is a crisis of success. Since the fifteenth century, ideas, customs and institutions that originated in Europe have spread around the globe. A very sober and far from Eurocentric historian of the world observes that 'the balance sheet of cultural influence is overwhelmingly one-sided . . . The teaching of Marx was long a force throughout twentieth-century Asia; the last non-European whose words had any comparable authority in Europe was Jesus Christ.'[1] In the 'creeping unity' that has seized humankind, writes J. M. Roberts, 'the language of democracy and human rights is now enlisted more widely than ever to pay at least lip service to western notions of what public life should be'. The 'pervasive influence of a civilization originally European' is evident not just in the technologies of modernization but also in 'certain master ideas and institutions'.[2] So – no longer a master race, just master ideas? Europeanization and Americanization are obviously competing variants of Westernization. But is 'globalization' also, at bottom, just a polite euphemism for Westernization? Is Roberts's 'creeping unity' of humankind in fact a creeping imperialism, through which we impose our Western values on others?

'Members of Congress, ours are not Western values, they are the universal values of the human spirit,' Tony Blair declared, to loud applause from his Washington audience in summer 2003.[3] But are they? And what does that mean? 'Western values' as we generally nowadays recognize them – democracy, human rights, free speech, the rule of law, etc – are, historically speaking, just a subset of the values embraced in the lands of the West. Nor has this long been the dominant subset. To be sure, today's 'Western values' have roots that can be traced far back, to ancient Athens, Jerusalem and Rome. The idea of the moral equality of all human beings, for example, appears in Christianity, blending elements from Judaism and Greek philosophy.[4] In his speech at St Mary's Church, Putney, in 1647, the Puritan Thomas Rainsborough returned to that Christian source, but made the leap from moral to civic equality. Yet only in the late seventeenth- and eighteenth-century Enlightenment did philosophers systematically elaborate what are recognizably today's Western values.

Our 'Western values' are, in large measure, Enlightenment values; yet throughout the next two centuries these were under fierce challenge inside the West itself. The philosopher Isaiah Berlin spent a good part of his life engaging with these often intellectually formidable enemies of the Enlightenment. For much of the twentieth century, millions of Europeans thought fascism or communism were better alternatives to liberal democracy. Adolf Hitler was also a European, and a Westerner. He was an anti-Western Westerner, but still a product of Western civilization. Like all attempts to harness values to places – 'American values', 'British values', 'central European values', 'European values', 'Asian values' – the claim for 'Western values' deliberately mistakes a part for the whole. In so doing, it mixes description and prescription.

Moreover, as soon as 'Western values' appeared in a shape we would recognize today, they carried the aspiration to go beyond the West, whether in the English Enlightenment universalism of Locke or the German Enlightenment universalism of Kant. All human beings should in principle, as of natural right, be treated as moral equals. So Enlightenment Westerners did claim the universality of human rights. However, it is quite another thing to say that these values were in fact universal, in the sense of being found in the history of all cultures. Rich and cognate notions – tolerance, pluralism, justice, obligations of the ruler to the citizen – can be discovered in the writings of Confucius, the fourth-century BCE Indian political writer Kautilya, or Islamic philosophers. Yet a careful enquiry into the universality of human rights, by Ludger Kühnhardt, finds very little evidence that any recognizable notion of individual human rights was present in these cultures, until it came to them from the West. Kühnhardt notes, for example, that the Chinese language did not have characters for the concept of 'human rights' until the nineteenth century.[5]

In short, what we habitually call 'Western values' are only a few of the values historically embraced in the West, even into very recent times. To associate the West constantly and exclusively with them is, at best, the highly selective claim of a wider Western patriotism. At worst, it's Western nationalism, in the generic, Orwellian meaning of nationalism that I have used in this book. Ever since these values were first articulated systematically, in the Enlightenment, their proponents have staked a claim for them to be accepted as universal. They are not, however, empirically universal. Historically, they were first institutionalized in the West and they came to most other cultures from the West. They go significantly beyond the human universals discovered in all cultures by anthropologists, and the liberal or pluralist elements to be found in most religions. They are now, if you will, just one major offer in the global market for values.

All this may seem rather academic, in the pejorative sense of the term. But for any country that has not always been part of the West – and that's most countries – it is not academic at all. A nice illustration comes from the end of the Cold War, which was also the true beginning of the early twenty-first-century crisis of the West. In December 1989, Soviet President Mikhail S. Gorbachev and American President George H. W. Bush were sitting in a Soviet naval ship, the *Maxim Gorky*, bobbing up and down in stormy seas off Malta. And what were they talking about, the two presidents, while the Soviet empire crumbled and the seas raged around them? About 'Western values'. Bush's secretary of state, James Baker, had raised the prospect of Germany being united on the basis of Western values. According to the Russian transcript, the conversation then went as follows:

Gorbachev: Aleksander Yakovlev asks: How come democracy, openness and the market are 'Western' values?
Bush: Because the USA and Western Europe have shared them for many years.
Gorbachev: But we share them too. These are, after all, values that belong to the whole of humanity.
Bush: But that wasn't always true . . .

After some more verbal swordplay, James Baker, the lawyer and consummate deal-maker, suggested cutting the difference:

Baker: Perhaps we could agree on the compromise that this positive process is on the basis of 'democratic values'?[6]

The lawyer saves the day. Yet perhaps Baker was wiser than he knew. His improvised suggestion points in exactly the right direction for today. All of us should abandon this muddled, vainglorious talk of 'Western values' or 'universal values', 'American', 'European' or, for that matter, 'Asian' values. Instead, we should say what we actually mean – modestly, plainly, concretely.

What are the basic terms of engagement that we, in the post-West, propose to the rest of the world? At the moment, there are two extreme positions, the Western triumphalist fundamentalist and the Western cultural relativist. The triumphalist fundamentalist posture is well captured in the opening of the Bush administration's 2002 national security strategy. 'The great struggles of the twentieth century between liberty and totalitarianism ended with a decisive victory for the forces of freedom,' it begins, with perfect accuracy and justified satisfaction, but then goes on '– and a single sustainable model for national success: freedom, democracy and free enterprise.' A single sustainable model? What titanic hubris. Even within the present spectrum of democratic capitalism there are many different models, with widely varying roles for the state as against free enterprise. If all the nations of the world successfully imitated today's American model, there would soon be no habitable world. Were America's profligate emissions of greenhouse gases to be matched by China, India, Russia and everyone else, we'd all be fried. 'Sustainable' is what it's not. And even if it were possible for the United Nations to be composed entirely of crypto-Americas, this would be deeply undesirable, on grounds of, so to speak, the biodiversity of world politics – not to mention sheer boredom.

The cultural relativist position is what I call Vulgar Huntingtonism (by analogy with Vulgar Marxism). It says: 'These values and institutions are peculiar to the West; we cannot expect Muslims, Confucians or even Orthodox Christians to share them; therefore we should not expect of them the respect for human rights, free speech, democracy and so forth that we expect among ourselves.' This is equally misguided. Twenty years ago, the West's 'realist' cultural relativists told us the Poles and Hungarians were not ready for democracy, because they had a different 'political culture'. That condescending judgement has been proved wrong since 1989. Then they told us the Orthodox countries of Europe were not ready for it. With truly heroic condescension, Samuel Huntington himself opined that 'Greece is not part of Western civilization', although, he conceded generously, 'it was the home of Classical civilization which was an important source of Western civilization'. Bad luck, Greece. 'In their opposition to the Turks,' Huntington explained, 'Greeks have considered themselves historically spear-carriers of Christianity.'[7] In the meantime, the Greeks, these blighted non-Western anti-Turkish spear-carriers, have been among the most eloquent advocates of largely Muslim Turkey joining the European Union. And Turkey is itself proving that it can consolidate an admittedly still very imperfect democracy with an Islamist party in power. As for Confucian Chinese being quite incapable of democracy: have these cultural relativists never visited Taiwan?

The right way lies between these two extremes. It can be described, without apology, as the path of freedom. Freedom not just for us but for all. However, this freedom we propose to all has to be clearly and even narrowly defined. In the terms popularized by Isaiah Berlin, this is 'negative' liberty: freedom from removable constraints, so long as removing them does not itself constrain the liberty of others.[8] In dealing with other countries and cultures, the constraints on which we should concentrate first are the most obviously acute and burdensome ones – those that no normal man or woman, in any known culture, would gladly endure if he or she had the chance to get rid of them. The more modest and precise is our definition of this freedom we want for others, the more likely it is to be accepted by them, rather than being rejected as arrogant Western imperialism.

Confucius can help here. Most of us – even us secular Europeans – probably know the so-called golden rule of Christian conduct on earth in the shorthand form: 'Do as you would be done by.' Or, in the King James Bible version of the original: 'Therefore all things whatsoever ye would that men should do to you, do ye even so to them; for this is the law and the prophets.'[9] To which George Bernard Shaw made a witty reply, that seems tailor-made for the dilemma of the post-West in today's world. 'Do not do unto others as you would that they should do unto you,' said Shaw. 'Their tastes may not be the same.'[10] Exactly so. But five centuries before Christ, Confucius formulated the injunction in a subtly different way. 'What you do *not* wish for yourself,' wrote Confucius, 'do *not* impose on others'[11] (my italics). Perhaps, taking our lead from Confucius, we can define our purpose thus: we aim to ensure that what other people do not wish for themselves is not imposed upon them.

At a time when Poland was still unfree, a Polish poet wrote this short poem, entitled 'Freedom':

What is freedom, ask the philosophers.
I too sometimes answer that it's
guaranteed liberties in the face of the power
of the state, or else I emphasize the strength
of convictions, the sovereignty of the soul and
loyalty to your own vocation. Yet even when
I'm unable to define the essence of freedom
I know exactly what it is to be unfree.[12]

This makes the essential point. There is always a question, even for wealthy people in free countries, as to how truly free you are as an individual. An American billionaire can still be a slave to convention, fashion, work, or his own desires. Some people in the former communist countries of central Europe have been disoriented and made unhappy by freedom. When the former East German communist party leader Erich Honecker was in prison in West Berlin, he received letters from his former subjects saying they had lived 'more quietly' under his rule.[13] But if you ask most East Germans, they certainly don't want his old regime back. There are also exceptional people who can find spiritual freedom in captivity. One of the most moving conversations I have ever had was with a young woman in Rangoon who told me how, in the miserable, overcrowded, half-starved conditions of a Burmese prison cell, she had found her way, through intensive Buddhist meditation, to *nirvana*. 'I thanked my jailers,' she recalled. 'I thanked them for helping me to reach *nirvana*.' But she didn't want to return to prison.

Freedom is elusive, difficult, risky, hard to define, let alone to achieve; but those who are unfree know exactly what unfreedom is. A Confucian no more enjoys having his nails pulled out under torture than a Christian. To see your daughter raped in front of your eyes by a militia gang is as soul-rending for a Muslim mother as for a Jewish mother. To feel your son slowly dying in your arms from hunger or AIDS is as unbearable for an African father as for an Indian father. So many people in the world still live, and die, in an unfreedom which we can be quite sure they do not want, simply because they are human and we are human.

What is now the most widespread form of basic unfreedom? Sixty years ago, when Roosevelt spelled out his 'four freedoms', and even thirty years ago, at the height of the Cold War, most of us would probably have answered 'dictatorships and the wars they cause'. Today, the answer must be extreme poverty. The first freedom towards which we should now work, if we want a free world, is Roosevelt's 'freedom from want'. This is also the field in which it is clearest what we – the thousand million rich and free – have to do.

Two large but very simple steps can lift hundreds of millions of our fellow human beings out of this kind of unfreedom. The first step is to practise what we preach: free trade. We should open our markets to their goods and cut our agricultural subsidies. This can only happen if America and Europe do it together. The second step is to increase aid. All rich and free countries should catch up with the exemplary Scandinavians and reach the target of giving 0.7 per cent of GDP, suggested by Lester Pearson, back in 1969, in a truly worthwhile Canadian initiative. But what states do is only half the story. All rich and free individuals should also donate more in private aid. Peter Singer, in his inspiring book *One World*, suggests that we should each aim to give 1 per cent of our annual income towards providing clean water, basic sustenance, shelter and medical care for the poorest of the poor. Anyone whose income is more than the average wage in a rich country can well afford that 1 penny from each pound we earn, or 1 cent from each Euro or dollar. Why don't we?

Some obvious reservations apply. We need to make sure our own farmers will not go to the wall in order to save the lives of African farmers. We have to see that aid is skilfully administered and doesn't stick to the wrong fingers along the way. The Great Aid Hike cannot and should not happen overnight. Yet in principle, the means to spread 'freedom from want' are right in front of our noses.

Working towards what Roosevelt called 'freedom from fear' is more complicated. Fear, unlike want, is a constituent part of all human lives. So what we're confronting here are only the causes of particularly acute fear, threatening basic human dignity and the most elementary human right: the right to life. Where do such threats now mainly come from? In the twentieth century, we spent most of our time worrying about states that were too strong: the 'Big Brother' regimes. There are still quite a few of them about – in Burma, in

North Korea, in several parts of Africa, and, in some respects, still the Chinese communist party-state.

In the early twenty-first century, however, we spend as much time worrying about states that are too weak. It's in failed states, such as Somalia and Rwanda, that people are murdered in large numbers just because of their ethnicity. It's in failed states, such as Afghanistan, that militant extremists and international terrorists find a congenial home. Then there's the danger of dictators, extremists or terrorists getting hold of the weapons of mass destruction which, thanks to the Western-led arms industry and arms trade, are ever more deadly and ever more widely available.

In a breathtaking example of American 'can-do' idealism, a former American ambassador, Mark Palmer, has proposed a campaign by the world's democracies to get rid of the world's last forty-four dictators over the next twenty years. 'The Community of Democracies', he writes, 'must adopt this common goal: All Dictators Out by 2025.'[14] It was actually forty-five dictators by his count when he started writing his book, but, while he wrote, Saddam Hussein was deposed by American and British military force. One down, forty-four to go? Palmer's work is mainly devoted to an admirable programme of non-violent means for encouraging the fall of dictators, and he says these should have been explored more thoroughly in the case of Iraq. However, he adds, in a slightly embarrassed formulation, 'I did personally favour invasion over a failure to act at all to oust Saddam Hussein'[15] – which, as he has himself just pointed out, is to pose a false alternative.

Palmer's contortions reflect the dilemma of many who care for other people's freedom as well as their own. We now face this question: is Western military intervention justified simply to remove a brutal dictatorship? If so, we should, logically, be urging our governments to prepare an invasion of Burma. Burma suffers under a military dictatorship at least as brutal as Saddam's, facing an opposition which already has the legitimacy of an overwhelming victory in democratic elections.[16] Now there are few things in the world that I would like more than to see the end of that loathsome Burmese junta, and Aung San Suu Kyi at last taking the place to which she was elected, at the head of a free Burma. But I'm afraid the answer to the question has to be 'no'. 'No' for Burma, and 'no' altogether.

Military intervention – preferably with explicit UN sanction, failing that with the support of a double majority (of democracies and of the country's neighbours), and, in very exceptional cases, even with a smaller coalition – can be justified a) where there is genocide taking place, as in Bosnia, Kosovo, Rwanda, and Iraq in 1988 but not Iraq in 2003; or b) where there is a real and present danger of a regime or terrorist group acquiring weapons of mass destruction which they are likely to use against us, their neighbours or their own people. How on earth we establish whether there is such a real and present danger is something we shall all have to wrestle with – especially after this claim was made about Saddam's Iraq, on the authority of secret intelligence, and turned out to be untrue. What qualifies as genocide is also a matter for the most serious debate.[17] But intervention is not justified simply to end a dictatorship.

There are good reasons why statesmen from the signatories of the Peace of Westphalia in 1648 to the authors of the UN Charter in 1945 set such store by respect for state sovereignty and non-intervention. If I think I'm justified in invading your country, you may equally well feel you're justified in invading mine. Or someone else's. President Putin plainly felt encouraged by America's unilateral action over Iraq to continue his oppression of Chechnya; and China felt it had a freer hand in Tibet. The road back to international anarchy is a short one.

Moreover, even if intervention is justified, for one of the reasons I've just given, what do we do when we're there? You may say: 'just give the country back to the people!' But which people, and how? What if, as often happens, there are several peoples in an ethnically fractured state? And so we enter the strange business of early twenty-first-century international occupations: Bosnia, Kosovo, East Timor, Afghanistan, Iraq. 'Nation-building' was the oddly nineteenth-century term first given to this enterprise; now the more modern and accurate 'state-building' is gaining ground. But are we any good at it? We're not. Of course it's early days, but I don't yet see a single example of a post-intervention international occupation which has successfully 'built' a self-governing free country. The two precedents usually quoted – Germany (West) and Japan – are the exceptions that prove the rule. Both were functioning nation-states before they were occupied. Both were occupied by just a few leading Western powers, which assumed total control following the unconditional surrender of regimes that had launched wars of aggression against them.

In our modern crypto-colonies, non-functioning, ethnically fractured states or parts of states are occupied by a multiplicity of national forces and international organizations, who rush to share power with hastily appointed or elected local elites. Power and legitimacy are hopelessly fragmented. Different international organizations pass the buck to each other; the locals pass the buck to the internationals, and the internationals back to the locals. The internationals keep changing, and half the participating governments want to get out as soon as they can. Corruption is rife, confusion endemic. Where we really had to intervene, in Bosnia, Kosovo, East Timor and Afghanistan, we must now stick with it, keep trying, and not sullenly withdraw, leaving the job half done. In Iraq, where we did not have to intervene, we none the less have promises to keep, and Europe has an even more vital interest than America in the outcome. But these are not good roads to freedom.

No, whether we look at its causes or its consequences, we conclude that military intervention must remain a last resort, only to be tried when all other means have failed. Armed intervention is, in itself, already a confession of failure. Both in principle and in practice it's better that people find their own path to freedom, in their own countries, in their own time, and, wherever possible, peacefully. But should we help these people as they fight freedom's battle? Most emphatically we should, by every non-violent means at our disposal. For we hold this truth to be self-evident: that those who love freedom must also want it for others.

We should urge our governments and companies to link trade and investment to respect for human rights, and other political and legal conditions which will vary from case to case. We should urge our parliaments to give more money to organizations like the American National Endowment for Democracy, the German party foundations and Britain's Westminster Foundation for Democracy, as they support those working for democracy in countries that do not yet have it. We can also give our own money or time to some of the myriad non-governmental organizations that help independent media, lawyers, women's groups, trades unions, students and political parties in places that are still unfree, or only partly free. Nor should we hesitate to expose these places to the full magnetism of our own freedom, through the internet, international broadcasting and scholarships for foreign students to study in our schools and colleges.

There's no room here for the false modesty of exaggerated cultural relativism. The Chinese students on Tiananmen Square gave pride of place to a model of the Statue of Liberty. One day, as the poet James Fenton prophesied soon after their demonstration was crushed by tanks, 'they'll come again / to Tiananmen'.[18] In the Chinese film *Balzac and the Little Chinese Seamstress*, a student banished to a remote mountain region during the Cultural Revolution approaches a doctor to ask him to perform an abortion on a friend. Instead of cash, he promises the doctor a volume of Balzac, in a classic Chinese translation. He shows him some sample lines he has written on the inside of his sheepskin jacket: 'My dear Christophe, you cannot know the delights of being free. To feel that all minds are free around you, yes, even the dunces, is an indescribable pleasure, as if the soul were swimming in endless skies.'[19] As the doctor reads these lines, he is moved almost to tears. It's good to be reminded by the Chinese that French is one of the great languages of liberty.

There is, however, a place for the true modesty of realism about our possibilities of influence. When we support the oppressed, dictators will always cry 'foul' and protest that this is 'intervention in our internal affairs'. The truth is that so long as the rulers of a state control their own frontiers, army, riot police and secret police, even the most powerful free countries in the world cannot topple them. All we can do is to give their own people the chance of toppling them or, preferably, negotiating them out of power. By our external assistance we are, as it were, just levelling up the playing field. By military intervention, we may bring an oppressed people freedom from the barrel of a gun. By these non-military forms of intervention, using our economic and 'soft' power, we do something slower and more open-ended, but in the end much better: we give them the chance to win it for themselves. It is, so to speak, not freedom itself we bring, merely the freedom to seize the possibility of freedom.

We also need to be modest about our ability to find all the right answers for other societies. What is it we want them to build? The shorthand answer generally given, especially by Americans, is Democracy with a capital D. Now liberal democracy is the best form of government yet discovered. But if you rush to a multi-party election without having first developed the underpinnings of liberal democracy – the rule of law, habits of good government, civil society, private property, independent media – you can end up with what Fareed Zakaria has called 'illiberal democracy'.[20] And if extremists win that election, you may find yourself with 'one man, one vote, once'. Some writers then leap to an opposite conclusion: that you have first to build the economic, legal and other foundations before 'topping out' with democracy. As with Spain under Franco, first make your bourgeoisie, then it's an easy step to bourgeois democracy. So the Chinese communists were right to put economic modernization before democratization, Gorbachev wrong to do it the other way round. But this is not self-evident. Actually, much of post-communist Europe has built the house of democracy from the roof downwards. A rather wonky building results, but it's still a freedom house.

The wiser conclusion, surely, is that it's not for us to say in what order others should do things. We can, and should, offer a toolbox of experiences in all aspects of transition, from how to write a constitution to how to deal with a difficult past, from demolishing nuclear silos to building a welfare system. But then it's up to them to decide. They should know best what is best for them. And if they don't, they must have the right to make their own mistakes. The Chinese house in 2025 will be different from an American house, and that is good – provided always that the essential moral and political minima are observed. And one further, vital task for the post-West is to lead the international debate about the definition of these universal minima of inalienable human dignity, on which there can be no compromise.

Democracy, like European union, is not an end in itself. It is a means to higher ends. What are these higher ends? Free people will differ about them too. My own shortlist comes from a prayer I chanced upon in one of my sons' old schoolbooks. It asks for 'freedom, good government, just laws and happy homes'. The first three

– freedom, good government and just laws – seem to me at once a more precise and a more inspiring formulation of our political goals than the blank Democracy. The fourth – happy homes – reminds us of the limits of politics:

> How small, of all that human hearts endure,
> That part which laws or kings can cause or cure.[21]

The recipe for human happiness is mysterious and cannot be purchased at Wal-Mart.

As I conclude this modest yet also hair-raising programme for a free world, I will confess to a nagging voice of doubt. This doubt, this Tiresias twinge, concerns the insatiable power of Western-style consumerism. If you visit a country like Burma, you see a miserable dictatorship but you also see a society which conserves in dress, custom and religion a very different, more traditional way of life. Only here and there do you notice the reversed baseball cap creeping in. Now Burma's dictators must go; but when they fall, the armies of Western-style consumerism will be waiting at the frontier, with their container-loads of tawdry goods, their cheap cigarettes called 'London', their sex shops, ready-made lifestyle packages and state-of-the-art techniques for the unceasing manufacture of new consumer desires. This invasion force is more irresistible than the Red Army, or even today's US Army, for it advances by asking what people want – and giving it to them. Then it makes them want more, and more, and more. This manufacturing of consumer desires is the exact opposite of the Buddhist ideal of transcending human desires. Which of the two will make more happy homes?

In any case, Western-style consumerism is unsustainable on a global scale. The earth cannot for ever bear more and more people demanding more and more. Yet how can economies grow without demand? If this is the underlying reality of the 'single sustainable model' then it will turn out to be not a model and not sustainable. All that remains will be the 'single', but that is itself undesirable, because humankind evolves through diversity. In this respect, too, as the West goes far beyond the West, it calls itself into question – as it often has before, and always should. Not only must we expect that the models of a free society that China, India, Africa or Latin America produce will differ from our own; we must actively hope that they will. An 'open society' inside a Western country does not mean the predominance of a single model; it means the constant, peaceful, regulated competition of many models. In this sense, we also need an open society of states.

So our ultimate objective is not that in 2047, on the four-hundredth anniversary of the Putney debates, some preppy Rainsborough from Boston should stand crowing from a hilltop: 'All dictators gone; world free; mission accomplished!' It's that a young woman in Teheran, Mombasa or Shanghai should adapt the old words of Thomas Rainsborough, in her own way, in her own country, in her own tongue, and say

For really I think that the poorest she that is on earth has a life to live, as the greatest he; and therefore truly, sir, I think it's clear, that every woman that is to live under a government ought first by her own consent to put herself under that government; and I do think that the poorest woman on earth is not at all bound in a strict sense to that government that she has not had a voice to put herself under.

What Can We Do?

A crisis of the West has revealed a great chance. Shall we seize it? Or will Europe half-heartedly pursue a half-baked dream of being a rival superpower to the United States, and frustrate its own better purposes as a result? Will Britain go on dithering, like a pensioner Hamlet? Will America yield to the temptations of predominant power, the rich go on living high and letting the poor die, the free remain indifferent to the misery of the unfree?

There's a wise motto for freeworlders: 'pessimism of the intellect, optimism of the will'.[1] Observe that its author did not say 'optimism of the heart'. The *will* is something active, defiant, striving. We expect the worst but work for the best.

One of the oddest things about our age of unparalleled democracy is that so many people feel so disillusioned with conventional politics that they don't even bother to vote. They say: 'We can't really influence what our politicians do and it doesn't matter that much anyway.' Wrong and wrong. It matters a lot. Most of us, the lucky thousand million, live relatively peaceful, comfortable private lives, in which, from day to day, we can happily ignore politics or ideologies; but in the meantime, our rulers are steadily demolishing the possibility that our children will do the same. Not that the people who govern us are generally scoundrels. Well, not utter scoundrels anyway. But half the time they really don't know what they're doing. The world is not safe in their hands. We must not leave it to them.

And we can influence them. In fact, there's never been a time when politicians tried so often and assiduously to find out, through opinion polls and focus groups, what the people really desire – and then to offer it, at least in slogans and promises. What is this 'public opinion' to which they are so nervously attentive? It's us.

Lenin's question 'What is to be done?' somehow suggests that, whatever the 'what', it's 'to be done' by someone else, by impersonal parties, governments or classes. Our question should be: 'What can *we* do?' The answer is: a lot. For a start, every time we hear someone holding forth, in the bar, office or family living room, about '*the* Europeans' or '*the* Americans' we can stop them and ask: '*Which* Europeans? *Which* Americans?' I hope this book has supplied ammunition for a good round or two. Every time we do this, we deflate just a little the dangerous myths of nationalism – British, French and American nationalism, but also what I've described as European nationalism. And we swing, if only by a thousandth of 1 per cent, that anonymous 'public opinion' recorded in the polls.

Those who write, broadcast or teach may even hope to swing a hundredth of 1 per cent. While I've been writing this book, many others have been arguing against the stupidity of Europe and America squabbling while the world burns. Political writing is, in this respect, unlike other kinds of writing. As a novelist or a poet, you always hope to be a unique voice. As a political writer, you also hope to express things differently, better, more vividly, but you are – or at least, should be – pleased, not distressed, when others are saying something similar; for what matters is that the right cause will prevail. When I listen to the chorus of fellow spirits on both sides of the Atlantic, I think it may. It's like hearing other people hacking away at the Berlin Wall to left and right of you – very heartening.

If we think our politicians are corrupt and useless, we can go into politics and get rid of them: locally, nationally or internationally. If we don't like old-fashioned party politics, which require us to live in half-truth, other forms of direct action are available. For example, we can give our time or money to pressure groups, charities and non-governmental organizations – the 'NGOs'. We have to pick with care: some are excellent, others useless. The best have a huge impact. What has been done to relieve the debt burden of the poorest countries was in large part a response to an NGO campaign. So was the international treaty to ban landmines. When Jody Williams, who won the

Nobel Peace Prize for her work in bringing that about, was asked how she did it, she replied 'e-mail'.

E-mail and the internet can empower us in ways that we've only just begun to explore. What I've called the democratization of political knowledge is one of the great advances of our time. With the erosion of official secrecy, and the genius of Google, we can know what our rulers are up to almost before they know themselves. And then, using e-mail, we can do something about it.

Not everything passes through virtual reality. I've argued that the future of civilized political life in Europe depends on making it possible for immigrants, especially Muslim immigrants, to feel at home in our post-Christian societies. At the moment, we're doing very badly. When an American Jewish friend talks of the 'moral incompetence' of Europeans in this respect, I wish I could disagree. Part of the answer is to change government policies but another part comes in the everyday reality of our human contacts with neighbours or colleagues. This is what determines whether people really feel at home. For the non-immigrant European there are multiple pitfalls. Offensive racism is one danger, but so is excruciating kindness: talking very slowly and clearly to the Indian or Moroccan postman as we tell him how glad we are to have him in our country. *Our* country? His country too. That matter-of-fact acceptance is increasingly the norm in cities like London, but elsewhere there is still a long way to go. And a little more cross-cultural knowledge would do no harm. How many non-Muslims know when or what Eid-ul-Fitr is?

Then there's development aid. I've said it before, but it bears repeating: if we want to be able to look ourselves in the face every morning, anyone who earns more than the average wage in a rich country should aim to give 1 per cent of his or her annual income to charities with a good track record in the developing world. We can afford it.

Meanwhile, who's for another demonstration? Whatever our view on the pros and cons of the Iraq War, we can surely agree that the massive anti-war protests on Saturday, 15 February 2003, in many of the capitals of Europe – but also in New York, San Francisco and Sydney – created a remarkable moment of popular political participation.

Right or wrong, this was better than apathy. But why is it that virtually all the large demos we see on international issues are against
American-led wars or arms deployments? Isn't there anything else we
need to shout against, or *for*? How about a simultaneous march,
across the whole of the post-West, against terrorism of all kinds? Or
another, organized at a critical moment in world trade negotiations, to
demand the kind of free trade that will benefit the world's poor?

These are just a few thoughts about what we can do.
Freeworldweb.net is a website for us to exchange ideas. We have
plenty of other places where we can talk and act. The main thing is to
refuse the illusion of impotence. There are many divisive walls in
today's world. There's the wall being built between Israelis and
Palestinians, which in places looks uncannily like the Berlin Wall.
There are the high walls of trade protectionism around both Europe
and the United States. But behind them are the biggest walls of all: the
mind-walls. If we raise our voices, these walls will come down. We
are many, and we have not spoken yet. It's up to us.

Maps

Money

Arms

People

Values

Freedom

Money

Canada 1.9%

USA 21.4%

Mexico 1.9%

Venezuela

Colombia

Peru

Chile

Brazil 2.8%

Argentina

Ireland

UK 3.2%

Portugal

Spain 1.8%

France 3.3%

Belgium

Netherlands

Germany 4.6%

Switzerland

Italy 3.1%

Austria

Norway

Sweden

Finland

Denmark

Poland

Czech Republic

Hungary

Greece

Romania

Russia 2.4%

Ukraine

Kazakhstan

Turkey

Israel

Algeria

Morocco

Nigeria

South Africa

Egypt

Saudi Arabia

Iran

Pakistan

India 5.7%

China 12.1%

Thailand

South Korea 1.7%

Vietnam

Bangladesh

Japan 6.9%

Philippines

Malaysia

Indonesia

Singapore

Australia 1.1%

New Zealand

Annual income per person
(international dollars)

Over $25,000

$15,000–$25,000

$5,000–$15,000

Under $5,000

The size of each national
block corresponds to
that country's share of
the world's gross
domestic product.

The shading indicates gross
national income per person.
Figures are for 2002,
calculated at purchasing
power parities.

All other
countries

Data source: World Bank

254

Arms

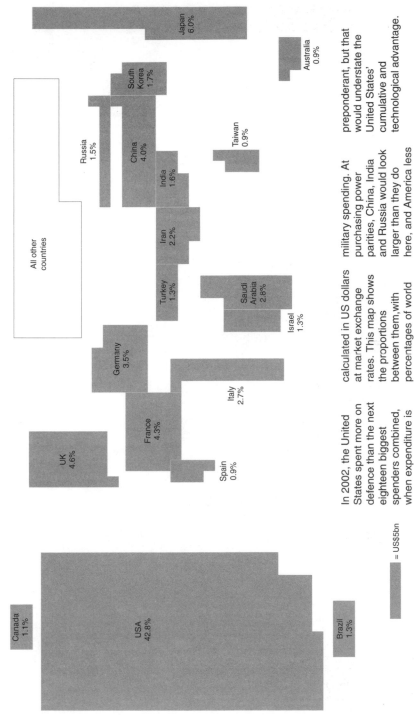

Canada
1.1%

USA
42.8%

Brazil
1.3%

UK
4.6%

France
4.3%

Spain
0.9%

Germany
3.5%

Italy
2.7%

Turkey
1.3%

Saudi
Arabia
2.8%

Israel
1.3%

Iran
2.2%

India
1.6%

China
4.0%

Russia
1.5%

All other
countries

South
Korea
1.7%

Japan
6.0%

Taiwan
0.9%

Australia
0.9%

= US$5bn

In 2002, the United States spent more on defence than the next eighteen biggest spenders combined, when expenditure is calculated in US dollars at market exchange rates. This map shows the proportions between them, with percentages of world military spending. At purchasing power parities, China, India and Russia would look larger than they do here, and America less preponderant, but that would understate the United States' cumulative and technological advantage.

Data source: SIPRI Yearbook

People

Country	%
China	20.4%
India	16.7%
USA	4.6%
Indonesia	3.7%
Brazil	2.9%
Pakistan	2.4%
Russia	2.3%
Bangladesh	2.2%
Nigeria	2.1%
Japan	2.0%
Mexico	1.7%
Philippines	1.3%
Vietnam	1.3%
Egypt	1.2%
Turkey	1.1%
Iran	1.1%
Ethiopia	1.1%
Thailand	1.0%

=10 million

This map draws countries proportionate to their percentage share of estimated world population in mid-2003. Only countries with a population over 10 million are shown.

All other countries

North Korea, South Korea, Taiwan, Malaysia, Australia, Burma, Cambodia, Sri Lanka, Nepal, Kazakhstan, Ukraine, Romania, Serbia & Montenegro, Uzbekistan, Afghanistan, Belarus, Czech Rep, Poland, Hungary, Syria, Iraq, Saudi Arabia, Yemen, Greece, Netherlands, Germany, Italy, France, Spain, UK, Belgium, Portugal, Cameroon, Uganda, Sudan, Kenya, Tanzania, Mozambique, Madagascar, South Africa, Malawi, Dem Rep of Congo, Zambia, Zimbabwe, Angola, Morocco, Algeria, Mali, Niger, Senegal, Burkina Faso, Côte d'Ivoire, Ghana, Canada, Cuba, Venezuela, Guatemala, Colombia, Ecuador, Peru, Chile, Argentina

256

Data source: CIA World Factbook

Values

This map shows findings of the World Values Survey along two key axes, from traditional values to secular-rational values, and from survival values to self-expression values.

Sometimes known as the Inglehart Values Map, after its author, Ronald Inglehart, it summarizes responses from interviews conducted in 1999–2001 with more than 120,000 people in eighty-one countries. The designated clusters, including Catholic Europe, Protestant Europe, Ex-Communist (marked by a dotted line) and English-Speaking, are part of his map.

Inglehart reports that the basic pattern has changed little over three successive rounds of the World Values Survey, covering the 1990s, although there is a tendency for all richer countries to move somewhat towards the upper right-hand corner of the map.

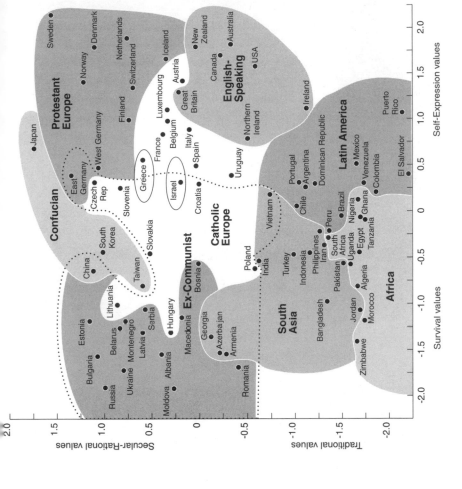

Source: Ronald Inglehart et al. (eds).,
Human Values and Beliefs:
A Cross-Cultural Sourcebook
(Mexico City: Siglo XXI, 2004)

Freedom

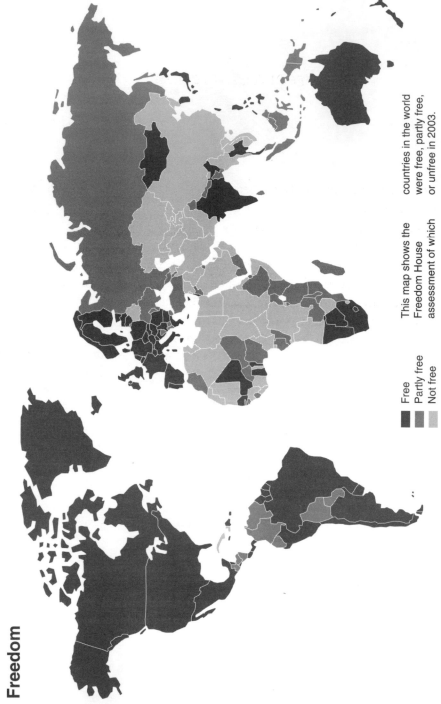

Free
Partly free
Not free

This map shows the Freedom House assessment of which countries in the world were free, partly free, or unfree in 2003.

Source: Freedom House

Freeworldweb.net

The end of a book is only the beginning of a conversation. Or, in this case, the continuation of a conversation which is already in progress along millions of different lines of communication across the world. The age of the physical book is very far from over, but websites can respond faster to change. Freeworldweb.net is a website where readers of this book in different countries, and anyone interested in its subject, can exchange reactions, information and ideas. I shall also post new material there from time to time.

TGA

Notes

These notes only give references for direct quotations in the text, numerical claims, and points where I have drawn very directly on other people's work. They occasionally make small but significant qualifications to statements in the text. They don't give references for non-attributable remarks made in private conversations. What use is it for you to read 'personal information' or 'conversation with the author' if I can't tell you who said it and when?

A CRISIS OF THE WEST

1. *Life's Picture History of Western Man* (New York: Time Inc., 1951), quotations from pp. 1–2 and 290.
2. Jean-Marie Colombani, 'Nous sommes tous Américains', *Le Monde,* 13 September 2001.
3. Quoted by Martin Walker, UPI's Chief International Correspondent, in a UPI report from Washington, 4 February 2003.
4. Charles A. Kupchan, 'The End of the West', *Atlantic Monthly,* 1 November 2002.
5. Robert Kagan, *Of Paradise and Power: America and Europe in the New World Order* (New York: Alfred A. Knopf, 2003), p. 3.
6. Note that these rankings are based on purchasing power parities. See the table, based on 2002 World Bank figures, in *Strategic Audit: Discussion Document, November 2003,* prepared by the British government's Strategy Unit, and available on <http://www.strategy.gov.uk> At market exchange rates, it would be first (America) and fourth (Britain) against third (Germany) and fifth (France).
7. *Libération,* 11 February 2003.
8. George Orwell, *Collected Essays* (London: Secker & Warburg, 1961), p. 281.

I JANUS BRITAIN

1. Quoted from the original manuscript in A. S. P. Woodhouse (ed.), *Puritanism and Liberty: Being the Army Debates from the Clarke Manuscripts, with Supplementary Documents* (London: Dent, 1938), p. 53. I have modernized the spelling of Rainsborough, sometimes given as Rainborough or Rainborow.

2. John Winthrop's 1630 'Model of Christian Charity', quoted in Daniel J. Boorstin, *An American Primer* (New York: Mentor, 1966), pp. 26–43, at p. 40.

3. Information on his younger brother and his sister from Richard L. Greaves and Robert Zaller (eds), *Biographical Dictionary of British Radicals in the Seventeenth Century* (Brighton: Harvester Press, 1982–4), entries on Thomas and William Rainsborough.

4. According to a search on <http://mapquest.com>

5. On the 350th anniversary of the Putney Debates, in-church speeches were delivered by the left-wing Labour politician Tony Benn and the Marxist historian Christopher Hill. The anniversary was also marked by a large conference in Washington, DC.

6. Figures from VSO Annual Report 2003, on <http://www.vso.org.uk>

7. Quoted from their website, <http://www.longview.com/ourcompany/>, accessed on 26 August 2003.

8. William Shakespeare, *King Richard II*, Act II, Scene 1.

9. I saw this in a German newspaper in the 1970s. I have unfortunately been unable to retrace it.

10. Quoted by Leszek Kołakowski in his *Main Currents of Marxism* (Oxford: Clarendon Press, 1978), vol. 1, p. 1.

11. John Major quoted in Jeremy Paxman, *The English* (London: Penguin, 1999), p. 142. What Orwell actually wrote was 'the old maids biking to Holy Communion through the mists of the autumn mornings', see George Orwell, *The Lion and the Unicorn: Socialism and the English Genius* (London: Secker & Warburg, 1941), p. 11.

12. Jeremy Black, *A History of the British Isles* (London: Macmillan, 1997), p. 325.

13. This is the conclusion of Robert Colls, *Identity of England* (Oxford: Oxford University Press, 2002), pp. 380–81. The location of Brunanburh has apparently not been established.

14. The 2001 Census put minority ethnic groups at 7.9 per cent of the total population, or one in twelve and a half. If one allows for subsequent growth, immigrants not covered by the Census, and asylum-seekers, one in twelve seems a fair conservative estimate.

15. See the results of the April 2001 Census on <http://www.statistics.gov.uk/cci/nugget.asp?id=273>

16. BBC News report, 29 January 2001, on <http://news.bbc.co.uk/1/hi/uk/1142546.stm>

17. As reported by Andrew Gimson in a fascinating series of articles in the *Evening Standard* on multi-ethnic London, this on 10 July 2001.

18. Philip Baker and John Eversley (eds), *Multilingual Capital* (London: Battlebridge Publications, 2000).

19. *Daily Express*, 8 May 2002.

20. Figures from the British Beer and Pub Association, *Facts 2003*. See <http://www.beerandpub.com>

21. John Major on the BBC *Today* programme, 18 September 2002.

22. William Shakespeare, *King Henry V*, Act IV, Scene 3.

23. Estimates from the Foreign Office website <http://www.fco.gov.uk> and *Social Trends 2000* (London: The Stationery Office, 2002). Official Spanish statistics record 105, 479 British citizens registered as resident in Spain on 31 December 2003, (<http://dgei.mir.es/en/general/balance_DGEI2003.pdf>). The real number of British people spending a large part of the year there is certainly larger.

24. A figure of 1.2 million is given in *The Observer*, 16 November 2003. The 2000 US Census puts the number of UK-born US residents at just over 600,000. The estimate for Americans living in the UK was given to me by the then Minister at the US Embassy in London, Glyn Davies, on 1 July 2003.

25. *Social Trends No. 32, 2002 Edition* (London: The Stationery Office, 2002), p. 217.

26. Estimate by the then Minister at the US Embassy in London, Glyn Davies, 1 July 2003.

27. *Newsweek*, 13 November 2001.

28. Intelligence^2 debate on 24 April 2003. The final vote was 188 for, 115 against, 26 don't knows.

29. Raymond Seitz, *Over Here* (London: Phoenix, 1998), p. 9.

30. Quoted from Trevelyan's hugely influential *English Social History* by Philip Bell in 'A Historical Cast of Mind: Some Eminent English Historians and Attitudes to Continental Europe in the Middle of the Twentieth Century', *Journal of European Integration History*, 1996, vol. 2, no. 2, pp. 5–19, at p. 12. Bell notes that Trevelyan's book sold nearly 400,000 copies between 1944 and 1949. J. H. Plumb commented in 1951: 'In many homes it must be the one and only history book. This work is not only a social history but a social phenomenon.' Scottish, Irish and, to a lesser degree, Welsh schoolchildren were taught rather different histories.

31. See J. C. D. Clark, *The Language of Liberty 1660–1832: Political*

Discourse and Social Dynamics in the Anglo-American World (Cambridge: Cambridge University Press, 1994).

32. See Norman Davies, *The Isles: A History* (London: Macmillan, 1999), pp. 7–8.

33. See Jeremy Black, *Convergence or Divergence? Britain and the Continent* (London: Macmillan, 1994), pp. 261ff.

34. Trade and foreign investment figures for 2001 in *UK International Priorities: A Strategy for the FCO* (London: The Stationery Office, 2003), pp. 37–8.

35. The Treasury estimates that 3 million jobs in the UK are linked, directly or indirectly, to the export of goods and services to the European Union. This figure is based on the assumption that the share of total UK employment associated with UK exports to the EU is equal to the total UK value added (GVA) generated by UK exports to the EU. Joseph P. Quinlan, *Drifting Apart or Growing Together? The Primacy of the Transatlantic Economy* (Washington: Center for Transatlantic Relations, 2003), calculates that 1.3 million British jobs depended on American affiliates in 2000.

36. See <http://www.lakenheath.af.mil/home.html>

37. Stated with some authority by a former head of the Joint Intelligence Committee, Sir Rodric Braithwaite, in *Prospect*, May 2003, pp. 20–23, at p. 21.

38. Reported on the BBC's *Today* programme, 31 October 2002.

39. Admiral James Woolsey, quoted on the BBC's *Today* programme and in *The Economist*, 26 April 2000.

40. The fourth largest at market exchange rates, but only the seventh using purchasing power parities. See the table, based on 2002 World Bank figures, in *Strategic Audit: Discussion Document, November 2003* prepared by the British government's Strategy Unit, and available on <http://www.strategy.gov.uk>

41. 'Aber dieses groteske Österreich ist nichts anderes als ein besonders deutlicher Fall der modernen Welt.' Robert Musil, *Tagebücher: Band 1* (Reinbek bei Hamburg: Rowohlt, 1983) p. 354. I am grateful to Malcolm Spencer for this reference.

42. Cartoon of 18 June 1940, see David Low, *Years of Wrath: A Cartoon History 1932–1945* (London: Victor Gollancz, 1986), p. 117.

43. *The Sun*, 15 May 2003.

44. Letter from John Church in *Daily Mail*, 3 January 1997. I owe the reference to Edwin Jones, *The English Nation: The Great Myth* (Stroud: Sutton Publishing, 2000).

45. William Shakespeare, *King John*, Act V, Scene 7.

46. Conrad Black, *Britain's Final Choice: Europe or America?* (London: Centre for Policy Studies, 1998).

47. Ibid., p. 27.

48. Robert Conquest, 'Toward an English-Speaking Union' in *The National Interest*, Fall 1999, pp. 64–70.

49. This is the definition by one of the main promoters of the idea of the Anglosphere, James C. Bennett. See his 'An Anglosphere Primer' from <http://www.pattern.com/bennettj-anglosphereprimer.html>

50. Gerard Baker, *Financial Times*, 20 March 2003.

51. The combined readership figure of 22.4 million is from the 2003 National Readership Survey, for the broadly 'Eurosceptic' *Sun*, *Daily Mail*, *Daily Telegraph*, *Times*, *Daily Express* and *Daily Star*, as against a total of 30.8 million for all national dailies. See <http://www.nrs.co.uk/open_access/open_topline/newspapers/newspapersJan03-Dec03_print.htm>

52. Ibid. For comparison, some 8.4 million read the broadly 'Europhile' *Daily Mirror*, *Guardian*, *Independent* and *Financial Times*.

53. Hugo Young, *This Blessed Plot: Britain and Europe from Churchill to Blair* (London: Papermac, 1999), p. 1.

54. *Guardian*, 16 September 2003.

55. William Shakespeare, *Richard II*, Act II, Scene 1. 'Pelting' means paltry.

56. Will Hutton, 'We must be at the heart of Europe,' in *The Observer*, 10 June 2001.

57. Will Hutton, *The World We're In* (London: Little Brown, 2002), p. 271 and *passim*.

58. Jonathan Freedland, *Bring Home the Revolution: The Case for a British Republic* (London: Fourth Estate, 1998).

59. Harold Macmillan, *Pointing the Way, 1959–1961* (London: Macmillan, 1972), p. 316.

60. Headlines in *The Sun*, 27 May 2003, *Daily Mail*, 16 May 2003, *Sunday Express*, 19 October 2003, *Daily Telegraph*, 15 May 2003.

61. See Eugene L. Rasor, *Winston S. Churchill 1874–1965: A Comprehensive Historiography and Annotated Bibliography* (Westport, CT: Greenwood Press, 2000).

62. Speech of 4 June 1940, in Robert Rhodes James (ed.), *Winston S. Churchill: His Complete Speeches 1897–1963* (New York and London: Chelsea House, 1974), pp. 6225–31, at p. 6231. (Subsequently referred to as: Rhodes James, *Churchill Speeches*.)

63. 'Let us therefore brace ourselves to our duty and so bear ourselves that if the British Commonwealth and Empire lasts for a thousand years men will still say "This was their finest hour"', speech of 18 June 1940, in Rhodes James, *Churchill Speeches*, pp. 6231–8, at p. 6238.

64. Entry for 4 December 1943, *Chips: Diaries of Sir H. Channon* (London: Weidenfeld & Nicolson, 1967), p. 381.

65. Speech of 3 April 1939 in Rhodes James, *Churchill Speeches*, p. 6094.

66. Speech of 19 May 1939 in Rhodes James, *Churchill Speeches*, p. 6126.

67. H. V. Morton, *Atlantic Meeting* (London: Methuen, 1943), p. 98.

68. Ibid., pp. 152–5.

69. See D. C. Watt, *Succeeding John Bull* (Cambridge: Cambridge University Press, 1984).

70. This remark, made to Clark Clifford, is quoted by Paul Addison in 'Churchill in the Twenty-First Century', a special issue of *Transactions of the Royal Historical Society*, 6th series, xii (2002), at p. 198.

71. Simon Jenkins in *The Times*, 30 October 2002.

72. Minute of the Roosevelt–Stalin meeting on 4 February 1945 by Charles Bohlen in *Foreign Relations of the United States: The Conferences at Malta and Yalta* (Washington: Department of State, 1955), p. 572.

73. Rhodes James, *Churchill Speeches*, p. 7381.

74. Rhodes James, *Churchill Speeches*, p. 7842.

75. Rhodes James, *Churchill Speeches*, p. 7836.

76. Rhodes James, *Churchill Speeches*, p. 7382 and, for 'France and Britain', p. 7485.

77. Quoted in Roy Jenkins, *Churchill* (London: Pan Books, 2002), p. 855.

78. Ibid., p. 855.

79. Konrad Adenauer, *Erinnerungen 1945–1963* (Stuttgart: DVA, 1987), p. 512.

80. 'I believe myself to be what is called a good European', broadcast, 21 March 1943, in Rhodes James, *Churchill Speeches*, p. 6758.

81. See David Reynolds, 'Rethinking Anglo-American Relations' in *International Affairs*, vol. 65, no. 1, pp. 89–111.

82. Eisenhower's diary, 6 January 1953, quoted in Anthony Seldon, *Churchill's Indian Summer: The Conservative Government 1951–55* (London: Hodder & Stoughton, 1981), p. 391.

83. Roy Jenkins, *Churchill* (London: Pan Books, 2002), p. 864, quoting Churchill's doctor Lord Moran. Jenkins notes that Moran is 'not always verbally reliable', but there is ample evidence that Churchill practised self-censorship in this respect while preparing for publication the final volume of *The Second World War*.

84. Ivan Krastev in *Die Zeit*, 14 August 2003.

85. Speech of 17 July 2003, available at <http://www.number-10.gov.uk/output/Page4220.as>

86. Quoted in Peter Riddell, *Hug Them Close: Blair, Clinton, Bush and the 'Special Relationship'* (London: Politicos, 2003), p. 137.

87. Quoted with phonetic accuracy in John Kampfner, *Blair's Wars* (London: Free Press, 2003), p. 121.

88. *New Labour: Because Britain Deserves Better* (London, 1997), p. 36. I owe this reference to Anne Deighton.

89. For example, in his speech to the Confederation of Indian Industry in Bangalore, 5 January 2002. <http://www.number-10.gov.uk>

90. As reported by a usually reliable source.

91. Speech on receiving the Charlemagne Prize in Aachen, 13 May 1999. <http://www.number-10.gov.uk>

92. Hugo Young, *This Blessed Plot: Britain and Europe from Churchill to Blair* (London: Papermac, 1999), p. 482.

93. Speech delivered at the Warsaw Stock Exchange, 6 October 2000. <http://www.number-10.gov.uk>

94. Speech to a joint session of both houses of Congress, 17 July 2003, <http://www.number-10.gov.uk/output/Page4220.as>

95. Remarks by the president on accepting the bust, 13 July 2001, quoted from 17 July 2001 news story on <http://www.ananova.com>

96. Peter Riddell, *Hug Them Close: Blair, Clinton, Bush and the 'Special Relationship'* (London: Politicos, 2003), p. 161.

97. He listed this as the top priority of British foreign policy in a meeting with British ambassadors on 7 January 2003. Text on <http://www.number-10.gov.uk> There also 'broadening its agenda'.

98. Diary entry for 7 March 2002, in Robin Cook, *The Point of Departure* (London: Simon & Schuster, 2003), p. 116.

99. The reference was to Colin Powell, US Secretary of State, not Jonathan Powell, Blair's Chief of Staff.

100. A witticism I first heard from the BBC's political editor, Andrew Marr.

101. The aide was Alistair Campbell, quoted in Peter Stothard, *30 Days: A Month at the Heart of Blair's War* (London: HarperCollins, 2003), p. 106.

102. Quoted in John Kampfner, *Blair's Wars* (London: Free Press, 2003), p. 350.

103. See the various drafts in Warren F. Kimball, *Churchill and Roosevelt: The Complete Correspondence*. Volume I (Princeton: Princeton University Press, 1984), pp. 86–109, at p. 94.

104. US Department of State, *Foreign Relations of the United States: The Conference at Quebec 1944* (Washington, DC: US Government Printing Office, 1972), p. 348.

105. *Wall Street Journal Europe*, 5/6 October 2001.

106. Remarks at the Cheltenham Literary Festival, 19 October 2003.

107. The parallel is sharply pointed out by Peter Riddell in his *Hug Them Close: Blair, Clinton, Bush and the 'Special Relationship'* (London: Politicos, 2003), p. 231. For Adenauer and de Gaulle's Placentia Bay in Reims, see Hans-Peter Schwarz, *Adenauer: Der Staatsmann 1952–1967* (Stuttgart: DVA, 1991), p. 755ff.

108. Tony Blair, conversation with the author, London, 3 September 2003.
109. The political editor of *The Sun*, Trevor Kavanagh, emphasizes that their readership has a large number of floating voters, by contrast with the solidly Conservative readership of the *Daily Mail* (conversation with the author, London, 1 July 2003). According to the 2003 National Readership Survey, the average daily readership of *The Sun* is just under 9 million. See <http://www.nrs.co.uk/open_access/open_topline/newspapers/newspapersJa no3-Deco3_print.htm>
110. Philip Gould, *The Unfinished Revolution: How the Modernisers Saved the Labour Party* (London: Abacus, 2001), p. 375.
111. Interview on BBC *Newsnight*, 14 November 2003.

2 EUROPE AS NOT-AMERICA

1. *Le Monde*, 26 February 2003.
2. Letter to the author from Dominique Strauss-Kahn, 23 July 2003, and background papers of the Round Table.
3. *Frankfurter Allgemeine Zeitung*, 31 May 2003. All following quotations also come from this source.
4. Oxford Union debate, 12 June 2003. My notes.
5. Claus Koch in *Merkur*, Sonderheft 9/10, September/October 2000, pp. 980–90, at p. 990.
6. In a television discussion on *Das philosophische Quartett*, ZDF, 30 March 2003.
7. At a press conference on 22 January 2003. For the full reference, see note 83 below.
8. One of many indignant responses by European intellectuals to Rumsfeld's 'old Europe' remark in the *Feuilleton* of the *Frankfurter Allgemeine Zeitung*, 24 January 2003.
9. Robert Kagan, *Of Paradise and Power: America and Europe in the New World Order* (New York: Knopf, 2003), p. 3. The book's US publication date was 5 February 2003. The original article appeared in *Policy Review* No. 113, June/July 2002.
10. Quoted in Tony Judt, *Past Imperfect: French Intellectuals 1944–1956* (Berkeley: University of California Press, 1992), p. 188.
11. According to the notes of the Italian journalist Paolo Valentino, who was present at the press conference where Berlusconi made these remarks, what Berlusconi said was: 'The Western world is bound to westernize and conquer people: we did it with the communist world and with parts of the Islamic world. Unfortunately, there is part of the Islamic world which is still 1400

years backwards. From this point of view, we must be conscious of the strength of our civilization, of its superiority and supremacy.' E-mail from Paolo Valentino to the author, 13 November 2001.

12. Oriana Fallaci, *The Rage and the Pride* (New York: Rizzoli, 2002), translated from the Italian in Fallaci's own inimitable English. 'Moslem invaders' on p. 177; 'Reverse Crusade' on p. 83.

13. See Denys Hay, *Europe: The Emergence of an Idea* (Edinburgh: Edinburgh University Press, 1957) p. 25. The battle is variously described as being of Tours or Poitiers, in 732 or 733.

14. Ibid., p. 83ff.

15. The preamble, drafted by Valéry Giscard d'Estaing, refers only to 'the cultural, religious and humanist inheritance of Europe', see *Draft Treaty Establishing a Constitution for Europe* (Brussels: European Convention, 2003), p. 5.

16. Estimates from *The Economist*. 6 March 2004.

17. See the reconstruction of his map in John Goss, *The Mapmaker's Art: An Illustrated History of Cartography* (New York: Rand McNally, 1993), p. 24. Eratosthenes appears to have placed the eastern frontier of Europe on the River Don. Only in the eighteenth century did the Urals come to be accepted as the conventional eastern frontier of the geographer's Europe.

18. Quoted by Giuliano Amato in Mark Leonard (ed.), *The Future Shape of Europe* (London: Foreign Policy Centre, 2000), p. 32.

19. Quoted in Jeremy Black, *Convergence or Divergence? Britain and the Continent* (London: Macmillan, 1994), p. 164.

20. The suggestive sub-title of Linda Colley's outstanding study of the formation of British national identity is 'forging the nation'; see *Britons: Forging the Nation 1707–1837* (New Haven: Yale University Press, 1992).

21. Rudolf von Thadden at a conference of the Collège d'Europe in Warsaw, 10/11 May 2003, drawing on remarks about French identity by Fernand Braudel.

22. Henry Kissinger, 'America at the Apex: Empire or Leader?' in *The National Interest*, Summer 2001, pp. 9–17, at p. 12.

23. Jean Lacouture in *Le Débat*, no. 125, May–August 2003, and Douglas Johnson in *Prospect*, April 2003.

24. See his article '1940: Fulcrum of the Twentieth Century?' in *International Affairs*, vol. 66, no. 2, pp. 325–50.

25. Quoted in Jean Lacouture, *De Gaulle: The Ruler, 1945–1970* (London: Harvill, 1991), p. 359.

26. I owe this reference originally to Robert Darnton, 'A Euro State of Mind', *New York Review of Books*, 28 February 2002.

27. Harold Macmillan, *Pointing the Way: 1959–1961* (London: Macmillan, 1972), p. 427.

28. De Boissieu's formal position was Deputy Secretary-General of the Council of the European Union.

29. Jacques Delors and Clisthène, *La France par l'Europe* (Paris: Bernard Grasset, 1988), p. 60. I owe this reference originally to Tony Judt, *A Grand Illusion? An Essay on Europe* (London: Penguin, 1996).

30. Dominique Noguez, 'Une langue si "easy"', in *Le Monde*, 8 August 2002.

31. Speech to the UN Security Council, 14 February 2003, on <http://www.france.diplomatie.fr.>

32. Dominique de Villepin, *Le cri de la Gargouille* (Paris: Albin Michel, 2002), pp. 9–10.

33. Allensbach poll reported in *Frankfurter Allgemeine Zeitung*, 19 March 2003.

34. This was the clear gist of an evening's conversation that I and another historian had with him about 'German identity' on 19 February 2002.

35. Quoted by William Horsley in a BBC report dated 17 September 2002.

36. Quoted by Michael Naumann in *Die Zeit*, 6 February 2003.

37. Peter Pulzer, by whom I originally heard this quoted, suggests it may be part of political folklore, like so many of the best political quotations. I would be grateful to any reader who can produce a source.

38. Peter Struck in the *Berlin Mitte* talkshow on ZDF, 13 February 2003.

39. Quoted in Timothy Garton Ash, *In Europe's Name: Germany and the Divided Continent* (London: Jonathan Cape, 1993), p. 114.

40. For 'colony' see, for example, the jacket copy of Egon Bahr, *Der deutsche Weg: Selbstverständlich und normal* (Munich: Blessing, 2003); for 'vassal', Christoph Bertram in *Financial Times*, 28 May 2003.

41. This and other quotations from my notes of our conversation in Berlin, 1 June 2003.

42. Angela Merkel, after-dinner remarks at a dinner in London, 10 June 2003.

43. Allensbach poll reported in *Frankfurter Allgemeine Zeitung*, 19 March 2003.

44. Ipos poll reported in *Le Monde*, 13 November 2003.

45. German Marshall Fund et al., *Transatlantic Trends* (Washington, DC, 2003), p. 9.

46. Figures from the Gallup International Millennium Survey of 1999 on <http://www.gallup-international.com>. Note that figures are for 'North America', presumably including Canada.

47. Pew Global Attitudes Project, *Views of a Changing World: June 2003*

(Washington, DC: The Pew Research Center for the People and the Press, 2003), p. 115.

48. Figures from a 1996 survey quoted in Andrew Kohut et al., *The Diminishing Divide: Religion's Changing Role in American Politics* (Washington, DC: Brookings Institution Press, 2000), p. 27.

49. Pew Global Attitudes Project, *Views of a Changing World: June 2003* (Washington, DC: The Pew Research Center for the People and the Press, 2003), p. 105.

50. Ibid., p. 108. However, the proportion of people who blame failure on the individual rather than 'society' is only a few percentage points lower in Britain and West Germany than in the US, ibid., p. T-53.

51. OECD figures quoted in *Financial Times*, 23 October 2003.

52. See Lawrence Mishel et al., *The State of Working America 2002–3* (Ithaca: Cornell University Press, 2003), pp. 411–16.

53. Here I follow Will Hutton, *The World We're In* (London: Little Brown, 2002), p. 149.

54. Quoted by Minxin Pei in 'The Paradoxes of American Nationalism', *Foreign Policy*, May/June 2001, based on figures from the World Values Survey.

55. Estimates for 2000 put gun ownership in the US at 83–96 per 100 inhabitants, compared to around 30 for France and Germany and 10 in Britain. Report by Stephen Castle in *The Independent*, 2 July 2003.

56. These figures are based on a British Home Office comparative study for the years 1998–2000, see <http://www.homeoffice.gov.uk/rds/pdfs2/hosb502.pdf> (Tables 1.1, 1.2).

57. Seymour Martin Lipset, *American Exceptionalism: A Double-Edged Sword* (New York: Norton, 1996).

58. See our co-authored response to Habermas and Derrida, 'Die Erneuerung Europas' in *Süddeutsche Zeitung*, 5/6 July 2003. This insight came from Dahrendorf.

59. See the fascinating Introduction to Peter A. Hall and David Soskice, *Varieties of Capitalism: The Institutional Foundations of Comparative Advantage* (Oxford: Oxford University Press, 2001), pp. 1–68.

60. Ibid., p. 21.

61. In 2001, the tax burden was 50.8 per cent in Sweden and 37.4 per cent in the UK. Data from OECD Revenue Statistics 2002, see <http://www.oecd.org/dataoecd/30/37/2401707.pdf>

62. See Minxin Pei, 'The Paradoxes of American Nationalism', *Foreign Policy*, May/June 2001, based on figures from the World Values Survey. Against 72 per cent of Americans, the figures were 74 per cent of the Irish, 71 per cent of Poles and 20 per cent of the Dutch.

63. Pew Global Attitudes Project, *Views of a Changing World: June 2003* (Washington, DC: The Pew Research Center for the People and the Press, 2003), p. 115.

64. All estimated demonstration numbers from the BBC, 17 February 2003. As usual, estimates of demonstration numbers varied widely.

65. The figure of half is taken from a poll reported in *The Australian* on 25 March 2003. Obviously the figures fluctuated.

66. Examples can be found in Peter A. Hall and David Soskice, *Varieties of Capitalism: The Institutional Foundations of Comparative Advantage* (Oxford: Oxford University Press, 2001), p. 22, and Adair Turner, *Just Capital: The Liberal Economy* (London: Macmillan, 2001), pp. 261–3.

67. See Peter A. Hall and David Soskice, *Varieties of Capitalism: The Institutional Foundations of Comparative Advantage* (Oxford: Oxford University Press, 2001), pp. 19–21 and *passim*.

68. Seymour Martin Lipset, *American Exceptionalism: A Double-Edged Sword* (New York: Norton, 1996), p. 289.

69. This and following figures from the excellent OECD website, <http://www.oecd.org>

70. Larry Lindsey in the *Financial Times*, 28 August 2003, quotes a 2003/4 figure of $311 billion for Medicaid against $105 billion for the NHS.

71. All figures from Budget of the United States Government, 'Table 3.1 – Outlays by Superfunction and Function: 1940–2009', accessed via <http://frwebgate5.access.gpo.gov/cgi-bin/waisgate.cgi?WAISdocID= 532133420880+8+0+0&WAISaction=retrieve>

72. I am most grateful to Ronald Inglehart for letting me have early sight of the latest version of the map, and for checking my account of it. He notes that the results are quite consistent over successive surveys. The results of the 1999–2001 surveys are published and analysed in Ronald Inglehart et al. (eds), *Human Values and Beliefs: A Cross-Cultural Sourcebook* (Mexico City: Siglo XXI, 2004).

73. Again, I am drawing on the authoritative work in Peter A. Hall and David Soskice, *Varieties of Capitalism: The Institutional Foundations of Comparative Advantage* (Oxford: Oxford University Press, 2001).

74. Article II-15 of the Charter of Fundamental Rights of the European Union, conveniently reprinted in *Draft Treaty Establishing a Constitution for Europe* (Brussels: European Convention, 2003), p. 82.

75. See John M. Evans et al., 'Trends in Working Hours in OECD countries', *OECD Labour Market and Social Policy – Occasional Papers, 45* (29 March 2001), pp. 7–30.

76. The figures for 2001 were USA 73.1 per cent, Germany 65.9 per cent, France 62 per cent, but note that Britain was close to the USA with 71.3 per

cent. See OECD, *Employment Outlook 2002; Statistical Annex*, p. 304.

77. OECD figures for 2000, Table B2 in 'Education at a Glance 2003', available via <http://www.oecd.org>

78. Ralf Dahrendorf has estimated the rough ratio of private giving as 100 for the US to 10 for the UK to 1 for continental Europe. Others argue that British and European giving is significantly higher than that.

79. According to *The Indian Programmer*, September 2001, 'a couple of thousand' programmers took up the German offer of 2000. See <http://www.theindianprogrammer.com/issues/germany revisited.htm>

80. Pew Global Attitudes Project, *Views of a Changing World: June 2003* (Washington, DC: The Pew Research Center for the People and the Press, 2003), p. 112.

81. German Marshall Fund et al., *Transatlantic Trends* (Washington, DC, 2003), p. 4. Note that 83 per cent of Americans agreed.

82. See, for example, his essay 'Warum braucht Europa eine Verfassung?' in *Die Zeit*, 28 June 2001.

83. Quoted from the transcript of his press conference on <http://www.defenselink.mil/transcripts/2003/t01232003_sdfpc.html>

84. Article entitled 'United We Stand' in *Wall Street Journal Europe*, 30 January 2003.

85. 'New Allies back US Iraq Policy', *New York Times*, 6 February 2003. The forceful advocate and drafter was Bruce Jackson, a Republican activist for Nato enlargement. For a critical account of his role see <http://www.prospect.org/print-friendly/print/V14/5/judis-j.html>

86. Report by Nicholas Watt in *The Guardian*, 15 February 2003. Straw later told me that he had initially thought of saying something like 'invaded' or 'occupied' in 1066 by the French, but *politesse* prevailed.

87. 34.3 million Americans claim Irish ancestry, almost nine times the population of Ireland (3.9 million). See <http://www.census.gov/Press-Release/www/releases/archives/facts for features/001687.html>

88. *Snění o Evropě*, written in 1986 and published in samizdat.

89. Jiří Dienstbier, *Od snění k realitě: vzpomínky z let 1989–1999* (Prague: Lidove Noviny, 1999).

90. Oswald Spengler, *Der Untergang des Abendlandes: Umrisse einer Morphologie der Weltgeschichte* (Munich: Beck, 1979) p. 3.

91. *Granta*, No. 11, 1984. The full title given there to Kundera's seminal essay on the fate of central Europe was 'A Kidnapped West or a Culture Bows Out'. The version published in *New York Review of Books*, 26 April 1984, bears a more cautious title, 'The Tragedy of Central Europe'.

92. Quoted from TCDS Bulletin, Graduate School, New School University (June 2003), p. 6. I owe this reference to Jacques Rupnik's excellent chapter

in Denis Lacorne and Tony Judt (eds), *Antiamericanism* (London: Hurst, forthcoming).

93. For example, 'I deem it very important that there should be clear functional links between the CSCE and the other existing European or *Euroatlantic structures*', speech to Foreign Ministers Council of the Conference on Security and Cooperation in Europe, Prague, 30 January 1992. <http://old.hrad.cz/president/Havel/speeches/index uk.html>

94. Quoted in an article by Steven Erlanger in the *New York Times*, 4 June 2000.

95. Report by Laurent Zecchini in *Le Monde*, 19 February 2003.

96. In *International Herald Tribune*, 22 February 2003.

97. André Glucksmann, *Ouest contre Ouest* (Paris: Plon, 2003).

98. Nicolas Bavarez, *La France qui tombe: Un constat clinique du déclin français* (Paris: Perrin, 2003), Alain Duhamel, *Le désarroi français* (Paris: Plon, 2003), Romain Gubert and Emmanuel Saint-Martin, *L'arrogance française* (Paris: Balland, 2003).

99. Quoted from my notes of the Intelligence[2] debate in London on 29 October 2003.

100. Jean-François Revel, *L'obsession anti-américaine: Son fonctionnement, ses causes, ses inconséquences* (Paris: Plon, 2002), Philippe Roger, *L'ennemi américain: Généalogie de l'antiaméricanisme français* (Paris: Seuil, 2002).

101. Conversation with the author, Washington, DC, 31 May 2001.

102. See Joseph P. Quinlan, *Drifting Apart or Growing Together? The Primacy of the Transatlantic Economy* (Washington, DC: Center for Transatlantic Relations, 2003). Unless otherwise indicated, all figures in the next three paragraphs are taken from that invaluable study.

103. Ibid., Executive Summary, p. iii.

104. See Pew Global Attitudes Project, *What the World Thinks in 2002* (Washington, DC: The Pew Research Center for the People and the Press, 2002), p. T-57.

105. Ibid., p. 22.

106. Ibid., p. 21.

107. German Marshall Fund et al., *Transatlantic Trends* (Washington, DC, 2003), p. 9.

108. Article II-11.4 of the *Draft Treaty Establishing a Constitution for Europe* (Brussels: European Convention, 2003), p. 17.

109. Hubert Védrine, 'The Europe of the Future', *Newsweek*, Special Davos edition, December 2002/February 2003, p. 34.

110. See above, note 5.

111. In the *Feuilleton* of the *Frankfurter Allgemeine Zeitung*, 24 January 2003.

112. In his introductory speech to the Convention on 26 February 2002, available on <http://european-convention.eu.int>

113. Quoted in Jean Lacouture, *De Gaulle: The Ruler, 1945–1970* (London: Harvill, 1991), p. 393.

114. Calculations for 2001 by Marton Benedek from figures provided by OECD Development Assistance Committee.

115. *Gazeta Wyborcza*, 8/9 February 2003.

3 AMERICA, THE POWERFUL

1. From my notes of that meeting, 31 May 2001.

2. Will Hutton, *The World We're In* (London: Little Brown, 2002), p. 365.

3. See Walter Russell Mead, *Special Providence: American Foreign Policy and How it Changed the World* (New York: Routledge, 2002), p. xvii and *passim*.

4. The point is made forcefully by Michael Lind in his *Made in Texas: George W. Bush and the Southern Takeover of American Politics* (New York: Basic Books, 2003), p. 145 and *passim*.

5. James Madison, Alexander Hamilton and John Jay, *The Federalist Papers* (London: Penguin, 1987), p. 113. This comes in Paper VIII, by Hamilton.

6. Quoted in Arthur M. Schlesinger, *The Disuniting of America: Reflections on a Multicultural Society* (New York: Norton, 1998), p. 29.

7. Entry on Steven Udvar-Hazy, founder of the aircraft leasing business ILFC, in <http://www.forbes.com/global/1999/1011/0220093a.html>

8. Irving Howe, *Celebrations and Attacks: Thirty Years of Literary and Cultural Commentary* (London: André Deutsch, 1979), p. 243.

9. Merrill D. Peterson (ed.), *Thomas Jefferson: Writings* (New York: Literary Classics of the United States, 1984), p. 98.

10. Quoted by Wolf Lepenies, in *La vie des idées dans le monde*, No. 4, June–July 2003. I'm more broadly indebted to Lepenies's article for this thought about the first European Union.

11. Goethe, 'Den Vereinigten Staaten'.

12. Rudyard Kipling remembered peeking through the eyes of the statue as a child, when it was exhibited in Paris before being shipped across the Atlantic. See Julian Barnes, 'Sentimental Journeys' in *Guardian Review*, 11 January 2003.

13. William H. McNeill, 'What we mean by the West' in *Orbis*, Fall 1997, pp. 513–24, at p. 520.

14. Ibid., p. 520.

15. *Life's Picture History of Western Man* (New York: Time Inc., 1951), p. 290.

16. Notes from a trip in December 2002. I drew on this material for my 'Anti-Europeanism in America', *New York Review of Books*, 27 March 2003.

17. The exact figure was 18 per cent. Quoted by Bruce Cole in *Wall Street Journal*, 24 November 2003.

18. Address at Independence Hall, Philadelphia, 4 July 1962, from <http://www.jfklibrary.org/jfk-independencehall-1962.html> The following quotation is from the same source.

19. See his *An Essay towards the Present and Future Peace of Europe*, first published in 1693.

20. Desmond King, *Making Americans: Immigration, Race and the Origins of the Diverse Democracy* (Cambridge, MA: Harvard University Press, 2000), p. 252.

21. For 1.5 million, ibid., p. 251; the 2000 Census counted 11.89 million Asian Americans, see <http://www.awib.org/content_frames/census2000.html>

22. The term used by the American scholar Richard Alba; see Desmond King, *Making Americans: Immigration, Race and the Origins of the Diverse Democracy* (Cambridge, MA: Harvard University Press, 2000), p. 261.

23. Projection from the *Statistical Abstracts of the United States, 1994*, cited in Stephen M. Walt, 'The Ties That Fray', *The National Interest*, Winter 1998/99, pp. 3–11, at p. 7.

24. As opposed to Rome, Georgia, or Rome, Iowa, or any of the ten American Romes that can be found on <http://mapquest.com>

25. E-mail to the author from Thomas W. Simons, 16 May 2002, quoted with his kind permission.

26. See Alistair Horne, *Macmillan: 1894–1956* (London: Macmillan 1988), p. 160.

27. See Joseph S. Nye, *The Paradox of American Power: Why the World's Only Superpower Can't Go It Alone* (New York: Oxford University Press, 2002), pp. 8ff. and *passim*.

28. Max Boot, 'America Acts the Grown-up', *International Herald Tribune*, 26 November 2002.

29. Quoted, without a reference, in two slightly different forms in Brendan Simms, *Unfinest Hour: Britain and the Destruction of Bosnia* (London: Penguin, 2001), p. 53 and p. 339. I have been unable to trace this back to an original source.

30. Poos is often quoted as having said 'the hour of Europe' had dawned during an EC 'troika' diplomatic mission to Yugoslavia on 28 June 1991. Like so many famous quotations in recent history, this one proves very difficult to trace back to a reliable source. Brendan Simms, *Unfinest Hour: Britain and the Destruction of Bosnia* (London: Penguin, 2001), p. 54, quotes it without giving a source. Mark Almond, *Europe's Backyard War: The War in the*

Balkans (London: Heinemann, 1994), p. 32, gives his source as ITV *News at Ten* on 27 June 1991, but no such news item appears on the ITN archive website, and the words Almond goes on to quote appear, in a slightly different form, in an item for 28 June (see note 31, below), where, however, Poos does not say 'the hour of Europe'. Laura Silber and Alan Little, *The Death of Yugoslavia* (London: Penguin, 1995), p. 175, have him saying 'the age of Europe has dawned', also without a source.

31. Transcript from ITN *News*, 28 June 1991. I owe this reference originally to Mark Almond, *Europe's Backyard War: The War in the Balkans* (London: Heinemann, 1994), p. 32.

32. Quoted in Brendan Simms, *Unfinest Hour: Britain and the Destruction of Bosnia* (London: Penguin, 2001), p. 54.

33. Quoted in Ivo H. Daalder, *Getting to Dayton: The Making of America's Bosnian Policy* (Washington, DC: Brookings Institution Press, 2000), p. 34.

34. Madeleine Albright, *Madam Secretary: A Memoir* (London: Macmillan, 2003), p. 382. The reference was of course to Neville Chamberlain's notorious 'Munich Agreement' with Adolf Hitler.

35. Richard Holbrooke, *To End a War* (New York: Random House, 1998), p. 364.

36. Sidney Blumenthal, *The Clinton Wars* (London: Viking, 2003), p. 667.

37. Both quotations in ibid., p. 670.

38. Gertrude Himmelfarb, *One Nation, Two Cultures* (New York: Vintage, 2001), p. 120. The book was first published in 1999.

39. Goldberg File, *National Review Online*, 31 July 2002.

40. Conversation with author, Washington, DC, 9 December 2002.

41. This and subsequent quotations from his acceptance speech at Aachen on 2 June 2000. The text can be found at <http://www.karlspreis.de>

42. Ipsos US Express poll, 3–5 December 2002. I am most grateful to Michael Petrou for arranging for the inclusion of these questions.

43. My notes of that meeting, Washington, DC, 31 May 2001.

44. See Colin Powell's article with that title in *Foreign Affairs*, January/February 2004.

45. Quoted from David Frum's lively portrait of *The Right Man: The Surprise Presidency of George W. Bush* (New York: Random House, 2003), p. 70.

46. For what they found, see the *Climate Change Review*, released by the White House on 11 June 2001, as the president left for Europe. See <http://www.whitehouse.gov>

47. See <http://www.whitehouse.gov/news/inaugural-address.html>

48. *Weekly Defense Monitor*, 28 June 2001, available at <http://www.cdi.org/weekly/2001/issue25.html#2>

49. *Washington Post*, 8 June 2001.

50. Quoted in Bob Woodward, *Bush at War* (New York: Simon & Schuster, 2002), p. 37.

51. Ibid., p. 46.

52. I owe this comparison to Michael Hirsh's illuminating *At War with Ourselves: Why America is squandering its chance to build a better world* (New York: Oxford University Press, 2003). Obviously this capacity did not – at this writing – extend to catching Osama bin Laden.

53. Bob Woodward, *Bush at War* (New York: Simon & Schuster, 2002), p. 176.

54. Ibid., pp. 179–80.

55. Quoted in Sidney Blumenthal, *The Clinton Wars* (London: Viking, 2003), p. 780.

56. Charles Krauthammer, *Washington Post*, 26 April 2002.

57. Issued on 17 September 2002. All quotations are from the version on the official White House website, <http://www.whitehouse.gov>

58. Partially declassified Presidential Decision Directive of 21 June 1995, available on <http://www.fas.org/irp/offdocs/pdd39.htm> I owe this reference to Melyvn P. Leffler, in his 2003 Harmsworth Inaugural Lecture at Oxford, entitled '9/11 and the Past and Future of American Foreign Policy'.

59. Conversation with a senior administration official, Washington, DC, 11 December 2002.

60. The letter, dated 26 January 1998, can be found on the Project's website, <http://www.newamericancentury.org>

61. This account, based on the recollections of former Treasury Secretary Paul O'Neill, comes from Ron Suskind, *The Price of Loyalty: George W. Bush, the White House and the Education of Paul O'Neill* (New York: Simon & Schuster, 2004), pp. 72–3.

62. Bob Woodward, *Bush at War* (New York: Simon & Schuster, 2002), pp. 49, 83–5.

63. Bush to Woodward, looking back on the Afghan war, ibid., p. 45.

64. And one of the six refers to Uzbekistan's desire to have immediate membership in Nato as its reward for supporting the war on terror. Ibid., p. 172.

65. Richard Perle, in *The Guardian*, 13 November 2002.

66. I explore this at greater length in 'Anti-Europeanism in America', *New York Review of Books*, 27 March 2003.

67. See Charlemagne, 'Divide and Rule', *The Economist*, 26 April 2003, quoting a senior administration official. Subsequently, when out of office, Richard Haass acknowledged that he was the source. E-mail to the author, 6 March 2004.

68. Richard Haass at a Ditchley Conference, 27–29 June 2003, quoted with his kind permission.

69. See John C. Hulsman, 'Cherry-picking as the future of the transatlantic alliance', in the web magazine *Open Democracy* (<http://www.opendemocracy.net>), 20 February 2003.

70. Editorial in *Wall Street Journal Europe*, 30 May/1 June 2003.

71. Draft Defense Planning Guidance, quoted in *New York Times*, 8 March 1992.

72. This particular formulation comes from his remarks at a Center for Security Policy 'Keeper of the Flame' award dinner, 6 November 2001, see <http//:www.defenselink.mil/speeches/2001/s20011106-secdef.html> He used the formula many times.

73. Conversation with a senior administration official, Washington, DC, 10 December 2002.

74. For the text of his triumphant remarks on the deck of the USS *Abraham Lincoln* see <http://usinfo.state.gov/topical/pol/terror/texts/03050112.htm>

75. Quoted in Ron Suskind, *The Price of Loyalty: George W. Bush, the White House and the Education of Paul O'Neill* (New York: Simon & Schuster, 2004), p. 96.

76. Pierre Hassner, *The United States: the empire of force or the force of empire?* Chaillot Papers No. 54 (Paris: Institute for Security Studies, 2002), p. 43.

77. This and following quotations from speech by George W. Bush in the Banqueting House, London, 19 November 2003. Text at <http://www.whitehouse.gov>

78. Alistair Horne, Macmillan's biographer, believes this often quoted remark to have been made at the time of the Profumo affair, but has never found an exact context. Letter to the author, 25 February 2004.

79. Quoted in *The Guardian*, 2 December 2003.

80. This is based on 2002 expenditure calculated at market exchange rates, in *SIPRI Yearbook 2003: Armaments, Disarmament and International Security* (Stockholm: SIPRI, 2003), pp. 305, 345–50. When using purchasing power parities, the United States only exceeds the next five powers, with China, India and Russia now coming before France and Britain (ibid., p. 305) but such a reckoning clearly understates its cumulative and technological advantage. I am most grateful to Marrack Goulding for drawing my attention to these careful calculations.

81. See Dana Priest, *The Mission: Waging War and Keeping Peace with America's Military* (New York: Norton, 2003), p. 70.

82. See, for example, the projections in Goldman Sachs, *Dreaming with BRICs: The Path to 2050*, Global Economics Paper No 99, on <http://www.gs.com>

83. See the British Foreign Office projections, based on Economist Intelligence Unit data, in *UK International Priorities: A Strategy for the FCO* (London: The Stationery Office, 2003), p. 16.

84. Thomas Jefferson writing to William Short, 28 July 1791, in *The Writings of Thomas Jefferson* (Washington, DC: Taylor & Maury, 1853), vol. III, pp. 273–9.

85. The nearest parallel one can find is early twentieth-century British liberal imperialism. This is trenchantly explored by Niall Ferguson in his *Colossus: The Price of America's Empire* (London: Penguin, 2004).

86. These words are spoken by Pastor Lorenzen in Chapter 23 of *Der Stechlin*.

87. Quoted in Niall Ferguson, *Colossus: The Price of America's Empire* (London: Penguin, 2004), p. 49.

88. Report by Frank Bruni in *New York Times*, 22 September 2001, quoted in Ivo H. Daalder and James M. Lindsay, *America Unbound: The Bush Revolution in Foreign Policy* (Washington, DC: Brookings Institution Press, 2003), p. 88.

89. Richard Perle, writing in Robert Kagan and William Kristol (eds), *Present Dangers: Crisis and Opportunity in American Foreign Policy* (San Francisco: Encounter Books, 2000), p. 335.

90. German Marshall Fund et al., *Transatlantic Trends* (Washington, DC, 2003), p. 7.

91. Pew Global Attitudes Project, *Views of a Changing World: June 2003* (Washington, DC: The Pew Research Center for the People and the Press, 2003), p. 27. There also the 76 per cent figure.

92. Figures quoted by the retiring Nato Secretary-General, George Robertson, on the BBC *Today* programme, 9 December 2003.

93. This and the following figures are from the Executive Summary in Joseph P. Quinlan, *Drifting Apart or Growing Together? The Primacy of the Transatlantic Economy* (Washington, DC: Center for Transatlantic Relations, 2003).

94. Walt Whitman, 'Song of Myself'.

4 THE NEW RED ARMIES

1. Introduction by Ambassador Francis X. Taylor to US Department of State, *Patterns of Global Terrorism 2001* (May 2002), available on <http://www.state.gov>

2. Quoted from section 2, 'Definitions' in US Department of State, *Patterns of Global Terrorism 2002* (April 2003), available on <http.//www.state.gov> The report notes that the US government has employed this definition 'for statistical and analytical purposes' since 1983.

3. The graph to 2001 is drawn as Figure 2 to an article, to which I am also otherwise indebted, by Charles Tilly, 'Violence, Terror and Politics as Usual', originally published in the *Boston Review*, summer 2002, and available on <http://www.bostonreview.net>

4. This and other 2002 figures in section 4, 'The Year in Review', of US Department of State, *Patterns of Global Terrorism 2002* (April 2003), available on <http://www.state.gov>

5. Attributed to an unnamed statistician by E. L. Jones, *The European Miracle: Environments, Economies and Geopolitics in the History of Europe and Asia* (Cambridge: Cambridge University Press, 1987), p. xii.

6. Speech at the UN Financing for Development Conference in Monterrey, Mexico, 22 March 2002, available on <http://www.whitehouse.gov>

7. National security strategy issued on 17 September 2002, section III. All quotations are from the version on <http://www.whitehouse.gov>

8. In his State of the Union address to Congress on 6 January 1941.

9. In *Newsweek*, special Davos edition 'Issues 2004', dated December 2003–February 2004.

10. The list in Francis Fukuyama, *The End of History and the Last Man* (London: Penguin, 1992), p. 49 seems to me arbitrarily short. I am most grateful to Jonathan Keates, and his disintegrating *Almanach de Gotha*, for help in augmenting it.

11. This and the following figures follow Larry Diamond, 'A Report Card on Democracy' in *Hoover Digest*, 2000, no. 3, pp. 91–100, at p. 91.

12. This covers the period from January to November 2003. Information from Freedom House, to be published in Adrian Karatnycky et al. (eds), *Freedom in the World: The Annual Survey of Political Rights and Civil Liberties 2004* (New York: Freedom House, forthcoming).

13. The difference is spelled out clearly by Larry Diamond, 'Universal Democracy?', *Policy Review*, June/July 2003, pp. 3–25, esp. p. 8.

14. Figures for 2003 from Freedom House. The methodology is explained in Adrian Karatnycky et al. (eds), *Freedom in the World: The Annual Survey of Political Rights and Civil Liberties 2003* (New York: Freedom House, 2003), pp. 691ff.

15. See the discussion later in this chapter, 'Rich North, Poor South', pp. 164–73.

16. See his *Development as Freedom* (Oxford: Oxford University Press, 1999).

17. This correlation was famously demonstrated historically by Adam Przeworski et al., *Democracy and Development: Political Institutions and Well Being in the World, 1950–1990* (Cambridge: Cambridge University Press, 2000), following an earlier suggestion by Seymour Martin Lipset. I

have increased their per capita threshold figures slightly, to take account of 2002 per capita GDP in purchasing power parity (PPP), as shown in Adrian Karatnycky et al. (eds), *Freedom in the World: The Annual Survey of Political Rights and Civil Liberties 2003* (New York: Freedom House, 2003), pp. 703–4.

18. National security strategy issued on 17 September 2002. All quotations are from the version at <http://www.whitehouse.gov>

19. Francis Fukuyama, *The End of History and the Last Man* (London: Penguin, 1992), pp. 39ff. The original article appeared in *The National Interest*, Summer 1989, pp. 3–18, entitled 'The End of History?' Note the question mark.

20. Kofi A. Annan, '*We the Peoples . . .*' *Nobel Peace Message* (New York: Ruder Finn Press, 2001), p. 43.

21. Samuel P. Huntington, *The Clash of Civilizations and the Remaking of World Order* (London: Touchstone Books, 1997), pp. 83ff. and *passim*.

22. Ibid., p. 209.

23. Joseph Stiglitz, *Globalization and its Discontents* (London: Penguin, 2002), p. 9.

24. Peter Singer, *One World: The Ethics of Globalization* (New Haven: Yale University Press, 2002), p. 10.

25. I owe this (real) example to Anthony Giddens, *Runaway World: How Globalization is Reshaping our Lives* (London: Profile Books, 2002), p. 6.

26. For 'post-modern' see Robert Cooper, *The Breaking of Nations: Order and Chaos in the Twenty-first Century* (London: Atlantic Books, 2003); for 'neo-medieval' see Jan Zielonka, (ed.), *Europe Unbound: Enlarging and Reshaping the Boundaries of the European Union* (London: Routledge, 2002), p. 13.

27. See his *Longitudes and Attitudes: Exploring the World before and after September 11* (London: Penguin, 2003), pp. ix–x.

28. See his *The Shield of Achilles: War, Peace and the Course of History* (London: Penguin, 2002).

29. See the quotation from Bernard Lewis's 1990 article 'The Roots of Muslim Rage' in Samuel P. Huntington, *The Clash of Civilizations and the Remaking of World Order* (London: Touchstone Books, 1997), p. 213.

30. Alfred Stepan and Graeme B. Robertson, 'An "Arab" more than a "Muslim" electoral gap' in *Journal of Democracy*, vol. 14, no. 3, July 2003, pp. 30–44.

31. United Nations Development Programme/Arab Fund for Economic and Social Development, *The Arab Human Development Report 2002* (New York: UNDP, 2002), p. 27. See also the 'freedom score'. No source is given for the freedom score, but it is clearly based on the Freedom House assess-

ments, as subsequently acknowledged in *The Arab Human Development Report 2003* (New York: UNDP, 2003), p. 28.

32. Ibid., p. 1.

33. Ibid., p. 2.

34. *The Arab Human Development Report 2003* (New York: UNDP, 2003), p. 25.

35. United Nations Development Programme/Arab Fund for Economic and Social Development, *The Arab Human Development Report 2002* (New York: UNDP, 2002), p. 85.

36. Ibid., p. 44.

37. Ibid., p. 52.

38. Albert Hourani, *A History of the Arab Peoples* (London: Faber & Faber, 2002), p. 449 and *passim*.

39. Thomas Friedman, *Longitudes and Attitudes: Exploring the World before and after September 11* (London: Penguin, 2003), p. 197.

40. Quoted by Clyde Prestowitz, *Rogue Nation: American Unilateralism and the Failure of Good Intentions* (New York: Basic Books, 2003), p. 14.

41. 'Strengthening the EU's Partnership with the Arab World', Memorandum to the Italian Presidency of the European Council from Javier Solana, Romano Prodi and Chris Patten, dated Brussels, 4 December 2003, section 3, 'Objectives'. <http://europa.eu.int/>

42. From the final version of the European Security Strategy adopted by the European Council in Brussels on 12 December 2003, and available on the EU website, <http://europa.eu.int/>

43. Régis Debray in *International Herald Tribune*, 24 February 2003.

44. United Nations Development Programme/Arab Fund for Economic and Social Development, *The Arab Human Development Report 2002* (New York: UNDP, 2002), pp. 37–8. According to estimates by the UN Economic Commission for Europe (Population Activities Unit, Indicators) the population of the EU of twenty-five countries in 2020 would be around 446 million.

45. Ibid., p. 30.

46. Lecture at St Antony's College, Oxford, 18 November 2003.

47. Quoted in Marc Lynch, 'Taking Arabs Seriously', *Foreign Affairs*, September/October 2003, p. 86.

48. Interview in *Muslim Democrat*, vol.5, no.1, November 2003, p. 8, downloaded from <http://www.islam-democracy.org>

49. See, for example, Pew Global Attitudes Project, *Views of a Changing World: June 2003* (Washington, DC: The Pew Research Center for the People and the Press, 2003), pp. 33–41.

50. Quoted in Marc Lynch, 'Taking Arabs Seriously', *Foreign Affairs*, September/October 2003, p. 93.

51. See the table compiled on the basis of data supplied by Ronald Inglehart from the World Values Survey in *The Arab Human Development Report 2003* (New York: UNDP, 2003), p. 19.

52. In fact, nearly two thirds of those living on less than $1 a day in 1999, according to World Bank figures. But the proportion is declining due to Asia's economic development.

53. Gerald Segal gives a figure of 33 per cent for China compared to 28 per cent for Europe and 0.8 per cent for the US, in his 1999 *Foreign Affairs* article, 'Does China Matter?', reprinted in Barry Buzan and Rosemary Foot (eds), *Does China Matter? A Reassessment. Essays in Memory of Gerald Segal* (London: Routledge, 2004), pp. 11–20, at p. 12. I'm grateful to Rosemary Foot for letting me have early sight of this volume.

54. Alice Amsden, *The Rise of "The Rest": Challenges to the West from Late-Industrializing Economies* (New York: Oxford University Press, 2001).

55. Quoted in David Hale and Lyric Hughes Hale, 'China Takes Off', *Foreign Affairs*, November/December 2003, pp. 36–53, at p. 46.

56. For China, see the chapter by Stuart Harris in ibid., pp. 54–70, at pp. 55–7. For India, see Stephen P. Cohen, *India: Emerging Power* (Washington, DC: Brookings, 2001), p. 27.

57. See the discussion by Stuart Harris in Barry Buzan and Rosemary Foot (eds), *Does China Matter? A Reassessment. Essays in Memory of Gerald Segal* (London: Routledge, 2004), pp. 57–8.

58. Henry Kissinger, *Does America Need a Foreign Policy? Toward a Diplomacy for the 21st Century* (New York: Free Press, 2002), p. 110.

59. See, for example, President Jiang Zemin, quoting Deng Xiaoping, in Orville Schell and David Shambaugh (eds), *The China Reader: The Reform Era* (New York: Vintage, 1999), p. 497.

60. Thus Avery Goldstein in G. John Ikenberry and Michael Mastanduno (eds), *International Relations Theory and the Asia-Pacific* (New York: Columbia University Press, 2003), pp. 57–106.

61. Quoted by Evan S. Medeiros and M. Taylor Frevel, 'China's New Diplomacy', *Foreign Affairs*, November/December 2003, pp. 22–35, at p. 32.

62. Henry Kissinger, *Does America Need a Foreign Policy? Toward a Diplomacy for the 21st Century* (New York: Free Press, 2002), p. 110.

63. Thus Barry Buzan in Barry Buzan and Rosemary Foot, (eds), *Does China Matter? A Reassessment. Essays in Memory of Gerald Segal* (London: Routledge, 2004), p. 159.

64. Henry Kissinger, *Does America Need a Foreign Policy? Toward a Diplomacy for the 21st Century* (New York: Free Press, 2002), p. 160.

65. Part of a presidential address made at the 'Voice of America' in October

1997, quoted in Orville Schell and David Shambaugh (eds), *The China Reader: The Reform Era* (New York: Vintage, 1999), pp. 479–87, at pp. 480–82.

66. See the European Commission's paper, dated 10 September 2003, on 'A maturing partnership – shared interests and challenges in EU–China relations', p. 16, on EU website <http://europa.eu.int/>

67. The figure for the US is cited by David Hale and Lyric Hughes Hale, 'China Takes Off', *Foreign Affairs*, November/December 2003, pp. 36–53, at p. 49. The EU figure of €47 billion is given in the paper cited in note 66 above, also for 2002.

68. This is the thrust of the argument made by Henry S. Rowen in an incisive paper, *The Growth of Freedoms in China* (Stanford University: Asia/Pacific Research Center, 2001).

69. Simon Leys, Introduction to his edition of *The Analects of Confucius* (New York: Norton, 1997), p. xxv.

70. See Henry S. Rowen, *The Growth of Freedoms in China* (Stanford University: Asia/Pacific Research Center, 2001), pp. 10–14.

71. I count *The Economist* and *Financial Times* as international rather than purely British or European papers.

72. The story is well told in Chris Patten, *East and West* (London: Macmillan, 1998), pp. 303–305.

73. See the European Commission's paper, dated 10 September 2003, on 'A maturing partnership – shared interests and challenges in EU-China relations', available on the EU website, <http://europa.eu.int/>

74. I follow here the assessment of Jeff Sachs, Director of the Earth Institute at Columbia University. See his 'Visiting Global Public Policies for Sustainable Development: A Transatlantic Dialogue', speech at the Atlantic Conference, 26 May 2003, on <http://www.earthinstitute.columbia.edu.>

75. UN Food and Agricultural Organization, *The State of Food Insecurity in the World 2003*, quoted in *International Herald Tribune*, 26 November 2003.

76. This figure is given in the *Human Development Report 1999* (New York: UNDP, 1999), p. 38. My attention was drawn to it by Peter Singer, *One World: The Ethics of Globalization* (New Haven: Yale University Press, 2002), p. 81, from whom I take the population figure of 600 million.

77. My notes of a panel discussion at the World Economic Forum, Davos, 2001.

78. I owe this thought to Peter Singer, *One World: The Ethics of Globalization* (New Haven: Yale University Press, 2002), at p. 151, drawing on the UNICEF 2001 report on *The State of the World's Children*.

79. I take this figure from the 2003 *Report of the Commission on Human*

Security, available on <http://www.humansecurity-chs.org/finalreport/index.html>

80. See *Human Development Report 1999* (New York: UNDP, 1999), p. 38.

81. See *Globalization, Growth and Poverty: Building an Inclusive World Economy* (Washington, DC/Oxford: World Bank/Oxford University Press, 2002), p. 2 and *passim*. This incisive report was written by Paul Collier, of St Antony's College, Oxford, and the aptly named David Dollar.

82. See *Human Development Report 2003* (New York: UNDP, 2003), pp. 1–3.

83. Conversation with Dov Zakheim, then in effect the chief financial officer of the Pentagon, Washington, DC, 25 July 2003.

84. See *Foreign Aid in the National Interest: Overview* (Washington, DC: US Agency for International Development, 2002), pp. 27–9.

85. See, for example, *Global Civil Society 2002* (Oxford: Oxford University Press, 2002), a yearbook launched by the London School of Economics in 2001.

86. Speech at the UN Financing for Development Conference in Monterrey, Mexico, 22 March 2002, available on <http://www.whitehouse.gov>

87. See *Foreign Aid in the National Interest: Overview* (Washington, DC: US Agency for International Development, 2002), pp. 29–30.

88. Report in *International Herald Tribune*, 10 September 2003. In April 2003, Congress approved $79 billion (a good part of which had already been spent by the Pentagon) for the Iraq War and initial post-war expenses; it approved a further $87 billion in September 2003.

89. Calculations for 2001 by Marton Benedek from figures provided by OECD Development Assistance Committee.

90. This and the figures in the next two paragraphs are taken from *Human Development Report 2003* (New York: UNDP, 2003), pp. 145–7.

91. The group was headed by Jeff Sachs. He summarizes their findings in a lecture on 'The Millennium Compact and the End of Hunger', Des Moines, Iowa, 16 October 2003, available on <http://www.earthinstitute.columbia.edu/about/director/index.html>

92. See *Globalization, Growth and Poverty: Building an Inclusive World Economy* (Washington, DC/Oxford: World Bank/Oxford University Press, 2002), p. 9.

93. *Human Development Report 2003* (New York: UNDP, 2003), pp. 155–6.

94. See *Make Trade Fair* (Oxford: Oxfam, 2002), p. 98ff. Available on <http://www.maketradefair.com>

95. *Human Development Report 2003* (New York: UNDP, 2003), p. 155.

96. There are two qualifications that need to be made here. First, where a

poor country has tariff-free access to the EU market, its agricultural producers can in principle benefit from the higher food prices inside the EU which result from the CAP. Second, where poor countries are net food importers, they benefit in the short term from the lower prices of subsidized food exports from the West. However, the much more damaging long-term effect of those subsidized exports is to undermine those countries' farm sectors. I am most grateful to Alex Duncan for drawing these points to my attention.

97. In practice, some import restrictions remain on bananas, rice and sugar. For the details, see <http://europa.eu.int/comm/trade/issues/global/gsp/eba/index_en.htm>

98. As reported in the Charlemagne column in *The Economist*, 21 June 2003.

99. Report in *New York Times*, 27 June 2002.

100. Fareed Zakaria, *The Future of Freedom: Illiberal Democracy at Home and Abroad* (New York: Norton, 2003), p. 174, gives a figure of $2 billion.

101. This figure is given by Joseph Stiglitz, *Globalization and its Discontents* (London: Penguin, 2002), p. 269.

102. See Adrian Karatnycky et al., (eds), *Freedom in the World: The Annual Survey of Political Rights and Civil Liberties 2003* (New York: Freedom House, 2003), p. 93.

103. Debt service to social spending figures are given by the Worldwatch Institute on <http://www.worldwatch.org/press/news/2001/04/26/>

104. Debt and cotton export figures are from the September 2003 Jubilee Research, *Real Progress Report on HIPC*, country entry on Benin. Available on <http://www.jubileeplus.org/analysis/reports/realprogressHIPC.pdf>

105. The BBC *Today* programme, 10 June 2003, reported a specific case of a Ghanaian tomato farmer forced out of business by EU-subsidized exports.

106. For this first Commitment to Development Index (CDI) see 'Ranking the Rich' in *Foreign Policy*, May/June 2003.

107. Fareed Zakaria, *The Future of Freedom: Illiberal Democracy at Home and Abroad* (New York: Norton, 2003), p. 173, gives a figure of 20,000 for 1990. I'm assuming their number has not decreased.

108. See *United Nations Chronicle*, on-line edition, vol. XXXVI, no. 3, 1999.

109. See <http://www.unfpa.org/6billion/ccmc/thedayofsixbillion.html> and UNPD, *World Population Prospects: The 2002 Revision*, on <http://www.un.org/esa/population/unpop.ht>

110. See <http://www.unfpa.org/6billion/> Every two fifths of a second is my timing of that counter.

111. *World Population Prospects: The 2002 Revision*, p. 1, available on <http://www.un.org/esa/population/unpop.ht>

112. Ibid., p. vii.

113. Thomas Malthus, *Essay on Population*, quoted in Amartya Sen, *Development as Freedom* (Oxford: Oxford University Press, 1999), p. 205. I follow Sen's argument.

114. Ibid., Table 9.1 on p. 206.

115. *Human Development Report 2003* (New York: UNDP, 2003), p. 227.

116. Ibid., p. 125. 'Water stress' is defined as consuming more than 20 per cent of your renewable water supply every year.

117. See Marq de Villiers, *Water Wars: Is the World's Water Running Out?* (London: Phoenix, 2001)

118. International Energy Agency, *World Energy Outlook 2002*, on <http://www.worldenergyoutlook.org/weo/pubs/weo2002/weo2002.asp>, p. 33.

119. See International Energy Agency, *World Energy Outlook 2002*, <http://www.worldenergyoutlook.org/wco/pubs/weo2002/weo2002.asp> and US International Energy Administration, *International Energy Outlook 2003*, <http://www.eia.doe.gov/oiaf/ieo/>

120. I say 'modern' because a primitive form of steam power was used earlier in China, but not in the piston-to-wheel form that contributed to the industrial revolution. I am grateful to David Faure for enlightening me on this point.

121. See World Bank, *Entering the 21st Century: World Development Report 1999/2000* (New York: OUP, 2000), pp. 87ff.

122. See the revealing account in ibid., pp. 94–7.

123. Here I follow Bjorn Lomborg, *The Skeptical Environmentalist: Measuring the Real State of the World* (Cambridge: Cambridge University Press, 2000), p. 261.

124. I follow the authoritative Intergovernmental Panel on Climate Change report, *Climate Change 2001*, available on <http://www.ipcc.ch/pub/reports.htm>

125. BBC news report, 5 March 2004, citing a report in the journal *Science*.

126. Munich Re, as reported on <http://news.bbc.co.uk/2/hi/americas/3308959.stm>

127. World Bank, *Entering the 21st Century: World Development Report 1999/2000* (New York: OUP, 2000), p. 100.

128. Quoted in Dinyar Godrej, *The No-Nonsense Guide to Climate Change* (London: Verso, 2001), p. 90.

129. Intergovernmental Panel on Climate Change, *Climate Change 2001: Synthesis Report*, <http://www.ipcc.ch/pub/reports.htm>, p. 5.

130. Ibid., p. 8.

131. Ibid., p. 9.

132. International Energy Agency, *World Energy Outlook 2002*, <http://

www.worldenergyoutlook.org/weo/pubs/weo2002/weo2002.asp>, p. 30.

133. *Globalization, Growth and Poverty: Building an Inclusive World Economy* (Washington, DC/Oxford: World Bank/Oxford University Press, 2002), p. 17.

134. Ibid., p. 17. These were 1998 figures, so may now be higher. 'European' presumably refers to the 1998 EU of fifteen countries.

135. Peter Singer, *One World: The Ethics of Globalization* (New Haven: Yale University Press, 2002), p. 21. A BBC report dated 29 September 2003 gives a figure of 16 per cent above 1990 levels, see <http://news.bbc.co.uk/2/hi/science/nature/3143798.stm>

136. John Steinbeck, *America and Americans* (New York: Penguin, 2002), pp. 377–8.

137. As reported in *Time* (international edition), 1 June 1992.

138. Sir John Houghton, quoted in the *New Statesman*, 1 December 2003.

139. See the table in Bill Emmott, *20:21 Vision: The Lessons of the 20th Century for the 21st* (London: Penguin, 2003), p. 267.

140. Presidential announcement on 14 February 2002, available on <http://www.whitehouse.gov/news>

141. US International Energy Administration, *International Energy Outlook 2003*, <http://www.eia.doe.gov/oiaf/ico/>, pp. 162–3. For the 7 per cent commitment level, see the table in Dinyar Godrej, *The No-Nonsense Guide to Climate Change* (London: Verso, 2001), p. 107.

142. Tony Blair, speech on sustainable development, 24 February 2003, available on <http://www.number-10.gov.uk>

143. See the report in *The Observer*, 22 February 2004.

144. Quoted in Dinyar Godrej, *The No-Nonsense Guide to Climate Change* (London: Verso, 2001), pp. 114–15.

145. See the exploration and extension of Freud's idea in Michael Ignatieff, *The Warrior's Honour: Ethnic War and the Modern Conscience* (London: Chatto & Windus, 1998), pp. 48ff.

146. Robert Cooper, *The Breaking of Nations: Order and Chaos in the Twenty-first Century* (London: Atlantic Books, 2003), p. 138ff.

147. Thomas Aquinas, *Summa Theologiae. Secunda Secundae*.

CRISIS AS OPPORTUNITY

1. As reported in *The Observer*, 22 February 2004.

2. See Chapter 25 of Niccolò Machiavelli, *The Prince* (London: Penguin, 1961), at p. 130.

3. See chapter 1 above, p. 28.

TWENTY YEARS AND A THOUSAND MILLION CITIZENS

1. Ian Buruma and Avishai Margalit, 'Seeds of Revolution', in *New York Review of Books*, 11 March 2004, summarizing the argument of their book *Occidentalism* (New York: Penguin, 2004).

2. These well-known lines appear in the poem 'To Althea, From Prison' by the seventeenth-century English poet Richard Lovelace.

3. The title of the autobiography of Ken Livingstone: *If Voting Changed Anything, They'd Abolish It* (London: HarperCollins, 1987). Livingstone was subsequently elected Mayor of London.

5 BRITAIN FINDS ITS ROLE

1. See Douglas Brinkley, 'Dean Acheson and the "Special Relationship": The West Point speech of December 1962', *The Historical Journal*, vol. 33, no. 3 (1990), pp. 599–608. Later, contemplating the resulting storm, Acheson commented ruefully, 'the first requirement of a statesman is that he be dull'.

2. Dictated by Bismarck on 9 November 1876; see Johannes Lepsius et al. (eds), *Die grosse Politik der europäischen Kabinette 1871–1914*, vol. 2 (Berlin: Deutsche Verlagsgesellschaft für Politik und Geschichte, 1922), no. 256, p. 88.

3. The story is told in my *In Europe's Name: Germany and the Divided Continent* (London: Jonathan Cape, 1993).

4. BBC News report, 11 February 2002, see <http://news.bbc.co.uk/2/hi/uk_news/education/1815073.stm>

5. Rudyard Kipling, 'The English Flag'.

6. I am treating the *Financial Times* as an international rather than a British daily paper.

7. Quoted in P. Williamson, *Conservative Leadership and National Values* (Cambridge: Cambridge University Press, 1999), p. 234.

8. Conversation with the author, London, 22 September 2003.

9. See Jennifer Jenkins, *The Phonology of English as an International Language* (Oxford: Oxford University Press, 2000), p. 1.

10. Václav Havel, conversation with the author.

11. Gisela Stuart, conversation with the author.

12. William Wordsworth, lines from 'It Is Not to Be Thought of, that the Flood' in *Poems Dedicated to National Independence and Liberty*.

13. George Orwell, *The Lion and the Unicorn: Socialism and the English Genius* (London: Secker & Warburg, 1941), p. 127.

6 WHAT EUROPE CAN BE

1. I owe this splendid formulation to my colleague Kalypso Nicolaïdis. She develops the notion in Kalypso Nicolaïdis and Robert Howse (eds), *The Federal Vision: Legitimacy and Levels of Governance in the United States and the European Union* (Oxford: Oxford University Press, 2001), p. 474.

2. The essay is reprinted in P. J. O'Rourke, *Holidays in Hell* (London: Picador, 2002), pp. 211–31, at p. 212.

3. I owe this imagery of induction to my colleague Adam Roberts, who explores it further in his forthcoming book on liberal international order.

4. See Helen and William Wallace (eds), *Policy-Making in the European Union* (Oxford: Oxford University Press, 2000), p. 33ff.

5. In *Frankfurter Allgemeine Zeitung*, 31 May 2003.

6. Quoted above, p. 111.

7. Quoted from the transcript, republished in facsimile as *Congress of Europe: The Hague 7–11 May 1948* (Strasbourg: Council of Europe, 1999), p. 16.

8. Bertolt Brecht, 'Kriegsfibel', Verse 69.

9. Eric Hobsbawm, *The Age of Extremes 1914–1991* (New York: Pantheon, 1994), p. 578.

10. See below, p. 242 and the report of the International Commission on Intervention and State Sovereignty, *The Responsibility to Protect* (Ottawa: International Development Research Centre, 2001).

11. German Marshall Fund et al., *Transatlantic Trends* (Washington, DC, 2003), p. 10. Of the 71 per cent who said they wanted the EU to become a superpower, 49 per cent changed their mind if this would involve greater military expenditure. In other words, only 36 per cent of all those asked supported the EU becoming a superpower with greater military expenditure.

7 UNCLE SAM

1. The speaker was George F. Will, Washington, DC, 10 December 2002.

2. De Gaulle's biographer, Jean Lacouture, confirms that de Gaulle almost certainly did make this often quoted remark, but cannot point to an exact source for it.

3. *Private Eye*, 28 November–11 December 2003.

4. Thucydides, *The History of the Peloponnesian War*, edited and translated by R. W. Livingstone (London: Oxford University Press, 1943), p. 267.

5. The full text is given in Caroline Kennedy, *A Patriot's Handbook: Songs,*

Poems, Stories and Speeches Celebrating the Land we Love (New York: Hyperion, 2003), pp. 644–5.

6. I owe this crisp formulation to the Independent International Commission on Kosovo, *The Kosovo Report: Conflict. International Response. Lessons Learned* (Oxford: Oxford University Press, 2000), p. 4. It is justified in detail in that report.

7. Thucydides, *The History of the Peloponnesian War*, edited and translated by R. W. Livingstone (London: Oxford University Press, 1943), p. 267.

8. William Blake, 'Auguries of Innocence'.

9. Here I am plagiarizing my own article, 'The Peril of Too Much Power', in the *New York Times*, 9 April 2002.

10. Rudyard Kipling, 'The White Man's Burden' (1899), a poem addressed to the United States on the annexation of the Philippines.

11. William Camden, *Remaines, concerning Britaine: But especially England, and the Inhabitants therof* (London: printed by Nicholas Okes for Simon Waterson, 1623), p. 5.

12. Conversation with the author, Washington, DC, 24 July 2003.

13. *Life*, 17 February 1941.

14. W. C. Sellar and R. J. Yeatman, *1066 and All That* (London: Methuen, 1999), p. 123. The book was first published in 1930.

8 TOWARDS A FREE WORLD

1. J. M. Roberts, *The New Penguin History of the World* (London: Penguin, 2002), p. 797.

2. Ibid., pp. 1174–6.

3. Speech to a Joint Session of Congress, 17 July 2003, <http://www.number-10.gov.uk/output/Page4220.asp>

4. This is eloquently explored by Larry Siedentop, *Democracy in Europe* (London: Penguin, 2000), p. 193f.

5. Ludger Kühnhardt, *Die Universalität der Menschenrechte* (Bonn: Bundeszentrale für politische Bildung, 1987), pp. 190, 300f. and *passim*.

6. Michail S. Gorbatschow (*sic*), *Gipfelgespräche: Geheime Protokolle aus meiner Amtszeit* (Berlin: Rowohlt, 1995), pp. 128–9.

7. Samuel P. Huntington, *The Clash of Civilizations and the Remaking of World Order* (London: Touchstone Books, 1997), p. 162.

8. See Isaiah Berlin, *Liberty* (Oxford: Oxford University Press, 2002), edited by Henry Hardy.

9. Matthew 7:12.

10. George Bernard Shaw, 'Maxims for Revolutionists: The Golden Rule', in

Man and Superman: a Comedy and a Philosophy (London: Penguin, 2004), p. 251.

11. *The Analects of Confucius* (New York: Norton, 1997), translated by Simon Leys, p. 55.

12. '*Wolność*' in Adam Zagajewski, *List. Oda do Wielości* (Paris: Instytut Literacki, 1983). The last word of the poem, '*niewola*', is more usually translated as 'captivity', but 'to be unfree' seems to me closer to the meaning in this poem.

13. See my *History of the Present: Essays, Sketches and Despatches from Europe in the 1990s* (London: Penguin, 2000), pp. 101–104.

14. Mark Palmer, *Breaking the Real Axis of Evil: How to Oust the World's Last Dictators by 2025* (Lanham: Rowman & Littlefield, 2003).

15. Ibid., p. 283.

16. See my 'Beauty and the Beast in Burma', *New York Review of Books*, 25 May 2000.

17. See the report of the International Commission on Intervention and State Sovereignty, *The Responsibility to Protect* (Ottawa: International Development Research Centre, 2001).

18. 'Tiananmen' in James Fenton, *Out of Danger: Poems* (London: Penguin, 1993), p. 41.

19. I am citing the lines as quoted (and retranslated) in the film, directed by Dai Sijie. They do not appear in the original book version, Dai Sijie, *Balzac and the Little Chinese Seamstress* (London: Vintage, 2002).

20. See Fareed Zakaria, *The Future of Freedom: Illiberal Democracy at Home and Abroad* (New York: Norton, 2003).

21. Samuel Johnson, lines added to Goldsmith's 'The Traveller'.

WHAT CAN WE DO?

1. This motto is often ascribed to the Italian Marxist Antonio Gramsci, who used it on the masthead of his journal *Ordine Nuovo*. In fact, Gramsci was popularizing words originally coined by the French author and pacifist Romain Rolland.

Acknowledgements

This book was made possible by an intellectual free world of colleagues and friends. I can name only some of them here, but I am profoundly grateful to them all.

At St Antony's College, Oxford, I would like to acknowledge first and foremost my colleagues at the European Studies Centre, for intellectual stimulation and congeniality, and, in the case of Janet Pearson and Ulli Parkinson, for invaluable administrative support. Marrack Goulding, Avi Shlaim, Rosemary Foot, David Faure, Robert Mabro, Steve Tsang, Eugene Rogan, Paul Collier, Alex Duncan, Alistair Horne and Dennis Anderson have commented on particular sections or enlightened me on specific points. I am also grateful to the Zeit Foundation Gerd and Ebelin Bucerius for its generous financial support. In the wider Oxford community, I owe specific thanks to Adam Roberts, Jennifer Welsh, Peter Pulzer and Mark Freedland.

My understanding of the United States has been deepened by my annual sojourns as a Senior Fellow at the Hoover Institution, Stanford University. I thank John Raisian, the Director, for getting me there in the first place, and all my Stanford friends for sharing with me their widely differing Americas.

A third source of regular stimulus has been my fortnightly commentary in *The Guardian* and an informal syndicate of newspapers across Europe and the Americas. I thank particularly Alan Rusbridger, and my confrères, too numerous to name, on all those papers. The *New York Review of Books* – arguably not just America's but Europe's finest intellectual journal – enabled me to make an illuminating trip exploring attitudes to Europe in the United States. My thanks go once again to Robert Silvers and Rea Hederman. On that trip, John and Leslie Earle arranged a memorable evening with their students in Lawrence, Kansas.

A major source for this book was conversations with leading politicians and officials. A few of them are identified in the notes. However, most of these conversations were on a non-attributable or private basis. I can therefore only offer a blanket vote of thanks to all who talked to me, discreetly and indiscreetly.

The typescript was read in first draft by this potent array of critical intelligences: Arnulf Baring, David Cornwell, Ralf Dahrendorf, John Fox, Pierre Hassner, Ian McEwan, Michael Mertes, Kalypso Nicoläidis, Aleksander Smolar, Timothy Snyder, Michael Taylor, Maurice Thompson, Tobias Wolff, my brother Christopher, my father and my wife. I believe it's a better book as a result, and I owe a very special debt of gratitude to each and every one of them.

For assistance on individual topics, I am grateful to Ronald Asmus, Dan Clark, Anne Deighton, Giles Fraser, Richard Haass, Judith Herrin, Trevor Kavanagh, Jonathan Keates, Jean Lacouture, Melvin P. Leffler, Noel Malcolm, Jacques Rupnik, Thomas W. Simons, Malcolm Spencer, Gisela Stuart and Paulo Valentino. Andrew Kohut was an incisive guide through the polling riches of the Pew Research Center for the People and the Press.

I enjoyed working closely with students from many countries on the research for this book. Glyn Prysor hunted down historical and political sources with a passion for accuracy that promises much for his future work as a historian. Marton Benedek was endlessly ingenious and helpful, particularly in his pursuit of American–European comparisons. As a Canadian, Michael Petrou took a sharply critical look at both Europe and America. Julia de Clerck-Sachsse surveyed the German debate, and shared with me some of her generation's views. John Crouch, Seth Green, Rachel Ziemba, Eric Weaver, Stefan Szwed and Dimitar Bechev participated in lively student debates, and helped me with specific points.

For the Values map, and its interpretation, I thank its begetter, Ronald Inglehart; for the Freedom map, Adrian Karatnycky and Christopher Walker at Freedom House. The idea for the proportional block maps originally came from a *Financial Times* version of a map in the *World Bank Atlas*, relating only to Money. It was my idea to do the same for Arms and People. Russell Birkett expertly translated the idea into graphic reality.

At Penguin, I am once again indebted to Stuart Proffitt for his meticulous and supportive editing, and to an impressive editorial and production team. At Rogers, Coleridge & White, Gill Coleridge has seen this book through every stage from idea to reality, with a calm and experienced eye.

Free World was chewed over most often and most enjoyably at a kitchen table. Deepest thanks to my wife, Danuta, for her patience and support, and to my frankest and warmest critics, my sons, to whom it is dedicated and for whom, in several different senses, it is written.

Index

OWLS TO ATHENS

By H. N. Turteltaub from Tom Doherty Associates

OWLS TO ATHENS

H. N. TURTELTAUB

A TOM DOHERTY ASSOCIATES BOOK   NEW YORK

OWLS TO ATHENS

Copyright © 2004 by H. N. Turteltaub

This book is printed on acid-free paper.

Edited by Patrick Nielsen Hayden

A Forge Book
Published by Tom Doherty Associates, LLC
175 Fifth Avenue
New York, NY 10010

www.tor.com

Forge® is a registered trademark of Tom Doherty Associates, LLC.

Library of Congress Cataloging-in-Publication Data

Turteltaub, H. N.
    Owls to Athens / H. N. Turteltaub.—1st ed.
        p. cm.
    "A Tom Doherty Associates book."
    ISBN 0-765-30038-9 (acid-free paper)
    EAN 978-0765-30038-6
    1. Menedemos (Fictitious character)—Fiction. 2. Sostratos (Fictitious character)—Fiction.
3. Greece—History—Macedonian Hegemony, 323-281 B.C.—Fiction. 4. Aegean Sea
Region—Fiction. 5. Merchant mariners—Fiction. 6. Athens (Greece)—Fiction. 7. Ship
captains—Fiction. 8. Cousins—Fiction. I. Title.

PS3570.U758O95 2004
813'.54—dc22

                                                                              2004050620

First Edition: December 2004

Printed in the United States of America

0 9 8 7 6 5 4 3 2 1

Every book of mine is for Laura.
This time I'm saying so right up front.

A NOTE ON
WEIGHTS, MEASURES, AND MONEY

I have, as best I could, used in this novel the weights, measures, and coinages my characters would have used and encountered in their journey. Here are some approximate equivalents (precise values would have varied from city to city, further complicating things):

1 digit = ¾ inch
4 digits = 1 palm
6 palms = 1 cubit
1 cubit = 1½ feet
1 plethron = 100 feet
1 stadion = 600 feet

12 khalkoi = 1 obolos
6 oboloi = 1 drakhma
100 drakhmai = 1 mina (about 1 pound)
60 minai = 1 talent

As noted, these are all approximate. As a measure of how widely they could vary, the talent in Athens was about 57 pounds, while that of Aigina, less than 30 miles away, was about 83 pounds.

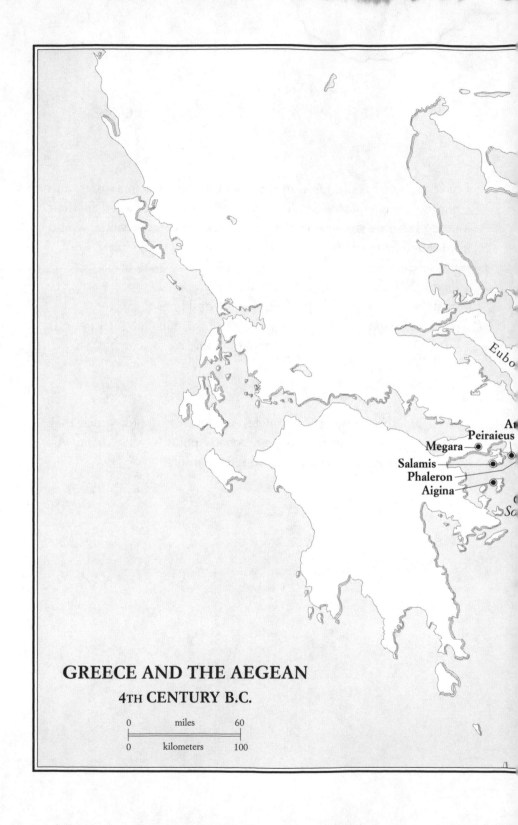

Eubo

At
Peiraieus
Megara
Salamis
Phaleron
Aigina
Sa

GREECE AND THE AEGEAN
4TH CENTURY B.C.

| 0 | miles | 60 |
| 0 | kilometers | 100 |

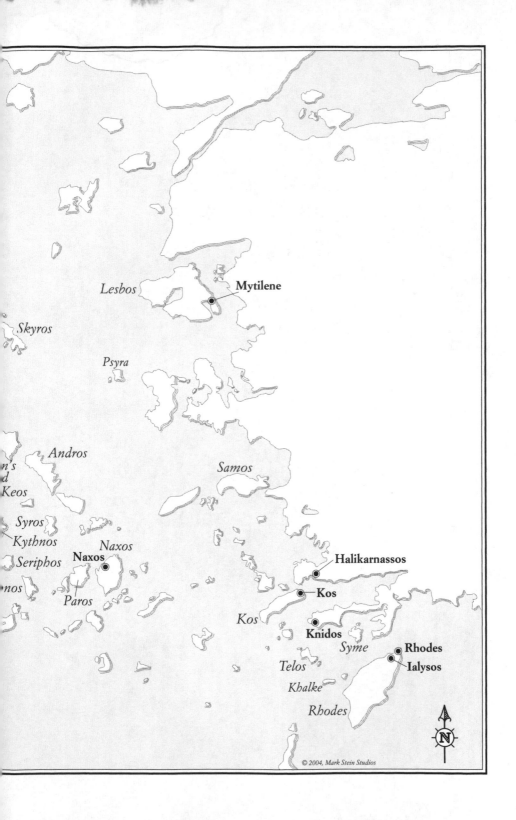

Lesbos

Mytilene

Skyros

Psyra

Andros

*n's
d*
Keos

Samos

Syros
Kythnos

nos

Seriphos

Naxos

Naxos

Paros

Kos

Halikarnassos

Kos

Knidos

Knidos

Kos

Syme

Rhodes

Telos

Ialysos

Khalke

Rhodes

© 2004, Mark Stein Studios

OWLS TO ATHENS

1

FROM THE MEN'S ROOM—THE ANDRON—MENEDEMOS
son of Philodemos watched the rain patter down in the courtyard of
his father's house. It dripped from the red roofing tiles at the edge of
the eaves. The drips had scored little grooves in the dirt; this was as
heavy a rain as Rhodes ever saw, and heavier than usual for so late in
winter. Spring—sailing season—would be here soon, but the skies
didn't seem to know it.

As if he were a caged animal, Menedemos rocked back and forth on
his stool. "I want to be away," he said to his cousin. "I want to be out
and *doing* things." He was a handsome man in his late twenties, muscular and well built though a little below average height, his face clean-
shaven in the style Alexander the Great had set.

His cousin dipped his head in agreement. Though Alexander was
sixteen years dead, Sostratos son of Lysistratos wore a full, rather
shaggy beard. He was a few months older than Menedemos, and
taller by a palm and a couple of digits. Sostratos didn't carry his
height well, though, and, thanks to his diffident manner, usually followed Menedemos' lead. Menedemos could be a great many things,
but hardly ever diffident.

"I wish it would clear out, too," Sostratos said. "If we get to Athens
early enough, we can see the plays at the Greater Dionysia." Like
Menedemos, he'd grown up speaking Greek with the Doric drawl of
Rhodes. But he'd studied philosophy at the Lykeion in Athens; like
those of many educated Hellenes, his accent these days had a heavy Attic overlay. "Tragedies, satyr plays, comedies . . ." He sighed longingly.

"Comedies nowadays are thin-blooded things," Menedemos said.
"Give me Aristophanes any time."

Sostratos tugged at the front of his chiton, as if wagging the enormous phallos a comic actor wore. "A lot of those jokes have got tired
in the hundred years since Aristophanes told them," he said.

"Then why can't the new poets come up with anything better?"

Menedemos retorted; this was an old argument between them.

"I think they can," Sostratos said. "Menandros, for instance, is a match for your precious Aristophanes any day."

"Oh, nonsense," Menedemos declared. "The old plays are the best ones."

"Maybe Menandros will put on a new one at the Dionysia," Sostratos said. "Then you'll see."

"See what?" Menedemos' father asked, coming up behind them.

"Hail, Uncle Philodemos," Sostratos said. "How are you today?"

"Not too bad, thanks," Philodemos answered. He was nearer sixty than fifty, his beard and hair silver, but he still held himself erect— exercise at the gymnasion had helped there. And he'd kept most of his teeth, which let him sound like a younger man.

"If we get to Athens in time for the Greater Dionysia, Menedemos may see what a fine comedian Menandros is," Sostratos said.

"Ah." Philodemos' voice encompassed the gray sky and the wet courtyard. "Nobody's going anywhere as long as the weather stays like this. Put to sea with clouds and fogs and who knows what and you're asking to wreck your ship."

"It should clear out soon, Father," Menedemos said.

"I doubt it," Philodemos replied.

Menedemos sighed. Had he said he expected bad weather to last, he was sure his father would have contradicted him there, too. They never had got on well. Menedemos thought his father was a stubborn old stick-in-the-mud. For his part, Philodemos was convinced Menedemos was a wild youth who had no respect for anything. Sometimes each seemed determined to prove the other right.

Philodemos also had another excellent reason for not getting along with Menedemos. Fortunately, he didn't know he had it. Menedemos was determined that he never find out.

Sostratos said, "Regardless of whether we get to Athens in time for the Dionysia, that is where we ought to take the *Aphrodite* this year."

"Oh, yes. I agree," Philodemos said. "That's where you'll get the best prices for the goods you brought back from Phoenicia last season."

Oh, yes. I agree. The words echoed sourly inside Menedemos' head. His father never would have been so quick to agree with *him,* or to admit it if he did. But Philodemos gave his nephew the approval he withheld from his son. Of the two young men, Sostratos was usually the one who was cautious and sensible. *The one who's boring,* Menedemos thought. That wasn't wholly fair. He knew as much. The thought formed all the same.

Voice sly, he said, "You're as eager to go back to Athens for the sake of your philosophical friends as you are for trade."

His cousin didn't even try to deny it, which spoiled the jab. Sostratos just dipped his head in agreement and said, "Of course I am."

"And what about you? Why are you so eager to go to Athens?" Menedemos' father asked him. He answered his own question: "You're eager on account of all the loose women there, that's why—all the bored, faithless wives who don't care about their husbands or about doing what's proper. You'd sooner hunt piggies than hares any day." With sardonic relish, he used the slang for a female crotch singed free of hair.

Menedemos gave back a bland smile. "Spearing them is more fun." That was slang, too, of an obvious sort.

Sostratos snorted. Philodemos rolled his eyes. He said, "Joke all you want about adultery now, but it's landed you in more trouble than anybody since Paris ran off with Helen."

That wasn't fair. Menedemos' father undoubtedly knew it wasn't fair. But it held enough truth to make it sting. Menedemos *did* make a hobby of seducing other men's wives, and he *had* found himself in trouble because of it. Trying to forestall any more of Philodemos' wit, he said, "Well, we won't stop in Halikarnassos on the way to Athens."

There was a husband in Halikarnassos who would kill him on sight—who almost had killed him a few years before. Menedemos hoped the fellow had perished when Ptolemaios laid siege to the city a couple of years before. He wished it had fallen and been sacked, but no such luck. Antigonos' older son, Demetrios, had quick-marched an army up from the southeast and relieved it.

Philodemos surely would have brought up Halikarnassos if he hadn't. Even though he had, his father leaped on it: "A terrible thing, when our firm can't do business in a polis because you outraged the wife of one of the leading citizens."

"She wasn't outraged, by Zeus," Menedemos said. "She loved every minute of it. Her husband, on the other hand . . ."

"No point in quarreling about it now." Sostratos did his best to make peace. "We can't change it. It's over. It's done. No man can step into the same river twice."

That was a philosophical tagline; Menedemos knew as much, even if he'd had less education than his cousin. If Philodemos knew, he didn't care. "I want to keep him from jumping into this river of adultery again," he said. Then he pointed at Sostratos. "And you, too, as a matter of fact."

Sostratos winced. In Ioudaia the summer before, he'd bedded an innkeeper's wife. Now he was tarred with the same brush as Menedemos—and Menedemos' father wasn't shy about using that brush to paint him black. "Sir, that's over and done, too," Sostratos said.

"Which means what?" Philodemos asked. "That you won't do it any more? I hope that's what it means, by the gods."

"I hope it does, too," Sostratos said. He'd enjoyed his little foray into adultery much less than Menedemos enjoyed *his* affairs. "I hope so, but who can know for certain? The future's a book that hasn't yet been unrolled."

Philodemos bristled. He wanted promises, not hesitation. Before he could say anything, though, someone knocked on the door. A house slave hurried over to see who it was. A moment later, the man came back to the andron and spoke to Philodemos: "It's your friend Xanthos, master."

Sostratos leaped off the stool where he'd been sitting. "Well, I'd better be getting back to my father's house," he said. Xanthos was honest and sincere and friendly—and deadly dull, never a man to use a word when an oration would do.

"Bring him in, Bryaxis," Philodemos said. "Bring him in out of the rain and fetch him some wine. *You'll* stay and talk with him, won't you, son?" He turned to Menedemos with appeal in his eyes.

"Stay and listen to him, you mean?" Menedemos said as the slave—and Sostratos—headed for the door. Now he had his chance to take revenge on his father for giving him a hard time about his habits—had it and used it. "No, thank you, sir. I have some things I need to do upstairs, and I'm afraid they won't keep. I'm sure Xanthos will have a great many—a very great many—interesting things to say. Farewell."

He left the men's chamber as Bryaxis brought Xanthos toward it. The other merchant, plump and gray-haired, waved to him. He waved back—and kept walking to the wooden stairway that would let him escape. Behind him, he heard Xanthos drone out a greeting to his father, and Philodemos' valiantly polite reply. Chuckling, Menedemos went on up the stairs.

Behind the closed doors of the women's quarters, his father's second wife and a slave woman were making cloth from wool. The frame of the loom creaked and rattled as Baukis worked. Menedemos had always found it impossible to think of her as his stepmother. How could he, when she was ten or eleven years younger than he was?

She said something to the slave, who answered. The closed door muffled sounds so that Menedemos could hear voices, but not words. Both women laughed. Menedemos wondered what sort of women's gossip had amused them.

He went on to his own room. It held a bed, a stool, and a chest of drawers. At the moment, with the shutters closed against the rain, it was dark and gloomy and dull. Menedemos didn't care. Anything—including a dull, gloomy room—was better than staying in the andron and listening to Xanthos rehearse a speech he was going to give in the Assembly or, worse yet, repeat a speech he'd already given there.

After a while, the rising and falling cadences of Xanthos' rather froggy baritone came from downstairs. Menedemos smiled to himself. Sure enough, his father's friend was in full rhetorical flight. Menedemos wondered how long his father would have to endure the drivel. Xanthos could go on for a couple of hours without noticing he was making people around him wish they were dead or he was dead or everyone was dead.

Instead of dying, Menedemos fell asleep. When he woke up, Xanthos was still going on. Menedemos yawned, stretched, and chuckled softly. Philodemos couldn't match him there, no matter how much he might want to. If he started to snore and fell off his stool down there in the andron, Xanthos might notice. On the other hand, he might be so carried away with his own eloquence that he didn't. Still, it was a chance a polite man wouldn't take.

And Philodemos *was* polite, especially to everyone but his son. Menedemos chuckled again. Now his father was paying the price for his good manners.

WHEN SOSTRATOS GOT OUT OF BED and opened the shutters, he blinked in delighted surprise. Yesterday's rain clouds had blown away. The sky was a brilliant, velvety dark blue, shading toward pink in the east. Something flew by overhead: by its skittering path through the air, probably a bat returning to wherever it would hide during daylight hours.

Sostratos went back to his bed and pulled the chamber pot out from under it. After he'd used the pot, he dumped it out the window into the street below. This early in the day, he didn't have to worry about splashing passersby with its contents. He stuck the pot under the bed once more, put on his chiton, and went downstairs for breakfast.

His father was already sitting out in the courtyard with a chunk of bread, a plate of olive oil into which to dip the bread, and a cup of unwatered wine. "Hail, son," Lysistratos said. He was Philodemos' younger brother, and a good deal more easygoing than Menedemos' father. "How are you today?"

"Not bad, thanks," Sostratos answered. "Yourself?"

"Tolerable, tolerable," his father said. "My bones ache when I get up in the morning, but that comes of living as long as I have." He smiled. "If I weren't alive, I don't suppose I'd ache at all."

"Well, no," Sostratos said. He went into the kitchen and came out with a breakfast identical to his father's. He was just sitting down beside Lysistratos when a slave girl emerged, yawning, from her little room. "Hail, Threissa."

"Hail, young master," she replied in accented Greek. As her name suggested, she came from Thrace. She was red-haired and snub-nosed, a few years younger than Sostratos himself. She yawned again, then went to get her own breakfast. Lysistratos wasn't a slaveowner who measured out his slaves' rations to the last grain of barley. Threissa would eat about what he and his son had had.

Sostratos and Lysistratos both followed her with their eyes. Lysistratos always contented himself with watching her: a man who slept with a slave girl in his own house was asking for trouble with his wife. Sostratos took her up to his room every now and again. Had she shown any sign of enjoying his attentions rather than simply enduring them as a slave had to do, he would have made love to her more often.

The first rays of the sun touched the roof tiles. A few birds began to sing. More would come to Rhodes later, as they returned from the south. Lysistratos said, "I wonder how long this weather will hold. If it stays good, you'll be able to put to sea before long."

"I hope so!" Sostratos exclaimed. The thought of sailing for Athens so excited him, he hardly noticed Threissa coming out of the kitchen with bread and wine.

His father chuckled. "Athens is your beloved, sure enough."

"I've never said otherwise," Sostratos replied. He laughed, mostly at himself. "I couldn't very well, could I?—not if I wanted to tell the truth, anyhow."

"I was sorry to have to bring you home from the Lykeion as soon as I did," Lysistratos said. "We needed a good toikharkhos, though, and you're the one in the family with far and away the best head for figures."

"No, that's Menedemos—or aren't you talking about women?" Sostratos asked innocently.

His father rolled his eyes. "You know I'm not. And you know I'm right, too."

With a sigh, Sostratos dipped his head. He *was* the one best suited to keeping track of the cargo a ship carried, and of how much money, to the obolos, every item brought. He did know as much. He was a good bargainer, too, though his cousin might have been even better.

All the same . . . He sighed again. All the same, he wished he could have gone right on studying in Athens. Some men were lucky enough—and rich enough—to be able to pursue the love of wisdom their whole lives long. He wasn't. He'd had to come back to Rhodes to help his family and make his own way in the world. Though five years had passed since that sorry day, he still felt as if he'd torn his heart out and left it behind when he sailed away from Peiraieus.

Most of him still longed to return. The rest . . . For the rest, it was too late. He'd quoted Herakleitos the day before at Uncle Philodemos' house. The Ionian philosopher had surely been right: you couldn't step into the same river twice. When you went back in, it wasn't the same river any more.

And I'm not the same any more, either, Sostratos thought. Knowledge for its own sake did still matter to him. It mattered very much; he hoped it would for the rest of his life. One day, he wanted to write a history of his times to rival those of Herodotos and Thoukydides. But he was more practical, more hard-headed, than the weeping, gangling young man who'd so unwillingly come back to Rhodes when Lysistratos summoned him. He'd been dealing with trade goods and money these past few years, and they'd inevitably left their mark on the way his mind worked.

He said, "Do you know, Father, there's a bit of me that dreads going back to Athens? I never would have imagined that."

"I can see why," Lysistratos answered. "If you're very much in love with a hetaira when you're a young man, do you really want to see her again twenty years later? Do you want to find out she's got fat and gone gray and lost a front tooth? Wouldn't you rather recall the beauty you knew once upon a time?"

"That's it," Sostratos agreed. "That's exactly it. How can Athens live up to the way I remember her?"

"She probably won't," his father said. "But it isn't the city's fault. Cities don't usually change that much, not in a few years. People are the ones who change."

"Yes, I was thinking the same thing." Sostratos didn't think the changes he'd seen in himself were necessarily for the better, but saw no point in mentioning that to Lysistratos. He feared his father wouldn't have agreed with him.

A sparrow fluttered down into the courtyard. Sostratos tossed it a scrap of bread. The little bird hopped over, cocked its head to one side as it examined the morsel, and then pecked at it. Satisfied, it snapped it up and flew away.

"You should have put some wine out for it, too," Lysistratos said, amusement in his voice.

"Put some wine out for what?" Sostratos' mother asked as she came out into the courtyard.

"Oh, good day, Timokrate," Lysistratos said. "Sostratos gave a sparrow some crumbs for breakfast, and I was saying it should have had wine, too."

"It probably wouldn't have been able to fly straight if it had," Timokrate said. She was in her early forties, gray beginning to streak her brown hair. Smiling at Sostratos, she said, "You always did like to feed the birds."

"Well, why not, Mother?"

"No reason at all," she said, walking toward the kitchen. "It's just funny how you haven't changed much through the years."

"Oh." That made Sostratos scratch his head. Here he'd been thinking he was a different man from the one who'd left Athens, and his mother still saw him as the same little boy who'd played in this courtyard back when Alexander the Great was alive. Which of them was right?

Timokrate came out with bread and wine, too. Smiling at her son and her husband, she took her breakfast back upstairs to eat in the women's quarters. Erinna, Sostratos' younger sister, had always chafed under the restrictions Hellenic custom placed on respectable women. She wanted to be out and doing things, not shut away inside a house. His mother seemed perfectly content to stay indoors most of the time. *People are different,* Sostratos thought with profound unoriginality.

Erinna had lived with her second husband, Damonax, for the past year (her first had died after they'd been married only three years). She wouldn't be going out of his house for a while, anyhow; their little boy, Polydoros, was just over a month old. Sostratos said, "I'm glad Erinna had a boy."

"So am I." Lysistratos dipped his head. "Both because it's better to have a boy and because . . ." His voice trailed away.

Sostratos finished the thought: "Because Damonax might have exposed it if it were a girl."

"Yes." His father dipped his head again. "Whether or not to rear a baby is a husband's privilege."

"I know. But Erinna would have been very unhappy if Damonax had decided not to raise it," Sostratos said. When his sister came back to live at the family home after losing her first husband, she'd fretted that she would never remarry and never have the chance to bear children. To have a child and then lose it at a husband's whim . . . That would have been cruelly hard.

"On the whole, your brother-in-law seems a pretty reasonable fellow," Lysistratos said.

"On the whole, yes," Sostratos said. "When it comes to olive oil, no. How many times do we have to tell him we're not going to fill the *Aphrodite* to the gunwales with the stuff and haul it to Athens? I thought you and Uncle Philodemos had made him understand why we can't do it."

"Oh, we did," his father answered. "But he can't be reasonable—or what we think of as reasonable—about that. He's got his own family's interests to worry about, too, you know. They still aren't all the way out of debt, and olive oil is what they've got to sell. And so . . ." He sighed and shrugged.

"It's good oil. I've never said it's not good oil. But it's not the right cargo for a merchant galley, not with the overhead costs we've got because of all the rowers we need." Sostratos sighed, too. "I almost wish we hadn't done so well with it last sailing season. Then Damonax could really see why we don't want anything more to do with it."

"Especially not going to Athens," Lysistratos said.

"Especially not going to Athens," Sostratos agreed. "I can't imagine a worse place in the world to try to bring in olive oil. They stopped growing grain there a couple of hundred years ago, by the gods, so they could plant more olive trees. They export oil; they don't import it. Zeus on Olympos, Father, at the Panathenaic Games they give the winners amphorai of olive oil—their own olive oil."

"We both know that. . . ." his father began.

"Damonax knows it, too," Sostratos said. "He studied at the Lykeion in Athens before I got there. How can he help knowing it?"

Lysistratos let out a sad little chuckle. "Well, son, when someone marries into the family, you don't just get the good. You get all the problems he brings with him, too. And Damonax and his family probably think of us as a bunch of stingy whoresons."

Sostratos dipped his head. "That's true. But there's a difference—*we're right*." He knew he was being silly. So did his father. They both laughed. But it wasn't as if he didn't mean it, too.

TWO DAYS OF BRIGHT SUNSHINE in a row made Menedemos want to rush down to the Great Harbor to make sure the *Aphrodite* was fully laden and ready to put to sea. His father said, "You don't want to go out too early, you know. Better to wait a few extra days than to get caught by the last big blow of winter."

"But others will be setting sail now," Menedemos protested. "I don't want them to get the jump on me."

"Some skippers always set sail sooner than they should," Philodemos said. "A lot of the time, they end up paying for it." Menedemos fumed. Watching him fume, his father smiled a thin smile and added, "I'm going down to the agora, to find out what the news is. I expect you to be here when I get back."

"Why don't you just hire a pedagogue to take me here and there, the way you did when I was seven years old?" Menedemos said bitterly. His father took no notice of that. He hadn't really expected that Philodemos would. But the look of smug satisfaction on his father's face when he left for the market square stung like sweat dripping onto a raw sore.

Fuming still, Menedemos went into the kitchen. Sikon the cook would listen to him grumble, or give him something tasty to make him forget about grumbling. But Sikon wasn't there. He'd probably gone to the agora, too, or to the harborside fish markets to see what he could bring home for the evening's supper. Barley porridge still simmered above a low fire. Menedemos had eaten some for breakfast. He'd hoped for something better now: tunny or octopus, perhaps. Those failing, he dipped out another bowl of porridge. His father would have complained about his eating at midmorning, too. *But Father's not here,* he thought, and ate. The porridge, bland stuff, tasted better for being illicit.

Splashes that had nothing to do with rain greeted his ears when he went back out into the courtyard. At the direction of Philodemos' second wife, a slave poured water from a hydria onto the flowers and herbs in the garden there. "Careful, now," Baukis told him. "Don't miss the marjoram."

"I won't, mistress." The slave turned the stream from the big, heavy water jug where she pointed.

"That's better," she said, and dipped her head. When she looked up again, she saw Menedemos. She smiled. "Hail."

"Hail," he answered gravely. "How are you?"

"Well enough. Glad of this sunshine," Baukis said.

"It is nice, isn't it?" Menedemos agreed. Nothings, commonplaces . . . but he could look at her while they talked. Here inside her own household, she went unveiled, of course. She was no great beauty, but, except for front teeth that stuck out, pretty enough—and, at seventeen, any woman seemed fresh and glowing and ripe. Her figure had certainly ripened, these past few years. When she'd wed Philodemos, she'd been hardly more than a girl, with hardly more than a girl's shape. No more.

"Will you be sailing soon?" she asked.

"Before long, anyhow," Menedemos said. "Sostratos wants to get to Athens as fast as he can, and I don't blame him. We'll put to sea as soon as Father decides the weather's likely to hold."

"I hope you have good fortune." Baukis watched his face, as he watched hers—as was only polite when two people talked. If her gaze traveled the length of him, as his now and then paused at her rounded bosom or at the sweet flare of her hips . . . If her gaze swung so, it was only in the most casual way, a way on which, for instance, the patient slave with the hydria could not remark.

"Thanks," Menedemos replied. His glances were every bit as circumspect. Philodemos raved because he made adultery a game. But he knew adultery with his father's young wife would be, could be, no game. He'd realized he might want her not long after his father wed her. Only since the autumn before had he known she might want him, too.

They'd kissed only once. They'd never done more than kiss. Whatever else Baukis wanted, she also wanted to make Menedemos' father a good wife. Lying with Menedemos might not merely cause scandal. It might cause murder.

Since she couldn't speak of love, she spoke of travel: "Athens must be a wonderful place."

"Sostratos knows it better than I do. It's his second home," Menedemos said.

The hydria gurgled dry. The slave sent Baukis a look of appeal. She tossed her head and tapped her sandaled foot on the ground. "Go fill it again, Lydos," she said. "You can see some of the plants here still need more water. With the rains lately, the cistern's nice and full."

"With the rains lately, the plants shouldn't need all that much water," Lydos said.

"They'll dry up if you don't keep them moist," Baukis said sharply. "And if *you* don't dry up, I'll find something for you to do that you'll like a lot less than watering the garden."

Muttering to himself in a language that wasn't Greek, the slave shouldered the hydria and carried it back toward the cistern. Had it been late summer, with the cistern dry, Baukis would have sent a slave woman to the well a few blocks away. Menedemos laughed to himself. Who could guess when the woman would have come back from the well? Men talked in the market square. Women gossiped around the wellhead.

For that matter, who could guess when Lydos would come back from the cistern—and it was only at the rear of the house? By the way he dragged his feet going there, he was in no hurry to get on with his work. But then, what slave ever was in a hurry, except maybe to go out and get drunk on a festival day?

Menedemos wasn't about to rush him, either. Now he could gaze his fill at Baukis . . . provided he didn't do it too openly. They still weren't alone. As if to prove that, Sikon the cook came into the house, his face a thundercloud—shopping for fish must not have gone well. He stormed into the kitchen and made a racket as he started on the day's baking. Maybe he was working out his anger. Maybe he thought that the noisier he was, the busier everybody would think he was. That was another slave trick old as time. The doorman was puttering around, too, and the slave women upstairs. In a household full of slaves, you could never count on being alone for very long.

Baukis took not quite half a step toward Menedemos. Then she stopped, a rueful—and more than a little frightened—smile on her face. She knew the risks of living in a house full of slaves as well as he did. They were lucky they hadn't been found out the one time their lips did touch.

We can't, she mouthed silently. They'd been saying that to each other ever since discovering they both wanted to.

I know, Menedemos mouthed back. They'd been saying that, too, each trying to convince the other, both trying to convince themselves.

The past two springs, when Menedemos had known he longed for Baukis but hadn't known they shared a longing, he'd wanted to flee Rhodes as soon as he could. Now . . . Now at least part of him wished he could stay and wait for a chance that might never come, a chance he might not take even if it did come. Hellenes agreed love was a mad, dangerous passion. What to do if one fell into it anyhow? On that, there was no agreement.

He started to mouth, *I love you,* but he couldn't even do that. Here came Lydos back with the water jug. He was still grumbling. Baukis had had her problems with the house slaves, and especially with the cook, but she was wise enough to affect not to notice this. All she said was, "Oh, good—that didn't take too long," and showed him the plants that still needed watering. As he bent to moisten the dirt around them, Baukis shot Menedemos another glance full of harried amusement.

And Menedemos could only dip his head. Had he fallen in love with any other wife in all of Rhodes . . . For a long time, he'd tried to make himself believe this hadn't happened. Life would have been much easier—much safer, too—if it hadn't. But the world was what it was, not what he wished it would be.

Lydos' second jar of water ran dry. He looked up at Baukis in mute appeal; the garden was almost done. She knew exactly what he was thinking. "Go get enough water to finish the job," she said.

"Oh, by the gods!" Lydos turned to Menedemos in appeal. "Young master—"

Menedemos tossed his head. "I can see the corner that's still dry," he said before Lydos could go any further. "My father's wife is right. If you're going to do something, do it properly. That's a lesson you learn at sea—or, if you don't, you pay for it."

Lydos let out a theatrical groan, as if Menedemos had just ordered him sold to the mines. When that failed to soften either Menedemos' heart or Baukis', he carried the hydria away again, moving like an old, old man whose joints pained him.

Baukis snorted. "It must be terrible for a man to be made into a slave."

"Yes, it is." Menedemos looked right at her, as if to say she had made him into hers.

She spent a lot of time indoors, which kept her skin fair. He watched, enchanted, the flush that rose from her neck to her cheeks to her forehead. *Stop that,* she mouthed.

She was right, of course. The more such foolish things he did, the likelier someone would notice: his father, which would be the worst disaster of all; or a slave, who might tell his father or extort who could guess what by threatening to tell; or even Sostratos, who'd puzzled over why Menedemos had been so eager to get away from Rhodes the past couple of sailing seasons.

As Baukis had, Menedemos snorted. His cousin, sometimes, thought too much for his own good. A more perceptive man, one who felt more and perhaps thought a little less, might well have realized what was wrong with Menedemos. Or maybe Sostratos needed to fall in love himself before he could recognize the symptoms in others. They weren't—or Menedemos hoped they weren't—something that could be known by reason alone.

He stole another glance at Baukis . . . and caught her stealing a glance at him. Their eyes met for a heartbeat, then jerked away. Hers went to the stairway leading up to the second story, his to the stone bench in the courtyard. He pointed. "Look—there's a wall lizard, soaking up the sun. *He* thinks spring is here."

The motion of his arm made the grayish-brown lizard dash to the edge of the bench, leap off, and disappear amongst the plants in the garden. Baukis said, "I'm glad to see it. They eat insects. Have you ever seen one with a grasshopper in its mouth?"

"Oh, yes." Menedemos dipped his head.

Talk of lizards was safe enough. When Lydos returned with the hydria, he couldn't have noticed anything the least improper. A sour expression on his face, the slave emptied the jar not far from where the little animal had taken shelter. It fled again, this time across the courtyard. It vanished into a crack in the mud-brick inner wall of the house.

Menedemos laughed. "Poor thing must have thought Deukalion's flood was sweeping down on it."

"Yes." Baukis gave Lydos a severe look. "You don't need to drown the plants, you know."

"Sorry." He sounded anything but.

"Be more careful next time," Baukis told him. His nod was so impatient, so perfunctory, that Menedemos would have called him on it if Baukis hadn't. But she did: "Be more careful, Lydos, or you *will* be sorry."

That got through. "Yes, mistress. I'll remember," the slave said, and this time Menedemos believed him.

"See that you do, because I'll remember, too," Baukis said. "Now go on." Lydos hurried away, carrying the hydria.

"You handled that very well," Menedemos said.

"Oh, slaves aren't so hard. I was dealing with slaves before I was married, too, you know," Baukis said. But then she checked herself. "*Most* slaves aren't so hard. On the other hand, there's Sikon."

"Yes." For a moment, Menedemos left it at that. Baukis and Sikon had feuded ever since she came to Philodemos' house. She wanted to be a good household manager, and was convinced he was trying to bankrupt the place with the fancy fish he bought. He wanted to turn out the best suppers he could, and was convinced she wanted everyone in the house to live on barley porridge, beans, and salt fish. The truth, as usual, lay somewhere in between—or so Menedemos thought, anyhow. He said, "Cooks are a law unto themselves, you know."

"Really? I never would have noticed," Baukis said tartly. But then she relented: "I suppose it is better not to be quarreling with him all the time."

They'd come to a tentative truce the autumn before. It had already held longer than Menedemos had expected. He said, "I'm glad you're not squabbling any more." That gave him another excuse to smile at Baukis. It gave her another excuse to smile back. And no one who saw them or listened to them could have noted anything out of the ordinary.

SOSTRATOS HELD HIS NEPHEW with exaggerated care, as if afraid Polydoros were about to leap from his arms and precipitate himself headfirst onto the dirt of the courtyard at Damonax's house. For all his care, both Erinna and a wet nurse hovered close by, ready to snatch the baby out of his inexperienced hands.

Trying to reassure them that he had some idea what he was doing, he said, "He sure looks a lot better than he did right after he was born."

His sister scowled. "What was wrong with him right after he was born?" she demanded in irate tones.

"He looked just fine, I'll have you know," the wet nurse added.

"All right. All right. Fine. I didn't mean anything by it," Sostratos said hastily. The women relaxed. Sostratos looked down at Polydoros. The baby was a healthy pink now, not the reddish-purple color he'd been. His head had been almost cone-shaped. It was much rounder now, and getting more so each time Sostratos saw him. Even his expression seemed more alert, less confused, than it had when he first came into the world.

Some things hadn't changed, though. Sostratos suddenly realized the cloths around the baby's middle were moist. He thrust Polydoros at the wet nurse and wiped his hands on his chiton.

"There, there," the woman told the baby. "We'll take care of that. Don't you worry about a thing." She carried him away.

When she came back, she sat down on a bench, slipped her chiton down from one shoulder, and gave Polydoros her breast. Sostratos watched the baby suck, as interested in the process as he was in the bare breast. He also listened to his nephew nursing; he hadn't realized it could be so noisy. He could hear every gulp Polydoros took. Then the baby swallowed wrong and choked. The wet nurse took him away from the breast and held him up against her shoulder, patting him on the back till he belched: a surprisingly large, surprisingly deep sound. Then she brought him down and let him nurse some more.

"You'll be sailing soon, won't you?" Erinna asked.

"What?" When Sostratos concentrated on something, he did so to the exclusion of everything else around him. He had to pause and make himself remember what his sister had said before he could dip his head and answer, "Yes, very soon, especially if the weather stays fine like this. Athens!" He couldn't hold the excitement from his voice.

"Athens." Erinna sounded resigned—or was it merely wistful? For her, leaving her husband's house was an adventure. Sailing off to another city? When she'd come back to Lysistratos' household after losing her first husband, she'd listened with endless fascination as Sostratos told her stories of the distant places he'd seen. With the circumscribed lives respectable women led among the Hellenes, listening was all she could do. She would never see distant places herself.

Sostratos eyed her with some concern. Like him, she'd always been on the lean side. Now, though, she still kept the flesh she'd put on while carrying Polydoros. To his eye, it didn't suit her frame: it seemed added on, not a natural part of her. "How are you, my dear?" he asked, hoping his worry didn't show.

"Tired," she answered at once. "After you have a baby, you feel as though someone's dropped a wall on you. I don't think you can help it."

"Oh, yes." The wet nurse dipped her head. "*That's* true, by the gods."

"What . . . What is it like? Having a baby, I mean," Sostratos asked hesitantly. As they often did, curiosity and decorum warred within him. This time, curiosity won.

Not that it got him much. Erinna only laughed. "It's not *like* anything," she said. "It's the hardest thing I've ever done. I think it's the hardest thing anyone can do."

"Oh, yes," the wet nurse said again, and then, softly, " 'What's it like?' Men!" She didn't have to worry about keeping Sostratos sweet.

"I can't very well know unless I ask, can I?" he said, stung by the scorn in her voice.

If he thought his question would get him less, he rapidly found himself wrong. "Men!" the wet nurse said again, this time not bothering to hold her voice down. "What you don't understand is, you can't know even if you do ask."

"Gorgia's right, I'm afraid." Erinna sounded sad. She knew of Sostratos' unrelenting itch to find out whatever he could. Sad or not, though, she tossed her head here. "Unless you had a baby yourself, you couldn't know what it was like. You're not . . . equipped for it." That made the wet nurse—Gorgia—giggle.

It made Sostratos angry, at least for a moment. "But—" he began. Then he spread his hands in defeat. "No, I suppose not, any more than you can understand what growing a beard is like." He scratched his own hairy chin. Most Hellenes of his generation, Menedemos among them, shaved their faces as Alexander had done. Sostratos thought his beard made him look like a philosopher. Maybe he was right.

Someone rapped on the front door. Erinna said, "That's Damonax—I know his knock." By the way one of the house slaves hurried to the entrance, he recognized his master's knock, too.

The door scraped as it turned on pivots set into the floor and the lintel above. The house slave spoke to Damonax in a voice too low for Sostratos to make out what he said. He didn't need to have studied logic to figure out what it must have been, though, for Damonax replied, "He *is?* Well, good. I've been meaning to talk with him for the past few days, anyhow."

Erinna's husband strode into the courtyard. He was a handsome man of above average height, though not so tall as Sostratos. Unlike his brother-in-law, he bore himself with the air of a man who knew he was somebody. His chiton was of fine, soft white wool. A gold ring on the index finger of his right hand flashed in the sun. Sostratos smiled to himself. Damonax looked and acted like a rich man, as befitted one whose wealth lay in land. But Sostratos knew whose family was really better off.

"Hail," Damonax said with a smile that showed off the teeth he took fastidious pains to keep white. "How are you today?"

"Fine, thanks." Sostratos held out his hand. "And you?"

"Couldn't be better." Damonax clasped it: a firm, manly grip. Like Sostratos, he'd studied at the Lykeion. Also like Sostratos, he flavored the Doric dialect of Rhodes with a strong Attic accent. "What do you think of your nephew these days?"

"That's obvious, O best one," Sostratos answered, looking toward Polydoros, who'd fallen asleep in Gorgia's arms. "He'll have the strength and beauty of divine Akhilleus and the wit of resourceful Odysseus."

Erinna sent Sostratos a sharp glance. She knew irony when she heard it. Damonax didn't, or didn't always. He complacently dipped his head and said, "Yes, I think so, too." He looked around. "Haven't they given you any wine? No olives or figs to munch on? What is this place coming to?"

Not wanting either his sister or Damonax's slaves to get in trouble, Sostratos spoke quickly: "I've been so busy admiring your son and talking with Erinna, I didn't even notice."

"Kind of you to say such a thing, best one, but really, there are standards," Damonax said. "Come into the andron with me, why don't you, and we'll set you to rights."

Sostratos would rather have gone on talking with Erinna, of whom he was fond, than gone with his brother-in-law. He had a pretty good idea why Damonax wanted to talk with him, and didn't anticipate a happy result. But he couldn't very well say no, not without a shocking breach of manners. Swallowing a sigh, he said, "Lead on, and I'll follow."

At Damonax's heels, he stepped up into the men's chamber. As in most houses, it was raised a step above the level of the courtyard and the other ground-floor rooms. No sooner had he perched on a stool than the slave who'd let Damonax into the house brought wine and olives. Damonax and Sostratos both poured a little wine on the floor as an offering to Dionysos.

When Sostratos drank, he raised an eyebrow. "My dear fellow! This can't be mixed any weaker than one to one. That's potent even at a symposion, but in the morning? Do you want your slaves to have to carry me home? What would people say?"

"One cup won't send you raging through the streets looking for women to ravish like a satyr," Damonax said easily.

Aren't you thinking of Menedemos? But, though that got to the tip of Sostratos' tongue, he didn't say it. He had more reasons to be loyal to his cousin than to his brother-in-law. He took a cautious sip from the cup—a big, deep piece of earthenware in the Spartan style, not one of the shallow, graceful, two-handled kylikes that didn't hold nearly so much. "The wine is very nice," he admitted. "Where's it from?"

Damonax's chuckle was self-deprecating. "Just a local vintage, I'm afraid."

Rhodes made good wine, good enough to export. But no one would confuse even her best with what the vintners of Khios or Lesbos or Thasos turned out. That Damonax served a Rhodian wine said his family's fortunes had declined. That he served a good Rhodian wine said either that they hadn't declined too far or that he still had good taste even if he needed to be more careful about indulging it these days.

Sostratos ate an olive. Spitting the pit onto the floor of the andron, he said, "These are tasty, too."

"Glad you like them, my dear," Damonax replied. "They're from the family farm." *Oh, a pestilence,* Sostratos thought. *I've given him an opening.* But Damonax didn't charge right into the breach like a soldier entering a besieged city. Instead, with another of his charming smiles, he asked, "Have you ever been out to the farm?"

"Why, no, O best one, I never have," Sostratos said.

"You must visit one day," Damonax said. "Do you good to see there's life on the land as well as here in the bustling polis. It's in the western part of the island, you know, between Ialysos and Kameiros— not far from the Valley of the Butterflies."

"Ah?" Sostratos pricked up his ears. "Now that I would like to see one of these days." Farm life interested him very little. For better or worse, he *was* a creature of the polis, of the agora. He was sure he would go mad in short order with only the same handful of faces to see and to talk to month after month, year after year; with news filtering in long after it was fresh, if it ever came at all. An interesting natural phenomenon, on the other hand . . .

Damonax smiled and dipped his head. "It's quite something. Myriad upon myriad of butterflies perching in the valley through the heat of summer. They cover the rocks, especially by the waterfall, like one of those carpets the Persians lay on the floor."

"The summer . . ." Sostratos sighed. "It's also the sailing season, you know. I'm likely to be away from Rhodes."

"They don't disperse over the island till the fall rains start, and you're usually home by then," Damonax said. "Why don't you pay me a call when you get back from Athens? That should be just about olive-harvest time, too. The oil from the first ones picked is always the best, you know, and if you're there to dip a barley roll into it when it comes out of the last settling pit. . . ." He smiled again, a voluptuary's smile.

"You tempt me," Sostratos said.

"Good. I mean to," Damonax answered. "The invitation is open, believe me. And when you see the oil pressed from the olives, when you taste it before it even goes into the amphora . . . Till then, you don't know what oil can be. Rhodian wine may not be of the very finest, but Rhodian oil is, by the gods. And we make some of the best of any farm on the island."

Now we come down to it, Sostratos thought unhappily. "No one has ever said you didn't, O marvelous one," he said.

His brother-in-law gave him a sour look, as any educated man would have done. Sokrates had been fond of using that salutation when he felt sarcastic, so that *marvelous* meant something like *marvelously foolish.* Damonax went on, "Your family has been most unreasonable about taking some of my olive oil aboard the *Aphrodite* this sailing season."

Sostratos didn't like quarrels. He especially didn't like quarrels with people with whom he had marriage ties. But he also didn't like problems with trade, and trade came first. Sighing, he said, "We've been over this ground before, you know—more than once, in fact—and you can pour lots of strong wine down my throat, but you still won't seduce me."

"If you'd only be reasonable—" Damonax said.

"No." Sostratos tossed his head. "I'm afraid you're the one who's being unreasonable, not me or my father or uncle or cousin. You do know where the akatos is going this spring?"

"Athens, of course," Damonax replied.

"That's right." Now Sostratos dipped his head in agreement. "And since you studied there, the same as I did, you'll have heard the phrase 'owls to Athens,' too, won't you?" He waited. When Damonax didn't answer right away, his voice got sharper: "Won't you?"

"Well . . . yes," Damonax said.

"And you'll also know what it means, isn't that so?"

His brother-in-law flushed angrily. "Don't play the game of elenkhos with me. You're not Sokrates, by the dog of Egypt!"

"All right, my dear. Fine. If you want me to spell it out for you, I will, alpha-beta-gamma." Sostratos let out an angry exhalation of his own. "'Owls to Athens' means taking something someplace where they don't need it. Athens doesn't need owls, because she already stamps them on her coins. And Athens doesn't need imported olive oil, because Attica already makes more of it than any other district in Hellas. Athens imports grain so she can grow more olives. You know that, too. You know it, but you don't want to think about it. What a lover of wisdom that makes *you.*"

"My family needs the silver the oil would bring," Damonax said. "It's very fine oil—*you* know that."

"I also know I haven't a chance of selling it in Athens, no matter how fine it is. They're glutted with what they make themselves," Sostratos snapped. "*And* I know it's not a proper cargo for a merchant galley anyhow—not enough profit even if it does sell." He held up a hand. "Don't tell me about last season, either. Yes, we made money, but we would have made more with other cargo we couldn't carry because of your big, bulky amphorai full of oil."

"What am I supposed to do, then?" Damonax demanded.

"What we've been telling you all along: put it in a round ship, where the crew is small and the overhead is low. Sell it someplace where they don't grow so much on their own—Kos, maybe, or Khios, or the cities up along the Thracian coast where the weather's cooler and they don't always get good crops."

His brother-in-law pooched out his lower lip and looked sullen. "You have no family feeling whatsoever."

"On the contrary." Sostratos tossed his head. "My first loyalty is to my father. My next loyalty is to Uncle Philodemos and Menedemos. If the only way I can help you is by hurting them—and, incidentally, myself—what would you have me do?"

"Go to the crows," Damonax said.

Sostratos got to his feet. "Good day," he said, and strode out of the andron.

Erinna knew something was wrong. "Where are you going?" she called to Sostratos as he stalked across the courtyard.

"Home." He pushed past a startled slave and out the front door to Damonax's house. Menedemos, no doubt, would have slammed it in his wake. Instead, Sostratos closed it as quietly as he could. As far as he was concerned, Damonax was the one in the wrong, and he wanted to do nothing to put himself there with his brother-in-law—or his sister. That didn't keep him from seething as he stormed away. Oh, no. On the contrary.

MENEDEMOS SPENT AS MUCH TIME as he could outside his father's house. For one thing, that kept him and Philodemos from locking horns. For another, it eliminated temptation, or at least the chance to do anything about temptation. And, for a third, he was a man who liked crowds and noise and excitement. Going to the agora was a lot more fun than sitting around watching flowers begin to bloom.

Potters and woodcarvers and leatherworkers cried their wares from stalls that had sometimes been in their families for generations. Jewelers showed off brass bracelets that gleamed like gold, beadwork necklaces, and silver rings. Farmers in from the countryside offered up grain and olive oil, olives in brine and vinegar, cabbages and lettuces, beets and mushrooms, eggs from ducks and hens. A dentist reached into a man's mouth with iron forceps to pull a rotted tooth while a crowd gathered round to watch and point and call advice. Hearing the victim groan, Menedemos thanked the gods his own teeth were sound.

A mountebank strolled through the crowd, juggling a stream of cups and balls and knives. Every so often, someone would throw him an obolos. He caught the little silver coins without losing control of everything he kept in the air. A grotesquely overmuscled strong man lifted a fellow of ordinary size over his head and tossed him about as if he weighed nothing at all. An artist of sorts perched on a stool in front of a patch of smooth-raked sand. For an obolos, he would use a long stylus to sketch a man's portrait in the sand. Menedemos watched him work. His strokes were quick and sure; he caught a man's essence with a minimum of wasted motion. Each portrait remained to be admired till the next customer gave him some silver.

"Here." Menedemos took an obolos out of his mouth and handed it to the artist. "Do me."

"Certainly, O best one." After popping the coin into his own mouth, the man smoothed the sand once more. The fellow whose portrait had been there muttered under his breath; his picture hadn't lasted long. A few lines delineated Menedemos' sharp chin, his straight nose and strong cheekbones, the eyebrows that were almost too bushy, and the hairline that had retreated perhaps a digit's width at each temple. After a couple of minutes, the sketch artist looked up. "Here you are, my friend: you."

"Looks like me," agreed Menedemos, who had often seen his image in a mirror of polished bronze. A poor man from the countryside, though, might have no true idea what he looked like till this fellow showed him.

As Menedemos turned away, someone just coming up peered at his portrait and said, "There's a good-looking fellow." He preened. Even though he was no longer a youth for suitors to pursue, he never got tired of praise.

Not far away, half a dozen men were arguing about what this year's campaigning season would likely bring in the wars among Alexander's marshals. "Mark my words, someone will triumph over all the rest," a gray-haired man declared.

"I don't know about that," a younger fellow said. "As soon as one of those polluted Macedonians looks like he's getting on top, the others gang up on him and pull him back down again. That sort of thing can go on for a long time."

Menedemos walked over to join them, saying, "It's already gone on for a long time. Alexander's been dead—what?—sixteen years now."

The men who were talking shifted a little to give him room. If a man couldn't hash things out with his fellow citizens in the agora, he couldn't do it anywhere. A stocky fellow of about Menedemos' age whose scars said he'd fought as a mercenary dipped his head. "That's right," he said. "Sixteen years, and we've still got Antigonos and Ptolemaios and Lysimakhos and Kassandros in the field against each other." He sounded cheerful—as long as the marshals brawled, mercenaries would never lack for work.

"And Seleukos," somebody else said. "Don't forget Seleukos, way off in the east. Antigonos tried to squash him a couple of years ago, but he couldn't do it."

"You're right," Menedemos said. "He's like a reveler who hears a symposion and invites himself in. I think the other four will have to keep an eye on him now that he's inside the andron, or he'll walk off with the furniture."

"Anybody old One-Eye can't beat is someone to keep an eye on, sure enough," said the man who looked like a mercenary.

"Alexander showed the world one man could lead the Hellenes— and the Macedonians, too," the gray-haired fellow said. "Now that he's proved it can be done, the marshals will keep banging away till only one's left standing, the way pankratiasts do at the Olympic Games."

"They'll try—that's certain enough," Menedemos said. "But they don't fight the way pankratiasts do. It's not one against one. They make treaties with one another—they make 'em, and then they break 'em. For one man to win, he'd have to defeat all the others at once, and nobody's managed it yet."

"Which probably means it can't be done," said the younger man who'd first disagreed with the older one. "Don't you see that, Xenomenes?"

"No." The man with gray hair tossed his head. "Fifty years ago, you would have told me nobody could ever rule all the Hellenes. Then Philip of Macedon went and did it, and Alexander held on to them afterwards. So I don't see why the same shouldn't hold true here."

That produced a thoughtful silence. Menedemos wondered what Sostratos would have had to say about it; his cousin was fond of such arguments, too. But he stubbornly stuck to his own view: "Maybe it can happen, but that doesn't mean it's likely to."

"Ha!" Xenomenes said. "Tell it to Antigonos, not me. He's the one the rest worry about the most—and they need to."

"Ptolemaios stung him a couple of years ago, taking away the southern coast of Anatolia," the man who looked like a mercenary said.

"But he's still got Phoenicia and a lot of the Hellenic cities along the west coast of Anatolia," Menedemos said. "That means he can still build up his navy—and he hires pirates, the same as he hires men to fight on land."

All the Rhodians muttered at that. Their polis lived by trade. They hated pirates, and used their navy to try to keep them down. Menedemos had fought them on each of his last two voyages. He had no use for a man who abetted them.

Neither did any of the others. One of them said, "If he hires pirates, he's liable to hire them against us one fine day, unless we do just what he tells us."

Menedemos pulled at the neckline of his tunic and spat into his bosom to turn aside the evil omen. Three other Rhodians did the same thing. Mournfully, Xenomenes said, "All we want to do is stay free and autonomous—well, *really* free and autonomous."

A lot of poleis that called themselves by those two proud names were free to do whatever the marshal controlling them said and autonomous of the rest of the marshals. Such was the level to which Hellenic independence had sunk in the past generation. Even Rhodes had briefly had a Macedonian garrison, but had expelled it after Alexander died. Now she truly was free and autonomous, able to do business with Ptolemaios and Antigonos alike—and with the other, more distant, marshals as well.

Xenomenes went on, "How can we hope to keep our freedom, though, if one of the Macedonians triumphs over the rest? He'd swallow us up, the same as he'd swallow everything and everybody else."

"But you're still assuming something you haven't shown: that one marshal *could* beat all the rest," Menedemos said. "Until you show that, it's like worrying about what would happen if an elephant fell out of the sky without showing how an elephant could fly in the first place."

The older man gave him a nasty look. Several of the other Rhodians laughed, which only made Xenomenes more irate. They argued about the marshals and whatever else came to mind for the next couple of hours. Every now and then, someone new would join the circle, as Menedemos had, or one of the men already there would wander off to do something else. Menedemos couldn't think of a better way to pass the time—unless it was keeping company with a woman, of course.

When he finally went back to his house, his father was waiting in the andron. Menedemos politely dipped his head and walked toward the stairs. He didn't feel like another argument now. But when Philodemos waved in a peremptory way, he had no choice but to stop and go over and ask, "What is it, Father?"

"How soon can the *Aphrodite* sail?" Philodemos rapped out.

Menedemos dug a finger into his ear, wondering if he'd heard straight. "How *soon* can she sail?" he echoed, half in disbelief.

"That's what I said, isn't it?" his father replied irritably.

"Yes, sir." Menedemos frowned in thought. "Loading her and rounding up a crew won't take more than a day or two. Wouldn't even be that long if we didn't need so many rowers. But most of them will be men who've pulled an oar in her before."

"Go ahead and get ready, then," Philodemos said. "The sooner, the better. Can't be too soon, by Poseidon's beard."

"Wait." Menedemos held up a hand. "Just a couple of days ago, you were complaining I wanted to go out too early to suit you. Why have you changed your mind all of a sudden?"

Before Philodemos could answer, a slave brought him a cup of wine. He poured out a small libation, then drained the cup. "Ahh!" he said, wiping his mouth on his arm, and then, "I'll tell you what made me change my mind: I just had another session with your cousin's brother-in-law, that's what. Zeus on Olympos!" By the way he looked around, he wished he had more wine.

"Papai!" Menedemos exclaimed. "I thought you'd persuaded him we weren't going to load the *Aphrodite* up with his olive oil, and that was the end of it."

"I thought the same thing," his father said. "I thought so, but I was wrong. The only way to persuade Damonax of anything is to clout him in the head with a rock. Even then, you have to keep clouting him, because the first wallop doesn't get through."

"Why can't he understand we won't make enough money with his oil for it to be worth our while? We've told him often enough," Menedemos said.

"I think he does understand," Philodemos answered, peering down into his winecup as if hoping it held more. "I don't think he cares, which isn't the same thing. He's convinced we owe him a living, regardless of what that does to *our* prospects."

"Well, Furies take him, then," Mcncdcmos said.

"That's just what I told him, when I saw I couldn't get through to him any other way," his father said.

"Good for you." Menedemos dipped his head in complete agreement. He and his father might—did—quarrel about a great many things. Neither of them, though, suffered fools gladly.

"And so, you see, that's why I want you to sail," Philodemos said now. "If you're gone, Damonax can't possibly nag me about loading oil onto the merchant galley—at least, not till next sailing season rolls around."

"I'll take care of it. You know I've been eager to go for a while now," Menedemos said. That was true. He couldn't squabble with his father if a couple of thousand stadia separated them. He couldn't make love to his father's wife if a couple of thousand stadia separated *them,* either. Part of him regretted that. The more sensible part—and the larger part, as well—knew nothing but relief. A slow smile stole over his face. *I'll make love to other men's wives instead,* he thought.

"I know what you're thinking," his father growled, and pointed an accusing finger at him. "You're thinking about adultery with all those loose Athenian women again, that's what. I can tell."

Menedemos hoped his father didn't see him wince. "I don't know what you're talking about," he said with such dignity as he could muster.

"A pestilence take me if you don't," Philodemos said. Menedemos did his best to look innocent. He was guilty of what his father had accused him of, yes. Next to what his father didn't know, though, that was as nothing.

The sooner he sailed for Athens, the better.

"*OIMOI!*" SOSTRATOS SAID IN DISMAY, and then switched from Greek to slow, halting, angry Aramaic: "My master, you are a thief."

Himilkon the Phoenician looked aggrieved. "Your servant cannot imagine why you would say such a thing," he replied in his own language, and then clutched his long robe with both hands, as if to rend the garment in dismay.

Sostratos went back to Greek: "Why? I'll tell you why. You've been quietly buying up papyrus all winter long, that's why, and the price you want for it is outrageous."

"If you do not care for that price, buy somewhere else." Himilkon's Greek, though gutturally accented, was better than Sostratos' Aramaic. In fact, he'd taught Sostratos what Aramaic he knew.

"I don't seem to be able to buy anywhere else," Sostratos said. "If I could, I would, believe me. But no one else has any, so I have to come to you." He glowered at the merchant from Byblos. "You knew the *Aphrodite* would go to Athens this season."

"You didn't keep it a secret, most noble one," Himilkon replied. "As soon as you came back from Phoenicia last fall, you started talking about how you planned to go to Athens and sell some of the goods you'd got. And even if you hadn't, how smart would I have to be to figure out that you would want to go west instead of east this time?"

Every word of that was nothing but truth and common sense. None of it made Sostratos any happier. If anything, he got more upset, saying, "You have no right to hold us for ransom like a pirate."

"For ransom? No, indeed." Himilkon shook his head. "I do not want to kill you if you do not pay. I do not want to burn down your house. All I want to do is what any merchant wants: I want to make a profit."

"You know Athens uses more papyrus than any other place in the world except maybe Alexandria—and they grow the stuff in Egypt," Sostratos said. "You want me to pay you your ridiculous price for it so the *Aphrodite* can sell it in the Athenian agora."

The Phoenician gave him a sly smile. "You can raise the price you charge for it, too."

"Not that far," Sostratos said. "We won't be the only ones selling it, you know. If we have to ask twice as much as anybody else just to get our silver back, we won't do a whole lot of business there."

"It won't be so bad," Himilkon said. "Remember, most papyrus comes through Rhodes—and if it came through Rhodes lately, I bought it. You'll have less competition than you think."

"But papyrus is always a luxury item. People don't have to have it," Sostratos said.

"Of course. But that's true of anything you'd carry on an akatos, wouldn't you say?" Himilkon tugged on the gold hoop he wore in his left ear, as if settling it more comfortably. He scratched at his curly black beard. "I fear the reason you are most upset with me, O best one, is that I have the advantage in this dicker."

Sostratos feared he was right. The Rhodian wasn't about to admit it. "No, indeed," he said. "We've made plenty of bargains where you had the advantage. Remember the peafowl a few years ago?"

"Oh, yes, I remember them very well," Himilkon replied. "And when you sailed to Great Hellas with them, how much of a profit did you squeeze out of the Italiote Hellenes?"

"Peafowl were unique, though. Papyrus is anything but," Sostratos insisted.

Himilkon's only response was a shrug. "If you don't care for the price I set, my master, you are welcome to sail for Athens without papyrus."

"All right." Sostratos got to his feet. He automatically ducked his head as he rose from his stool; Himilkon's ramshackle harborside warehouse had shelves that stuck out at odd angles and a low ceiling. On the shelves lay packets and bales and jars of goods from all around the Inner Sea and from lands far to the east and north: the Phoenician dealt in many things besides papyrus. Sostratos, at the moment, didn't care. He said, "Always a pleasure talking with you, O marvelous one. Farewell."

He turned to go. Sometimes the best bargains were ones you didn't make. He'd taken several steps toward the door before Himilkon, in a voice full of pain, called, "Wait."

"Why?" Sostratos asked. "What more do we have to talk about?" He'd hoped the Phoenician would stop him, but he hadn't counted on it. Sometimes the only way to keep a dicker alive was to show you weren't afraid to kill it, too. Sometimes. Judging when . . . Judging when was what made a merchant.

"If you're going to be . . . difficult, I suppose I can get by with less than three drakhmai, three oboloi for a roll of twenty sheets," Himilkon said. "A little less, mind you."

"I should hope so," Sostratos said. "One drakhma, two oboloi is a more usual price—that's only a bit more than a third of what you were trying to squeeze out of me."

"That's the price when everyone is bringing lots of papyrus into Athens," Himilkon said. "Since most Egyptian shipping comes through Rhodes, and since I've been buying up the stock since last fall, it isn't likely to be so cheap this season."

"So you say now," Sostratos said. "But all we need to worry about is one round ship from Alexandria sailing straight for Athens. Their main cargo is always grain, but their captains carry other things, too, to make extra on the side, and papyrus is something that always brings them a nice profit."

"It could bring you a nice profit, too," Himilkon said, doing his best to make the idea sound tempting.

Sostratos refused to show he was tempted. "It *could*," he said pointedly, "if you gave me room to move on the price. Otherwise . . ." He tossed his head.

The Phoenician clapped both hands to his face in melodramatic dismay. "And you called *me* a thief! I suppose you expect me to lose all the profit I expected to make from getting the papyrus in the first place."

"You won't get any if you make it too expensive to be worth my while," Sostratos said. "And you have to leave me room to push up the price and make my own profit in Athens. If I can't charge a halfway decent price for it, nobody will buy any from me. I might as well not bring it if I can't sell it."

Himilkon said something pungent in Aramaic. Sostratos said something else, just as pungent, in the same language to remind Himilkon he understood. They yelled at each other in Greek. Himilkon edged his price down by a couple of oboloi. Sostratos laughed scornfully. The Phoenician, looking harassed, came down again.

That made Sostratos come up—by an obolos a roll. Himilkon bawled as if a branding iron were searing his flesh. Sostratos ignored the theatrics, which only made Himilkon more theatrical. "You want my wife and my children to starve!" he shouted.

"You want *me* to starve," Sostratos retorted.

Himilkon came down again—and then again. He was discovering the papyrus he'd bought did him less good than he'd expected. If he didn't sell it to Sostratos, to whom would he sell it? Rhodes boasted only two or three scribes, who among them wouldn't use in five years what he'd accumulated. As long as Sostratos made it plain he would go to Athens without papyrus if the Phoenician didn't meet his price, he had a good chance of getting it.

And he did. In the end, Himilkon sold him the writing material for one drakhma, four oboloi the roll: less than half of what he'd first proposed. Sostratos knew he would still have to hope papyrus was in short supply in Athens. That would let him bump up his selling price to the point where he made decent money. If it wasn't . . .

If it's not, he thought, *the* Aphrodite *might as well be carrying Damonax's olive oil, for all the profit we'll show on papyrus.* But then he tossed his head. Olive oil was heavy and bulky and took up lots of room. Papyrus wasn't, and didn't. *And I'd sooner haggle with scribes and writers than with oil merchants any day.*

2

BRIGHT MORNING SUN SPARKLED OFF SEAWATER IN THE
Great Harbor at Rhodes. Menedemos stood at the stern of the
Aphrodite, steering-oar tillers in his hands. He was ready to leave on
the instant, even if the akatos remained tied up at the quay. "We've got
all our cargo, don't we?" he asked Sostratos, for the third time since
they'd come to the merchant galley at dawn.

"Yes, we're fully laden," his cousin answered. "That is, unless Damonax's slaves come rushing up with a couple of hundred amphorai of
olive oil at the last instant."

"They'd better not, by the dog!" Menedemos said. "Your precious
brother-in-law doesn't think we're sailing till day after tomorrow, does
he? Let his slaves bring the oil then—and let 'em lug it back when they
find out we're gone."

"That will be a good joke—then," Sostratos said. "We'll hear about it
when we get home. Our fathers will hear about it right away, I'm sure."
He sighed. "Family." By the way he said it, he meant it for a curse.

Up on the quay, Menedemos' father said, "Looks like your crew is
still a couple of men light."

Family, Menedemos thought, in much the same way as Sostratos
had said it. Aloud, he replied only, "Yes, Father." Turning to his
keleustes, he said, "They should be here any moment now, shouldn't
they, Diokles?"

"They should have been here already, skipper," the oarmaster answered unhappily. Diokles was sun-browned, in his mid-forties, with
the broad shoulders and callused hands of a man who'd spent a lot of
years pulling an oar. "I told 'em to show up early. If they're having a
last carouse and holding us up, I'll make 'em pay once they do come
aboard, you see if I don't."

Menedemos wouldn't have wanted Diokles angry at him. Yes, he was
somewhere between fifteen and twenty years younger than the oarmaster, but Diokles had courage to spare and a formidable physique his

loincloth displayed to good advantage. Most of the time, Diokles was as good-natured as any man could be. When he wasn't, though . . .

"Ahoy, the *Aphrodite*!" The hail came from the base of the pier. A barefoot man also wearing only a loincloth—surely a sailor—hurried up toward the merchant galley. "Ahoy!" he called again. "Looking for another rower?"

"Hail, Teleutas." Now Menedemos sounded unhappy. In a low voice, he asked Diokles, "He's not one of the men you're waiting on, is he?"

"He sure isn't," Diokles answered at once. "He always shows up at the last minute, looking for whatever he can get."

"Do we want him aboard?" Sostratos said. "He *is* a thief, even if he hasn't stolen from his crew, and he's no braver than he has to be."

"I know. I know," Menedemos said. "He works as little as he can get away with, too. But he's *here,* and the other fellows aren't."

Sostratos gnawed his lower lip. Diokles looked as if he'd bitten into bad fish. Menedemos felt the same way. But neither his cousin nor the keleustes said no. With a sigh, Menedemos waved Teleutas on. The sailor grinned and came down the gangplank and onto the *Aphrodite.* He had his own pillow to protect his backside from the hard rower's bench where he'd soon perch.

A quarter of an hour later, one of Diokles' chosen men wove his way up to the akatos. Watching him, Menedemos hoped he wouldn't fall off the pier and into the sea. He made it down the gangplank and aboard the *Aphrodite,* though Sostratos had to grab him to keep him from falling flat on his face on the poop deck.

Up on the wharf, Lysistratos laughed. He'd seen plenty of sailors board their ships in that condition. So had Philodemos, but Menedemos' father looked disgusted, not amused. The glance he shot his son said he thought Menedemos made a habit of getting that drunk as soon as he put Rhodes under the horizon. That wasn't fair, or true, but Menedemos knew his father wouldn't listen if he said so.

He turned his attention to the sailor instead. "Hail, Nikodromos," he said, his voice as sweet as unmixed Ariousian from Khios. "Take your place, my dear—we're going to sweat the wine out of you."

"Whatever you want, skipper," Nikodromos said grandly. He found an empty rower's bench and sat down—almost fell down again.

"Maybe we ought to wait for one more man," Sostratos said. "The shape he's in, he'll foul the stroke till noon."

"We'll survive it, and so will he," Menedemos answered. "He'll sober up faster by working than any other way." His chuckle was thoroughly nasty. "And he'll be sorrier about it than he would be any other way, too."

"We won't make much of a show leaving the harbor if he's too sozzled to keep time," Sostratos said.

Menedemos gnawed on the inside of his lower lip. That got home. He liked to leave Rhodes with every bench manned, and with the oars rising and falling as smoothly as if the *Aphrodite* were a five in the Rhodian navy. Most of the sailors had pulled oars in a navy five or a smaller trireme at one time or another, so the hope was by no means forlorn. With Nikodromos drunk, though, he wouldn't be able to look like a warship today.

He was still wondering whether to change his mind when somebody else—not a sailor, but one of the harborside loungers who might be found in any port around the Inner Sea—ran along the pier calling, "I thought you were already loaded here, but there's a troop of slaves carrying amphorai headed this way."

Menedemos and Sostratos exchanged glances of consternation. "Damonax!" they said together. So did their fathers, up on the quay. Menedemos realized he'd just had his mind made up for him. "Cast off!" he called, and the linen ropes that bound the *Aphrodite* to the wharf came in at bow and stern. He dipped his head to Diokles. "Let's get moving, best one."

"Right you are, skipper." The oarmaster held up a small bronze square on a chain and a little mallet with which to strike it. He raised his voice till it carried all the way to the bow: "You ready, boys?" The rowers set themselves at their oars, staring back at him and waiting for the word of command. He smote the square, at the same time calling out, "Rhyppa*pai*!"

The rowers all pulled, even Nikodromos. Diokles clanged the square again, and also used his voice to give the stroke. "Rhyppa*pai*!" At the last syllable, the men pulled. "Rhyppa*pai*!" The *Aphrodite* slid forward, a little farther, a little faster this time as she began to gain momentum. "Rhyppa*pai*! Rhyppa*pai*!"

"Farewell! Safe voyage!" Lysistratos called from the end of the quay. Menedemos' father didn't say anything, but he did wave. Menedemos lifted one hand from the steering-oar tillers to wave back.

Sostratos peered over the *Aphrodite*'s stern, back toward the quay she'd just left. "Oh, my," he said a couple of minutes later. "Here come those slaves—and to the crows with me if Damonax isn't with 'em."

"Tell me what's going on," Menedemos said. "I can't look over my shoulder right now." The merchant galley shared the calm but crowded waters of the Great Harbor with several fishing boats and a couple of round ships. Menedemos chuckled. "Wouldn't do to take my eye off where I'm going and ram somebody when I wasn't looking, eh?"

"I should hope not," Sostratos said. "The damages a jury would vote if you did something like that . . ." He shivered at the idea. "I don't even want to think about it."

"Well, neither do I," Menedemos said, steering toward the narrow outlet at the north end of the harbor. "And we won't have to—if you do your job and tell me what's happening back there."

"All right." But then, maddeningly, his cousin paused again. "Sorry," Sostratos said after a moment. "A round ship just passed between us and the quay, so I couldn't see. Now I can. The slaves have set down their amphorai, and Damonax is saying something to our fathers. Whatever it is, he's upset—he's pounding his fist into the palm of his other hand. A teacher of rhetoric couldn't do it any better."

"Won't make an obolos' worth of difference with my father," Menedemos predicted.

"Looks as if you're right," Sostratos said. "Uncle Philodemos is just standing there, tossing his head again and again. What's that line in the *Iliad* where Akhilleus has been praying to Zeus that Patroklos should drive Hektor away from the ships of the Akhaioi and come back safe himself? Zeus hears, but—?"

"'The father granted him the one prayer, but tossed his head at the other,'" Menedemos quoted at once; he knew Homer well.

"Thank you, my dear. That's just the line I wanted," Sostratos said. "The only difference is, your father's not granting any of Damonax's prayers. And Damonax is getting madder and madder, too. Now he's cupping his hands in front of his mouth—he's going to try to shout to us."

Thin and faint across the widening stretch of water, Menedemos heard, "Ahoy, the *Aphrodite*! Come back and pick up some cargo!"

"Shall I answer him?" Sostratos asked. "I could yell back to the pier, I think."

"Not a word!" Menedemos said. "Put a hand behind your ear and pretend you can't make out what he's saying." Sostratos did. He wasn't the greatest actor, but across four or five plethra of seawater he didn't have to be.

Damonax yelled again. This time, Menedemos really did have trouble making out what he was saying. Sostratos kept that hand behind his ear. He started to laugh. So did several of the rowers, who also looked back at where they'd been. "Don't foul up the stroke, you whipworthy rascals!" Diokles shouted at them. "Poseidon's prick, you're clumsy enough already."

"What's so funny?" Menedemos asked.

"My brother-in-law's jumping up and down on the wharf, like a three-year-old when you tell him he can't have another piece of honey cake," Sostratos answered.

"Somebody ought to give him a good thrashing, the way you do with a three-year-old who has a fit when you tell him he can't have another piece of honey cake," Menedemos said.

"That would be nice," his cousin agreed. "He's right by the edge of the pier now. Maybe he'll fall in. Maybe your father—or mine—will help him fall in." Menedemos waited in eager anticipation. But then Sostratos tossed his head. Disappointment in his voice, he went on, "No such luck. The slaves are picking up the jars of oil and taking them away, and Damonax is going with them."

"Too bad," Menedemos said. "I'd have loved it if he went into the drink instead."

"I just hope he doesn't take it out on Erinna, that's all." Sostratos sighed. "Family."

"Family," Menedemos echoed, and gave all his attention back to the *Aphrodite*. A big, beamy round ship was bearing down on her, great square sail full of the breeze from out of the north, hold full of grain or wine or—irony—olive oil. The round ship was about as maneuverable as an avalanche. Like the *Aphrodite*, like any ship around the Inner Sea, she had eyes painted at her bow, but how much good did they do when she couldn't get out of her own way? And Menedemos would have bet the round ship's goose-headed sternpost had more brains than the man handling her steering oars.

Menedemos pulled the port-side steering-oar tiller toward him and pushed the starboard tiller as far away from him. Graceful as a dancer, the *Aphrodite* swung to port and slipped past the lumbering round ship. Sailors on the round ship's deck waved as the merchant galley glided by. Most of the *Aphrodite*'s crew were too busy to wave back.

Long fortified moles to the east and north protected the Great Harbor of Rhodes from storms. The opening between them was only a couple of plethra wide. Side by side with a little fishing boat from whose crew Sikon might buy the evening's opson, Menedemos steered the akatos out of the harbor and onto the open sea.

As SOSTRATOS DID EVERY SAILING SEASON, he discovered how much the *Aphrodite*'s motion changed when she left the calm waters of the harbor and braved the Inner Sea. Before, all he'd noticed was the forward thrust each time her oars bit into the water. Now the light chop made her pitch up and down as her bow rode over the waves and down into the troughs between them.

Sostratos' stomach felt as if it were lurching in the same way as the akatos. Gulping, he hoped the barley porridge he'd had for breakfast would stay down. He looked forward from the poop deck. A few sailors were similarly greenish, but only a few. That was how things usually went. Sostratos gulped again.

"Use the rail if you've got to give it back, boys," Menedemos said, on the whole in a kindly way. "The bilges get foul enough without adding puke to the mix." He lowered his voice to ask, "Are you all right, Sostratos?"

"I'll be all right in a few days," Sostratos answered. "I wish this didn't happen every sailing season, but it does. I need a few days to get my sea legs, that's all."

"You look a little paler than usual," Menedemos said.

"I'll be fine in—" Sostratos stopped, gulped once more, clapped a hand to his mouth, and took two quick steps over to the rail. Breakfast did not stay down, but he put it neatly in the sea. "A pestilence," he wheezed when he could speak again. "Been a long time since I've actually gone and heaved."

"Happens to a lot of people," his cousin said, with the ease of one whom seasickness didn't bother. "Maybe now you're over it, the way some pregnant women are when they throw up in the morning."

"I hope so!" Sostratos spat to get the vile taste out of his mouth. Spitting didn't do much good. He dipped some wine from an amphora carried for the crew. Rinsing his mouth with that helped more. He spat out one mouthful, then swallowed another. His stomach didn't rise in immediate rebellion, which he took as a good sign.

Once the *Aphrodite* was well out of the Great Harbor, Menedemos took half the men off the oars, letting them row from every other bench. He'd started out with all forty benches filled for the sake of swank. Out on the open sea, he usually used eight or ten men on a side, and rotated the crew every couple of hours. That way, he could have fresh men rowing when he really needed them: escaping or fighting pirates, pushing forward against a headwind, or clawing away from the shore in case of storm.

The merchant galley rounded the northernmost tip of the polis—and the island—of Rhodes. Sostratos pointed to the marble temple of Demeter, whose gleaming white bulk stood out from the swarm of red tile roofs. "Our houses are somewhere not far from there," he said. "I wish I could pick out mine, but it's just another roof from here."

"I'm not sorry to be gone," Menedemos said. "I suppose I even owe your brother-in-law a vote of thanks."

"For what?" Sostratos said, and then, "Oh! You mean for nagging our fathers?"

"I sure do. If he hadn't got my father good and mad, we'd still be stuck in Rhodes, playing knucklebones and twiddling our thumbs. The biggest reason we got to sail so soon is that our fathers wanted him to shut up and go away."

"I know," Sostratos said. "And I'll give you another reason to be grateful to good old thick-headed Damonax. Without him, we wouldn't have had a chance to get up to Athens soon enough to catch the Greater Dionysia, and now we do. I tell you, my dear, you haven't lived till you've seen the theater in Athens. There's nothing like it in any other polis in the world."

"I'm looking forward to it," Menedemos said. "That is one of the reasons I wanted to sail—not the only reason, mind you, but one of them."

"The tragedies will probably be revivals," Sostratos said, "but I keep telling you there are some good comic poets still writing."

As usual, his cousin said, "Give me Aristophanes any day. I'll believe anybody can match him when I see it, and not till then."

That could have started another argument, had Sostratos let it.

Instead, he only smiled and shrugged. Menedemos was loyal to Aristophanes as he was loyal to Homer. Argument wouldn't change that. In both poetry and drama, Sostratos had more modern tastes. Argument wasn't likely to change that, either.

Once well clear of the northern tip of Rhodes, Menedemos swung the *Aphrodite* to port, so that she headed west. Sostratos peered north, toward the haze-shrouded Karian coast. As with Rhodes, the rains of fail and winter had left it bright with greenery. When the merchant galley came back at the end of summer, the sun would have baked it sere and brown. Minor islands—Syme, Khalke, Telos—lay ahead. They too looked green and inviting. Sostratos had trouble imagining duller places to live, though.

"Think this breeze will hold, Diokles?" Menedemos asked.

"Reckon it ought to, skipper, for a while, anyway," the oarmaster replied.

"Well, let's get some use out of the sail, then." Menedemos raised his voice to call out to the crew: "Lower the sail from the yard."

The men hurried to obey. Using the brails—lines that ran from the top of the merchant galley's square sail to the bottom—they quickly spread it, then swung the yard from the starboard bow back to the stern at the port side to take best advantage of the wind. The sail, sewn together from small pieces of linen, filled with air. The mast creaked a little as it took the force of the wind. The *Aphrodite*'s bronze ram, greened from all its time in the sea, dug deeper into the water.

"Seeing all the squares the brails and the seams make on the sail always makes me think of geometry lessons," Sostratos said. "What can we prove from the figure before us? What is the area of this rectangle or that one?"

"Geometry lessons." Menedemos shuddered. "All I remember when I think of them is the schoolmaster with his stick. He drew blood sometimes, the polluted rogue."

"I didn't get hit all that often," Sostratos said.

"No—you were the one who always had his lessons straight," Menedemos said. "The other boys in the class didn't love you for it."

"I know." Sostratos sighed. "I've never had any trouble understanding being disliked for doing things wrong. Who wants a bungler around? But having people hate you for doing what's right, doing what you're supposed to—that always seemed unfair to me."

"You made the rest of us look bad," his cousin said.

"You should have paid attention, too, then," Sostratos said. "Those lessons weren't that hard."

"Not to you, maybe," Menedemos said. "As far as I was concerned, the master might have been speaking Aramaic. Perimeter and hypotenuse and isosceles and I don't know what all else." He took a hand off the tiller and held it up. "And don't you start explaining them to me, either. I don't have to worry about them any more."

Sostratos' ears burned. He *had* been on the point of launching into a geometry lesson. Like most of what he'd studied, mathematics had come easy for him. That it hadn't for Menedemos and the other boys still perplexed him. But if it wasn't a matter of their not studying, not paying attention, what was it?

He'd hardly posed the question in his own mind before Menedemos said, "Some of us are good at some things, others at others. You soaked up lessons the way a soft cloth soaks up water. But you won't claim you're better than I am at figuring out how people work, I hope."

"Oh, I might claim it, but it wouldn't be true," Sostratos said. "You have the edge on me there." He plucked at his beard. "I wonder why that should be."

"People would be boring if everybody were just like everybody else," Menedemos said. "We'd all go around like *this*"—he looked very severe and stiffened his body till he almost seemed cast from bronze—"as if we were so many Spartan hoplites all in a line in the phalanx."

Laughing, Sostratos said, "Why couldn't you make us all into pretty girls? But if we were all pretty girls, what would be the point of chasing one?"

"There's always a point to chasing pretty girls." Menedemos spoke with great conviction. But even joking with Sostratos hadn't made him stop paying attention to the *Aphrodite* and the breeze. "Swing the yard forward a little more," he called to the sailors.

As the men made the adjustment and the stays creaked, Sostratos asked, "Do you think we can go all the way to Knidos today?"

His cousin looked ahead. Knidos lay at the end of a long spit of land jutting west into the sea from the coast of Karia. At last, regretfully, Menedemos tossed his head. "If we'd put to sea earlier in the day, I do believe I'd try it, and sail on by the stars if we weren't there by sunset.

As things are, though, it's too much to ask of the sailors on their first day out. We'll put in at Syme."

"All right." Sostratos would have done the same himself. Sometimes, though, Menedemos liked to push things. Sostratos pointed to the little island ahead. "Will you use that bay in the south where we put in a few years ago?"

"No, I was thinking of anchoring at the town on the north coast," Menedemos answered. "It's not much of a town, I know, but in a way that's all the better. The men can go into a tavern without being tempted to run off and desert."

"Gods know that's true," Sostratos agreed. "Nobody in his right mind would want to desert at Syme. No matter what you were trying to escape, what could be worse than staying there the rest of your days?"

Menedemos considered that. He didn't need long to shudder. "Nothing I can think of," he replied.

LITTLE FISHING BOATS COMING BACK from their day's work bobbed around the *Aphrodite* as her bow anchors went into the sea in front of the town of Syme. The town lay on a sheltered bay of the island with which it shared a name. Most of the fishing boats beached themselves, the men aboard them hauling them farther out of the water than oars could drive them. Menedemos had beached the merchant galley in the sheltered bay of which Sostratos had spoken. He didn't feel like doing it here. If trouble came, he wanted to be able to get away in a hurry. He couldn't very well do that with a beached ship.

"These folks are probably all right," Diokles said, bearing down just a little on the word *probably*.

"I know," Menedemos said. "If two or three other ships were here with us, I think I'd run her up onto the sand. This way . . . no. When fall came and we didn't get back to Rhodes, somebody could come after us, and they might say, 'The *Aphrodite*? Oh, no, she didn't put in here. She must have come to grief somewhere else.' Who could give 'em the lie? I don't *think* they'd do that, mind you, but why tempt 'em?"

"You get no arguments from me, skipper," the keleustes said. "*Why tempt 'em?* is just right, far as I'm concerned."

Up and down the length of the *Aphrodite*, sailors stretched and twisted, working kinks out of muscles they hadn't used all winter. Some of them rubbed olive oil onto their blisters. Teleutas, who happened to be back by the poop deck, rubbed something else on them instead, from a small flask he'd stuck under his bench. Menedemos sniffed. "Isn't that turpentine?" he asked, his eyebrows leaping in surprise.

"That's right," the sailor said.

"Doesn't it burn like fire?" Menedemos said.

"It's not so bad," Teleutas answered. "It hardens the flesh instead of making it soft, the way oil does. I was talking with an Epeirote sailor in a tavern. He said they use it up there, and I thought I'd give it a try."

"Better you than me," Menedemos said.

Another rower, a former sponge diver named Moskhion, asked, "Can we take the boat and go ashore, skipper? We can buy ourselves some wine and some better grub than we've got on the ship here. Maybe there's a brothel in town, too."

"I don't know about that," Menedemos said. "This isn't what you'd call a big place, and ships don't put in here all that often. But yes, you can go find out, if you have a mind to."

The merchant galley towed her boat behind her, on a line tied to the sternpost. The boat was new. She'd lost the old one the sailing season before, on the way back to Rhodes from Phoenicia. When two pirate ships attacked off the Lykian coast, a sailor had cut the old boat loose to help the *Aphrodite* fight them off. And so she had—but she hadn't been able to go back and recover the boat.

Soldiers pulled the new boat alongside the akatos and clambered down into her. She carried half a dozen oars—small ones, compared to the nine-cubit sweeps that propelled the *Aphrodite*—and could hold a dozen men. The sailors briefly argued over who would row her back to the ship for the next group, then set off for the town of Syme.

"Are you going ashore?" Sostratos asked.

Menedemos tossed his head and mimed an enormous yawn. "Not likely, my dear. I might never wake up again. What about you?"

"I'm tempted," his cousin answered. "After all, Syme's less than a day's sail from Rhodes. You can see this place any time you look west. Even so, I've never been into the town."

"Yes, and we both know why, too: it's not worth going into," Menedemos said.

"Too true." Sostratos thought for a moment, then shrugged. "I live in Rhodes. I've stayed in Athens. I've visited Taras and Syracuse—poleis that *are* poleis, if you know what I mean. I'm sorry, but I can't get excited about Syme. This is one step up from a village—and a small step, too."

"That's the way I feel about it," Menedemos said. "Well, if we're going to stay aboard ship, shall we have supper? What Syracusan wouldn't be jealous of our feast?"

Sostratos laughed. Syracuse was famous for its fancy cooking. Some cooks from the Sicilian city had even written books of their favorite recipes for opson, recipes full of rare, expensive fish, spices from all around the Inner Sea and beyond, and rich cheeses. The *Aphrodite* carried coarse, hard barley rolls for sitos and olives and onions and hard, crumbly, salty cheese for opson to go with it. If the crew wanted fish as a relish, they had to put lines over the side and catch it themselves.

The rough red wine in the amphorai was a suitable match for the rest of the meal. Menedemos could think of no worse condemnation. "This stuff almost makes you want to drink water," he said.

"Drinking water isn't healthy," Sostratos said.

"You think this wine is?" Menedemos returned. "You can taste more of the pitch on the inside of the jar than you can of the grapes." He sipped again, and pulled a face. "Of course, considering what the grapes *do* taste like, maybe that's just as well."

"It's not supposed to be anything special. It's just supposed to be wine," his cousin said. "And even if it isn't the best stuff Dionysos ever made, it won't give you a flux of the bowels, the way water would."

"Well, that's true." Menedemos flipped a couple of more drops of wine onto the poop deck. "My thanks, great Dionysos, for arranging that we don't get the galloping shits from wine—for we'd surely drink it even if we did."

"That's peculiar praise for the god," Sostratos said, smiling. "But then, Dionysos is a peculiar sort of god."

"How do you mean?" Menedemos asked.

"Just for instance, Homer doesn't say much about him," Sostratos answered. "He talks much more about the other Olympians—even Hephaistos has a couple of scenes where he's the center of attention, but Dionysos doesn't."

"That's true," Menedemos said thoughtfully. "There is that passage in the sixth book of the *Iliad,* though. You know the one I mean:

'*I* would not fight with the gods who dwell in the heavens.
For not even the son of Dryas, mighty Lykourgos,
Could stay at strife for long with the gods who dwell in the
　　heavens.
He once drove off the attendants of madness-bringing Dionysos
Near sacred Nyseion: they all
Let their mystical gear fall to the ground. Dionysos, afraid,
Plunged into the salt sea, and Thetis received him into her bosom
While he feared. For the man put him in great terror through his
　　shout.'"

"Yes, that's probably the place where the poet talks most about him," Sostratos said. "But isn't it strange to have a god who's a coward?"

"Dionysos did have his revenge later," Menedemos said.

"But that was later," Sostratos reminded him. "Can you imagine any of the other Olympians, even Aphrodite, leaping into the sea on account of a mortal man's shout?"

"Well, no," Menedemos admitted.

"And Herodotos says Dionysos came from Egypt, and Euripides says he came out of India, and just about everyone says he came from Thrace," Sostratos said. "None of the rest of the Olympians is foreign. And some of Dionysos' rites . . ." He shivered, though the evening was fine and mild. "Give me a god like Phoibos Apollo any day."

"Dionysos' rites on Rhodes aren't so bad," Menedemos said.

"No, not on Rhodes," his cousin agreed. "But Rhodes is a tidy, modern, civilized place. Even back on Rhodes, though, they get wilder if you leave our polis and the other towns and go out into the countryside. And in some of the backwoods places on the mainland of Hellas . . . My dear fellow, Euripides knew what he was talking about when he wrote the rending scenes in the *Bakkhai.*"

"That's a play I've only heard about," Menedemos said. "I've never seen it performed, and I've never read it."

"Oh, you must, best one!" Sostratos exclaimed. "If we're lucky, maybe they'll revive it in Athens while we're there. It's . . . quite something. I don't think there's ever been another play that shows the power of a god so strongly."

"If a freethinker like you says that, I suppose I have to take it seriously," Menedemos said.

"It's a marvelous play," Sostratos said earnestly. "And the poetry in the choruses is almost unearthly, it's so beautiful. No one else ever wrote anything like it—and Euripides never wrote anything else like it, either."

Menedemos respected his cousin's judgment, even if he didn't always agree with it. "If I ever get the chance, I'll see it," he said.

"You should," Sostratos said. "In fact, you ought to find someone who has a copy and read it. There are bound to be a few in a polis the size of Rhodes—and of course there'll be more than a few in Athens."

"If I ever get the chance," Menedemos repeated. He spat an olive pit into the bay. From the shore came the noise of raucous song. He grinned. "Sounds like the men are having a good time. I hope Syme's still standing in the morning, what there is of it."

"It should be," Sostratos said. "They were in Rhodes yesterday, and they only just put to sea. They shouldn't have that urge to tear places to pieces—it's too early in the voyage."

The crash that followed on the heels of his words could only have been an amphora shattering. Menedemos sighed and said, "Let's hope nobody broke that over anybody's head." He got out his himation. Sailors prided themselves in going about in nothing but a chiton regardless of the weather, but a mantle also made a good blanket. He wrapped himself in the rectangle of thick woolen cloth and lay down on the poop deck.

Sostratos did the same. As he twisted and turned, trying to get comfortable, he said, "We've been sleeping in beds all winter long. Bare planks aren't so comfortable any more."

"It's not too bad," Menedemos said, cradling his head in his arms. "If it were raining, now . . ." He yawned. He wasn't really that sleepy; he was trying to convince himself as well as Sostratos. It must have worked, for the next thing he knew the eastern horizon glowed pink and gold. He yawned and stretched. Something in his back crackled. He got to his feet.

Sostratos still lay there snoring. Given the chance, he usually slept later than Menedemos. He didn't get the chance today—Menedemos stirred him with his foot. Sostratos' eyes flew open. "What was that for?" he asked blurrily.

"Time to get up. Time to get going," Menedemos answered. When he was awake, he was *awake.* "We've got a full day's sailing ahead of us." Sostratos groaned and pulled the himation up over his head. Menedemos stirred him again, less gently this time. He drew another groan from his cousin, who emerged from the mantle like a tortoise poking its nose out of its shell. "Come on, my dear," Menedemos said cheerfully. "Like it or not, rosy-fingered dawn has found us."

Like an old, old man, Sostratos stood up. "I don't like it," he said.

WATERED WINE AND BARLEY rolls dipped in olive oil helped reconcile Sostratos to being awake. At Diokles' command, the rowers backed oars. They pulled hard, as if eager to get the *Aphrodite* away from Syme as soon as they could. None of them had a bandaged head, so Sostratos supposed that amphora the evening before hadn't fractured a skull.

"Let's get in a little practice," Menedemos said. "At the oarmaster's command—starboard oars hold the backstroke, port oars forward."

"Port oars . . . forward!" Diokles bawled. The rowers obeyed quite smoothly. The *Aphrodite* spun, turning almost in her own length. When her bow pointed north, out to sea, the keleustes called, "Both sides . . . forward!" The akatos sped away.

Sostratos spent the first couple of hours of the day's sailing arguing with Menedemos. "Why do you want to stop at Knidos?" he asked.

"Uh, to trade?" When Menedemos sounded most reasonable, he also sounded most annoying. So it seemed to Sostratos, anyhow.

"Very well, O best one: to trade. And what will they have in Knidos to trade?" Sostratos never stopped to wonder if, when he sounded most like Sokrates, he also sounded most annoying.

"Well, the usual run of things they have there," Menedemos replied.

"Exactly—the usual run of things," Sostratos agreed. "If we were going somewhere besides Athens, that might be good enough. But since we *are* bound for Athens, why waste the time at Knidos? Why not head straight for Kos? Koan silk is special enough to do well anywhere. The rich Athenians will like it, and so will the Macedonian officers in Kassandros' garrison."

"Koan silk isn't so special as we thought it was," Menedemos said.

"That stuff I got in Sidon last summer, that stuff from out of the east, puts it in the shade. I didn't think even the gods could weave cloth like that."

"Neither did I," Sostratos admitted. "But the trader had only that little bit of it, and we got a good price for it from Ptolemaios' brother, Menelaos. As far as the Athenians are concerned, Koan silk is the best there is. And so, we ought to stop at Kos."

"Why not Knidos *and* Kos?" Menedemos asked.

"Because we probably won't find anything in Knidos that's worth taking to Athens. And because, if we stop at every ordinary polis between here and Athens, we'll never get there in time for the Greater Dionysia."

His cousin took his right hand off the steering-oar tiller and wagged a finger at him. "That's the real reason you want to hurry. You hardly care about trade at all. What kind of merchant does that make you?"

"One who likes drama," Sostratos said. "Don't you?"

"Of course I do, but I like profit more," Menedemos said.

"So do I," Sostratos said. "And I'm telling you there's not enough profit in Knidos to make stopping there worth our while."

"I'm the captain, by the dog of Egypt," Menedemos said. "If I want to stop at Knidos, I cursed well will."

"I'm the toikharkhos," Sostratos retorted. "If you won't listen to me when it comes to cargo and money, why bring me along?"

They went round and round and back and forth. They did it in a low voice, neither showing too much excitement, for neither wanted the crew to know how seriously they disagreed. Every so often, Menedemos would break off to steer the ship or call an order to the men handling the sail. Then he would turn back to Sostratos and start up again. When he said, "I'm the captain," for the fourth time, Sostratos really did lose his temper.

"Yes, you're the captain. *Euge!* for you," he said. "But what's the rest of the crew supposed to do when the captain is an idiot?"

"Don't tell me how to sail the ship," Menedemos snapped.

"I'm not. I'm trying to tell you *where* to sail her, which is a different matter altogether. Where has to do with what we buy and sell, and that's my business. Let me ask it another way: can we make Kos by sundown if this wind holds?"

Menedemos looked as if he wanted to say no. He wanted to, but he couldn't. Sostratos would know he was lying. They could make Kos even if the wind died, but that would strain the rowers. Sostratos could see why Menedemos wouldn't want to make them work too hard on the second day out from Rhodes.

"Perhaps you'd sooner go to Halikarnassos—the strait between Kos and mainland isn't even close to a hundred stadia wide," Sostratos said sweetly.

His cousin gave him a harried look, and muttered, "Oh, shut up." Thanks to his affair with that prominent citizen's wife, he couldn't set foot in Halikarnassos without the risk—the likelihood—of getting killed. After a moment, though, he glared at Sostratos. "Maybe the fellow got killed in Ptolemaios' siege summer before last."

"Yes, O marvelous one, maybe he did," Sostratos said. "On the other hand, maybe he didn't. Do you care to take the chance?"

For a moment, he wondered if he'd made a mistake. Menedemos took an appalling number of chances, and enjoyed doing it. Here, though, he tossed his head, which only proved how serious the prominent Halikarnassian had been about sending him across the Styx. He glanced longingly in the direction of Knidos, which lay dead ahead, but then pulled the steering-oar tiller in his left hand a little toward him and pushed the steering-oar tiller in his right away from him. The *Aphrodite* swung slightly to port, so she would skirt the peninsula at whose tip Knidos sat.

"We'll go to Kos," Menedemos said. "Are you happy now? Will you quit nagging me? If I had a wife and she pestered me like that, I'd make her sorry for it."

"I think it's a good business decision," Sostratos said.

"I know you do," Menedemos answered. "I'm not nearly sure I agree with you, but you win this time. You're stubborn as a donkey, do you know that?" He looked Sostratos up and down. "The resemblance doesn't end there, either."

"Thank you so much, my dear," Sostratos said. His cousin took no notice of him, but concentrated—most ostentatiously concentrated—on steering the ship. Stung, Sostratos made his way past the grunting, sweating rowers and the rest of the *Aphrodite*'s crew to the merchant galley's tiny foredeck. Whenever he stood up there, he thought of the peafowl the *Aphrodite* had carried west to Great Hellas three years before. They'd made good money on the birds from rich Italiote Hellenes, and from a richer Samnite visiting Taras who'd bought the peacock. They'd made good money, yes, but Sostratos hoped he never saw another peafowl as long as he lived.

He also thought of Aristeidas, who'd spent so much time up here doing lookout duty. But the sharp-eyed sailor's bones lay in Ioudaia. Sostratos pounded a fist down on the rail. The robbers there could easily have killed him, too.

Like most of the cities of southwestern Anatolia, Knidos was nominally free and autonomous. Also like most of them, it held a garrison of Antigonos' soldiers. A couple of war galleys—big, beamy fives, full of rowers and marines—patrolled in front of the harbor. Sostratos wondered if one of them would come rushing out to investigate the *Aphrodite*. He wouldn't have been surprised. Antigonos' men were no less arrogant than those who followed Ptolemaios or Kassandros or Lysimakhos or, he supposed, Seleukos. The Macedonian marshals ruled the civilized world. Poleis like Rhodes, poleis that really were free and autonomous, were few and far between nowadays.

To Sostratos' relief, the fives kept prowling back and forth, back and forth. He didn't *think* one of their skippers would have been highhanded enough to plunder the *Aphrodite*. That would have offended Rhodes. He didn't think so, but he was just as well pleased not to have to find out.

Also to his relief, the wind blew more from the east than from the north as the merchant galley made her way up through the channel between the mainland and the little island of Nisyros to the west. Menedemos kept eight men on each side at the oars to help the sail propel the ship through the water. Had the wind turned against the *Aphrodite,* he would have had to raise the sail to the yard and put more men on the oars to make any decent headway: either that or tack like a round ship, and almost as slowly as a round ship would have.

I wish there were a way to get closer to the wind than a square sail can, Sostratos thought. After a moment, though, he shrugged. He'd sailed from Sicily to Phoenicia, and he'd never seen any other kind of rig. That was all too likely to mean no other kind was practical. He tried to imagine a different way to mount a sail, tried and felt himself failing.

Kos climbed up out of the sea ahead. Menedemos pointed to some tumbledown ruins on the southwestern coast. "I wish Astypalaia were still the Koans' main town," he said. "We'd be almost there already."

"I wouldn't want to live in what was left of a polis after a Spartan sack *and* an earthquake," Sostratos said. "The town they have now is better situated all the way around—it looks right across the channel to

Halikarnassos. And it's laid out in a sensible grid like Rhodes, so a stranger has some chance of finding his way around. The streets in the old city were probably tracks that wandered wherever they wanted."

"Every word you say is true, my dear," Menedemos replied. "But Astypalaia's right here in front of our noses, and we've still got some traveling to do before we get to the polis of Kos."

Ptolemaios' galleys prowled in front of Kos. Antigonos' warships patrolled in front of Halikarnassos. Sostratos supposed they clashed every so often. At the moment, they were leaving one another alone, for which he was duly grateful.

The sun was just setting as the *Aphrodite* came to the harbor. Before the akatos could enter, one of Ptolemaios' fives hurried up to look her over. The war galley's banners displayed the eagle of the lord of Egypt. "Heave to!" an officer at the bow shouted.

"*Oöp!*" Diokles called to the rowers, and they rested at their oars.

"What ship are you?" the officer demanded. "Where are you from, what are you carrying, and where are you bound?"

"We're the *Aphrodite,* out of Rhodes and bound for Athens," Sostratos answered. The war galley's flank loomed up out of the water like a wooden wall. She had twice the freeboard of the akatos; her deck stood six or seven cubits above the surface of the sea. A ripe stench wafted out of her oarports. She had two rowers on each thranite and zygite oar, a single man on each bottommost, or thalamite, oar. All the rowers were enclosed under the decking that held marines and kept missiles from striking home. It had to be like an oven in there. Sostratos wondered how often they swabbed out the bilges. Not often enough, by the stink.

"A Rhodian, eh?" the officer said. "What firm?"

"That of Philodemos and Lysistratos," Sostratos said.

The officer turned his head and spoke to some of the men behind him. One of them must have vouched for the firm's existence, for he grunted and asked, "What's your cargo?"

"Crimson dye, ink and papyrus, beeswax, embroidered linen, Rhodian rose perfume . . ." Sostratos replied, thinking, *And no olive oil, gods be praised.*

"All right. Pass on, Rhodian," the officer on the war galley said. "You know, you look like a pirate at first glance."

"Really?" Sostratos raised an astonished eyebrow. "No one's ever told me that before." Behind him, half a dozen sailors snickered and snorted. Ptolemaios' officer scratched his head, as if wondering whether the Rhodian was making sport of him. Too late, Sostratos realized he should have swallowed his sarcasm. Diokles smote the bronze square. The rowers bent their backs. The *Aphrodite* slid toward the harbor. After a long, worrying moment of sitting quiet in the water, the war galley resumed its patrol.

"Come back here a moment, O best one, if you'd be so kind," Menedemos called from the poop deck. Sostratos came. He came with all the eagerness of a small boy summoned to a whipping by his father, and for the same reason. But all Menedemos said was, "You'd do better not to crack wise when that fellow's ship could sink us without even noticing she'd done it."

"Yes, my dear," Sostratos said meekly. Still, he couldn't help adding, "I'm not the only one who's ever done such a thing, you know."

"Are you talking about *me*?" Menedemos demanded in disbelieving tones.

That was too much. "Yes, by the dog, I am talking about you," Sostratos said.

Menedemos reached out and poked him in the ribs. He jumped and squawked. Menedemos laughed. "Got you!" he said. "Got you twice, in fact. I know I've let my tongue run freer than it might have every now and again. That still doesn't mean it's a good idea, whether I do it or you do."

"By the dog," Sostratos said again, this time in an altogether different tone of voice. "Maybe you're growing up."

His cousin looked aggrieved. "Is that a nice thing to tell someone?"

"Some people would think so," Sostratos answered. "But then, they'd already be grown up, so I wouldn't need to say it to them." This time, his cousin looked genuinely affronted, which made him feel a little better.

WHEN MENEDEMOS WOKE UP in a bed, he needed a moment to remember where he was. Hearing Sostratos' snore coming from another bed no more than a cubit away reminded him the two of them had taken a room at an inn not far from the harbor at Kos. Menedemos yawned, scratched, and sat up. Then he scratched again, more earnestly. He hoped he hadn't shared the bed with little guests who hadn't paid for it.

Sunlight slid through the shutters over a narrow window—and poured through a couple of broken slats. Menedemos stood up and used the chamber pot under the bed. Sostratos twisted so that one of those sunbeams fell across his face. He threw up a hand, which sufficed to wake him. "Good day," he said around a yawn of his own.

"And a good day to you." Menedemos held out the pot. "Here. I was going to boot you out of bed anyhow, as soon as I finished using this."

"Thanks. I'm so sorry to disappoint you." Sostratos used the chamber pot, then carried it over to the window. "Coming out!" he called as he opened the shutters. He poured the slops into the street below. An irate yelp said somebody might not have moved fast enough at his warning. He turned back to Menedemos. "Do you suppose the innkeeper will have bread for breakfast?"

Menedemos shrugged. "If he doesn't, we can stop at a bakery or buy something from someone on the street. And then—on to Pixodaros'."

"Pity he couldn't have seen that silk we sold to Menelaos," Sostratos said. "I wonder what he would have made of it."

"He would have made money, that's what," Menedemos said. "But he couldn't have matched that silk. None of the Koan weavers can. If it ever starts coming out of the east regularly, they'll have to find another line of work, because what they make doesn't come close."

"You get no arguments from me. I wouldn't have believed it if I hadn't seen it with my own eyes, but I did." Sostratos headed for the door. "Now the question is, will I see breakfast with my own eyes?"

The innkeeper was munching on a barley roll when the two Rhodians walked into the main room. "No, I don't sell breakfast," he said when Sostratos asked. "You can buy some wine from me, though."

Menedemos tossed his head. "Why do that now and then something to eat later on?" he said. "Come on, Sostratos—we'll get 'em both in the same place." His cousin didn't disagree. The innkeeper's glare burned into their backs as they walked out onto the street.

Pixodaros' house was only a few blocks away, across the street from a brothel full of pretty boys. The slave who opened the door at the silk dealer's exclaimed in surprise: "The Rhodians!" He bowed very low, then went on in accented Greek, "You not come back last year, master think something bad happen."

"No, we're fine," Menedemos answered. "We sailed east last year instead of west, that's all. Not much point coming to Kos when you're bound for Sidon, is there?"

The slave shook his head. "No, sir, none at all. You come in. You both come in. My master, he be glad to see you." He stood aside to let them through the doorway, then hurried past them into the house, calling, "Master, master! The Rhodians is here!"

"Are they?" Menedemos heard Pixodaros say. He had an accent, too: just enough to make someone notice he hadn't been born a Hellene. "Well, that's very good news indeed. Fetch them some wine and something to go with it, Ibanollis."

"Ibanollis," Sostratos murmured, fixing the name in his memory. "Ibanollis. Ibanollis." Menedemos knew his cousin had it now. He relied on Sostratos' memory more than he cared to admit, even to himself.

Out came Pixodaros: a plump, prosperous-looking Karian with a luxuriant black beard just beginning to show streaks of gray. "Hail, Rhodians," he said, bowing to Menedemos and Sostratos before stepping forward to clasp their hands. "Very good to see you again. I feared for your safety: going out on the wine-dark sea is a risky business."

Menedemos smiled. Pixodaros surely used the Homeric epithet to show that, even though he came from barbarian stock, he'd been grafted on to the tree of Hellenic culture. "We're well, as I told your slave," he replied; he wouldn't try to pronounce Ibanollis' name. "We sailed east last year, that's all. *You* seem to be doing splendidly for yourself."

"I'm lucky," Pixodaros said with un-Hellenic modesty. But it was true. He went on, "If my master had had children who lived . . ." He shrugged broad shoulders. Old Xenophanes had died childless and left his business to the slave—a freedman now—who'd been his right-hand man. Had the Hellene had a son—or even a daughter with a husband—Pixodaros would have stayed a slave himself instead of owning slaves. "Come." He waved the Rhodians toward the andron. "Drink wine with me. Eat olives and cheese and bread. So you went east, did you?"

"Yes, to Sidon, and I went down into Ioudaia from there," Sostratos said.

"Well, well. You Hellenes have always had itchy feet, haven't you?" Pixodaros said. "Me, I'm here, and I like being here just fine." Ibanollis came in with a wooden tray with wine and snacks on it. He poured wine for his master and for the Rhodians. Pixodaros spat an olive pit onto the ground, then asked, "Tell me, O most noble ones, did you see any . . . unusual silk while you were in Phoenicia?"

Menedemos and Sostratos looked at each other. "You know of the silk that comes out of the east, then?" Menedemos said.

"I have heard of it. I have not seen it," the Karian answered. "I have heard it is finer than any we make on Kos. Is this true?"

"It is, I'm afraid," Menedemos said. "It's so fine and thin and smooth, it might almost be another fabric. Do you know Zakerbaal son of Tenes, the Sidonian cloth merchant?"

"I have heard his name, but I have never done business with him," Pixodaros replied. "He is the man who had this eastern silk?"

"That's right." Menedemos dipped his head. "I bought twelve bolts from him, paying more than two and a half times their weight in Koan silk. And I sold all twelve bolts to Ptolemaios' brother, Menelaos, at Cypriot Salamis, for a hundred and eight minai of silver." Had Pixodaros been ignorant of Zakerbaal, he would have been tempted to say he'd given the Phoenician merchant even more. But the truth might get back here, and that truth was impressive enough by itself.

It certainly impressed Pixodaros. "By Zeus Labraundeus!" he muttered—Zeus of the double-headed axe, with his cult center at Labraunda, was a leading Karian god. The silk merchant gathered himself. "I find that hard to believe."

"My cousin speaks the truth," Sostratos said. "Give us any oath you please, and we will swear it. You know us well enough to know we don't swear lightly, either."

By Pixodaros' expression, he did know that, and didn't like it. His next question was one that had also occurred to Menedemos: "How much of this new eastern silk will come to the lands around the Inner Sea?"

"I don't think anyone can say yet," Menedemos answered. "Till I got to Sidon, I hadn't even heard of it. I suppose that, since you sell silk yourself, word would have come to you sooner than to most people."

"Yes, I would think so." The Karian emptied his cup, then filled it again. A sigh made his wide shoulders sag. "All I can do is keep selling what I make. No matter how fine this other stuff may be, I know mine is good, too. Anyone who wants it will still have to pay the proper price." He looked a challenge at the two Rhodians.

"Well, best one, when we were here two years ago, we worked out a bargain for silk and dye and perfume," Menedemos said. "That suited us well enough. How did your side of it work out?"

"Not bad," Pixodaros said. "Will you expect the same rates again?"

"Certainly," Sostratos said.

"Why shouldn't we?" Menedemos added.

"Because, if you went to Phoenicia, you got the crimson dye yourselves," Pixodaros answered. "You paid less for it than you would have if you'd bought it in Rhodes."

"But we had the cost of bringing it back ourselves," Menedemos countered. "That isn't cheap, not with the *Aphrodite.*"

"And we got attacked by pirates off the Lykian coast," Sostratos said. "The dye almost didn't get here. *We* almost didn't get here."

"Oimoi!" Pixodaros exclaimed. "Tell me your story."

Menedemos and Sostratos told it together. As usual, Menedemos did most of the talking. He couldn't be quite so dramatic as he would have liked, for he knew his cousin would add a dry correction or two if he strayed too far from the facts. Even without embellishment, the story was a good one.

When the Rhodians finished, Pixodaros clapped his hands and said, *"Euge!* I am glad to see both of you here and safe."

"Believe me, we're glad to be here and safe," Sostratos said. "But now you see why we charge what we charge for the crimson dye."

Although Menedemos dipped his head in agreement, he sent Sostratos an annoyed look. This wasn't the time to start banging away at business again. Sostratos should have smiled and told another story, or a joke, or something of the sort. Menedemos reached for the oinokhoe and poured his winecup and his cousin's full again. Dickers had a rhythm to them, no less than tunes on the kithara. Make one go too fast and it would come out wrong, just as a tune would. Sostratos didn't always have a feel for that.

To make sure this bargain went as it should, Menedemos asked, "Has any news from Athens reached Kos this sailing season?"

Pixodaros hesitated for a fraction of a heartbeat before tossing his head. Menedemos had seen that response before from barbarians who wanted to seem as Hellenic as they could. Their first impulse was to shake the head, as most foreign folk did, and they needed that tiny moment to catch themselves and remember Hellenes did things differently. The Karian answered, "No, not yet. Ships are only beginning to put to sea this spring, and none from Athens has come here yet."

Sostratos asked, "Has any ship bound for Athens been here to buy silk?"

That was a legitimate question. Menedemos would have asked it if Sostratos hadn't beaten him to it. This time, Pixodaros tossed his head without hesitation. "No, you are the first," he replied, and smiled a sly smile. "Maybe I should charge you more, because I know you'll make more there."

Sostratos jumped as if stung by a wasp. "That's not just!" he exclaimed.

"He's joking, my dear," Menedemos said. "He wanted to startle you, and he did."

Pixodaros' smile got wider, showing strong, white teeth—he didn't look as if he were one who'd suffer miseries on that account as he got older. "I know it is not just, my friends, and I would not do it. But startling a friend every now and again—you should have seen the look on your face." He laughed out loud.

"Oh." Sostratos looked foolish. But then he managed a small, self-deprecating laugh. He didn't get angry, or at least didn't show anger, for which Menedemos was glad. In his own way, Sostratos was a good bargainer, but he could forget himself. Not here, though.

"Shall we see some silk now?" Menedemos asked, his voice casual. "If it's up to your usual standard—and I'm sure it will be—shall we forge the same sort of bargain as we did two years ago?"

"I think so," the Karian freedman replied. "I made money on it, and I gather you gentlemen did, too." He raised his voice. "Ibanollis! The Rhodians are ready to look at the silk now. Bring the best we have."

"I do," Ibanollis said. "You wait one little bit."

The silk was very good, some of the finest and most transparent Koan weavers made. But it could not match the eastern cloth Menedemos had got from Zakerbaal the Sidonian. Merchants always looked disappointed at the quality of goods they were offered: that was part of the role they played. Here, though, Menedemos and Sostratos had no trouble seeming unimpressed, and Menedemos knew they would have had a hard time acting blasé about this silk if they hadn't seen the other.

Pixodaros sensed they weren't putting on their indifference, too. He said, "You remind me of men going home to ugly wives from the house of a beautiful hetaira. Is this eastern silk really *that* splendid?"

"I'm afraid it is, O best one," Menedemos said soberly. "For its kind, though, what you have here is excellent." He felt like a man praising an ugly wife for the way she managed a home.

With a sigh, Pixodaros said, "Well, I can hope the eastern silk stays in the east for the rest of my life." He suddenly looked anxious. "You do still want to make this bargain, don't you?"

"We wouldn't have come here if we didn't," Sostratos reassured him. "For now, Koan silk is the finest cloth we can get, and it will have a ready market in Athens."

"For now," the Karian muttered under his breath. Menedemos wished his cousin hadn't tacked that on, even if it was true—perhaps especially because it was true. Pixodaros made himself straighten his shoulders, as a Hellene might have done. "I do still have the finest silk made around the Inner Sea." He spoke as if reminding himself as well as the Rhodians.

"Of course you do," Menedemos said soothingly. "We're always pleased to do business with you. Sostratos said it—that's why we're here." Pixodaros smiled. Even so, he had to be wondering how long he and his could stay prosperous. Through his son's lifetime? Through his own? Or only another year or two? Menedemos thought it would be longer than that, but he didn't know. He wouldn't have wanted to do business with that kind of risk hanging over him. By all the signs, neither did Pixodaros. But he didn't have that worry, and the freedman did.

When they left Pixodaros' house, maybe that sense of relief was part of what made Menedemos look across the street. "You know what I'm going to do?" he said. "I'm going to have a go at the boy brothel there. Want to come along?"

"No, thanks," Sostratos said. "I don't much fancy boys."

"Neither do I, usually," Menedemos said. "I feel like it today, though."

"Have fun. I'll see you back at the inn, then," Sostratos said.

The brothelkeeper was a fat Phoenician with a curled beard. His Greek held a guttural accent. "At your service, my master," he said. "Take your pick." He waved at the youths in the main room. Had they been women, they would have been spinning to earn him extra money. Some of them wore silk tunics, as women might have (Menedemos wondered if it was Pixodaros' silk). Others were naked.

Menedemos pointed to a youth of about fifteen with less paint on his face than most of the boys wore. "Him, I think."

"Hearkening and obedience," the whoremaster said with a bow. "Sadyattes, go with the man."

A Lydian, Menedemos thought as the slave got to his feet. "Come with me," the boy said, sounding more resigned than alluring. The room to which he led the Rhodian was small and gloomy, with no furniture but a bed, a stool with a small jar on it, and a chamber pot. It smelled of sweat. Sadyattes pulled his chiton off over his head. He was a little pudgier and a little hairier than Menedemos had expected. *Perfection is for the gods,* Menedemos thought. *He'll do.* Still sounding resigned, Sadyattes asked, "What do you want?"

"Nothing fancy—just the usual," Menedemos said.

"All right." Instead of bending over straightaway, the slave reached for the jar. "Will you use some olive oil first? It's . . . easier that way."

Menedemos pulled off his own chiton. "Well, why not?" he answered. "Go ahead—put some on me." The brothel boy obeyed, gently pushing back his foreskin as he rose. Sadyattes' fingers were skilled and knowing. "Now turn around," Menedemos said after a little while. The boy did. Menedemos took his pleasure. Sadyattes gave no sign of taking any of his own, but boys seldom did. Menedemos patted him on the backside, then gave him an obolos. "Here. You don't need to tell that fellow with the fancy beard you got this."

"I thank you, most noble one." The slave put the little silver coin in his mouth.

Whistling, Menedemos left the boy brothel, which was more than Sadyattes could do. When he got back to the inn, Sostratos asked, "How was it?"

He thought a moment, then shrugged. "Nothing fancy," he said. "Just the usual."

"RHYPPA*PAI*!" DIOKLES CALLED. "Rhyppa*pai*! Rhyppa*pai*!" The rowers bent their backs; some of them grunted with effort at each stroke.

Sostratos looked toward the Anatolian mainland, which slowly crawled past to starboard. Then, deliberately, he looked to port again.

A smooth horizon seemed to rise and fall less than a corrugated one. As if to show how much he approved of that, he said, "I don't like the Ikarian Sea."

"No, eh?" Menedemos grinned at him. "Why am I not surprised?"

"Because it's got some of the roughest water anywhere in the Inner Sea?" Sostratos suggested. He gulped and silently told his stomach to stay where it belonged. For the moment, it seemed willing to listen to him.

His cousin chuckled. "And all the time I thought it was because you sympathized with Ikaros, who came crashing down somewhere around here."

"As a matter of fact, I do sympathize with Ikaros," Sostratos said. "I sympathize with Daidalos, who after all made his son's wings, even more. What's wrong with pursuing knowledge, I'd like to know?"

"People ought to pursue good sense first," Menedemos said.

"Really?" Sostratos raised an eyebrow. "And how can a man have any idea of what good sense is without knowledge? Suppose you tell me that."

"Oh, no, you don't." Menedemos tossed his head. "You're trying to lure me into a philosophical discussion. No thanks, my dear; I don't want to play."

"Not even when you started it?" Sostratos made a reproachful clucking noise. "For shame. You remind me of a man who starts arguments in taverns and then ducks out before the fists fly."

"I'd rather talk about where we put in next," Menedemos said. "That has money attached to it."

"So it does." Sostratos pointed north. "We're bound for Samos and then, I thought, for Khios. With the fine wine they make there . . ."

"As a matter of fact, I was thinking of passing up Khios altogether and going straight on to Lesbos," Menedemos said.

"You were?" Sostratos gaped. That came like a thunderbolt from a clear sky. "By the dog of Egypt, why? We can bring Ariousian from Khios to Athens and make a splendid profit. There's no better wine in the world than Ariousian."

"Yes, and don't the Khians know it?" Menedemos replied. "With what they charge, we have to bump up our prices so high, hardly anyone can afford to buy from us."

"That's the point of having an akatos," Sostratos said. "For bulk

goods, we could take out a round ship and not have to pay all our rowers."

"Lesbos makes good wines, too," his cousin said. "Not quite up to
Ariousian, I admit, but plenty good enough for the *Aphrodite* to carry.
And Lesbos has something Khios doesn't."

"What?" Sostratos demanded; he couldn't think of anything.

But Menedemos could: "Truffles. They grow close by Mytilene, and
they're always best in the springtime. Tell me the rich Athenians and
the Macedonian officers in the garrison won't want truffles."

Sostratos couldn't, and he knew it. "Truffles," he murmured, intrigued in spite of himself. "Isn't that interesting? I have to hand it to
you, my dear—they never would have occurred to me. Still . . . I hate
to spend the extra time on the way."

"On account of the Greater Dionysia?" Menedemos asked, and
Sostratos dipped his head. Menedemos took a hand off the steering-
oar tiller to shake a reproachful finger. "Profit first, best one. Profit
first, drama second."

"Normally, that's a good rule," Sostratos said. "But the Greater
Dionysia is special."

"I'll tell you what's special," Menedemos said. "The clink of the
owls the Athenians'll lay down for truffles and good Lesbian wine is
special, that's what."

"I know we have to make money." Sostratos said it with more than
a little shame in his voice. A *kalos k'agathos,* a proper Hellenic gentleman, lived off the land he owned and looked down his nose at trade.
Damonax professed being that kind of gentleman. As Sostratos had
seen, though, his brother-in-law didn't despise the money from trade,
especially when his family needed it—which they did a lot of the time.

"Well, then, act like you enjoy it." Menedemos didn't mind being a
merchant—or, if he did, he hid it well, perhaps even from himself. "If
it weren't for people like us, all the *kaloi k'agathoi* would be sitting
around on bare floors scratching themselves, because who'd sell 'em
all the things that make life worth living? Nobody, that's who."

"Getting the chance to see strange places *is* part of what makes being
a merchant worthwhile," Sostratos admitted. "And I've never been to
Mytilene, so"—he dipped his head—"all right. If that's what you want
to do, we'll do it. You know, that polis wouldn't be here today if the
Athenians hadn't changed their minds during the Peloponnesian War."

"When did the Athenians ever do anything *but* change their minds?" Menedemos asked, more than a little scornfully.

"They would have massacred the city after it rose up against them, and they sent off a trireme with orders to do just that," Sostratos said. "But then they had second thoughts, and they sent another ship after the first. The rowers on the first ship dawdled; they didn't like what they were doing. The other ship hurried. Even though it started a day behind, it got there just in time to stop the slaughter. Mytilene's worth seeing, just on account of that."

Menedemos laughed. "If that's what interests you, all right. The other thing that makes me want to go to Lesbos is the word of mouth." He leered. Diokles chuckled.

Sostratos said, "Is it true, what they say about Lesbian women? Did they really invent that particular vice there? From what I've heard of Sappho's poetry, she doesn't talk about it."

"With that funny Aiolic dialect they speak there, half the time it's hard to tell *what* they're talking about," Menedemos answered. "But if you mean, did they invent sucking a man's prong, well, Aristophanes sure thinks so."

"That doesn't mean it's true," Sostratos said. "Aristophanes says all sorts of things that aren't so."

His cousin ignored him. Menedemos seldom wasted a chance to quote from the comic poet, and proved no exception now: " 'You seem to me to be the lambda among the Lesbians,' he says. And there's that modern poet, what's-his-name—Theopompos, that's it—too:

> 'Not to mention this old method, repeated
> Through our mouths
> Which the children of the Lesbians
> Found.' "

"That's not proof—it's only assertion," Sostratos said.

"You want proof, find a friendly girl on Mytilene," Menedemos answered. "She'll measure the hypotenuse on your triangle. See, I remember some geometry after all."

He and Diokles both found the joke very funny. For some reason Sostratos couldn't fathom, he did, too. He tried to think rationally about a pretty girl from a brothel drawing triangles in the sand and talking in learned tones about the theory the godlike Pythagoras had proved—and the harder he tried, the harder he laughed.

"You're absurd," he told his cousin.

"Thank you," Menedemos answered, which for some reason made them both laugh more than ever. At last, Menedemos said, "On to Lesbos, then."

"On to Lesbos," Sostratos agreed. After a while, he asked, "What are truffles supposed to cost? Have you got any idea?"

Menedemos tossed his head. "Whatever we have to pay, we charge more in Athens, that's all. So far as I know, they don't grow truffles there, so they'll pay."

"Well, yes, certainly," Sostratos said. "But I've never traded for them before. I'd like to have some idea of how to tell good ones from bad, and how much I ought to pay for each grade. The more I know beforehand, the better the bargains I can hope to make."

"Ask at some of our stops on the way up to Mytilene," Menedemos suggested. "The closer we get to Lesbos, the more likely the merchants in the market squares are to have dealt in 'em."

"That makes good sense," Sostratos said. "Yes, that makes very good sense. How did *you* come up with it?"

"Talent," Menedemos said airily. "Pure talent."

Few things irked Sostratos more than having his cousin refuse to rise to one of his gibes. "There must be a rational explanation instead," he said.

Menedemos blew him a kiss. "You're so sweet," he purred. "Sweet as vinegar."

"Oh, *lesbiaze,*" Sostratos said. The verb, derived from the alleged proclivity of Lesbian women for such things, set him and Menedemos—and Diokles, and some of the rowers, too—laughing all over again.

3

MENEDEMOS STEERED THE *APHRODITE* TOWARD THE harbor at Mytilene. Part of the polis sat on a little island in the middle of the harbor. The rest lay on Lesbos proper, to the north of the islet. A modern wall of gray stone protected the portion of Mytilene on the Lesbian mainland. Like Rhodes, that part of the city was built on a grid; a glance told Menedemos the streets on the little island, the older part of Mytilene, ran every which way.

"I keep waiting for a war galley to come boiling out and ask what we're doing here," Sostratos said.

"That happened at Samos, but not at Khios," Menedemos said. "My guess is, we're far enough inside Antigonos' dominions that people don't worry so much about a lone galley."

"People in Antigonos' dominions don't worry so much about whether we're pirates, either," Sostratos said. "They might want to hire us if we turn out to be raiders, but they don't care about sinking us."

"From everything I've seen and heard, old One-Eye cares about himself first, last, and always, and to the crows with everything else," Menedemos said. "If he can get some use out of pirates, he's all for them. If he can't, he doesn't worry one way or the other."

Diokles pointed to a quay not far from the bridge joining the old part of Mytilene to the new. "There's a good place to tie up, skipper," he said.

"Yes, I see it," Menedemos agreed, and swung the merchant galley slightly to port. He eased her up alongside the jutting pier, then dipped his head to the oarmaster.

"Back oars!" Diokles called. A couple of strokes killed the bit of forward momentum the *Aphrodite* had left. The keleustes grunted in satisfaction. *"Oöp!"* he said, and the rowers rested. "Ship oars!" he added. As they obeyed, sailors tossed lines to waiting longshoremen, who made the akatos fast to the pier.

"What vessel? What cargo?" asked one of the men on the quay. In

Aiolic fashion, he put the accent on each word as far forward as it could possibly go.

"We're the *Aphrodite,* out of Rhodes," Menedemos answered. His Doric drawl seemed even more foreign here than it did in the Ionic-speaking towns the merchant galley had visited on her way north. "We've got Rhodian perfume, papyrus and ink, Koan silk, crimson dye and beeswax and balsam and embroidered linen from Phoenicia—things of that sort."

"And what are you looking for here?" the local asked.

"Wine, of course," Menedemos said, and the fellow dipped his head.

Sostratos added, "And truffles. Can you give us the names of a couple of dealers?"

The Mytilenean looked elaborately blank. "By the gods, Hellenes are a greedy folk," Sostratos muttered. He took an obolos out of his mouth and tossed it to the longshoreman.

As soon as the fellow caught it, his manner changed. "I can give you one sip right now," he said. *A sip?* Menedemos wondered, and then remembered that Aiolic used *s* instead of *t* in front of *i*. The longshoreman went on, "And that's steer clear of Apollonides. He adulterates what he sells."

"Thanks, friend," Sostratos said. "Knowing whom to stay away from is as important as knowing whom to go to."

"Try Onetor," the local suggested, "and after him Neon. Onetor's brother, Onesimos, sells wine. Neon and Onetor are both honest, more or less, but Onetor is more likely to have the best truffles than Neon is."

Now Menedemos gave him an obolos. The longshoreman was effusive in his thanks. In a low voice, Sostratos said, "We'll do some more checking before we deal. This fellow may not know what he's talking about, or else he may be Onetor's cousin, or Neon's, and get a cut of whatever business he brings in."

"I know that," Menedemos answered, also quietly. "We'll ask around in the agora. Still, we've got a place to start."

Like sparrows scattering when a jay fluttered down to peck at seeds, the longshoremen drew back as a swaggering soldier in a swirling red cape strode up the quay toward the *Aphrodite.* He was wide through the shoulders, at least as tall as Sostratos, and looked taller because of the crested and brightly polished bronze helm he wore. His eyes were gray; his close-cut beard had big red streaks in it. When he spoke, the Macedonian that poured from his lips made Aiolic dialect seem straightforward by comparison.

Menedemos stood there dumbfounded, wondering how to tell him he was speaking gibberish. Sostratos undertook the job: "I'm very sorry, O best one, and I do not mean to offend you, but I cannot follow what you say." He made his own speech as Attic as he could: that was the dialect people who learned Greek were most likely to follow, and to use.

After an incomprehensible Macedonian oath, the soldier tried again. This time, he managed intelligible Greek, asking, "What ship be ye here? Where be ye from? What might ye carry?" Menedemos told him. He followed Doric Greek about as well as Sostratos' almost-Attic, and asked another question: "Whither be ye bound?"

"Athens." Sostratos spoke before Menedemos could. By the way his tongue caressed the city's name, he longed for it as Menedemos might have longed for one of the women who lived there.

"Athens, eh?" The Macedonian dipped his head, smiling a little, and said something more in his native speech. He turned and marched down the pier, his rawhide boots thudding on the sun-baked, bird-splashed planks.

"What was that last bit?" Menedemos asked Sostratos.

"It sounded like, 'Maybe I'll see you there,'" his cousin answered.

"It sounded like that to me, too, but that's not likely, is it?" Menedemos said. "He's Antigonos' man, and Athens belongs to Kassandros."

"They don't love each other," Sostratos agreed.

"We probably heard it wrong," Menedemos said. "I'd almost rather listen to a Thracian than a Macedonian. At least Thracian's a real foreign language, and you know ahead of time it won't make any sense to you. When you hear Macedonians talking, you pick up a word now and then, and you hear other bits that sound like they ought to make sense, but then you listen a little longer and you realize you don't know what in Tartaros they're talking about."

"Usually it's something like, 'Surrender right now. Give me your silver,'" Sostratos said. "Macedonians aren't very complicated people."

As unobtrusively as he could, Menedemos kicked him in the ankle, saying, "You're pretty simple yourself, to scoff at them where the Lesbians might hear you and blab. We want to do business here, not get in trouble."

"You're right, my dear. I'm sorry. I'll be more careful." Sostratos was much more ready than most Hellenes to apologize when in the wrong. That made Menedemos have a hard time staying angry at him, but also roused faint contempt. Did his cousin have no self-respect?

Diokles asked, "Are you young gentlemen going to an inn tonight, or will you sleep aboard ship?"

"Good question." Menedemos turned to Sostratos. "How about it? Do you feel like a bed tonight, with maybe a slave girl in it to show us what women in Lesbos are famous for?"

"We'd probably get better lodgings at the house of the Rhodian proxenos here." Sostratos eyed the setting sun. "Too late to send anybody to his house this evening. Tomorrow would do better for that, and so I'd just as soon sleep here tonight."

After a moment's thought, Menedemos dipped his head. "You make good sense," he said. "All things considered, you usually do."

"Thanks—I think," Sostratos said. "I *am* fairly good at being right. One of the things I've found, though, is that it's much less useful than people think."

"That's a what-do-you-call-it—a paradox," Menedemos said. "What's wrong with being right?"

"For one thing, a good many questions aren't important, so whether you're right or not really doesn't matter very much," Sostratos said seriously. "For another, being right annoys people a lot of the time. They think you think you're better than they are, when all you truly think is that you're more accurate."

Menedemos had watched Sostratos look down his nose at him and at other people too many times to be altogether convinced by that. Saying so, though, would have sparked a quarrel. Instead, he got himself a couple of barley rolls, some olives, and some dried fish. "Why don't you pour us some wine?" he said. "This won't be much of a supper, but it'll keep us going."

His cousin got out their cups. "We'll eat better at the proxenos' house than we would at an inn," he said. "The only thing innkeepers know how to do is to fry whatever you bring them in hot oil." Sostratos dipped wine from an amphora of the rough red the crew drank, then diluted it with water from another jar.

"You're bound to be right about that," Menedemos said as Sostratos gave him his cup. "I've had some ghastly suppers in inns."

"Who hasn't? Only men who never travel," Sostratos said. "And this is another one of those places where, even if I am right, so what?" He took a sip of wine, then fixed a supper for himself. "You see? My being right didn't even get you to bring out any food for me, though I poured your wine."

"Well, now you've embarrassed me," Menedemos said, which was true; he knew he should have taken sitos and opson for Sostratos as well as himself. "I'm just lazy and useless, that's all." He hung his head.

"If you were on the stage, they'd throw cucumbers and squishy apples at you, the way you overact," Sostratos said. Menedemos snorted, though Sostratos was probably right again.

WHEN SOSTRATOS WOKE UP on the *Aphrodite*'s poop deck, he needed a moment to remember in which city's harbor the ship lay. Kos? Samos? Khios? No, this was Mytilene, on Lesbos. The wind blew from the north, and carried the city stink of dung and smoke and sweat and garbage from the part of the polis on Lesbos proper straight into the harbor. When Sostratos was inside a city, he stopped noticing the smell after a while. Going out to sea, though, reminded him of it whenever he came back to port.

He sat up, rubbing his eyes. The eastern sky, the sky above the Anatolian mainland, was gray with advancing dawn. Menedemos still snored beside him. That seldom happened; more often than not, Menedemos woke before him. And Diokles still slept sitting up on a rower's bench, leaning against the planks of the ship's side. Sostratos rubbed his eyes again, wondering whether to believe them—he couldn't remember the last time he'd got up ahead of the keleustes.

He got to his feet and walked, naked, to the rail to ease himself. Even one man moving about gave the merchant galley a small but perceptible motion, enough to rouse both Menedemos and Diokles. "Hail," Menedemos said. "Not such a sleepyhead as usual, eh?"

"Oh, go howl!" Sostratos said. "Sleeping later than you do doesn't make me a lazy wretch."

"No, eh? Since when?" Menedemos got out from under his himation. He too didn't bother with clothes while sleeping: he used his wadded-up chiton for a cushion. He came over and stood beside Sostratos.

Diokles stood up and stretched. Sostratos said, "I still think you'd be more comfortable if you lay down when you slept."

The oarmaster tossed his head. "That may be fine for other people, but not for me. I got used to sleeping sitting up when I pulled an oar, and nothing else has felt right since. I have no quarrel with what anybody else does, and I don't see why anyone else should have a quarrel with what I do."

"I have no quarrel with it," Sostratos said. "It just seems strange."

Menedemos grinned impishly. "And when you have a girl, Diokles, do you sit up and put her on your lap?"

"Sometimes," Diokles replied, unruffled. "It's as good that way as any other, don't you think?"

"It's pretty good any which way." Menedemos turned to Sostratos. "Now that would be something useful for philosophers to do, my dear: figure out which way it's best, I mean."

"It's as Pindaros says—custom is king of all," Sostratos answered. "Besides, what one man likes most, another likes least. So who can say what *best* is?"

"If you go to a brothel, the girls charge you most for riding you like a racehorse," Diokles said. "They must think that's the best."

"Not necessarily," Sostratos said. "They might charge more because they have to do the most work that way. If they just bend forward, the man behind them is thrusting home with his spear, and they don't need to do much at all."

Menedemos laughed. "Well, this is an interesting way to start the morning. More fun than breakfast, I will say."

From gray, the eastern sky went to pink, and then to gold. The sailors who'd spent the night on the *Aphrodite* instead of going into Mytilene to drink and wench got up one by one. Before long, they were arguing about the best way to do it. They got no answer that would have satisfied a scholar at the Lykeion, but they had fun, too.

After a barley roll dipped in olive oil and a cup of watered wine, Sostratos said, "Shall we find the agora and see what we can learn about wine merchants and truffle sellers?"

"Sounds good to me." Menedemos tilted his head back and emptied his cup. He wiped his mouth on the back of his hand. "Let's go."

They walked up the gangplank and down the quay. As they passed a longshoreman, Sostratos asked him where the market square was. The Mytilenean might have been stricken with an advanced case of idiocy. He scratched his head, pulled at his lower lip, frowned, and generally gave the impression of a man who had a hard time remembering his own name, let alone anything harder. Sostratos didn't need to have read Hippokrates to know how to cure that malady. As he had with the other longshoreman, he gave the man an obolos. Sure enough, silver proved the proper drug. Intelligence blossomed on the Mytilenean's face. He pointed north into the part of the polis on Lesbos and gave quick, confident directions, finishing, "You can't miss it."

"I hope not," Sostratos muttered as they crossed the bridge.

"Up this street here, did he say?" Menedemos asked.

"That's right," Sostratos answered. He could see the grid of the city in his head, and see which way they should go. He'd needed years to realize most people couldn't do that.

The wind blew strongly out of the north. Menedemos said, "A good thing we're not coming up to Lesbos today. We wouldn't get anywhere fast."

"No, we wouldn't." Sostratos stopped and rubbed at his eyes: the breeze had blown a speck of dust into them. More dust swirled past. "Here's a town where the Hippodamian grid isn't everything you wish it were," he said, rubbing again. "They shouldn't have made the streets all run north-south and east-west. The north wind just races down these long, straight avenues."

"If you're going to have a grid—" Menedemos began.

Sostratos tossed his head. "No, no. If they'd rotated it through half a right angle, then it would be fine; the wind would be blocked. The way things are, though, it's . . . unpleasant."

"It sure is." Now his cousin paused to rub at his face and get some grit out of his eye. "Miserable wind. I'm glad we don't live here all year around."

"I wouldn't want to live anywhere but Rhodes," Sostratos said, counting street corners so he'd know when to turn.

"Not even Athens?" Menedemos asked slyly.

Sostratos had to think about that. He had to think so hard, he almost lost track of the corners. At last, though, he tossed his head. "No, my dear, not even Athens. It's a wonderful place to study, and the theater is the finest in the world, but it's not what it was in the time of Perikles and Sokrates and Platon. The people have lost too many wars, and they know it. They still call themselves free and autonomous, the way so many poleis do these days, but it's nothing a Rhodian would recognize as freedom. And what they call democracy . . ." He tossed his head again. "Demetrios of Phaleron runs things for Kassandros, and there's a Macedonian garrison to make sure nothing unfortunate happens."

"And if anyone says anything Demetrios doesn't like, he disappears?" Menedemos asked.

"Sometimes—not always, I admit," Sostratos replied. "Demetrios studied philosophy himself, and he makes a mild tyrant—a tolerable tyrant, if you don't mind the contradiction. Things could be worse there. But they could be a lot better, too. And we turn . . . here, I think. This must be the temple to Hera that fellow in the harbor was talking about." He swung to the left.

"I'd say so," Menedemos agreed, and followed him. He pointed down the long, straight street. "And I'd say that's the agora ahead."

"Looks like it. Sounds like it, too." Sostratos couldn't help smiling. All over Hellas, market squares were the same, even if they looked different. The agora was the beating heart of a polis, not just the place where men bought and sold things but also where they gathered to gossip and trade news. "Sidon and Jerusalem weren't like this."

"I don't know about Jerusalem—I wasn't there—but Sidon certainly wasn't, and not just because I didn't speak the language," Menedemos said. "The Phoenicians didn't care about gathering and talking things over the way we do."

"Neither did the Ioudaioi." Sostratos ran his fingers through his hair and flicked at his beard to get rid of any crumbs that might have clung there. "But now we're among Hellenes."

"You bet we are." Menedemos threw back his shoulders and strutted into the agora as if all the Mytileneans—none of whom had ever seen him before—should have known exactly who he was. Hurrying along behind him, Sostratos couldn't help laughing softly. His cousin always made a procession, even if it was a procession of one. *This will be a procession of two,* Sostratos thought, and also put his best foot forward.

And people *did* look up from their buying and selling and arguing when the two Rhodians walked into the market square. "Hail, friends!" Menedemos said loudly, his Doric accent helping him stand out when most other men spoke sibilant, oddly stressed Aiolic. "We're off the *Aphrodite,* the akatos from Rhodes that came in yesterday. We're bound for Athens, and we're looking for fine wine and truffles and whatever else we can find that the rich Athenians might like."

Half a dozen hands shot up. "Here, come see what I've got," merchants called. As Sostratos and Menedemos made their way through the crowd towards a wineseller's stall, a fellow whose main stock in trade seemed to be linen goods thrust something at them and said, "What do you think of this?"

"A rock?" Sostratos said. At the same time, Menedemos said, "A chunk of wood?"

That made them both stop and take a closer look. Sostratos took the chunk—it was a little smaller than a man's fist—from the linen-seller and hefted it. "It *is* stone," he said. "But you're right, Menedemos—it looks like wood."

Chuckling, Menedemos said, "Well, that gryphon's skull we found a couple of years ago was bone that seemed turned to stone. Maybe this is what it ate."

Sostratos didn't laugh now. He dipped his head. "Maybe it is." He turned to the Mytilenean who'd shown it to them. "This came from the western part of your island, isn't that so?"

"Why, yes, best one," the local said in surprise. "But how did you know that?"

"Theophrastos, with whom I studied in Athens, comes from Lesbos. He talks about this wood turned to stone, though I've never seen it before. He's even written a book called *On Petrifaction.*"

"By the dog!" Menedemos said. "I've heard of books about some odd things, but that may be the strangest one yet."

"Would you like to buy this chunk of, ah, petrified wood?" the linen-seller asked. "Five drakhmai doesn't seem like much, does it?"

"For a rock?" Sostratos said. "You're joking, O marvelous one." Thinking of the gryphon's skull pained him, as it always did. But it wasn't the sort of pain a rock that looked like—or perhaps was—a chunk of wood could assuage.

Sensing as much, the Mytilenean looked disappointed. "The way you were throwing those big words around, I figured you'd think five drakhmai was cheap."

"Well, friend, you'd better try some new figuring," Sostratos said. "I might buy it if you name me a halfway reasonable price. On the other hand, I might not, too. A lump of woody rock isn't something you *have* to have unless you're planning on bashing in a rascally linen-seller's brains."

"Ha!" Menedemos said. "I like that."

By the way the local chuckled, he thought it was funny, too. "You're a clever fellow, Athenian. What do you say to three drakhmai, then?"

"I say two things," Sostratos answered. "The first is, I'm no Athenian."

"You talk like one," the linen-seller said.

"I studied there, but I'm from Rhodes." Sostratos was more pleased than not that his accent could be taken for Attic. He wasn't pleased enough to pay three drakhmai. "The other thing I say is, farewell." He and Menedemos started on their way.

"Wait!" the linen-seller said. "What would you pay?"

"I might give you three oboloi, if I happened to feel generous," Sostratos said. "I certainly wouldn't give you any more than that."

"Three *oboloi*?" The Mytilenean looked as if he'd just taken a big swig of vinegar, thinking it wine. Sullenly, he thrust the lump of wood that was also a lump of stone toward Sostratos. "Take it, then, if you want it. Have a good sime."

Sostratos wondered if he ought to take it at any price. But it left him too curious to walk away. He gave the linen-seller three little silver coins and took the wood made stone from him. The Mytilenean looked much less dour with money in his hands. "What will you do with that?" Menedemos asked as they went through the agora.

"I don't know. I'll probably take it back to Rhodes and keep it as a curiosity," Sostratos answered. "Not much point showing it off in Athens—as I said, Theophrastos and the other natural philosophers already know about this kind of thing." He plucked at his beard, considering. "That means I'll put the three oboloi on my own personal account, not the firm's."

"I wasn't worrying about that," Menedemos said. "Nobody'll get excited about half a drakhma."

"Oh, I know. But it's only fair," Sostratos said. "If you bent a woman forward for three oboloi, you wouldn't charge that to the firm. You'd better not, anyhow."

"I might, if I didn't have somebody like you watching me," Menedemos said.

"Better I should catch you than your father," Sostratos said, at which his cousin looked as sour as the linen-seller had a little while before. He went on, "Let's see if we can find out about wine merchants and people who sell truffles, shall we? That's why we're here, after all."

They had to spend a drakhma and a half, an obolos at a time, to find out what they needed to know. That bothered Sostratos less than it might have, for he'd expected nothing different. They also spent a few oboloi for fried octopus: a fellow with a brazier emitting an irresistible smell strolled through the agora.

Collecting names wasn't hard. Two Sostratos heard often were those of Onesimos and his brother, Onetor. From that he concluded the longshoreman at the quay probably had been doing his best to talk about men who might actually help. That left him relieved and a little surprised. He'd spent far more than two oboloi other places and achieved far less.

The Rhodians also got one more name: that of Phainias son of Poseides, the Rhodian proxenos at Mytilene. Sostratos gave a youth an obolos to go tell Phainias they would like to call on him and to bring back his reply. A quarter of an hour later, the youngster found him and Menedemos in the agora. Panting a little, he said, "Best ones, he already knew your ship was here. He invites you to supper this evening, and says you may sleep at his home if you care to."

Beaming, Sostratos gave him another coin. Beaming, the youth ran off. Beaming, Menedemos said, "He knows how to *sound* like a proxenos, by Zeus. Now we'll see what sort of table he sets."

WHEN ONE OF HIS HOUSE SLAVES LED Menedemos and Sostratos into his courtyard, Phainias bowed himself almost double. "Welcome, welcome, three simes welcome, most noble ones!" he exclaimed. He was about forty, his hair thinning at the temples, though his smooth-shaved face helped him look younger. He'd probably been a striking youth; now a double chin and the beginnings of a pot belly said he didn't get to the gymnasion often enough. Bowing again, he went on, "You're in-trepid, the two of you. I didn't expect to see Rhodians so early in the sailing season."

"If we go out first, we're more likely to reap the profit," Menedemos said. Politely, he added, "Is there anything of yours we can take on to Athens?"

Phainias tossed his head. "Thank you. That's most kindly meant, but no. I deal in olive oil, after all, and there's not much point shipping that there."

Menedemos shot Sostratos a glance that said, *This fellow can see that. Why can't your polluted brother-in-law?* By Sostratos' expression, he was thinking the same thing. Menedemos looked around the court-yard. "Handsome place you have here," he said. Bees buzzed above flowers and herbs in the garden. A fountain splashed gently. A bronze Artemis, half life size, stood on a column drawing a bow.

"You're too kind, best one," Phainias said. As he spoke, a slave woman came out of the kitchen and picked some chervil from the gar-den. Menedemos smiled at her. Maybe Phainias would tell her to keep his bed warm tonight.

Sostratos didn't seem to notice the woman. His mind still on busi-ness, he said, "Another reason we're out early is to get to Athens be-fore the Greater Dionysia."

"Ah, you want to go to the theater, do you?" Phainias smiled. "I don't blame you a bit. As long as you're bound for Athens, you may as well have a good sime." As Sostratos spoke a Doric flavored with Attic, so Phainias' Aiolic dialect had the same overlay: he was plainly an edu-cated man. Every so often, though, his own speech pattern showed through. He went on, "I'll do everything I can to send you on your way quickly."

"You're a prince of proxenoi, O best one," Menedemos said— flattery, yes, but flattery with a lot of truth in it. Like any proxenos, Phainias represented and helped another polis' citizens in his native city. That could entail considerable effort and expense. Some men took on the job for the sake of its prestige and then scanted it. Phainias looked to want to do it right.

He bowed again at Menedemos' compliment. "You're very kind, most noble one, as I told you a moment ago. Come into the andron, if you please. We'll have some wine, some supper, some more wine—not a real symposion, mind you, but you can go to bed happy if that's what you're looking for. Does it please you?"

"It pleases very much." Menedemos answered quickly, before Sostratos could. His cousin's shoulders went up and down in a tiny shrug. Sostratos seldom cared to go to bed happy with wine. *Well, too bad,* Menedemos thought. *I feel like it, and he can go along.*

"This is a very fine andron," Sostratos said when they stepped up into it—like most, it was raised half a cubit or so above the level of the courtyard and the other rooms. Slaves were taking away stools and setting out couches for a more formal supper. A mosaic of colored pebbles decorated the floor. The walls were painted red up to the height of a man's shoulder, and ocher above that. Several lamps—some pottery, others bronze—hung from bronze chains fixed to the beams of the ceiling. Menedemos didn't think he'd seen anything fancier this side of Taras, and the Italiote Hellenes indulged themselves far more extravagantly than did their cousins who lived round the Aegean.

"Stretch out. Relax. Make yourselves at home," Phainias said, and leaned on his left elbow on one of the couches.

Again, Menedemos and Sostratos exchanged glances. At home, they almost always ate sitting on stools. So did most Hellenes. So did Phainias himself, or he wouldn't have had to move couches into the andron for the supposed pleasure of the Rhodians.

The wicker frame of Menedemos' couch creaked under his weight as he settled himself on it. For a moment, he thought he would go right through it and end up on the floor with a bump. That would have been a lovely way to ingratiate himself with his host. But the couch held. He smiled at the Rhodian proxenos. "Very nice."

"Very nice indeed," Sostratos echoed. He sounded a little too hearty, like a usually prim man paying inexpert court to a hetaira. As he leaned on his elbow, he looked out of place, too.

Two slaves brought in wine, water, a mixing bowl, and cups. Phainias asked, "Well, gentlemen, does one of wine to two of water suit you, or would you like some other mix?"

"That's fine," Menedemos said. Sostratos dipped his head. Menedemos added, "We thank you again for your kindness." One of wine to two of water was a little on the strong side, but only a little—not even Sostratos could possibly object to it, as he might have if Phainias had proposed a one-to-one mixture.

Phainias and the two Rhodians poured out small libations before drinking. Sostratos raised his cup in salute. "To our host!" he said, and drank. So did Menedemos. Sostratos took another, more thoughtful, sip. "This is very fine. Is it Lesbian?"

"It is indeed," Phainias answered. "You're in the market for wine, aren't you?"

"We sure are," Menedemos said. "From whom did you get it?"

"Why, from Onesimos son of Diothemis," the proxenos said. "He lives two doors down from me."

"He's the Onesimos whose brother sells truffles?" Menedemos asked, and Phainias dipped his head. The Rhodian asked, "Does Onetor also live close by here?"

"On the next street north," Phainias said.

"Would it put you to too much trouble to invite them here so we could get to meet them?" Menedemos asked. "If it *would* be difficult, best one, just tell me no. I don't want to impose on your kind hospitality."

"No bother to me," Phainias said. "I like Onesimos fine. I don't know Onetor so well, but he seems a good enough fellow. Let me go ask my cook if he can add a couple of guests at the last minute. You know how it is, I'm sure: the man who runs the kitchen thinks he runs the house, too."

"Oh, yes." Menedemos dipped his head, thinking of Sikon. So did Sostratos, though his family's cook wasn't such a domineering tyrant.

The proxenos got to his feet and left the andron. A moment later, a shriek came from the direction of the kitchen. Menedemos and Sostratos grinned at each other. Phainias returned a couple of minutes later, looking somewhat the worse for wear. "It's all settled," he declared. "I've sent slaves out to invite the two brothers." He dipped a fresh cup of wine from the mixing bowl. "Now what will happen is, neither of them will be able to come on such short nosice, and Kandaules will brain me for making him cook too much."

"My experience is, there's no such thing as too much opson," Menedemos said.

Sostratos looked alarmed at that forthright announcement of gluttony, but Phainias only smiled. "Yes, I've seen that myself," he said. "Here, would you like some more wine?"

"Thanks, best one." Menedemos held out his cup.

So did Sostratos. Phainias was dipping wine out of the bowl for him when a slave hurried to the front door. "Master, Onesimos is here," he called.

"Good, good," Phainias said. "Bring two more couches into the andron—quick, quick, quick. His brother's coming, too, or I hope he is."

Onesimos son of Diothemis was a tall, dour man of middle years, with a long face, a big nose, one front tooth that had gone black, and some of the hairiest ears Menedemos had ever seen. "Good to meet you both," he told the Rhodians, his voice a rumbling bass. "If I remember right, I did business with your fathers ten or twelve years ago."

"I wouldn't be surprised, most noble one," Menedemos said. "Lesbian wine is famous, and our firm has always liked to carry the best."

A pair of harassed-looking slaves brought in couches. Onesimos had just reclined on one when somebody rapped loudly on the front door. Onetor son of Diothemis came in a minute later. He was a couple of digits shorter than his brother, and shiny bald where Onesimos' iron-gray hair, like Phainias', was only just beginning to recede at the temples. But for that, they looked much alike; Menedemos wouldn't have cared to guess which was the elder.

"Nice to meet you, Rhodians," Onetor said. His voice was deep, too, but not quite so deep as Onesimos'. He dipped his head to Phainias. "And very nice of you to invite me. We should get to know each other better."

"Just what I was thinking," Phainias replied. "And supper and wine and maybe some business thrown in make a pleasant excuse for doing exactly that."

"We might do business ourselves, you know, you and I," Onetor said. "Truffles can give olive oil their flavor if they soak in it."

"That's an interesting thought," Phainias said.

"That *is* an interesting thought." Menedemos and Sostratos spoke together. Menedemos wondered how much rich, jaded Athenians might pay for oil with such an exotic flavoring. Sostratos must have been thinking the same thing, for he said, "We might do business with you, too, Phainias."

"I'd like that, best one—as long as you don't haggle too hard." The proxenos chuckled. The slave woman at whom Menedemos had smiled brought in a tray with loaves of wheat bread on it. He smiled again. She gave him a quick smile in return as she set a loaf on the low table in front of his couch. Phainias said, "That can wait, though. For now, we should enjoy our supper without worrying about such things." Another slave set bowls of oil on the table to go with the sitos.

Like any Hellene with manners, Menedemos and Sostratos ate bread with their left hands. Sostratos said, "Good oil, most noble one—and I know a little about what makes good oil, for my sister's husband exports it from Rhodes."

But not this year, not with us, Menedemos thought.

"I wouldn't give guests anything but my best," Phainias said.

"Very good oil," Onetor agreed. "If you were to steep truffles in an amphora or two of this oil, you could pour it into little lekythoi afterwards, and sell each one for a nice price."

"So you could." Menedemos gave the Mytilenean a thoughtful nod. "Meeting you may be a profitable pleasure for all of us."

"You certainly know the right words to say." Onetor seemed less intense than Onesimos, who concentrated on his food to the exclusion of everything else. "*Kaloi k'agathoi* look down their noses at profit, but the world would grind to a halt without it, and soon, too."

"My cousin and I were saying the same thing not long ago," Sostratos said.

"Just because you've got a fancy pedigree, that doesn't mean you're not a fool," Onetor said.

"Here comes the opson," Phainias said. If anything could distract from talk of profit, that was likely to do the trick. As a slave brought in a big tray, the proxenos went on, "Kandaules has baked belly-pieces from a lovely great tunny he bought at the fish market this afternoon."

"Oh, Demeter." Onesimos could speak after all—and reverently, too.

"I wish I were like that fellow from Kythera," Menedemos said. "What's his name, Sostratos? You know the one I mean—the chap who used to stick his hand in boiling water and drink hot things all the time so he could snatch opson from the platter and eat it when it was still too hot for anybody else to touch."

"Philoxenos," Sostratos said.

"Philoxenos! That's who he was, all right," Menedemos said. "You must be doing well for yourself, Phainias—there's some poet or other who says belly-pieces from a fat tunny are something a poor man never sees."

"That's Eriphos, I think." Sostratos came up with the name even when Menedemos hadn't asked for it.

Phainias said, "I *am* doing pretty well for myself, thanks. Good of you to nosice." Few Hellenes who were doing well hid it or failed to boast of it. The only reason Menedemos could see for modesty was fooling a tax-collector.

Savory steam rose from the tunny. Menedemos didn't—quite—burn his hand when he took a piece from the platter. He didn't—quite—burn his mouth when he tasted it. When he said, "Mm, that's good," he did talk with his mouth full. All the other compliments that rose were similarly muffled, so he knew not the least embarrassment. The only complaint he might have made was that he got a little less tunny than he would have liked. But he understood that, too: Kandaules suddenly had to feed more guests than he'd expected.

But then a slave came in with a bowl of stewed eels wrapped in beet leaves, and he stopped worrying about getting enough opson. Sostratos said, "Surely Rhodes has no finer proxenos in any polis around the Inner Sea!" He was talking with his mouth full again, but nobody seemed to mind.

A honey cake sprinkled with walnuts finished the supper. Onetor said, "You're a prince of hospitality, Phainias. You can put me in a cart and roll me home, because I've eaten too much to walk."

"Glad you enjoyed it, my friends," Phainias said as the slaves cleared away what little hadn't been eaten. They brought in wine and water and the mixing bowl once more.

"Did you get that jar from me?" Onesimos asked.

"Of course, best one," Phainias said. "Would I serve anything else? Before supper, the Rhodians and I were drinking one-to-two. Does that please you?"

Onesimos dipped his head. Onetor said, "Anything stronger and rolling me home wouldn't do. You'd have to carry me instead."

Since it wasn't a formal symposion, they didn't bother with the small taste of neat wine first or the prayer to Dionysos that went with it. There were no flute-girls or other entertainers. The Rhodians and Mytileneans just drank and talked and drank and talked. Phainias' slaves poured wine for them, kept the mixing bowl full, and added oil to the lamps.

Much of the talk, not surprisingly, revolved around politics. Phainias and Onetor admired Antigonos, whose garrison held Lesbos. Onesimos, by his occasional comments, despised all the Macedonian marshals. "Unfortunately, they won't go away," Sostratos said.

"Maybe they'll all kill each other off, with not one of them left alive," Onesimos said. "Gods grant it be so."

"Even if it is, some cousin or lieutenant general will rally their armies, and the wheel will start to turn again," Sostratos predicted. "Such things will go on as long as there are men and battles." That made Onesimos look more dour than ever.

It didn't make Menedemos particularly happy, either, but he thought his cousin was right. He said, "I wish I could like Antigonos more than I do."

"He's the best of the Macedonians, far and away," Phainias said.

"It could be, most noble one, and I would not quarrel with my host even if his kindness were far less than you've shown Sostratos and me," Menedemos said. "Still, I'd be lying if I said I was altogether happy with old One-Eye. He's too friendly with pirates to let a seaman be comfortable praising him."

"They don't trouble us," Onetor said.

That was the answer, right there in a nutshell. Menedemos knew as much. The Mytileneans overlooked evil that didn't touch them. But then he realized he and Sostratos did the same thing. He hadn't worried much about brigands on land till his cousin had to cross Phoenicia and Ioudaia to get to Engedi by the Lake of Asphalt. Thinking about troubles that didn't usually touch one was more trouble than it was worth for most people.

After a while, Onesimos got to his feet, saying, "Pleasure to make your acquaintance, Rhodians. I hope we can do some business. I'd better head on home now." Gait a little unsteady, he made his way toward the front door.

As soon as he was out of earshot, Phainias spoke in a low voice: "His wife nags him if he stays out too late."

Onetor chuckled. "My brother's wife nags him even if he doesn't stay out too late. From what he says, that's all she ever does."

"I wonder what she would say," Sostratos remarked.

"Who cares?" Onetor said. "She's only a woman, after all." He drained his cup. "I'd better go home, too, though, while I sill remember the way."

"Shall I send a slave along with a torch?" Phainias asked.

"Not when I'm just going around the block. Thanks for the kind of-fer, though, best one, and thanks for invising me over," Onetor said. "You and the Rhodians should think about truffle-flavored oil."

"We will," Phainias said, and Menedemos and Sostratos both dipped their heads.

Once Onetor had left, Menedemos told Phainias, "I don't think we'll last much longer, either." Sostratos' yawn showed he agreed.

"Here—we've got beds waising for you, most noble ones," the Rho-dian proxenos said. "Come with me, and I'll show you." He took a lamp off its chain to light his way to the back part of the house. Menedemos and Sostratos followed. Menedemos planted his feet with care, not wanting to step in a hole he didn't see and fall down. Phainias pointed ahead. "These two rooms here."

Menedemos suspected they'd been storerooms till the Mytilenean's slaves brought in the beds. That didn't bother him. Phainias was doing the Rhodians a favor by putting them up at all. He wasn't an innkeeper; he didn't have guests often enough to keep rooms permanently ready for them.

Now lamplight spilled out from under the doors. Phainias said, "The night's a little on the chilly side, my friends, so I hope you sleep warm. I'll see you in the morning."

He headed for the stairs. "Which room do you want?" Menedemos asked Sostratos.

"I'll take the one on the left," his cousin answered, and went in.

When Menedemos opened the other door, he wasn't surprised to find a slave woman sitting on the bed. He did grin to find he'd ended up with the woman he'd noticed before. "Hail, sweetheart," he said. "Are you supposed to help me sleep warm?"

"That's right, sir," she answered, her Aiolic accent flavored with something else—she wasn't a Hellene by birth.

"What's your name?" Menedemos asked.

"People here call me Kleis," she said. "It will do. I'm used to it. They can't say the one I was born with."

She would have come from somewhere on the Anatolian mainland, Menedemos guessed. She had a round face, a strong nose, very black hair and eyes, a bit of dark down on her upper lip. He thought she was two or three years older than he—just on the other side of thirty.

"Well, Kleis," Menedemos said, "is it all right?" Some slave women hated giving themselves to men. Menedemos knew a few men who enjoyed taking them all the more because they hated it. To him, they were more trouble than they were worth.

But Kleis nodded—another proof she was no Hellene. "Yes, it's all right," she said. "What else have I got to do for fun?" She stood up and pulled her long chiton off over her head. Her breasts were full and heavy, with big, dark nipples.

Menedemos took off his tunic and bent his head to them—first one, then the other. She made a small, wordless noise, down in her throat. Smiling, Menedemos straightened. "I hope it'll be fun." He slid an arm around her waist, which was surprisingly slim. "Let's find out." They lay down on the bed together.

SOSTRATOS DREAMT SOMETHING HAD FALLEN ON HIM, so that he couldn't move his legs. Had he been in an earthquake? Had sacks of grain, piled high waiting to go aboard a round ship, toppled and pinned him down? He didn't know. He couldn't remember. He only knew he was trapped.

He opened his eyes—and stared into the face of a sleeping woman, only a palm or so from his own. Her bare thigh, warm and soft, was draped over his. No wonder he couldn't move—but he hadn't been dreaming about such a pleasant trap.

Her eyes opened, too. They were greenish blue, the hair that framed her freckled face foxy red. Like Threissa back on Rhodes, she came from the lands north of the Aegean. "Good day, Gongyla," Sostratos said. "Did I make a noise and wake you? I was having a strange dream."

She shook her head. "No, sir. I don't think so." She sounded like Threissa, too, though she was several years older. "I just woke up, I think."

"All right." Sostratos shifted on the narrow bed. Gongyla took her leg off his. His hand brushed her breast. He let it rest there, and idly, hardly even noticing what he was doing, began to tease her nipple with thumb and forefinger.

"So early?" she said, frowning a little.

He hadn't really been thinking about having her, but he was still on the randy side of thirty. Her question decided him. "Yes, why not?" he said. A slave woman never had an answer to that. Sostratos did his best to warm her up. He wasn't sure his best did the job, as he had been the night before.

She still sulked even after he gave her a couple of oboloi. Menedemos would either have ignored that or jollied her into a better mood. Sostratos, not callous enough for the one, tried the other, saying, "You have a pretty name."

"Not mine," Gongyla said. "You Hellenes took mine, gave me this one." By the way she scowled at Sostratos, he might have done it personally.

"But it's a famous name among us," he said.

"Famous? How?" Her eyes called him a liar.

"Gongyla—the first Gongyla I know of—was a friend of the great poet Sappho, here on Lesbos perhaps three hundred years ago." Sostratos wasn't sure exactly when Sappho had lived, but this Gongyla wouldn't know, either.

"Who remembers so long? How?" the slave woman asked.

"People wrote down Sappho's poems," Sostratos answered. "That's how they remember them—and the people in them."

"Squiggles. Marks." Gongyla couldn't read. Sostratos would have been astonished had she proved literate; even among Hellenes, few women were. She brushed back a lock of coppery hair that had fallen down onto her nose. Not least for its strangeness, red hair fascinated and attracted Sostratos. Gongyla frowned in thought. "But these squiggles, these marks, they make this name remembered?"

"That's right." Sostratos dipped his head.

"Maybe something to wrising after all," the Thracian woman said; her Greek had an Aiolic accent, too. "I just thought it was for keeping track of oil and money and things like that." She hesitated, then asked, "Is Kleis in this Sappho's poems, too?"

"Yes—she was the poet's daughter."

"A woman poet?" Gongyla noticed the feminine endings.

"That's right," Sostratos said again.

"How funny." Gongyla got out of bed, pulled the chamber pot out from under it, squatted over the pot, and then put on her chiton. Sostratos also pissed into the pot. Then he got dressed, too. He noticed Gongyla eyeing him as he might have examined some bird he'd never seen before that chanced to perch in the *Aphrodite*'s rigging. "You know strange things. Many strange things," she remarked.

"Yes, that's true," Sostratos agreed. Most people noticed; not many noticed it as soon as Gongyla had.

Someone knocked on the door. "You in there, my dear?" Menedemos called. "You doing anything you don't want to stop just now?"

"No, we've taken care of that," Sostratos replied.

"Have you? How . . . efficient," Menedemos said. "Well, in that case come out and have some breakfast."

"All right." Sostratos' stomach growled. Waking up in bed with a woman had kept him from noticing how hungry he was. *Appetites and appetites,* he thought.

He opened the door. When Menedemos got a look at Gongyla, he started to laugh. "Now I understand," he said. "You've got a weakness for redheads. I saw as much with that Keltic girl of yours back in Taras a few years ago."

"I wouldn't call it a weakness," Sostratos said with dignity. "More of a . . . taste." He waited for his cousin to make an Aristophanic pun on that.

But Menedemos just said, "Come on. Have some porridge and some wine. Then we can go talk to Onesimos and Onetor. Do you want to go together to each of them in turn, or shall we beard them separately?"

"I'd just as soon do them separately, if it's all the same to you," Sostratos answered as they walked toward the andron. "We'll save time that way. You can haggle over wine as well as I can, and I'll dicker with the truffle-seller."

Menedemos chuckled. "I might have known you'd want to split things like that. Don't spend so much time asking Onetor questions about truffles that you forget to buy any."

Phainias was already eating breakfast in the men's chamber when Sostratos and Menedemos walked in. "Hail, best ones," the proxenos said. "Good day to you both." He used the dual number in talking about the two Rhodians. It seemed natural in his speech, but would have been hopelessly old-fashioned on Rhodes. "I hope you passed pleasant nights."

"I bent Kleis like a lioness on a cheese grater," Menedemos said.

Phainias laughed. Sostratos wondered where his cousin had come up with that figure of speech, then realized it probably came from Aristophanes. He said, "I enjoyed myself with Gongyla, too. Do you name all your slave women after people from Sappho's poems?"

"You're clever for spotting that," Phainias said. "Not everyone does."

"I didn't," Menedemos said. "But you're right, most noble one—he is a clever fellow."

The Rhodian proxenos went on, "As a matter of fact, I do. Makes it easier for me to remember what to call them. I don't think I'm the only one on Mytilene who does the same thing, either."

"It's efficient," Sostratos said, borrowing Menedemos' word. "Makes perfectly good sense to me." A male slave came in with porridge for him and Menedemos. Salt fish and bits of chopped olive livened up what would otherwise have been a bland bowl of barley mush. Sostratos dug in with a horn spoon. Between bites, he asked, "You said Onetor's house was around the block from you?"

"That's right," Phainias answered. "Go one street north, then turn left, Onetor lives in the third house on the left-hand side of the street."

"One street north, left, third house on the left." Sostratos dipped his head. "Thanks. I'll remember that."

"He will, too," Menedemos said. "And if we come back here next year, he'll still remember it then." He sounded half proud, half wary about Sostratos' memory.

"I'm not a trained monkey," Sostratos said. "You don't need to show me off."

"Nothing wrong with keeping track of things in your head," Phainias said. "I only wish I were better at it."

Once Sostratos had finished breakfast, he said, "I'm going to head over to Onetor's. We're up and the sun's up, so he ought to be up, too."

When he went north from Phainias' house, the breeze blew straight down the street and straight into his face. He was glad he had to walk only one block before turning. Then the houses on the north side of the east-west street shielded him from the worst of the wind. He ran his fingers through his hair, trying to look as neat as he could.

At the third house on the left, he knocked on the door. "Who's there?" someone called from within.

"Is this the house of Onetor son of Diothemis?"

"That's right. Who are you?"

"I'm Sostratos son of Lysistratos, one of the Rhodians Onetor dined with last night. I'd like to talk business with him."

"Wait a minute." The door soon opened. A redheaded Thracian slave—a man—stood aside to let Sostratos in. "My master is finishing breakfast in the andron. He asks if you've eaten."

"Yes, thanks," Sostratos replied. The Thracian led him through the entry hall and into the courtyard. Onetor put down a winecup to wave to him. He waved back, saying, "Hail, most noble one."

"Hail." Onetor raised the cup to his lips once more. "I've got a headache from last night," he said. "A little more wine will take the edge off it. Are you hungry? We have plenty."

"I ate with Phainias," Sostratos said. "I hope I'm not too early for you."

"Oh, no. Don't be silly, best one." Onetor tossed his head. "The sun's in the sky, so anybody who's not ready for business has only himself to blame. I'm no pampered Persian slugabed, to crawl out from under my blanket at noon. My wife was working in the garden sill you knocked. I'm sure she's finding something to do upstairs now."

"Good. That's all right, then. . . . Oh, thank you." A slave came into the andron with a cup of watered wine for Sostratos. He took a sip, then went on, "Tell me about truffles, if you'd be so kind."

"What do you want to know? Grades, prices, that sort of thing?"

"Not yet. I was hoping you'd just tell me *about* them. They don't grow on Rhodes, and I'd like to know as much as I can, both so I can tell my customers more and because I'm a curious sort myself."

"Yes, I nosiced that at Phainias' last night," Onetor said. "You've got that Attic way of talking. Did you study at the Academy?"

"No, at the Lykeion, under Theophrastos," Sostratos answered. "That's another reason I'm interested: Theophrastos makes a specialty of plants, so I always like it when I get the chance to add to what he taught me."

"Well, all right," Onetor answered. Sostratos would have been surprised if he'd refused; few people could resist talking about what they did for a living. The truffle-seller continued, "You may or may not have heard they grow underground."

"Yes, I did know that," Sostratos said. "I've also heard they grow best after rainy seasons where there's plenty of thunder."

"I've heard that, too, but I don't believe it," Onetor replied. "I've never seen it make one bit of difference. If there isn't much *rain* in a rainy season, that's another story. They don't do so well then, but what crop does?"

"Fair enough," Sostratos said. "That certainly stands to reason. What sort of soil do they prefer?"

"Sandy, usually—you often find them close by the seashore."

"*How* do you find them?" Sostratos asked. "You can't just dig at random on a beach."

Onetor hesitated, then seemed to decide it was safe to answer. "If there were truffles on Rhodes, I don't think I'd tell you," he said. "You might turn into a compesitor. But I've never heard of them there, either, so I suppose I can say something about that, anyhow. For one thing, there's a certain kind of grass—we call it truffleleaf—that grows above them. That gives me a clue where to look."

"What does this grass look like?" Sostratos asked. Onetor smiled and didn't say a thing. "All right, all right—forget I wanted to know," Sostratos told him. "You said that was one thing. What's another?"

"When I'm out hunsing truffles, I have help," Onetor said.

"What kind of help?"

Again, Onetor didn't answer. Sostratos realized he'd learned about as much as he was going to. A dog wandered into the andron: a flop-eared mutt with its tongue lolling out. Onetor scratched it under the chin and behind those floppy ears. Its tail wagged frantically.

"Friendly beast," Sostratos remarked.

"Porpax? Yes, I'd say so." Onetor scratched the dog again. It tried to jump up into his lap. "Careful, you silly thing," he said, fending it off. "You'll make me spill wine on myself."

"You named him after the handle of a shield?" Sostratos said. It was a fairly common name for a dog. "Does he shield your house from burglars?"

"He makes a good enough watchdog, yes," Onetor said. As if to prove it, Porpax barked, though he didn't seem to want to go after Sostratos. The Rhodian, in fact, wondered if he was too friendly to make a proper watchdog, if he wouldn't fawn on the thieves when he was supposed to bite. Onetor said, "He has other uses, too."

"Such as?"

Sostratos didn't mean anything by the question; he was just making conversation. But, once more, Onetor declined to answer. The smug way he didn't answer made Sostratos wonder if Porpax was somehow connected to the truffle trade. That struck him as unlikely, though— why would a dog want anything to do with fungi? Porpax ran off, yapping.

The slave came back, this time with a bowl of barley porridge and a spoon. Sostratos tossed his head. "No, thanks," he said. "As I told your master, I had breakfast before I came here."

But Onetor said, "Try this anyhow, most noble one. It has some shaved truffles in it, to give you a notion of the flavor."

"In that case, I will," Sostratos said. The first thing he noticed was the rich, almost meaty aroma rising from the porridge. When he tasted it, his eyebrows flew upwards. He knew he shouldn't show how impressed he was. Sometimes, though, a man simply couldn't help himself. If he'd said he didn't care for the flavor, Onetor would have known he was lying, "That's . . . very fine," he managed at last, and ate up the porridge as fast as he could.

"Glad you like it," Onetor said. "I wouldn't want you to buy without knowing what you're gessing."

"I can see why," Sostratos said, a little ruefully, or maybe more than a little. He'd known truffles were expensive. Now he understood the reason. He wondered just how much Onetor would try to squeeze out of him.

"Do you think you'd be interested in taking my goods to Athens?" the truffle-seller asked.

"I'm sure I'd be interested," Sostratos answered. "Whether I can afford them is likely to be a different question."

Onetor grinned at him. He *could* grin; he wasn't nearly so gloomy as Onesimos. He said, "For top grade, I charge three simes the truffles' weight in silver. I don't haggle. If you want them, that's what you'll pay. You won't find anybody cheaper in Mytilene, and you won't find anybody with better goods."

Any trader could say that. From the frequency with which Onetor's name had come up in the agora, he *was* the leading truffle dealer in town. Sostratos supposed he could charge six or eight drakhmai in Athens for each drakhma's weight of truffles. But there might be a better way. "Do you have to have silver?" he asked. "Or can we trade goods for goods, and both resell at a profit?"

"That depends," Onetor said. "What have you got?"

"Papyrus and ink from Egypt . . ." Sostratos began. Onetor tossed his head. Sostratos said, "I did expect those would do better in Athens. I've also got Koan silk, which is worth its weight in silver, too."

"It's pretty stuff, but I'm not interested in it," the truffle-seller said. "Kos isn't that far from here; silk's fairly common on Lesbos."

"All right, best one," Sostratos said. "I have fine beeswax from Ioudaia—"

"Anyone can find beeswax," Onetor broke in. "All you have to do is know how not to get stung."

"The *Aphrodite* carries fine wine from Byblos, with a bouquet as sweet as Ariousian's," Sostratos said. "I'm not making that up. We carried Ariousian to Great Hellas a few years ago, and this wine has a nose to match it."

"Let everything be as you say, most noble one, and it sill wouldn't matter much to me," Onetor replied. "Onesimos is the wine merchant in the family. He might be interested in this vintage from far away, but I'm not, except maybe to taste a cup. What else have you got on that akatos?"

"Embroidered linen cloth from Mesopotamia," Sostratos said. "Fine perfume from Rhodes, the island of roses. And genuine balsam from Engedi on the Lake of Asphalt in Ioudaia, the finest balsam in the world."

"Balsam, eh?" Onetor scowled. "What do you want for that? It's something I might be able to get rid of here on Lesbos."

"They sell it in Ioudaia for twice its weight in silver," Sostratos answered.

"Somesimes they sell it here in Hellas for twice its weight in silver, too," Onetor said pointedly.

"Not always," Sostratos said, just as pointedly. "And if I paid twice its weight, and I did, I'm not going to let it go for no profit. If you buy it from me, you won't sell it at your buying price, either."

"All that may be true—if you paid what you say you paid. But who knows about that?" Onetor sent Sostratos a sour stare. "Merchants are born liars."

"No doubt you would know, being one yourself," Sostratos said. Onetor's expression got blacker. Sostratos gave him a polite seated bow. "We can go on insulting each other, best one, or we can do business. Which would you rather?"

Now the Mytilenean frankly stared. "You're a cool customer, aren't you?"

"I try to stay cool, and I would like to be a customer," Sostratos replied. "Shall we talk about balsam and truffles, or shall we go on and on about what a thief each of us thinks the other one is?"

To his surprise, Onetor started to laugh. "You *are* a cool customer, Furies take me if you're not. All right, my dear, let's talk about trading truffles for balsam, and just how much balsam you'll give for a drakhma's weight of my fungi. Maybe perfume, too, now that I think of it."

Sostratos hadn't expected anyone to be interested in balsam till he got to Athens. But he had a good notion of the most he could hope to get for it there. That, clearly, was less than he could get for truffles. Because Onetor had annoyed him, he named an outrageous price to open the dicker. As he'd hoped, the truffle-seller bawled like a castrated colt. Sostratos came down, but, because he'd started so high, he came down to a price he still liked.

Onetor had made a mistake, setting the value of his truffles so firmly as the dicker started. He'd made it plain he wouldn't come down, but he couldn't very well go up from the three drakhmai of silver for each drakhma's weight of truffles, either. Sostratos was more flexible, and took advantage of that when haggling over both the balsam and the perfume. At last, he and the Mytilenean settled on prices that left neither of them too dissatisfied.

"While we're talking here, my cousin is dickering with your brother," Sostratos remarked.

"I hope Onesimos comes out of the deal with all his fingers and toes," Onetor said. "If Menedemos is anywhere near as sharp as you are, best one, he's too good for us poor fellows who stay in one polis all our days."

"You give me too much credit, most noble one," Sostratos murmured, not at all displeased at Onetor's flattery. "And," he went on truthfully, "you don't give yourself enough. I think this is a bargain where we'll both end up showing a nice profit."

"I wouldn't mind," Onetor said. "For a while there, I thought you were going to talk me out of my skin and sell it in the Athenian agora."

"Who's your prettiest hetaira here? I'd get a better price for hers," Sostratos said. Onetor laughed. The Rhodian asked, "Can you have your truffles ready this afternoon? I'll have sailors bring the balsam and perfume here then, if that pleases you."

"It pleases me fine. And if you're going to get an amphora or two of Phainias' oil and flavor it with truffles, you might also want to arrange to buy lekythoi here in Mytilene so you can sell the oil from the small jars. Kallikrates son of Kalligenes can probably sell you enough of them to do the job without making you wait."

Sostratos wondered if this Kallikrates would give Onetor a kick-back, but getting away in a hurry did matter. "I'll talk with him," he said. "Where's his pottery?"

"Not far from here. Phainias can give you directions; he buys all his amphorai from Kallikrates," Onetor said. That made Sostratos feel better. If the Rhodian proxenos bought from Kallikrates, the man was likelier to be reputable.

When he and Menedemos met at Phainias' house, he found his cousin jubilant. "We'll take Lesbian to Athens along with the Byblian," Menedemos said. "Do you know what I did? Do you know?" He was almost beside himself with glee.

"No," Sostratos replied, "but I suspect you're going to tell me."

"I traded him ten jars of Byblian for thirty of his best," Menedemos said. "Ten for thirty! Can you believe it?"

"*Euge!*" Sostratos and Phainias both spoke together. The proxenos went on, "How did you pry such a bargain out of Onesimos? He's one of the singiest men I know."

"You won't tell him?" Menedemos asked.

"By Zeus, best one, I won't," Phainias promised. "It would go against my duty as proxenos—and besides, Onesimos should deal in vinegar, he's so sour."

"Well, I thought so, too," Menedemos said. "We were talking about wine, and I made sure we tried his Lesbian before he sent a slave down to the harbor to bring back my sailors with a jar of Byblian for him to sample. We'd had quite a bit of his wine before then, in fact. He thought he was getting me drunk and pliable. I had something else in mind, though."

"I think I know what," Sostratos said. "You *are* a sly rascal."

"Why, thank you, my dear." Beaming, Menedemos turned back to Phainias. "When the slave and the sailors got back with the Byblian, we broached the amphora. What you need to know about Byblian is, it has the most wonderful bouquet in the world. Maybe Ariousian is as nice on the nose coming out of the jar, but I can't think of any other wine that is." He sniffed and smiled and went on, "When Onetor got a whiff of it, he was so excited, he almost looked happy."

"He *must* have been excited," Phainias said.

"Oh, he was, all right. He was practically panting to make the deal, as a matter of fact. And then we tasted the Byblian, and that didn't queer things, the way I feared it might."

The Rhodian proxenos still wore a puzzled expression. Sostratos explained: "Byblian is a funny wine. It's much nicer to the nose than it is to the palate. But if Onesimos had drunk a lot of his own Lesbian beforehand—"

"That's right. That's exactly right," Menedemos broke in. "Once you've had a few cups of wine, it all tastes pretty much the same unless it's real donkey piss. And Byblian's not *that* bad; it just doesn't have a flavor to match its bouquet. So when I sipped and praised it to the skies, Onesimos couldn't tell I was giving it more than it deserved."

"He usually deals in local wines, not ones from as far away as Byblos, so he wouldn't know that about your vintage," Phainias said.

"Which is what I was hoping for, and which is what happened," Menedemos said happily. "He knows plenty about his own little corner of the business, and so he thought he knew everything about all of it."

Sostratos said, "When Sokrates was defending himself before the Athenians, that was his complaint about artisans generally."

"Since his jury was probably full of them, he was foolish to complain about them to their faces," Menedemos said. Before Sostratos could rise to that, his cousin continued, "Me, I don't want to get tangled up with the law in Athens any which way. Things are more complicated there than anywhere else in Hellas, I think."

"It's a big polis, far bigger even than Rhodes," Sostratos said. "It's no wonder everything's more complicated there." Having said that, he couldn't very well go back and start a quarrel over Menedemos' gibe about Sokrates. Menedemos grinned at him. He pretended not to notice, which only made Menedemos grin more.

Phainias said, "You people who do business in so many poleis are a wonder to me. How do you keep everything straight?"

"I don't even try," Menedemos said. "I just count on Sostratos. He knows what all the various laws and customs are, who coins heavy drakhmai and who light, what's good in each town and what's not worth having, and so on."

"I already said he was a clever fellow," the proxenos replied. "I would say you're not bad yourself, and I would be right about that, too."

"Menedemos is so clever, he even thinks he can talk me into doing his share of the work," Sostratos said. "But *I'm* clever enough to see that, and not to let him get away with it . . . too often."

"Too bad!" Menedemos said with great feeling.

"Go howl," Sostratos replied. He and his cousin and Phainias all smiled. After a good day of trading, why not?

4

"COME ON, YOU LUGS," DIOKLES CALLED AS THE *APHRODITE* slid away from its mooring at Mytilene. "Put your backs into it. It's not like you're going to get heatstroke today."

"You're right about that," Menedemos said from his station at the steering oars. The day was cool and overcast, the sky so gray he couldn't find the faintest trace of the sun. It was, in fact, the sort of weather his father had warned him about while arguing against putting to sea too soon. Once more, he reminded himself he owed Sostratos' nuisance of a brother-in-law thanks for getting his father to change his mind. That wasn't something Menedemos himself had ever had much luck doing.

Sostratos said, "If it stays like this, we're liable to have an interesting time navigating today. Sailing from here to Athens, we'll be crossing one of the wider landless stretches of the Aegean."

"It won't be that bad," Menedemos said, hoping he was right. "We'll have Psyra, west of Khios, to sight on as we go west, and Skyros and Euboia should be coming up over the horizon by the time Psyra drops out of sight astern."

"True—as long as the weather doesn't get any worse than this," Sostratos said. "If it starts raining, though, or if a fog rolls in . . ."

Menedemos spat into the bosom of his tunic to avert the omen. After a moment, his cousin did the same. Bad weather was the main reason ships seldom put to sea from the middle of autumn to the beginning of spring. Storms were the most dramatic worry, but fog and mist might have been more dangerous. Not being able to tell where you were or to recognize landmarks till too late . . . What could be more terrifying?

Diokles said, "Even in the fog, we've got wind and wave and casting the line to keep us safe. Between knowing how deep the sea is and seeing what sort of stuff the lead brings up when it does touch bottom, we ought to have a pretty fair notion of where we are."

"That's right," Menedemos said loudly, aiming his words not only at

Sostratos but at the crew as well. He didn't want the men worrying he'd end up in Byzantion when he was aiming for Athens. He also didn't want them worrying he'd tear the belly out of the akatos on a rock he didn't see soon enough. He didn't want to worry about that himself, though he knew it could happen if he wasn't careful.

Maybe Sostratos didn't want to worry about that, either. He changed the subject, saying in a sly voice, "Are you slipping, best one? You haven't said a word about either Phainias' wife or Onesimos'."

"I never saw Phainias'," Menedemos answered. "And he gave us girls, so going after her wouldn't have been sporting of me, would it?"

"That hasn't always stopped you," Sostratos observed.

He was right. Not caring to admit it, Menedemos said, "I *did* get a look at Onesimos', as a matter of fact. She was about *this* tall"—he held the palm of one hand flat against his chest, just below the level of his nipples—"and about *this* wide"—he took both hands off the tillers to stretch his arms wide—"so as far as I'm concerned Onesimos is welcome to her."

The listening sailors laughed. Sostratos said, "She'd be not far from our age, wouldn't she? Do you suppose she was that fat when he wed her?"

"I wouldn't know, and I don't much care to find out," Menedemos answered. "More women are like that than you'd think. They can't get out to the gymnasion to exercise, the way men do. They just stay inside the women's quarters and nibble all day long. Some men like them that way, too. For all I know, Onesimos is happy with her. But she wasn't what I wanted."

A line of pelicans flew by, not far from the ship. Menedemos admired their great white wings. He wondered if one of them would glide down to the water and scoop out a fish with its long, pouched beak, but none did. Sostratos also followed them with his eyes. He remarked, "They really do have heads shaped like axes, don't they?"

"So they do!" Menedemos said; in Greek, the two words were very close in sound. "I never thought of that before." He thumped his forehead with the heel of his hand, wondering why not.

Sostratos said, "I can imagine the first couple of Hellenes who ever saw pelicans. One of them turns to the other and says, 'What's *that?*' And the second fellow goes, 'I don't know, but it's got a head like an axe.' And the name would have stuck."

"Do you suppose that's how it happened?" Menedemos asked, intrigued.

"I don't know. I can't prove it. But I wouldn't be surprised," his cousin answered. "Things like that must happen when people run into beasts they've never seen before. They have to call them *something,* and they try to find a name that fits. I'll bet that's how those big beasts that live in the Nile got called river-horses."

"Hippopotamoi," Menedemos said thoughtfully, and dipped his head. "I'll bet you're right."

Diokles spoke up: "Sometimes people will make a joke of things, too. After all, what do we Hellenes call those big birds that live in the Egyptian desert, the ones that run faster than horses and kick like mules?"

"Strouthoi," Menedemos and Sostratos replied together. They both started to laugh, for in Hellas the more common meaning for the word that also meant *ostrich* was *sparrow.* Menedemos said, "I can just see the first fellow who went down to Egypt and got a good look at one of them. He'd turn to his friend and he'd say, 'By Herakles, that's the biggest sparrow I ever saw.' "

"I think Egypt did that to the first Hellenes who went there," Sostratos said. "We made up names that kept us from showing how impressed we were. Why else would we have called those tall stone monuments *obeliskoi?"*

"Well, they do look like skewers, don't they?" Menedemos said. "We could have called them *phalloi* instead, easy enough."

"You're right," Sostratos said. "*I* hadn't thought of that." His grin was lopsided and wry. "Maybe it's just as well they have the name they do."

The sun didn't come out. The clouds didn't go away. Every so often, the *Aphrodite* made her way through mist or drizzle. Even when Menedemos wasn't trying to peer through the spatters of moisture, visibility stayed bad. He sent a lookout to the foredeck, doing all he could do avoid unpleasant surprises.

"I wish we still had Aristeidas," Sostratos said.

"So do I," Menedemos said. "It's not your fault we don't, you know."

"Whom would you blame, then?" his cousin asked.

"How about the polluted Ioudaioi who tried to rob you?" Menedemos suggested.

"I didn't shoot enough of them," Sostratos said morosely.

"My dear, you couldn't have shot more than you did, not unless you were twins—and maybe not then. If you hadn't shot as many of them as you did, you and Moskhion and Teleutas would have got killed, too. Would that have made you happier?"

"I didn't shoot enough of them," Sostratos said again, and then, very low, "Teleutas." He looked disgusted.

Menedemos suspected his cousin wouldn't have been nearly so upset if Teleutas hadn't come back from the trip to Ioudaia. He'd liked Aristeidas much better than the other sailor himself, too. He couldn't hash that out with his cousin now, not with Teleutas pulling an oar less than ten cubits away. What he did say was, "You did the best you could. You did the best anyone could. You have no blood-guilt on your head. You committed no sin. You weren't Oidipous, slaying his father at a crossroads. You should stop tormenting yourself about it."

Sostratos started to answer, then checked himself. At last, after a long pause, he said, "That makes good logical sense. I try to be a logical man. Therefore, it should make me feel better. Somehow, though, it doesn't, or not very much."

"You mind if I say something, young sir?" Diokles asked, not missing a beat as he gave out the stroke.

"Please," Sostratos said.

"I'm no philosopher, so maybe I've got it all wrong," the oarmaster said. "If I do, I expect you'll tell me. But it seems to me this logic stuff is only good for what you've got in your head, if you know what I mean. When it comes to what's in your heart and your belly and your balls, logic goes out the window like a full pisspot."

"Much truth in that," Menedemos said.

"Some truth in it, certainly—but only some, I think," Sostratos said. "If we don't use reason to rule our passions, though, what are we but so many wild beasts?" He didn't add, *or so many adulterers,* as he probably would have before meeting that Ioudaian innkeeper's wife. *That's something,* Menedemos thought.

"No doubt you're right," Diokles said. "But I don't reckon we can rule everything all the time. We wouldn't be people if we could."

"We *should* be able to," Sostratos said stubbornly.

"That's not what Diokles said, and you know it," Menedemos said.

His cousin sighed. "So it isn't." Sostratos looked out to sea, as if he'd had enough of the argument.

Menedemos looked out to sea, too, for different reasons. With the overcast and the spatters of rain, all he had to gauge direction were the waves and the breeze. He couldn't find the sun, and neither Lesbos nor Psyra rose above his contracted horizon. He hated sailing under conditions like these. Navigation was somewhere between a guess and a bad joke. If the sea had been calm, he could have sailed in circles and never known it. He wasn't doing that now—he was pretty sure he wasn't, anyhow—but he hoped he wasn't veering too far to the west or south. The one would only take him out of his way. The other might cause a meeting he didn't want with Psyra or even Khios.

"What do you think of our course?" he asked Diokles.

The oarmaster checked the breeze with a spit-wet finger, then looked over the side—the sea, reflecting the gray of the sky, was anything but wine-dark today—to eye the waves. "Feels about right to me, skipper," he replied at last. "Can't say much more than that, not with the weather the way it is. Soon as it clears out, or soon as we get close to land, we'll know where we're at."

"That's true," Menedemos said. "What I don't want is to get too close to land too soon, if you follow me."

"Oh, yes." Diokles dipped his head. "Grounding a galley to dry out her timbers is all very well, if she's not too heavily laden to get her afloat again afterwards. But going aground when you don't want to, or ripping out her belly on a rock you never saw—that's a whole different business."

"Yes." Menedemos wondered what his father would say if he wrecked the *Aphrodite*. Actually, he didn't wonder—he knew, at least in broad outline. In something like that, the small details were unlikely to matter.

He tried to look every which way at once: dead ahead; to port and to starboard; astern past the boat, which bobbed in the chop behind the akatos. No suddenly looming land. No piratical pentekonter driving out of the mist and straight toward the *Aphrodite*. No trouble anywhere. He worried all the same.

When he said that out loud, Diokles dipped his head again. "A good thing you do, too. You're the skipper. Worrying's your job. Gods protect me from a captain who doesn't."

SOSTRATOS SPENT a lot of time doing lookout duty up on the *Aphrodite*'s cramped foredeck. Part of that was expiation for Aristeidas, the best lookout he'd ever known. Part of it was a sensible desire to keep the merchant galley safe, combined with the knowledge that a toikhar-khos was just cargo—or, more likely, ballast—as long as she sailed on the open sea. And part of it was the chance to watch birds and fish and other creatures at the same time as he was doing something useful.

Flying fishes leaped from the water and glided through the air be-fore returning to their proper element. A black-capped tern folded its wings, dove into the Aegean, and came out with a silvery fish writhing in its beak. The flying fishes had most likely gone from water to air to keep from becoming prey. The tern had gone from air to water to turn fish into prey.

It didn't get to enjoy its catch. A gull chased it and made it drop the sprat before it could gulp it down. Moskhion had come up to the fore-deck to check the forestay. He pointed at the gull, which grabbed the stunned fish from the surface of the sea and greedily gobbled it up. "Might as well be a Macedonian."

"Why?" Sostratos said. "Because he'd sooner live off the work of others than work himself? Me, I was thinking of him as a pirate."

"Six oboloi to the drakhma either way, young sir," Moskhion an-swered. Dolphins leaped from the water and then dove back in with hardly a splash. The former sponge diver's face showed unalloyed pleasure as he pointed to them. "I love dolphins. I think they're the most beautiful fish there are."

"I love dolphins, too. What seafaring man doesn't?" Sostratos said. "And they *are* beautiful, no doubt about it. But they're not fish."

"What?" Moskhion scratched his head. "What are they, then? Cab-bages?" He laughed at his own wit.

Smiling, Sostratos said, "They're no more cabbages than they are fish."

The sailor started to laugh again, but the mirth faded from his face as he studied Sostratos'. Moskhion frowned. Some men, when they heard an opinion they'd never met before, wanted nothing more than to wipe it from the face of the earth. *So the Athenians served Sokrates,* Sostratos thought. Moskhion wasn't of that school—not quite. But he wasn't far removed from it, either. He said, "Why, what else can dol-phins be but fish? They live in the sea, don't they? They haven't got any legs, do they? If that doesn't make 'em fish, what does?"

"Being like other fish would make them fish," Sostratos said. "But as my teacher's teacher, a lover of wisdom named Aristoteles, pointed out, they aren't like other fish. That means they have to be some different kind of creature."

"What do you mean, they aren't?" Moskhion demanded. "I just showed you how they were, didn't I?"

"Seaweed lives in the sea and hasn't got any legs," Sostratos said. "Does that make it a fish?"

"Seaweed?" As if humoring a madman, Moskhion said, "Seaweed doesn't look like a fish, young sir. Dolphins do."

"A statue may look like a man, but is a statue a man? If you ask a statue to lend you a drakhma, will it?"

"No, but half the men I know won't, either," Moskhion retorted, and Sostratos had to laugh. The sailor went on, "How *is* a dolphin different than a fish? Just tell me that, if you please."

"I can think of two important ways," Sostratos answered. "You must know that, if you keep a dolphin in the sea and don't let it come up for air, it will drown. Any fisherman who's caught one in a net will tell you that. And dolphins bring forth their young alive, the way goats and horses do. They don't lay eggs like fish."

Moskhion pursed his lips and scratched at the corner of his jaw. "They're *funny* fish, then. You're right about that much, I expect. But they're still fish." He went down from the foredeck into the waist of the ship.

Sostratos stared after him. The sailor had asked for reasons why dolphins weren't like fish. He'd given them. What had it got him? Nothing—not a single, solitary thing. "Funny fish," he muttered. Sokrates had crossed his mind a little while before. Now the Athenian sage did again; Sostratos thought, *If he had to deal with people like that, no wonder he drank hemlock. It must have seemed a relief.*

Moskhion hadn't been rude or abusive. He'd even gone through the forms of reasoned argument. He'd gone through them . . . and then ignored them when they produced a result he didn't like. As far as Sostratos was concerned, that was worse than refusing to argue at all.

From his station at the stern, Menedemos called, "If you're going to be a lookout, my dear, kindly look ahead, not toward me."

"Sorry," Sostratos said, reddening. He gave his attention back to the sea.

He wondered whether, a moment later, he would have to scream out, *Rock!* and give his cousin just enough time to steer the merchant galley out of harm's way. If he were telling the story in a tavern—and especially if Menedemos were telling it in a tavern—it would go that way. But he saw no rocks. He saw little of anything: only gray sky above and gray sea below. He wished he could see farther out to sea, but, unless Menedemos' navigation was far worse than he feared, it mattered much less on this broad reach of the Aegean than it would, say, down in the Kyklades. In those crowded waters, you could spit over the side and hit an island no matter where you were.

Darkness fell with no special drama. Light oozed out of the sky. At Diokles' command, the rowers shipped their oars. Men who weren't rowing brailed up the sail. Anchors splashed into the sea. Menedemos ordered lamps lit and hung from the stempost and sternpost. He said, "If some idiot's sailing on through the night, we ought to give him at least a chance to see us."

"Did I argue?" Sostratos replied.

"Not about that." Menedemos paused to dip up a cup of the rough red wine the crew drank aboard ship. "But Moskhion's been going on about how you tried to tell him dolphins aren't fish."

"By Poseidon's prick, they *aren't!*" Sostratos yelped. "Ask any man who's studied the issue, and he'll tell you the same thing."

"Maybe so, O best one, but any sailor, it seems, will tell you you're out of your mind," Menedemos replied.

"It's the *Apology* of Sokrates all over again: men who know one thing well think they know all things well because of their little piece of knowledge."

"More than a few of our sailors have been fishermen, too," Menedemos said. "If they don't know fish, what do they know?"

"Not much, in my opinion." But Sostratos spoke in a voice not much above a whisper. He did remember he wouldn't be wise to anger the men. With an odd mix of amusement and annoyance, he watched his cousin's relief that he remembered.

He too drank wine, and ate an uninspiring shipboard supper. He almost thought of it as a Spartan supper. Then he remembered the horrid black broth served in the Lakedaimonians' messes. Contemplating that nasty stuff made an opson of olives and cheese and an onion seem far more palatable.

The clouds and mist remained after full night came. "Too bad," Sostratos said, wrapping himself in his himation. "I always like looking at the stars before I go to sleep."

"Not tonight." Menedemos was also making himself as comfortable as he could on the poop deck.

"I wonder what they really are, and why a few of them wander while the rest stand still," Sostratos said.

"Those are questions for gods, not men," his cousin replied.

"Why shouldn't I ask them?" Sostratos said. "Men should ask questions, and look for answers to them."

"Go ahead and ask all you like," Menedemos said. "Getting answers to *those* questions is a different story, though."

Sostratos wished he could have quarreled with that. Instead, he sighed and dipped his head, saying, "I'm afraid you're right. Until we find some way to reach out and touch the stars, we'll never be able to find out what they are or why they shine."

"Well, my dear, you don't think small—I will say that," Menedemos replied with a laugh. "How do you propose to touch the stars?"

"I haven't the faintest idea. I wish I did." Sostratos yawned. "I haven't the faintest idea how I'm going to stay awake any more, either." The next thing he knew, he wasn't.

When he woke, the sky was getting light. It wasn't the rosy-fingered dawn of which the poets wrote, though: no pink and gold eastern sky, no sunbeams darting up from the sea. Only a sullen gray like that of the day before made night withdraw.

Menedemos was already up. "Good day, my dear," he said. "Here you've gone and taken away the fun of giving you a good kick, the way I was about to."

"So sorry to deprive you of your simple pleasures." Sostratos got to his feet and stretched to work the kinks out of his back. Rubbing his eyes, he added, "I'm feeling pretty simple myself right now."

Up and down the length of the *Aphrodite,* sailors were rousing. Diokles had already got up from the rower's bench where he'd spent the night. He seemed as well rested as if he'd slept in the bedchamber of the Great King of Persia. "Good day, young sirs," he called to Sostratos and Menedemos.

"Good day," Sostratos said. "We should pass through the strait between Euboia and Andros before sunset, shouldn't we?"

"I hope so," the oarmaster said. "If we're anywhere near where we ought to be, and if our navigation today's halfway decent, we ought to manage that."

"And if we don't, everyone will blame me." Menedemos made a joke of it, where a lot of captains would have been deadly serious. Pointing up toward the clue-obscuring sky, he said, "I do have an excuse for not guiding us to within a digit's breadth of our perfect path."

"No arguments, skipper," Diokles said. "I expect you'll get us where we're going. If I didn't think so, I'd be a right idiot to sail with you, wouldn't I?"

After barley rolls dipped in oil and washed down with watered wine, sailors slowly spun the capstans and brought up the anchors. As soon as they were stowed, the sail came down from the yard. It billowed and flapped and then filled with wind. Menedemos steered the ship west-southwest.

"I hope it's west-southwest, anyhow," he said with a wry grin. "It's my best guess."

"Warmer than yesterday, I think," Sostratos said. "Maybe the clouds and mist will burn off as the sun gets higher."

Little by little, they did. The sun came out, first through clouds still thick enough to let a man look without pain at its disk and then more strongly. The sky went from gray to a hazy blue: still not quite the weather for which Sostratos would have hoped, but definitely better. The horizon stretched as the mist faded.

"Land ho!" a rower called. "Land to port and astern."

"That's Psyra, I think," Sostratos said, shading his eyes to peer east.

Menedemos laughed. "It had better be. Otherwise we're really lost."

Not too much later, Sostratos spotted Skyros off the starboard bow. He felt proud of himself. His eyes were no better than anyone else's—indeed, he knew they were worse than those of several sailors. But knowing where Psyra was let him do a geometry problem in his head and figure out about where Skyros ought to be.

And then, as the day continued to clear and the horizon to extend, several sailors pointed dead ahead at almost exactly the same time. "There's Euboia!" they called.

"Good," Menedemos said. "We're about where we're supposed to be. If anything, we're a little farther west than I thought we were. We *will* get through the strait between Euboia and Andros today, and then it's on to Athens."

"On to Athens!" Sostratos couldn't have been happier if his cousin had said . . . He thought about that, then grinned. He couldn't have been happier if Menedemos had said *anything* else.

As the strait neared, Menedemos ordered weapons and helmets served out to the crew. The men set bronze helms, most of them un-crested, on their heads. The sailors not at the oars hefted spears and swords and belaying pins. The rowers stashed their weapons under their benches where they could grab them in a hurry.

"I hope this is all a waste of time," Menedemos said. "But a lot of you men were along a couple of years ago, when that pirate tried to board us. We fought off the polluted son of a whore. If we have to, we can do it again."

I hope we can do it again, he thought. He glanced over to Sostratos, waiting for his cousin to start mourning the gryphon's skull the pirates had carried away with them. But Sostratos didn't say a thing. Maybe he'd learned to accept the loss. More likely, he'd learned Menedemos would come down like a rockslide if he started complaining about the gryphon's skull.

Fishing boats fled the *Aphrodite* with even more alacrity than usual. Teleutas laughed and said, "With all the ironware and bronze we're showing, they're *sure* we're pirates now." His helmet jammed down low on his forehead and a fierce grin on his narrow, homely face made him look like a man who would sooner steal than work.

I know he steals, Menedemos reminded himself. *Sostratos caught him at it in Ioudaia. If he ever steals on the* Aphrodite, *he's gone.* But Teleutas had never got caught doing that. No one on the merchant gal-ley had complained of a thief. Maybe he had too much sense to steal from his fellow Hellenes. For his sake, Menedemos hoped so.

The channel between the islands was less than sixty stadia wide. Menedemos sailed the *Aphrodite* right down the middle of it. He was close enough to land to see sheep kicking up dust in the hills above the beach on Euboia, and to see one of those little fishing boats go aground at the mouth of a stream on Andros. He and the whole crew kept close watch on inlets and rocky outcrops—those were pirates' fa-vorite hiding places.

Today, though, everything seemed as peaceful as if no one had ever thought of taking robbery to sea. When Menedemos said that out loud, Sostratos tossed his head. "Don't believe it for a moment, my dear," he said. "Somewhere up in those hills—probably more than one place up in those hills—a pirate lookout is watching us and thinking, *No, more trouble than they're worth.* And that's all that's keeping us safe."

Menedemos didn't need long to decide his cousin was right. He said, "Well, I wish the lookout who loosed that last pirate ship against us in these waters would have thought the same thing."

"So do I," Sostratos said. Menedemos cocked his head to one side, waiting for him to say more. Sostratos caught him waiting and laughed. "I've said everything I can about the gryphon's skull."

"Till the next time you do," Menedemos gibed.

Sostratos laughed again, on a different note. "Maybe you're right. I hope not, but maybe. I think we *are* going to make it out of this channel."

"It's not very long," Menedemos said. "We only seem to take forever going through it."

"Oh, good," Sostratos said. "I thought I was the only one who felt that way."

"No, indeed, best one, and I'm not ashamed to admit it," Menedemos said. "After all, we're passing through a place where we've already had trouble. If you think I'm not nervous about the passage, you're daft. I don't like fighting off pirates any better than you do."

"You do it well," Sostratos said. "If you didn't, we'd be slaves now, or dead."

"For which I thank you," Menedemos said, "but I've already had more practice than I ever wanted." He turned his head from one side to the other. Now the coastline of Andros was swiftly falling off to the southeast, that of Euboia to the northwest. "We're through it now for sure. Anyone who wants to come after us will have a long chase, and we're not that much slower than a pirate ship."

Sostratos pointed west. "There's the headland of Laureion, with Helen's island in front of it. Attica!"

"Yes, Attica," Menedemos agreed dryly. "We limped into Sounion at the cape there a couple of years ago, too, if you'll remember, to bury our dead after the fight."

His cousin flushed. "So we did. But we're not limping now. And we haven't been robbed of what was our main reason for coming to Athens." He pointed a thumb at himself before Menedemos could speak. "Yes, I know I just mentioned the skull—but it was in the context of what we were talking about."

"Context." Menedemos rolled his eyes and addressed some invisible audience: "He takes one look at Attic soil and starts babbling about context. What'll he be like when we actually set foot in Athens? Odds are, no one will be able to understand his Greek at all."

"Oh, go howl!" Sostratos pointed back toward the southeast, not at Andros but up into the heavens. "What would you say the phase of the moon is?"

Menedemos looked over his shoulder to see the moon, white and pale in the late-afternoon sky. "First quarter—perhaps a day after."

"That's what I thought, too." Sostratos beamed. "That means it's the seventh or eighth of Elaphebolion. The Greater Dionysia starts on the tenth. We're going to make the festival."

"Good," Menedemos said. "I like the theater as well as the next fellow—unless the next fellow happens to be you, maybe—but I also know we have to do business. I keep hoping you'll remember that, too."

"How could I possibly forget, having you to remind me?" Sostratos spoke with such surpassing sweetness, anyone who didn't know him would have been sure he meant every word and was grateful.

Menedemos, who knew Sostratos as well as any man alive, was sure his cousin meant every word and wanted to push him over the rail. With a sweet smile of his own, he said, "All right, then. As long as we understand each other."

"We usually do." Again, Sostratos sounded altogether acquiescent. Again, Menedemos was not deceived. But then his cousin grew serious. "Do you think we can round Cape Sounion today, perhaps go all the way to Anaphlystos harbor?"

After studying the sun, Menedemos tossed his head. "What I think is, we'll be lucky to get *to* Sounion. More likely, we'll lie up in one of the little bays on Helen's island." Sostratos looked as if Menedemos had just kicked a puppy. Relenting a little, Menedemos added, "Even so, we should have no trouble reaching Peiraieus tomorrow."

Sostratos brightened. Menedemos had known his cousin would. He could have said the ship would spend the night in Persia—or, for that matter, in Tartaros—as long as he also said it would get to the harbor of Athens the next day. Sostratos said, "I wonder why Helen is tied to so many islands. There's another one, to the west, that's supposed to be where she first slept with Paris on the way to Troy."

"That I don't know," Menedemos said. "To tell you the truth, I haven't worried about it much, either. When I think about Helen, I'd rather think about why Paris wanted her than why they remember her on islands."

"But everyone knows why Paris wanted her," Sostratos said. "The other question's much more interesting, because it doesn't have an obvious answer."

"That makes it *more* interesting?" Menedemos said. Sostratos dipped his head. They stared at each other in perfect mutual incomprehension.

The *Aphrodite* reached an inlet at the north end of Helen's island as the sun slid behind the highland of Cape Sounion. The island ran from north to south, and was much longer than it was wide. No polis stood anywhere on it, nor even a village. Sheep and goats wandered the low, rolling ground, cropping grass and bushes. As darkness spread over sea and land, herdsmen's campfires glowed like golden stars off in the distance.

No one came up to the ship to ask for news or give any of his own. That saddened Menedemos. "The shepherds think we'll grab 'em and sell 'em into slavery," he said.

"We wouldn't," Sostratos said.

"No, of course not. Couldn't very well sell 'em in Athens even if we did grab 'em," Menedemos said. "I wouldn't care to enslave free Hellenes anyway—if the herders *are* free Hellenes and not already enslaved like Eumaios the swineherd in the *Odyssey*."

"They don't know where we're from or where we're bound," Sostratos said. "For all they can tell, we might be Tyrrhenians who'd sell them in the slave markets at Carthage."

"I know. That's what bothers me," Menedemos said. "Even so close to Athens, people worry about pirates and raiders."

"These are sorry times, when men think of themselves first and everything else only afterwards," Sostratos said, but after a moment he ruefully tossed his head. "When didn't men think of themselves first?

After the Peloponnesian War, the Thirty Tyrants made themselves hateful. And before that, Themistokles had to trick most of the Hellenes into fighting Xerxes by Salamis."

"Athenians both times," Menedemos remarked.

"Oh, yes," his cousin said. "Athens has shown the world more of man at his best and worst than any other polis in Athens. But thinking of yourself first goes back to long before Athens was such a great city. Look at Akhilleus in the *Iliad.* How many strong-greaved Akhaioi died because he stayed in his tent after his quarrel with Agamemnon?"

"Well, but Agamemnon was in the wrong, too, for taking Briseïs away from Akhilleus." Menedemos held up a hand before his cousin could speak. "I know what you're going to say next. You'll say that was Agamemnon putting what *he* wanted ahead of what the Akhaioi needed. And he did."

Sostratos looked disappointed at not having an argument on his hands. He glanced up at the moon. So did Menedemos. It seemed brighter and more golden now that the sun had left the sky. Sostratos said, "In the city, they're getting ready for the festival. And tomorrow we'll be there! I don't know how I'm going to sleep tonight."

He managed. Menedemos had to wake him in the morning. But Sostratos didn't complain, not when Menedemos said, "Rise and shine, my dear. Today we're going to Athens."

"Athenaze," Sostratos echoed dreamily. Then he said it once more, as if for good measure: "To Athens."

"Oöp!" DIOKLES CALLED, and the *Aphrodite*'s rowers rested at their oars. Sailors tossed lines to longshoremen in loincloths, who made the akatos fast to the quay. Just hearing the harbor workers brought Sostratos a thrill. What educated man didn't want to sound as if he came from Athens? And here were these probably illiterate laborers, using the dialect of Plato and Euripides. They were speaking commonplaces, but they sounded good doing it.

Or so Sostratos thought, anyway. In the broad Doric of Rhodes, one of the sailors said, "Who do those fellows think they are, anyhow? Slaves could do their jobs, but they talk like a bunch of toffs."

Menedemos pointed up one of the long, straight streets of Peiraieus. "At least this town is laid out sensibly," he said.

"This is one of the first places Hippodamos of Miletos designed,"

Sostratos answered. "Perikles had him do it. That would have been thirty years or so before he laid out the polis of Rhodes."

"Did he do anything with Athens proper?" Menedemos asked, peering toward the great buildings of the Athenian akropolis thirty-five or forty stadia inland.

"I'm afraid not," Sostratos said. "I wish he would have. The streets there are the wildest tangle anybody's ever seen. The Athenians take pride in being able to find their way around—except when they get lost, too."

His cousin pointed to the base of the pier. "Here comes an officer to question us." Indeed, the fellow looked splendid in crested helm and crimson cloak thrown back over his shoulders—as splendid as Antigonos' man, almost identically dressed, had at Mytilene. Menedemos went on, "Now, for half a drakhma, is he a Macedonian or an Athenian?"

Sostratos looked the man over. He was of average height, on the lean side, with dark hair, an olive complexion, a thin face, and ironic eyebrows. More than anything else, those eyebrows decided Sostratos. "Athenian."

"We'll know in a moment," Menedemos said. "Wait till he opens his mouth. If we don't have any trouble understanding him, you win. If he starts spewing Macedonian at us, I do."

"What ship are you, and where are you from?" The officer asked the usual questions in perfectly intelligible Attic Greek. Menedemos grimaced. Sostratos hid a smile.

"We're the *Aphrodite,* out of Rhodes," he answered, as he seemed to do whenever the akatos pulled into a new port.

"Ah. Rhodians." The officer brightened. "You'll be friendly to Ptolemaios, then."

Kassandros, who'd ruled Athens for the past decade through Demetrios of Phaleron, was friendly to Ptolemaios. Sostratos dipped his head, not wanting to disagree openly. "We try to be," he answered. "But then, we're neutral, so we try to be friendly to everybody."

"I see." The Athenian looked less happy. "Where did you stop on your way here?"

"Kos," Sostratos said, which pleased the fellow—Kos belonged to Ptolemaios—and then, "and Samos and Khios, both briefly, and then Lesbos. We have Lesbian wine for sale, and Lesbian truffles, too."

"I . . . see." The officer's pinched face was made for frowning. The last three islands belonged to Antigonos, with whom Kassandros was anything but friendly. After a moment's sour thought, the man decided to make the best of it, asking, "What's the old Cyclops up to? Did you see anything interesting along the way?"

"*I* didn't." Sostratos turned to his cousin. "Did you, Menedemos?"

"Can't say that I did," Menedemos answered. "He has war galleys in the harbors and on patrol, but then he would, especially after Ptolemaios took so much of the southern coast of Anatolia away from him a couple of years ago. Ptolemaios laid siege to Halikarnassos, too, remember, but it didn't fall." He sounded disappointed.

Sostratos knew why. The officer didn't. He said, "Yes, I do recall that. It was Antigonos' son Philippos who relieved the town, wasn't it?"

"No, the other son, the older one—he's named Demetrios, too," Sostratos said.

That got a grunt from the Athenian. He served Demetrios of Phaleron. Maybe he didn't love him. After the grunt, he asked the next inevitable question: "What are you carrying besides wine and truffles?"

"Koan silk," Sostratos said. The officer approved of Kos.

"Rhodian perfume," Menedemos added. That was safe, too.

"Papyrus and ink," Sostratos said. Papyrus came from Egypt, while the ink was Rhodian.

"Beeswax," Menedemos said. Beeswax could come from anywhere under the sun. "Embroidered cloth. And crimson dye from Sidon."

Sidon belonged to Antigonos, but he didn't say the *Aphrodite* had been there. He let the officer assume the Rhodians had got it in their home polis rather than going to Phoenicia themselves—which, in connection with their stops at other places belonging to Antigonos, might have made the fellow more suspicious. As things were, the officer said, "All right. I hope you have a profitable time trading here. You do know you'll have to change your silver for Athenian owls?"

"Yes, best one," Sostratos said, at the same time as Menedemos was saying, "Yes, most noble one." Neither of them looked at the other. Money-changers charged a fat commission for their services. They kept some for themselves; the polis got the rest. Both Rhodians intended to evade Athenian law as much as they could. Plenty of people in any polis worried more about the weight of the silver they got than whether it bore the Athenian owl or the rose of Rhodes.

As the officer turned to go back down the pier, Sostratos said, "Excuse me, best one, but is Iphikrates son of Leon still the Rhodian proxenos here?"

The Athenian tossed his head. "No, he died two, maybe three years ago. Protomakhos son of Alypetos represents your polis here these days."

"Not a name I know," Sostratos said. Menedemos dipped his head in agreement. Sostratos went on, "Is his house here in Peiraieus, or does he live up in Athens?"

"He's in Athens, not far from the theater," the officer replied, which made Sostratos' heart leap with joy and, by Menedemos' expression, made his cousin fight back laughter. The Athenian added, "He deals in marble and other stone himself. He has a good name in the city."

"Glad to hear that," Sostratos said.

As the soldier did leave the quay, Menedemos' swallowed snickers broke free. "The proxenos has a house by the theater!" he said. "I'm sure your heart's breaking because we'll have to walk all the way into Athens to meet this Protomakhos. A pig dreams of swill, a sheep dreams of clover, and you—you dream of a house by the theater in Athens. And now your dream's come true."

Sostratos wanted to tell him he was talking nonsense—wanted to, but knew he couldn't. He gave back a rather sickly smile. "We really ought to go meet the fellow, don't you think?"

"I don't know." Menedemos sounded both judicious and dubious. "I was thinking of selling our goods at the marketplace right here in Peiraieus, and so we won't—"

"What?" Sostratos yelped. "Are you out of your mind? They sell timber and oil and wheat here, not the kind of. . . ." He fumbled to a stop when his cousin started laughing again, this time harder than ever. Sostratos sent him an aggrieved stare. "Oh. You're having me on. Ha. Ha, ha. Ha, ha, ha." That wasn't laughter. He repeated the empty syllables to show how funny he thought the joke was.

Menedemos set a hand on his shoulder. "I'm sorry, my dear. I truly am. I just couldn't resist. The look on your face—"

"Couldn't resist?" Sostratos said. "You didn't even try."

"Well, maybe not." Menedemos gauged the sun. "Do you think we've got time to go into town today and find this Protomakhos, or would we do better waiting till tomorrow?"

Sostratos looked at the sinking sun, too: looked at it and let out a long, mournful sigh. "Tomorrow would be better," he said, "and you have no idea how much I wish I could tell you otherwise." And then, suddenly, he snapped his fingers. "No, I take it back—we'd better go now."

"And how have you talked yourself into that?" Menedemos asked, amused.

"Simple. Tomorrow's either the ninth or the tenth of Elaphebolion." His gaze swung to the ripening moon, which announced the date. "I think it'll be the tenth. If it is, it's the first day of the Dionysia. There'll be a big parade and all sorts of other things going on, and nobody will want to do any business. That's why we ought to meet Protomakhos today."

His cousin thought it over. "Well, when you're right, you're right. We'd better go. Diokles, keep enough men on board and sober tonight to make sure none of these clever, light-fingered Athenians walks off with the akatos."

"I'll take care of it, skipper," the oarmaster promised. "You can count on me."

"I know. I do," Menedemos said. "And now I'd better get moving. Look at Sostratos there, shifting from foot to foot like a comic actor about to shit himself."

"I am not!" Sostratos said indignantly, and made sure he did *not* rise up onto the toes of his left foot. "I'm just . . . eager."

"That's what boys say when they shoot too soon the first time they visit a brothel," Menedemos retorted. Sostratos yelped again, even more indignantly than before. His cousin laughed and clapped him on the shoulder. "Let's go, then."

Even setting foot in Peiraieus was enough to excite Sostratos. He made himself hurry past the long colonnade that housed the harborside market. Most of the port wasn't worth looking at: nondescript houses and shops, mud-brick with red tile roofs. Some of them were whitewashed, rather more weren't. The goods on display were of the cheap, flashy sort he might have seen in any good-sized polis around the Inner Sea. But the people were speaking Attic Greek. Even the barbarians in business in Peiraieus, of whom there were a good many, spoke Attic flavored by their foreign accents. Hearing it made Sostratos smile.

Menedemos pointed. "What's that temple? It sure stands out amongst all this boring stuff."

"That's the sacred enclosure of Athena and Zeus," Sostratos answered. "Both deities are portrayed in bronze. Athena's holding a spear; Zeus has a rod in one hand and a Victory in the other. There's also a fine painting of Leosthenes and his family by Arkesilaos. That's new; the statues aren't."

"Leosthenes?" Menedemos frowned. "I can't place the name."

"The Athenian general who fought the Macedonians right after Alexander died, when we were just going from boys to youths," Sostratos said. "He beat them a couple of times up in Boiotia, but they won the war."

"All right. I remember that," Menedemos said. "I couldn't have come up with his name if you'd handed me to a Persian torturer, though." He pointed off to the right, toward the east. "And what's that big thing?"

"That's the fortress at Mounykhia, the harbor next door," Sostratos told him. "It's full of Kassandros' Macedonians."

"It would be, wouldn't it?" Menedemos said.

"What? You don't suppose the Athenians would line up with Kassandros if he didn't hold them down?" Sostratos did his best to sound artfully shocked. His cousin chuckled. He went on, "If there weren't any Macedonians around, Athens—and all the other poleis in Hellas—would go back to squabbling amongst themselves, the way they did before Philip put his foot on them."

"Not *all* the other poleis."

"What do you mean?"

"Thebes isn't there any more. Alexander destroyed it."

"That's true," Sostratos said. "I've heard people are starting to live on the site, though. One of these days, it'll be a city again."

"I suppose so," his cousin said. They walked on through Peiraieus and up toward Athens through the Long Walls joining the port to the great city. Menedemos nodded to the soldiers on the walls. "They'd be more Macedonians, wouldn't they?"

Sostratos eyed the men. "Probably. They're bigger and fairer than most Athenians, anyhow. But Demetrios of Phaleron is the glove to Kassandros' hand: what Kassandros wants done, Demetrios does. So they may be Athenians doing the Macedonians' bidding."

"I thought these walls would be more impressive," Menedemos said. "They aren't that tall, and they aren't that strong."

"They were first built in Perikles' day, and generals then knew less about besieging cities than they do now, so the works didn't have to be that strong to serve," Sostratos answered. "They were strong enough to keep the Spartans out. Athens wasn't stormed at the end of the Peloponnesian War. The Spartans starved her into surrender, and then made the Athenians pull down a stretch of the walls afterwards."

Menedemos looked around. "Built up again," he observed.

"Oh, yes," Sostratos said. "The Athenians did that as soon as they thought they could get away with it." His gaze went this way and that, too. The road up from Athens wasn't much to look at: only a dirt track, with grass and bushes on either side. Even so . . . "Walking this road, Menedemos . . . Walking this road is special. Perikles traveled on this road. So did Aiskhylos and Sophokles and Euripides. So did Thoukydides—and Herodotos, too, though he wasn't born here. Sokrates walked this road, and Platon, and Aristoteles. And now—Sostratos and Menedemos."

Menedemos went off behind a bush to ease himself. When he came back, he said, "Aristophanes might have pissed on that very same bush. What an honor!" He batted his eyes like a youth playing coy.

"To the crows with you," Sostratos said. "I try to talk about what coming to Athens means to me, and what do I get? Filthy jokes!"

"Aristophanes lived here, too, and the other comic poets, though you didn't bother mentioning *them*," Menedemos said. "Are you going to tell me comedy isn't part of what Athens stands for?"

"There's a time and place for everything," Sostratos replied, a weaker comeback than he'd thought he might give. Reluctantly, he dipped his head to his cousin. "All right. You have a point—of sorts."

"Thank you. Thank you so much!" Menedemos cried.

"Enough," Sostratos said. His cousin only laughed at him. He clicked his tongue between his teeth. He might have known that would happen.

But Menedemos wasn't a complete scoffer. Pointing up to the akropolis, he said, "That's the temple to Athena the Maiden, isn't it?"

"Yes, that's the Parthenon, sure enough," Sostratos answered. The sinking sun shone brilliantly on the white marble and on the painted blues and reds and yellows of the Panathenaic frieze.

"I've seen a lot of temples in my time," Menedemos said, "but that one's as fine as any."

Sostratos dipped his head. "I think so, too. We'll have to make a trip up there so you can see the cult statue. It's all gold and ivory, five or six times as tall as a man. There's nothing like it except the great Zeus at Olympia—and Pheidias made that image, too."

"All gold and ivory." For a moment, Menedemos sounded as piratical as any Lykian. Then his thoughts turned to those a trader might have: "I wonder how much of the gold stuck to Pheidias' fingers."

"Perikles' enemies charged Pheidias with that, and with putting his own face on one of the details of the ornamentation of the statue of Athena, and all manner of other things, for Perikles, of course, was his patron, and by striking at Pheidias they could embarrass the man through whom he did what he did," Sostratos said.

"Well? What happened?" Menedemos sounded interested in spite of himself.

"He didn't steal any of the gold. Perikles had warned him he might be challenged, so he made the gold plates for the statue easy to re-move. When the Athenians took them down and weighed them, they found that none of the metal entrusted to him was missing. But then they started shouting, 'Impiety!' when they found out he'd put his por-trait on one of the warriors on Athena's shield—that's what I was talk-ing about before."

"Men do that sort of thing all the time nowadays," Menedemos re-marked.

"I know, but this was more than a hundred twenty years ago, and they didn't then," Sostratos said. "And some say Perikles' face was there with his. Some say Pheidias had to leave Athens. Others say he was made to drink hemlock, like Sokrates later." He shuddered. So did Menedemos. They'd watched a man die of hemlock. It wasn't so neat and tidy as Platon made it out to be. Sostratos went on, "I don't think they killed him, but I can't prove it. Too long ago now—no one who knew the truth is left alive."

The walls of the polis of Athens loomed ahead. They were taller and more formidable than the Long Walls. All the traffic coming up from Peiraieus and going down to the port funneled through a single gate. A man leading a donkey with half a dozen amphorai lashed to its back came out of Athens toward Sostratos and Menedemos. An old man leaning on a stick went into the city ahead of the Rhodians. Guards asked him a question or two, then waved him forward.

One of the guards held up a hand. Sostratos and Menedemos dutifully stopped. In purest Attic, the guard said, "Who are you? What's your business here?"

"We're merchants from Rhodes," Sostratos answered. "We hope to do business in Athens. Right now, we're looking for our polis' proxenos."

"Pass on." The gate guard stood aside.

"This isn't quite the city proper," Sostratos said, pointing ahead after they went through the gate. "There's another wall up there, perhaps ten or twelve plethra farther along."

"Yes, I see it over the roofs of the houses and shops," Menedemos said.

"We have two choices for a gate there. One will bring us into the city north of the Pnyx, the other to the south," Sostratos said.

"What's the Pnyx?" his cousin asked. "Is it worth seeing?"

"It's where the Assembly meets—or rather, where it did meet till a few years ago," Sostratos replied. "These days, the people come together at the theater." He didn't point out—no telling who might be listening—that the Assembly's meetings were much less important than they had been during the great days of Athens. These days, Demetrios of Phaleron or Kassandros' officers or the Macedonian marshal himself decided what went on here. The people's voice was stifled.

"Doesn't sound that interesting, not to look at," Menedemos said. "Let's use the south entrance—that's the shorter way to the akropolis and the theater, isn't it?"

Sostratos dipped his head. "That's right. You do remember your way around."

"Some," Menedemos said. "It's been four or five years—that trading run where I met the charming lady in Halikarnassos, remember?"

"I'm not likely to forget," Sostratos said. "It wasn't the lady who was so memorable—"

"It was to me," Menedemos broke in.

Sostratos overrode him: "It was her husband. I don't know whether she will or not, but he'll never forget you."

"I'm probably not the only one he's got to worry about." Menedemos stepped up the pace. "Come on. There's the gate. I can see it. Hurry up, won't you? We do want to find the proxenos' house before the sun goes down."

You do want to change the subject, Sostratos thought. *You don't like getting reminded about outraged husbands. You didn't even mention him—only his wife. Whose wife will you go after here?* That was one question whose answer he hoped he wouldn't learn. He caught up with his cousin. They reached the gate side by side. A yawning guard waved them through without a word. On they went, into Athens.

MENEDEMOS DID HIS BEST not to stare like a back-country farmer coming for the very first time into a town big enough to boast a wall. It wasn't easy. On his last visit to Attica, he'd spent most of his time in Peiraieus. He'd been determined not to seem impressed there, too. Sostratos had almost had to drag him up to Athens to look around.

The first thing that struck him was how *big* a polis it was. Rhodes was a good-sized city in its own right, but it didn't come close to this one. Syracuse, in Sicily, was supposed to have been a match for Athens years before, but endless civil strife had taken its toll there. These days, only Alexandria deserved mention in the same breath—and Alexandria drew its wealth from all of Egypt, while Athens relied on Attica alone . . . Attica, and the wits of its citizens.

And, large as it was, Athens seemed even grander and more impressive. Menedemos' eyes kept rising to the akropolis. "They put everything they had into this, didn't they?" he murmured.

"That's what Thoukydides says," Sostratos answered. Plainly quoting, he went on, " 'For if the city of the Lakedaimonians were deserted, but the temples and the foundations of the buildings were left, after a long time had gone by there would be great disbelief at their power.' Then he says, 'But if this same thing happened to the Athenians, their power would likely be reckoned twice what it is, from the visible appearance of their city.' "

"Well, I've got to hand it to the old boy," Menedemos said. "He hit that one square in the middle of the target. This place is"—he looked around again, trying to come up with a phrase that fit—"a possession for all time." Sostratos smiled at that. "What's the matter now?" Menedemos asked indignantly. "Did I say something funny? I didn't mean to."

"Not funny, O best one—just . . . fitting," his cousin replied. "That's what Thoukydides intended his history to be: a *ktema es aei.*" He said the words for *possession for all time* in a very old-fashioned way; Menedemos supposed that was how Thoukydides had written them. Sostratos added, "His history is a hundred years old now, so it looks as if he's getting what he wanted."

"That's true," Menedemos said. "Here's hoping somebody remembers us after we're a hundred years gone."

"Yes. Here's hoping." Sostratos' voice had an edge to it.

Menedemos wondered what he'd done to irk his cousin. He didn't want to offend Sostratos without meaning to; that took the fun out of it. Then he remembered Sostratos aspired to write history, too. Clapping him on the shoulder, Menedemos said, "Don't worry about it, my dear. A hundred years from now, they'll be talking about Sostratos and Thoukydides, not the other way round."

"You're a splendid flatterer. I hope I have wisdom enough to know when I'm being flattered, though," Sostratos said.

"I don't know what you're talking about," Menedemos said. Sostratos snorted. Menedemos turned serious again: "When should we start asking Athenians where the proxenos' house is?"

"Not yet, by the dog," Sostratos replied. "Wait till we get to the theater. Then we have some chance of getting a straight answer. If we ask now, most of these abandoned rogues will take our oboloi, spin us a pretty set of directions that lead nowhere, and go their way laughing at how they suckered the hicks from out of town."

"Charming people," Menedemos said.

"In many ways, they are," his cousin said. "In many ways, mind you, but not all. They're out for themselves, first, last, and always. So are most Hellenes, of course—"

"I was just going to say that," Menedemos put in.

"Yes, but you wouldn't tell a stranger fancy lies for the sake of an obolos and a laugh," Sostratos said. "A lot of them would. They take being out for themselves further than most Hellenes do. They take almost everything further than most Hellenes do, for good and for ill. You don't have to be fast to live in Athens, but it helps."

"How did *you* manage, then?" Menedemos asked. His cousin was a great many things, but never fast, not the way he'd meant.

"For one thing, I learned to talk more like an Athenian," Sostratos answered. "For another, I kept company with lovers of wisdom, who are—mostly—a different breed."

"Oh," Menedemos said. That made a certain amount of sense, but only a certain amount. "Why are the philosophers different? Have they figured out how to live without money?"

"Some of them have, by choosing not to care about a lot of the things most men go after money to buy," Sostratos said. Menedemos tossed his head. That way wasn't for him. He liked his comforts too well. Sostratos continued, "But a lot of men who can study philosophy and history their whole lives long are the ones who can afford to do that from the start. They don't need to worry about an obolos here and an obolos there, because they come from rich families. They've got more silver than they can spend if they live to be ninety."

That edge returned to his voice. Menedemos remembered how bitter he'd been when his father called him home from Athens. "Well, my dear, if we get rich enough, you can walk away from the trading business and spend all your time at the Lykeion again," he said.

"Too late for me," his cousin said. "I've been out in the world too long; I could never be indifferent to money—or take it for granted, the way a lot of philosophers do. And do you know what really irks me?"

"Tell me," Menedemos urged. Every so often, Sostratos had to let out what ate at him or go wild.

"They don't know how lucky they are," he said now. "Remember, I told you I met that Hekataios of Abdera in Jerusalem when we were in the east last year? He was writing a history in Alexandria, and he found out the Ioudaioi had a role to play in it. So what did he do? He headed for Jerusalem to see what he could find out about them. He didn't worry about the money—he just *did* it. I was so jealous, I wanted to wring his scrawny neck. There I was, worrying about what I could sell and what I might buy, and he took his own sweet time wandering around asking questions—when he found someone who spoke Greek to answer them, that is."

"You're the one who learned Aramaic," Menedemos said.

Sostratos answered in that language, something so harsh and guttural and evil-sounding that three or four passersby spun around to stare at him. Menedemos didn't think Sostratos noticed. Returning to Greek, he went on, "Yes, I'm the one who learned Aramaic, and I probably learned more about the Ioudaioi than Hekataios did, too. And much good it did me, because he's the one who gets to write the book and be remembered."

Slyly, Menedemos said, "You're the one who laid the innkeeper's wife."

His cousin gave him a bleak laugh. "So I am. That didn't work out, either. Afterwards, we both ended up unhappier than we would have if we'd never gone to bed together."

"Yes, I know. That's too bad. It's not supposed to work that way." The only times Menedemos hadn't enjoyed adultery were the ones when the woman's husband had found out.

Sostratos didn't answer him now. They walked on through the narrow, winding, smelly streets of Athens. When Menedemos couldn't see the magnificent buildings of the akropolis or those at the edges of the agora off to the northwest, the city seemed just another polis, an oversized one, but nothing out of the ordinary in the way most of its people lived. After doubling back from yet another dead end, he wished it, like Peiraieus, boasted a neat Hippodamian grid of streets.

No such luck, though. He and Sostratos had to scramble out of the way when a woman called, "Coming out!" from a second-floor window and emptied a chamber pot into the dirt street below. Flies started buzzing around the stinking puddle. A man wearing a himation in front of the Rhodians shouted curses at the woman, for the slops had splashed him. When she ignored the hard words, he flung a rock at the window. It rattled off a wooden shutter, breaking two of the slats. He went on his way, contented. From the safety of the upstairs room, the woman screeched her own curses at him. Now he ignored her.

"Welcome to life in the big city," Sostratos said with a wry chuckle, although a scene like that could have happened in any Hellenic polis, regardless of size.

"It missed us, and we didn't walk in it afterwards," Menedemos said. "Past that, who cares?" They walked on for a little while, then turned onto a wider street that went more directly east. Menedemos pointed ahead. "Those curved rows of seats ahead—that has to be the theater."

"Yes, that's right." Sostratos dipped his head. "And do you see the big stretch of tile roof beyond them?"

"Not very well. You're taller than I am." Menedemos jumped in the air, which made a couple of Athenians goggle. "All right—yes, it's there. What is it?"

"That's the Odeion," his cousin answered. "Perikles had it built to house the musical contests at the Panathenaic Games. It's so big, it has ninety pillars inside holding up the roof. People say it's modeled after the tent Xerxes lived in when he invaded Hellas, but I don't know if that's true or just a story."

"If it's not true, it's a *good* story," Menedemos said. "Can't ask for more than that."

"I can *ask* for the truth," Sostratos said, a little stiffly. "Whether I can find it after more than a hundred years is liable to be another matter."

"I didn't mean anything by it," Menedemos said. His cousin walked on without answering. *I've gone and put his back up,* Menedemos thought unhappily. Sostratos got much too touchy much too fast when it came to historical questions, though in other areas he would put up with more than most Hellenes did. Instead of trying to jolly him along, Menedemos waved to a passing Athenian. "*Oê!* You, there!"

"What do you want?" the fellow asked.

"Can you tell us how to get to the house of Protomakhos the marble merchant? He's not far from the theater, is he?"

"Yes, I know where his house is," the Athenian said, and said no more. Menedemos had expected nothing else. He gave the man an obolos. Popping the coin into this mouth, the Athenian continued, "It's close by the temple of Dionysos, at the southwestern corner of the theater precinct. It's on the left side of the street as you go south. I forget whether it's the second or third house there, but you can knock on doors and find out."

"Thanks," Menedemos said.

"Any time, buddy." The Athenian stuck his tongue in his cheek, as if to say, *Any time you pay me:* he might have been going after the obolos he'd just got.

"Can we find it with those directions?" Menedemos asked as the local went on his way.

"We can find the right street, I think, or at least narrow it down to two or three," Sostratos answered. "And somebody on one of those streets ought to know where to find Protomakhos' house. We might not even have to spend any more silver."

"Ha! I'll believe that when I see it," Menedemos said.

A gray stone wall around the holy precinct kept him from getting more than a glimpse of the roof of the temple of Dionysos. That roof was of red tiles, like those of most of the nearby houses. These, though, were faded by the sun and cracked and weathered by who could say how many freezes and rainstorms. The temple had stood there a very long time.

Menedemos pointed to a street that headed south just beyond the temple. "Shall we try this one?"

"Why not?" Sostratos replied. "If we're wrong, we can't be far wrong. The Athenian said second or third house down, didn't he?"

"That's right," Menedemos said. When they came to the second house, he knocked on the door.

Several dogs inside the house started howling: not little yapping lap-dogs, but Kastorian hunting hounds with big, deep voices. Menedemos found himself hoping whoever was in there wouldn't open the door. He let out a sigh of relief when all he got was a hoarse shout: "Who's there? What do you want?"

"Is this the house of Protomakhos son of . . . uh . . . ?"

"Alypetos," Sostratos supplied.

"No," the voice said over the baying of the hounds. "He lives next door, one house down."

"Artemis be praised for that," Menedemos muttered as they went on to the next house. "If they'd opened the door to that last place, those dogs might have eaten us alive."

"We wouldn't have been alive for long," Sostratos said, relentlessly accurate. "And how would you like to live next door to that racket all the time? I like my peace and quiet. If it were me, I'd be tempted to throw some poisoned meat over the wall and get rid of a few of those beasts."

"It's not just the racket, either." Menedemos held his nose. "I know cities can't help being smelly places, but I don't fancy dog shit in my nostrils all day long. There'll be more flies, too, especially when the weather warms up."

"Would you rather stay at an inn, then?" Sostratos asked.

Menedemos sighed and tossed his head. "No, we're here." He knocked on the door. Again, someone on the inside asked who he was. He gave his name and Sostratos', adding, "This is the house of the Rhodian proxenos, isn't it?"

The door opened. The man standing there had to be Protomakhos himself. He was about fifty, broad-shouldered, a little thick in the belly but still vigorous, with a face that would have been strikingly handsome but for a nose that had met a mishap somewhere and bent to the left. "Come in, friends," he said. "Use my house as your own for as long as you're in Athens. I've heard of your fathers. If you match them, you won't be doing bad. Try to ignore the smell from next door; Demotimos raises hunting dogs."

"Thank you very much," Menedemos and Sostratos said together. Protomakhos stood aside to let them in. *A beginning,* Menedemos thought. In he went, Sostratos at his heels.

5

"WE THANK YOU AGAIN FOR YOUR GENEROUS HOSPITAL-ity," Sostratos told Protomakhos over breakfast the next morning. Menedemos, who was also spooning up barley porridge and sipping watered wine in the andron, dipped his head in agreement.

"My pleasure, best ones." Protomakhos took a swig from his cup. The wine he served was no Ariousian, but it would do; it was a good deal better than what the *Aphrodite* carried for sailors to drink. The Rhodian proxenos went on, "I don't know how much you'll get done for the next seven days or so, what with the Greater Dionysia starting today. You'll be paying your rowers for getting drunk in the god's name."

Menedemos stirred at that, as if he hadn't thought of it till now. Maybe he hadn't. Sostratos had. It distressed his thrifty soul, but the alternative was missing the festival—and missing the plays that went with it. "We'll just have to make the best of it, most noble one," he said. "I'm not sorry your house is so close to the theater."

His cousin almost choked on his wine. Protomakhos chuckled. "Aha! So you *did* come for the plays. I wondered, but coming right out and asking is rude. Yes, this isn't a bad place to start from if you fancy drama."

"I hope Menandros offers a comedy this year," Sostratos said.

"He's supposed to be working on one," Protomakhos said. "I don't know if he's finished it."

"Oh, I hope so," Sostratos said. "I'm trying to convince Menedemos that comedy doesn't start and stop with Aristophanes."

"*I* laugh at Menandros' plays," Protomakhos said. "I don't see how you can help it, not unless you're dead."

Sostratos glanced at Menedemos, to see how his cousin would take that. Menedemos was too polite to come right out and disagree with his host. Instead, he changed the subject: "I'll enjoy the plays, I'm sure. I'll also enjoy the rest of the festival for the god's sake. Nothing wrong with plenty of wine, or with women who have license to be loose for a few days."

"There's some of that at this festival, but less than at Dionysiai in other places," the Rhodian proxenos warned. "In fact, there's less of it than there was at the smaller festivity last month. I don't want you fellows to have the wrong idea and get in trouble because of it."

"I already knew as much, having spent some time here," Sostratos said. "We do appreciate your care for us." Menedemos didn't look as if he appreciated it at all, but Sostratos didn't remark on that.

Protomakhos said, "If you want to watch the parade into town from the Academy, you'd do well to head for the agora now. It fills up fast, with slaves as well as citizens. If you care to try your luck with women, that'll be your best chance—unless you feel like going out at night, that is."

"Shall we?" Menedemos asked.

"Why not?" Sostratos said. "If we're going to give ourselves to the god, we should do it in fullness."

"That's the spirit," Protomakhos said.

"Will you come, too, best one?" Sostratos asked him.

He tossed his head. "I'll wait till the procession gets to the temple of Dionysos here to pay my respects to the god. I'm an Athenian, you know, and not a young one. I've seen the Dionysia . . . well, a good many times by now. This part is always the same."

"All right." Sostratos nudged Menedemos. "Come on. Hurry up. We don't want to get there and find out we're too far away from the Street of the Panathenaia to see anything."

"I'm coming, I'm coming." Menedemos turned to Protomakhos. "I'm usually the one who has to hustle him along, you know. But he wants to see this, and so. . . ." He made as if to pour himself another cup of wine. When Sostratos rolled his eyes and let out an exasperated sigh, his cousin laughed and got to his feet.

People were already out in the streets when they left the Rhodian proxenos' house. A lot of the women looked like respectable wives and matrons: they weren't all slaves and poor folk by any means. Now Sostratos was the one who laughed.

"What's so funny?" Menedemos asked.

"You," Sostratos told him. "You're so busy turning and looking at them all, you can hardly walk, and you haven't got any idea which ones to smile at first."

"I don't get to see a crowd of them like this very often," Menedemos answered. "Most honest women who can afford it spend most of their time indoors, so I'm enjoying the . . . the variety."

"If you stare any harder, the Athenians will decide you're a bumpkin from Akharnai who's never come into the big city before," Sostratos said. Menedemos made a face at him—Aristophanes had written a comedy about Akharnaians—but kept on looking around at all the pretty, fairly pretty, and even not so pretty women who'd come out to celebrate the festival.

People were already passing cups of wine back and forth. Sostratos drank when somebody thrust one at him. The wine was neat and not very good. He took a small sip, then passed it to Menedemos. After drinking, Menedemos gave a woman the cup. Her smile showed two black front teeth. Menedemos didn't speak to her after that. He hurried on with Sostratos toward the agora. Phalloi decorated the streets, some of clay, some of wickerwork, some with cloth-covered wicker frames decorated with ribbons.

Athens' great market square lay on the flat ground northwest of the akropolis. The Street of the Panathenaia, a rutted dirt track, ran through it from northwest to southeast. Athens' public buildings bounded the southern and western sides: the mint and a couple of fountains on the south, along with a covered colonnade that was not only full of people but had them clambering up to the roof like monkeys. On the west stood the generals' headquarters, the round Tholos, which housed the rotating executive committee of the Council of Elders; the Bouleuterion, where the whole Council met, and the Royal Stoa, which also had people climbing its columns and up onto the roof.

The agora itself was filling rapidly. Skythian constables, shouting in bad Greek, fought to keep the crowd from packing the Street of the Panathenaia and blocking the procession. Everyone struggled to get as close as he could. Sostratos was an uncommonly large man. Menedemos wasn't, but he was an uncommonly good wrestler. They got closer than most.

Sostratos pointed northwest, toward the Dipylon Gate and the

Academy beyond the wall. "The god's boat will come from that direction," he said.

Menedemos dug a finger in his ear. "The god's what? The noise is
dreadful, isn't it? I thought you said 'boat.' "

"I did. You'll see," Sostratos said. Someone trod on his toe. *"Oimoi!"*
he exclaimed. Like any sailor, he always went barefoot. That had disadvantages in a crowd.

"Sorry, pal," said the fellow who'd stepped on him.

"You're lucky he's not like some of those harlots," Menedemos said.
"You know the kind I mean: the ones who have FOLLOW ME or something like that written backwards on the bottom of their sandals in
metal, so they leave the words in the dust of the street as they walk
along. No fun at all if that comes down on your foot."

"No, it wouldn't be," Sostratos agreed. Thoughtfully, he went on, "I
imagine the trade they'd bring in would vary from polis to polis, depending on how many men in each place can read. They'd do better
here or in Rhodes than up in Macedonia—I'm sure of that."

"Only you—" Menedemos said, and then had to stop, for he was
laughing too hard to go on. He needed some little while before he
could continue. "Only you, my dear, could think of a whore and think
of how much money she might make and why, and not of how she
makes her money."

"I know how they make their money," Sostratos said. "The other is
something I hadn't thought about before." He started to say that made
it more interesting, but checked himself. It did, to him, but Menedemos
had already shown he would make him sorry if he said anything like
that.

Flutes and drums and other instruments resounded, out beyond the
northern edge of the agora. Heads swung in that direction. An Athenian stepped out into the Street of the Panathenaia to get a better look.
One of the Skythian slave constables shoved him back into the crowd,
shouting, "What you t'ink you does? How selfis' is you?" Like a lot of
barbarians, he couldn't pronounce some of the sounds of Greek. Having tried to learn how to say the gutturals of Aramaic, Sostratos had
more sympathy for him than he would have before.

Unlike the Athenian, Sostratos was not only close to the Street of
the Panathenaia but also tall enough to see over the crowd. Beside

him, Menedemos twisted to look past the few people in front of him and now and then jumped in the air to get briefly above them. Once he too came down on Sostratos' toes. *"Papai!"* Sostratos said in pain and annoyance. "Have *you* got FOLLOW ME on the bottoms of your polluted feet?"

"Sorry." His cousin didn't sound sorry at all. He jumped up again. This time, he missed Sostratos when he landed.

"Here they come!" The words raced through the crowd.

Some of the dancers at the head of the procession were dressed as satyrs, with tight-fitting goatskin costumes, horsetails, erect phalloi as long as a man's forearm, and snub-nosed masks that put Sostratos in mind of the way Sokrates was said to have looked. They shouted lewd suggestions at the pretty women they saw, sometimes aiming their phalloi at them like spears. Some of the women shouted lewd suggestions of their own; the Dionysia, even in the toned-down version of it celebrated at Athens, was a time when restraint went out the window.

Behind the satyrs came maenads in torn, ragged tunics that suggested they'd been running wild on the mountainsides. Some of them carried thyrsoi, the ivy-tipped wands of Dionysos. Others bore smoky, crackling torches. Still others had tambourines. To the accompaniment of that jingling music, they called, *"Euoiii! Euoiii!"*—the cry of the god's followers.

Menedemos nudged Sostratos. "By the god of wine, what's *that*?"

"I told you," Sostratos answered. "That's the boat of Dionysos."

The ancient wooden image of the god, slightly above life size, was indeed pulled down the Street of the Panathenaia in a boat by a team of captering satyrs. The planking almost concealed the four large wheels on which the landboat rolled. Except for those wheels, it seemed perfect in every respect, from painted eyes and ram at the bow to goose-headed sternpost. Two more satyrs, these playing flutes, shared the boat with the image of Dionysos. A wreath of leaves crowned the god's head, as if he were enjoying a symposion. His right hand held more greenery, symbolic of fertility and renewal.

"That's . . . very strange to see," Menedemos said as the boat drew near. "What's the point to this parade, anyway?"

"You mean, besides just celebrating the god?" Sostratos asked, and his cousin dipped his head. Sostratos said, "Back about two hundred fifty years ago, the little town of Eleutherai, up on the border with

Boiotia, became part of Attica. To symbolize the joining, they paraded this very statue from Eleutherai to the temple at the foot of the Athenian akropolis—it has to be more than two hundred stadia from Eleutherai down to here. Now they just take the image out of the temple and up to the Academy, a little outside the walls, the day before the Dionysia and then have this procession bringing it back on the day the festival starts."

Rattling and creaking, the boat went by. The image of Dionysos smiled its secret smile. Sostratos had seen that expression on old statues of youths here in Athens and elsewhere around the Inner Sea. The smile seemed particularly fitting for a god whose rituals were so wrapped in mystery.

Behind the boat came a chorus of boys singing Dionysos' praises. Their leader walked backwards in front of them, directing the hymns. He'd come all the way from the Academy like that. Sostratos wouldn't have wanted to try it; he feared he would have fallen on his fundament, probably right about here, where the most people could see him do it and laugh. That thought had hardly crossed his mind before one of the boys, a very handsome one, coughed loudly from the dust the boat of Dionysos kicked up. He went scarlet to the roots of his hair. The leader of the chorus pulled a horrible face, which could only have made the boy feel worse. People would remember a public mistake like that for years.

"Poor fellow," Menedemos murmured. "I wouldn't mind consoling him."

"I'll bet you wouldn't, and I know just how," Sostratos said.

Menedemos laughed. "The festival of Dionysos is for things like that." He looked around. "I'd rather do it with a woman, though."

"I expect you'll have your chance," Sostratos said. "You'll have your chance to gorge on meat today, too. Here come the sacrificial animals."

Guided along by herdsmen, cattle and sheep shambled down the Street of the Panathenaia. Sheep bleated. Cattle lowed and swung their heads from side to side, uneasy in the presence of so many people. Once Dionysos' image returned to its temple, the god would get the beasts' fat-wrapped thighbones while the spectators shared the rest of the meat.

More big phalloi ended the procession. As the men who carried them went by, the Skythian constables stopped holding back the

crowd. Men and women streamed down the Street of the Panathenaia
after the parade. Some of them waved jars of wine and passed them
back and forth. Others sang snatches of Dionysiac hymns.

"Come on," Sostratos said. "Let's head for the temple. We can get
our share of beef or mutton, and take it back to Protomakhos' house."

"Or even piggy," Menedemos said, and Sostratos made a face at
him for the vulgarity.

One constable after another stood aside. The whole packed agora
tried to funnel itself into the Street of the Panathenaia. The result, of
course, was that nobody moved very fast. Sostratos said, "Well,
Menedemos, we won't get to the temple in a hurry . . . Menedemos?"
He looked around. That might have been his cousin kissing a woman
ten or twelve cubits behind him. On the other hand, it might not.
Quite a few couples were embracing in the crowd, and those ten or
twelve cubits were so packed with humanity that he got only a very
partial glimpse of that one. He shrugged and took a few steps south
and east, toward Dionysos' temple. Sooner or later, he'd get there. As
for Menedemos—he could celebrate the Dionysia any way he chose.

A fairly pretty woman breathed wine fumes up into Sostratos' face
as she tilted her head back to get a good look at him. "Are you really as
tall as that?" she asked, and hiccuped.

"Of course not," he answered gravely. "I'm standing on stilts. I always do."

She looked down at his feet to see if he was joking. *How much wine
has she had?* he wondered. A couple of beats slower than she should
have, she laughed. "You're a funny fellow," she said. "And you're tall."
She might have noticed it for the first time. Sending him a look intended for alluring but in fact more bleary, she added, "I like tall."

If he wanted his own Dionysiac adventure, he suspected he could
find it. He didn't, or not with her. He said, "Look at that big, handsome Macedonian over there. He's got his eye on you." When the
woman turned her head, Sostratos pushed his way through the crowd,
as far from her as he could go. By the time she looked back, he wasn't
there any more. He feared she would come after him. If she did,
though, she never caught up.

A step here, three there, half a dozen there, he made his way back
into the built-up part of Athens. A young man who'd already poured
down too much wine leaned over a low wall puking it up again. A man

and a woman—no, they weren't Menedemos and anyone, Sostratos noted with relief—ducked into a house, or perhaps an inn. A woman whirled through the crowd, dancing and clicking castanets. She stood on tiptoe to kiss Sostratos on the cheek, then spun away before he could put his arms around her.

Even before he got to the temple, Sostratos heard the frightened lowing and bleats from the animals as they smelled the blood of those already sacrificed. Soon he could smell it himself: a heavy, rusty odor that penetrated all the other stinks of the city.

More slave constables kept things orderly in the temple precinct as people queued up to get their gobbets of meat. The butchery was crude. The only requirement was for all the pieces to be of about the same size, so that one person in line didn't take away more than another. Some people got a fine chunk, some a piece full of gristle and fat. That was just luck, luck and where one happened to stand in line.

Flies buzzed all around, more of them every minute as the stream of sacrifices yielded ever more offal and blood. If they'd lit only on refuse, it wouldn't have been so bad. But, of course, they came to rest wherever they pleased. One landed on the soft flesh between Sostratos' left eyebrow and eyelid. He tossed his head like a spooked horse. The fly hummed away. He swatted at it with the palm of his hand, but missed. A moment later, another bit him on the back of the calf. He slapped his leg. The fly squashed under his fingers. He wiped his hand on his chiton and took a step toward the temple, feeling a little better for having killed one bug.

Ancient, gnarled olive trees gave shade from the warm spring sun as the queue snaked forward. The trees were surely at least as old as the temple itself—and it was in such bad repair, a new building would have been needed to do Dionysos justice. A northerly breeze rustled through the gray-green leaves overhead. Peeping birds hopped and fluttered from branch to branch. Sostratos hoped they were eating some of the flies.

"In the name of the god, here is meat from the sacrifice," a priest said, and handed a piece to the woman in front of Sostratos.

"In the name of the god, I thank you for it," she replied, and carried it away.

Sostratos took her place. The priest gave him a piece of about the same size. "In the name of the god, here is meat from the sacrifice." He sounded bored. How many times had he said the same thing today?

"In the name of the god, I thank you for it," Sostratos said. How many times had the priest heard that? As many as he'd spoken his own ritual phrase, surely.

As Sostratos took his chunk of meat away, the priest turned to the next man. "In the name of the god . . ." Sostratos did a little surreptitious poking and prodding at the meat. It seemed a pretty good piece. He took it back to Protomakhos' house. On the way, he heard a scuffle, an angry shout, and then the rapidly fading sound of running feet. Someone probably wouldn't get to eat the sacrificial portion for which he'd stood in line so long.

The proxenos' cook was a Lydian named Myrsos. He too poked at the meat, more assuredly than Sostratos had done. "This is a good piece, most noble one," he said in almost unaccented Greek. "It is better, I think, than the one my master brought home. Will your—cousin, is it?—also bring me a chunk?"

"My cousin, yes. I don't know. We got separated in the crowd," Sostratos answered. If Menedemos had found a woman who pleased him, he might not come back for some little while. To put that thought out of his mind, Sostratos asked, "What will you do with the meat you have?" That he seldom ate meat made him more curious.

"I shall make a *kandaulos,* a Lydian dish," Myrsos told him. "The ingredients are boiled meat, bread crumbs, Phrygian cheese, anise, and a fatty broth in which to simmer them all. It is a famous delicacy among my people, and you Hellenes have come to relish it, too."

"I've heard of it," Sostratos said. "Doesn't Menandros mention it in *The Cook*? How does it go?

'Rich fool of an Ionian, making his thick soups—
Kandaulos, food that rouses lust.' "

"It is a thick soup, yes, sir," Myrsos answered. "I hadn't heard those verses before, and I don't think it rouses lust."

"If Menedemos thought it did, he'd bring you back a whole cow," Sostratos said.

The Lydian smiled. "He's a young gentleman—and so are you." His own hair held more than a little gray. He went on, "Whether it rouses lust or not, it *is* tasty. And, after I serve the master and you Rhodians,

I'll be going out into town myself tonight, to see if I can find a friendly lady. I'd do the same thing even if I weren't eating *kandaulos,* too."

"Yes, anything can happen on the first night of the Dionysia, can't it?" Even if the festival wasn't so wild here as elsewhere, Sostratos had some warm memories of his own earlier stay in Athens. He said not a word about Myrsos' supper plans. Cooks always ate as well as the people for whom they worked.

Menedemos came back to Protomakhos' house late that afternoon. He did contribute a piece of meat to the *kandaulos.* He smelled of wine and looked pleased with the world. "Protomakhos can say what he wants. It's a Dionysia, all right," he declared, splashing water from the fountain in the courtyard on his face and over his head. "If you can't find a woman today, you're not trying very hard. I wonder how many babies born this winter won't look like their mothers' husbands."

"Sometimes it's better not to ask a question," Sostratos observed.

"You say that? *You?*" Menedemos gave him an owlish, half-sozzled stare. "The fellow who never once leaves off asking things?"

"I say it, yes. Some questions should be left quiet. If you don't believe me, think about Oidipous, lord of Thebes. His flaw was following the truth too far. It's possible. It's not common, but it's possible."

"All right, my dear. I'm not going to argue with you now, that's for sure. I'm in no shape for it. You'd tear me limb from limb." Menedemos belched softly.

"Was that you I saw kissing a woman in the agora, just after the parade went by?" Sostratos asked. "The crowd had already swept us apart, so I wasn't sure. If it was, you didn't waste any time at all."

"Yes, that was me," Menedemos answered. "We found someplace quiet—well, out of the way, anyhow—and had a good time. And then I met a slave girl with hair as yellow as a golden oriole's feathers. You probably would have liked her, Sostratos; you seem to fancy barbarians who look out of the ordinary."

"I do like red-haired women," Sostratos admitted. "I gather you liked this blonde pretty well."

"About this well." Menedemos held his hands a couple of palms apart. Sostratos snorted. His cousin went on, "And I had a bit of wine—well, maybe more than a bit—so I thought I'd come back here, lie up for a while, have some supper, and then go see what things are like tonight. They'll be wilder, or I miss my guess."

"Probably," Sostratos said. "Do remember, though, the theater opens tomorrow morning as soon as it's light. Three days of tragedies, then one of comedies."

"Yes, yes." Menedemos mimed an enormous yawn. "I'll probably have to use twigs to prop my eyelids open, but so it goes." He paused to sniff. "Mm—that must be the *kandaulos*. I'd rather smell it cooking than the dogs next door, by Zeus. And . . . I wonder if Sikon knows how to do up a *kandaulos*. With meat from a sacrifice, that would be a fancy dish he could fix without making my father's wife yell at him because the ingredients are so expensive."

"They do quarrel, don't they?" Sostratos said.

"It's better than it used to be, but even so. . . ." Menedemos rolled his eyes. The yawn that followed looked genuine. "I am going to sleep. Have one of Protomakhos' slaves bang on the door before supper, will you?" Without waiting for an answer, he headed off toward the room the Rhodian proxenos had given him.

He automatically thinks I'll do what he tells me. Sostratos kicked at a pebble in the courtyard. Menedemos had always thought that, ever since the two of them were children. Most of the time, he'd been right. That gift for getting other people to do what he wanted made him a good skipper. It could also make him very annoying. Sostratos did tell a slave to wake his cousin before supper. Then he went to the kitchen and dipped out a cup of wine. Maybe drinking it would soothe his feeling of being used.

He was sitting on an olive-wood bench in the courtyard when Protomakhos came downstairs. The Rhodian proxenos looked smug and happy. *Were you celebrating the Dionysia with your wife?* Sostratos wondered. That wasn't the sort of license the festival ordained, but it somehow seemed more satisfying.

"Hail," Protomakhos said. As Menedemos had, he sniffed. "Ah, *kandaulos*. Smells good, doesn't it?"

"It certainly does," Sostratos said.

They ate supper just before sundown, with lamps brightening Protomakhos' andron. To Sostratos' disappointment, Menedemos had emerged before the slave came to rouse him. Sostratos wouldn't have minded his cousin getting bounced out of bed. Menedemos looked toward the kitchen. "If that Lydian soup tastes as good as it smells . . ." he said.

It did. If anything, it tasted even better than it smelled. Sostratos couldn't remember the last time he'd eaten anything so rich and filling. "If we had meat all the time, we'd get too fat to show ourselves in the gymnasion," he said, "but oh, wouldn't we be happy?"

"Nothing satisfies like it," Menedemos agreed. "Well, nothing you can eat, anyhow."

Myrsos brought out a honey-cake full of layers of flaky dough for a sweet. It too was very fine. As he set the cake before the men in the andron, he said, "I'm off to join the festival, master." He wasn't asking permission. He was telling Protomakhos what he intended to do.

"Enjoy yourself. I'll see you in the morning," Protomakhos replied. A man who tried to keep his slaves at work all the time and didn't let them make merry now and again would have trouble with them in short order. The Rhodian proxenos plainly knew as much.

Menedemos got to his feet after finishing a piece of cake. "I'm going to see what's out there in the night, too," he said. "How about you, Sostratos? Never know what sort of girl you might run into on a festival night."

"I know. Every other comedy, it seems, uses that in the plot these days," Sostratos said. "A young man meets a girl when she's out of the house for a festival—"

"When else is he likely to meet her?" Protomakhos said. "When else is she likely to be out of the house?"

"True enough, O best one, but it's done so often, it's getting trite," Sostratos said. "Either he meets her when she's out, or he gets her alone and has his way with her without even realizing she's the girl he loves, or—"

The Rhodian proxenos broke in again: "These things do happen. That happened with a cousin of mine, as a matter of fact, and Menandros and the other comedians didn't dream of half the mess it caused between his family and the girl's."

"Oh, yes. Certainly," Sostratos said. "If it didn't happen, you couldn't write plays about it and expect anyone to take you seriously. But doing the same thing over and over again shows a lack of imagination. That's what I think, anyhow."

"What I think is, you still haven't said whether you're coming out with me," Menedemos said.

"Not right now, anyhow," Sostratos answered. "Maybe I'll go out into the streets later on. Maybe I'll go to bed, too. You snoozed this afternoon. I didn't."

"I intend to go to bed," Protomakhos said. "I've got too many years on me to head out after wild revels."

Menedemos' raised eyebrow said Sostratos was a young man behaving like an old one. Sostratos' raised eyebrow said he didn't care what his cousin thought. He waited to see whether Menedemos would mock him out loud and start a quarrel. Menedemos didn't. He only shrugged and started out of the andron.

"Shall I have a slave get you up in time to go to the theater tomorrow?" Protomakhos called after him.

After a long pause in the doorway for thought, Menedemos reluctantly dipped his head. "Yes, most noble one, please do," he said, and then left.

Protomakhos did go off to bed a little later. Sostratos sat by himself in the andron, now and then sipping wine and listening to Athens enjoy itself around him. Off in the distance, several women called out, *"Euoiii! Euoiii!"* and then burst into drunken laughter—playing at being maenads. Much closer, a man and a woman moaned and then gasped. By the soft thumps accompanying those sounds, they were probably making love up against a wall.

I wish I could go out and have a good time like Menedemos, without second thoughts, instead of staying off to one side and observing. Sostratos picked up his cup once more, only to find it empty. *Sometimes I can—every once in a while. Why not now?* He shrugged. The only answer he could find was, he didn't feel like it. *If I don't feel like doing it, I wouldn't be having a good time if I did.*

A woman giggled, right outside the house. "Come on, sweetheart," a man said. "We can lie here on my himation."

She giggled again. "Why not?"

Why not? Sostratos could almost always find reasons why not. Finding reasons why came harder for him. He couldn't find one now, and so he stayed where he was, listening to songs and laughter and revelry— and the dogs next door howling—as Athens celebrated the Dionysia. At last, with a shrug, he went back to the little room Protomakhos had given him. With the door closed, not much of the noise outside came in.

Drifting toward slumber, Sostratos thought, *No wonder I want to write a history one day. What else am I but a dispassionate observer, watching from the edge of the action?* Herodotos had been like that, with a passion only for indulging his curiosity. Thoukydides and Xenophon, on the other hand, had made history as well as writing it. *Maybe I will, too, one of these days.* With that hope filling his mind, he fell asleep.

It was still dark when a slave pounded on the door the next morning. The racket made Sostratos spring out of bed, his heart thuttering, afraid he'd been caught in the middle of an earthquake. Still naked, he'd taken two steps toward the door before reason routed blind panic. "I'm awake," he called, and the pounding stopped. He went back to the bed to put on his chiton. The pounding started again, this time one door over. Sostratos smiled. His cousin would like it no better—indeed, would probably like it less—than he had.

He opened the door and walked to the andron, where Protomakhos was breakfasting on bread and oil and watered wine. "Good day," the proxenos said. "Have something to eat, and then we'll go over to the theater. We'll get there before sunup, which ought to mean choice seats."

"That seems good to me," Sostratos said. A slave moving with the slow, quiet care of a man with a hangover brought him bread and oil and wine, too.

Menedemos came into the andron a couple of minutes later. He moved much as the slave had. "Good day," he said softly, as if the sound of his own voice might pain him.

"Good day," Sostratos and Protomakhos said together. Sostratos asked, "And how was your night of roistering?"

"Enjoyable—then. I'm paying for it now," Menedemos answered. When the slave brought him breakfast, he picked at the bread but gulped down the wine. After a little while, he dipped his head. "*That's* better, by the dog of Egypt. Takes the edge off the headache."

Protomakhos rose from his stool. "Good. Let's head for the theater, then." Sostratos followed eagerly. Menedemos followed, too, but with a small groan.

They picked their way through the morning twilight. The entrance lay only a few blocks north and east of Protomakhos' house. People streamed towards it from all over the city, even this early. Accents far from Attic said more than a few of them had come a long way to see the day's plays.

When they got to the theater, Protomakhos handed the attendant a drakhma, saying, "This is for the three of us."

"Certainly, best one," the man said, and stood aside to let them by.

"You didn't need to do that," Sostratos protested. "We wanted to buy your seat, to show in a small way how grateful we are for your kindness."

"Don't worry about it," Protomakhos replied. "What is a proxenos for but to show his guests the sights of his own polis?"

"Thank you very much," Sostratos said. Menedemos dipped his head as if afraid it would fall off if he weren't careful. He hadn't said more than two or three words since leaving the proxenos' house. He did look better than he had when he first came into the andron. Along with the wine, the cool, crisp air of early morning was helping revive him.

The two Rhodians and Protomakhos made their way down toward the orkhestra, the outthrust, semicircular area where the chorus danced and sang. The narrow stone aisle had transverse grooves cut in it to help keep feet from slipping. The slope was one in eight, steep enough to make falls a danger.

"This should do pretty well," Protomakhos said, and stepped off the aisle to sit down on a stone bench. Sostratos and Menedemos followed. The benches were all the same, with a raised portion for spectators' backsides and a lower part behind it where the people in the next row back could rest their feet.

Women had their own section in the theater, off to the left by the Odeion. That area had been added on after the Odeion was built, for it fit around the corner of Perikles' great structure. Looking toward the women seemed to make Menedemos recover better than wine or fresh air had done, even though many of them wore veils against the prying eyes of men.

Protomakhos looked that way, too. "In my great-grandfather's day, this was a place for men only," he remarked.

"I like it better this way." Yes, Menedemos was coming back to life.

Sostratos asked, "Do you know, best one, just when they did begin to admit women to the theater?"

The proxenos tossed his head. "They've been coming as long as I can remember. That's all I can say for certain."

"Someone ought to know something like that." Sostratos clicked his tongue between his teeth. "I wonder who."

Pointing to a stone chair in the center of the very first row, Protomakhos said, "That's where the priest of Dionysos Eleutherios sits. If anyone could tell you when the custom changed, he's probably the man."

Sostratos started to get up and go down to him then and there, but Menedemos took hold of his arm, saying, "He has other things to worry about right now, my dear."

"I suppose so," Sostratos admitted. "But I'm liable to forget if I don't ask when something first occurs to me."

"You?" Menedemos laughed. "You don't forget anything. If you ever found out the name of Perikles' dog, you'd remember it till the end of time."

He was right. But when Sostratos said, "That's different," he knew he too was right, though he would have been hard pressed to explain the difference between the two kinds of memory.

But Menedemos was also right in saying the priest had other things on his mind. The gray-bearded gentleman kept bouncing out of his chair to talk with one or another of the magistrates sitting in the first row, and with the high-ranking Macedonian officers who also got some of those prime seats—a sure sign of how much, or rather how little, Athenian freedom and autonomy were worth these days.

Protomakhos said, "If you're interested, there's Demetrios of Phaleron." He pointed to one of the dignitaries in the front row. The Athenian who served as Kassandros' governor was younger than Sostratos had thought him on his previous stay in Athens—about forty-five. He was also strikingly handsome; that Sostratos had recalled accurately.

With a chuckle, Menedemos said, "Even if we're not interested, he's still Demetrios of Phaleron." Protomakhos blinked. Sostratos groaned. Yes, his cousin was starting to feel better, and he half wished Menedemos weren't.

In came the chorus of boys, singing the same hymns they had during the procession the day before. Following them, this time on a small cart instead of the wheeled boat in which it had ridden down the Street of the Panathenaia, was the ancient wooden statue of Dionysos.

As he did every year, the god would watch the plays put on in his honor.

A couple of dozen youths coming of age this year marched out into the orkhestra behind the chorus. A magistrate presented each of them with a suit of hoplite's armor. They were the sons of Athenians who'd died in battle for their polis. That custom went back a long way. The youths got loud applause as they took their seats at the front of the theater. Most of their fathers would have fallen fighting the Macedonians who dominated the polis now. Cheering them was one way to show what people felt about the occupiers.

"Look!" This time, Protomakhos pointed up at the great buildings of the akropolis behind them. "The sun has risen. Won't be long before its rays get down here, too."

"One more argument the world is round," Sostratos said to Menedemos. "If it were flat, the sun would rise at the same time everywhere. But naturally a high spot on the sphere catches the light coming around the edge of the curve before a lower one can."

"I'm sorry, best one, but that's much too much like thought for so early in the morning," Menedemos replied. Sostratos sniffed.

Menedemos waved to a wineseller. The fellow waited in the aisle till Menedemos drained the little earthenware cup, then refilled it from the jar he carried at his side like a sword. Other hucksters went up and down the aisles with raisins and dried figs and little honey cakes and sausages and onions and chunks of cheese. Sostratos said, "The worse the play is, the better the business the men with the food will do."

"Seems only fair." Menedemos peered down toward the raised skene behind the orkhestra. "We're close enough to the stage to hit the actors with onions if they're very bad." Then he looked over his shoulder at all the thousands of people sitting behind him. "And we're close enough to the skene for all of them back there to hit *us* with onions if the actors are very bad."

Protomakhos laughed. "Anyone would know you've gone to a few plays in your time, most noble one, even if you've never come to the theater at Athens before."

"Are they going to put on revivals the first day?" Sostratos asked. "That's how they did it when I was a student here."

The proxenos dipped his head. "Yes, that's right; that custom hasn't changed. They're reaching back a long way this year, too. This is

Aiskhylos' series of Theban plays—*Semele, Xantriai, Pentheus,* and the satyr play, *Dionysos' Nurses.*"

Sostratos whistled. "Those must go back more than a hundred fifty years—before Perikles' day. The *Pentheus* treats the same episode as Euripides' *Bakkhai,* doesn't it?"

"Yes." Protomakhos dipped his head again. "Euripides' play has put all the others about Dionysos in the shade. But Demetrios of Phaleron is khoregos for these. Not only is he rich enough to do a first-class job, he's also an antiquarian, so it's no surprise that he'd put on something nobody's seen for a long time."

"This should be interesting." Sostratos leaned forward on the bench.

So did Menedemos. For a moment, that surprised Sostratos. But his cousin, after all, was the one who didn't have modern tastes. And Aiskhylos, with un-Hellenic modesty, had called his own work crumbs from the banquet of Homer.

Out came the first actor, to set the scene: a messenger, talking about the report that Kadmos' daughter Semele was with child—the child who would be Dionysos. A townsman of Thebes answered him. They went back and forth. "Only two actors," Menedemos whispered to Sostratos.

"Yes, that's right," Sostratos whispered back. "Sophokles introduced the third speaking part."

"Aiskhylos, they say, introduced the second," Protomakhos put in. "Before his time, it was just one man going back and forth with the chorus." Sostratos dipped his head; *hypokrites,* the word that meant *actor,* came from the verb meaning *to answer.*

A chorus of the women who would wash the newborn child after its birth danced out into the orkhestra, singing. The performers were, of course, male, as was the actor who portrayed Semele; women did not take part in plays. With masks and the actors' remarkable control over their voices, Sostratos did not feel or even notice the lack.

He *did* notice how stiff and formal and old-fashioned the chorus' steps and gestures were. Sure enough, Demetrios of Phaleron was an antiquarian, and was doing his best to stage the play as it might have appeared in Aiskhylos' day. Even the musical accompaniment seemed unusually slow and spare. That fascinated Sostratos, and made him feel as if he'd been swept back in time. Aiskhylos' splendid poetry didn't hurt there, either. But not all the audience reacted the same way.

A shout rang out from the back of the theater: "Come on, you stupid geezers! Shake a leg!"

Protomakhos laughed. "Everyone's a critic, or thinks he is."

The second choral interlude brought more catcalls. Apparently a good many people, used to things as they were, didn't care about—or for—things as they had been. *Everything stays in the present in their minds,* Sostratos thought sadly. *No wonder it took so long before Herodotos came up with the idea of investigating the past in any systematic way.*

Semele ended with the death of Dionysos' mother under the thunderbolt of Zeus—and with the apparent death of the god, too. *Xantriai,* which followed, took its name from the chorus of wool-carding women who defended Semele's name against the gossip and slander about her union with Zeus. Hera, Zeus' consort, appeared to stir up the Thebans against Zeus' newest offspring and the infant god's mother.

"Here's something out of the ordinary," Sostratos murmured to Menedemos: "an outraged *wife.*" His cousin made a face at him.

Aiskhylos' *Pentheus* did cover the same ground as Euripides' *Bakkhai:* the return of the full-grown god to Thebes, King Pentheus' attempt to suppress and arrest him, and Pentheus' horrible death—his rending—at the hands of Dionysos' maenads, who included Agaue, the king's own mother. Sostratos thought Euripides' play, which he knew well, did more interesting and thought-provoking things with the old familiar story; the *Bakkhai* hadn't become famous for nothing. But Aiskhylos was a magnificent poet in his own right, too.

Like any satyr play, *Dionysos' Nurses* let the audience recover from the full force of the tragedies they had just watched. It was loud and lewd and foolish, with satyrs with jutting phalloi in pursuit of the women who had reared the infant Dionysos. Comedy had sprung from the same roots, but grown in a different direction. Satyr plays, indeed, had grown very little, changing hardly at all from the days when drama was something new in Hellas.

After the satyrs capered off the stage for the last time, the actors in the company and in the chorus came out to take their bows. The applause was loud and generous; they'd delivered their lines and danced and sung as well as anyone could want. Then Demetrios of Phaleron stood up; the production had been his. He looked up and out at the vast crowd and bowed as the performers had done.

He also drew cheers from those who had liked the plays—and

louder ones here and there, cheers Sostratos suspected of coming from members of his claque. But, unlike the actors and chorus members, he didn't come off unscathed. "Don't serve us stale fish the next time!" shouted someone not far from the Rhodians.

"Your plays were even more boring than you are on the stump!" another man yelled from far up in the theater. He had lungs like a smith's goatskin bellows, for Sostratos heard him plainly.

Some of the jeers that rained down on Demetrios had nothing to do with the plays he'd just presented. "How does it feel being Kassandros' catamite, you wide-arsed effeminate?" an Athenian shouted.

"He won't answer—it's like farting at a deaf man," somebody else said. That jerked a startled laugh out of Sostratos; the usual phrase, of course, was *shouting at a deaf man*. Somehow, though, the theater precinct seemed to give license to everyone, not just the performers.

"To the crows with Kassandros!" another man cried. "Athens should be free!" Those words brought shouts of agreement from the crowd. Here and there, men shook their fists at Demetrios.

"He has nerve," Menedemos murmured.

Sostratos dipped his head. Despite the insults raining down on him, the lord of Athens stood there smiling and waving and bowing to the crowd, as if they were nothing but praise. "Of course, he also has the Macedonian garrison behind him," Sostratos observed.

"Yes, you're right," Protomakhos said. "We've already spent too many lives and too much treasure. If we rose against Demetrios of Phaleron, Kassandros' men would slaughter us. And the truth is, the Macedonian could have a much nastier puppet. So . . . We yell, but that's all we're likely to do."

The Rhodian proxenos was right. After getting the abuse out of their systems, the Athenians filed from the theater peaceably enough. The sun had traveled across the sky, and was low in the west. Menedemos said, "My rear end is as petrified as that lump of wood turned to rock you bought in Mytilene, Sostratos." He rubbed at his haunches, and he was far from the only man doing so.

"Sitting on a stone bench will make you feel it," Sostratos agreed. He turned to Protomakhos. "Meaning no disrespect to your stock-in-trade, O best one."

"My bottom's sore, too," Protomakhos said. "No such thing as soft stone."

"Will there be another trilogy tomorrow, or will the modern tragedies be separate from one another?" Menedemos asked.

"Almost certainly single plays," Sostratos answered. He turned to Protomakhos. "Who was the last tragedian who tried a trilogy?"

"To the crows with me if I remember," the proxenos said. "Nobody writes them these days, because all the tragedians know they'd never find a khoregos who could afford to produce a whole trilogy. Demetrios of Phaleron can, but you have to know he's spending his patron's silver, not just his own. Finding a khoregos who can afford to put on even one tragedy is hard enough, but three and a satyr play?" He tossed his head.

"Say what you will about Demetrios, but I enjoyed the plays," Sostratos said. "I enjoyed the staging, too. That has to be what it was like in the old days."

"Yes: splendid and a little clumsy at the same time," Protomakhos said.

"They knew they were splendid. They didn't know they were clumsy, didn't know and didn't care," Sostratos said.

"But *we* know," Menedemos said. "That makes watching the plays different for us from what it would have been for them. We know what they turned into. By the dog, we *are* what they turned into."

Sostratos started to answer that, but then checked himself. After a few steps, he started over: "You'd better be careful, my dear. Every once in a while, you say something that shows you're much more clever than you usually let on."

"Who? Me?" Menedemos was used to mockery from Sostratos. He didn't seem to know what to make of praise. After a startled blink, he turned it into a joke, saying, "Believe me, I'll try not to let it happen again."

Protomakhos laughed. "Anyone can see at a glance you two like each other pretty well."

That offended both Sostratos and Menedemos. They both indignantly denied it—so indignantly, they started laughing, too. Sostratos said, "Oh, yes. We get on fine . . . whenever I don't feel like strangling this thick-skin, which I do about half the time."

"Only half?" Menedemos bowed to him. "I must be getting better. And I haven't said a word about how often I wish I could pitch you over the rail."

They came down the little street south of the temple of Dionysos, the one that opened onto the street where Protomakhos lived. A couple of women came up the street from the other side of the theater. They had been chattering. When they saw the Rhodians and Protomakhos, they drew their veils up higher and fell silent.

One of them hurried past the men. The other turned down the same street. She walked on without a word. In a low voice, Protomakhos murmured, "My wife."

"Oh." Sostratos discreetly didn't look at her. He did glance at Menedemos. To his relief, his cousin had developed an apparently absorbing interest in some swallows circling overhead. Chance meetings after festivals were the wine and opson of the plots of modern comedies. In real life, though, they were liable to cause trouble—especially with Menedemos' taste for adultery.

Protomakhos knocked at the door. A slave opened it. Protomakhos' wife went through first. The men followed. Now Menedemos couldn't look up at birds. Was he eyeing the woman's hindquarters and the way she moved her hips when she walked? Or was he simply looking straight ahead, as anyone might do? Sostratos would have believed that of anyone else. Put his cousin, even accidentally, around a married woman, and who could say what might happen?

Protomakhos' wife behaved with perfect propriety: she pretended the men with her husband didn't exist. Menedemos didn't watch her as she went over to the stairway and, presumably, up to the women's quarters. Sostratos was jumpy enough to mislike the way Menedemos didn't watch her.

"I'll go see how Myrsos is doing with supper," Protomakhos said, and headed for the kitchen.

Menedemos let out a small, soft sigh. Sostratos felt ice run up his back. He was as frightened as if he'd heard an owl in daylight: more so, in fact. He could, if he worked at it, dismiss his fear about the owl as superstition. But he knew what that sigh meant. Out of the side of his mouth, he hissed, "She's our host's wife. Do try to remember that."

"Yes, my dear," Menedemos said in a way that proved he'd barely heard. "Doesn't she have the most exciting walk you ever saw? With a walk like that, she must be a handful and a half in bed."

"You're a handful and a half all the time," Sostratos replied in something not far from despair.

Menedemos only smiled at him. Protomakhos came out with a

smile on his face, too. "Oysters, Myrsos said," the Rhodian proxenos reported. Menedemos' smile got wider. Now Sostratos' despair was unalloyed. Why had the cook chosen this of all nights to do up a supper widely thought to be aphrodisiac?

As dusk fell, the sounds of revelry again floated over the walls and into Protomakhos' house. The Athenian scooped another oyster out of its shell. "I may go out myself, see what kind of a good time I can find," he said. "I've been sitting in the theater all day. I don't want to sit all night, too. How about you boys?"

"Us?" Menedemos said. "We're just a couple of of stick-in-the-muds tonight, I'm afraid. We'll all go to the theater tomorrow, though, eh?"

You're no stick-in-the-mud, Sostratos thought. *You just don't feel like leaving the house to hunt.* Protomakhos noticed nothing amiss. "Yes, the theater," he said. "I'll be the one with the thick head come morning, I expect."

The proxenos left, a hunter's smile on his own face. Menedemos yawned. "I think I'll go to bed," he said.

"Do you?" Sostratos said tonelessly.

"Yes. I'm tired." His cousin sounded perfectly innocent. That only made Sostratos more suspicious.

But what could he do except go to bed himself? He intended to stay awake as long as he could, to listen and make sure Menedemos stayed in his own room. Sleep sneaked up on him, though. The next thing he knew, a slave was pounding on the door. "Time to get up for the theater, sir," the man said.

"To the crows with . . ." But Sostratos, by then, was resigned to being awake. He got out of bed, eased himself, and went to the andron for breakfast. Protomakhos and Menedemos were already there. "How are you today?" Sostratos asked.

"Well, thank you," the proxenos replied.

"Just fine," Menedemos added with a smile. That could mean anything or nothing. Sostratos devoutly hoped it meant nothing.

He perched on a stool. The slave who'd awakened him brought him barley porridge and watered wine. "Eat up," Protomakhos said, showing no ill effects from whatever carousing he'd done the night before. "The sooner we get to the theater, the better the seats we'll have."

Sostratos watched his cousin as he spooned up the porridge. Menedemos showed nothing out of the ordinary. Had he gone upstairs

and tried to seduce Protomakhos' wife? If he'd tried, had he succeeded? Whatever had happened, the woman hadn't gone to her husband with a tale of rape or attempted rape. That was something. But
what had Menedemos done? Were they in danger of being summarily
evicted or worse? Menedemos' bland expression was proof against
Sostratos' curiosity.

As soon as Protomakhos finished breakfast, he got up. So did
Menedemos. Sostratos joined them. Protomakhos said, "Well, now
we'll see how our modern poets stack up against Aiskhylos."

"Bet on Aiskhylos," Menedemos said.

"I like some of the modern work," Sostratos said. Protomakhos
dipped his head.

Menedemos said, "As far as I'm concerned, you're both welcome to
it. Most modern tragedians think they have to be different to be clever,
and most of the differences are no good. That's how I see it, anyhow."

"Some truth to that, certainly," Protomakhos said. "Only some,
though, I think, O best one. Some of the poetry that's written nowadays is very fine."

Sostratos went into the theater prepared to agree with the proxenos.
This time, despite Protomakhos' protests, he and Menedemos paid for
their host's seat. Protomakhos responded by chasing a honey-cake
seller up an aisle to buy some of his wares for the Rhodians. As soon as
he was out of earshot, Sostratos said, "Please tell me you didn't."

"Didn't what?" Yes, Menedemos was too innocent by half.

"You know what. Make a play for the proxenos' wife. You know
you were eyeing her. You admitted it. Her walk!" Sostratos clapped a
hand to his forehead.

"All right. I'll tell you I didn't make a play for her." Menedemos
leaned over and kissed him on the cheek. "But, my dear, am I telling
you the truth?"

Before Sostratos could find any answer for that, Protomakhos came
back with the honey cakes. Sostratos sat there eating and licking his
fingers . . . and worrying. He didn't stop worrying even when the plays
started. Maybe his own glum mood made him less receptive to them
than he would have been otherwise—or maybe Menedemos had a
point, and they really weren't very good. Over that day and the next,
about half the tragedies he saw imitated old models so closely, he wondered why their poets had bothered setting pen to papyrus. The others

were definitely new, which did not, to his ear, mean they improved on their predecessors.

One of those innovative plays, a *Dolon* by an Athenian named Diomedon that ran on the third day of the tragedies, left Menedemos furious. "That was an outrage," he kept saying as Sostratos and he and Protomakhos left the theater. "Nothing but an outrage."

"How? In the way the poet treated Odysseus?" Sostratos thought he knew what was bothering his cousin.

And he proved right. Menedemos dipped his head. "The way he mistreated Odysseus, you should say. You know the story in the *Iliad,* I hope?"

"Yes, my dear," Sostratos said patiently. "I haven't your passion for Homer, but I do know the poems. Odysseus and Diomedes are out spying for the strong-greaved Akhaioi, and they run into Dolon, who's spying for the Trojans. They run him down, he begs for his life, but they kill him instead of holding him for ransom."

"That's close, but it's not quite right, and the differences are important." Menedemos was still fuming. "In the *Iliad,* Dolon begs Diomedes for his life, and Diomedes is the one who sends him down to the house of Hades. But what did this so-called tragedian do? He made *Odysseus* into the villain, that's what. He had him string Dolon along, swear a false oath to him that he wouldn't be hurt if he talked, and then, once he told all he knew, what does the poet have Odysseus do? He makes him turn to Diomedes and say, 'Truth is wasted on the foe,' and *then* Diomedes kills Dolon! That isn't *right.*"

Protomakhos said, "Best one, poets have been showing Odysseus as a treacherous conniver at least since the days of Sophokles. And you can't deny that that's part of his character in the epics."

"I don't deny it," Menedemos said earnestly. "That is part of his character. But it's not the *only* part, and the tragedians do him wrong by making it out to be all of what he is. Odysseus is *sophron:* he gets the most out of the wits he has. He's not so great a warrior as Akhilleus, but he has more sense in one toe than Akhilleus does in his head."

"That isn't saying much," Sostratos put in.

"Well, no," Menedemos agreed. "Odysseus, though, is the man who can do everything well. He outwits Polyphemos the Cyclops, he can build a boat or a bed, he fights bravely whenever he has to, he can plow a field, and he's the one who, at Agamemnon's assembly, keeps the Akhaioi from giving up and sailing home."

"You admire him," Protomakhos said.

"Who wouldn't admire a man like that?" Menedemos said. "Except a tragedian who thinks he knows more about him than Homer does, I mean."

"Don't you think modern poets are entitled to take what they need from the *Iliad* and *Odyssey*?" Sostratos asked. "We'd be missing a lot of our tragedy if they didn't, you know."

"Taking what they need is one thing. Of course they can do that," Menedemos replied. "Deliberately twisting what they take, though, turning it into the opposite of what it was . . . That goes too far. And I think that's what this Diomedon did. You notice the judges didn't give him a prize. Maybe they felt the same way."

"Your cousin has strong views," Protomakhos said to Sostratos.

"He's a free Hellene. He's entitled to them," Sostratos replied. "We don't always agree, but we have fun arguing."

"What did you think of *Dolon*?" the proxenos asked him.

"I'd forgotten it was Diomedes who killed him in the *Iliad*," Sostratos confessed. "That being so, I think this poet may have gone a bit too far myself."

"Ah, well," Protomakhos said with a shrug. "You Rhodians have been luckier in your government lately than we have. I can see how an Athenian might want to write a play about a clever, devious politician who stops at nothing to get what he wants."

"Oh!" Sostratos' eyes widened. "You're telling me this isn't just about Odysseus. It's about Demet—"

Menedemos stepped on his foot. "If it *is* about Demetrios of Phaleron," he hissed, "how big an idiot are you for shouting it to the housetops? Do you want Macedonians breaking down Protomakhos' door in the middle of the night to haul you away and see how many interesting things they can do to you—and to our host—and to *me*?" To him, plainly, the last was most important.

But he was just as plainly right. Sostratos admitted as much, adding, "Even so, it does make me more inclined to forgive *Dolon*."

"Well . . . maybe," Menedemos said grudgingly. "I still don't care for what it did, but our kind host has shown a reason why."

"Comedies tomorrow," Sostratos said. "You won't have to worry about ferreting out nasty political messages there."

"I wouldn't have had to worry about ferreting them out in Aristophanes' day, either," Menedemos said. "He came right out and shouted them in people's faces."

"We can't get away now with what he did then," Protomakhos said. "He couldn't get away with it, either, by the end of his career. Look at *Ploutos*. It's about wealth, but it's not about, or not very much about, the people of the time. It looks forward to the kinds of comedies poets write nowadays, in fact."

"The kinds of comedies people write nowadays . . ." Menedemos muttered.

"He's not much for them," Sostratos told Protomakhos. "I told him to wait till he'd heard one by Menandros. I certainly hope he's finished the piece you said he was working on."

"I don't know one way or the other," the Rhodian proxenos replied. "We'll find out tomorrow."

"So we will." Sostratos sounded cheerful.

"So we will." Menedemos sounded anything but.

At supper that evening, Protomakhos made no remarks about going out to celebrate the Dionysia. Menedemos didn't urge him to go out or ask questions about whether he would. Sostratos hoped that meant his cousin really hadn't seduced or tried to seduce the proxenos' wife. Menedemos enjoyed making him nervous almost as much as he enjoyed adultery.

The next day dawned chilly, with a nasty wind whipping down from the north. Protomakhos wrapped himself in a himation before heading for the theater. It was cold enough to tempt Sostratos to do the same, but he didn't. Menedemos acted as if the weather had nothing to do with him. "Aren't you fellows going to freeze?" Protomakhos said.

"We're sailors," Sostratos replied. "When was the last time you saw a seafaring man in anything but his chiton?"

"Have it your way," Protomakhos said. "But if your teeth chatter too loud to let me hear the lines, I'll be annoyed at you."

They got splendid seats. The cold weather kept lots of people indoors till after sunup. Sostratos' teeth *did* chatter. He clamped his jaw tight as he could to keep Protomakhos from noticing.

Out swaggered the actors for the first comedy. They didn't wear big phalloi strapped to their waists, as they would have done a couple of generations before. Their masks were more realistic, less burlesqued, than they would have been in earlier times, too. Indeed, little except the play itself distinguished them from tragic actors, and some performers worked in both types of drama.

Their play, unfortunately, did not distinguish itself. The verse limped—a couple of times, badly enough to make Sostratos wince. Even by the loose standards of comedy, the plot was stupid. And the jokes fell flat. As the dancers of the chorus twirled out to separate one act from another—they didn't also sing, as they would have in Aristophanes' time—Menedemos turned to Sostratos and said, "How does a play this bad ever get produced?"

"I don't know," Sostratos answered. "But I'll give you an even more frightening thought, if you like."

"What's that?" Menedemos sounded as if he doubted Sostratos could come up with one.

But Sostratos did: "Just remember, only Dionysos knows how many *worse* comedies were written, comedies not even a maniac would want to bring to the stage."

His cousin shuddered. "You're right. That *is* frightening."

As the play dragged on, the audience grew more and more restless. People shouted at the actors. They threw onions and squash and cabbages. One of the actors, after nimbly dodging a squash, turned to face the crowd. In smoother verse than the comic poet had given him, he said,

> "If you think these lines are hard to listen to,
> Remember—we have to bring them out."

He got a bigger laugh for his own words than he had for the poet's. The vegetables stopped flying.

"So much for this comic poet's reputation," Sostratos murmured.

"Yes, but the other question is, how much has the actor hurt himself with his quick tongue?" Protomakhos said. "Some people won't want to hire him now, afraid he'll step out of character again."

At last, mercifully, the comedy ended. The one that followed was better—but then, bad wine was better than vinegar. Menedemos said, "I don't think Aristophanes has much to worry about this year."

Sostratos would have liked to argue with him. He knew he couldn't, not by what they'd seen so far. But then the herald announced the third and final comedy: "*Kolax,* by Menandros!"

"Now you'll see something worth seeing," Sostratos said.

"Not a bad title: *The Flatterer,*" Menedemos said. "But what will he do with it? If he makes a hash of it the way these last two fellows did . . ." He leaned back and folded his arms across his chest, as if challenging Menandros to impress him.

To Sostratos' vast relief, the poet did not disappoint. His portrait of a flatterer was alarmingly realistic; the strutting soldier against whom the title character played came from a breed all too common since Alexander's time. And his cook might have been Sikon, straight from Menedemos' household.

He certainly sounded as full of himself as Sikon did:

"A libation! You—the one following me—give me the sacrificer's
    portion.
Where are you looking?
A libation! Come along, my slave Sosias. A libation! . . . Good.
Pour! Let us pray to the Olympian gods and
Olympian goddesses: to them all, male and female.
Take the tongue! On account of this, let them give salvation,
Health, enjoyment of our present good things,
And good fortune to us all. Let us pray for that."

Everything ended happily, as it was supposed to in comedy, with the flatterer arranging for the soldier to share the girl's favors with her neighbor. The play got more applause than the other two put together. Turning to Menedemos, Sostratos asked, "What did you think?"

"That . . . wasn't bad." Menedemos sounded oddly reluctant, as if he didn't want to admit it but couldn't help himself. "No, that wasn't bad at all. It wasn't Aristophanes—"

"It's not supposed to be Aristophanes," Sostratos broke in.

"I was going to say that very thing, if you'd given me the chance," his cousin said with some irritation. "It's not Aristophanes, but I enjoyed it. You were right. There. Are you happy now?"

"Yes," Sostratos said, which disarmed Menedemos. He went on, "I was pretty sure I would like it—I've always enjoyed Menandros' comedies. But I could only hope you would. I'm glad you do."

"If it doesn't win the prize for comedy, someone's been spreading silver amongst the judges again," Protomakhos said.

"We've had that happen a few times at Rhodes, too," Sostratos said. Menedemos made a nasty face to show what he thought of it. Sostratos asked, "How common is it here? I remember rumors in my student days."

"I've seen more really bad choices these past ten years than I can ever remember before," the Rhodian proxenos answered. "I suspect that has to do with . . ." He shrugged. "Well, you know what I mean."

Sostratos didn't, not at first, but he also didn't need long to figure out what Protomakhos meant. "Lots of things for sale these days?" he asked casually, not mentioning Demetrios of Phaleron by name: he'd learned his lesson.

Protomakhos dipped his head. "You might say so. Yes, you just might say so."

But then the head of the panel of judges cupped his hands in front of his mouth and called, "The winner of the prize for comedy this year is *The Flatterer,* by Menandros!" People who hadn't left the theater cheered and clapped their hands. A thin man of about thirty-five sitting in the second row stood up, waved rather sheepishly, and then sat down again.

"He can do better than that," Protomakhos said, clucking in disapproval. "He's been winning prizes for ten years now. He ought to show that he thinks he deserves them." He shrugged. "Well, no help for it. And we'll be going back to our regular lives in a couple of days. The Dionysia comes only once a year."

"I'm glad we got here in time for it, though," Sostratos said. "Now Menedemos and I can start thinking about making enough profit to cover all these idle days." He looked north and west, toward the agora. "We'll do it."

6

XENOKLEIA CLUNG TO MENEDEMOS AND WEPT IN THE darkness of her bedchamber. "What are we going to do?" she wailed—but quietly, so no sound seeped out through the door or the shutters. "The Dionysia ends after tonight, and I'll never see you again."

Kissing her, he tasted the salt of her tears. He'd thought she would show better sense; she had to be three or four years older than he was, somewhere on the far side of thirty. He tried to make light of things: "What do you mean, you'll never see me again, sweetheart? Don't be silly. All you'll have to do is look down from that window into the courtyard, and there I'll be. My cousin and I are going to stay in Athens most of the summer."

She cried harder than ever. "That's even worse," she said. "I'll see you, but I won't be able to talk to you, won't be able to touch you. . . ." She did, very intimately. "You might as well let a starving man see a banquet but keep him from eating."

That was flattering and alarming at the same time. He'd thought he'd found an affair with which to enjoy himself at the Dionysia. But Xenokleia thought she'd found . . . what? A lover to carry her away, as Paris had carried off Helen? If so, she was due for disappointment. *And* you *may be due for trouble,* Menedemos told himself. "There's something you need to do," he said to her.

"What? This?" Her hand closed on him again. He felt himself starting to rise. Had he met her a few years earlier, they would already have been coupling once more. He needed a little longer between rounds than he had in his early twenties.

But, despite the distraction, he tossed his head. "No, dear. Sometime soon, you need to seduce your husband. Put on something saffron and make up your face. When he takes you, stretch your slippers up toward the roof." He knew he was quoting from the oath in *Lysistrate,* but Aristophanes had said it better than he could.

"You tell me that *now*? When we're like *this*?" Xenokleia seized his hand and set it on her bare breast. Though she and Protomakhos had a married daughter and a young grandson, her breasts were as firm and upstanding as a younger woman's—she probably hadn't nursed her baby herself.

Menedemos knew she was angry. He also knew he had to risk that anger. "I do, darling," he said seriously. "If you happen to be with child, he'd better be able to think it's his."

"Oh." To his relief, Xenokleia's anger evaporated. She sighed. "After you, he'll be moldy salt-fish after mullet."

"You're sweet," he said, and, poising himself above her, stretched her feet up toward the roof, though she wasn't wearing slippers. Afterwards, she started to cry again. "Don't do that," he told her, running a hand along the sweet curve of her hip. "It was fun. We enjoyed it. Remember that. Forget the rest."

"It's *over*." Xenokleia wept harder than ever.

"Maybe we'll find another chance, if your husband goes to a symposion or something," Menedemos said. "But it was good—for what it was—even if we don't."

"For what it was." Xenokleia plainly didn't like the sound of that. "I wanted it to be . . ." She sighed. "But that's not going to happen, is it?"

"No." Menedemos was, in his own way, honest. "And even if it did, after a while you'd decide you would rather have kept this. Believe me, my dear—you would."

"You don't know how little this is," Xenokleia said. To someone like Menedemos, who associated an Attic accent with wisdom and authority, her words carried extra weight because of the way she said them. She said, "If I do take Protomakhos to bed, he's liable to fall over dead from surprise."

"Do it anyhow," Menedemos told her. No matter how much weight her words held, he remained sure of what this situation needed. "And besides, love—who knows? If you make him happy, maybe he'll make you happy, too."

Xenokleia's voice held only vinegar. "Not likely! All he cares for is his own pleasure. That's why . . ." She didn't go on, not with words, but squeezed him tight.

"You could teach him, you know. I think he can learn if you do. He's not a stupid man. Friendly women taught me," Menedemos said.

Protomakhos' wife stared at him, her eyes enormous in the darkness.

She laughed again, this time on a different note. "Funny that an adulterer should give me advice about how to get on better with my husband."

"Why?" Menedemos asked, stroking her. "He's going to be here. I'm not. You should have all the fun you can, no matter where you get it."

"You mean that," Xenokleia said wonderingly.

Menedemos dipped his head. "Yes, of course I do."

" 'Of course,' " she echoed, and laughed once more. "No wonder you get so many women—don't try to tell me this is the first time you've played this game, because I know better. You're too good at it, much too good. But you really do want everybody to have a good time, don't you?"

"Well, yes," Menedemos said. "Life's a lot more enjoyable when you do, and a lot of the time you can, if only you'll work at it a little. Don't you think so?" Now he squeezed her, and bent his head to tease her nipple with his tongue.

Her breath sighed out. "If you keep doing that, I won't ever want to let you go, and I have to, don't I?"

"I'm afraid so." He kissed her one last time, put on his chiton, and slid downstairs without a sound. The bedroom door closed softly behind him.

He peered out across the courtyard from the darkness at the bottom of the stairway. No slaves stirring. Good. He hurried over to the little chamber Protomakhos had given him. He'd almost got there when a churring nightjar swooping low after a moth flew in front of his face and made him recoil in alarm.

"Stupid bird," Menedemos muttered. Here was the door. He let out a sigh of relief. He'd made it.

He worked the latch, opened the door, stepped inside, and closed and barred it behind him. The room was inky black. No lamp was lit, but he needed none to find the bed. He'd taken one step toward it when a deep voice spoke from out of the gloom: "Good evening, son of Philodemos."

Menedemos froze. Ice climbed his spine faster than a squirrel racing up a tree. If Protomakhos had caught him sneaking back to his chamber, that was almost as bad as catching him in bed with Xenokleia. "I—I can expl—" he began, and then broke off as wit started to penetrate the first shock of terror. "Furies take you, Sostratos!" he burst out.

His cousin laughed softly, there in the darkness. "I just wanted you to think about a big radish up your arse, or whatever else Protomakhos might choose to do with you if he caught you with his wife."

"Think? No!" Menedemos tossed his head. "What you wanted me to do was fall over dead from fright, and you almost got your wish." His heart still thumped as if he'd run from Marathon to the city. But that wasn't exertion he felt; it was the dregs of panic.

"Had you done nothing wrong, you wouldn't need to fear," Sostratos pointed out.

"When I was a little boy, my mother could talk to me that way," Menedemos said. "I'm not a little boy any more, and my mother's dead. And even if she were still alive, you aren't her."

"Someone needs to talk sense into you," Sostratos answered, "or scare it into you if talking doesn't work. Our own host—"

"Now that the Dionysia's over, his wife and I are probably done, so stop fretting," Menedemos said. "If he didn't neglect her, she wouldn't have looked at me, would she?"

"He doesn't," Sostratos said.

"And how do you know that?" Menedemos jeered. "I know what Xenokleia told me."

"And I know what I saw the first day of the Dionysia, while you were still chasing other women through the city," Sostratos retorted. "What I saw was Protomakhos coming downstairs from the women's quarters with the look of a man who's just enjoyed himself with a woman. How much truth was his wife telling you, do you suppose?"

"I . . . don't know." Menedemos muttered to himself. Xenokleia had certainly sounded convincing—but then, she would have, wouldn't she? He tried to rally: "For all you know, Protomakhos bedded a slave girl, not his wife—if he bedded anybody at all."

"The only married men who sleep with slaves in their own houses are fools," Sostratos said, "Are you going to tell me Protomakhos is that kind of fool?"

"You never can tell," Menedemos replied, but he knew the response was weak. As he'd said to Xenokleia, he didn't think her husband was any kind of fool; by all the signs, the stone merchant was a very clever man. That being so, he went on, "I already told you—whatever happened between Xenokleia and me, which is none of your business—"

"It is if what you do lands us in trouble in Athens," Sostratos broke in.

"It won't, because we're through. I told you that," Menedemos said. "Now kindly get out of my room, where you had no business coming in the first place." As Sostratos pushed past him—almost walked into him—going to the door, Menedemos added, "And don't think I'll forget this, either, because I won't. I owe you one, and we both know it."

"I quiver. I shudder. I quake." Sostratos opened the door and closed it behind him. He didn't slam it; that would have drawn attention to them. A moment later, his own door opened and then closed. The bar thudded into place.

Menedemos barred his door again. He lay down, wondering if he'd sleep after the fright Sostratos had given him. He also wondered how many lies he'd heard from Xenokleia. He'd told more than a few lies in his time to end up in bed—or leaning against a wall, or sitting on a stool, or in any number of other postures—with a woman. Having a woman lie to him for the same reason was—he thought—something new.

Why had she? To get sympathy? To make him angry at Protomakhos? He shrugged. It wasn't likely to matter now. *It had better not,* he told himself. The Dionysia was over. Starting tomorrow, he would get down to business. And, no matter how enjoyable Xenokleia had been, he looked forward to it. He yawned, wiggled, stretched . . . and slept.

When he woke the next morning, rain was pattering down on Protomakhos' courtyard. It was late in the season, but not impossibly late. He was glad the *Aphrodite* already lay tied up at Peiraieus; sailing in the rain was asking for trouble.

Menedemos and Sostratos emerged from their rooms at the same time. They both hurried to the andron. The Rhodian proxenos was eating bread and oil when they came in. "Good day, best ones," he said after swallowing a bite. "The herbs and flowers will grow later than usual and better than usual this year."

"And we'll get muddy," Menedemos said, looking down at his feet. They already had. A slave brought breakfast for him and his cousin. "I thank you," he murmured, and began to eat.

"Fewer people will come to the agora on a day like today," Protomakhos said. "You might want to stay here and take it easy till the rain eases up."

Though Menedemos, for several reasons, wouldn't have minded at all, Sostratos spoke up before he could: "Many thanks, most noble one, but we'd better go down to the ship and bring up some of our goods. If you could set aside a storeroom or two for them, we'd be in your debt even more than we are already. Much easier to do business out of Athens than to have to go back and forth to the akatos."

"You're diligent," the proxenos said approvingly. "Men who work even when they don't have to often go far. Let me talk to my steward, and we'll see just which space we can set aside for you. You'll have all you need, I promise you that."

As the two Rhodians started down toward Peiraieus in the rain, Menedemos said, "By the dog of Egypt, Sostratos, I wasn't going to sneak up to Xenokleia with her husband in the house. You didn't have to drag me away by the ear like that."

"So you say now," his cousin replied. "For one thing, I didn't want to take the chance. For another, we *do* need to get to work."

"While it's raining?" Menedemos skirted a puddle in which something nasty bobbed.

"What's the easiest way to steal a victory?" Sostratos answered his own question: "To move faster than your foe. Look at Alexander, time and again. Look at Antigonos, when he used a forced march to fall on Eumenes before Eumenes even knew he was anywhere close by."

"I'm not planning on spearing any Athenian merchants, only prying silver out of them," Menedemos replied. Sostratos was in no mood to listen to banter. More often than not, Menedemos could lead his cousin. Today, he had to follow in Sostratos' muddy wake.

They left Athens and made their way down to the great polis' port between the Long Walls. The soldiers on those walls wrapped themselves in cloaks and capes and himatia. They still looked miserable up there. Menedemos felt pretty miserable himself. He was mud-splashed almost to the knee. So was Sostratos, but he ignored it. When Menedemos complained, all his cousin said was, "We've both got hats back at the *Aphrodite*. They'll keep the rain out of our eyes when we go up to Athens again."

"Hurrah," Menedemos said sourly. "I've never yet seen a hat that will keep my legs dry, though. Almost makes me want to wear trousers like a Kelt."

"Barbarous garments," Sostratos said, which was certainly true, and then, "Besides, do you want to have wet, muddy wool flopping and flapping on your calves and thighs?" That was not only true but sensible—very much like Sostratos to manage both at once.

Few people were on the road down to Peiraieus, or, for that matter, coming up from the port, either. Without Sostratos' dragging him out of Protomakhos' house, Menedemos wouldn't have been on the road, either. He glumly squelched along. To his relief and more than a little to his surprise, Sostratos didn't nag him about seducing Xenokleia—not that she'd taken much seducing. Since it was also very much like his cousin to nag, he wondered why Sostratos was holding back now. He didn't wonder enough to ask, though; that probably would have got Sostratos going.

They were already in the port and close to the wharves when Sostratos sighed and remarked, "I do sometimes wonder, my dear, if you'll ever learn."

Of course I learn. I can talk women into bed who would have ignored me when my line was rougher a few years ago. Menedemos came within a digit of saying that out loud. But it would have started the quarrel he didn't feel like having, and so, reluctantly, he swallowed the words. He gave back a soft answer instead: "Look, you can see the *Aphrodite*'s mast and yard from here. I hope everything's been all right while we were celebrating the Dionysia."

"Diokles would have sent word up into Athens if he'd run into real trouble," Sostratos said. He was right again. He was also successfully distracted, which made Menedemos even happier.

Menedemos waved to the *Aphrodite* as he and Sostratos came up the pier toward the merchant galley. Someone aboard the akatos waved back. Squinting through the rain, Menedemos called, "That you, Diokles?"

"It's me, all right," the oarmaster answered. "I know the two of you well enough by your size next to each other." Menedemos was most of a head shorter than Sostratos. Not caring to be reminded of it, he glowered at his cousin as if it were Sostratos' fault. The oblivious Diokles went on, "Everything's fine here, young sirs."

"That's good news," Menedemos and Sostratos said together. Menedemos added, "Nobody got in trouble celebrating the festival?"

"Not so you'd notice," Diokles replied. "Somebody—I forget who—lost a tooth in a tavern brawl. A few more men got black eyes and such, and we've been gobbling cabbage like you wouldn't believe to fight our hangovers."

"I've never found it does much good," Menedemos said. "Well-watered wine the next morning works better."

"We've done that, too," Diokles said. Teleutas, who was—as often happened—lounging around not doing much, let out an indignant squawk. Diokles dipped his head. "Oh, yes—Teleutas says he had his pouch slit at a brothel. Only a couple of drakhmai lost, though, if he did. He'd just gone through most of his pay on wine before he got himself a woman."

The sailor squawked again. "What do you mean, if? It happened just like I said."

Diokles shrugged. "I wasn't there." Menedemos and Sostratos looked at each other. They shrugged in unison. Teleutas was a less than reliable witness. He'd proved as much many times over. Smiling slightly, Sostratos muttered something under his breath. Menedemos couldn't make out what it was, but had a pretty good idea: amusement that an occasional thief should complain of theft.

"We're going to take some of our goods up to the proxenos' house in Athens proper," Menedemos said. "That way, Sostratos and I can do business without running back here whenever we sell something."

Sostratos ducked under the poop deck, emerging with the leather sacks that held beeswax, papyrus, embroidered cloth from the east, and the truffles they'd got in Mytilene. "These are all light," he said. "I can take them myself."

"I haven't got a whole lot of sailors here, skipper," Diokles said worriedly. "If you don't want to be going back and forth all day, you'll need to hire some of these harborside loungers and scroungers."

"What do you think, Sostratos?" Menedemos asked. "You handle the silver."

His cousin was a slow man with an obolos, one of the things that made him a good toikharkhos. He dipped his head now without the least hesitation. "Yes, we'd better do it," he said. "The point of bringing things up into Athens is that we shouldn't be going back and forth all the time. Pay them three oboloi each, four if they squawk—this isn't an all-day job, or one that takes any skill."

"Right," Menedemos said. A drakhma—six oboloi—a day would keep a man fed and housed, though not in fancy style. The way prices kept rising nowadays, though, he wondered how much longer that would stay true. But there was a worry for another time. Now he cupped his hands in front of his mouth and shouted: "Hauling work! Half a day's pay! Who wants to bring home some silver?"

Some of the layabouts wanted a drakhma even for a half day's hauling work. One of them said, "You don't know how expensive things are here, stranger. This is Athens, after all, not some little polis where nothing ever happens."

"We're from Rhodes," Menedemos snapped. "We know what a drakhma's worth, by the dog of Egypt—and when things happen in our polis, they happen because *we* choose them." That got home to the toplofty Athenian. Menedemos went on, "If you won't take four oboloi"—he'd quickly discovered he couldn't get anyone to take three—"well, hail, friend. Will you or won't you?"

"I will," the fellow said, "but that doesn't mean you're not a cheapskate."

Menedemos batted his eyes, as if he were a youth teasing a suitor. "You say the sweetest things, my dear," he murmured—he'd had plenty of practice at that role in his younger days.

"Cistern-arsed effeminate," the Athenian said under his breath, a sneer right out of Aristophanes. It wasn't quite loud enough to make Menedemos notice it and run the man out. When they started back up towards Athens, he did set the fellow to hauling jars of wine on a carrying pole, the heaviest work he had.

"We've got quite a parade here," Menedemos remarked as they started away from the waterfront. "All we need is some rattling chains and we could be taking slaves to the market."

"I'm glad we're not in that business—too risky," Sostratos said. "Selling a barbarian every now and again is all right, I suppose, but you're asking for trouble if you do it too often."

"I'm not arguing," Menedemos said. "I never wanted to be a slave trader, either. Oh, maybe once in a while, if the chance comes up, but I wouldn't care to make a habit of it. People look down their noses at men who buy and sell other men. I do myself. I don't quite know why—we couldn't very well live the lives of free Hellenes if we didn't have plenty of slaves to labor for us—but people do."

"Most of the men who buy and sell slaves aren't the sort the better classes care to deal with—except when they need a new serving woman or workman or what have you," Sostratos said. "That's part of it, I think. And the other part is, we all know what can happen to us if an enemy sacks our polis. Not all slaves are barbarians. Hellenes say they don't enslave their fellow Hellenes, but it happens. Look what Alexander did to Thebes. Look what happened to the Athenians who went to Sicily during the Peloponnesian War."

A middle-aged man carrying several lekythoi full of truffle-flavored olive oil looked up at that. "My great-grandfather went to Sicily to fight against Syracuse," he said. "He never came home. I don't think he was killed in battle, so he likely died in the mines. His wife was pregnant with my grandfather when he sailed away. They almost exposed the baby. If they had, I wouldn't be here."

Sostratos said, "Disasters happen more and more often these days, too. Generals are better at taking cities by storm than they used to be—we talked about that when we first came up between the Long Walls, remember, Menedemos? And the Macedonian marshals are always at war with one another, so poleis keep falling."

Menedemos imagined Rhodes falling to the forces of Ptolemaios or Antigonos—most likely the latter, since his home polis got on well with the lord of Egypt. Would slave dealers swarm to the city, to batten on the disaster? Of course they would. They always did. Imagining misfortune befalling his polis was as much as he could do. He couldn't envision himself enslaved.

No? he thought. *You didn't have any trouble those couple of times when pirates attacked the* Aphrodite. *You knew you were fighting for your life and for your freedom then.*

Once they got into Athens again, they couldn't move so fast. That was only partly because the winding streets were full of Athenians intent on their own business, though they were. But the real problem was the swarm of boys who had as much fun with the procession of men carrying trade goods as their parents had had with the Dionysiac procession not long before. In fact, the boys—some in chitons, others naked despite the chilly, rainy weather—had even more fun, for they could dart out and disrupt this parade.

"Here, you little wretch, stop that!" Menedemos' hand smacked against the wet, bare backside of a boy of perhaps eight who'd almost tripped up two men carrying jars of expensive Byblian. Because the backside—and the hand—were wet, the swat sounded amazingly loud. The boy jumped and yelled and cursed Menedemos with a fluency some of the *Aphrodite*'s sailors couldn't have matched. His own hand clapped to the afflicted part, he scurried away, agile as a lizard.

"*Euge!*" Sostratos said. "Maybe you'll make some of the other scamps think twice."

"By Zeus, I hope so," Menedemos said. "Somebody needs to."

His cousin pointed ahead. "There's the theater—you can see the seats set into the side of the slope that leads up to the akropolis. We're getting close to Protomakhos'."

"Good," Menedemos said. "When we get there, I'm going to have one of his slaves heat up some water in the kitchen and pour it into a basin. Then I can wash my feet and warm them up, too."

"That's a good idea," Sostratos said. "Protomakhos had better have two basins."

"If he doesn't," Menedemos said, "I go first." He never noticed the look Sostratos sent him. He was used to going first. He almost always had. And he saw no reason at all why he shouldn't keep right on doing it.

SOSTRATOS AND MENEDEMOS TRUDGED UP the long ramp toward the akropolis. The sun shone down out of a bright blue sky—the rain had blown out to sea. The backs of Sostratos' calves twinged, for the ramp was steep, and he had scant occasion to climb slopes aboard ship, especially carrying a lekythos of truffle-flavored oil. Menedemos grumbled under his breath. He was a far better athlete than Sostratos—he'd almost gone to the Olympic Games a few years before as a sprinter—but this told on him, too.

"Why couldn't Demetrios' man have met us someplace where we didn't have to pretend we were mountain goats?" he muttered.

"It's all right," Sostratos said. "I would have brought you up here sooner or later so you could get a good look at the buildings and the paintings and the statues. There's no other place like this in all the civilized world. Not even Corinth's akropolis comes close. And besides, we're almost there by now, and the way down will be easy."

"Ah. That's true." Menedemos brightened.

The Propylaia, the gateway into the akropolis, loomed in front of them. Half a dozen simple Doric columns supported the entranceway. The space between the two middle ones was wider than the other gaps. People coming in and going out passed through that space. To the right of the gateway stood the temple of Athena of Victory; to the left the Pinakotheke, a dining hall with seventeen couches and some of the grandest paintings in Athens. "They have a portrait of Alkibiades in there," Sostratos said. "Lots of other paintings, too."

"Didn't Alkibiades spend most of his time getting Athens into trouble?" Menedemos asked.

"Yes, and the rest getting her out again," Sostratos replied.

Past the Propylaia stood a stone pillar with a phallos and a bearded face: a Herm like the ones at crossroads or in front of many houses. This one was bigger than most, but otherwise ordinary. Menedemos paid it no special notice. Sostratos hadn't thought his cousin would.

"Do you know who carved that Herm?" he asked slyly.

Menedemos looked it over. "No. Should I?" he said. "Whoever he was, he wasn't anything special, for I've seen plenty of better work."

"He wasn't anything special as a stonecarver, no," Sostratos admitted, "but he was in other ways: Sokrates made that."

"Oh." Menedemos gave it a second look, then shrugged. "Well, I can see why he never got rich."

"Scoffer! Come on. We're supposed to meet Demetrios' man by the Parthenon."

They hurried along side by side. Sostratos had a horror of being late and offending Demetrios' servitor. But he stubbed his toe on a stone, stumbled, and almost dropped the lekythos. Menedemos caught him by the elbow. "Steady, my dear. You don't want to have to bring the fellow back here and say, 'Lick this patch of ground if you want the true flavor.' No point to being like Euripides, is there?"

"Euripides? What are you going on about now?" Sostratos knew he sounded cross. He hated being clumsy, especially in front of his graceful cousin.

"Don't you know Aristophanes' *Frogs*?" Menedemos chuckled. "When Dionysos goes down to the house of Hades to bring back a good tragedian, Aiskhylos and Euripides square off. And Aiskhylos sinks Euripides like a round ship full of dear Protomakhos' marble, for he shows you can fit, 'He lost his little bottle of oil,' into the metre of any of Euripides' prologues."

"Oh. I'd forgotten that one, yes." Sostratos knew and liked Euripides better than Aristophanes. He mentally started the prologue to *Iphigeneia in Tauris*. Sure enough, the phrase fit right in. *Meleagros?* Yes again. *Clever Melanippe?* No doubt about it. Aristophanes knew his versifying, all right. Sostratos decided to gibe at his cousin, not the comic poet: "I thought you called Protomakhos' wife 'dear,' not the man himself."

Menedemos just grinned and stuck out his tongue, as if he were the Gorgon on the bottom of a drinking cup. "Here's the Parthenon. Where's this Kleokritos we're supposed to meet?"

"I can't pull him out from between my gum and my cheek like an obolos, you know," Sostratos said. "Now he'll be the one who's late, and he'll have to do the apologizing to us instead of the other way round."

"Don't hold your breath," Menedemos said. "The next Athenian— or even slave in Athens—I hear saying he's sorry about anything will be the first. These people are the rudest I've ever run across." Even as he spoke, his head tipped back so he could get a better look at the frieze above the entrance to the temple. He clicked his tongue between his teeth in reluctant approval. "Rude or not, though, they knew what they were doing when they made this place."

"Yes." Sostratos dipped his head. "Pheidias was in charge again, though this was too much work for him to do by himself."

The reliefs, freshly painted, might have been carved yesterday, not more than a century before. Flesh tones and robes of yellow and red stood out from the deep blue background. Horses seemed about to bound forward. So did centaurs. Pointing to them, Menedemos said, "I used to think they were creatures out of myth."

"So did I," Sostratos said. "Now that I've seen a gryphon's skull, I'm not so sure as I used to be."

A bent-backed, white-bearded man leaning on a stick came out of the Parthenon and made his slow, painful way past the Rhodians. Menedemos said, "Can we go inside? You've talked about the statue of Athena ever since we left Rhodes."

"Why not? We shouldn't stay long, in case Kleokritos comes, but the image was made to be admired."

When they went inside and left the sunlight behind, their vision needed a little while to adjust to the dimness. A broad central aisle was separated from a narrow outer one at the sides and back of the sanctuary by columns set on two levels. That interior colonnade led the eye to the great cult statue at the far end of the shrine.

Sostratos had seen it before. Even so, his breath came short. Beside him, Menedemos stopped in his tracks. "Oh," he said softly. It wasn't really a word: just an expression of amazement and awe. One small step at a time, he approached the statue of Athena. Every so often, he would say, "Oh," again. Sostratos didn't think he knew he was doing it.

The image of the goddess had to be twenty-five cubits tall, or even a bit more: say, seven times as tall as a man. Everything that would have been flesh on a living woman was of ivory, the pieces so cleverly joined that Sostratos couldn't tell where one left off and the next started. Athena's robes, her triple-crested helm, and her hair were covered in thin sheets of glittering, shimmering gold.

It shimmered all the more because a shallow pool of clear, clean water in front of the statue reflected light from outside up onto it. The slightest breath of air—perhaps even the Rhodians' footfalls—stirred the surface of the water, and stirred the reflected light, too.

Athena held a winged Victory in her right hand. Next to her might, the Victory seemed tiny. Sostratos had to remind himself it was several digits taller than he. The goddess' left hand rested on and supported a great shield. Somewhere on the shield were the portraits of Perikles and Pheidias that had landed the sculptor in so much trouble. Sostratos thought he might find Perikles if he searched. Other images had given him a notion of what the great leader of Athens looked like. Pheidias? He tossed his head. Was a man truly immortal if no one recognized him?

Between the shield and Athena's left leg, a great serpent coiled and reared. The scales of its back were picked out in gold, those of its belly in ivory.

Sostratos and Menedemos stood at the far edge of the reflecting pool, staring up and up and up at the statue. After a long, long silence, Menedemos said, "Well, my dear, you were right, and I'm not ashamed to admit it. We haven't got anything like *this* at home. I'm glad I've seen it. If I hadn't . . . well, what point to coming to Athens if I hadn't?"

"The core of the statue is of wood," Sostratos said. "All told, a couple of hundred minai of gold cover it—and the ivory, of course. It—"

His cousin held up a hand. "Never mind the details. I don't want to know. I see what it is, and that's enough."

"Really?" Sostratos said. "I think knowing how it's put together makes it more marvelous, not less."

"You would," Menedemos said.

They might have squabbled then, but someone called to them from the direction of the entrance: "Are you fellows the Rhodians I'm supposed to meet?"

Sostratos and Menedemos both turned. A man stood silhouetted in the bright doorway. "Kleokritos?" Sostratos asked.

"That's me," he answered. Sure enough, he didn't say he was sorry for being late. Sostratos and Menedemos walked away from the statue to greet him. They both kept looking back over their shoulders at it. Kleokritos laughed under his breath. He was about thirty-five; his clean-shaven face helped him seem younger. He spoke a pure Attic Greek, and looked like a Hellene. Even so, Sostratos wondered whether he was free-man or slave. Few free Hellenes would have subordinated themselves to another man as he had to Demetrios of Phaleron. *Not my worry, gods be praised,* Sostratos thought. After the introductions and small talk, Kleokritos went on, "So you fellows have something special to sell, do you?"

"I should say so." Sostratos held up his little bottle of oil—and made very sure he didn't lose it. "Olive oil flavored with Lesbian truffles."

"Is that so?" Kleokritos had sharp, foxy features. He might have suddenly spied a duck swimming near the edge of a pond. "Yes, the boss might like something like that. You realize you'll have to give me a taste? I'd look like a proper fool buying something like that without making sure it is what you say it is."

"Certainly, O best one." Sostratos pulled the stopper from the jar. He hid the nervousness he felt. He'd shaved the truffles he'd got from Onetor fine as he could, to make them give up the most flavor, but he hadn't tasted the oil since. *You should have, you fool.* He wished it had had longer to sit. If it were little more than ordinary olive oil to the tongue . . .

Kleokritos plunged a forefinger into the jar, then stuck the digit in his mouth. When he assumed the expression of a fox that had just dragged a duck out of a pond, Sostratos knew the oil was all it should be. "Well, well," Kleokritos said, and then again: "Well, well."

"You see," Menedemos said.

"Yes, I do." Kleokritos dipped his head. "May I have another taste?" Sostratos held out the lekythos to him. He smacked his lips. "That's quite something, isn't it? I don't suppose your price will be cheap, either."

"Truffles cost several times their weight in silver," Sostratos pointed out.

"Oh, yes. I know. Demetrios has bought them now and again." Kleokritos licked his finger clean, tidy as an Egyptian cat. He sighed. "Suppose you tell me what you have in mind. Let's see how loud I scream."

"A mina a jar." Sostratos never would have had the nerve to ask such an outrageous price if he hadn't seen Demetrios' production of Aiskhylos' plays. Just being able to present a trilogy and a satyr play bespoke extraordinary wealth. Putting them on so sumptuously be-spoke not only wealth but a certain willingness to spend it freely.

"A pound of silver, you say?" Kleokritos took Sostratos and Menedemos by the elbow. "Come, gentlemen." He led them out of the Parthenon, into the sunshine once more. *Then* he screamed, loud enough to make a couple of passersby whip their heads around in alarm. "There," he said. "I didn't want to profane the shrine with that. You're robbers, not Rhodians."

"Sorry you think so," Menedemos replied. "I'm sure Kassandros' top officers wouldn't—Macedonians are made of money, near enough. We wanted to give Demetrios the first chance at our oil, but. . . ." He shrugged regretfully.

Kleokritos flinched. Sostratos smiled to himself. So there *was* fric-tion between Demetrios of Phaleron and the Macedonians for whom he ruled Athens. That didn't surprise Sostratos. He probably could have sold the news to Antigonos or Lysimakhos. On the other hand, maybe not. Who was to say they didn't already know?

"Best ones, surely you see your price is beyond the moderate, be-yond what is reasonable." Kleokritos not only sounded like an Athen-ian, he sounded like one who'd studied at the Academy or the Lykeion.

As smoothly as if they were performing in a play at the theater,

Sostratos and Menedemos tossed their heads together. "I'm sorry, most noble one, but that isn't how things look to us," Sostratos replied. "When you think about what we paid for the ingredients, and the risks we took bringing them to Athens—"

"Oh, come now!" Kleokritos said. "This polis is safe and strong under the leadership of Demetrios and the protection of Kassandros."

So that's the formula they use, is it? When I write my history, I'll have to remember it, Sostratos thought. Aloud, he said, "I have no quarrel"—*no public quarrel*—"with what you say about the polis. But sailing on the Aegean is a risk, and no small one. My cousin and I were attacked by pirates less than two years ago between Andros and Euboia. We were lucky enough to fight them off, but they stole some of our most valuable cargo."

Menedemos stirred at that. It might not have been strictly true of the gryphon's skull, not in monetary terms. Sostratos didn't care. Who could set a true price on knowledge?

Kleokritos sighed. "My principal *will* want this lovely oil. I have no doubt of that. But he does not care to be held for ransom. I'll give you sixty drakhmai the lekythos. What do you say?"

"We say it's time to talk to Kassandros' officers," Menedemos replied, and Sostratos dipped his head. With a nasty smile, Menedemos added, "Perhaps they'll invite Demetrios to supper and let him have a taste."

"You are a nasty, wicked wretch," Kleokritos said. Menedemos bowed, as at a compliment. Demetrios of Phaleron's man muttered under his breath. At last, he said, "Exactly how many lekythoi of truffle-flavored oil have you got?"

Menedemos looked to Sostratos. Sostratos had known his cousin would. "Seventy-one," he said: as usual, he had the number on the tip of his tongue.

After some muttering and counting on his fingers, Kleokritos said, "I'll give you a talent for the lot of them."

"Sixty minai of silver, eh? You *are* talking of Athenian weight?" Sostratos asked, and Kleokritos impatiently dipped his head. Now Sostratos murmured as he flicked beads on a mental counting-board. In a low voice, he told Menedemos, "Eighty-four drakhmai, three oboloi the lekythos, more or less. What do you think?"

"It should do," Menedemos answered, also softly. "Unless you think we can squeeze him—or maybe the Macedonians—for more?"

"No, let's make the deal. It gives us a better chance to work on selling other things to other people." Sostratos waited to see if Menedemos would argue. When Menedemos didn't, he turned to Kleokritos. "We accept."

"Good. *That's* settled, then," Kleokritos said. Sostratos thought so, too. That talent—less what the new ingredients had cost—would pay the crew for three months. No, longer than that, he realized: he paid the sailors in Rhodian coinage, which was lighter than what the Athenians minted. Kleokritos asked, "Do you have all the oil at Protomakhos' house?"

"No, not all," Sostratos answered. "We didn't know we would sell it all to the same man. We can bring the rest up from Peiraieus tomorrow, and you can pick it up tomorrow afternoon or the next day. Does that seem good to you?"

"Yes. I expect I will come day after tomorrow," Kleokritos replied.

Menedemos said, "At Protomakhos' house we also have wine from Lesbos and wine from far-off Byblos. The Lesbian I expect you will know. Of the Byblian I will say only this: its bouquet is a match for Ariousian's. Ask among people you know if you don't believe me. They'll tell you I speak the truth."

They might also tell him the wine's flavor didn't match its aroma—but Menedemos hadn't said anything about that. Kleokritos said, "I will ask. And, of course, I will ask my principal if he wants to add to his cellars. If he declines"—Demetrios of Phaleron's man shrugged—"then I wish you good fortune selling your wine to someone else." He let out a dry chuckle. "I doubt you will have too much trouble disposing of it."

"Good wine generally does find a home," Sostratos agreed.

Kleokritos chuckled. "In any town with a Macedonian garrison, good wine—or even bad wine—has to work hard not to find a home." He started back toward the ramp that led down into the main part of Athens. Over his shoulder, he added, "I'll see you day after tomorrow, best ones. Hail."

"Hail," Sostratos and Menedemos said together. Once Kleokritos was out of earshot, Menedemos went on, "He'll buy wine, too. I don't know about day after tomorrow, but he will." He sounded confident as could be.

"Yes, I think so," Sostratos replied. "He's plainly eager for fancy food and drink—he may want some truffles, too. If his cook can do a *kandaulos* like Myrsos', think how fine it would be with truffles flavoring the broth."

"Makes my mouth water," Menedemos said. "Part of me hopes we don't sell them all. If we bring some home to Sikon and your cook, we can enjoy them ourselves."

Sostratos thought about teasing him over putting personal pleasure before profit. He couldn't, not in good conscience, not when he felt the same way himself. He said, "I wish I could see Demetrios having a use for beeswax."

"Are you worrying about that already?" Menedemos asked. A little sheepishly, Sostratos dipped his head. His cousin made a face at him. "Don't be foolish. You haven't even started talking to sculptors yet. There's bound to be some vain Athenian or swaggering Macedonian who thinks this polis can't live without a bronze statue of him, and that's what beeswax is for."

"I know, but I can't help fretting," Sostratos said.

Menedemos laughed. "Really, my dear? I never would have guessed. You're probably fussing about the balm from Engedi, too, even though the next physician you talk to will be your first."

With such dignity as he could muster, Sostratos replied, "I don't have to admit that, and I don't intend to, either."

"You just did, I think," Menedemos said, and laughed harder than ever. He went on, "You haven't seen any scribes, either, but I'd bet you're worrying about our papyrus and ink."

"No. That not," Sostratos said. "I can always sell papyrus in Athens. This polis uses more of it than any other three in Hellas, and that includes Rhodes and Alexandria. I am a little worried about the price I'll have to charge because Himilkon gouged me—outsmarted me, really, but gouged me, too. But I will be able to sell it, and the ink will naturally go with it."

They strolled out through the Propylaia and started down the ramp. Kleokritos was already near the bottom. He didn't need to slow down to sightsee; he could come up here whenever he liked. Menedemos looked back toward the Parthenon. "If anyone were ever to sack this place . . ."

"Bite your tongue!" Sostratos exclaimed. "Even the Macedonians think Pheidias' image of Athena's worth more as art than it would be as booty, and they're the greediest men in the world. If they leave it alone, anyone would—I hope."

"Well, so do I," Menedemos said. "What's that phrase your pet historian used—'a possession for all time'? It suits the statue, too."

Sostratos tried to imagine the austere Thoukydides as his—or anyone else's—pet. He felt himself failing. Wanting to get in a jab of his own, he said, "I'm sure you aim to be the one who sells our rose perfume to all the hetairai of Athens."

"Somebody's got to do it," Menedemos said cheerfully. "They pay well."

"Make sure you get it in silver, not in something I can't enter in the ledgers," Sostratos said.

His cousin leered. "Enter, indeed!" Sostratos winced. He'd left himself open for that, and Menedemos had wasted no time taking advantage of it. "I know the difference between owls and piggies, best one," Menedemos added. "If I get any of the other, it'll be along with the drakhmai, not instead of them."

"All right. Knowing you, though, I did think I ought to make sure," Sostratos said. Maybe he wasn't being fair; Menedemos did separate business and pleasure . . . most of the time. Shading his eyes, Sostratos peered southwest. "You can see all the way down to the sea from here. If my eyes were good enough, I could pick out the *Aphrodite* among all the other ships tied up in Peiraieus."

"A hawk couldn't do that, not from here," Menedemos said.

"And even if it could, it wouldn't care," Sostratos agreed. "But we ought to be able to make our sight keener."

"How?"

"I don't know. I wish I did. Cupping a hand behind your ear makes you hear better. Cupping both hands in front of your mouth makes your voice louder. We ought to be able to do *something* to help our eyes."

"We ought to be able to do all sorts of things we can't," Menedemos said. "I'd like to be able to get it up ten times a day, for instance."

"If you could, you'd never do anything else," Sostratos said.

"Who'd want to do anything else if he could do that instead?"

"You *are* a shameless wretch," Sostratos said. Menedemos grinned and dipped his head. After an exasperated snort (and how many exasperated snorts had Menedemos forced from him?), Sostratos went on, "The arts let us do things we could never do without them. We can span rivers with bridges. We can sail the seas. We can make temples like the Parthenon. Why shouldn't we be able to stretch our sight?"

"Because we don't know how," Menedemos answered. Sostratos had built a beautiful, flawlessly logical argument—but one that broke to pieces like a cheap pot when Menedemos dropped a hard, sharp-cornered fact on it. "We ought to be able to fly, too. Birds can. Bats can, and butterflies. Why not people?"

"Ikaros and Daidalos did, if you believe the myth," Sostratos said.

Menedemos was more inclined than Sostratos to take myths and legends seriously, but not this one. "It's only a wish, not a truth, and you know it as well as I do," he said. "Every so often, some poor fool who thinks it's the truth makes himself a set of wings and goes up onto a roof or a cliff and jumps off. If he's lucky, he breaks his ankle. If he's not, he breaks his stupid neck or smashes himself flat as a flapjack. Am I right or am I wrong?"

"Oh, you're right, best one, no doubt about it—for now." Sostratos fell back on the only argument he could: "But we may learn things we don't know now. The alphabet lets memory reach further than it could before. Iron was plainly a new thing in Homer's day—he calls it 'difficultly wrought.' Because it's both hard and cheap, we can do things with it we couldn't with bronze alone. Maybe some artisan will figure out how to stretch our sight or make us fly, too."

"Well, maybe," Menedemos said. "I'm not going to hold my breath, though." He made a little hop from the end of the ramp onto the dirt of the southeastern corner of the agora. "I *am* going to head back to Protomakhos'."

"You're hoping he's not there," Sostratos said in dismay.

His cousin tossed his head. "Not in broad daylight. The slaves would notice, and they'd likely blab. Tonight, though . . . We'll have to see what he does." He hurried away. As Sostratos followed, he wondered whether clouting Menedemos over the head with the lekythos he carried would knock any sense into him. Off the evidence he had, probably not. *Too bad,* he thought. *How I wish it would.*

MENEDEMOS BOWED to Kleokritos. "Here is the oil, most noble one," he said, pointing to the lekythoi lined up in Protomakhos' courtyard.

"Ten rows of seven jars, plus one. May Demetrios and his friends enjoy them."

"That's a fine-looking phalanx," Demetrios of Phaleron's man said with a smile. He gestured to a couple of the men who followed him. Most of them looked to be laborers hired for the day to carry the jars of oil. These two were different: both were better dressed and brighter looking than their comrades. They carried nice-sized leather sacks. *More of Demetrios' retainers,* Menedemos judged. Kleokritos went on, "They have your silver for you."

"Good," Menedemos said.

"As soon as I make sure it's the proper amount, you are more than welcome to the oil," Sostratos added.

Kleokritos' smile vanished. "You're not going to count out six thousand drakhmai!" he exclaimed. "We'd be here all day. You don't think I'd cheat you?"

"Of course not, O best one," Sostratos said suavely. Menedemos knew his cousin was lying. Kleokritos likely knew it, too. But Sostratos gave him no excuse to protest, continuing, "You have every right to count the jars of oil—and to open and taste them, too, if that seems good to you. And I don't need to count so many coins. Protomakhos, may I borrow your scale?"

"Certainly," the Rhodian proxenos replied. At his order, a slave brought out a huge balance. Another, grunting, carried a stone weight. "One talent," Protomakhos said. "Being in the stonecutting business, I find such large weights useful. This one balances perfectly against the standard talent the officials in charge of weights and measures keep in the Tholos. If you want to go over there, I'm sure the metronomoi will show you that."

"Never mind," Kleokritos said sourly, to the obvious relief of the slave carrying the weight. "Set it on one pan of the balance, and I'll set the silver on the other."

The slave put the weight on the pan. The men with Kleokritos who had the money set their sacks on the other pan. The scales did not balance. Kleokritos turned a dull red. He took a stout leather wallet from his felt and started feeding coins from it onto the scale: a drakhma, a tetradrakhm—four times as heavy—a didrakhm, another fat tetradrakhm. Altogether, he had to load on more than fifty drakhmai before the weight finally rose.

"There!" he snarled. "Are you happy now?"

"Certainly, most noble one," Menedemos said. "I know it must have been an accident." This time, he was the one doing the lying. He didn't want to embarrass Demetrios of Phaleron's man any more than he had to. *What a coincidence, though,* he thought, *that Kleokritos happened to have enough money with him to make good the error in case we challenged him.* Without the scales, he and Sostratos never would have noticed the payment's being light by less than one part in a hundred, but half a mina of silver was a tidy sum of money by itself. "Still, we do want things to be right, don't we?"

"Right," Kleokritos said. That wasn't agreement. It was anger coming out in one word. Demetrios' man said not a word about wine, Lesbian or Byblian. He barked at the Athenians he'd hired. They hurried to pick up the lekythoi and left Protomakhos' courtyard not so much to escape it as to get away from Kleokritos.

"You boys have more nerve than I would," Protomakhos said once Kleokritos was gone, too. "I wouldn't risk offending Demetrios of Phaleron."

"I like that." Sostratos' voice cracked in indignation. "His man tries to cheat us, but we're the ones who have to worry about offending him. Where's the justice in that?"

"He's not talking about justice, my dear. He's talking about power," Menedemos said. "In a polis like this, they come from different places. You ought to know that—you lived here for a while."

"It's good to see one of you understands, anyhow," the proxenos said. "Walk soft. If you get in trouble with Demetrios, I won't be able to do much for you."

"We'll be careful," Menedemos said, thinking, *He doesn't know about Xenokleia, or he wouldn't want to warn me.* He knew which upstairs window looked out from her bedroom. He carefully didn't glance that way. No point making Protomakhos suspicious when he wasn't already. Sostratos' gaze held irony. Menedemos pretended not to notice.

"You'll *probably* get away with this without anyone saying a word," Protomakhos said.

"Because we're right?" Sostratos asked.

"No—I already told you that's got nothing to do with it," Protomakhos answered. "But you're Rhodians. Ptolemaios doesn't want to offend Rhodes, Kassandros doesn't want to offend Ptolemaios, and Demetrios of Phaleron won't do anything to offend Kassandros. If you came from Samos or Mytilene or some other place Antigonos holds, you'd be wise to get out of Athens before Kleokritos and Demetrios could take their revenge, for they would."

"Power again," Sostratos murmured. Protomakhos dipped his head. Menedemos eyed Sostratos with a mix of respect and pity. His cousin *could* learn, and learn quickly. But he had to reason everything out, one step at a time. He seldom used his heart or his belly to gauge how things worked. It had to be his mind or nothing.

"Tomorrow," Menedemos said, "tomorrow I'll take a couple of jars of perfume into the agora and I'll start shouting about how wonderful it is. Some of the better hetairai are bound to have slaves out shopping for them. Once a slave girl gets a sniff, she'll take word back to her mistress. Then I'll see if I can do business with her."

The Rhodian proxenos laughed. "What sort of business do you aim to do?" He gestured lewdly.

"Don't you start, if you please," Menedemos said. "Sostratos was giving me a hard time about taking it out in trade, too."

"I don't want you giving the hetairai a hard time," Sostratos said, "at least not in exchange for the firm's merchandise. If you're going to be firm, do it on your own time and pay for it."

Protomakhos winced, though he was the one who'd started the puns. *I won't have to pay for it if I do it with a wife and not a hetaira,* Menedemos thought. But, with Xenokleia the wife in question, that was much better left unspoken.

Turning to Sostratos, Protomakhos asked, "And what will you be doing while your cousin's out having a good time?"

"I've still got truffles to sell, and I've got the Byblian and Lesbian," Sostratos answered. "I think the first thing to do is try to sell the wine to some of Kassandros' Macedonian officers. Everybody knows how thirsty Macedonians are, and everybody knows how much money they've got, too."

The proxenos chuckled. "That's a good combination, all right. I wish you both good fortune, and you"—he pointed to Menedemos—"can take that any way you please."

"I know I can sell perfume," Menedemos said. "Whether I get to do any buying . . ." He shrugged. "I'll find out."

"You two won't need the scales any more, will you?" As Protomakhos had a moment before, he used the dual number in referring to
Menedemos and Sostratos. That grammatical form was common in
Homer's Greek, much less so in modern Attic. By using it, Protomakhos
implied the Rhodians were a natural pair. Menedemos' eyes flicked toward Sostratos. Sostratos was looking his way, too. Both of them, evidently, were trying to decide whether they wanted to be part of such a
pair.

Distracted, Menedemos had to make himself remember the question. "No, O best one. We do thank you for the use of them, though."

"I ought to charge you the extra you got from Kleokritos as commission." Protomakhos smiled to show he didn't mean that seriously.

"Take it," Menedemos said at once. "You've shown us all sorts of
kindnesses. The least we can do is pay you back a little." Sostratos
looked wounded, but set his face to rights so quickly that Menedemos
didn't think the proxenos noticed. Menedemos knew his cousin had
less simple generosity than he did himself: one more thing that made
Sostratos a good toikharkhos.

Protomakhos, meanwhile, tossed his head. "No, no. That's kind of
you, but I couldn't possibly. I'm here to help you Rhodians, not to take
your money."

Menedemos didn't insist. That might have offended the proxenos.
He resolved to do something nice for Protomakhos before leaving
Athens. *After all, his wife has done something nice for me.*

Now Menedemos let his eyes slide across the windows of the upper
story. He didn't linger at the one belonging to Xenokleia's bedchamber.
He knew better than to do anything so foolish. He hoped Xenokleia
knew how to keep her mouth shut—and how to keep her demeanor
from giving anything away, too. Life *would* get more difficult if she
didn't. He tried not to contemplate how much more difficult it might
get. Sostratos was also better than he at brooding over things that might
go wrong.

No disaster had struck by the time the two Rhodians set out the
next morning. "Have fun in the agora," Sostratos told Menedemos.

"People would talk if I did it there," Menedemos replied. Sostratos
spluttered and choked, spraying watered wine. Protomakhos laughed
out loud.

When Sostratos could speak again, he said, "You're trying to sell to hetairai, and I to Macedonian officers. I may make more money, but you'll have more fun."

"You never can tell," Protomakhos said. "Some of those Macedonians are as wide-arsed as any Athenian effeminate."

"I'm sorry, best one," Sostratos said. "No matter what a Macedonian officer's idea of fun may be, no Macedonian officer is mine."

Menedemos made his way to the agora through morning twilight. He didn't have a stall, of course, or even a tray slung around his neck to hold his goods. He did have lots of little jars of perfume in a leather sack, a brash manner, and a loud voice—and he got there early enough to stake out a spot by the Street of the Panathenaia, where lots of people would surely pass by.

The sun touched the buildings of the akropolis—and, to the north, the top of the hill called Lykabettos. That one was sharp and conical and useless as a fortress, or for anything else Menedemos could see. For that matter, the akropolis itself couldn't come close to sheltering all the people of Athens, not any more. In the old days, he supposed it might have.

He reached into the sack and pulled out a jar. "Fine perfume from Rhodes!" he called. Selling this, his Doric drawl wouldn't hurt him. "Sweet-smelling rose perfume from Rhodes, the island of roses!"

A woman with the rough hands and bent back of a laundress said, "Can I have a sniff?" He yanked out the stopper. Sniff she did, and then smiled. She asked, "How much do you want for a tiny little jar like that?" She knew how to haggle—the first thing she did was disparage Menedemos' goods.

He told her.

Her jaw dropped. After that moment of astonishment, she got angry. "You're having me on!" she said, and shook a fist in his face. He wouldn't have wanted to brawl with her; she looked formidable. "I don't make that much money in a month!"

"I'm sorry, my dear, but that *is* the price," Menedemos said.

"Then you're a polluted thief!" she exclaimed.

He tossed his head. He didn't want her saying that. "No, indeed," he told her, "for this jar"—he balanced it on the palm of his hand—"holds a lot of labor. The roses have to be grown and picked, the sweet-smelling petals plucked, the lot of them boiled down into an essence and mixed with fine oil—I don't know all the details, for the perfumers keep them secret. But I do know that everyone who does that labor has to be paid, too, and that's what you see in the price I charge."

She didn't call him a liar. She did say, "It's a cursed shame when honest folk can't afford something nice, I'll tell you that. Who's going to buy at your price? Those bastards who run the polis and suck our blood, that's who, them and brothelkeepers and fancy whores. Furies take the lot of 'em, and you, too." She flounced off without giving Menedemos a chance to answer.

He didn't know what he could have said to her. The people she'd named *were* the ones who could afford what he was selling. Hetairai weren't exactly whores—they entertained the men they chose, not the men who chose them—but their entertainment involved, or could involve, going to bed with their clients, so they weren't exactly *not* whores, either.

Oh, rich merchants could buy perfume, too. On the one hand, though, how likely were they to be honest? And, on the other, they were more likely to buy it for hetairai than for their wives. Wives would always be there. A man had to work to make a hetaira want to stay with him. He had to work, and he had to spend silver.

"Perfume!" Menedemos called again. As the sun lit up the market square, more and more people came in. "Fine perfume from Rhodes, the island of roses! Sweet perfume no sweet woman should be without!"

Another woman who'd plainly lived a hardscrabble life—and, after all, what other sort would be out shopping for herself?—asked him what he wanted for his wares. He gave her the same answer he'd given the laundress. She squalled louder than if he'd hiked up his chiton and waggled his private parts in her face. There were men who did that sort of thing to amuse themselves. Menedemos thought it was in poor taste, but what could you do?

Yet another woman came up to him, this one dressed in a long tunic of fine white wool. "Hail," she said. "May I smell your perfume?" Her Greek held a faint accent.

"Of course," he answered politely. She looked and sounded like the slave of someone prosperous—exactly the sort of person he was looking for. He pulled out the stopper and held the jar out to her.

She leaned forward. Her nostrils flared as she inhaled. "Oh, yes," she said softly. "That is very fine. What price do you ask?" When he told her, she didn't flinch. "Let me speak to my owner. She may well buy. Stay here. I will return."

"Who *is* your owner, sweetheart?" Menedemos asked.

"Her name is Potheine, Rhodian," the slave woman said. "If you came from Athens, you would know the rich and famous men who have had her as their companion." *Companion* was what *hetaira* had first meant; the masculine form of the word, *hetairos,* still did mean that and nothing more. In the feminine, there were companions . . . and then there were companions.

Menedemos asked, "And who are you?" Showing he cared about a slave might make her urge his case more strongly to her mistress.

"Me?" She seemed surprised at the question. "They call me Threitta here." That was Attic for *Thracian.* She wasn't redheaded like the slave in Sostratos' household, but, with light brown hair and hazel eyes, she was fairer than most Hellenes.

"Well, Threitta, I hope you hurry to your famous mistress for me," Menedemos said. To make sure she did hurry, he gave her three oboloi. He asked for nothing in return—not a kiss, not a promise that the girl would urge the hetaira to buy the perfume. He'd found a free gift usually worked better than one where the dangling strings were obvious.

The slave girl took the little silver coins and hesitated, waiting for him to tell her what he wanted. When he said nothing more, she stuck the coins in her mouth. "You have an interesting way of doing business," she remarked.

"Thank you," Menedemos said, though he wasn't sure that was praise. Threitta nodded—which would have proved she wasn't a Hellene born, had he had any doubts—and vanished into the still-swelling crowd in the agora. Menedemos tried to keep track of her, but it was like trying to keep track of one raindrop in a storm. He blinked, and then he couldn't find her any more.

He went back to calling about the perfume and its virtues. Threitta might not be—probably wasn't—the only hetaira's slave in the market square this morning. Menedemos didn't much care to whom he sold perfume. He cared only about selling it and getting his price.

By the time Threitta came back, he had sold a jar to a plump man who insisted so loudly that he was buying it for his wife, he convinced Menedemos he was lying through his teeth. Some people never did figure out that the best way to lie was not to trumpet the untruth all over the landscape but to pass it off lightly or, indeed, to keep quiet about it. *Why should I care who gets the perfume?* Menedemos thought. *It's not my business, or it wouldn't have been unless that fool made it so.*

When Threitta returned to the agora, Menedemos didn't notice her till she'd got within a few paces of him. He had an excuse: her companion drew all eyes his way. The blond, long-mustached Kelt was taller than Sostratos, handsome, wide-shouldered, narrow-waisted: he looked like a pankratiast, or perhaps more like a demigod. His eyes were the color of Egyptian emeralds. He stared through Menedemos as if the Rhodian didn't exist.

"Hail," Menedemos said to Threitta. "Who's your . . . friend?"

"Bolgios is Potheine's body-servant," she answered.

I'll bet he is. That's quite a body. Menedemos didn't say it, though it quivered on the tip of his tongue. "I see," was all that came out.

Threitta went on, "He has the money for you. My mistress wants five jars of perfume."

Sure enough, Bolgios thrust out a fat leather sack that clinked when Menedemos took it. The Kelt's hand, the back of it thatched with little hairs like wires of finest gold, was as enormous as every other part of him. It could have swallowed Menedemos', as a father's swallows that of his toddler son when they go walking together. No one would have dreamt of robbing such a brute.

"Let me count the silver," Menedemos said. The bag felt as if it held about the right amount of silver—just under two minai.

Bolgios' eyes flashed green fire. "Are you after calling my mistress a cheat, now?" he asked: a musically accented snarl.

Menedemos quailed before few men. If he said yes to that, though, he knew the barbarian would tear him limb from limb. "By no means," he answered, as politely as he could. "But anyone can make a mistake. There might even be an owl or two too many in here. I don't want anything that shouldn't be mine, but I do want everything that should."

Bolgios stood there, considering. At last, grudgingly, he nodded. Yes, he'd wanted to wreak a little havoc. Now he had to accept the idea that he wouldn't get the chance. "You speak as a proper man might," he allowed. "Count the silver."

Menedemos did, making piles of coins, ten drakhmai to the pile. "It is as it should be," he said at last, and hoped he didn't sound too relieved.

"He gets nothing above what he should?" Bolgios asked Threitta. Maybe the Kelt didn't know how much Potheine was supposed to pay. Maybe he just had trouble counting.

"No." The Thracian woman shook her head. "All's well." Bolgios grunted. That all was well plainly disappointed him.

"Here is the perfume." Menedemos handed Threitta the little jars. "I hope your mistress has pleasure from them." He smiled his most charming smile. "If I could, I would like to meet her and thank her for her business."

"She is not looking for clients now," Threitta said. "She has all she needs."

And she had Bolgios. When Menedemos made his request, the barbarian stiffened. Menedemos could almost see the hair rise at the back of his neck, as it might have on a dog just before the beast bit. Was Bolgios sleeping with Potheine? Menedemos couldn't tell. Was he jealous of any other man who did? Of that the Rhodian had not the slightest doubt. He didn't try to sweeten Threitta and get her to change her mind, as he might have done if she'd come back to the agora by herself.

She and the enormous Kelt went off side by side. Thanks to Bolgios' height and bright blond head, Menedemos had no trouble tracking them as they wandered through the market square. Again, he wasn't the only one following Bolgios with his eyes. An elephant parading through the agora might have drawn more attention. Then again, it might not.

Gathering himself, Menedemos took up his call again: "Fine perfume from Rhodes, the island of roses! Perfume fit for Athens' finest hetairai!" He didn't know Potheine was one of those, but anybody who'd been able to buy Bolgios couldn't be poor. He sold several more jars before the day was done. Maybe that extra line he'd tacked on to the pitch helped.

7

SOSTRATOS HAD BEEN TO A FAIR NUMBER OF SYMPOSIA
in his day. Nothing, though, prepared him for this one down in Mounykhia. He'd heard things about the kinds of parties Macedonians
threw. Now he was seeing them at first hand. If he wanted to sell wine
to the men from the north who held Athens for Kassandros, he'd discovered, he also had to drink wine with them. If, once he got back to
Protomakhos' house, he remembered a quarter of what was going on
around him, he would have stories to dine out on for years to come.

If I get back to Protomakhos' house, he thought muzzily. *If I don't
pass out here, or maybe fall over dead here.* Not least because Macedonians were so powerful, everyone accepted that they really were Hellenes, even if a proper Hellene could make out only about one word in
three of their dialect. Like the barbarians Demosthenes had accused
them of being a generation before, though, they drank their wine neat.
And so, perforce, did the people who drank with them.

The symposion wasn't in a proper andron, but in a big chamber in
one of the Macedonians' barracks halls inside their fortress at Mounykhia. Sostratos' couchmate was a tetrarkhos—a man who com-
manded a quarter of a phalanx: an important officer—named Alketas.
A black-bearded rowdy of about forty, he was the fellow who'd been interested in buying Byblian.

He gave Sostratos a shot in the ribs with his elbow. "Not a bad bash,
eh?" he bawled—he could speak perfectly good Greek when he felt
like it (and when he wasn't too drunk to remember how).

"Well . . ." Sostratos said, and said no more. He couldn't even tell
Alketas he'd never seen anything like it, because this wasn't the first
Macedonian carouse in the occupiers' seaside fortress he'd had to at-
tend.

Alketas looked at his cup. "But, my dear, you're not *drinking*!" he
exclaimed. He shouted for a slave. How the poor slave heard anything

through the din filling the room baffled Sostratos, but he did. Alketas pointed to the enormous mixing bowl in the middle of the floor. Why the Macedonians bothered with a mixing bowl was also beyond Sostratos, since they didn't mix their wine with water. The slave plied the dipper and filled the Rhodian's cup, then brought it back to him.

Even the bouquet of neat wine seemed plenty to make his head spin. And, under Alketas' watchful gaze, he had to take a long pull at the cup. The neat wine (not anything he'd sold the tetrarkhos) was almost thick enough to chew, and sweet as honey. He could feel it snarl when it crashed down into his stomach. He didn't want to get too drunk, but around Macedonians there often seemed little choice.

Two couches over, an officer between Sostratos' age and Alketas' had already drunk himself unconscious. He sprawled on his back, his arm, like a corpse's, dangling down to the floor. His cup sat forgotten on his belly. The fellow who shared the couch with him grabbed for it but missed—he only knocked it over. Wine red as blood soaked the blind-drunk man's tunic as if he were dreadfully wounded. He never stirred. *He'll feel wounded come morning,* Sostratos thought.

Off in a corner, a frightened-looking flute-girl played. She seemed to hope no one noticed her. Considering some of the things that might happen if the Macedonians did, Sostratos couldn't blame her. A scarred veteran who'd surely marched with Alexander, his skin burnt almost Ethiop black by years of sun, was drumming with bare palms on the table by his couch. His pounding rhythm had nothing to do with the love song the flute-girl was playing.

Another percussive rhythm came from a few couches past the veteran. Two younger Macedonians were sitting face-to-face, taking turns slapping each other. *Whap!* One's head would jerk to the side as he was struck. Then he would slap the other fellow. *Whap!* Every once in a while, they would pause for a bit and, laughing uproariously, drink more wine. Then they would start again. *Whap! . . . Whap!*

"Do you Macedonians often play that game?" Sostratos asked Alketas.

"What?" The officer said. Sostratos pointed at the two men matching slap for slap. Alketas eyed them for a little while, then said, "No, I've never seen that before." He watched a little longer. "Looks like fun, eh? Want to try it?"

"No, by the dog!" Sostratos exclaimed. He was willing to do a lot of things to sell wine. Getting his brains rattled again and again, though, went too far.

"Suit yourself," Alketas said with a broad-shouldered shrug. "I was just trying to liven things up. Pretty dull symposion so far, isn't it?"

"That's not the word I'd use, most noble one," Sostratos replied. With neat wine buzzing through his veins, he had trouble deciding which word he would use, but *dull* definitely wasn't it. A soldier had hiked up another flute-girl's tunic and bent her forward onto the couch. He stood behind her, thrusting hard. That sort of thing could happen at a lot of symposia. Sostratos wasn't shocked, though he'd never before heard a man shout out a war cry at the moment he spent himself.

Four Macedonians began singing a raucous song in their own dialect. One by one, most of the other men in the room joined them. The swarthy veteran gave up his drumming. The two men who were slapping each other didn't stop, but they did sing between blows. The din was indescribable—and, to Sostratos, incomprehensible.

Alketas started howling at the top of his lungs. He paused only once, to nudge Sostratos again with his elbow and shout, "Sing!"

"How can I?" the Rhodian answered. "I don't know the words. I don't even understand them."

"Sing!" Alketas said again, and gave himself back to the song. It seemed to go on forever. From snatches Sostratos picked up here and there, he gathered it was a battle song that came from a Macedonian civil war several generations earlier. The irony made him want to laugh, but he didn't. The civil war the Macedonians were fighting now spanned most of the civilized world. The one they were singing about had been some tribal brawl as likely as not to have gone unnoticed by the true Hellenes to the south.

Of course, it wasn't as if those true Hellenes hadn't had plenty of faction fights of their own, both between cities and within them. Sostratos sighed and sipped at his wine; raising the cup gave him an excuse for not singing. Faction fights were the curse of Hellas. All the men, all the groups, all the poleis were so jealous of their rights and privileges, they refused to acknowledge anyone else's. He wondered what the answer was, and whether there was an answer. If so, Hellenes had never found it.

Four more flute-girls swayed into the room. They wore short

chitons—chitons that would have been short even on men—of filmy Koan silk. The silk was thin enough to let Sostratos see they'd singed off the hair between their legs. Alketas forgot his Macedonian war song. Sostratos thought his eyes would bug out of his head.

The flute-girls stayed in the open space in the middle of the room, where none of the symposiasts could grab them without leaping off his couch. A moment later, the din from the Macedonians redoubled, for a troupe of dancing girls followed the musicians, and the dancers wore nothing at all. Their oiled skin gleamed in the light of lamps and torches.

"Now we're getting somewhere!" Alketas whooped. He turned to Sostratos. "Things are finally picking up a little, eh?"

"Yes," Sostratos said politely. *Yes, if you like getting blind drunk and rumpling slave girls,* he added to himself. By all the signs, the Macedonians liked nothing better. One of the dancing girls did a series of flips. An officer jumped up and caught her in midair—not the least impressive show of strength Sostratos had ever seen. As if they'd rehearsed it, she wrapped her legs around his midsection. To the cheers of his comrades, he carried her back to his couch. They went on from there.

A couple of other Macedonians also grabbed girls for themselves. Dancing was all very well, they seemed to say, but other things were more fun. That deprived the men who would have been content to watch the dancers for a while of some of their enjoyment, but the Macedonians wouldn't have been what they were if they'd spent much time worrying about other people's feelings.

The two men who'd got into the slapping match paid no attention to flute-girls, naked dancing girls, or anything else. *Whap! . . . Whap!* Sostratos wondered how long they'd stay at it. Till one gave up? In that case, they might be here a long, long time. *Whap! . . . Whap!* If they'd had any brains when they started, they wouldn't by the time they were through.

"Come here, sweetheart!" Alketas beckoned to one of the dancers. She came, probably not least because the meaty, hairy arm with which he'd beckoned had on it a heavy golden armlet. He shifted on the couch so his feet came down onto the floor and splayed his legs apart. "Why don't you make me feel good?"

"That's what I am here for, my master," she said, and dropped to her knees. Her head bobbed up and down. Sostratos wondered what she was thinking. Had she been born a slave and known no other life?

Or had some misfortune brought this fate upon her? She spoke Greek like a Hellene.

Alketas put his hand on her head, setting her rhythm. Her dark hair spilled out between his fingers. He grunted. She pulled away, gulping and choking a little. "That was fine," the Macedonian said. "Here." He gave her a fat, heavy tetradrakhm, an enormous fee for what she'd done.

"Thank you, most noble one," she said. She had nowhere obvious to store the coin, but it disappeared nonetheless.

Alketas pointed to Sostratos. "Take care of my friend here, too."

"Yes, sir." She dipped her head, which probably meant she *was* a Hellene. Looking at Sostratos, she asked, "What would you like?"

"What you did for him," Sostratos answered with dull embarrassment. He didn't like performing in public, but he also didn't want to take the girl outside into the darkness and have Alketas laugh at him. He was, after all, trying to sell the man more wine.

"Shift a little, sir, if you please," the girl said. Sostratos did. She knelt in front of him and began. For a little while, his embarrassment kept him from rising. That would have made Alketas laugh at him, too; the Macedonians enjoyed sneering at effete Hellenes. But then the pleasure her mouth brought led him to forget embarrassment and everything else except what she was doing. As the tetrarkhos had, he pressed her head down on him and groaned when she brought him to the peak.

Afterwards, he gave her a didrakhm: a compromise between the usual price of such things and his desire not to seem too stingy after the Macedonian's extravagant generosity. Again, she made the coin vanish even though she was naked.

Sostratos turned to Alketas to talk about Byblian. Before he could, a brawl broke out. This was no game—the Macedonians overturned couches as they pummeled each other. One smashed a cup over the other's head. More men leaped into the fight, not to break it up but to join it. More crockery smashed. Howls of pain mingled with howls of glee.

Alketas yelled something in Macedonian. He turned to Sostratos and went back to intelligible Greek: "Now we're getting somewhere!"

"Are we?" Sostratos said. Alketas didn't even bother answering. He flung himself into the fray, fists and feet flying. A cup whizzed past

Sostratos' head and shattered on the frame of the couch behind him. He wished he were somewhere, anywhere, else. Wishing did as much good as it usually did.

"GOOD DAY, BEST ONE," Menedemos said, stepping into Protomakhos' andron. The sun was just coming up. The day promised to be warm and clear. A roller, a jackdaw-sized bird with a blue-green head and breast and a chestnut back, perched on the roof tiles across the courtyard. Its croaking call put Menedemos in mind of a crow's, but no crow ever wore such gorgeous feathers.

"And to you," the Rhodian proxenos replied. He pointed to the mixing bowl. "Have some wine. A slave will bring you porridge in a moment."

"Thanks." Menedemos dipped out a cup for himself. He raised it in salute. "Health to you." When he drank, he raised an eyebrow. "This is a strong mix, especially for the morning. Is there a reason?" Protomakhos didn't seem the sort of man to start out the day by getting pie-eyed, but more than one cup of this wine would do the trick. Menedemos sipped cautiously. As the proxenos had said, a slave brought him breakfast.

"I should say there is." Pride rang in Protomakhos' voice. The pull he took at his cup wasn't cautious in the least. "I'm going to be a father."

"Congratulations, best one! That's very good news indeed. May it be a son." Menedemos spoke as naturally as he could. Part of the good news he saw was that Xenokleia must have slept with Protomakhos recently enough for him to be sure *he* was going to be a father. Menedemos wasn't nearly so sure of that himself, but Protomakhos' opinion was the one that mattered.

"I hope so. We had a son, years ago, but he died before his first birthday." Protomakhos' smile faded. "So many children do. You know you're taking a chance loving them, but you really can't help it when they smile at you. And then they sicken, and. . . ." He spread his hands. After another sip of wine, he went on, "We have our daughter, too, who's married and gone to her husband's household. Do you know, I think I'll rear this child even if it turns out to be a girl, too."

"Good for you," Menedemos said. "Not many families raise two daughters."

"I know it's seldom done," Protomakhos replied. "But with so many years between the two of them, I can afford it." He started to raise his cup once more, then stared down into it, a bemused expression on his face: he seemed taken by surprise to find it empty. Even after he filled it, though, the bemusement remained. "Women are funny," he remarked, apropos of nothing in particular.

"Oh, yes," Menedemos said. He'd never thought much about the custom of exposing unwanted infants up till now. It was just something people did when they needed to. To put a baby that might be *his* out for the elements, though . . . He knew a startling amount of relief that Protomakhos had said he wouldn't.

If the proxenos hadn't poured down that first cup of strong wine so early in the day, he might not have gone on. But he did: "For a while now, my wife and I have done what we could to make sure she *wouldn't* conceive. Lately, though, she decided to try to have another child. I was glad enough to go along—more fun finishing inside than spilling seed on her belly. More fun than her prokton, too, though I don't suppose everyone would go along with me there."

"Some men probably wouldn't," Menedemos said. "Me, I agree with you." Xenokleia hadn't had *him* take any of those precautions. A good thing she'd managed to get Protomakhos to abandon them without rousing his suspicions.

"A son," the Rhodian proxenos murmured. "I'm very fond of our grandson—don't get me wrong—but a son is something else. I hope I live to see him out of boyhood." He shrugged. "That's in the hands of the gods, though, not in mine."

"Yes." Menedemos snapped his fingers. "Do you know what, best one? Your grandson will have an uncle or aunt who's younger than he is."

Protomakhos stared, then guffawed. "You're right, by the dog! I hadn't thought of that."

Sostratos came into the andron, yawning and looking red-eyed and bleary. "Hail," Menedemos said. "Another long night with the Macedonians, my dear?"

His cousin dipped his head—cautiously, as if it hurt. "Afraid so. This symposion wasn't quite so bad as the one a couple of weeks ago where it turned into a free-for-all at the end, but it was bad enough." A slave poured him a cup of wine. "I thank you," he said, but he blinked when he raised the cup to his lips. "Have we got swilling Macedonians *here* today? This can't be weaker than one to one, and that's too potent for first thing in the morning."

"I have my reasons for a strong mix," Protomakhos answered, and explained what they were.

"Oh." Sostratos blinked again, this time in surprise of a different sort. To Menedemos' relief, his cousin had the sense not to look at him. Sostratos went on, "That's splendid news. Congratulations!"

"For which I thank you." The Rhodian proxenos raised his cup in salute. "And on account of which I say, drink up!"

Menedemos was happy enough to pour down the rest of his wine. No matter what Sostratos said about him, he wasn't a man who usually started out the day drinking hard. If he had been, he would have worried more about it. As things were, he knew he could get away with it once in a while.

And Sostratos also drained his cup. He said, "Maybe some more wine going down will ease the headache I have from what I drank last night. By Dionysos, you drink more wine with Macedonians than you can hope to sell them. It feels like that, anyhow." He held his head in both hands.

"They're paying our prices," Menedemos said. His cousin— gingerly—dipped his head. Menedemos went on, "And you've sold them some truffles, too. You can't eat those faster than they buy them."

"I wish I could, for they're better than food has any business being," Sostratos said. "But I am glad I've made the sale. Demetrios of Phaleron does seem to be annoyed enough at us not to want to buy any more of what we've got."

"I told you that would happen," Protomakhos said.

"It's not Demetrios," Menedemos said. "He probably wouldn't know our names if you gave him over to a Persian torturer. It's that polluted Kleokritos—he's paying us back by not paying us any more."

"Many goodbyes to him!" Sostratos said. "A man who thinks he's been cheated because we caught him cheating us . . . I'm just as happy not to deal with a man like that."

"No one has challenged Kleokritos in a long time," Protomakhos said. "He's not used to it. Demetrios of Phaleron has held Athens for

Kassandros for ten years now. We've spoken of this—he hasn't been so harsh as he might—but he *might,* and no one wants to find out if he would. I admire your courage for standing up to his man."

"That didn't even occur to me," Sostratos said. "I just wanted things to be *right.* Too many cheats running around loose. We fall foul of these petty chiselers every trading run, it seems. They try to gouge us out of a few drakhmai here and a few drakhmai there, and then when we catch them at it they seem surprised—no, not surprised, angry—we're making a fuss. But if anybody tried to do *them* out of half an obolos, they'd scream bloody murder."

Menedemos rose from his stool and set a hand on his cousin's shoulder. "Well, my dear, we spoiled Kleokritos' fun, and we're unloading the things he might have bought on the Macedonians. I'd say that's a good revenge."

"Good enough," Sostratos agreed. "But I'd be happier if we didn't need to take revenge on him."

"I'm going back to the storeroom and get myself some more perfume," Menedemos said. "Then to the agora. No drunken Macedonians have been buying what I peddle."

"You haven't brought back any lewd tales for us," Protomakhos said. "Not much luck with the hetairai?"

With a shrug, Menedemos answered, "Well, best one, there's luck, and then again there's luck. I've sold a lot of perfume, and sold it at good prices. But I've dealt with the women through their slaves, and I haven't lain with any of them. Who knows, though? I may yet."

He hurried off to get the perfume. Behind him, Sostratos' voice floated out of the andron: "If Menedemos sees a pile of horse turds, he's sure he'll find a team hitched to a chariot around the next corner, just waiting for him to hop on and ride."

Protomakhos laughed. Menedemos started to turn around and shout at Sostratos for talking about him behind his back. But then he checked himself. What his cousin had said wasn't an insult, and *was* true. Menedemos always did hope for the best. Why not? Some people expected the worst, to shield themselves from disappointment. As far as Menedemos was concerned, that wasn't living; it was only existing and waiting to die. He wanted to go through life aiming higher than that.

A slave barred Protomakhos' front door after he left. By now, he knew the way to the agora well enough not to need to look up at the great frowning bulk of the akropolis to get his bearings. Turn here, turn there, don't go down the street with the baker's shop at the corner because it's a dead end and you'll only have to turn around, pick up a rock before you come by the shoemaker's place so you can fling it at his polluted hound if the beast runs up snarling again.

The sun was already shining on the agora by the time Menedemos got there. He'd put on his petasos. The wide-brimmed hat would help keep Helios from cooking his brains inside his skull. That wasn't why he grumbled. Showing up later than he had been doing meant other hucksters had already staked claims to the choicest spots.

Well, no help for it. He found a place not far from the Painted Stoa, on the north side of the agora. "Fine perfume from Rhodes!" he called, holding up a jar. "Sweet rose perfume from Rhodes, the island of roses!"

Even as he made his sales pitch, though, his eyes kept going to the paintings and other memorials in the shadows under the covered colonnade. No one but people who couldn't afford it seemed interested in his perfume. About halfway through the morning, curiosity got the better of him. *It's like the Parthenon,* he told himself. *Not much point coming to Athens if I don't see this.*

Most famous of the paintings on wooden panels was the one of the battle of Marathon by Polygnotos. There were the Athenians (and the Boiotians from Plataia) driving back the Persians toward their ships, which were manned by bearded, long-robed Phoenicians. Other panels showed Athenians fighting Spartans; Theseus and more Athenians fighting the bare-breasted Amazons in ancient days; and the Akhaioi just after the fall of Troy, with the Trojan women, Kassandra among them, captive before Aias. Shields preserved against time and verdigris by a coat of pitch hung between the panels—they came from the Spartan citizens who'd surrendered on the island of Sphakteria when the Peloponnesian War had been going well for Athens.

After seeing what there was to see, Menedemos bought a little fried octopus and a cup of wine. Then he went back to crying the virtues of Rhodian perfume. He didn't sell any all that day. Somehow, though, he cared much less than he'd thought he would. Seeing the Painted Stoa had given him a profit of a different sort.

SOSTRATOS WINCED WHEN HE LEFT ATHENS BY THE PEOPLE'S GATE and headed east toward the base of Mount Lykabettos. Up till now, he'd never gone back to visit a lover after leaving. Returning to the Lykeion, though, felt exactly like that. He'd spent the happiest days of his young life there. Then he'd had to go. Now he was coming back, yes, but he wasn't the same person as he had been when he reckoned the place the center of his life. Herakleitos had had it right. You couldn't step into the same river twice. The river wasn't the same the second time, and you weren't the same, either.

As they had for at least three centuries, youths learning the use of arms and armor paraded on the flat land of the Lykeion, between the olive groves. Some of them, probably, were young men who'd received their panoplies in the theater at the Dionysia now recently past. A drill-master's voice pursued the epheboi: "Left! . . . Left! . . . No, you clumsy fool, *that's* not your left! . . . Left!" Sostratos smiled. Those same irate shouts had been part of the background while he studied here.

After a moment, his smile faded. Would the Athenian phalanx ever amount to anything again? Or would Athens be nothing more than a counter Kassandros and the rest of the Macedonians shoved back and forth across their gaming board? Things weren't as they had been a hundred years before, when this polis came close to becoming the lord of Hellas—and when Macedonia was full of backwoods bumpkins who battled among themselves and were hardly ever seen in Hellas proper.

Macedonia, of course, remained full of backwoods bumpkins who battled among themselves. Now, though, they did it over almost the entire reach of the civilized world, from Hellas east all the way to Persia and beyond. Sostratos dimly remembered having a similar thought at one symposion or another. Was this an improvement? He formed that question intending the answer to be, *certainly not.* But if the Macedonians weren't battling among themselves, wouldn't Hellenes be doing it in their place? From everything the Rhodian knew of his people's history, that seemed altogether too likely.

He got a glimpse of other men walking about, too, those under and among the olive trees rather than out in the open. They weren't marching under the direction of a drillmaster, either, obedient to a single will. They all traveled together, all searching—as free men should—for knowledge and truth.

"Peripatetics," Sostratos murmured. That was what Aristoteles had called the men who studied with and under him, for they walked about—*peripateo* was the verb in Greek—discussing one philosophical topic or another. The name lived on under Theophrastos, Aristoteles' nephew and successor.

Seeing the scholars, Sostratos suddenly wanted to turn and run back towards Athens. *I studied here,* he thought. *I studied here, and now I'm coming back as a tradesman.* The leather sack of papyrus he carried in his left hand all at once seemed to weigh fifty talents. *They'll recognize me. They'll remember. Won't they think of me as respectable women think of a widow who's had to turn to whoring to keep food on the table for herself and her children?*

He made himself keep walking toward the gray-branched, pale-leaved olive trees. Some of the Athenian epheboi would have a harder time going into battle than he did going forward now.

The man doing most of the talking there under the trees was a dapper fellow in a fine chiton with a himation elegantly draped over one shoulder. His hair and beard were white, his back still straight and his eyes still sharp and keen even though he had to be well up into his sixties. When Sostratos saw him, he almost fled again. *Oh, by the gods, that's Theophrastos himself! Too soon, too soon! I wasn't ready yet.*

Theophrastos was saying, "And speaking of the ridiculous, there is the phrase, 'A big fish is a poor nobody.' This is said to have first been used by the kitharist Stratonikos against Propis of Rhodes, who sang to the kithara. Propis was a large man, but one without much talent. It packs a lot of insult into a few words, for it says that Propis was large, was no good, was a nobody, and had no more voice than a fish."

A couple of the younger men with Theophrastos scribbled notes on waxed tablets. Stratonikos' insults were famous wherever Greek was spoken. Not so long before, in Cyprian Salamis, one of them had cost him his life.

"We should, however, commonly distrust what people commonly say," Theophrastos went on. "I know for a fact that, while the gibe did indeed originate with Stratonikos, it was in fact aimed at Simykas the actor, and taken from the old saw, 'No rotten fish is large.' Now one moment, my friends, if you please." He turned to Sostratos, who was coming up through the olive trees. "Yes, my good fellow. You wish . . . ?"

I can't run away. They'll all laugh at me if I do. Only that thought nerved Sostratos to keep walking forward. "Hail, Theophrastos, wisest of men," he said, and knew some small pride that his voice wobbled only a little.

"Hail." Theophrastos cocked his head to one side. "I've heard your voice before, friend—to the crows with me if I haven't. And I do believe I've seen your gangling frame as well. You're a Rhodian. You studied here. You were interested in . . . let me see . . . history and natural philosophy, as I recall. You're . . . Sostratos son of . . ." He snapped his fingers in annoyance. "Your pardon, please. I've had too many students over too many years. I can't recall your father's name."

"It's Lysistratos, sir," Sostratos answered. Some of the young men who'd been with him at the Lykeion were still here, still learning. How he envied them!

"Lysistratos, yes." Theophrastos dipped his head. "I was sad when you had to leave us. You had a good head on your shoulders." Sostratos blinked. Suddenly he felt as if he were walking on air. Theophrastos . . . said *that* . . . of him? The older man went on, "Do you now hope to return to your studies, then? You would be welcome."

"Thank you," Sostratos whispered. "Thank you more than I can say, most noble one, but no." That last word was one of the hardest he'd ever had to say, for all of him wanted to scream, *Yes!* "I have come to sell you—"

Several of Theophrastos' students giggled. A couple of them laughed out loud. Sostratos' cheeks felt afire. Of course these bright young men would mock anyone who had to make his living by trade. Their wealth let them spend all the time they wanted here, without worrying about making a living. Unfortunately, Sostratos *did* need to worry about that.

"Let him finish, please," Theophrastos said. "A man must live. Yes, Sostratos? You are selling . . . ?"

Was that courtesy harder to bear than the students' scorn? Sostratos didn't know. But if the ground had opened beneath his feet and dropped him down to the house of Hades, he wouldn't have been sorry to escape the dreadful moment. He had to force out the answer through lips that didn't want to say it: "Papyrus, O best one."

"Papyrus?" Now Theophrastos forgot all about the young men who'd been strolling with him. He hurried forward, an eager smile on his face. "Are you really? By the dog of Egypt, that's wonderful news! We were running low, and I wondered when we'd ever see any again.

You are a friend in need!" He stood on tiptoe and kissed Sostratos on the cheek.

Several of his students hurried up, too, all of them exclaiming about how much they needed papyrus. "Have you got ink, too?" one of them asked.

"Yes, I do." Sostratos hoped he didn't sound too cold: that young man had been one of those who'd laughed hardest when he said he'd come to the Lykeion on business. Now that he turned out to have something this rich, pampered fellow wanted, he rated politeness—at least till his back was turned.

I don't belong here any more, Sostratos realized, and the pain of that realization tore into him like knives, like fire. *They've gone their way, I've gone mine, and I can't turn around, go back, and pick up where I left off. If I write my history—no, when I write my history, it will have to be from the perspective of a man of affairs, not from that of a lover of wisdom.*

Tears stung his eyes. He turned away for a moment, to keep Theophrastos and the others from seeing them. *I could have done this. Even Theophrastos thinks I might have done well if I had. I could have—but I won't.*

Theophrastos tugged at his arm. "Come back to the residence, my dear," he said. "I don't want to let you get away. Let's make this deal as quickly as we can, so that, if we find anything worth knowing, we will be able to set it down for posterity." He waved to his students. "We are done for the morning, my friends. We shall return to the nature of the ridiculous another time."

"I was almost here a couple of years ago, in a different capacity," Sostratos said, and told Theophrastos about the gryphon's skull and its loss.

His old teacher seemed less impressed, less interested, than he'd expected. With a shrug, Theophrastos said, "These peculiar bones do turn up now and again, I admit. My own view of them, though, is that they are more the province of temples and priests than of students of philosophy."

"Why?" Sostratos asked. "Isn't learning that the gryphon was in fact a real beast and not something out of a legend a worthwhile addition to natural philosophy?"

"It would be, yes, if the bones demonstrated that beyond conceivable doubt," Theophrastos said dismissively. "But, since they are so often ambiguous—to say the least—and since we don't have them here before us, this is surely but one of many possible interpretations. Wouldn't you agree?"

He smiled, as if sure Sostratos couldn't do anything but agree. Without the gryphon's skull in hand, Sostratos could only smile back. Had he had the skull, Theophrastos might have said the same thing. What old bones meant didn't seem to interest him much. If Theophrastos *had* said the same thing, Sostratos would have been tempted to break the skull over his head.

As things were, he had to get his revenge another way. They walked back to a medium-sized house where the Lykeion had its home; it was not far from the house of the polemarkhos, the Athenian official in charge of military affairs—a man whose job was much less important than it had been in days gone by. A slave brought wine as they sat on a stone bench in the courtyard. Theophrastos said, "And what do you want for the papyrus you were kind enough to bring us?"

He'd already made the mistake of admitting the Lykeion badly needed the writing material. And he'd made the mistake of putting Sostratos' back up. The sympathy Sostratos might have felt—*had* felt—for the place where he'd studied flickered and blew out when Theophrastos showed no interest in even hearing much about his stolen gryphon's skull. And so he answered, "Four drakhmai a roll, most noble one."

"What?" Theophrastos yelped. "That's robbery! A lot of the time, it costs only a third of that."

"I'm sorry, best one," Sostratos replied. "I confess I was robbed by the supplier who sold it to me"—which was true—"and I can't hope for a profit on less"—which was less than true.

"Robbery," Theophrastos repeated.

"I'm sorry you feel that way," Sostratos said. "I do have to live, as you said yourself. If you can't meet my price, I'd better talk to the folk at the Academy. I wanted to come to you first, out of the affection I felt for this place, but. . . ." He shrugged.

"The Academy?" Theophrastos looked like a man smelling bad fish when he heard the name of Athens' other leading school. "You wouldn't deal with them? Nothing they turn out is worth writing down, anyhow." Sostratos only shrugged. Theophrastos glowered at him. "Well, it's plain to see you haven't kept all the ideals we tried to inculcate in you."

Sostratos shrugged again. Theophrastos turned red. Sostratos got his price.

PROTOMAKHOS WAVED A FAREWELL TO HIS HOUSE SLAVES, and to Menedemos and Sostratos. "Hail, all," he said. "I'll be back eventually, with wreaths and ribbons on my head and a torchbearer lighting my way home. My head will ache tomorrow morning, but the time I have tonight should make it all worthwhile." Out the door he went.

One of his slaves said to another, "And he'll wake everybody up when he gets home, banging to be let in."

"Isn't that how it always goes?" the second slave replied. They both used Greek. Maybe they'd been born into slavery and knew no other tongue, or maybe they came from different lands and had only Greek in common.

Menedemos didn't care how much noise Protomakhos made when he came reeling home after a symposion. He cared only that the Rhodian proxenos was leaving the house and wouldn't be back for hours. With any luck at all, he could sneak up to Xenokleia's room.

"Don't be stupid," Sostratos whispered as they stood in the courtyard.

"I wouldn't think of being stupid," Menedemos answered, also in a low voice. "Stupid people get caught."

"What can you get from her that you can't get in a brothel?" Sostratos asked.

"Enthusiasm—and you know it," Menedemos replied.

His cousin turned away. Menedemos took that to mean that Sostratos did indeed know it. Whether it might also mean that Sostratos didn't approve regardless of whether he knew it or not . . . Menedemos didn't bother worrying about that. He ran his hand along the side of his jaw. He'd shaved in the morning, so his face was smooth. That was good. If he rubbed olive oil on his cheeks now and started scraping away, the house slaves would be bound to wonder why.

Protomakhos' cook served the Rhodians nice white barley rolls for sitos and some sort of fish baked in cheese for opson. The cheese helped obscure what sort of fish it was, which probably meant it wasn't anything fancy. After supper, Menedemos said, "Myrsos wouldn't have tried getting away with that if his master were here."

"It wasn't bad," Sostratos said.

"No, it wasn't bad, but it wasn't up to what we've been getting when Protomakhos eats with us," Menedemos said. "The cook got to put a few oboloi into his own mouth. Or else dear Protomakhos said, 'I'm not going to be here tonight, so don't bother spending much on supper.' "

"He wouldn't do that!" Sostratos exclaimed in dismay. "I don't think he would, anyhow. No, he wouldn't—the wine was the same as we always have here."

"Was it?" Menedemos considered. "Yes, I suppose it was. But if he had an open jar, dipping some out is nothing." Their couches sat close together in the andron; they could talk without fear of being over-heard.

"You're just looking for reasons to dislike him so you'll feel better about sneaking upstairs to lie with his wife," Sostratos said.

Now Menedemos turned away. That held more truth than he cared to admit. He yawned and spoke in a loud voice, one he wanted Pro-tomakhos' slaves to hear: "I'm going to bed early tonight. I had a busy day in the agora, and I'm beat."

"Suit yourself," Sostratos said, and then, in lower tones, "Shall I bar your door—from the outside?"

"Funny. Very funny," Menedemos said sourly. "You should write comedies. You'd run your precious Menandros straight out of business."

"I have no more idea how to write a comedy than . . . than I don't know what," Sostratos said. "What I don't want to have to do is figure out how to write a tragedy."

Having got the last word, he went to his own room. He didn't slam the door behind him. That might have shown the slaves he and Menedemos had been quarreling. Menedemos knew his cousin wasn't showing restraint for his sake. Sostratos was showing it so they wouldn't get in trouble doing business in Athens. But the reason didn't matter much. That Sostratos was showing restraint did.

Menedemos went to his own room and closed and barred the door. He blew out the lamp. No one outside could tell he wasn't going to bed. He even lay down on the wool-stuffed mattress. The bedframe creaked, taking up his weight. He caught himself in a yawn. If he really did fall asleep here . . . *Sostratos would be delighted,* he thought, *but Xenokleia wouldn't.*

Not wanting to give his cousin the chance to gloat would have been reason enough to stay awake, even without the other. He waited and waited and waited. He wished moonlight spilled under the door to help him gauge the passage of time, but the room faced the wrong way and the moon hadn't risen anyhow. And, for this, darkness was better.

When he judged enough time had gone by to leave him likely the only one awake down here, he got out of bed and tiptoed to the door. Halfway there, he paused to yawn. Everyone else might be—had better be—asleep, and he was sleepy. *Then why are you doing this?* he asked himself. *Why don't you just lie down again and get up in the morning?*

He stopped in the middle of the dark room. He'd never really wondered about why before. That sort of question was much more likely to occur to Sostratos than to him. The answer that formed in his mind was, *Because I can. Because I always have when I saw the chance.*

Was that reason enough? Sostratos, surely, would have said no. But Sostratos lay in the room next door. He was probably tight-lipped with disapproval even in his sleep. Menedemos thought of Xenokleia's waiting arms. He hoped Protomakhos' wife wasn't asleep. If she was . . . *If she is, I'll feel like a proper idiot when I sneak back down the stairs. And oh, how Sostratos will laugh when he finds out in the morning!*

Menedemos silently slipped the bar from the brackets that held it in place. He opened the door. It scraped a little as it swung on the dowels that held it to the lintel and to a flat stone with a mounting hole set into the rammed-earth floor beneath it. Menedemos stepped out into the courtyard, closing the door behind him. He looked around. Everything was quiet and still. After the absolute darkness inside his bedchamber, starlight seemed full-moon bright.

Heart thudding in the mix of anticipation and fear he always found so intoxicating, he tiptoed toward the stairs. Up he went. One, two, three, four, five . . . The sixth step creaked. He'd almost frightened himself to death discovering that the first time he sneaked up to Xenokleia's bedroom. Now he took a long step up from the fifth stair to the seventh and went on his way, silent as a lion stalking its prey. No lions on Rhodes, of course, but they still prowled the Anatolian mainland not far away.

The upper landing. To the right around the corner. His heart pounded harder than ever. If anyone discovered him here, no excuse could be good enough. His prokton puckered. *How* big were those radishes with which Athenians were allowed to punish adulterers?

But then he forgot about radishes, forgot about fear, forgot about everything. For faint, flickering yellow lamplight spilled out from under Xenokleia's door. She *had* been waiting for him! He hurried forward and tapped on the door, ever so lightly, with the nail of his forefinger.

Footsteps inside. Xenokleia opened the door. Menedemos' jaw dropped. She stood there naked and smiling, holding the lamp. "Come in," she whispered. "Hurry."

As soon as he did, she blew out the little flame. Darkness descended like a thick blanket. "I wanted to see more of you," Menedemos murmured.

"Too dangerous," Xenokleia answered. He muttered, but she was doubtless right. She reached out, found his hand, and set it on the soft, firm flesh of her breast. "Here I am."

"Oh, yes, darling." He squeezed.

She hissed and took an involuntary step back. "Be careful," she said. "They're sore. I remember they were the other times I got pregnant, too."

"Sorry." Menedemos pulled his chiton off over his head. "I'll be *very* careful. I promise."

Xenokleia laughed, but only for two or three heartbeats. Then she said, "We'd better hurry. We can't know for sure when he'll come home."

"I know." Menedemos remembered jumping out a window in Taras when a husband who'd quarreled with his brother returned from a symposion hours before he should have. The Rhodian found the way to Xenokleia's bed even in the dark. Why not? He'd been there before.

He kissed her. He caressed her. He teased her breasts, and didn't do much more than tease them. His hand glided down between her legs. When they joined, she rode him like a racehorse. That kept his weight from coming down where she was tender. He went right on stroking her secret place after they joined. Some women found that too much; others thought it was just enough. By the way Xenokleia arched her back and growled deep in her throat, she was one of the latter.

Her final moan of delight was almost loud enough to make

Menedemos clap a hand over her mouth. He was glad he'd roused her. He didn't want her rousing the household slaves. But then his own pleasure burst over him, and he stopped worrying about that or anything else.

She sprawled down onto him, careless of her sore breasts. He ran a hand along the sweat-slick curve of her back. After a kiss, he asked, "Is the baby mine?"

"I don't know for certain," Xenokleia answered. "I did what you said—that was clever, and I can't say it wasn't. So I can't know—but I can tell you which way I'd bet."

"Ah." So far as Menedemos knew, he hadn't left any cuckoo's eggs in other nests before. He still didn't know, not for sure. But if his seed wasn't stronger than that of a man more than twenty years older . . . Then it wasn't, and Protomakhos would have himself a legitimate child.

Xenokleia kissed him again. Then she said, "You'd better go downstairs."

"What I'd rather do is—"

She tossed her head. "That would take a while now, and we may not have the time." She was right—right that it would be risky, and right that his lance would need a bit to stiffen from boiled asparagus to iron. *If we'd met five years earlier . . .* But then, how long did Protomakhos need between rounds? Days, certainly. *Poor old fellow,* Menedemos thought with a young man's heartlessness.

The Rhodian found his chiton by the door and slipped it on. He opened the door. "I hope we find more chances," he whispered as he stepped out.

"So do I," Xenokleia called after him. He shut the door. She barred it after him. As he tiptoed downstairs—again skipping the creaky one—he thought, *Good. At least I kept her sweet. She won't tell tales to her husband. Her being pregnant will help keep her quiet, too. She won't want him wondering whether the baby's his.*

He looked out across the courtyard from the darkness at the bottom of the stairs. All quiet. Quick as a lizard, he scurried to his room and closed the door behind him. A long sigh of relief. No Sostratos here now. No Protomakhos lying in wait, either. *I got away with it again.*

He lay down on the bed. He hadn't fallen asleep before someone— no, not someone; Protomakhos—pounded on the front door. "Let me in! Let me in!" he shouted—no, sang. How drunk was he? Drunk enough, evidently. *How lucky am I?* Menedemos wondered. Lucky enough, evidently. And Xenokleia had been right—a second round would have been a disaster. *It would have been fun anyhow,* Menedemos thought as a slave padded across the courtyard to open the door for Protomakhos. In came the proxenos, still singing loudly, if not very well. Despite the racket, Menedemos yawned, twisted, stretched . . . slept.

A CLOTH MERCHANT TOSSED HIS HEAD. "Sorry, friend," he said, and his regret seemed genuine. "That's very pretty work you've got there, and very fine work, too. I don't say anything different, so don't you get me wrong. But to the crows with me if I know who would want it, and I don't care to buy what I'm not sure I can sell. I don't want to get stuck with it. I'd have thrown my silver away."

"Thank you for looking at it," Sostratos said, carefully refolding the embroidered linen he'd bought on his way to Jerusalem. He'd heard the same response from several other cloth dealers. He'd bought the linen because the embroidery work—a hunting scene with hares crouching beneath thornbushes and red-tongued hounds trying to get them out—was astonishingly vivid and colorful, far better than anything of the sort he'd seen in Hellas. The Phoenician who'd sold it to him told him it came from the east, from Mesopotamia. Because it was so beautiful, he hadn't imagined he would have any trouble selling it. But it was also unusual, which made some people leery of it. Sostratos asked, "Do you know of someone in your business who might be more inclined to take a chance?"

"Sorry," the cloth merchant repeated, and tossed his head again. "You know what I would do if I were you, though?"

"Tell me."

"I'd try to sell it to some rich man who likes hunting. He'd have the money to buy it, and he might figure out something to do with it— hang it on the wall of his andron, maybe, so his friends could admire it at his symposia."

That was a good idea—or it would have been a good idea for an Athenian merchant. A local man would have dealt here for years. He would have customers in mind when he saw something like the cloth.

Sostratos didn't. He was a stranger here, and the Athenians were strangers to him. "Strangers . . ." he murmured.

"What's that?" the cloth merchant asked.

"Nothing, O best one, nothing really," Sostratos answered. "But I thank you very much for your suggestion."

"I hope you *can* unload that. It's very pretty, no doubt about it," the Athenian said. "But it wouldn't come cheap for me, and I don't want to spend my owls on something where I might not get 'em back."

"All right. Hail." Sostratos walked out of the fellow's shop and into the brilliant sunlight of the very first days of summer. It would have been even hotter in Rhodes, but it was plenty warm enough here. Sostratos' shadow was a black puddle around his feet. Down in Egypt, he'd heard, shadows got shorter still at solstice time, till they all but disappeared. *If you measured the difference in the angle of a noontime shadow on the same day here and at Alexandria, and if you knew exactly how far it was from here to there, you could use geometry to figure out how big the world is.*

You could . . . if you knew. But no one did, not with the needed precision. Sostratos sighed. *So many things we don't know.*

One of the things he still didn't know was where he would sell the embroidered cloth. But now, thanks to the dealer, he had an idea. He was glad he'd put on his petasos before visiting this fellow. Otherwise, he would have wanted to double back to Protomakhos' house to get one. If he walked down to the seaside with his head uncovered, his brains might cook before he got there. He hadn't cared to go to Peiraieus in the rain, squelching through mud. He didn't much care for a long walk in baking heat, either.

He laughed at himself. *You want it to be sunny but mild all the time.* After a moment's thought, he dipped his head. *Yes, that is what I want.* Nothing was wrong with wanting it, as long as he understood that wanting it didn't mean he'd get it.

He wasn't bound for Peiraieus today, but for Mounykhia, where the great fort housing Kassandros' men dominated the skyline. "What do you want?" demanded a guard with a long spear. That was what Sostratos thought he said, anyhow; he used Macedonian dialect so broad as to be almost unintelligible to someone who spoke one of the more usual varieties of Greek.

"I want to see Alketas the tetrarkhos, if you please." Sostratos answered as clearly as he could, and did his best to use Attic—the guard would be more used to that, and more likely to understand it, than Sostratos' native Doric.

And the fellow dipped his head to show he did follow. "Who be you?" he asked.

"Sostratos son of Lysistratos, a Rhodian. I've sold Alketas wine. I have something else here he might care to see."

"Wait. No go. No come. Wait." The Macedonian tapped the ground with the iron-shod butt of his spear to make sure Sostratos got the message. Then he disappeared into the bowels of the fortress. Sostratos waited. Sweat dripped off him. A bee buzzed close. He took off his hat and whacked at it. It flew away. He put the hat back on, first carefully checking to make sure the bee wasn't inside. Just as he was starting to grow impatient, the sentry returned. "*Now* you come," he said.

He led Sostratos past an exercise yard where soldiers were practicing under the watchful eye and iron lungs of an underofficer. "Lower—spears!" the man bellowed. Down they came. They were so long, several ranks of spearheads projected out past the first rank of men—one reason a phalanx was so hard to oppose. How did a foe get through that hedgehog of spears to the soldiers behind it? The Persians never had found an answer, not from Marathon all the way to Alexander's time. The closest they'd come was hiring Hellenes to fight for them. In the end, that hadn't worked, either.

The motion had looked smooth enough to Sostratos, but the underofficer flew into a rage, screaming abuse at the men in Greek and then going into Macedonian when he ran out. Sostratos didn't get all of that, but it certainly sounded inflammatory. The soldiers looked hot and tired and resigned—even amused—about the underofficer's curses.

"You come," the guard said again. He lowered his spear from vertical to horizontal so he could take it down a corridor. A slave coming the other way yelped and flattened himself against the mud-brick wall to keep from getting spitted. The Macedonian laughed. The corridor opened out onto another, smaller, yard. The guard pointed. "There."

In the courtyard, Alketas stood talking with Dionysios—the commander of the fortress—and two other officers. He waved when he saw Sostratos. "Hail, Rhodian!" he boomed.

"Hail," Sostratos replied. "How are you today?"

"Couldn't be better," the Macedonian replied. "What have you got today? Have you come up with more wine from interesting places?"

In a way, Sostratos hated selling fine wine to someone like Alketas. Like as not, he'd pour it down neat, and get his tongue too numb to savor it after the first couple of gulps. A man who drank to get drunk and not to enjoy what he was drinking deserved to swill something one step above vinegar. Selling him Lesbian and Byblian was almost like pouring them straight into a chamber pot. On the other hand, as Sostratos couldn't ignore, it was much more profitable.

Today, that issue didn't arise. "Not wine," Sostratos answered. "I've got something to decorate your quarters, if you're interested."

"Oh-ho!" Alketas made curving motions with his hands. "Is she a blonde?" The Macedonians with him laughed.

Sostratos gave back a dutiful smile. "*Something,* I said, O best one, not *someone.* No, what I have is ... this." He unfolded the embroidered cloth and spread his arms to display it.

All four Macedonians stared in admiration at the hunting scene. Dionysios said, "That comes out of Mesopotamia, doesn't it?" He was the oldest man there, his hair thin on top and more gray than brown.

"Yes, most noble, it does. I got it in Ioudaia, farther west," Sostratos replied. "How did you know?"

"I saw the like going through that country with the Alexander," Dionysios said. Greek could show a man's special status by tacking the article on in front of his name. And who better deserved special status than Alexander?

If he were alive today, he wouldn't even be fifty. Sostratos thought for a moment, then dipped his head. That was right, even if it seemed unbelievable. He'd been thirty-three when he died, and he was sixteen years dead. This graying general, certainly not a young man but still far from ancient—he was probably younger than Sostratos' father—had likely been older than the King of Macedonia he'd served. That was a very curious thought.

"What do you want for it?" Dionysios asked now. "Those things don't come cheap, I know—not unless you steal 'em. But that's a fine one, and I wouldn't mind having it on my own wall."

"He brought it for me," Alketas said indignantly. Macedonians stood on very little ceremony among themselves.

"I wouldn't mind having it, either," said a third soldier, a fellow with only three fingers on his left hand. And the fourth officer, a foxy-faced, auburn-haired man who looked more Thracian than Macedonian, also dipped his head.

"I'll give you fifty drakhmai for it," Dionysios said. "I know you wouldn't take less."

In fact, Sostratos would have been glad to get so much. The Phoenician trader had added the cloth to a lump of beeswax to get an extra bottle of Rhodian perfume. But the foxy-faced man waited only a heartbeat before saying, "I'll give you sixty."

"Sixty-five, by Zeus!" Alketas exclaimed.

"Seventy!" said the officer with the missing fingers. The Macedonians glared at one another.

Sostratos? Sostratos smiled.

The soldiers kept bidding up the price of the embroidered hunting scene. In between the numbers they shouted, they yelled abuse at each other, first in Greek and then, as their tempers kindled, in the broad Macedonian dialect they'd grown up speaking. As with the underofficer in the other courtyard, Sostratos understood little of that; what he could make out seemed fouler than any insults in common use in Greek.

In due course, the officer with the missing fingers said, "One mina, eighty drakhmai." He waited. Sostratos waited. The other Macedonians glowered, but none of them bid again. The officer beamed. He made a fist with his good hand and thumped his chest with it. "Mine!" He might have been three years old.

Sullenly, Alketas said, "I don't care how pretty it is. Nothing's worth that kind of silver if it doesn't have a smooth little piggy to screw." Since his last offer had been only ten drakhmai lower, that struck Sostratos as a case of the fox's complaining the grapes were sour after he found he couldn't get them.

"Mine!" repeated the officer with the missing fingers. He reached out to take the cloth from Sostratos.

The Rhodian didn't give it to him. "Yours when I have my silver," he said.

"Wait," the fellow told him, and hurried away. He came back carrying a leather sack, which he thrust at Sostratos. "Here. Go ahead and count them."

Sostratos blinked. He couldn't remember the last time a customer gave him that kind of invitation. He hefted the sack. It felt about right. With a shrug, he replied, "Never mind, most noble one. I trust you." The Macedonian beamed. Sostratos gave him the square of embroidered linen. His smile got wider. He was happy. Sostratos was happy, too. The only unhappy people were the other three Macedonians, the ones the officer had outbid. And they, Sostratos knew, would get over it.

ADRASTOS THE DYER WAS A FAT PHRYGIAN WHO WORE A SAFFRON chiton with a crimson border, as if to show what he could do. His shop was in Peiraieus—not far from where the *Aphrodite* was tied up, in fact. When he glowered at Menedemos, his bushy eyebrows came together to form a single black bar across his forehead. "*You* have crimson dye for sale?" he said suspiciously, his Attic Greek good but flavored by the guttural accent of his Anatolian homeland. "I have never seen anyone but Phoenicians selling it up till now—unless you bought it from them and plan to gouge me to make up for what you paid."

"Not at all, my good fellow," Menedemos answered, doing his best not to wrinkle his nose against the stink of stale piss clinging to the dyeshop. They all smelled that way; no one knew a better bleach than urine. Menedemos went on, "I did buy my dye from a Phoenician, as a matter of fact."

"Ha! I knew it," Adrastos said.

Menedemos held up a hand. "Please, O best one—you didn't let me finish. I bought it from a Phoenician dyemaker in Sidon when I took my akatos east last year. Because of that, I can charge what the Phoenicians usually do—no middleman's markup, as you feared."

"From Sidon, eh?" The dyer still sounded suspicious. "What dyemaker did you deal with there?"

"Tenashtart son of Metena," Menedemos answered. "Do you know him?"

"I have never met him. I have not traveled to Phoenicia, and I do not think he has ever come to Athens, though I've heard he's traveled to Hellas," Adrastos said. "But I know of him, and of his firm." He tugged at his curly black beard. "If you had not dealt with him, I do not think you would know of him."

"Here is a jar of dye I bought from him." The Rhodian set it on the counter between them. "I can sell you about as much as you want, at prices as good as you'll get from any man of Sidon or Byblos."

The Phrygian picked up the jar, holding it on one plump palm and slowly turning it with his other hand. "Truly, this is the very style of jar Tenashtart uses." He yanked out the stopper and sniffed. The dye had a nasty reek from the shellfish of which it was made, though Menedemos marveled that Adrastos could smell anything through the pungent odor of urine permeating his shop. The dyer nodded, and then, as if to show he really had learned Hellenic customs, dipped his head, too. Menedemos hid a smile; he'd seen other barbarians do the same. Adrastos said, "It does appear to be the true crimson dye. May I test it with a scrap of cloth?"

"Please do, most noble one," Menedemos told him. "That's why I brought it."

Adrastos poked the corner of a rag into the jar, then pulled it out. He studied the deep red color. "Yes, that's Sidonian crimson, sure enough. It's not as good as what Tyre used to make before Alexander sacked the town. Tyrian crimson was brighter, and wouldn't fade no matter what. Such a color! I was just a youth getting started in my father's business—you would have been a little boy then. You don't see the like any more. The men who knew how to make it are dead, or else they're slaves doing something that's got nothing to do with dye. This isn't bad for what you can get nowadays, but it doesn't come up to Tyrian." He sighed.

Menedemos would have thought he was trying to beat the price down, but other men who knew about the dyes the Phoenicians made had told him the same thing. "Is it good enough for you to want it?" he asked.

"Oh, yes," Adrastos said. "As long as I can get a decent price, that is." He named one.

"That's not decent. That's *in*decent!" Menedemos yelped. "You want me to give it away." He named his own, considerably higher, price.

Adrastos howled like a wolf. "Any Phoenician tried to charge me that, I'd fling him into a vat of piss." He sent Menedemos a speculative look, as if wondering how the Rhodian would look all wet and dripping.

"Some people," Menedemos remarked, "think they're the only ones who work a trade. In a polis the size of Athens, I can always sell to someone else."

"Sell, certainly. Steal from honest folk with your prices? Not likely!" Adrastos said.

They traded more insults. The Phrygian came up a little. Menedemos went down a little. They both knew ahead of time about where they would end up. As they drew closer to that point, they haggled harder. Finally, Menedemos said, "Have we got a bargain?"

"Yes, Rhodian. I think we do." The dyer stuck out his hand, which was stained with crimson and saffron and woad and other dyes. Menedemos clasped it. Adrastos asked, "And how soon can I have the dye?"

"My ship is tied up here in Peiraieus," Menedemos said. "Let me walk over, and I'll get it for you. You'll have the silver waiting?"

"Oh, yes. The world would squeak to a stop if not for silver," Adrastos answered. "I pay what I say I'll pay. You don't need to worry about that."

When some men told Menedemos he didn't need to worry, he worried harder than ever. The Phrygian didn't strike him as being one of that sort, though. Yes, Adrastos dressed gaudily, but how else was a dyer supposed to show off his skill? The man's shop was neat and clean. He couldn't help the way it smelled, not in the business he was in. And the owls he gave Menedemos wouldn't stink. With a smile at that conceit, Menedemos said, "All right, O best one. I'll be back in a little while with the dye, then."

He hurried toward the quays, dodging past a fisherman carrying a basket of sprats, some of them still wiggling a little; another fisherman with a basket of eels for customers who could afford better than sprats; a naked sponge diver, his eyes blood-red from staying open in the sea, a couple of sponges under his arms; a gray-haired, unveiled woman selling little cheese pies; a shaven-headed Egyptian sailor coming out of a brothel with a sated smirk on his face; and a net-seller or -mender all draped with his wares. Flies buzzed. Sparrows hopped around, pecking at this and that. A dog with half its left ear missing gnawed a length of pig gut a sausage-seller must have thrown away. It growled when Menedemos walked by. He raised a leg to kick it if it tried to bite, and it shrank back in fear.

As Menedemos neared the pier to which the *Aphrodite* was tied, someone called his name. He turned. There was Sostratos, waving. Menedemos waved back and said, "Hail! What are you doing here? I thought you'd be up in the city."

"I sold some ink to a fellow who thinks he's the next Euripides, and then found I'd got rid of all the jars we'd brought up to Protomakhos' house." Sostratos looked disgusted with himself. "I hate making mistakes like that."

"Reminds me you're human," Menedemos said.

By his cousin's expression, Sostratos didn't care to be reminded. But he also recalled enough humanity to stay polite, which he didn't always. He asked, "How about you?"

"I just sold some crimson dye to a dyer whose shop can't be more than three or four plethra from the *Aphrodite*," Menedemos said. "Got a decent price for it, too."

"How much?" Sostratos asked. Menedemos told him. He dipped his head. "Yes, that's not bad," he agreed. "Nothing to make Kroisos the Lydian king jealous, but not bad."

"Kroisos collected taxes and tribute," Menedemos said. "We have to earn our money."

"So we—" Sostratos broke off and pointed out to sea. "By the dog of Egypt!" he whispered. "Will you look at that?"

Menedemos looked. There approaching the harbor was an immense fleet of war galleys and transports. He started to count them, but rapidly gave up. There had to be well over a hundred. He and Sostratos weren't the only ones who'd spotted them, either. Everywhere, people on the street and on the quays stopped whatever they were doing and pointed out to sea like Sostratos.

"Who do you suppose they are?" Sostratos asked in a small voice.

"You said it yourself—'by the dog of Egypt,'" Menedemos answered. "They have to belong to Ptolemaios. Otherwise the Athenians and Kassandros' men would be trying to shut the harbor against them and beat them back, and they're not."

They certainly weren't. A couple of Kassandros' Macedonians waved to the officers on the deck of an approaching war galley—an immense ship, at least a six, with two men per oar on all three banks of oars. One of the men on the galley waved back. His red cloak clung to his shoulders; the breeze blew from off the sea.

Blowing from off the sea, it carried the stench of the galleys to the shore. Menedemos made a face. *"Pheu!"* he said in disgust. "That's a worse reek than the one I came away from at Adrastos' dyeshop."

"A lot of men packed close together on a lot of warships, without much water for washing." Sostratos, as usual, wanted to get to the bottom of things. Usually, that was a virtue. Today, it irritated Menedemos.

"I know, my dear," he said. "No matter what you may think, I'm not a fool. And whatever the reason, that's a horrible stink."

Transports started tying up wherever there was room along a pier. Naked sailors tossed lines to longshoremen, who made the ships fast. Gangplanks thumped out onto the quays. Soldiers tramped along the gangplanks, up the quays, and onto dry land. They wore their helmets and corselets and carried both spears and shields. The longshoremen got out of their way as fast as they could.

"They look ready for business, don't they?" Sostratos said.

"They sure do," Menedemos answered.

"I don't understand," Sostratos said. "Is Ptolemaios going to help Kassandros garrison Athens? If he is, will Kassandros move some of his men somewhere else? To the north, say, to fight against Lysimakhos? There's been no rumor about any of this." By the way he sounded, he took that as a personal affront.

But he wasn't the only one puzzled. The Macedonians who'd waved to the approaching fleet came up to the closest column of soldiers. One of them asked a question. Menedemos couldn't make out the words, but it had to be something like, *What's going on here?*

Quite casually, an oncoming soldier lowered his long spear—it was more than twice the height of a man—and thrust it into the Macedonian's gut. His companion stared in astonished disbelief. Before he could do anything but stare, another soldier speared him. Both men let out bubbling wails of anguish as they crumpled, their blood spilling into the dust. They died without ever knowing why.

"Forward, men!" called an officer with the soldiers. "Now we take hold of this place."

Forward they came, sandals thumping. And, as they came, they shouted out their war cry: "Demetrios son of Antigonos! *Eleleu!* Demetrios son of Antigonos!"

Menedemos and Sostratos gaped at each other as the column pounded past. That wasn't Demetrios of Phaleron the soldiers were shouting for. It was Demetrios the son of Antigonos the One-Eyed, Macedonian marshal and deadly foe to Ptolemaios and Kassandros both. However he'd done it, his men were swarming into Peiraieus— and, for all Menedemos knew, into Mounykhia, too—in what looked like overwhelming numbers.

8

SOSTRATOS HAD NEVER THOUGHT HE'D BE CAUGHT IN THE storming of a city. He looked around for some place where he and Menedemos might hide—looked around and saw nothing. He didn't want to break and run. That would draw the invaders' attention to him, and they were all too likely to serve him as they'd served Kassandros' officers.

Some people did run away. Demetrios son of Antigonos' soldiers didn't pursue them. And some people came pelting down toward the wharves to find out what was going on. Even more than most Hellenes, Athenians were insatiably curious.

One of the war galleys, a great fearsome six, drew near the shore. A very tall man wearing a gilded, high-crested helm, a gilded corselet, and a crimson-dyed cape draped over his back stood near the bow. Sostratos pointed toward him. "That has to be Demetrios," he said.

"I don't know if it has to be, but I'd think it probably is," Menedemos answered.

"His father is supposed to be a big man. His cousin Polemaios was a big man. We saw that when he was aboard the *Aphrodite* a couple of years ago. It must run in the family," Sostratos said. "And besides, who else but Demetrios would wear such a fancy outfit?"

Closer and closer came the war galley, till it was within easy bowshot of the shore. Sostratos wondered if it would run aground. Demetrios' soldiers formed a perimeter along the shoreline to keep anyone from coming *too* close, but a good archer could have shot at the ship from beyond it. He could have, that is, if he'd found room to draw his bow. The crowd of gawkers grew thicker by the minute. Sostratos and Menedemos both used their elbows to keep from getting squashed together like olives in brine.

The man at the bow of the six waited a few minutes more, to let the crowd build further. Then he cupped both hands in front of his mouth and called, "Hail, people of Athens! Hail, *free* people of Athens. I am Demetrios son of Antigonos."

"Told you so," Sostratos whispered.

"Hush," Menedemos whispered back, and Sostratos did.

Demetrios dropped his hands for a moment to gaze out at the Athenians, and to let them see him. The war galley was close enough to the shore for him to show off not only his size but also his good looks. He was about Sostratos' age, ruddy like so many men from the north, with a long, straight nose and a forward-thrusting chin.

"Hail!" he said once more, in a ringing baritone. "My father has sent me here on what we both hope will be a mission that makes you Athenians happy. What I aim to do is very simple. I aim to set the city free, to throw Kassandros' garrison out of Mounykhia, and to give you back your own laws and your old constitution. And, by Athena, that's *all* I aim to do."

He stopped. He waited. The Athenians looked at one another. A quick gabble of conversation broke out. A few people said that couldn't possibly be *all* Demetrios and Antigonos wanted from Athens. More, though, burst into delighted cheers. "*Euge* for Demetrios!" they shouted, and, "To the crows with Demetrios of Phaleron!" and, "Furies take Kassandros and all who follow him!" Some few of them had brought weapons. They threw them down now, in token of surrender.

Out on the galley, Demetrios raised a hand. "Men of Athens, I promise I will not set foot in your polis until Kassandros' garrison is gone. I hope and expect it will be soon, for I have wanted to see Athens for many years."

Cheers rang out, and more shouts of praise for Demetrios. Out of the side of his mouth, Sostratos said, "He may not come into Athens himself till then, but you notice he didn't say anything about his soldiers."

"Oh, yes," Menedemos replied. "I'm just glad you were selling ink to some fellow who fancies himself a poet, and not wine or truffles to Kassandros' officers over at their fortress. You'd be trapped there if you were."

"*Oimoi!*" Sostratos exclaimed. "I hadn't thought of that, but you're right."

Demetrios shouted, "Let word go into the city—in fact, I will send it—that I would speak with whatever representative Demetrios of Phaleron will send to me. For he must surely see that his time in Athens is past, that the polis now lies in my hands, and that I *will* liberate it in accordance with my father's orders."

"Let's take care of our business here and then get back up to Athens as fast as we can," Sostratos said. "I don't know if we'll have the chance much longer."

"That makes more sense than I wish it did," Menedemos said. "I hope Demetrios' men don't take it into their heads to plunder the *Aphrodite.*"

"How do you propose to stop them if they do?" Sostratos asked bleakly.

"We can't," his cousin replied, which was exactly what Sostratos thought. "That's why I hope they don't."

The two Rhodians hurried to the merchant galley. When they got there, they found the normally unflappable Diokles in a fragile state. "By the gods, young sirs, when I saw those soldiers on the quays, I thought we were going to be *somebody's* opson. Maybe I'm wrong. I hope I am. But . . ." He shuddered. "Those were a bad few minutes there till Demetrios started talking. The Athenians ate that up, didn't they? He can charm the birds right out of the trees."

"Sooner or later, though, we'll find out whether he's telling the truth," Sostratos said.

"There is that," the oarmaster agreed. "What do we do now? Sit tight and hope he is?"

That was Menedemos' decision, not Sostratos'. "Yes, I think we do," Menedemos answered. "We'd have to leave more than half the crew behind if we try to sneak out now, and who knows if Demetrios' fleet will let anybody leave? If he was telling even part of the truth, we'll be all right."

"If anybody does give us trouble, we should shout out at the top of our lungs that we're Rhodians," Sostratos said. "Plundering Athenians is one thing for Demetrios' men—up till now, Athens has been on Kassandros' side, and Kassandros and Antigonos are enemies. But Rhodes is a neutral. Demetrios has to be—well, he'd better be, if he's smart—leery about offending her."

Menedemos dipped his head. "Right you are, best one! That makes good sense, and I'm not sure I would have thought of it myself."

"We've got a toikharkhos with a good head on his shoulders," Diokles said. Sostratos grinned; Diokles' good opinion mattered to him. Then he remembered that Theophrastos had said the same thing. The philosopher's good opinion mattered to him, too. Did it matter much more than the keleustes'? Sostratos tossed his head. If that didn't show how much he'd changed since his student days, he couldn't imagine what would.

He got the ink, and helped Menedemos carry the jars of crimson dye to Adrastos' shop. Menedemos took the dyer's money without counting it. Showing silver now could be dangerous.

"Let's head back up to the city," Sostratos said. "The farther away from all these soldiers we get, the better I'll like it." His cousin was in many ways a daredevil. Sostratos wanted to throttle Menedemos for taking up with their host's wife. He seemed to have got away with it, but what if Xenokleia had gone straight to Protomakhos after his first advances toward her? Trouble, that was what. And what if her baby ended up looking like Menedemos? Trouble again, perhaps, though not till the next visit to Athens. But Menedemos showed no desire to play dangerous games with Demetrios' soldiers. For that, at least, Sostratos was grateful.

Back toward Athens they went. The way up to the city was more crowded than Sostratos had ever seen it. He wasn't surprised. He and Menedemos couldn't have been the only ones who wanted to get away from the newly arrived Macedonians. Demetrios' name was on everyone's lips. Somewhere up in front of them was the dividing line between people who knew Antigonos' son was seizing control of the harbors of Athens and those who didn't. As traders traveling from city to city, Sostratos and Menedemos had often been news-bringers, on the very edge between those who knew and those who wanted to find out. Not today; their stop at Adrastos' had let others get ahead.

They hadn't gone far before hoofbeats thundered behind them. Raucous voices shouted, "Make way! Make way for the envoys of Demetrios son of Antigonos!" The cavalrymen raced past at a fast trot. At that rate, they might get to Athens before any of the people on foot.

Menedemos sighed as the horses went by. "I wish I'd done more riding," he said.

"Not me." As far as Sostratos was concerned, that was as much daredeviltry as his cousin's taste for sleeping with other men's wives. "I may admire a man who can stay on a horse's back, but that doesn't mean I want to imitate him very often. It's a long way down, the ground is hard, and what have you got to hold on with? Your knees. No, thanks."

"You were the one who hired a donkey to go exploring when we were in Italy," Menedemos pointed out.

"That was a donkey," Sostratos said, nobly resisting the temptation to add, *And you're another one.* "It was small, and I'm pretty large. My feet were almost dragging in the dust when I got astride it. It walked. It didn't trot or gallop."

"And besides, you were curious then," Menedemos said. Sostratos didn't dignify that with a reply, especially since it was true.

On they went. Sweat poured off Sostratos; he wished he'd drunk some wine, or even water, before setting out from Peiraieus. Who could guess what Demetrios' men were doing back there, though? He looked over his shoulder. No great cloud of black smoke rose into the sky. They hadn't started burning for the sport of it, anyhow. Demetrios had said he'd come to liberate Athens. Of course, the difference between what a general said and what he did was all too often enormous.

Sostratos and Menedemos had almost got back to Athens when they saw Demetrios' horsemen again, this time coming the other way. Along with the soldiers rode a worried-looking civilian who looked none too happy on horseback. Sostratos caught a snatch of conversation: a cavalryman said, "Don't worry, O best one. I'm sure we'll work something out."

"I wonder what that means," Menedemos said.

"Maybe Demetrios son of Antigonos hasn't got a Persian torturer waiting for Demetrios of Phaleron after all," Sostratos replied.

"Maybe." Menedemos laughed a nasty laugh. "Or maybe he wants Demetrios of Phaleron to *think* he hasn't got a torturer waiting for him."

"It could be," Sostratos admitted. "The Macedonians play the game for keeps. Kassandros has had it all his own way here in Athens for a long time, and so has Demetrios of Phaleron. If the other Demetrios has trouble finding reasons to give him a hard time, I'm sure plenty of Athenians could suggest some."

Once the Rhodians got into the city, Sostratos found out how right he was. Athens bubbled like grape juice fermenting into wine. For ten years, people had had to keep quiet about what they thought. That was what tyranny did. It had been a genteel tyranny, but tyranny it was nonetheless. Now . . .

Now, going through the city toward Protomakhos' house, Sostratos heard a lot of what people must have been thinking and not saying. "Furies take Demetrios!" was popular. So was, "To the crows with Demetrios!" Someone said, "One of Demetrios' pals cheated me on a house. I couldn't do anything about it for a long time, but I'll get even now." Somebody else added, "There's a lot of polluted villains who'd better run before we catch 'em and hamstring 'em!" Maybe he was speaking metaphorically. On the other hand, maybe he wasn't. Had Sostratos been a man who'd enriched himself during Demetrios of Phaleron's years in power, he didn't believe he would have cared to linger in Athens to find out.

No MATTER WHO RULED ATHENS, business had to go on. Menedemos went back down to Peiraieus the day after Demetrios son of Antigonos' men took the port, to make sure the *Aphrodite* stayed safe. "No trouble here, skipper," Diokles reported. "The soldiers are under good discipline, and they aren't plundering."

"That's a relief," Menedemos said, and brought some more perfume up into Athens.

He was haggling with a hetaira's slave in the agora the following day when a single sentence swept across the market square: "He's gone!"

"Demetrios of Phaleron?" Menedemos asked.

"Couldn't be anyone else," the slave woman answered. She was middle-aged and plain, but her face glowed. "Maybe things will be better here now."

"I hope so," Menedemos said, thinking, *On the other hand, maybe they won't.* He muttered to himself. That was something more likely to occur to Sostratos. But nobody who'd watched Alexander's Macedonian marshals bang one another back and forth had an easy time believing any one of them could solve a polis' problems just by appearing and snapping his fingers. However much they wanted to be, the marshals weren't gods. About Alexander himself, Menedemos wasn't so sure.

As he and the slave went on dickering, details followed that first exciting breath of rumor. From what people said, Demetrios son of Antigonos had granted Demetrios of Phaleron a safe-conduct up to the border of Boiotia, which remained in Kassandros' hands.

"Too bad," the woman said. "I wanted him up on a cross."

"What did he do to you?" Menedemos asked.

"Oh, he didn't do anything to me," she answered. "But he's been sucking up to the Macedonians for years, and I'm sick of it."

"I see," Menedemos said. "But isn't Demetrios son of Antigonos a Macedonian, too?"

"Well, what if he is?" the slave woman asked in return. "He said we're going to be free, so of course I'd rather see him than Demetrios of Phaleron."

She herself was unlikely to be free no matter which Demetrios called the shots in Athens. Would the polis be free? She certainly seemed to think so. By the excited chattering all around, so did a lot of the Athenians. To Menedemos, their optimism only proved they hadn't been free for a long time, and weren't very good at gauging what promises were worth. Demetrios son of Antigonos would promise anything to win the Athenians over, just as Menedemos might to coax a girl into bed. Delivering afterwards? That was liable to be a different story.

Menedemos shrugged. The only thing he could do now was try to stay out of the way of Macedonian soldiers, no matter which marshal they claimed as their master. He went back to haggling with the slave woman. At last, they reached a price that satisfied both of them. She went off to get the silver from her mistress.

She came back with it herself, instead of bringing along an enormous Keltic body servant. Menedemos thought that wise. Before long, soldiers loyal to Demetrios son of Antigonos would be coming into the agora. They were liable to react to an enormous Kelt the way hounds reacted to a boar.

Sure enough, Demetrios' soldiers did enter the agora later that afternoon. They seemed more travelers than warriors, though. Some of them gaped at the buildings lining the south and west sides of the market square. Others craned their necks to peer up at the even more magnificent buildings of the akropolis. A whiff of panic swept through the agora when they first appeared. As soon as the merchants found out they weren't intent on rapine and murder, the panic blew away. The Athenians started trying to sell them things instead.

So did Menedemos. He held up one of his little jars. "Perfume! Fine perfume from Rhodes, island of roses! Make some Athenian girl glad to see you when you give her perfume!"

A soldier came over to him. "How much?" he asked. Menedemos

told him. He scowled, then tossed his head. "You've got to be joking, pal. I can pay a platoon of Athenian girls to be glad to see me for that kind of money."

"Ah, but the ones you get with this are worth a platoon of the ordinary sort," Menedemos said.

"Some are better in bed than others, sure," the soldier said, "but none of 'em's *that* much better." Menedemos did not make a sale.

When he got back to Protomakhos' house as the sun was going down, he found Sostratos had news: "They've dug a trench around the fortress in Mounykhia. None of Kassandros' men gets out."

"You think the fortress will fall?" Menedemos asked.

"I don't see how it can do anything else," his cousin answered. "No sign of Demetrios son of Antigonos in Athens yet, either. Maybe he does keep promises. Wouldn't that be strange?"

"I wish he would come," Menedemos said. "We've still got some wine and truffles and perfume left. He's Antigonos' son. He can't be poor. Maybe he'll buy things now that the other Demetrios has fled."

"Maybe he will, or maybe his officers will," Sostratos said. "I certainly hope so. Right at the moment, they're besieging some of our best customers."

"Rude of them, isn't it?" Menedemos remarked.

Sostratos raised an eyebrow. "That's one way to put it, yes."

The Rhodians kept trying to do business in Athens, but nobody seemed eager to spend much silver—or perhaps to show much silver—till people saw what sort of master Demetrios son of Antigonos would make. The siege of the fortress at Mounykhia went on. Every so often, a few men came in or went out during brief truces. People said Dionysios, the commander, was dickering with Demetrios over surrender terms. Menedemos had no idea how the people who said that knew it, but say it they did.

Demetrios didn't need all the soldiers he'd brought along to maintain the siege. He sent others west to Megara, to take that polis away from Kassandros. In the earlier days of Hellas, Megara was a prominent polis, but the rise of Athens eclipsed it. Its walls didn't hold Demetrios' men out for long. Only pleas from Athens to spare a former rival kept the city from being plundered.

Protomakhos, who brought word of that to Menedemos and

Sostratos, went on, "Demetrios has some sense of what looks good in the eyes of Hellenes. That's probably why he spared the place."

"That's more than his father does," Sostratos said. "Antigonos is like a shark. He'll bite off your leg first and worry about what you think of it later."

"So I've heard," Protomakhos agreed. "But Demetrios is smoother than that. He asked Stilpon the Megaran philosopher if any of his men had robbed him, and Stilpon answered, 'No, I haven't seen anybody carrying away any knowledge.'"

Menedemos and Sostratos laughed. Menedemos said, "Demetrios didn't stop *all* the plundering, from what I've heard. His men might have left the Megarans their immovable property, but they did steal most of the slaves in the town, maybe for themselves, maybe to resell to dealers."

"I heard the same thing," the Rhodian proxenos said. "As Demetrios was heading out of Megara, he told Stilpon, 'I leave this a city of free men.' And Stilpon answered, 'I should say you do, for you've taken all our slaves.'"

"Talking back to the man who's just captured your city takes nerve," Menedemos said. Protomakhos dipped his head.

Sostratos asked, "If Demetrios has left Megara, where's he going?"

"That I don't know," Protomakhos answered. "Wherever he can give his foes—and his father's—the most trouble, is my guess."

But that guess proved wide of the target. Sostratos was the one who found out what Antigonos' son had been up to after leaving Megara. A few days after Protomakhos brought the news of Demetrios' departure, Sostratos said, "He's gone to Patrai, or rather, just outside of Patrai."

"To Patrai!" Protomakhos exclaimed. "That's well west of Corinth, isn't it?—on the north coast of the Peloponnesos. What made him go there?"

"Not 'what,' O best one—'who,'" Sostratos answered. Something in his voice made Menedemos look up sharply. His cousin wasn't looking his way, but out of the andron and across the courtyard. Still, Menedemos sensed that Sostratos was really talking to him as he continued, "It seems Kratesipolis invited him to pay her a call."

Menedemos knew the name. Still, he thought it best to let Protomakhos be the one who responded. Respond the Rhodian proxenos did: "The woman who was ruling Sikyon, not far from Patrai, not long ago?"

"That's the one." Sostratos dipped his head. "She's the widow of Alexandros son of Polyperkhon, and she's still supposed to be a famous beauty."

"Polyperkhon didn't amount to much, did he?" Menedemos remarked. No one could possibly have argued with him; the Macedonian officer, a man of the generation of Antigonos and, indeed, of Philip of Macedon, had ruled varying chunks of Hellas since not long after the death of Alexander the Great, but he'd never managed to make himself a major player in the wars of the Macedonian marshals.

"No, my dear, but the story's about his daughter-in-law—and about Demetrios," Sostratos said. "He went after her like a hound after a hare. He dashed off to Patrai with just a few officers, and when he got there he set up his tent well apart from theirs. He wanted to have a . . . private visit with Kratesipolis."

"He's a young man, isn't he? The age of you two Rhodians, more or less?" Protomakhos chuckled reminiscently. "When you're that age, a lot of the time, your spear stands and you just *have* to flesh it in piggy—or you think you do, anyhow."

Now Menedemos was the one who gazed out at the courtyard as if it were the most fascinating thing in the world. If Protomakhos suspected . . . But he didn't seem to. Sostratos' voice still held that sharp edge as he went on, "Demetrios almost paid for his folly with his neck, too. Some of Kassandros' men got word he was there, and he barely escaped them when they came to call."

The story wasn't about adultery. How could it be, with Kratesipolis a widow? But it was about a man doing something stupid on account of a woman and almost dying on account of it. Just for a heartbeat, Menedemos' gaze flicked toward Sostratos. His cousin looked almost indecently smug. Yes, he'd enjoyed telling it, sure enough.

Blind—fortunately—to the byplay, Protomakhos said, "Maybe Demetrios has learned his lesson. Maybe he'll come back here and finish off the siege down at Mounykhia. By Zeus, I hope so. Business won't get back to normal till he does."

"I hope he does, too," Sostratos said. "But somebody who's mad for women like that, he's liable to keep right on doing crazy things as long as he lives." No, he wasn't looking at Menedemos. But he was talking to him.

"Well, I won't say you're wrong," Protomakhos replied. "Whether he's mad for women or not, though, the way he got into our harbors shows he's a pretty good general."

"That's true," Sostratos said. "The way he relieved Ptolemaios' siege of Halikarnassos a couple of years ago, too."

He got in another jab there, though again not one Protomakhos would notice. Menedemos couldn't think of Halikarnassos without thinking of the trouble he'd wound up in there on account of that merchant's wife. He glanced over to Sostratos once more. His cousin had had things all his own way lately when it came to giving. Menedemos knew that was his own fault; his affair with Xenokleia had given Sostratos plenty of openings. But that didn't mean Menedemos wouldn't enjoy revenge. Oh, no, it didn't mean that at all.

DEMETRIOS' MEN PUMMELED the fortress at Mounykhia with dart- and stone-throwing engines. Trapped inside the fort, Dionysios and the garrison fought back as well as they could. But they were badly outnumbered, and the catapults made going up on the battlements worth a man's life. A few days after Megara fell, Demetrios' men stormed the stronghold. The Macedonians inside threw down their weapons when they saw they couldn't hold off their foes; Demetrios' soldiers took Dionysios alive.

And then, instead of garrisoning the fortress at Mounykhia themselves, Demetrios' men started tearing it down. That impressed Sostratos more than anything else they'd done. "Maybe Demetrios really means it when he says he wants Athens to be free and independent," he remarked at supper the day after the fortress fell. "Who would have believed that?"

"Not me," Protomakhos said, nibbling at an eel. "I just thought we'd go from one foreign overlord to the next. How about you, Menedemos?"

"Me? I just hope we'll be able to get some business done now," Menedemos said. "I let Sostratos worry about the political side of things. He's the one who enjoys fretting over things he can't change."

That held more venom than Menedemos usually used to charge his words. Sostratos wondered what he'd done to irritate his cousin. He couldn't think of anything. He'd just been himself . . . hadn't he?

Before he could fix on anything he might have done, Protomakhos said, "They say Demetrios will finally enter the city day after tomorrow to address the Assembly and make everything official."

This time, Sostratos didn't quibble about what *they,* whoever they were, might say. What the proxenos reported sounded too likely for him to quarrel with it. Sostratos did ask, "Is there any way a foreigner could join the Assembly when Demetrios speaks to it? I'd love to hear that with my own ears."

"I doubt they'll be taking roll, not for a meeting like this," Protomakhos replied.

"I was thinking the same thing," Sostratos said eagerly. "Want to come, Menedemos?" He tried to sound as friendly as he could.

His cousin started to toss his head, but then shrugged instead. "Well, why not?" he said. "A lot of the people I'd want to see would be at the meeting anyhow."

The Assembly met in the theater, not far from Protomakhos' house. The proxenos and the two Rhodians left his home early, as they'd done to see the tragedies and comedies. Even so, the theater was already more than half full by the time they got there. For one thing, admission to the Assembly was free. For another, after so long obeying Demetrios of Phaleron and, through him, Kassandros, the Athenians seemed eager to reclaim their freedom. That struck Sostratos as a good omen.

As the dawn brightened and the sun finally rose, a man strode importantly across the stage. People pointed at him and exclaimed to one another. Sostratos nudged Protomakhos. "Who is that? I don't recognize him."

"That's Stratokles, by Zeus," Protomakhos answered. "Demetrios could have started better."

"Why?" Sostratos pricked up his ears at the hint of scandal. "Who is he? What has he done?"

"He's a debauched, arrogant buffoon," Protomakhos said. "He played at politics before Demetrios of Phaleron's day, and none too well. He used to keep a hetaira named Phylakion. One day she brought back some neck bones and brains from the agora for a supper, and Stratokles said, 'Here are the things we political men play ball with.'"

Sostratos made a disgusted noise. Menedemos said, "Lovely fellow!"

"Isn't he?" Protomakhos dipped his head. "And then there was the time the year after Alexander died, when the Macedonians beat our fleet off Amorgos. Stratokles got word of the sea fight first somehow, and told everyone it was a victory. He put on a garland and proposed a sacrifice to the gods and a distribution of the meat. Then a couple of days later the truth reached the polis. Everyone started cursing him, and he said, 'Why blame me when I made you happy for two days?' "

"Lovely fellow indeed," Sostratos said.

He would have said more than that, but Stratokles spoke then: "Men of Athens, it is my great privilege to present to you our liberator from years of loathsome tyranny, Demetrios son of Antigonos!" He might have been a rogue, but he owned a ringing baritone voice that filled the theater without effort.

Demetrios came out to stand beside him. They made an odd pair, for the Athenian was short and squat, while Demetrios, who had a godlike physique, towered head and shoulders above him. "Hail, people of Athens!" he said, and his voice also outdid Stratokles'. "Antigonos, my father, is concerned for the freedom and autonomy of all poleis of Hellas, and especially for those of Athens, the greatest and most famous polis of them all."

That won him a warm round of applause. The Athenians were no more immune than anyone else to hearing themselves praised. Demetrios went on, "This being so, my father has ordered me to restore to you your ancient democratic constitution, which tyrants have trampled on for far too long."

More applause, a great roar of it. Sostratos clapped his hands along with the rest. He lived in a democratic city, and thought well of democracy. But he couldn't help wonder what sort of strings Antigonos and Demetrios would attach to the restoration.

"My father has also told me to tell you he is pleased to send you 150,000 medimnoi of wheat from Anatolia for your storehouses and your bakeries," Demetrios said. "And he will also send you timber enough to build a hundred triremes and restore your fleet to the glory it once enjoyed."

Amid the rapturous cheers from the Athenians all around, Menedemos muttered, "Ha!" Sostratos dipped his head. Rebuilding a navy took more than timber. It took skilled rowers by the thousands. Where would Athens find them? How would she pay for them? Demetrios said nothing about that. And triremes were the small change of fleets these days, anyhow. Fours, fives, and sixes—all full not only of rowers but also of equally expensive marines—did the bulk of the work. Some of Demetrios' promises were less extravagant than they seemed.

That might have occurred to the two Rhodians. It didn't seem to have crossed a single Athenian's mind. *Well, that's their worry, not mine,* Sostratos thought. He hoped it *wouldn't* be the Athenians' worry, but feared and expected it would.

As the applause faded, Demetrios bowed to the assembled people of Athens and stepped back, leaving the stage to Stratokles again. The orator said, "With our first decrees as men free once more, let us praise the great Antigonos and Demetrios for liberating us from the hateful yoke of Demetrios of Phaleron and Kassandros, his puppetmaster!"

More cheers rang out. Demetrios son of Antigonos looked artfully astonished, as if he hadn't imagined Stratokles would propose such a thing. "See how modest he is!" someone behind Sostratos exclaimed.

Sostratos had other ideas. He glanced over at Menedemos, who was also looking his way. "Put-up job," Sostratos mouthed. His cousin dipped his head.

"May it be propitious," Stratokles continued: the opening formula for a decree. "Let us set up gilded statues of Antigonos and Demetrios in a chariot, the said statues to stand near those of Harmodios and Aristogeiton in the agora so that one pair of liberators may regard the other. Do I hear an opposing voice?"

No one spoke in opposition. The decree passed without a single mutter. Sostratos thought it extravagant, but shrugged mental shoulders. Harmodios and Aristogeiton were credited with helping to overthrow the tyranny of Hippias and usher in democracy at Athens two hundred years earlier. Anyone who'd read Thoukydides, as Sostratos had, knew things weren't nearly so simple. But, by now, what the Athenians believed was at least as important as what had really happened.

And—statues! Whoever was making those gilded statues would need beeswax to coat his mold and take the fine detail he would sculpt. "Beeswax," Sostratos muttered. "Beeswax." He didn't want to forget.

Stratokles hadn't withdrawn. "May it be propitious," he said again.

"Let us reward our liberators with honorary crowns valued at two hundred talents of silver, to show the world that the Athenians' gratitude is not to be despised or taken lightly. Do I hear an opposing voice?"

Again, Demetrios looked modest and surprised. Again, no one dissented. Again, the decree passed by acclamation. Sostratos slowly dipped his head. Athens would pay, and pay plenty, for the privilege of liberation. Even for a polis as rich as this one, two hundred talents was a lot of money.

"May it be propitious," Stratokles said once more, and Sostratos wondered what was coming next. He didn't have to wait long: "Let us consecrate an altar to Antigonos and Demetrios, this altar to be known as that of the Saviors. And let us consecrate another altar where Demetrios first came down from his chariot and set foot on the soil of Athens, that one to be known as the altar of the Descending Demetrios. And let the chief priest who serves the altar of the Saviors henceforth give his name to the year, as the arkhon does now. Do I hear an opposing voice?"

There stood Demetrios. No matter how abashed he looked, his men had just driven Kassandros' out of Athens. He said he'd set the city free. What could he do if he changed his mind? *Anything he wants to,* Sostratos thought. The Athenians no doubt thought the same way. Stratokles heard no opposing voices. The decree—one servile enough to make Sostratos faintly sick to his stomach—passed without a single protest from the Assembly.

And more followed. The newly free—or so Demetrios had named them—people of Athens voted to add to the ten tribes among which they divided up their citizens two more, to be named Antigonis and Demetrias. They voted to hold annual games in honor of Demetrios and his father, with sacrifices and a procession. And they voted to include the portraits of Antigonos and Demetrios on the ceremonial mantle offered to Athena in the Parthenon every five years, "along with the images of the other gods," as Stratokles said. Like the ones that had come before, those motions passed without dissent.

That seemed to be all of them. As if to prove it was, Demetrios stepped forward once more. He bowed. "Men of Athens, I thank you for your generosity, and I know my father thanks you as well," he said.

Sostratos fought down a strong urge to retch. That hadn't been generosity. It had been the most revolting display of sycophancy he'd ever seen. No one, he was sure, had ever flattered even the Great Kings of Persia like this. But now the Athenians, who'd beaten the Persians at Marathon, at Salamis, and at Plataia, who'd preserved liberty for all of Hellas, wriggled on their bellies to kiss the dust through which Demetrios had walked. And they called that freedom! No, he didn't want to retch. He warned to cry.

Demetrios went on, "You have been kind to my father and me. Because you have, we shall also be kind to you, in the ways I have promised and in any other ways that seem good to us."

How the Athenians cheered! Demetrios practiced that abashed smile once more. Or maybe it wasn't so practiced. Maybe all this praise heaped on him really had turned his head. He surely couldn't have heard anything like it before. Yes, he was Antigonos' right-hand man, but Antigonos, by all accounts, was not a man one could safely flatter—he had wit enough to see through it. Nor was he one one to spoil his sons, either Demetrios or Philippos.

Sokrates had to drink hemlock here, Sostratos thought. He shivered. Two years before, he'd watched Polemaios drink hemlock. Dying of the drug was neither so neat nor so philosophical as Platon made it out to be. *But now the Athenians have found a sweeter poison.*

Stratokles moved that the meeting adjourn. That drew no more argument than any of his other motions had. The people of Athens streamed out of the theater, by all appearances well content with what they'd done. The morning remained young.

As long as he and Menedemos were in the midst of the Athenians, Sostratos said nothing. All his cousin said was, "Well, well." That could have meant anything. Sostratos knew what he thought it meant. He agreed, too.

Protomakhos was also conspicuously quiet as he and the Rhodians made their way back to his house. Once inside, he led them to the andron and called for wine. Then, making sure none of his slaves was in earshot, he spoke in low, intense, furious tones: "You young fellows, you come from a polis with a democracy that really works, isn't that so?"

"Yes," Sostratos said. Menedemos dipped his head.

The Rhodian proxenos took a long pull at his winecup. Then he went on, "Me, I'm not a youth any more. I'm old enough to remember how democracy is supposed to go. I recall the days before Philip of

Macedon won at Khaironeia and put all of Hellas under his boot. People then cared about the way things went. They cared about doing what was right, doing what was best. They cared about something besides bending over and showing Demetrios how wide their arseholes were." A disgusted look on his face, he drained the cup and dipped it full again.

Sostratos said the only thing he could think of that might make the Athenian feel a little better: "You haven't had a real democracy here for quite a while, most noble one. Maybe, now that this is done, your people will get the hang of it again."

"Do you think so?" Protomakhos asked morosely. "I don't. Stratokles got to play the sycophant today, but plenty of others haven't had the chance yet. They'll take it. And they'll take revenge on everybody who backed Demetrios of Phaleron, too. You wait and see. If Kleokritos didn't go over the border with his master, I wouldn't lay an obolos on his chances of living to grow old. Would you?"

"Well, no," Sostratos admitted. The proxenos was all too likely to be right. Whenever one faction ousted another, the first thing it usually did was get its own back against its rivals. Sostratos could have gone into detail about that; he'd read Herodotos and Thoukydides and Xenophon. But few Hellenes needed to read the historians to understand what their folk were capable of. Protomakhos almost certainly hadn't. Hellenes who knew themselves, knew their own kind, could see what was coming.

Menedemos said, "As long as the city doesn't break out in civil war"—he might have been talking about a pestilence—"we'll do all right. And so should you, best one," he added, pointing to Protomakhos. "They'll probably want to buy lots of slabs of marble to inscribe the decrees they passed today."

"Yes, I suppose they will." Protomakhos seemed less than delighted at the prospect. But then he brightened, a little. "If they are going to buy them, they may as well buy them from me."

"That's the spirit!" Menedemos dipped his head. He seemed perfectly friendly toward the dealer in stone. Knowing how . . . friendly Menedemos had been with Protomakhos' wife, Sostratos found that bemusing. He knew Menedemos shouldn't jeer at the man he'd cuckolded, but his cousin was proving an even better actor than he'd expected.

With an effort, Sostratos wrenched his thoughts away from adultery. *Commerce,* he told himself. *Think of commerce.* Turning to Protomakhos, he asked, "Do you know who's likely to do the statues of Antigonos and Demetrios in their chariot? I'd like to see him as soon as I can—that will be my best chance to sell all the beeswax I got in Ioudaia."

"*Euge,* my dear!" Menedemos exclaimed. He beamed at Sostratos. To Protomakhos, he said, "Isn't my cousin the cleverest fellow?"

Oh, yes, Sostratos thought. *You like my wits well enough when I turn them toward ways of making us money. But when I use the same logic to point out how you might want to choose a different road for your own life, you don't want to hear me. But what's more important in the end, silver or satisfaction?* He clicked his tongue between his teeth. Menedemos, no doubt, would define *satisfaction* differently.

Protomakhos played the diplomat: "Both you Rhodians are doing well for yourselves. As for sculptors, my guess would be they'll choose Hermippos son of Lakritos. He trained under the great Lysippos, and he's the best in the polis nowadays."

"Lysippos was a fine sculptor, sure enough," Sostratos said. "There's that Herakles of his back in Rhodes—people admire it."

"Oh, that one," Menedemos said. "I know the one you mean. Yes, he could make bronze and marble breathe, sure enough."

"I've seen some of his work, too," Protomakhos said. "Hermippos isn't quite in the same class, but he does well enough."

Sostratos almost remarked on that, but held his peace. People would admire Lysippos' work for generations; his name would live on. For every Lysippos, though, how many men did well enough to make a living, perhaps even well enough to gain some reputation while they were alive, but would be utterly forgotten five years after earth covered them? Others besides Thoukydides had written about the Peloponnesian War. What scribe copied their works these days? Before long— if it hadn't happened already—mice would nibble the last papyrus roll that held their histories, and then they would be gone. Other bards besides Homer must have sung. Who remembered them?

Are you sure you want to write a history? Sostratos wondered. *If you don't write it, you'll surely be forgotten,* he answered himself. *If you do, you have a chance of living on. Any chance is better than none.*

He dragged his mind back to the business at hand. "Where does this Hermippos have his shop?" he asked Protomakhos.

"Just north and west of the agora," Protomakhos replied. "The Street of the Panathenaia divides, one road going to the Sacred Gate, the other to the Dipylon Gate. Hermippos' shop is on the road to the Dipylon Gate, a couple of plethra past the boundary stone that marks the quarter of the Kerameikos."

The next morning, Sostratos got his lump of beeswax out of the prox-enos' storeroom and made his way up the street leading to the Dipylon Gate. To his relief—and more than a little to his surprise—he found Hermippos' shop without much trouble. The sculptor was an excitable little man in his thirties, with broad shoulders and big hands. "No, you thumb-fingered idiot, *this* way! How many times do I have to tell you?" he shouted at a harried-looking apprentice as Sostratos came up. He glowered at the Rhodian. "And what do *you* want?"

"Hail, Hermippos," Sostratos said, eyeing the work in progress: an armored Athena in marble, a competent piece but with nothing about it to draw the eye back for a second look. Protomakhos had gauged the man well. "Are you going to be making the gilded statues of Antigonos and Demetrios?"

"Why do you want to know?" the sculptor asked suspiciously. "I don't need any new 'prentices; the one I've got gives me enough headaches. And if you think you can wangle some kind of kickback from me for the commission, to the crows with you. I've got it straight from Stratokles."

"You misunderstand, O best one," Sostratos said, instantly glad he didn't have to deal with Hermippos every day. "I have fine beeswax to sell you."

That got Hermippos' notice. "You do, eh? Let's see it. Some people would try to sell me cow turds and call 'em wax."

"No cow turds," Sostratos said. "Here." He took the lump out of the sack. "See for yourself."

"Hmm. *Hmm.*" Hermippos looked pleased in spite of himself. He reached out to feel of the beeswax as Sostratos set it on the counter. Sostratos watched his hands in fascination. He had long, elegant fingers, but they bore the scars of countless burns and cuts. His palms were nearly as callused as those of a rower. The pale blotches of burn scars went most of the way up his forearms. Hermippos nipped off a tiny piece of wax with the nails of his thumb and forefinger so he could taste it as well. After smacking his lips, he dipped his head. "Yes, that's the genuine article. I've had people try to sell me tallow, too, the abandoned temple-robbers."

"I don't play those games," Sostratos said. "I'll get the best price I can, but I sell top-quality goods."

"I've never heard anybody who doesn't say that." Hermippos turned to his apprentice. "Do something useful for a change—give me a chisel."

Muttering, the young man obeyed. Sostratos wouldn't have wanted to work for Hermippos. He also wouldn't have wanted to be Hermippos in a sculptor's studio, working side by side with someone he constantly abused. Too many lethal implements were too handy. What was to keep that apprentice from driving that chisel into his back or picking up a hammer and smashing in his skull? Only the fellow's own self-restraint, and Hermippos seemed to enjoy flaying that every time he opened his mouth.

The sculptor thrust the chisel into the beeswax again and again, grunting with effort. He finally grunted one last time and, without a word of warning, tossed the chisel back to the apprentice. Taken by surprise, the fellow dropped it on his foot—fortunately, not point-down. He yelped anyhow. "Just be more careful next time," Hermippos snapped. He gave Sostratos another grudging dip of the head. "You didn't hide any rocks in there to make it seem heavier than it is."

"No," Sostratos said. "I made the same check when I bought it from a Phoenician."

"You weren't born a fool, then." Hermippos raked his apprentice with a glance. "Unlike some people I could name." He took a deep breath. "All right, Rhodian. You've got it. I want it. How much are you going to try to gouge me for?"

"Four minai," Sostratos answered.

"What?" Hermippos howled. "Why, you cistern-arsed, dung-eating catamite! Furies take you! I could buy a slave for that. Maybe I should. I'd get more use from him than I do from this two-legged donkey here." He jerked a thumb over his shoulder at the apprentice.

Sostratos sent the harried youngster a sympathetic glance. The apprentice's lips moved silently. *Squeeze him,* he mouthed. *He needs the wax.* Nothing on Sostratos' face showed that he'd seen. Inside, though, he smiled. Hermippos' bad temper was going to cost him money.

"I'll give you a mina and a half, and you ought to be glad to get that much," the sculptor growled.

"No. Good day." Sostratos picked up the lump of beeswax and made as if to go.

He didn't miss the look of alarm that flitted across Hermippos' face. "Well, two minai," Hermippos said. Sostratos didn't put down the beeswax. He started to walk away. "Two and a half!" Hermippos called. Sostratos kept walking. "All right, three, then!" the sculptor cried.

That was enough to make Sostratos stop. He ended up selling the wax for three minai, seventy-five drakhmai. When Hermippos went to get the silver, Sostratos told the apprentice, "I'll gladly give you five drakhmai for the tip. Come to the house of Protomakhos, near the theater."

"I wish I could say I didn't need it, but Hermippos doesn't pay me well enough to make that anything but a lie," the young man said. "I'll be there. I—" He broke off, for Hermippos came back with the silver just then. Sostratos carefully counted it, but the sculptor hadn't tried to cheat him. He headed back to Protomakhos' house well pleased with himself, even if he was paying a small commission.

"PERFUME FROM RHODES!" Menedemos held up a jar in the agora. "What man could resist a woman who wears perfume from Rhodes, the island of roses? Fine perfume from Rhodes!"

Plenty of people seemed able to resist his sales pitch. They walked past as if he didn't exist. He'd seen that only in the very largest and most sophisticated poleis: Rhodes, Taras, Syracuse, and now here in Athens. Most places, people stopped and listened to the pitch even if they didn't intend to buy. What else did they have in the way of entertainment? Things were different here, though. Athenians had more choices available than people in most towns did. They'd seen too many men trying to sell too many different kinds of things. Unless they felt like buying—which no one at the moment seemed to—one more didn't much interest them.

Several of Demetrios' soldiers strolled through the agora, looking now here, now there. They spoke a wide variety of Greek dialects; Menedemos wondered how they understood one another. One of them, a handsome, well-built man in the early years of middle age, broke away from his friends and came over to Menedemos, saying, "Hail, Rhodian. We've met before."

Menedemos hated people who introduced themselves like that. This fellow did look familiar, but. . . . He snapped his fingers. "Euxenides of Phaselis!" he exclaimed, recognizing the man—he'd taken Euxenides from Rhodes to Miletos a couple of years before. "By the dog, O best one, so we have. You're one of the best carpenters I've ever seen. That steering oar you made . . . What are you doing in Athens?"

"Making catapults. That's what I do best," Euxenides answered. "I'll tell you, the Athenians have junk, too. They won't, though, not when I'm through." His Greek, though basically a Doric dialect like Menedemos', held overtones of hissing and sneezing; Phaselis, on the southern coast of Anatolia, was a town inhabited by both Hellenes and Lykians.

"Isn't a catapult a catapult?" Menedemos asked.

All of Demetrios' soldiers laughed. "Hear the civilian!" Euxenides exclaimed, a smile on his face. "No, indeed, my friend. There are two main types—flexion machines, which are bent like overgrown bows, and torsion engines, which use twisted skeins of hair or sinew for their hurling force. Torsion engines throw harder and throw farther, but most of what they've got here are the old-fashioned flexion type. I'll fix that, by Hephaistos . . . if I can lay my hands on enough sinew." That made him look worried. Then, suddenly, he pointed at Menedemos. "You're a merchant. You wouldn't happen to know who might have a supply, would you?"

"Sorry, but no," the Rhodian answered. "If I wanted sinew, though, I'd go to a butcher, or maybe to a priest after sacrifice."

"About what I aim to do," Euxenides said.

"Did you stop just to say hail, or can I really sell you some perfume?" Menedemos asked. "If you've got a sweetheart or a hetaira you want to impress, there's nothing better."

"Haven't been in town long enough to latch on to a woman," Demetrios' officer replied. "I like it here, though. I wouldn't mind settling down if I have the chance."

"They'll never let you become a citizen. They're even fussier about that here than they are in most poleis," Menedemos warned.

Euxenides of Phaselis only shrugged. "I don't mind. From what I've seen, they treat resident aliens well here. They'd better—they've got a lot of them. I don't care if I can marry an Athenian girl or not, and I *really* don't care if I get to vote in the Assembly." His chuckle had a nasty edge. "Besides, who knows how long the Assembly will stay in business this time around, anyhow?"

He could see that. Menedemos could see it, too. He wondered why the Athenians couldn't see it for themselves. They'd gone without democracy for only about fifteen years all told. Was that long enough to turn them into blind men and fools? Evidently.

Euxenides said, "I owe you and your cousin a good turn. You could have turned me over to Ptolemaios' men when you stopped in Kos. You likely would have picked up a nice little reward, but you didn't do it. So what can I do for you?"

"Can you put our names in Demetrios' ear?" Menedemos asked. "We still have some luxury goods he might fancy—truffles from Mytilene, Lesbian and Byblian wine, things of that sort. If he gets any truffle-flavored olive oil from Demetrios of Phaleron's house, the other Demetrios bought that from us."

"I'll do it," Euxenides said at once. "My pleasure. Where are you staying?"

"At the house of Protomakhos, the Rhodian proxenos, a little south of the theater. It's not hard to find—at least not by the standards of this place."

"Oh, yes." Euxenides dipped his head. "Phaselis isn't easy for strangers, either, but Phaselis is a little town. You get lost here, you can stay lost for days. Good thing my sense of direction works." He turned to go. "Farewell, Rhodian. I won't forget to mention you to the big boss."

"Thanks." Menedemos hoped the soldier meant it. Too many people promised to do something like that and then forgot about it as soon as they turned a corner. Menedemos shrugged. He'd made the effort. If Euxenides delivered, splendid. If he didn't . . . Well, Menedemos and Sostratos were no worse off.

After crying his perfume in the agora till close to sundown—and selling two jars to a greasy fellow who wouldn't say what he did, but who looked like a brothelkeeper—Menedemos made his way back to Protomakhos' house. The proxenos wasn't there, which raised Menedemos' hopes of sneaking up to Xenokleia's room after dark. But Sostratos returned a few minutes after he did, and Protomakhos a few minutes after his cousin. *Oh, well,* Menedemos thought.

Sostratos looked pleased with himself. "I've been going through the polis talking with physicians," he said. "Sold a lot of balsam of Engedi today."

"*Euge,*" Protomakhos said.

"*Euge,* indeed," Menedemos added. "How much more could you have sold if you didn't fritter away time talking shop with the physicians?"

Reddening, Sostratos said, "I learn things talking with them. It doesn't cost a lot of time, and one day I might help a sailor who gets sick or hurts himself." He enjoyed playing the role of a physician aboard the *Aphrodite.* How much good he did was a different question. But then, how much good any physician did was often a matter of opinion. Fortunately, most of the rowers were young and healthy, and didn't need much in the way of medical care.

"Nothing wrong with talking shop," Protomakhos said. "I've picked up enough chatting with builders and sculptors that I sometimes think I could run up a temple or carve the cult statue to go inside it. Odds are I'm wrong, but I do think so."

"Menedemos would sooner talk shop with hetairai," Sostratos said slyly.

"I'd rather talk about their business than about the best cure for chilblains or hammertoes, yes," Menedemos said. "If you don't think the one is more interesting than the other, that's your affair."

"There's a time and a place for everything," Sostratos said. "I don't think about piggies every moment of every day."

Protomakhos wagged a finger at him. "I'd say you're too hard on your cousin, O best one. From what I've seen of Menedemos, he doesn't chase women every hour of the day and night like some men I've known."

A long, long silence followed. Sostratos looked at the ceiling. Menedemos looked at the floor. At last, several heartbeats later than he should have, Sostratos said, "Well, you may be right."

"I'm sure I am." Protomakhos, to Menedemos' vast relief, seemed to notice nothing amiss. He went on, "I know how kinsfolk can be. My brother and I still quarrel whenever we set eyes on each other, and as for one of my brothers-in-law. . . ." He rolled his eyes.

"Brothers-in-law! *Oimoi!* By the dog, yes!" Sostratos exclaimed, and started telling the proxenos about some of the things Damonax had done and had wanted him to do. Protomakhos listened sympathetically, and the awkward moment passed. Menedemos had never before been praised for his moderation with women by a man he was cuckolding. He'd thought he was hardened to most of the things that could happen, but this embarrassed him. It was like being praised for honesty by a man whose house you'd just robbed.

Three days later, the Rhodians and Protomakhos were about to sit down to supper when someone pounded on the door. "Who's that?" Protomakhos said in annoyance. "Whoever it is, why did he have to pick now, when I can smell the fish cooking?"

"Some people have no consideration," agreed Menedemos, who'd been able to indulge his passion for opson no less than other passions, and far more openly.

But instead of some bore who wanted to gossip with Protomakhos—Menedemos thought of the Athenian equivalent of his father's long-winded friend, Xanthos—it was Euxenides of Phaselis. "Hail, Rhodians," he said. "Are those the best tunics you've got? They'll have to do, I suppose. Demetrios bids you to supper, and I'm to take you there. Come along with me, the both of you."

"You kept your word!" Menedemos blurted.

"Sure I did," Euxenides said. "You did right by me, so the least I can do is right by you. Come on. We don't want to keep him waiting."

"Let's go," Sostratos said. "Just let me grab the truffles I still have. . . ."

Euxenides impatiently shifted from foot to foot while Sostratos did. Protomakhos said, "All that lovely opson, and only my wife and me to eat it." He didn't sound disappointed; he sounded like a man with a gods-given excuse to make an opsophagos of himself.

Out the door Euxenides of Phaselis went, the two Rhodians in tow behind him. Though Euxenides had been in Athens only a few days, he moved confidently through its labyrinth of streets. When Menedemos remarked on that, the soldier shrugged and said, "I told you, I've always had a good sense of direction."

After that, Menedemos waited for him to get lost. But he didn't. He brought the Rhodians to a large house north of the akropolis. Hulking Macedonians in full armor stood guard in front of the door. One of them said something to Euxenides. Menedemos couldn't follow it. Euxenides of Phaselis not only did, he answered in the same dialect. The bodyguards stood aside.

As Euxenides led the Rhodians inside, he remarked, "This is where Demetrios of Phaleron lived before he, ah, decided to move elsewhere."

"Wait here just a moment, best ones," a slave said in the entry hall. He hurried away, then returned. "All right, come ahead." As Menedemos entered the courtyard, he got a fleeting glimpse of a very pretty girl hurrying to the stairway. He wondered just what she and Demetrios had been doing. Beside him, Sostratos let out a warning cough. Menedemos sent his cousin a hurt look. Killing himself by jumping from a high place would end quicker and hurt less than letting the son of a Macedonian marshal catch him sniffing after a mistress.

Demetrios son of Antigonos lounged on a couch in the andron with a cup of wine. "Hail, Rhodians," he said when Euxenides presented Menedemos and Sostratos to him. He was very large and very strong and, up close, perhaps the handsomest man Menedemos—a handsome fellow himself—had ever seen. As the Rhodian had noted in the theater, he had a man of action's thrusting chin. With it went a voluptuary's wide-lipped, sensual mouth; a long, straight nose and prominent cheekbones; a mane of light brown hair; and eyes green as marble. "Forgive me for not rising," he went on, "but I'm getting over a fever."

"Yes, I saw her just now as she was going away," Menedemos said blandly.

Sostratos coughed again, this time in horror. But Demetrios threw back his head and laughed. "Very neat," he said. "That's the sort of crack my father would make." His voice, when he wasn't using it to fill the theater of Dionysos, was extraordinarily smooth and musical. The gods had blessed him with all they could give a man. He waved Menedemos and Sostratos to couches on either side of his own, and Euxenides to another. A slave brought them wine. "I found several amphorai of Thasian in Demetrios of Phaleron's cellars," Antigonos' son told them. "Coming from the north myself, I'm partial to northern vintages."

The wine was sweet as honey—so sweet, in fact, that Menedemos wondered if it had honey mixed into it. The vintners of Thasos some-times did that. It was also neat. Sostratos said, "Most noble one, could we please have a mixing bowl and some water? Otherwise, your men may have to carry us back to our host's house."

Demetrios laughed again. "As you wish, though mixing wine seems as silly to me as drinking it neat does to you. If I want water, I'll drink water; if wine—wine. Some of one, some of the other? Who needs that?"

Menedemos wanted to fuss at Sostratos for acting like a little old woman. He thought about continuing to drink his wine without added water. That, he feared, would only make his cousin look worse. And Demetrios was a large man, and used to neat wine. Menedemos himself was much smaller, and used to drinking it mixed. Getting hope-lessly plastered while his host stayed sober would do nothing to im-prove him in the Macedonian's eyes. And so, when Sostratos mixed one part wine to two of water—a little on the strong side, no doubt in def-erence to Demetrios, but only a little—Menedemos sipped along with his cousin. Euxenides of Phaselis drank his Thasian without water. He was a soldier, though, and by now surely used to Macedonian ways.

They chatted for a while. Demetrios had a lively wit, and a gift—if that was what it was—for puns that made Menedemos cringe and even forced a couple of groans from Sostratos, who was also formidable in such sports. "If you think I'm bad, you should hear my father," Demetrios said with a reminiscent smile. "Strong men run screaming when he gets started—you'd best believe they do."

His affection for Antigonos seemed altogether unfeigned. He was one of the most powerful men in Hellas—no, in the whole civilized world—yet he remained fond of and obedient to his father. To Menedemos, who'd been striking sparks with *his* father ever since his voice began to change, that seemed very strange.

As twilight thickened outside, a slave lit more torches and lamps in the andron, holding darkness at bay. Another slave carried in a tray piled high with some of the finest, whitest loaves of wheat bread Menedemos had ever seen. They were still warm from the oven, and so light and airy the Rhodian marveled that they didn't float off the tray and hang in the air like dandelion fluff. The olive oil in which the diners dipped their sitos was some of the truffle-flavored stuff Menedemos and Sostratos had sold to Demetrios of Phaleron.

"Mighty fine," Euxenides of Phaselis said, ripping another loaf to pieces so he could soak up more of the precious oil.

"It is, isn't it?" Demetrios son of Antigonos agreed complacently. "The other Demetrios bought it, but I'm the one who gets to enjoy it." The glow in his eyes showed how much he enjoyed it. He seemed to enjoy everything that came his way—food, wine, women, acclaim. And yet he was also a solid soldier—more than a solid soldier—and had displaced his cousin, Polemaios, at Antigonos' right hand. He probably enjoyed soldiering, too.

Menedemos knew he was jealous. He also knew how foolish such jealousy was. A monkey could be jealous of Aphrodite's beauty, and it would do the animal no more good. Not only did Demetrios have his multifarious gifts, he also had the chance to make the most of them. Like almost all men, Menedemos needed to devote the larger part of his energy just to getting by from day to day. What he might have done got lost in what he had to do.

Back in Ioudaia, Sostratos had despised Hekataios of Abdera for being able to travel as he pleased and having the leisure in which to write history . . . and for not knowing how lucky he was. Menedemos' sympathy when he heard about that had been distinctly muted. Now, though, now he understood.

"Have you got more of this oil?" Demetrios asked, licking his fingers.

"Sorry, but no," Menedemos said, while Sostratos, whose mouth was full, tossed his head. Menedemos went on, "Your, ah, predecessor bought all we brought here."

"Demetrios of Phaleron is a man of taste; no way around that," Demetrios son of Antigonos said. "Clever fellow, and a nice fellow, too. Pity he chose the other side and not my father's. I wonder where he'll turn up next, and what he'll do there. As long as he's not working against Father's interests, I wish him well."

He sounded as if he meant it. Menedemos doubted he could have been so dispassionate about an enemy. But he hadn't heard too many Athenians who truly despised Demetrios of Phaleron. Yes, they were glad to see their ancient democracy restored (though some of the decrees they'd passed made it look as if they'd forgotten the point of ruling themselves). But the general opinion was that Kassandros' puppet could have been worse. For a man who'd ruled as a tyrant for ten years, the verdict could have been far harsher.

Having swallowed, Sostratos said, "We have no more oil, O Demetrios, but we do have truffles from Lesbos. Your cooks can shave them, if you like, and steep the shavings in oil. Or they can cook the truffles themselves, if you'd rather."

"If *I'd* rather?" Demetrios laughed another of his easy laughs. "Don't you find, in your households, that the cooks think they're the lords and everyone else their subjects? Mine certainly do. Myriads of soldiers jump to obey my orders, but if I tell a cook to steam a fish and he's intent on baking it, I'll have baked fish for supper that night."

"Oh, yes," Menedemos said. "My father's cook has been squabbling with my stepmother ever since Father remarried a few years ago."

"My family's cook isn't quite so temperamental as Menedemos'," Sostratos said. "But there are times when he has a whim of iron; no doubt about it."

"After supper, talk to my servants. I'll buy whatever truffles you have left," Demetrios said. "Let the men know I want them. You'll get a fair price, I promise."

Now Menedemos didn't look at Sostratos. Still, he was sure his cousin was as delighted as he was. Demetrios' servants would have to buy after orders like that, and would have to pay a price better than just fair. Demetrios was one of the richest men in the world. To him, a silver drakhma counted for less than a bronze khalkos did for most mere mortals—hardly even small change.

More slaves brought in course after course of opson: stewed eels, steaks cut from the belly of a tuna, roast dogfish. There were also smoking beef ribs. They obviously came from an animal butchered on purpose; they weren't the gobbets handed out at random after a sacrifice. Menedemos occasionally ate pork, but he didn't think he'd had deliberately butchered beef before.

Maybe his surprise showed on his face, for Demetrios said, "We Macedonians live lives closer to those of Homer's heroes than most Hellenes do. We're meat-eaters, for we have broader lands on which to pasture cattle."

"I wasn't complaining, most noble one," Menedemos replied. "Is that cumin in the sauce?" He smacked his lips. "Tasty."

"I do believe it is, and black pepper from Arabia, too," Demetrios said.

After the ribs came fruit candied in honey and a cheesecake simi-larly sweetened. "A splendid supper," Sostratos said. "We thank you for your kindness."

"My pleasure." Demetrios' smile fairly glowed. He had charm; no doubt of that. After a sip from his cup of wine, he went on, "And where does Rhodes stand amidst all the confusions of the world that's taken shape since Alexander died?"

It seemed nothing but a casual, friendly question. Menedemos an-swered it the same way: "We're neutrals, and happy to be neutral. We have no quarrel with anyone."

Euxenides of Phaselis spoke up: "The Rhodian certainly speaks the truth for himself and his cousin, Demetrios. They carried me the same as they would have carried one of Ptolemaios' men a couple of years ago."

"Good. That's good." Demetrios' smile remained charming. But he went on, "What was true a couple of years ago could be less true now, though. And it isn't easy to stay neutral when one is a small polis in a world of large . . . powers." What had he almost said? Kingdoms? None of Alexander's squabbling marshals claimed a crown for himself, though all of them were kings in everything but name.

"So long as we do business with everyone, and so long as we stay free and autonomous, we'll hold on to our neutrality," Sostratos said.

"Oh, yes. So long as." Demetrios' voice also stayed silky-smooth. "But when you do the bulk of your business with one fellow, well, nat-urally your other neighbors wonder just how free and autonomous you truly are. Athens, after all, claimed to be free and autonomous before I liberated her."

Rhodes did much more business with Ptolemaios' Egypt than with the lands of any other marshal . . . including Antigonos. And Antigonos' lands were near neighbors to Rhodes. Menedemos didn't care for the turn the conversation had taken, especially since he doubted whether Athens was any freer or more autonomous now than before her "libera-tion."

Sostratos said, "Surely, most noble one, you can't be thinking of Rhodes. Why, we've built ships for your father's fleets. If that isn't how a proper neutral behaves, I don't know what would be."

"Just so." Menedemos beamed across Demetrios' couch toward his cousin. Nobody could match Sostratos when it came to bolstering arguments with good, solid facts. His cousin was so logical, so rational, disagreeing with him seemed impossible.

And Demetrios didn't disagree with him. Smiling still, Antigonos' son said, "I do hope you can see, my friends, that free and autonomous poleis like Athens and Rhodes can sometimes need protection against those who would try to force them into leaning in an . . . unfortunate direction."

"Not being an Athenian, I would not presume to speak for Athens," Sostratos said. "As far as Rhodes goes, since only we Rhodians choose how we lean or if we lean, the question doesn't arise."

"I certainly hope it never will," Demetrios said. "That could be . . . very unfortunate indeed."

Was he giving them a warning? It sounded like one. Menedemos said, "I'm sure all my fellow Rhodians will be glad to know of your concern."

"Oh, good. I hope they are." Demetrios turned his head and shouted for more wine. Out it came: that splendid Thasian, thick and sweet and potent even when mixed. No one worried about anything as abstract as neutrality for the rest of the evening.

9

SOSTRATOS WAS HAGGLING OVER THE PRICE OF BALSAM OF Engedi with a physician named Iphikrates when the front door to the Athenian's house opened and his slave—he seemed to have only one—led a moaning man, his face gray with pain and one hand clasped to the other shoulder, into the courtyard. "He hurt himself," the slave said in bad Greek.

"Yes, I see that," Iphikrates said, and then, to Sostratos, "Excuse me, O best one. We'll get back to this in a bit."

"Of course," Sostratos answered. "Do you mind if I watch?" He was no physician and never would be, but he was avidly curious about matters medical—and, because that made him the closest thing to a healer aboard the *Aphrodite,* the more he learned, the better.

"Not at all." Iphikrates turned to the patient. "What happened to you?"

"My shoulder," the man said unnecessarily. He went on, "I was repairing a roof, and I slipped, and I fell, and I grabbed at the edge of the roof with one hand, and the arm tore out of the socket."

Iphikrates dipped his head. "Yes, I would have guessed at a dislocation by the way you carry yourself. This is something I can relieve. My fee is four oboloi—in advance. Patients, once treated, have an unfortunate tendency toward ingratitude."

The injured man took his hand off his shoulder and spat little silver coins into it. "Here," he said. "Fix it. It hurts like blazes."

"Thank you very much." Iphikrates set the coins on the stone bench where Sostratos was sitting. He called to his slave: "Fetch me the leather ball, Seuthes."

"I bring him." The slave—Seuthes—ducked into the house, returning a moment later with a small, sweat-stained leather sphere.

"What will you use that for?" Sostratos asked, fascinated.

"Who's he? He talks a little funny," the patient said.

"He's a Rhodian," Iphikrates said, while Sostratos thought, *They can still hear that I'm a Dorian.* Iphikrates looked back to him. "You'll see in a moment." He told the man with the dislocated shoulder, "Lie down here on your back, if you please."

"All right." Grunting, his face twisting at each incautious movement, the man obeyed. "What now?" he asked apprehensively.

"Take your other hand away. . . . Yes, that's good." Iphikrates sat down on the ground beside the patient. Seuthes handed him the leather ball. He put it in the patient's armpit and held it in place with his heel, slipping his leg in between the other man's arm and his body. Then he grasped the man's forearm with both hands and jerked and tugged at the arm. The patient let out what would have been a blood-curdling shriek if he hadn't been gritting his teeth. Sostratos leaned forward on the bench to see better.

Another jerk and twist. Another scream from the injured man, this one less muffled. "I *am* sorry, best one," Iphikrates told him. "I have to find the best angle to—" He jerked once more, without warning, in the middle of the sentence. A sharp *pop!* rewarded him. The patient started to cry out again, then broke off and sighed in relief instead. Iphikrates beamed. "There! That's done it."

"Yes, I think so." The other man warily sat up as Iphikrates took the ball and his foot away. "It still hurts, but nothing like the way it did. Thanks, friend."

"My pleasure." Iphikrates sounded as if he meant it. "Always good to get something I can cure. For another four oboloi, I can give you a dose of poppy juice to ease the pain."

His patient thought it over, but not for long. "Thanks, but no. That's almost half of what I make in a day. I'll drink more wine, and put less water in it." Not being a Macedonian, he didn't even think about drinking his wine with no water at all.

"Suit yourself," Iphikrates said. "Drink enough wine and it will dull the pain, though not so well as poppy juice does. I take it you don't want me to put that arm in a sling or to bandage it to your body so it's less likely to pop out again?"

"You can put it in a sling for today, if you like," the injured man said. "I'm not going back to work now. But if I don't go tomorrow, how am I going to eat? Nobody will feed my family and me if I don't."

"All right, best one. I understand that—who doesn't?" Iphikrates said. "But be careful with that arm, and use it as little as you can for the next month or so. You have to give the shoulder as much of a chance to heal as you can. If you permanently weaken the joint and muscles, it can start popping out all the time, and then where will you be?"

"Halfway to Hades' house," the other man replied. "I understand you, too. But"—he shrugged with his good shoulder—"I have to take the chance. Who can save money on a drakhma and a half a day?" He got to his feet. Iphikrates fixed him a sling from a length of cloth that looked as if it was hacked out of an old chiton. The patient dipped his head. "Thanks again. Doesn't hurt too bad. My wife and son will be surprised to see me home so early. Farewell." He walked out the door without a backwards glance.

Turning to Sostratos, Iphikrates sighed. "You see how it is? Here is a patient I can actually help—and any physician knows how many he can't help at all—but my treatment is likely to go for naught, simply because the man can't afford to give the injured member proper rest. If I had an obolos for every time I've seen that, I wouldn't need to dicker so hard with you, for I'd be rich."

"You did very well there. I've never seen that trick with the leather ball before," Sostratos said. "There's a physician on Rhodes who uses an elaborate contraption with winches to fix dislocated joints."

"Oh, yes—the skamnon," Iphikrates said. "Some in Athens use it, too, and charge extra for it. I could, but I've never seen that it works better than simpler methods, or even as well as they do. The point, after all, is—or should be—helping the patient, not making yourself seem impressive."

"It looks more like an instrument of torture than anything else," Sostratos said.

"It isn't pleasant for the man who's strapped into it," the physician said. "Even so, I would use it if I thought it gave good results. But since it doesn't—no. Now, where were we?"

"Right at two drakhmai for each drakhma's weight of balsam," Sostratos answered. "I really can't go lower than that, not considering what I paid in Ioudaia. And you'll know, most noble one, if you've bought balsam of Engedi before, that you won't get a better price from anyone, even a Phoenician."

Iphikrates sighed. "I wish I could call you a liar and a thief and beat you down some more, for I'm not made of money myself. But I have bought balsam before, and I know you're telling the truth. You're an odd sort of merchant, you know: most traders bluster and make claims I know to be false, but you don't seem to."

"You don't use the skamnon when you could," Sostratos said. "Maybe we aren't so different."

"You would get a better price for your balsam from some of those who do," the physician said. "By making themselves seem so splendid and so knowledgeable, they extract bigger fees from their patients than I do. But, whether they seem knowledgeable or not, they get no better results. And, as I say, results are the point of the exercise."

"I can make enough money to suit me at two drakhmai for each drakhma's weight," Sostratos said. "Does it seem good to you to buy at that price?"

"It does," Iphikrates replied. "I will pay you twenty drakhmai for ten drakhmai by weight of balsam. That will last me for some time—perhaps even until I find another more or less honest merchant."

"For which I more or less thank you," Sostratos said. Both men chuckled. The Rhodian went on, "You'll have scales to weigh out the balsam?"

"Oh, yes." Iphikrates dipped his head. "I couldn't get by without them, not with the remedies I compound. I keep it with the medicines—that room back there. Why don't you wait for me here for a moment? I'll get the silver, and then we'll settle accounts."

"Certainly." Sostratos hid a wry smile. Iphikrates had called him more or less honest, but wouldn't let him go unwatched into the room with the drugs. Sostratos wasn't offended. Some medicines were valuable even in small, easy-to-conceal amounts. Iphikrates didn't know him well enough to be sure he wouldn't steal. He wouldn't have let the physician wander unattended through the family warehouse, either.

Iphikrates returned with a fistful of silver. "Come along," he said. He opened the door to let Sostratos go in ahead of him.

After the bright sunshine of the courtyard, the Rhodian's eyes needed a few heartbeats to adjust to the gloom inside. His nostrils flared when he breathed in. The room was full of scents: spicy mint; the sharpness of ground pepper; the dark, heavy odor of poppy juice; delicate frankincense and bitter myrrh; vinegar; wine; something that tickled the nose (was that hellebore?); olive oil, familiar from the kitchen and the gymnasion; and others Sostratos could not name. The scales stood on a small table, next to a heavy alabaster mortar and pestle and a bronze spoon. Sostratos sniffed again. "You must enjoy working here," he remarked.

"What? Why?" Iphikrates frowned, not following him.

"The smells, of course," Sostratos said.

"Oh." The physician sniffed with the air of a man who hadn't for quite some time. "To me, you understand, they're just the odors of work. That's a shame, isn't it? Here." He set ten owls in one pan of the scale. It sank down. He handed Sostratos the spoon. "Put your balsam on the other pan till they balance."

As Sostratos did, the balsam of Engedi added its own sweet fragrance to the rest of the odors in the room. Iphikrates smiled. Sostratos added a little more, scraping the sticky stuff from the bowl of the spoon with his thumbnail. Down came the pan with the balsam. He waited to see if he needed to put on a bit more yet, but the two pans could hardly have been more even.

"Well judged," Iphikrates said. He took the drakhmai off the scale and handed them to Sostratos. "And here are ten more besides," he added, giving the Rhodian the other coins as well. "I thank you very much."

"And I you, O best one," Sostratos replied. "I admire physicians for doing so much to relieve the pain and suffering that are a part of every life."

"You're gracious, Rhodian—more gracious than my profession deserves, I fear," Iphikrates said. "You saw me at my best a little while ago. That man had an injury I know how to treat. But if he'd come to me coughing blood or with a pain in his chest"—he set a hand on his heart to show what kind of pain he meant—"or with a lump in his belly, what could I do for him? Watch him and take notes on his case till he either died or got better on his own, as Hippokrates did. I couldn't cure him of any of those things, or of a myriad more besides."

"I've seen Hippokrates' writings," Sostratos said. "My impression was that he treated patients with all sorts of conditions."

"He *tried* to treat them," Iphikrates answered. "Whether his treatments did an obolos' worth of good is liable to be a different story. No man can be a physician without having his own ignorance shoved in his face a dozen times a day. You have no idea how frustrating it is to watch a patient die from something that seems minor—and that surely would be, if only I knew a little more."

"Oh, but I do," Sostratos said. Iphikrates looked dubious till he explained: "I've seen men aboard the *Aphrodite* die of fever after belly wounds that looked as if they ought to have healed in a few days. Can you tell me why that happens?"

"No, and I wish I could, because I've seen it, too," the physician said. "Life is fragile. Cling to it tightly, for you never know when it may slip away." With that reassuring piece of advice, he sent Sostratos on his way.

AFTER THE FIRST MEETING of the Assembly, the one that voted Demetrios son of Antigonos honors that might have embarrassed one of the twelve Olympians, Menedemos didn't go back. He'd seen all he cared to see, and more than he could readily stomach. He would have expected Sostratos to keep going whenever he could, but his cousin also stayed away from the theater. That one session, evidently, had been plenty for him, too.

Protomakhos, on the other hand, kept going whenever the Assembly convened. Menedemos couldn't blame him for that. He was, after all, an Athenian. He had an interest in the proceedings that the Rhodians lacked. He also had the right to speak and the right to vote.

One morning not too long after Menedemos and Sostratos sold Demetrios their truffles, Protomakhos returned from the theater with the expression he might have worn if he'd stepped barefoot into a big pile of dog turds right outside the house. Menedemos had come back from the agora to get some more perfume, and was on his way out when Protomakhos stormed in. His host's revolted look couldn't be ignored. "By Zeus, O best one, what's wrong?" Menedemos asked. He didn't *think* Protomakhos would look that way if he'd just found out Xenokleia was unfaithful, but he wasn't sure.

To his relief, the Rhodian proxenos wasn't glowering at *him*. Protomakhos said, "You were there when Demetrios first came into Athens."

"Yes," Menedemos said: simple agreement seemed safe enough.

"You saw how we debased ourselves, heaping honors on him and on his father."

"Yes," Menedemos said again.

"And, no doubt, you didn't think we could sink any lower," Protomakhos went on. He threw back his head and laughed. "Shows what you know, doesn't it?"

"Oh, dear." Menedemos feared he could guess where this was going. "What did Stratokles do now?"

"It wasn't Stratokles," the proxenos answered. "We have more than one flatterer in our polis. Aren't we lucky?" He didn't sound as if he thought the Athenians were lucky.

"Who, then?" Menedemos asked.

"An abandoned rogue named Dromokleides of Sphettos," Protomakhos said. "Sphettos is a village on the far side of Mount Hymettos, here in Attica. Hymettos has good honey; Sphettos has troublemakers. This Dromokleides proposed that Demetrios be given the same honors as Demeter and Dionysos whenever he visits Athens."

"*Oimoi!* That's pretty bad," Menedemos said. "Doesn't he realize there's a difference between being named after a god and being one yourself? I can see why some people say Alexander was a demigod— look at everything he did. But Demetrios? I'm sorry, but no."

"You have some common sense, Rhodian," Protomakhos said sadly. "That's more than I can say for the Assembly."

"You mean they *passed* this resolution?" Menedemos said in dismay.

"They certainly did." Protomakhos shouted for wine. As a slave hurried to get some, the proxenos turned back to Menedemos. "I'm sorry, best one, but I have to wash the taste of this out of my mouth. Join me?"

"Thanks. I will. I don't blame you a bit," Menedemos said. "And did Demetrios look all shy and abashed, the way he did when Sostratos and I came with you?"

"*He wasn't even there,*" Protomakhos replied. "Dromokleides did it anyway. I suppose Demetrios will hear about it sooner or later, when he gets out of bed with whatever woman he's got in there with him now." Menedemos remembered that pretty girl he'd glimpsed when he and his cousin dined with Demetrios. But Protomakhos hadn't finished. As the slave came back with wine—he'd included a cup for Menedemos, too—the Rhodian proxenos went on, "That wasn't the only decree our new Perikles passed today. By the dog, no!—not even close."

He paused to let the slave pour the cups full. The wine couldn't have been weaker than one to one. The slave had done a good job of gauging his master's mood. Menedemos said, "Do I want to know the rest?"

"Probably not, but I'm going to tell you anyhow—misery loves company," Protomakhos said. "They're going to rename the month Mounykhion Demetrion, in honor—honor? ha!—of the victory Demetrios won at Mounykhia. They're going to call the odd day between the end of one month and the start of the next that happens sometimes when you don't know just when the new moon is—they're going to call that a Demetrion, too. And you know the Dionysia you went to? It's not the Dionysia any more, by Zeus. From now on, it's going to be the Demetria." His larynx worked as he emptied his winecup. Then he filled it again.

Menedemos sipped more slowly, but he was hardly less troubled. "That's . . . laying it on with a shovel, isn't it?" he said. "I hope Demetrios has the sense not to take any of this twaddle too seriously. If he starts believing he's a god on earth . . . Well, that wouldn't be so good—for him or for anyone else." Demetrios *had* struck him as being on the vain side. He was glad it was Athens' worry, not his or Rhodes'.

"You can see that—you've got sense," Protomakhos said. *Sostratos doesn't think so,* Menedemos thought. *And neither would you, if you knew Xenokleia might be carrying my child.* Since the proxenos, fortunately, didn't know that, he continued, "I can see it, too. Men like Stratokles and Dromokleides?" He tossed his head. "And I still haven't told you the worst."

"There's more yet? *Papai!*" Menedemos said. "Come on, then. Let me hear it. After ninety-nine lashes, what's the hundredth?"

"Just so. As part of an offering, we Athenians are supposed to consecrate some shields at Delphi. There's been a disagreement over how best to do it. So Dromokleides, that worthless arse-licker, put forth a motion that the people of Athens should choose a man who would sacrifice, get good omens, and then approach Demetrios—approach the savior god, is how the motion puts it—and get his oracular response on how best to perform the consecration. And whatever he says, that's what Athens will do. *And the motion passed.* Someone's probably busy cutting the letters into stone right now."

"Oh, dear," Menedemos said again. That wasn't enough. "Oh, my." That wasn't enough, either. He finished his wine in a hurry and poured himself some more. That might not have been enough, either, but it was on the right track.

"We won at Marathon," Protomakhos said bitterly. "We won at Salamis. We fought Sparta for a generation. I was just going from youth to man when we gave the Macedonians all they wanted at Khaironeia. That would have been around the time you were born. We lost, but we fought hard. We gave it everything we had. Even Leosthenes stood up against the Macedonians after Alexander died. And now *this*? It makes you want to cry." By his anguished expression, he meant it literally.

Menedemos set a hand on the Rhodian proxenos' shoulder. "I'm sorry, best one," he said; on matters political, he could and did sympathize with Protomakhos. "Times are hard nowadays."

"Furies take all the Macedonians—Demetrios and Antigonos, Kassandros, Lysimakhos, Ptolemaios, Polyperkhon, all of them!" Protomakhos burst out. *It's the wine,* Menedemos thought. *This is too strong a mix, and it's having its way with him.* But Protomakhos didn't sound the least bit drunk as he went on. "This could happen to Rhodes, too, you know. If one of the marshals ever gets inside your walls, you'll bend over backward—bend over forward—to keep him happy, too."

That made Menedemos take a swig from the cup he'd refilled. He spat into the bosom of his chiton to turn aside the evil omen. "May that day never come," he said. If it did, he feared Protomakhos was right. Flatterers lived everywhere, and none of the Macedonian marshals— with the possible exception of Antigonos—had shown himself immune to praise.

"We said the same thing, Rhodian. Don't forget that," Protomakhos replied. "What you wish for and what you get too often don't match." He eyed the little jars of perfume Menedemos had set down so he could drink some wine. "I'm sorry I burdened you with this. Go on back to the agora and make yourself some silver."

"It's all right," Menedemos said easily. "Don't worry about it. You've shown Sostratos and me every kindness." *More than you know, in fact.* "The least I can do in return is lend an ear."

"Nice of you to say so," Protomakhos told him. "What I say is, the two of you have been the best guests I've had since I became proxenos. I'll be sorry when you go back to Rhodes, and you're welcome in my home any time."

"Thank you very much." Menedemos took a long pull at his wine to help hide any blush he might be wearing. He wasn't immune to embarrassment. Hearing such praise from a man whose wife he'd bedded made him feel foolish, not to mention guilty. But showing what he felt would only land him in trouble, and what Protomakhos had to say then would be anything but praise.

For now, the Rhodian proxenos remained oblivious. "I tell you only what you deserve," he said.

Menedemos finished his wine, took up the perfume, and left Protomakhos' house in a hurry. He didn't want to betray himself, and he didn't want to lacerate his conscience any more, either. As he threaded his way through Athens' twisting streets toward the agora, he wondered why it troubled him. It hadn't during his affairs in Halikarnassos and Taras and Aigina and any of several other towns. Why here? Why now?

You've been listening to Sostratos for too long, and he's finally started rubbing off on you. But Menedemos tossed his head. It wasn't that simple, and he knew it. Part of it was that he'd come to know and to like Protomakhos, which he hadn't with any of the other husbands he'd outraged. Part of it was that he remained unsure how much of what Xenokleia said about Protomakhos was true and how much invented to spur on her new lover.

And part of it was that seducing other men's wives was a sport that was starting to pall. The thrill of sneaking into a strange bedroom seemed smaller. The risks seemed bigger. And he'd come to realize that what he got from the women, while better in its way than what he got in a brothel, wasn't exactly what he wanted, or wasn't all of what he wanted.

Maybe I need a wife. The thought so surprised him, he stopped short in the middle of the street. A man behind him who was leading a scrawny donkey loaded down with sacks of grain or beans let out an indignant squawk. Menedemos got moving again. His father had started talking about looking for a bride for him. Up till this moment, he hadn't taken the idea seriously himself.

And Father has the woman I really want—and I think she wants me. Menedemos muttered under his breath. For the past several sailing seasons, he'd done his best to leave thoughts of Baukis behind when Rhodes dropped below the horizon. Some things he *would* not do, no matter how tempting. He hoped he wouldn't, anyhow.

He wondered why she drew him so. She wasn't spectacularly beautiful, even if she did have a nice shape. The only thing he could think of was that he'd got to know her even before he first found her attractive.

She'd been a person to him, a person he liked . . . and then he'd noticed her sweet hips and rounded bosom (considerably sweeter and more rounded now than when she'd come into the household as a girl of fourteen). He whistled tunelessly. Could that make such a difference? Maybe it could.

Here was the agora. He'd got to it without noticing the last half of his journey. He tried to put Baukis out of his mind—tried, but didn't have much luck. He made an unhappy noise, down deep in his throat. Even he knew how dangerous falling in love could be. And it would have been dangerous even if she weren't his father's wife. Like any Hellene, he reckoned falling in love a disease. It was, in many ways, an enjoyable disease, but that didn't improve the prognosis. Of course, the prognosis for anyone who fell in love with his stepmother—even if she was years younger than he—was bad.

The hurly-burly of the market square came as a relief. With people chattering and chaffering all around him, Menedemos couldn't keep his mind on his own worries. Somebody said, "I wonder how the world could have existed before Demetriozeus created it. I suppose all our ancestors were just figments of his imagination."

"Fig-sucking figments," somebody else replied, and added another obscenity on top of that.

Menedemos laughed. Not all the Athenians were impressed with what the Assembly had voted, then. That was a good sign. He almost paused to talk politics with the men who'd jeered at the latest decree. Then he decided to keep walking instead, for he realized they likely wouldn't want to talk to him, not when his accent proved him a foreigner the instant he opened his mouth. A man could say things to his friends that he wouldn't to a stranger.

Someone was selling garlic in the place where Menedemos had been selling perfume. That made him laugh again. Unlike Sostratos, who was given to prolonged sulks, Menedemos had trouble staying gloomy for long. He found another spot, one not far from the statues of Harmodios and Aristogeiton in the middle of the agora. Most Athenians believed the two young men had liberated them from tyranny a couple of centuries before. From what Sostratos said, that wasn't how things had really happened. Even nitpicking Sostratos, though, couldn't deny that what people believed often helped shape what would happen next.

"Fine rose perfume from the island of roses!" Menedemos called.

For this, as opposed to politics, his Doric drawl was an asset. He held up a perfume jar in the palm of his hand. "Who wants sweet-smelling Rhodian perfume?"

As usual, all sorts of people came up to him and asked how much the perfume cost. Also as usual, most of them retreated in dismay when he told them. And some of them got angry when they found out. A woman who'd brought a basket of eggs into the city from a farm or a village out beyond the walls exclaimed, "How *dare* you sell anything that expensive? How do you think it makes people who have to worry about every obolos feel?" That she was there and unveiled and sun-browned and wearing a tunic full of patches and mends said she was one of those people.

Shrugging, Menedemos answered, "In the fish market, some people buy eels and tunny and mullet. Others buy sprats or salt-fish. Some people wear golden bracelets. Others have to make do with bronze."

As soon as the words were out of his mouth, he wished he hadn't chosen that example. The woman with the basket of eggs wore a bronze necklace. The day was warm, and the cheap piece of jewelry had left a green mark on her sweaty skin. But her reply took a different tack: "But there's *something* for poor people there, anyhow. Where can I find perfume somebody like me could buy? Nowhere. All I can do is envy the fancy whores who get it."

He shrugged again. What could he say to that? She wasn't wrong. Before he found any words, she turned her back and strode away in magnificent contempt. He bit his lip. He couldn't remember the last time a mere woman—especially one he wasn't bedding—had made him feel ashamed.

"I'm allowed to make a living, too," he muttered. But, because the *Aphrodite* carried only luxury goods—the most profitable sort—he dealt for the most part with rich men and the occasional rich woman. He and Sostratos were rich themselves, or rich enough. He too often took for granted the life he led. He never had to worry about where his next meal was coming from, or to agonize over whether to spend an obolos on food or rent. Neither did anyone he knew. Even the family slaves had . . . enough.

But life wasn't so simple, wasn't so pleasant, for most Hellenes. If it had been, they wouldn't have had to buy sprats for opson when they could afford anything better than olives or a little cheese. They wouldn't have worn clothes as sorry as that egg-seller's. They wouldn't have exposed so many infants, and they wouldn't have been so thin.

She rubbed my nose in what's real, the Rhodian thought ruefully, *and it doesn't smell anywhere near so sweet as my perfume.*

But if he didn't sell that perfume, he *would* find out what being poor was like—find out from the inside. And so he went back to calling out its virtues. And, before too long, a man whose double chin and bulging belly said he didn't have to worry about hunger bought three jars. "Two for my hetaira," he said, winking, "and one for my wife, to keep her sweet."

"You're a fellow who knows how to handle women, O best one," Menedemos replied: partly a merchant's flattery, partly one man talking to another. The plump Athenian, who had a slave following him like a dog, didn't haggle very hard over the price. He didn't have to worry about every obolos, either. Drakhmai rang sweetly in Menedemos' hands as the other fellow paid him.

The Athenian strutted off. His slave, who hadn't said a word all through the dicker, carried the perfume. The rich man would have lost dignity if he'd been seen carrying it himself. The woman with the basket of eggs hadn't been shy about carrying it herself. But then, she didn't have so much dignity to lose.

Menedemos made another sale not long before he would have gone back to Protomakhos' house. The day turned out to be quite nicely profitable. And yet, as the sun sank down toward the Pnyx and he did head back to the proxenos' home, he found himself less happy than he would have liked.

SOSTRATOS RAN HIS TONGUE over his lips, savoring the sweetness of what he'd just eaten. "That may be the best honey cake I've ever had, most noble one," he told Protomakhos. "My compliments to your cook."

"Very fine indeed," Menedemos agreed.

"Myrsos is a fine cook. I'd be the last to say otherwise," Protomakhos replied. "Still, I don't think this cake would have turned out so well anywhere but Athens. The clover honey from Mount Hymettos is the best in the world."

"You've mentioned it before. I certainly won't quarrel with you, not after tasting it," Menedemos said. "Delicious."

"Yes." Sostratos snapped his fingers. "Do you know, my dear, we could get a good price for it back in Rhodes."

His cousin dipped his head. "You're right. We could. Not only that, we should."

"Do you recall who sold you this honey?" Sostratos asked Protomakhos.

Looking faintly embarrassed, the proxenos tossed his head. "I'm afraid I don't. You'd do better to ask Myrsos. He buys the food along with cooking it. As long as he doesn't bankrupt me, I give him free rein."

"A sensible attitude," Menedemos said. "If you have the silver, why not eat well?" That sounded very much like him, though Sostratos wondered whether his father's second wife would agree. By what Menedemos had said, she'd locked horns with the cook at his house more than once. But then his cousin surprised him by adding, "The ones I feel sorry for are the people who can't afford fine opson or good wine or honey like this—and there are so many of them." Sostratos sometimes worried about the plight of the poor, too, but he hadn't imagined they'd ever entered Menedemos' mind.

Protomakhos said, "That is too bad for them, but I don't know what anyone can do about it."

"Neither do I," Menedemos said. "No one seems to want to do much of anything. They're only the poor, after all." Sostratos scratched his head. Such pungent sarcasm wasn't his cousin's usual style at all. What had happened to turn his thoughts into such channels? Sostratos didn't want to ask in front of Protomakhos, but his bump of curiosity itched.

Since he was also curious about Hymettos honey, he went into the kitchen to talk to Myrsos. The Lydian cook was munching on a piece of honey cake himself. He looked not the least bit abashed. Other slaves might have their rations carefully measured out—though Protomakhos, like Sostratos' father, wasn't that strict—but cooks always ate at least as well as the men they served.

Myrsos proved less informative than Sostratos would have liked. "I bought it from a woman in the agora," he said. "She had a big pot of it, and the scent told me it was good. I'm sorry, but I don't know her name."

Sostratos didn't want to wander the agora sniffing one pot of honey after another. He deplored inefficiency. His nose might also prove less sensitive, less educated, than Myrsos'. The cook evidently knew just what he wanted in honey. Sostratos didn't. He took a couple of oboloi out from between his teeth and the inside of his cheek. Like anyone else, he'd mastered the art of eating without swallowing his small change—though he'd heard of a miser who'd poked at his turds with a stick to get back an obolos that accidentally went down his throat. "Anything else you can recall about the woman?" the Rhodian asked, holding out the spit-shiny coins.

"No," Myrsos said regretfully, which made Sostratos think him honest. "I will say, though, that physicians often use honey in their medicines, to hide the nasty taste of herbs and such. You might ask one. Some will use the cheapest, of course, but others will want to have the best."

"That's a good idea," Sostratos said, and gave him the money.

He went back to Iphikrates' house the next morning. The man had bought the best balsam; he might well use the best honey, too. "Hail, best one," Iphikrates said. "I just prepared a first-rate salve for hemorrhoids."

"Lucky you," Sostratos murmured.

"There's no part of the body that can't go wrong," the physician said. "What brings you back here? Have you figured out some new way to pry silver out of me? I warn you, it won't be easy. I haven't got a whole lot more to spend."

"As a matter of fact, no," Sostratos answered. "I was wondering if you use Hymettos honey—and, if you do, from whom you buy it."

"Ah." Iphikrates dipped his head. "Now I understand. Yes, I do use Hymettos honey. It costs more than honey from other places, but the flavor is worth it. So you think it's worth exporting, too, do you?"

"If I can get a decent price for it," Sostratos said. "Who sells it to you?"

"A fellow named Erasinides son of Hippomakhos," Iphikrates answered. "He keeps bees over by the mountain, and doesn't come into the polis all that often. You can either wait for him and hope he does, or else go out and pay a call on him. If you go, you'll want to take some people with you to carry back the jars of honey, or else hire a donkey."

"Oh, yes," the Rhodian said with a smile. "I do know something about that."

Iphikrates chuckled. "I suppose you might. Probably more fun than making a salve to smear on somebody's poor, sore prokton, too."

"I hope you don't use honey from Hymettos in *that,*" Sostratos said.

"Well, no," the physician replied. "Not much point to it. Although, considering how some people who come to see me *get* their hemorrhoids . . ."

"Never mind," Sostratos said hastily. Iphikrates laughed out loud. Sostratos went on, "Tell me whereabouts along the mountain this Erasinides lives. I'd rather not spend hours wandering the slopes calling out his name." He made Iphikrates repeat the directions several times to be sure he had them straight.

As in any city, plenty of men in Athens hired donkeys by the day. Sostratos arranged that afternoon to pick one up early the next morning. For an extra couple of oboloi, the Athenian who owned the animal agreed to let him use some baskets with lids he could tie down and enough rope to lash them to the donkey.

"I'm used to tying knots aboard ship," Sostratos said. "This will be something different."

"You'll manage." The man with the donkey sounded confident. *Of course he sounds confident,* Sostratos thought. *He wants to make sure he gets as much money out of me as he can.*

The Rhodian took the donkey as the sun was just beginning to touch the buildings on the akropolis. The owner even helped him fasten the baskets to the animal. When he tugged at the lead rope, the donkey brayed out a complaint, but it came along.

It kept complaining all the way through the city and out into the countryside. Sostratos grew sick of its bellows and brays. He thought about whacking it, but feared that would only make it louder, so he refrained. A man leading a quiet donkey from Mount Hymettos toward the city grinned at him as they passed and said, "Enjoy your songbird."

"Thanks," Sostratos answered sourly. The horrible noise spoiled his delight in what would have been a pleasant walk.

Mount Hymettos lay about thirty stadia southeast of Athens: an hour's journey. With the donkey being obstinate and loud, it seemed three times as long to Sostratos. He hardly noticed the fine, warm morning, the neat vineyards, the olive groves with fruit steadily ripening, the watered garden plots full of every sort of vegetable.

As the road began to climb, the donkey complained more and

more. Finally even Sostratos, a patient man, had had enough. He picked up a stout branch that had fallen from an olive tree, broke off a few twigs, and whacked the branch into the palm of his hand. The donkey was far from young. It must have seen that gesture before, for it suddenly fell silent. Sostratos smiled. He kept on carrying the stick. The donkey kept on being quiet.

By what Iphikrates had said, Erasinides lived about halfway up the mountain, not far from the marble quarries that were Hymettos' other claim to fame. Sostratos looked for a Herm cut from red stone at a crossroads, and let out a sigh of relief when he spotted the pillar with Hermes' face and genitals carved on it. "Up this road to the left," he told the donkey. It didn't like going up, but the threat of the stick kept it from making a big fuss.

Faint in the distance, the sound of picks clanging on stone came to the Rhodian's ears. Someone shouted. Sostratos couldn't make out the words, but recognized the tone: that was a boss giving workers orders. Some things didn't change no matter where you were, or in what trade. Even in Ioudaia, where the very language was different, people in charge sounded just as peremptory, just as impatient, as they did in Hellas.

Brush and scrub lined the track—it hardly deserved the name of road any more. Every now and then, it opened out to show a farm. The farther away from the main road out of Athens Sostratos got, the smaller and meaner the farms seemed. The Rhodian wondered how many generations of men had worked them. *As many as there are,* he thought, *no fewer.*

Bees buzzed. At first, Sostratos hardly noticed. When he did, he grinned: he took them as a sign he'd come to the right place. He also wondered what nectar they found to sip in this sun-blasted summer, when most of the fields and meadows were yellow and dry. Something, he supposed, or the bees wouldn't have been out at all.

Another shabby little farm, this one with only a tumbledown ruin of a barn. Just a couple of stadia to go to Erasinides' place—*if I'm on the right track. I think I am. Zeus, I hope I am.* And then Sostratos forgot about bees, about honey, about Erasinides—about everything except the hound baying like a wolf as it loped toward him. It wasn't much smaller than a wolf, either, and no tamer.

The donkey let out a squealing bray that Sostratos forgave. It jerked the lead rope out of his hand and started to run. The dog, though, paid no attention to it. The dog wanted Sostratos. Maybe it thought he was coming to rob the farm. Or maybe it simply craved the taste of human flesh. He wouldn't have been surprised, not with those great yellow teeth and that wide, red, slavering mouth.

If he ran like the donkey, the hound would pull him down from behind. Only his certainty of that kept him from turning and fleeing. Instead, he set himself, hefting the stick he'd picked up to beat the donkey. *One chance,* he told himself. *That's all I get.*

Baying, the dog sprang at him. He swung with all his might—and caught it right on the end of the nose. Those fearsome, deep-throated howls changed as if by magic to yips of agony.

"Here, you polluted monster!" Sostratos shouted. "See how you like it!" He walloped the hound again, this time in the ribs.

Now yelping, the dog ran from Sostratos faster than it had run toward him. Now furious, he ran after it. When he saw he wasn't going to catch it, he bent down, picked up a rock, and threw it. It caught the dog in the rump and brought forth another shrill howl of pain.

"Here now! What do you think you're doing?" A farmer came out of the house, brandishing a staff.

"Driving away your gods-detested hound." Sostratos picked up his stick again. He was angry enough to be ready for a fight if the other man wanted one. "That's what you get for letting the monster run loose. If it comes at me again on my way back to Athens, I'll kill it."

Plenty of men were fiercer than he. But he was larger than most, and only half the age of the farmer, whose scraggly hair and beard were white. The man shook a fist at him, but then retreated into his dwelling. The dog peered out from the ruins of the barn. It didn't seem to want to have anything more to do with the Rhodian. That suited him down to the ground.

He went back after the donkey, which had moved faster without his guidance than it ever had with it. It didn't seem to think him a hero for driving off the dog. Instead, it might have blamed him for bringing it near the hound in the first place. On he went, up the western slope of Mount Hymettos.

"Is this the farm of Erasinides son of Hippomakhos?" he called to a man chopping weeds with a mattock.

The farmer jerked his thumb up the road. "Next farm uphill, stranger, on the left-hand side of the track."

"Thanks." Sostratos plodded on. So, unhappily, did the donkey. Erasinides' farm was noticeably greener than the ones he'd been passing. He soon saw why: a spring bubbled out of a cleft in the rocks a few cubits from the farmhouse. Channels led the water here and there.

Sostratos knelt by the stream to wash his head and hands, take a drink, and water the donkey. As he got to his feet, drops dripping from his beard, a stocky, middle-aged man came out of the barn and said, "Hail, friend. Do something for you?"

"Are you Erasinides?" Sostratos asked. The farmer dipped his head. Sostratos gave his own name and said, "The physician Iphikrates tells me he buys his honey from you. I'd like to do the same."

"Iphikrates is a good man. He doesn't think he knows it all, the way some physicians do," Erasinides said. "Where are you from, friend, to speak such an . . . interesting Greek? Sounds like the Doric bits you hear in tragedy."

"I'm from Rhodes," Sostratos answered. He knew his accent had been heavily influenced by Attic. He wondered what Erasinides would make of the way Menedemos spoke. "Do you have honey for sale?"

"Oh, yes." But the Athenian seemed in no hurry to haggle. "Nine ships from Rhodes, under Tlepolemos," he murmured: not quite quoting the *Iliad*'s Catalogue of Ships, but showing he knew it. "Did Rhodians speak oddly then, too, do you suppose?"

"I don't know, best one," Sostratos answered. Erasinides, plainly, wanted to chat before getting down to business. Rustics often did. "We think our accent the usual one, you know, and everybody else's strange."

"Is that a fact?" Erasinides' laugh showed that, if it was a fact, it was an amusing one. "Must come of being a long ways off from Athens, I expect."

With Athens' present prominence, he had a point. But he was the sort who would have said the same thing had he lived up in Thessalia, which had its own backwoods way of speech. Sostratos said, "Custom is king of all"—Pindaros' poetic truth quoted by Herodotos. Bees buzzed around a patch of clover next to Erasinides' barn. Pointing that way, Sostratos asked, "Do you gather your honey from wild bees, or do you keep your own hives?"

"Oh, I have my own," Erasinides replied. "Collecting wild honey's like trying to build a house out of driftwood—you'll come up with some, but never enough to suit you."

"Do you get stung when you take the honeycombs?" Sostratos asked.

The farmer dipped his head. "Now and again. I wear a petasos with the thinnest veiling I can get, to keep 'em off my face. Past that"—he shrugged—"I pick the stings out, and I go about my business. They don't much bother me. Some folk aren't so lucky. I had a neighbor, a fellow named Ameinokles, who'd wheeze and gasp and have trouble breathing whenever he got stung."

"You *had* a neighbor?" Sostratos said.

"That's right." Erasinides dipped his head again. "It happened once too often, poor fellow. His throat closed up and he . . . strangled to death, you might say."

Sostratos wondered what Iphikrates could have done about that. Nothing, all too likely. As Erasinides had said, the physician didn't try to hide his own ignorance. Sostratos said, "Do you put the honey in jars all the same size?"

"Oh, yes. I didn't used to, but it's better for business when I do. I buy lekythoi from a potter I know. I can get 'em cheap—he makes lots of oil flasks, because people always need 'em, either to hold olive oil at home or—the fancy glazed ones—for funeral offerings. I don't buy those, on account of they cost more."

"How much for a jar?" Sostratos asked.

"Twelve drakhmai."

That wasn't far from what the Rhodian had expected. Over an hour or so, pausing for politics and women and bees and wine and mean dogs and whatever else came to mind, he haggled Erasinides down to eight drakhmai the lekythos. He paid in shiny Athenian owls; the farmer made it plain he had no use for perfume or balsam or anything else the *Aphrodite* had brought to Athens. Erasinides helped him pack the lekythoi into the baskets on the donkey's back, and gave him straw to stuff between them to keep them from breaking.

"Thank you kindly," the farmer said as he left. "You Rhodians seem a goodly folk, even if you do talk funny."

On the way past the farm with the fearsome hound, Sostratos gripped his stick tightly. The dog didn't bother him. He kept going, down off the mountain and back toward the whirl that was Athens.

*   *   *

"WAIT A MINUTE," Menedemos said. "Isn't Demetrios already married?"

The man who'd given him the news, a sausage-seller named Kleon, dipped his head. "That's right," he said. "He married Phila a long time ago—Antipatros' daughter, you know, the one who'd been married to Krateros before." He had an engagingly ugly face, which he now twisted into an engagingly lewd leer. "But she's a lot older than Demetrios, and Antigonos had to talk him into marrying her for the sake of her blood and her connections. This time, maybe he wants to have some fun."

All through the Athenian agora, people were buzzing with the news. "He certainly does like to have his fun," Menedemos said. "That little call he paid to have fun with what's-her-name—Kratesipolis—almost cost him his neck." *By the dog!* he thought. *I sound like Sostratos. Demetrios is too wild even for me. Who could have imagined that?* He went on, "So who is this new woman? Eurydike, you said her name was?"

"That's right, my dear," Kleon answered. "Her blood's as blue as the sky. She's descended from Miltiades, the hero of Marathon. She used to be married to Ophelis, the King of Kyrene west of Egypt, but she came back to Athens after he died."

"Phila, Kratesipolis, and now Eurydike," Menedemos said musingly. "Demetrios must like widows."

"Well, they already know how." Kleon leered again. "You don't have to teach 'em, the way you do with maidens. Besides, it's not like Demetrios is going to be faithful to this one, any more than he has to any of the others."

"No, I suppose not," Menedemos said. "He sure hasn't up to now." He remembered the pretty girl he'd glimpsed at Demetrios' house. Demetrios could do anything he wanted. Menedemos sighed. That sounded marvelous.

Kleon said, "I just wonder if he's going to be cheap about it, or if he'll throw a feast and sacrifice animals and give away meat and wine." Like most of the Athenians Menedemos had met, he kept his eye on the main chance. As now: he thrust his tray at Menedemos, asking, "You going to buy something, or are you just going to stand around and gab?"

"Here," Menedemos handed him an obolos. Kleon gave back a

sausage link. It was so full of garlic and fennel, Menedemos needed a couple of bites to be sure it was made from pork. If the meat wasn't so fresh as it might have been, the spices kept him from noticing.

"Sausages!" Kleon shouted after sticking the coin in his mouth. "Get your sausages! Demetrios gives his to Eurydike, but I've got sausages for everybody!"

Menedemos snorted. No wonder Aristophanes had written a sausage-seller into his *Knights*. The only thing redeeming Kleon's vulgarity was that he seemed as unaware of it as a dog licking its privates. He went on crying his wares and making crude cracks about Demetrios' wedding. A good many Athenians laughed, too, and several of them bought his wares.

Holding up a little jar of perfume, Menedemos called, "Fine scent from Rhodes! Eat Kleon's sausages and don't stink afterwards!" Kleon shot him an obscene gesture. With a laugh, he returned it.

The Rhodian soon went back to his usual sales pitch. The other made a good joke, but wasn't likely to draw anybody who could afford the perfume. *Too bad,* he thought.

He kept on calling. A couple of women and one man stopped and asked him how much he wanted for the perfume. When he told them, they beat hasty retreats, as did most would-be customers. The man proved abusive. Menedemos gave at least as good as he got, as he had with Kleon.

A man selling wine by the cup strolled through the agora. On a warm day like this, he did a brisk business. Menedemos waved to him and spent another obolos. The wine was a long way from the best the Rhodian had ever drunk, but he'd expected nothing better. No one sold Ariousian or Thasian or Lesbian for an obolos. This cooled him and quenched his thirst, which was all he'd had in mind.

Another woman came up to him. She wasn't far from his own age, and wasn't bad-looking: slim, dark-haired, bright-eyed, with fine white teeth. He smiled and said, "Hail, my dear. How are you today?"

"Well, thank you," she answered. Her Greek, though fluent, had an accent that proclaimed it wasn't her native tongue. Menedemos' hopes soared—that probably meant she was a slave, perhaps the slave of someone prosperous. She asked, "For how much are you selling your perfume?" When he told her, she didn't flinch. All she said was, "Can you come with me to my mistress' house?"

"That depends," Menedemos said. "Who is your mistress, and can she afford to buy?"

"She can afford to buy," the slave woman said gravely. "Her name is Melite, and she is not the least renowned hetaira in Athens."

"I'm sure she's the honey of the city," Menedemos said. The slave began to nod agreement—again proving herself not a Hellene by birth—but then made a face at him. He gave back an impudent grin; the hetaira's name sounded like the word for honey.

"Will you come?" Melite's slave asked again.

"I'd love to," Menedemos answered. The woman sent him a sharp look. He stared back, as innocently as if the remark couldn't have been taken more than one way. After a moment, she shrugged and started out of the agora. Scooping up the perfume jars on the hard-packed ground by his feet, Menedemos followed.

Melite's house was nothing special on the outside, but Hellenes, no matter how prosperous, didn't make a habit of displaying what they had. The more they showed off, the likelier someone was to try to take away what they'd worked so hard to get. The man who opened the door for the slave and Menedemos wasn't so ferocious-looking as the Kelt who served Menedemos' earlier customer, but the Rhodian wouldn't have cared to quarrel with him: his broad shoulders and thick arms said he could take care of himself in a brawl, and his flat nose said he'd been in a few in his time. He and the slave woman exchanged a few words in a language that wasn't Greek. The way he looked at her told Menedemos not to bother her in his sight.

The woman went upstairs. Even in a house Melite owned, she lived in the women's quarters. She came downstairs with the slave, veiled as if she were altogether respectable. But, just for an instant, the breeze blew the veiling aside. Menedemos exclaimed in surprise: "Oê! You were at Demetrios' when my cousin and I came to supper."

"That's right." Melite dipped her head. "You didn't see me for long, then or now."

"No, I didn't." Menedemos smiled his most charming smile. "But I remembered you. You're worth remembering."

"I thank you for saying so." To Menedemos' disappointment, the hetaira sounded more amused than impressed. She went on, "I hope you will not be angry when I tell you one of the things I have seen is that men—especially young men—will say almost anything if they think it will give them a better chance to take a woman to bed."

"I don't know what you're talking about," Menedemos answered, deadpan. The slave woman snorted. Her mistress laughed out loud. With a bow to Melite, Menedemos continued, "My dear, one of the things you will also have seen is that telling the truth often works best. I *was* telling the truth when I said I recognized you."

"So you were." Melite didn't give him another glimpse of her face. She used the veil as a hoplite used a shield, interposing it between his eyes and her features, leaving him guessing about what she was thinking. He believed her voice still held amusement when she said, "Whether you recognized me or not, though, you need to understand I am not looking for a new . . . friend. I have as many as I care to."

"I'm sure you do, if you can count Demetrios among them." Menedemos spoke as if her warning bothered him not in the least. That too was how the game was played. No matter how he spoke, though, he couldn't help remembering that when Sostratos sold Koan silk to a hetaira in Miletos a couple of years before, she'd paid him silver and given him herself. Menedemos didn't care to think his bookish cousin could outdo him with women. He didn't care to think it, but here it might be true.

Melite said, "Demetrios plays with women the way a child plays with soldiers carved from wood. Because he is who he is, he can do that. But no woman would put up with it from an ordinary man."

Menedemos drew himself up to his full height, which was considerably less than Demetrios' godlike stature. "If you were to know me, you would find I am no ordinary man, either."

"Oh? Would you also give me golden bracelets and necklaces and rubies and emeralds for a single night, the way Demetrios did?" Melite asked.

Backtracking, Menedemos answered, "I didn't claim I had Demetrios' money. But I would give silver in due measure. And I would give you something I daresay Demetrios didn't."

"Would you?" the hetaira said. "And what is that?"

"Joy."

She cocked her head to one side, studying him. He could feel her eyes, even if they remained indistinct behind the veiling. "You *are* brash," she said. Menedemos bowed again, though he wasn't sure she'd paid him a compliment. She went on, "One of the things a hetaira does not do is talk about her friends. That is how and why they stay friends with her."

Hetairai, as Menedemos knew perfectly well, were no more immune to gossip than any other people. Still, he didn't really care to learn how Demetrios reverenced Aphrodite. He was more interested in paying his own respects to the goddess.

But when Melite said, "Is it not true that you came here to sell me perfume, not yourself?" he decided he wouldn't worship Aphrodite in her company.

A grin let him put the best face on it he could. "My dear, I would never be so rude as to charge you for *that*," he said. Both the hetaira and her slave laughed then. Menedemos held out a jar of perfume. "For *this*, on the other hand . . ."

"Let me smell it," she said. He undid the stopper and handed her the jar. She sniffed. "That *is* sweet," she admitted, returning it to him. "What is your price? For the perfume, I mean, not for anything else." When he told her, she gasped in artfully simulated anger. "That's robbery!"

"Your slave didn't think so, when I told her the same thing in the agora," Menedemos replied.

"What does a slave know?" Melite said with a scornful toss of her head. The glare she aimed at the barbarian woman said her slave should have known enough to keep her mouth shut. The slave looked as if she wanted to vanish into thin air. Melite gave her attention back to Menedemos. "Anyhow, that's much too much. I'm not made of silver. I'll give you half of what you asked."

"No." Menedemos shoved the stopper back into the jar. "You will have bought perfume before, I'm sure. You know what it's worth. And what perfume is finer than essence of Rhodian roses?"

Melite sent him a sly, sidelong look. "Half what you asked, then— and what you asked for earlier."

With real regret, he tossed his head. "I'm sorry—I *am* sorry—but no. Business is business, and pleasure is pleasure, and I would be a fool to mix them. I'm not just in business for myself—I have my cousin and my father and my uncle to think of. How would I explain the owls I ought to have?"

"Gambling losses?" she suggested, with the air of a woman who'd made such suggestions many times before. "You can always explain such things if you use a little wit. Who would know?"

But Menedemos answered, "I would." Melite's shoulders slumped, ever so slightly. The Rhodian went on, "Family counts for more than half an hour of fun. Family lasts." His lips quirked again. "Family, you're stuck with."

"If you say so." Melite's tone showed she had a different opinion. She pointed to the perfume. "What I say is, you still want too much." She named a new price, higher than her first offer but still much lower than Menedemos'.

"No," he repeated. "I didn't give you a price much too high to begin with. I can haggle well enough when I need to, but I don't always haggle for the fun of it; I'm no Phoenician. I've told you what I need. If you don't feel like paying it, I'll go back to the market square."

"Maybe I should have taken you to bed at the start," Melite said thoughtfully. "Then you might not have been so stubborn." She came up again.

Now Menedemos moved down, just a little. He had left himself some room to maneuver. He sold her four jars of perfume at a price as good as he'd got in Athens. Melite went upstairs for the money herself; she didn't trust the slave woman to bring it. She gave Menedemos a mix of coins from all over Hellas, a mix that said not all her friends were Athenians. Some of the coins were lighter than the Athenian standard; others, like the turtles from nearby Aigina, were heavier. Overall, he thought it evened out. Sostratos would probably have insisted on finding a scale and weighing every drakhma and tetradrakhm from other poleis. Menedemos didn't intend to bother.

Melite spoke to her slave, who carried away the jars of perfume she'd bought. To Menedemos, the hetaira said, "Now I can smell like roses the rest of my life."

"May it be long," he answered politely. "Have you a sack I can use to carry this silver back to the Rhodian proxenos' house where I'm staying?"

"Of course." Melite called after the slave woman, telling her to fetch one. Then she said, "For someone like me, I wonder whether long life would be gift or curse."

"Why would you want to die?" Menedemos asked in surprise.

"You're young, you're beautiful, you're healthy, and you can't be poor if you just spent so much money on perfume."

"But when I get older, when my looks fade?" Melite sounded genuinely worried. "I bought the perfume because I think it will earn me more in the long run. But if I don't get rich now, what will I do if I'm still alive in twenty years? I won't be able to do this any more; men won't want me. Maybe someone will marry me, but more men make promises to hetairai than ever keep them. I don't want to end up a washerwoman or something like that, fretting over every obolos and going hungry half the time. In your trade, no one will care if you go gray or get wrinkled. Me? It's a different story."

She wasn't the first woman Menedemos had heard who was alarmed about losing her looks. Hetairai, though, depended on theirs more than most women. Even so, looks weren't all that counted for them. He said, "If you sing well, if you quote from poetry and plays, if you make men feel good about themselves while they're with you, all that will stave off the evil day."

"It helps," Melite agreed. "Still, though, if a man has a choice between a sweet young thing who can sing and quote and do everything else a hetaira should do and a dumpy older woman, where will he go? That works for me now, but I've seen women who were famous once trying to sell themselves to slaves for a couple of oboloi so they could buy sitos." She shivered. "Death is better than that, I think."

Menedemos thought of his father and uncle, who no longer put to sea. They weren't sitting around waiting for death to overtake them, though. They were still busy with the family firm. But Melite was right: what they looked like had nothing to do with how well they could carry on. Briefly, Menedemos wondered what he would be like if he reached his father's age. He felt his imagination failing. The only thing he was sure of was that he wouldn't be eager to go to his tomb. He didn't think Melite would, either, no matter what she said now.

Here came the slave woman with a cloth sack. Menedemos dumped the silver into it. He dipped his head to Melite. "Farewell."

"And to you," she replied. "I hope you go back safe to Rhodes."

"Thanks," he answered. "I hope you do well here. I hope the perfume helps."

"It will—for a while." Melite shrugged. "After that? Who knows?"

The slave led Menedemos to the door. Neither he nor Melite said anything about her. Who worried over whether a slave did well? No one doing well ever became a slave in the first place.

On his way out of Melite's home, Menedemos suddenly stopped: so suddenly, he might have turned to marble like a man who'd seen Medusa's head; so suddenly, one foot stayed up in the air, almost but not quite completing a step. That last thought wasn't quite true. If your polis fell, anything might happen to you, no matter how well you were doing. Anything at all.

SOSTRATOS WENT INTO THE STOREROOM at the back of Protomakhos' house. The room was nearly empty. Hardly any wine, little perfume, only a few jars of crimson dye, and a few rolls of papyrus remained. The silver he and Menedemos had earned for their goods, and the honey and other bits of merchandise they'd acquired here in Athens, already lay aboard the *Aphrodite*. Sostratos smiled a slow, pleased smile. He knew what they'd spent. He knew what they'd made. He knew they would go home with a solid profit for this journey.

Menedemos came in behind him, perhaps to look things over, too; perhaps to make sure he wasn't someone else who aimed to pilfer what remained here. Over his shoulder, Sostratos said, "Hail."

"Oh. It's you. Hail," Menedemos answered, which showed what he'd been thinking. "Everything safe here?"

"Safe enough," Sostratos said. "And it seems to me we've done about as much as we can do here in Athens. We aren't likely to make enough from now on to cover the cost of our rowers day by day."

"Are you sure?" Menedemos asked, and then waved his hand. "Forget I said that. Of course you're sure. You don't tell me things like that unless you're sure. You want to head back to Rhodes, then? It's earlier than I expected to leave."

"Which only means the weather is likely to stay good," Sostratos said. "Don't you want to be somewhere else before Demetrios starts wondering how much money we've made and whether he can get his hands on it?"

"He wouldn't do that. We're Rhodians. His father would skin him if he angered Rhodes . . . wouldn't he?" But conviction leaked from Menedemos' voice, sentence by sentence. When he laughed, it was sheepishly. "Who knows what Demetrios might do if he set his mind to it?"

"That's how it seems to me, too. We have good reasons to go. To the crows with me if I can find any good reason to stay," Sostratos said.

Menedemos looked back over his shoulder. No one from Protomakhos' household stood within earshot. "Xenokleia . . ." Menedemos whispered.

Sostratos tossed his head. "Any *good* reason, I said. If she's not a bad reason, I've never heard one."

"She wasn't bad at all," his cousin said. "I still don't know if she was telling the truth about her husband, but I don't much care, either. *She* wasn't bad."

There were times when Sostratos could have gleefully strangled Menedemos. His cousin knew that, and just as gleefully exploited it. And so, instead of losing his temper now, Sostratos reminded himself of that. He said, "Do you truly think the woman is reason enough to stay here, when measured against all the reasons we have for leaving?"

"Well, no, not when you put it like that," Menedemos admitted.

"All right, then," Sostratos said. "If we're agreed, I'll go down to the harbor and bring back enough sailors to carry our leftovers to the *Aphrodite.* This has been a soft cruise for the men. They've been able to live it up—"

"As much as you *can* live it up on a drakhma and a half a day," Menedemos put in.

"True. But all they've been buying are food and wine and women. They don't have to worry about lodging or anything like that," Sostratos said. "I'm sure Diokles will know which taverns they favor."

As Sostratos walked between the Long Walls, he kept looking back toward Athens and the marvelous buildings on her akropolis. He sighed. He'd done more than sigh after his father sent word he had to leave the Lykeion and come home to Rhodes. He'd wept bitter tears every step of the way down to Peiraieus. Not now. He'd changed in the years since then. He wasn't sure the change was for the better, but he was sure it was real. His visit to his old haunt, his talk with Theophrastos, had shown him the life of the Lykeion, however marvelous he'd thought it while younger, didn't suit him any more.

Demetrios' soldiers swaggered through the streets of Peiraieus. When the *Aphrodite* first came to Athens, Kassandros' soldiers had done the swaggering. Aside from the master they served, Sostratos saw little difference between one set of Macedonians and mercenaries and the other.

Demetrios had proclaimed the liberation of Athens, and had even torn down the fortress of Mounykhia to show he was serious, but Athenians still got out of the way in a hurry when Macedonian soldiers came by.

So did Sostratos. He didn't want trouble with Demetrios' men. No great warrior himself, he knew what was too likely to happen if trouble somehow started. He sighed again, this time in relief, when he reached the quays without hearing a shout of, "What do you think you're doing, skinny?" or anything of the sort.

Diokles waved as Sostratos came up the pier toward him. "Hail, young sir," the keleustes said. "You'll be planning to sail soon, won't you?"

Sostratos started. "How did you know that?"

"You've taken up just about everything we brought here to sell," Diokles answered. "By now, you've had it a while. Either you've got rid of it all, or else there'll be some odds and ends left to bring back to the ship. One way or the other, what's the point to staying around any longer?"

"Odds and ends it is," Sostratos said. "I'll need some sailors to haul them here, and then we'll head for Rhodes."

The oarmaster dipped his head. "Suits me. I haven't had much to do since we got here, and I'm tired of sitting around and rusting. I don't enjoy staying drunk for a week at a time the way I did when I was younger, and I can't screw as often as I used to, either. I'm ready to go to sea."

He was so very ready, he tramped up to Athens himself with Sostratos and some sailors, and didn't complain about shouldering a carrying pole and helping to haul a jar of Byblian back to the *Aphrodite*. Most of the time, that would have been beneath his dignity.

Before sailing, Sostratos checked the silver stowed under the poop deck. He smiled when he finished. Everything was as it should have been. He was ready to see Rhodes again, too—and how better than coming home with a nice profit?

10

FROM HIS STATION ON THE RAISED POOP DECK OF THE *Aphrodite,* Menedemos looked forward toward the bow. "Are we ready?" he called to the rowers waiting at the oars.

No one said no. Two of the crewmen were Athenians, new men hired to take the place of a pair of Rhodians who'd fallen in love with women here and decided not to leave. The newcomers had known enough to bring cushions for the rowing benches, so they probably had a fair notion of what they needed to do. Menedemos' eyes flicked to the quay. Yes, the mooring lines had been loosed and brought aboard the akatos. And yes, the anchors were raised and stowed near the bow. Satisfied with the last-minute check, he dipped his head to Diokles.

The oarmaster raised his bronze square and the little mallet with which he hit it. "Back oars!" he shouted, and smote the square to set the stroke.

Grunting, the men at the oars got to work. *Clang! . . . Clang! . . . Clang!* The first few strokes hardly moved the merchant galley. Menedemos had expected nothing different, especially with the ship's timbers heavy with seawater because she hadn't been dragged up onto the beach and dried out.

As Diokles had been going to sea since Menedemos was a little boy, he'd doubtless expected nothing different, either. He railed at the rowers anyhow: "Come on, you worthless lugs! Put your backs into it! You're not lotos-eaters any more—no more lying around or drinking or screwing and getting paid for it. Now you've got to earn your silver. Let's see you *work,* by the dog!"

Little by little, the *Aphrodite* slid away from the pier, picking up speed with each stroke as she backed out into the harbor. Menedemos glanced over to the quay again to make sure an irate Protomakhos wasn't rushing up to scream, "Adulterer!" at the last moment. Some women couldn't keep a secret (neither could some men, but

Menedemos chose not to dwell on that). Xenokleia, though, seemed to have stayed quiet long enough.

Harborside loungers and sailors aboard round ships, fishing boats, and some of Demetrios' war galleys watched the akatos pull away from the quay. Menedemos caught Diokles' eye. "Let's give them a little show, shall we?" he said.

"Right you are, skipper." The keleustes knew what Menedemos had in mind. He raised his voice to carry all the way up to the bow: "At my order, portside rowers keep backing oars, starboard switch to normal stroke. Ready? . . . *Now!*"

Menedemos helped the turn with the steering oars. The *Aphrodite* spun through half a circle almost in her own length, so that her bow faced out to sea and her stern the quays she was leaving. Diokles ordered both sets of rowers to switch to normal stroke as the turn neared completion; Menedemos finished it with the steering oars alone, and guided the merchant galley out into the Saronic Gulf.

A couple of men aboard one of Demetrios' sixes patrolling the harbor waved to the *Aphrodite,* complimenting her on a smart maneuver. As soon as his course suited him, Menedemos took his right hand off the starboard steering-oar tiller and waved back. One of those men wore an officer's cloak. Praise from someone who didn't have to give it was doubly welcome.

"We'll do better next time," Diokles promised, and glowered at the rowers. *"Won't we?"* He turned it into a threat.

"I'm sure we will," Menedemos said. The oarmaster played the villain's role. Menedemos, by contrast, could be the easygoing one, the one who sometimes took the edge off Diokles' strictness. He enjoyed that role more than he would have liked playing the harsh taskmaster himself.

The breeze came from off the land. "Unbrail the sail and let it down from the yard," Menedemos said. The sailors leaped to obey. Down came the big square sail, brails and bracing lines cutting it into squares. It flapped two or three times before filling with wind. Once it did fill, Menedemos took more than half the men off the oars. Even the ones who stayed at their benches didn't row; they only waited to make sure the breeze didn't suddenly slacken. The *Aphrodite* wasn't in such a hurry that she needed to speed along under wind and oars both.

"You're too cursed soft on them, skipper," Diokles growled as he lowered his bronze square and mallet. He looked back toward Menedemos so the sailors couldn't see his face; as he did so, he winked. Menedemos couldn't smile back, not without giving the game away to the men. Instead, he glared at Diokles, much more severely than the remark really warranted. The keleustes winked again, to show he understood what Menedemos was doing.

Salamis and the crowded waters where Great King Xerxes' fleet had come to grief more than a hundred seventy years before lay to starboard. Only a few fishing boats bobbed in the channel between the island and the mainland of Attica today. Menedemos had no trouble filling it with triremes in his mind's eye, though. Neither Xerxes' sailors nor the Hellenes they faced knew how to build anything bigger and stronger back in those distant days. *What a few fives and sixes might have done!* Menedemos thought.

Had he wanted to know more about Salamis than he did, he could have asked Sostratos, who was doing lookout duty up on the tiny foredeck. His cousin would have quoted from Herodotos, and probably from Aiskhylos' *Persians* as well. Not feeling like being overwhelmed, Menedemos didn't ask.

Aigina, a larger island, rose from the water almost dead ahead. The *Aphrodite* had stopped at the polis there a couple of years before. Having seen it, and having seen what sort of business merchants did there, Menedemos didn't care to pay a second visit. Beyond Aigina, blued and blurred by haze and distance, lay the northeastern corner of the Peloponnesos. Menedemos was content—more than content—to let it stay in the distance.

He pulled the steering-oar tiller in his left hand toward him and pushed the one in his right hand away. The *Aphrodite* swung gently to port, heading along parallel to the coast of Attica, which ran generally south and east toward Cape Sounion.

Mild chop in the Saronic Gulf made the merchant galley roll a bit. Menedemos wondered if his cousin would lose his breakfast after a long spell ashore, but Sostratos seemed fine. A handful of sailors did lean over the rail to feed the fish, including one of the newly hired Athenians. The rest of the rowers ribbed the men with touchy stomachs. There were always some in every crew.

Menedemos enjoyed the motion. He'd had enough of steady ground under his feet. He wanted to be reminded he was aboard a ship. Going out to sea again felt good. He drew in a great lungful of fine salt air. "Wonderful to get the city stink out of my nose," he said.

"That's the truth," Diokles agreed. "I'm sick of smelling shit."

The breeze freshened. The sail thrummed, taut with wind. The *Aphrodite* skimmed over the sea; a long creamy wake trailed out behind her and behind the boat she towed. Menedemos took the last rowers off the oars. When the wind pushed her along like this, he didn't have to worry about anything more. With a wind like this at her back, even a round ship performed . . . respectably.

Of course, a round ship trying to make her way up to Athens had to tack against the wind, and had a sorry time of it. The long, sleek merchant galley arrowed past a couple of those unfortunates, who had to make reach after sideways reach to go a little distance forward.

"Even if we were heading the other way, we could fight through the wind," Menedemos said.

"For a while, anyhow," Diokles said. "You go straight into the teeth of a stiff breeze for too long, though, and you'll break your rowers' hearts."

Menedemos dipped his head. The keleustes was right. An akatos could do things a round ship couldn't hope to. All the same, a captain who thought the men at the oars were made of bronze like the legendary Talos, and so would never tire, was doomed to disappointment if not to danger.

The sun slid across the sky. The wind never slackened. Glancing now and then toward the coast of Attica to port, Menedemos marveled at how fast it slid by. Ahead, the Saronic Gulf opened out into the broader waters of the Aegean. The three westernmost islands of the Kyklades lay to the east: Keos, Kythnos south of it, and Seriphos farther south still.

A sailor took Sostratos' place on the foredeck. Menedemos' cousin came back toward the stern. He climbed the steps up to the poop and stood a couple of cubits away from Diokles. "Where do you aim to stop tonight?" he asked Menedemos.

"Normally, I'd say Keos or Kythnos," Menedemos answered. "With this wind . . . With this wind, I'm tempted to see if I can't make Seriphos. That wouldn't be a bad day's run, would it?"

"No." But Sostratos sounded less than happy.

"What's the matter?" Menedemos asked.

"If we put in at Kythnos, we might pick up some cheese there," Sostratos said. "We could sell it for a profit in Rhodes—Kythnian cheese is famous all over Hellas."

"Hmm." Menedemos considered. "Well, all right, my dear, we'll do that, then," he said. "We're not in any enormous rush to get home. And Seriphos isn't anything much. It's so rocky, people say the Gorgon looked at it."

"That's because it's connected with Perseus," Sostratos replied. "It's supposed to be where he and his mother Danaë washed up after Akrisios, her father, put them in a big chest and set them afloat. And he's supposed to have shown the Gorgon's head there, too, and turned the people to stone."

"It's also supposed to be a place where the frogs don't croak," Menedemos said.

"We wouldn't have heard them at this season of the year, anyhow," Sostratos said, which was true. He went on, "And we can't sell frogs, croaking or otherwise, or chunks of rock. Good cheese, on the other hand . . ."

"I already said yes," Menedemos reminded him. He changed course a little, till the stempost covered the island of Kythnos from where he stood. "Now I'm aimed straight for it. Are you happy?"

"I'm positively orgiastic, O best one," Sostratos answered.

"You're positively sarcastic, is what you are," Menedemos said. Sostratos dipped his head; that was something he could hardly deny.

The wind held all day. The *Aphrodite* raced past the tiny islet of Belbina, which lay eighty or a hundred stadia south of Cape Sounion. A few sheep ambled over Belbina's steep, meager fields; except for a shepherd or two, the island was uninhabited. Kythnos still lay dead ahead.

In weather like this, sailing was joy, not drudgery. Rowers hung fishing lines over the side of the ship, some of their hooks baited with bits of cheese—cheap cheese. Every so often, one of them would let out a yip of triumph and haul in a flying fish or a sea bream or a goby: something he could cook over a charcoal brazier and enjoy for his opson.

Kythnos swelled ahead. It was greener than Seriphos to the south, but not much. Sheep and goats wandered the hills in back of the island's one small town, which faced west, back toward Attica and the Peloponnesos—*toward civilization,* Menedemos thought unkindly.

Kythnos the town boasted no developed harbor. A visiting ship could either beach herself nearby or anchor in front of the town. At Menedemos' order, the anchors splashed into the sea. After so long immersed, the *Aphrodite* wouldn't gain much from a night or two out of the water. Once back in Rhodes, she would come out of the sea till spring.

"All yours," Menedemos told his cousin. "Here's to cheese."

WHEN SOSTRATOS LISTENED to the people of Kythnos talk the next morning, he felt as if he'd somehow traveled back through time. They spoke Attic Greek, but a very old-fashioned Attic, saying *es* for *eis* (into), *xyn* for *syn* (with), and any number of other things that had vanished from the speech of Athens itself more than a hundred years before. Hearing them, he might have been listening to Aiskhylos . . . had Aiskhylos chosen to talk about cheese and the sheep and goats from whose milk it was made.

He supposed the Kythnians spoke that way because, even though they were only a day's sail from Athens, not many ships bothered coming into the harbor here. The locals were isolated from the wider world. If change came, it came only slowly.

A breeze from off the mainland—not so strong as the one that had driven the *Aphrodite* here but still brisk enough—ruffled Sostratos' hair as he made his way toward the agora. After Athens, Kythnos seemed ludicrously small; it might have been a toy town, made for children to play with. That didn't keep him from getting lost once. There were enough houses to box him in to where he wasn't sure whether he needed to go right or left to find the market square, and he guessed wrong. He had to give a man with several missing front teeth an obolos for directions, and then had to ask him to repeat himself, for his dialect and the missing teeth made him hard to understand.

In the agora, people displayed fish and woolen cloth and cheeses. The fish were for other Kythnians. The cloth struck Sostratos as nothing special. The cheeses . . . The cheeses were as fine as Kythnos' reputation would have led him to believe, than which there was little higher praise.

And the prices proved amazingly low. Sostratos had to work to keep astonishment off his face when a fellow who'd piled wedge after wedge of delicate, creamy goat's-milk cheese on a little table behind him asked no more than a Rhodian cheesemaker would have for something only a quarter as good. The local, an anxious-looking man with large, rabbity eyes and a wen on one cheek, took his surprise for anger rather than delight. "I can come down a little, best one," the man said hastily, even before Sostratos made a counteroffer. "Don't go away, please."

Sostratos collected himself. "Well, all right," he said, as if he didn't really want to stay. "Maybe I won't, as long as you're reasonable."

"I can be very reasonable, sir, very reasonable indeed," the cheesemaker replied.

He meant it, too. Sostratos was almost embarrassed to haggle with him. It felt like stealing from a helpless child. Sostratos knew he could have forced the Kythnian lower than he finally did. He didn't have the heart to do it. He consoled himself by thinking he would still make a good profit on the cheese, even if he bought it at this slightly higher price.

Another man two stalls over sold a sharp, crumbly sheep's-milk cheese for prices similarly small. Again, Sostratos could have bargained harder. He knew Menedemos would have squeezed every obolos possible from these men, scorning them for fools because they didn't understand how splendid their cheeses were.

Dickering with some merchants, even most merchants, Sostratos bargained as ferociously as he knew how. Phoenicians, Athenians, that truffle-seller up in Mytilene—they were all out for themselves, just as he was. These men, though . . . They seemed pathetically grateful that he would give them any silver for their cheeses.

"Owls," the man with the crumbly cheese murmured, almost in awe, when Sostratos paid him. "Aren't they pretty? Most of the time, you know, we just swap stuff back and forth amongst ourselves. I get me a few owls, though, and who knows? I may even go across to Attica"—he didn't say *to Athens,* which might have been beyond his mental horizon—"and, and *buy* things."

"That's what money is for," Sostratos agreed.

"It is, isn't it?" To the Kythnian, it seemed a new idea. A Karian farmer a hundred stadia from the nearest tiny town could hardly have been more distant from the kind of trading Sostratos did than was this fellow Hellene only a long day's sail from Athens, the beating heart of the civilized world.

Suppressing several sighs, Sostratos went on through the agora. His only problem was choosing the best of the best. One man gave him a sample of a hard yellow cheese that made him raise his eyebrows. "I don't think I've ever tasted anything quite like this," he said.

"I wouldn't be surprised, O stranger," the Kythnian said with modest pride—no one here seemed to display more than modest pride. "It's made from cow's milk."

"Really?" Sostratos said, and the cheesemaker dipped his head. "How . . . unusual." Few Hellenes, especially south of Boiotia (whose very name was associated with cattle), kept cows. Sheep and goats were far more common, for they were valuable for their wool as well as for their milk.

"Do you like it?" the local asked.

"It's not bad," Sostratos answered; no matter how pitiful he thought the Kythnians, he couldn't make himself sound *too* enthusiastic. "What do you want for a wedge?"

He wasn't surprised when the cheesemaker named a price higher than any of the others had given him. Another reason few cows dwelt in this part of Hellas was that they took more fodder for the amount of milk they yielded. Despite that, for an exotic cheese like this what the Kythnian wanted wasn't bad at all. Sostratos haggled a little harder than he had with the other men, but only a little. Before long, he and the cheesemaker clasped hands to seal the bargain.

"I thank you very much," the fellow said. "Some of my neighbors think I'm daft for keeping a cow, but I guess I've shown them."

"Maybe you have." Sostratos would never have let one relatively small sale go to his head like that, but he was a Rhodian, used to dealing all over the Inner Sea. To a Kythnian, for whom a major journey meant walking from his farm to this little town—it surely didn't deserve to be called a polis—showing some drakhmai to his neighbors might be a triumph of sorts.

Sailors from the *Aphrodite* helped Sostratos carry the cheeses back to the akatos. One of them was Teleutas. With a sidelong glance Sostratos' way, he said, "You'd better get us back to Rhodes in a hurry. If you don't, we'll eat up your profits."

The other sailors laughed. Sostratos didn't. He knew Teleutas better than he wanted to. "By the dog of Egypt, if even a crumb of cheese goes missing before we get home, you'll *swim* back to Rhodes," he ground out. "Do you understand me?"

"Easy, young sir," one of the other sailors said. "He was only joking."

Teleutas' grin didn't quite reach his eyes. "That's right," he said. "Nothing's going to happen to them."

"It had better not," Sostratos told him. "Because *I'm* not joking."

An oppressive silence cloaked the working party till they got down to the beach. Even the men who rowed them and the cheeses back to the *Aphrodite* noticed it. "Somebody fart in somebody else's face?" one of the rowers asked when no one said a word as the boat glided toward the merchant galley.

"You might say so, Moskhion," Teleutas answered. "Yes, you just might say so." He eyed Sostratos again, smirking slightly.

Sostratos glared back. "If we need another sailor in a hurry, I expect we can find one even in a gods-forsaken place like this," he said.

Moskhion looked horrified. He said, "I wouldn't maroon anybody in this miserable dump."

"If we had a thief aboard, I'd maroon him anywhere," Sostratos replied. Moskhion shut up and started rowing again. He'd gone with Sostratos into Ioudaia the year before. He couldn't very well forget the gold ring Teleutas had stolen from a local there. No one had ever proved—no one had ever even claimed—Teleutas stole while aboard ship. Had that been proved, or even claimed, Teleutas wouldn't have sailed with the *Aphrodite* this spring.

He gave no more smirks now. He looked out at the sea and at the akatos and said not a thing. Without a doubt, that was the best thing he could have done. Had he given Sostratos any more lip, he would have gone out of the boat and into the water of the harbor. Sostratos had no idea whether Teleutas could swim. At the moment, he was too angry to care.

When they came alongside the *Aphrodite,* the sailors in the boat passed chunks of cheese to the men in the merchant galley. "Here, we'll put them in leather sacks," Menedemos said. "We've got a good many left from the trip up to Athens, and they'll keep out salt water and vermin." He grinned. "All the vermin that don't walk on two legs, anyhow."

Several sailors aboard the akatos laughed. Nobody from the ship's boat did. Teleutas looked as if he were about to, but he changed his mind even without a scowl from Sostratos. After all the cheese went onto the *Aphrodite,* Sostratos and the sailors scrambled up over the rail and into the low waist of the ship.

His cousin waited till the two of them were—mostly—out of earshot of the crew before asking, "What's wrong, my dear? You look ready to bite a belaying pin in two, but I see you came back with plenty of cheese."

"Oh, the cheese is fine. The cheese is better than I expected it to be, in fact," Sostratos said, still seething. "But that polluted Teleutas . . ." The story poured out of him; he finished, "I wish he never would have come aboard the *Aphrodite* in the first place."

"Well, unless he does come right out and steal, we're stuck with him till we get back to Rhodes," Menedemos answered. "Next year, though, tell him to go howl when he asks to go with us again."

"By the dog, I will," Sostratos said. "I wish I had this spring. He's nothing but trouble. Even when he doesn't do anything wrong, he always makes it seem he's just about to. You have to keep an eye on him every minute."

"Many goodbyes to him, then," Menedemos said. "We'll pay him off when we get home, and that'll be the end of it. When he comes around whining for work next spring, tell him to bend over and—"

"I understand you, thanks," Sostratos said hastily.

"Good. That's settled, then." Menedemos liked things neat and tidy. He liked them that way so much, he sometimes assumed they were when they weren't. Here, though, Sostratos agreed with his cousin. Menedemos asked, "Anything else we need to do here on Kythnos?"

"I don't think there's anything else *to* do on Kythnos," Sostratos said.

"Ha! Wouldn't be surprised if you're right. I know I don't want their water; we've got enough, and I remember how nasty and brackish it was when we stopped here a couple of years ago with Polemaios aboard." Menedemos turned to Diokles. "Everybody's aboard and ready to row?"

"Everybody's aboard, skipper," the oarmaster answered. "A few of the boys are still nursing headaches from too much wine, but they can probably row."

"Sweating'll be good for 'em," Menedemos said with the airy

confidence of a man who wasn't hung over at the moment. "Let's get out of here, then. I don't think we can make Paros with the daylight we've got left, but we ought to get to Syros without much trouble."

"Sounds about right," Diokles agreed. He turned and started shouting at the crew. They hurried to take their places at the oars and by the lines that would lower the sail from the yard. "Rhyppa*pai*!" Diokles called. "Rhyppa*pai*! Rhyppa*pai*!" The men began to row. The *Aphrodite* made her way out of the harbor.

Sostratos was glad to go. To Menedemos, every trading run, every island, every town seemed a new adventure. Sostratos liked the travel for what he could learn, but there wasn't much to learn about Kythnos. And the more he saw of other places (even Athens, and who could have imagined that?), the better Rhodes looked. Rhodes was home, and they were on their way.

MENEDEMOS SWUNG THE *APHRODITE* to port. Kythnos was longer than it was wide; to go east from the island's single town, one had to round a headland at either the northern or southern tip of the island. He'd chosen the latter. To catch the wind abeam, the sailors swung the yard from the port bow back. They'd started the motion only a heartbeat after he started the turn, and finished it at about the same time. He smiled to himself. He hadn't even had to give an order.

"Pretty day," Diokles remarked as they swung past the headland, and it was. The sun shone warm and bright in the blue, blue sky, though it no longer stood so high as it had at the start of summer. The Aegean was a deeper blue, or rather several deeper blues. Kythnos, on the merchant galley's left hand, added variety: brown soil, gray rock, streaks of greenery amid sun-dried yellow.

Other islands of the Kyklades dotted the horizon: everything from black rocks with the sea foaming around them, good for nothing but tearing the bottom out of a ship that came upon them unawares, to Syros and Paros and Naxos in the east, Siphnos in the southeast, and rocky Seriphos and Melos beyond it due south.

Gulls and terns wheeled overhead, skrawking and mewing. They often attended ships; what was garbage to men was opson to them. An osprey folded its wings and plunged feet first into the sea two or three plethra from the merchant galley. It came up again a heartbeat later, flapping strongly to get back into the air. Its talons clutched a writhing fish.

"When terns dive in, gulls steal from them," Sostratos said. "But who's going to steal from an osprey?"

"No one in these waters, by Zeus," Menedemos answered.

"I wonder what the fish was," Sostratos said. "I wonder if the bird chose it because it likes that kind of fish, or just because it chanced to be swimming near enough to the surface to be seen."

Menedemos laughed. "I wonder, O best one, if there's any limit to how many questions you can dream up. If there is, you haven't touched it yet."

His cousin looked wounded. "What's wrong with curiosity? Where would we be without it? We'd be living in mud huts and trying to knock hares over the head with rocks, that's where."

"Two more questions," Menedemos said, "even if you did answer one of them." He wondered how angry—and how entertaining—Sostratos would get at the tweaking. He didn't tease his cousin as much as he had when they were younger; Sostratos had got better at holding his temper, and so offered less amusement now.

He held it this morning, saying, "I have one question more: what difference does it make to you?"

"None, really. I was just curious." Menedemos made a face, realizing he'd delivered himself into Sostratos' hands.

"Thank you, my dear. You just proved my point for me." Sostratos could have said more and worse. That was small consolation to Menedemos. What his cousin *had* said was plenty: plenty to make his ears heat, plenty to make Diokles laugh softly. For the next little while, Menedemos gave exaggerated attention to steering the ship—which, at the moment, needed little steering. He'd lost the exchange; he knew he'd lost it; and he hated losing at anything. That he'd lost it through his own foolish choice of words only made losing more annoying.

But he couldn't stay irked for long, not with the breeze filling the sail and thrumming in the rigging, not with the gentle motion of the ship and the soft splashing as the ram at her bow cut through the water, not with . . .

Thinking of the ram brought him up short. "Serve out helmets and weapons to the crew, Diokles," he said. "More pirates in these waters, Furies take 'em, than fleas on a scavenger dog. If they want us, we'd better make sure they get a hard fight."

Since the akatos had had to fight off pirates each of the past two sailing seasons, Diokles couldn't very well disagree. In fact, he dipped his head and said, "I was going to do that anyway pretty soon."

Before long, with bronze pots on their heads and swords and spears and axes in their hands, the men on the *Aphrodite* looked piratical themselves. The merchant galley was beamier than a pentekonter or hemiolia, but the crews of fishing boats and round ships weren't inclined to make such fine distinctions. They never had been. Now, though, they fled with as much haste as Menedemos had ever seen. Fishing boats smaller than the neat little craft the merchant galley towed behind her rowed away with the men in them pulling as hard as if they crewed a war galley charging into battle. Two different sailing ships heeled sharply to the south as soon as their sailors spied the *Aphrodite.* They wanted to get as far away from her as they could, as fast as they could.

"If standing behind the sail and blowing into it would help them go faster, they'd do that, too," Menedemos said with a laugh.

"They'll be hours beating their way back up to their old course against the wind," Sostratos said.

"Too bad for them," Menedemos said.

"Hard to blame them," Sostratos said. "When taking chances can get you sold into slavery or murdered and tossed over the side, you don't do it. If we believed in taking chances, we wouldn't have armed ourselves."

He wasn't wrong. Even so, Menedemos said, "You know, there are times when you squeeze all the juice out of life."

"There are times when I think you want just enough juice to drown yourself," Sostratos replied.

They scowled at each other. Menedemos yawned in Sostratos' face to show how dull he thought Sostratos was. Sostratos turned his back, walked over to the rail, and pissed into the wine-dark sea. Maybe that was general contempt; maybe he was getting rid of juice. Menedemos didn't inquire. Sostratos set his chiton to rights and stalked up to the foredeck, back very stiff.

Diokles clucked in distress. "The two of you shouldn't quarrel," he said. "The ship needs you both." He used the dual, implying Menedemos and Sostratos were a natural pair.

Menedemos was steering the ship. He couldn't turn his back on Diokles, no matter how much he wanted to. At the moment, he would sooner have given his cousin a good kick in the fundament than been yoked to him in the Greek language as part of a pair. *Sanctimonious prig,* he thought.

For the rest of the day, none of the sailors seemed to want to come near either him or Sostratos. The men walked on tiptoe, as if the *Aphrodite*'s planking were covered with eggs and they would be whipped if they broke one. Songs, jokes, the usual chatter—all disappeared. Only the sounds of wind and wave remained. The merchant galley had never been so quiet.

Too stubborn and too proud to make any move toward Sostratos, Menedemos stayed at the steering oars the rest of the day. Slowly, slowly, the island of Syros drew near. It was even more desiccated than Kythnos. The *Aphrodite* had stopped here, too, a couple of years before. Menedemos remembered the verses from the *Odyssey* wherein Eumaios the swineherd praised the island from which he'd come. He also recalled Sostratos' comment: that the praise proved Homer a blind poet.

He angrily tossed his head; he didn't want to think about Sostratos at all. Doing his grim best not to, he steered the merchant galley around the northern tip of the island (which, like Kythnos, was taller than it was wide) and down toward Syros town on the eastern coast. The town sat inside the curve of a little bay. The harbor was fine; had the island of Syros had more in the way of water and people and crops, the harbor could easily have supported a real city. As things were, it mattered about as much as nice eyebrows on an ugly girl.

Because only a few fishing boats and the occasional ship going from somewhere else to somewhere else used the harbor, no one had bothered to improve it with moles and piers. The *Aphrodite* sat in the bay a couple of plethra from the town. Her anchors plopped into the water to hold her fast.

By the sun, an hour or so of daylight remained. Sostratos called for sailors to row him ashore. "Where do you think you're going?" Menedemos demanded.

"There's a temple to Poseidon here," Sostratos answered. "There's supposed to be a sundial in it made by Pherekides, who taught Pythagoras. It may be the oldest sundial in Hellas. While we're here, I'd like to take a look at it. Why? Are you planning to sail off without me?"

"Don't tempt me." But Menedemos gestured gruffly toward the boat. "Go on, then. Be back by dark."

Sostratos pointed to the handful of houses that made up the town. "If you think I'd stay there, you're—" He broke off.

You're even stupider than I thought you were. That was what he'd been on the point of saying, that or something like it. Menedemos' resentment flared anew; he conveniently forgot all the equally unkind thoughts he'd had about Sostratos. "On second thought, stay away as long as you please," he snapped.

He watched the boat take his cousin to the shore, watched Sostratos talk with an elderly local and take an obolos out of his mouth to give the fellow, watched the graybeard point uphill and to the north, and watched Sostratos hurry off in that direction. He also watched the men who'd rowed Sostratos ashore disappear into a wineshop.

"Skipper, what will you do if the young gentleman has trouble?" Diokles asked. "Going off on your own in a strange place isn't always the smartest thing you can do."

"How could there possibly be a problem?" Menedemos answered. "Sostratos seems sure it's safe, and he knows everything. If you don't believe me, just ask him."

Diokles gave him a reproachful look. "Most of the time, the two of you"—he used the dual again, perhaps to drive home his point, perhaps to annoy Menedemos—"have pretty good sense. But when you don't, you really don't." Most of the time, he would have added something like, *meaning no disrespect.* Today, he didn't bother.

Menedemos pointed to the boat, which lay on the beach. "What am I supposed to do when that's there?"

Unfazed, the oarmaster replied, "Find some sailors who can swim, and make sure they're good and ready."

That made better sense than Menedemos wished it did. Muttering under his breath, he strode the length of the galley, asking men if they could swim. Less than half the crew could, which didn't surprise him, though he knew how himself. "We'll wait till half an hour after sundown," he said. "If Sostratos isn't back by then . . ."

But he was. Menedemos spied his long, angular form with a curious mixture of resentment and relief. After brief confusion when Sostratos didn't see the sailors, he went into the wineshop and brought them out. They weren't too drunk to row him back to the *Aphrodite.*

"And how was your precious sundial?" Menedemos asked after his cousin scrambled back into the akatos.

"It seemed remarkably like . . . an old, decrepit sundial." Sostratos looked and sounded sheepish.

"Eat some supper and then lay your old, decrepit bones down on the planks." Menedemos spoke gruffly, like a father annoyed at a way-ward child. That was how he felt. Again, how Sostratos felt about him never entered his mind.

Resentment sparked in Sostratos' eyes, but he seemed to decide he couldn't disobey sensible advice like that without looking a proper fool. He wrapped himself in his himation. Before long, he was asleep. If he spoke very little to Menedemos . . . *I don't much want to talk to him right now, either,* Menedemos thought, just before sleep also over-took him.

SOSTRATOS LOOKED DOWN at the waxed wooden tablets on which he'd kept the accounts of the trading run to Athens. As long as he paid at-tention to those, he didn't have to worry about Menedemos. That, at the moment, suited him fine.

Clang! Clang! The keleustes' bronze square beat out time for the rowers. The wind had died. The sail was brailed up tight to the yard. The *Aphrodite* glided east from Syros across a dead-calm sea, pro-pelled by ten grunting, sweating rowers on each side: every other bench had a man in place.

"Sail ho!" called the lookout on the foredeck. "Sail ho off the port bow!"

That made Sostratos look up from his accounts. The lookout was pointing northeast. Sostratos stood up to see farther. Before long, he spied the sail, too. He shaded his eyes with his hand to cut the glare from the morning sun.

Nor was his the only head to swing that way. After a few heartbeats, a sailor said, "That's a round ship. Nothing to worry about." He was right. That huge sail and broad, beamy hull could only belong to one of the merchantmen that hauled grain and lumber and cheap wine and oil and other bulk commodities around the Inner Sea. The only way a round ship could endanger the akatos was by colliding with her.

Once the sailors saw the ship to the northeast was no threat, they went back to whatever they'd been doing. Sostratos was tired of going over the accounts. He already knew them well. Keeping an eye on the round ship also let him avoid having anything to do with his cousin.

Because the *Aphrodite*'s sail was brailed up against the yard, the round ship's crew needed longer to spot her than they would have otherwise. When they did, they swung their bow away from her. They couldn't very well run, not on this windless day. Their ship would have had trouble outrunning a clam.

From his place on the poop deck, Menedemos said, "If I were ever tempted to turn pirate, a time like this would do it. That fat sow can't flee, can't fight, and can't hide. She's just sitting there, waiting to be taken."

"I wonder how much loot she's got," Teleutas said wistfully—or was it hungrily? Sostratos couldn't tell, though he was always ready to think the worst of the sailor.

Menedemos spoke sharply: "We're Rhodians. Remember it. We knock pirates over the head when we get the chance. We don't play that game ourselves."

"Only kidding, skipper," Teleutas said. "You were the one who brought it up, you know."

And so Menedemos had—but he'd made it plain he was talking about something contrary to fact. He *wasn't* really tempted to turn pirate. Was Teleutas? Sostratos wouldn't have been surprised. But Teleutas, as usual, had an excuse just plausible enough to keep him out of trouble.

Sostratos stowed the account tablets in a leather sack. Then he went back to the poop deck. "Hail, young sir," Diokles said, not changing his rhythm a bit as he beat out the stroke for the rowers. Menedemos didn't say anything. He kept his hands on the steering-oar tillers and his eyes on the sea. Sostratos might not have been there.

But Sostratos finally had something he could talk about without starting a fight. "That Teleutas," he said in a low, angry voice. He couldn't stand the sailor, but was grateful to him in a curious way.

And, sure enough, Menedemos dipped his head. "He's a piece of work, isn't he?" he agreed. "You were right about that. I wouldn't be surprised if he's been a pirate now and again."

"Neither would I," Sostratos said. "I *will* turn him away if he tries to sail with us next year."

"Suits me." Menedemos suddenly seemed to realize he was talking with Sostratos instead of shouting at him. He tried to glue the scowl back on his face, but had less luck than he might have wanted. Instead, he gave Sostratos an odd, grudging half smile. "Hail."

"Hail, yourself," Sostratos answered in those same grudging tones.

"We're . . . stuck with each other, aren't we?" Menedemos said.

"We seem to be," Sostratos said. "If we were married, we could divorce. Since we're tied by blood . . . well, you said it. We can make the best of it or the worst, but we *are* stuck."

"I saw you going over the accounts," Menedemos said. Sostratos dipped his head. His cousin went on, "Just how well did we do?"

"Do you want it to the obolos, or will the nearest drakhma do?" Sostratos asked in turn. "If it's to the nearest drakhma, do you want it in Athenian owls, or shall I convert it to Rhodian currency?"

Menedemos stared at him. Sostratos looked back, deadpan. Menedemos took a hand from the steering-oar tillers to point an accusing forefinger at him. "Oh, no, you don't. You can't fool me, you abandoned rogue. You almost did, but not quite. You're having me on, and I'm smart enough to know it."

Sostratos named a sum in Athenian drakhmai. Then he named a larger sum in lighter Rhodian drakhmai. He added, "That assumes we can convert currency without paying any fees, the way we did in Athens. Silver is silver, no matter what the people who run a polis think. If we do have to pay the fee, what we make goes down by two percent, in which case it would amount to"—he named one more sum—"in Rhodian drakhmai, of course."

"You aren't having me on. You couldn't be making that up." Now Menedemos sounded uncertain. For his part, Diokles looked as if he couldn't believe his ears.

"Go through the accounts yourself if you don't believe me," Sostratos said, knowing Menedemos wouldn't. He couldn't resist adding another barb: "Our fathers will, of course."

"So they will." Menedemos seemed disenchanted with that prospect, too. He said, "When we get back to Rhodes, we're Philodemos' son and Lysistratos' son again. One of the reasons I like going to sea is that I can be my own man away from Rhodes, not just my father's son."

"Something to that, I suppose." But Sostratos spoke more for politeness' sake and to keep from starting another quarrel than from conviction. His own father was more easygoing than Uncle Philodemos.

Of that he had no doubt, or that Philodemos tried much harder to run Menedemos' life than his own father did with him. Still, Sostratos remained convinced Menedemos would have had a smoother time of it if he didn't push back so hard against Uncle Philodemos. He'd tried saying as much now and again, but Menedemos, as usual, didn't want to listen.

"I can't wait till next spring," Menedemos said now. "I want to get away, to be free, to be myself."

Sostratos had never had any trouble being himself in Rhodes. If the number of wives Menedemos had seduced in the polis was any indication, he hadn't had all that much trouble there, either. One more thing his cousin wouldn't want to hear. Sostratos did say, "I can see why you're eager to be gone, but I'm glad you don't sound desperate, the way you did when we left Rhodes a couple of years ago."

He'd thought that safe enough. No matter what he'd thought, he proved wrong. Without warning, Menedemos' face turned into a slammed door. Sostratos' cousin suddenly started talking in monosyllables—when he talked at all. For most of the next two or three hours, he just kept quiet. Sostratos didn't think Menedemos was angry at him again, but Menedemos was plainly angry about something.

Partway through that unnerving silence, Sostratos asked, "What did I say that was wrong? Tell me what it is, and I'll apologize for it."

"It isn't anything," Menedemos said tightly. "It isn't anything at all."

He wasn't telling the truth. He didn't even come close to telling the truth. That couldn't have been more obvious. Just as obvious, though, was that he didn't want Sostratos poking and prodding at whatever he hid. Most of the time, Sostratos would have kept on poking and prodding anyhow. Being who and what he was, he might not even have noticed that Menedemos was holding something back. After the quarrel with his cousin, though, he found himself more alert to Menedemos' moods, and pushed it no further.

He did send an inquiring glance Diokles' way. Maybe the oarmaster had some notion of what was troubling Menedemos. But Diokles, after making sure Menedemos wasn't looking at him, only shrugged a tiny shrug. Maybe he knew and couldn't say with Menedemos listening. More likely, Sostratos judged, he wasn't sure what troubled him, either.

Little by little, as Menedemos realized Sostratos wasn't going to pry any more, he came out of the shell into which he'd retreated. He smiled. He laughed. He cracked jokes. But he gave no hint of why he'd gone into the shell in the first place.

PAROS AND NAXOS, which lay side by side, were the two largest and wealthiest islands in the southern Kyklades. They were both much better watered than the barren, rocky islands farther west in the chain. Vineyards, olive groves, and fields of wheat and barley—fallow at this season—flourished on them. And they both enjoyed great mineral wealth, too. Parian marble was famous all around the Inner Sea. The stone of Naxos had a smaller reputation, but it was also quarried on the western slopes of the mountains that jutted up at the heart of the island.

Menedemos brought the *Aphrodite* in at the polis of Naxos, on the northwestern coast. The crew moored the merchant galley next to a round ship that was taking on blocks of marble bigger and heavier than a man could carry. A wooden crane was carefully swaying them aboard the ship. Menedemos watched in fascination; if the fellow in charge of the crane made a mistake, or if a rope broke, one of those blocks would tear right through the ship's bottom. It would end up on the floor of the harbor and the round ship would end up sunk.

"Easy! Easy!" the boss called to the workers—probably slaves—straining at the capstan. "Lower away! A little more . . . A little more . . . Hold on! Now once more, a quarter of a turn . . . There!"

The block went down into the round ship's hold. Sailors down below there must have freed it from the securing lines, for one of them called up something to a man on deck, who waved to the crane operator. At his command, the crane swung back to another block waiting on the quay. Its crew made the block fast. Before going any further, the boss carefully checked the rope that would lift the chunks of marble. That block could wreck the quay if it fell, too, or smash a man to a red rag.

Only after the last block had swung into the hold did Menedemos call, "*Euge!*" to the man in charge of the crane.

"Thanks, friend," the fellow replied. His shoulders sagged for a moment as he allowed himself a sigh of relief. Then, straightening, he went on, "And thanks even more for not bothering me when I was busy there."

"You're welcome," Menedemos said. "I could see you needed to pay attention to what you were doing."

"Some people don't care. By the dog, a lot of the whipworthy rascals don't care." Anger blazed in the boss' voice. "They've seen you, and that matters to them, so of course the thick-heads think it must matter to you, too. And if something goes wrong and you wreck a ship or crush a man, what do they do? They point and they gape and they laugh, that's what. To Tartaros with all of them!" He spat on the quay.

More fire to him than I thought. Menedemos asked, "How did you get into your line of work?"

"About how you'd expect: I learned it from my father, same as he learned it from his," the Naxian answered. "Some of the things Grandpa did, and *his* father . . ." He tossed his head. "We know a lot more about pulleys now than we did a long time ago, I'll tell you that."

"You're right." Menedemos' gaze went to the top of the *Aphrodite*'s mast, where a pulley block helped sailors raise and lower the yard. Little fishing boats, still made the way they had been from time out of mind, offered no such advantages. Aboard them, raw muscle power was the only thing that counted.

"Good talking to you, friend. Safe trip to wherever you're going." With a wave to the Rhodian, the crane boss turned back to his crew. At his shouted directions, they broke the crane down into lengths of lumber and ropes and carried the pieces back into the polis of Naxos. Menedemos hadn't realized the big, impressive device was so easily portable.

"I wonder how much a crane could lift," Sostratos said.

"Why didn't you ask the man in charge of that one?" Menedemos said.

"You seemed more curious than I was," his cousin answered.

Menedemos thought nothing much of that till he remembered how his complaints about Sostratos' unending curiosity had helped spark their quarrel. He supposed he could have started another one if he'd risen to the remark. Instead, he answered, "Watching somebody who really knows what he's doing—no matter what it is—is always a pleasure."

"Yes, I think so, too," Sostratos agreed. "Are you planning to stay and do business here in Naxos?"

"It would only be luck if we found anything worth hauling back to

Rhodes," Menedemos answered. "I do want to refill our water jars, though. This is the place to do it. What we've got is hot and stale and hardly worth drinking, and I've never heard of anybody coming down with a bad flux from drinking the water here."

The sailors he sent into town with the water jars laughed—giggled, in fact—as they went. Some of them patted at their hair or dragged wood or bone combs through it. Carrying water was usually women's work. That accounted for the sailors' silliness. Hoping they'd meet pretty women at the wellhead accounted for their primping.

In due course, the sailors came back with fresh water. "Hail, girls!" someone called from the waist of the *Aphrodite.* Menedemos thought it was Teleutas, but he wasn't sure. Whoever it was, he infuriated the men with the jars. They didn't seem sure who'd called out to them, either, which was probably lucky for him.

One of the water-carriers said, "Go ahead and laugh, you polluted catamite. We saw real women, honest women, women who aren't whores. We didn't just see 'em, either. We talked with 'em, and they answered back."

The other sailors with jars up on their shoulders dipped their heads in agreement. Menedemos didn't know how the jeering sailor felt about that. As for him, he was inclined to be jealous. Hellenes didn't get many chances to meet honest women to whom they weren't related. By the way the sailors acted, they'd made the most of this one.

"Where will we pass the night tomorrow?" Sostratos asked.

Menedemos shrugged. "I was thinking of spending it at sea. There's no good stopping place halfway between Naxos and Rhodes. We've been this way before. You know the choices as well as I do—some really miserable little islands."

He waited for his cousin to grumble and complain, but Sostratos only shrugged. "All right with me. I don't mind a night on the planks, especially when we'll probably be home for good the next night."

"Oh." Menedemos knew he sounded almost disappointed. *Am I looking for another quarrel with Sostratos?* he wondered. *I hope not.* "Home for good." He tasted the words, finding them not altogether to his liking. "I won't be sorry to sail away when spring comes back."

"I don't suppose I will, either." Sostratos looked west and a little north—back in the direction of Athens. "And yet . . ." He sighed. "Visiting Athens, seeing it again, after I had to leave, reminds me that

Rhodes really *is* my home. Too late to make a philosopher out of me; I've been chasing profit too long."

"Nothing wrong with profit," Menedemos said. "Without it, merchants couldn't operate. And without merchants, where are philosophers? Squatting there straining to take a shit, that's where." He wasn't sure whether Aristophanes *had* said that about men who loved wisdom, but it was something the comic poet might have said.

"Oh, yes. I had that same thought in Athens, though I didn't put it so . . . elegantly," Sostratos said.

Was that praise, or was he being snide? Menedemos couldn't tell. He wondered whether his cousin was sure. With a shrug, he clapped Sostratos on the shoulder. "Stuck with being a trader, eh? And stuck with being a Rhodian? Well, I suppose there are worse fates." He could think of plenty of them. What he didn't know was if any were better.

Sailors who hadn't hauled water began clamoring to go into Naxos. Unlike Kythnos and Syros, this was a real city, with plenty of taverns and plenty of brothels to choose from. Like an indulgent father—not a breed with which he was personally familiar—he waved them away from the *Aphrodite.*

"Some of them will come back to Rhodes without an obolos to put in their mouths," Sostratos said.

"Shall I tell them not to drink and roister?" Menedemos asked. "Would they listen if I did?"

"I can think of more than one family back home that would thank you if you did." But Sostratos sighed. That wasn't what Menedemos had asked, and he knew it. With another sigh, he went on, "No, they wouldn't heed you. That's too bad."

"No doubt, but I don't know what to do about it," Menedemos said. "As a matter of fact, I was thinking of going into a tavern myself tonight."

"You were?" Sostratos sounded as if he were confessing to some particularly nasty vice. "By the dog, why?"

"Always a good idea to pick up some news of what lies ahead," Menedemos replied. "If pirates are out in force in the waters east of here, I'd sooner find out in a wineshop than the hard way. And besides"—he grinned at Sostratos—"I'm sick and tired of the wine we've got on board."

"Your second reason's a disgraceful excuse, and I hope you know it," his cousin said severely. "Your first one, on the other hand . . . I'll come with you. Two sets of ears might pick up something one misses."

They set out just before the sun dipped below the western horizon. The twelve daylight hours shrank every day as summer waned, while those of the nighttime stretched. The wineshop they chose lay only a couple of streets in from the harbor. A dried grape vine hung over the door said what kind of place it was. So did the raised voices and discordant snatches of song floating out through the doorway. Some men hadn't gone to the tavern for gossip. They'd gone to squeeze what merriment they could from wine.

Menedemos and Sostratos both coughed when they went inside. Torches filled the room with smoke. Soot stained the mud brick of the walls and the rafters above those torches. Olive-oil lamps on a few tables and on the stone-topped counter at the back of the room added the stink of hot grease to the smoke. And—Menedemos wrinkled his nose—someone in the not too distant past had given back his wine. That stink wasn't strong enough to drive the Rhodians out of the tavern, but it was there.

"Hail, friends!" The man who ran the place had the falsely jovial air so many tavernkeepers assumed. He was a scrawny little fellow with enormous ears. When he didn't remember to smile and be cheerful, his narrow face relaxed into what looked like a permanently sour expression. Menedemos had seen the like on other taverners, on men who ran brothels, and on those who made their living overseeing slaves. This fellow put the smile back on and asked, "Where are you boys from?"

"Rhodes," Menedemos answered.

"We're on our way back there now from Athens," Sostratos added.

"Wine?" the tavernkeeper said. Menedemos and Sostratos both dipped their heads. The Naxian set two big, deep mugs on the counter. A round opening cut in the gray stone let him plunge his long-handled dipper into the amphora waiting below. He filled the cups, then held out his hand. "Two oboloi each."

The Rhodians paid. Menedemos sloshed out a small libation. When he drank, he sighed. As far as the wine went, he could have done better staying aboard the *Aphrodite.* He felt Sostratos' ironic gaze on him, but refused to acknowledge it.

"Out of Athens, are you?" a gray-haired man with a big nose said. "What's really going on there? We heard Demetrios was out, and then we heard Demetrios was in. Somebody doesn't know what he's talking about, that's plain."

"There are two different Demetrioi," Menedemos said.

"That's right." Sostratos dipped his head. "Demetrios of Phaleron is out; he's fled to Kassandros. And Demetrios son of Antigonos is in. He's knocked down the fortress of Mounykhia that Kassandros' men were using, and he's given back—he says he's given back—the Athenians' old constitution."

"Is that what's happened? No wonder I was confused," the gray-haired man said. Menedemos was ready to take him for a fool, but then a shrewd look crossed his face and he asked, "What have the Athenians given him, if he's given them their old laws?"

Now Sostratos was the one who didn't want to go into detail. "They've voted him many honors," he said, and would have let it go at that.

Even here in the middle of the Aegean, he doesn't want to embarrass Athens, Menedemos thought with amusement. *He* didn't care if he made the polis they'd left look bad. Since he didn't, he told the men in the tavern some of the sycophantic degrees the Athenian Assembly had passed.

Some of them laughed. The gray-haired man with the big nose said, "You're making that up. They'd never sink so low. This is *Athens* we're talking about, not some miserable little polis in the middle of nowhere."

"By Zeus, by Athena, by Poseidon, I'm telling you the truth," Menedemos said.

"He is." The melancholy in Sostratos' voice made him sound all the more convincing. "We were in the Assembly with the Rhodian proxenos when many of these decrees were proposed, and we saw and heard them passed. I wish I could tell you otherwise, O men of Naxos, but to do so would be a lie."

Menedemos thought such philosophical-sounding language would put the Naxians' backs up. Instead, it seemed to impress them. "Who would've reckoned the Athenians, of all people, would turn out to be wide-arsed?" the tavernkeeper muttered—an epitaph for the polis if ever there was one.

The gray-haired man dipped his head. "That's right. We didn't wiggle *our* backsides at Antigonos like that when he brought is into his Island League. Sure, there's a cult for him on Delos now, but that's only polite these days. The rest of the nonsense the Athenians did . . . *Pheu!*" He turned away in disgust.

Sostratos started to say something in response to that, then visibly checked himself. What could he say? The Naxian hadn't said anything he hadn't thought himself. Instead, he gulped down his wine and shoved the cup across the counter to the taverner. That worthy held out his hand. Not till Sostratos paid him did he refill the cup.

"Hearing news like that out of Athens makes me want to pour it down, too," the tavernkeeper said. "Not that Demetrios and Antigonos are bad," he added hastily (after all, they still ruled Naxos), "but it's a shame to see a city that was so great grovel like a cur dog."

"Grovel like a cur dog," Sostratos echoed bitterly, and took a long pull at the wine he'd just bought.

"He's trying to make you want to get drunk," Menedemos said in a low voice.

"He's doing a good job of it, too," Sostratos said. But he didn't upend the cup to drain it as fast as he could. Every so often, his natural urge toward moderation served him well.

Menedemos' natural urges did not run in that direction. As the captain of a merchant galley, though, he had to be prudent regardless of his natural urges. He asked, "Has anyone come into Naxos from the east in the past few days? What are things like between here and Rhodes? Is it quiet, or are pirates prowling the seas?"

The gray-haired man spoke up again: "It's been pretty quiet, from what I've heard. My brother-in-law's a fisherman, and he's headed that way lately hoping for tunny. He hasn't had a whole lot of luck with the fish, but he's never said anything about spotting trouble on the sea."

"Thank you, friend," Menedemos said. "I'll gladly fill your cup for you again, if you like." The Naxian dipped his head. Menedemos gave the taverner two oboloi. The fellow plied his dipper. The gray-haired man lifted the newly full cup in salute. Menedemos politely returned the gesture. They both drank. Menedemos knew he wasn't sure to be safe on the way back to Rhodes, not till he came within sight of the polis. But he was also glad to be sailing with good news and not into the teeth of bad.

*   *   *

PEERING EAST FROM THE FOREDECK, looking for the first sight of Rhodes, Sostratos jerked as if stung. "Ship ho!" he called urgently. "Ship ho, dead ahead! I just see a hull and rowers—no sail!"

That meant, or could mean, trouble. Sostratos waved toward the stern to make sure Menedemos had heard him. Menedemos waved back to show he had. He ordered a full complement to the oars.

Sostratos stared out to sea. Whatever the other ship was, she was drawing closer in a hurry. She'd probably spied the *Aphrodite*'s sail—which sailors were now brailing up—before anyone aboard the akatos noticed her. That she was some sort of a galley had been plain from the moment Sostratos set eyes on her. The question now was, what sort? A hungry pirate ship would come bounding across the waves like that. So would a Rhodian war galley, patrolling against pirates. The *Aphrodite*'s lean lines didn't fool only fishing boats and round ships, which sometimes proved embarrassing.

Still, I'd rather clear things up with a Rhodian war galley than fight off a hemiolia full of cutthroats, Sostratos thought. He anxiously peered ahead. So did all the sailors not straining at the oars.

Suddenly, painfully, Sostratos wished Aristeidas still lived. The lynx-eyed sailor would have known exactly what to make of that other galley. Sostratos and the rest of the men with only average eyesight had to wait till she came nearer—which meant, till she became more dangerous if she was a pirate.

"I think . . ." A sailor spoke hesitantly, then with growing conviction: "I think she's showing three banks of oars."

Sostratos squinted. He pulled the skin at the outer corner of one eye taut, closing the other. That sometimes helped him see farther and more clearly. Sometimes . . . The galley *did* have more than one bank of rowers. Did she have three?

"I . . . think you're right," Sostratos said after a few more heartbeats. He let out a sigh of relief, and the heartbeats after that didn't come faster on account of fear. A ship with three banks of oars was bound to be a war galley, not a piratical hemiolia or bireme. He watched the sailors relax their grip on weapons, too. They wouldn't have to fight for their lives and their freedom today.

From the stern, Menedemos asked, "Is that the *Dikaiosyne,* come to pay us another call?" The *Justice* was the Rhodian navy's first tri-hemiolia, an idea Menedemos had had. She was lighter and swifter than an ordinary trireme, just as a hemiolia was lighter and swifter than an ordinary ship with two banks of oars. Both classes could quickly re-move the thranite rowing benches aft of the mast, and could stow the mast and yard on the decking where they had been.

After another glance across the narrowing gap of water, Sostratos tossed his head. "No," he answered. "She's an ordinary trireme." Her mast was down, but he could see that all three banks were manned from bow to stern.

"Ah, well," Menedemos said. "One of these days, I'd like to take a trihemiolia out and see what she can do. Seems only fair, when there wouldn't be any if I hadn't thought of them."

The officer who'd captained the *Dikaiosyne* had done so not least because he was rich enough to have the leisure to go pirate-hunting without needing to worry about making a living. Here, for once, Sos-tratos fully sympathized with his cousin. Just as having to work for a living had kept Menedemos from command of a trihemiolia, so it had kept Sostratos himself from finishing his studies at the Lykeion. *I am what I am now, and I've made the best of it,* he thought. *But still I per-sist in wondering—what would I have been, what would I have become, if I could have stayed?*

An officer in a red cape strode up along the trireme's deck to the bow. He cupped both hands in front of his mouth and shouted across the blue, sun-sparkled sea: "Ahoy, there! What ship are you?"

"We're the *Aphrodite,* out of Rhodes and bound for home," Sos-tratos shouted back.

"The *Aphrodite,* eh? Tell me what firm you belong to and where you were headed when you left this spring."

"We sail for Philodemos and Lysistratos," Sostratos answered, re-flecting that Rhodes wasn't too big to keep everyone from knowing everyone else's business. "And we went to Athens. We're on our way back from there now. You do know Demetrios Antigonos' son has run Demetrios of Phaleron and Kassandros' garrison out of Athens?"

"Yes, we've heard that," the officer said. As his ship came up along-side the *Aphrodite,* Sostratos spied her name—*Iskhys*—painted above one of the eyes at her bow. *Strength* was a good name for a war galley.

Thanks to the trireme's greater freeboard, the Rhodian officer could peer down into the merchant galley. "You haven't got much aboard there. What's your cargo?"

"Well, we've got honey from Mount Hymettos and cheeses from Kythnos," Sostratos told him. "Mostly, though, we're bringing back a fine crop of Athenian owls."

"You'll change them back to Rhodian coins, of course," the officer said.

"Of course," Sostratos agreed, hoping he wouldn't have to. He would rather have seen the two percent Rhodes took on changed money go into the coffers of the firm of Philodemos and Lysistratos.

"Safe journey back to Rhodes," the man on the *Iskhys* said. Sostratos waved his thanks, thinking the trireme would go on its way. But before it did, the fellow added, "I'll check with the customs men to make sure you got back all right."

He waved to his keleustes, who got the war galley moving again. As she glided away, the stench from her rowers, who worked in the closed-in area below the deck, filled Sostratos' nostrils. But the stench from the officer's words revolted him even more. The man had sounded polite enough, but what he meant was that he would check up on the *Aphrodite* after the *Iskhys* got back from her patrol. And *that* meant Sostratos would have to change his money, or some large part of it, or else face endless trouble from the Rhodian authorities. Two percent of the gross—a considerably larger part of the profit—had just taken flight.

"Would you come back here, my dear?" Menedemos called. He sounded polite, too, but Sostratos wasn't deceived. His cousin left most of the financial arrangements to him, but Menedemos wasn't altogether ignorant of the way money worked. He couldn't be, not if he wanted to make a living as a merchant. He knew what the conversion fee would do to their profits.

"What was I supposed to tell him?" Sostratos asked as soon as he ascended to the poop deck. "He could see we weren't carrying wine or oil or statues or slaves or anything of the sort. He'd figure out we had silver instead."

"Cursed money-changers are worse than vultures," Menedemos grumbled. "They sit behind their tables and flick the beads on their counting-boards with eyes cold as winter. I don't think there's one of them who has a soul. And they'll try to steal more than two percent if we don't watch them like hawks, too."

"I'll watch them," Sostratos promised. "I know their tricks. No false weights; no thumbs on the scales; none of their games. I promise."

"That's better than nothing." Menedemos' tone suggested it wasn't good enough. He didn't snarl at Sostratos the way he might have, but he didn't sound delighted, either. Since Sostratos himself was less than delighted, he couldn't blame his cousin. Menedemos went on, "Hide as much of the silver as you possibly can. If we're paying two percent on part of it, that's better than paying two percent on all of it."

"I already thought of that," Sostratos said.

"Good. I wasn't sure you would. Sometimes you're . . . more honest than you need to be."

"I'm honest with our customers, especially the ones we deal with year after year," Sostratos said. "As far as I'm concerned, that's only good business." It also fit who he was, but he didn't make that argument; Menedemos would have jeered at it. He did add, "Anyone who lets the government know exactly how much silver he has is a fool, though."

"I should hope so," Menedemos said. "We've earned it. Those bunglers would only squander it."

Sostratos dipped his head. Then he ducked under the poop deck. There wasn't much room to hide things on an akatos, but still, if you knew what you were doing. . . .

11

PHILODEMOS COULDN'T HAVE LOOKED MORE DISGUSTED
if he'd practiced in front of a mirror of polished bronze. "Waste of silver," he grumbled. "As if what passes for a government in this polis
will do anything worthwhile with the money it mulcts from us. Better
we should have kept it."

"Yes, Father." Menedemos sounded as resigned as he felt. He'd
known his father would be disgusted that they'd had to pay money-
changing fees. "We didn't have to hand over two percent of everything: we managed to hide a good part of the silver."

"*Euge!*" But Philodemos sounded sarcastic, not pleased. "You
shouldn't have had to pay any of it."

"Just the roll of the dice," Menedemos said. "That officer on the
Iskhys warned he was going to check on us. If he followed through and
found we hadn't paid an obolos, that would have been worse."

"Furies take him!" his father snarled. "Who was the long-nosed
snoop, anyhow? Did you recognize him?"

Menedemos tossed his head. "No, I didn't." Philodemos rolled his
eyes, as if to ask the gods why they'd given him such a purblind son.
Stung, Menedemos said, "I'm sorry, Father. Maybe Sostratos did."

"Maybe so. I can hope he did, anyhow. At least your cousin's not a
blind man."

That did worse than sting. Nothing else Philodemos did hurt as
much as his praising Sostratos. Menedemos knew his cousin had certain virtues he lacked. What his father couldn't seem to see was that he
also had virtues Sostratos lacked. Sostratos himself admitted as much.
But Sostratos' approval wasn't what Menedemos had been struggling
to win since he was a toddler . . . had been struggling to win, and too
often hadn't won.

Abruptly, his father changed course: "And what do you make of
Demetrios son of Antigonos? How dangerous is he?"

"If you're his enemy, very dangerous," Menedemos answered. "We should have seen that a couple of years ago, when he raised Ptolemaios' siege of Halikarnassos for his father."

"Halikarnassos," Philodemos muttered, and Menedemos knew his father was thinking of his misadventures there, not Demetrios' adventures. The older man asked, "Did he restore the Athenian democracy, as we've heard here?"

"He restored it, yes, not that the Athenians know what to do with it any more." Menedemos told of the extravagant honors the Athenian Assembly had conferred upon Demetrios and Antigonos.

"Those are true? Genuine?" Philodemos demanded. "Not just rumors?"

"By the dog, Father, they're true," Menedemos said. "I went to the Assembly with the Rhodian proxenos, and I listened to the decrees being passed myself."

"Disgusting. Disgraceful," Philodemos said. "I had heard of some of those, and thought they were a pack of lies put out to blacken the Athenians' name—and Demetrios', for accepting what he doesn't deserve. They and he must be blind to shame."

"I wish they were rumors," Menedemos said. "I think the Athenians took Demetrios by surprise. I think they turned his head, too. You could almost see him thinking, *Oh, I must be marvelous after all!*"

"He's young—he's around your age, isn't he?" By the way Menedemos' father said it, no one of about his age had any business being allowed to run loose without a pedagogue following him around, let alone being entrusted with anything important like captaining a merchant galley or seizing a polis from a powerful foe.

Menedemos wanted to make a hot retort to that. But he was the one who'd said Athenian sycophancy had turned Demetrios' head. Philodemos hadn't had to say it, or even to suggest it. *I'm doing Father's work for him,* Menedemos thought in dismay. What he did say was, "He's going to be formidable, Demetrios is. He's already formidable, as a matter of fact. He took Kassandros' men by surprise when he brought his fleet to Athens, and he took their fortress by the harbor neat as anyone could want."

"What do you suppose he'll try to take next?" Philodemos asked.

"He'll come east from Athens," Menedemos said. "He'd almost have to. Antigonos' two most dangerous foes right now are Ptolemaios and Seleukos, the one in Egypt, the other in Mesopotamia and points east. But which one Antigonos will send him after . . . Well, old One-Eye may know, but no one else does."

"I say Seleukos." Philodemos stuck out his chin. "He's the upstart amongst the Macedonian marshals. Kassandros and Lysimakhos and Ptolemaios and Antigonos all have their places. Seleukos, though, he's trying to bring an extra couch into the andron for a symposion. Antigonos won't let him get away with that if he can help it."

"Makes good sense to me, Father." Menedemos would have guessed Antigonos and Demetrios would go after Ptolemaios because he was closer and held lands along the coast of the Inner Sea, on which coast Hellenes clustered like frogs around a pond. But Philodemos' arguments were also cogent—cogent enough that quarreling about them seemed more trouble than it was worth. Besides . . . "We'll all know next spring."

"So we will." Philodemos' chuckle was on the grim side.

"You've been asking me questions about Athens and our other stops," Menedemos said. "What's been going on here in Rhodes while I was away?"

"Here in Rhodes?" The question seemed to take his father by surprise. Philodemos paused and thought, then said, "Well, I do believe we've finally got the last of the damage from the flood repaired. The priests offered a bullock in thanksgiving at the temple of Dionysos near the agora, and I brought home a pretty nice piece of beef."

"That *is* good news, Father—that you got some good meat and that things are finally fixed." Nine years before, Rhodes had suffered through a storm the likes of which not even the oldest citizens recalled. Along with driving rain, hailstones weighing up to a mina pounded the polis. Some people were killed outright when struck by them, others badly hurt. To make things worse, the storm came late in the rainy season. The drains had been neglected, and soon clogged up. That meant the rapidly rising waters couldn't get out through the city walls.

Rhodes was shaped like a basin, with a good deal of difference between high ground and low. The low ground, by the agora and the temple of Dionysos, went under; even the temple of Asklepios was threatened. People clung to roofs and statues and the tops of shade trees to escape the raging waters.

At last, part of the western wall of the city had given way, allowing the flood to spill out into the sea. Things could have been worse. Had

Rhodes been a city largely built of mud brick like Athens, many more houses would have collapsed and many more people on rooftops would have drowned. Even as it was, though, more than five hundred perished.

"Is it really nine years since that happened?" Menedemos asked. "It doesn't seem so long ago."

To his surprise, his father laughed. "Well, son, maybe you're turning into a man after all," Philodemos said. "That's one of the signs: when all that's past starts squeezing together in your memory. You were born half a lifetime ago for me, but there are times when it feels like just a couple of years." He tossed his head in slow wonder. "By the dog, there are times when it feels like just a couple of months ago."

"Not to me," Menedemos said. From his own perspective, his life was very long indeed—what, for a man, could seem longer? If twenty-eight years didn't equal eternity, what did? And yet somehow, as his father said, the nine years since the great flood had compressed into what felt like not much time at all. As he got older, would twenty-eight years crumple the same way? He didn't think it was likely, but he wasn't quite ready to call it impossible, either.

His father took a meditative sip of wine. "Time's a funny business. Now, if the philosophers wanted to do something useful instead of just standing around listening to each other's fancy talk, they'd figure out how things like that worked. But don't hold your breath. It isn't likely."

"Sostratos went back to the Lykeion in Athens," Menedemos remarked.

"Did he?" Philodemos said. "What did he think?"

"His time stretched instead of shrinking—he found he didn't belong there any more," Menedemos answered. "He sold the philosophers papyrus and ink at an outrageous price and made 'em pay it."

That made Philodemos grin in approval unalloyed. "Good for him!" he exclaimed. "I can't think of a surer way to prove you've beaten your past."

Menedemos didn't know whether his cousin had beaten his past or simply moved away from it. He didn't think Sostratos was sure, either. Again, though, he saw no point to contradicting his father. He asked, "How are things here inside the house? Are your wife and Sikon still quarreling whenever you turn your back?"

"Things aren't perfect there," Philodemos answered. "Baukis will still give the cook a hard time every now and then. And I'm sure Sikon sometimes buys fancy, expensive fish just to spite her. But they do get on better than they did. They aren't at war *all* the time, and they don't fight so hard when they do lock horns." By the relief in his voice, he was thoroughly glad of that, too.

So was Menedemos, who said, "Good. I always hated getting stuck in the middle when they started shouting at each other. And they'd both get offended when I didn't take their side."

"Oh, yes!" Philodemos dipped his head. "That's happened to me, too. Hasn't been so bad lately, though, gods be praised."

"Good," Menedemos repeated, and meant it. He asked his father no more about Baukis. Even though they lived in the same house, too much curiosity about the older man's wife would have been unseemly. It might also have roused Philodemos' suspicions, and that was the last thing Menedemos wanted.

One of the first things he wanted was Baukis. He'd known as much for years. He hadn't done anything about it, no matter how much he wanted her—in fact, precisely because he wanted her so much. He hadn't, and hoped he wouldn't. He'd been fighting this lonely, silent battle ever since the knowledge of his desire first flowered in him. *And I'll win, too.*

It would have been easier—it would have been much easier—to be confident of that, and, indeed, to want to win, if he hadn't begun to realize Baukis wanted him, too. He gulped down his wine, not that wine would help.

SOSTRATOS FELT as if he'd been riding this miserable donkey forever. In point of fact, he hadn't set out from the city of Rhodes more than a couple of hours earlier. He'd left around noon, and the sun wasn't even halfway down the southwestern sky. His brain was sure of the time. His backside and his inner thighs would have argued differently.

He'd probably come about eighty stadia, heading south and west. He'd passed through Ialysos not long before. Along with Lindos and Kameiros, Ialysos had been one of the three main settlements on the island of Rhodes before they joined together to build the polis of Rhodes. Ialysos never had been a polis, not in the proper sense of the word. It wasn't a city, but a community of villages with a well-sited fortress on the nearby high ground. All those villages had shrunk in the hundred years since the polis of Rhodes became the most important place in the northern part of the island—indeed, the most important place on the island as a whole. But they persisted, like an old, decrepit olive tree that kept sending out green shoots whenever the life-giving rains came.

Ahead, the ground rose toward steep hills and then, farther southwest, toward Mount Atabyrion, the highest peak on Rhodes. Damonax's farm and olive groves—about whose products Sostratos knew more than he'd ever wanted to—lay near the lower edge of the steeply rising ground. It was good country for olives: not so near the coast that flies ruined the crop, but not high enough to let cooler weather damage it, either.

Before Sostratos got to Damonax's farm, he was glad he'd decided to hire the donkey instead of walking. It wasn't so much that he'd shifted the pain from his feet to his hindquarters. But when a farm dog came rushing up, yapping and growling, the donkey lashed out with a clever hoof and knocked the dog sprawling. When it got up again, it retreated even more rapidly than it had advanced. Its yelps were music to Sostratos' ears.

"What a good fellow!" he exclaimed, and patted the donkey's neck. He didn't think that meant much to the beast. Getting off and letting it crop the lush green grass by the side of a creek counted for more.

A couple of pigs with ridges of hair down their backs nosed through garbage by Damonax's farmhouse. A nanny goat tied to a tree had nibbled the grass around it down to the ground and had stood on her hind legs to devour all the shoots and tender twigs she could reach. Chickens scratched and clucked between the farmhouse and the barn.

Out of the barn came a middle-aged, sun-browned man in a short chiton and stout sandals. He scratched at his shaggy beard—a beard worn not in defiance of fashion like Sostratos' but seemingly in ignorance of it—and crushed something between his thumbnails. Only after he'd wiped his hand on his tunic did he call, "If you've come to pick olives, you're still a few days early, and you know you're supposed to bring your own pole to knock the fruit off the trees."

Sostratos' gaze went to the olive grove. Sure enough, the olives were ripening on the branches, getting darker and fuller of oil. He turned back toward the overseer. "I'm not here for the olive harvest. I'm Sostratos son of Lysistratos, Damonax's brother-in-law. You must be Anthebas."

"That's me, young sir. Hail, and pleased to make your acquaintance," Anthebas answered. "I beg your pardon for not knowing you by sight. I was, uh, expecting someone grander." He dug the toe of one of those sandals into the dirt to show his embarrassment.

Someone better groomed and all perfumed, he means—someone like his boss, Sostratos thought without much anger. Sliding down off the donkey, he let out a sigh of relief and rubbed at his hams. Anthebas sent him a chuckle and a sympathetic smile. Sostratos said, "Damonax and my sister and their son *are* here?" That was what the slaves had said back in Rhodes. If they'd been wrong, or perhaps lied for the sport of it, his fundament would get even sorer on the way back.

But Anthebas dipped his head. He pointed to the farmhouse. "Oh, yes, sir. They're in there. Would you like me to take care of your donkey?"

"If you'd be so kind." Sostratos went over to the door and knocked on it.

He'd wondered if his brother-in-law would let him in himself. But Damonax didn't carry rusticity so far. One of his slaves, a man Sostratos had seen in Rhodes, did the honors. Unlike Anthebas, who spent all his time out here, this fellow recognized the new arrival. Bowing slightly, he said, "Hail, O best one. Welcome, in my master's name. Please come in."

"Thank you, Atys," Sostratos said, and the Lydian slave beamed as he stood aside, proud to have his own name remembered.

Though Sostratos didn't say so, the farmhouse struck him as cramped and dark, especially compared to the fine home where Damonax lived while staying in the city. It was simply one room after another to form a square; it wasn't built around a courtyard as all city houses above the level of shanty were. That contributed to the gloom, for the only light in the rooms came through the windows, which were small and partly covered by shutters. Sostratos wondered why anyone would choose to live in such an uncomfortable place when he didn't have to.

"Hail, most noble one!" There was Damonax, handsome and elegantly turned out as always. "Good to see you." He stuck out his hand.

Sostratos clasped it. Damonax's grip said he was holding back strength. Sostratos hoped his said he didn't care about such petty games. "How's your son?" he asked. "How's my sister?" He could ask that, where inquiring after Damonax's wife would have been rude.

"They're both very well, thank you," Damonax replied. "Polydoros seems a very healthy little boy, for which the gods be praised." He was a man of no great piety—which didn't bother Sostratos, who wasn't, either—but spoke with the air of someone taking no chances. Since so many children didn't live to grow up, Sostratos couldn't blame him.

A wail from another room declared something had happened that the very healthy little boy didn't care for. "How *do* you get used to living with all the noise a baby makes?" Sostratos asked with genuine curiosity.

"It was hard at first, when he cried so often," Damonax said. "Now, though, his mother or a slave takes care of it, and it doesn't bother me too much."

That hardly seemed fair to Erinna. On the other hand, if caring for a baby wasn't woman's work, what was? Sostratos muttered to himself, caught between loyalty to his sister and expectations about the way things were supposed to work.

Damonax asked, "And how did you find Athens?"

"Oh, you sail north and west from Cape Sounion, and there it is," Sostratos answered blandly. His brother-in-law stared, then let out an undignified snort. Sostratos went on, "Seriously, it could be better. You'll have heard that Demetrios son of Antigonos drove out Demetrios of Phaleron?"

"Oh, yes, and restored the Athenians' old democratic constitution, and knocked the fortress of Mounykhia flat. That all sounds promising."

"I suppose it would. But have you heard how the Athenians paid him back for liberating them?" Sostratos asked. Damonax tossed his head. As Menedemos had with his father, Sostratos told him, finishing, "You see."

"Oh," Damonax said, and then, as if conscious that wasn't enough, "Oh, dear. I'd . . . hoped for better from them." If that wasn't an expression of philosophical restraint, Sostratos had never heard one. Damonax asked, "Did you get out to the Lykeion?"

"Yes." Sostratos hoped the one-word answer would keep Damonax from asking any more questions about that.

No such luck. His brother-in-law inquired, "And how's old Theophrastos?"

"He doesn't seem to have changed much from when I studied there," Sostratos replied truthfully. "He remembered me." He could say that with more than a little pride.

"Good. Good." Damonax set a possibly friendly hand on his shoulder. "And what did he think of your . . . going into commerce?"

To the crows with you, my dear, Sostratos thought, shaking off the hand. *If I weren't in commerce, if my family didn't make a good living from it, you wouldn't have been able to use Erinna's dowry and the money we made from your oil last year to pay off the debts on this land. The way you talk, though, I might have been keeping a brothel full of pretty boys.*

He caught himself before any of that passed the gate of his teeth. He didn't want to quarrel with Damonax (though he had to remind himself he didn't): not only would it ruin this visit to the farm, but it also might make life harder and less pleasant for Erinna. That being so, he smiled back and answered, "He said he understood it was necessary for me to help support my family." Now, with a certain malice, he set *his* hand on Damonax's shoulder, as if to say his brother-in-law was part of the family he supported.

"Er—yes." Damonax's smile went fixed. He took the point—took it and didn't care for it. Sostratos had hoped he wouldn't. Damonax changed the subject in a hurry: "Let me show you to your room."

That was unexceptionable. Sostratos dipped his head and followed his brother-in-law. The chamber was small and cramped, with barely enough room for a bed. It did boast a south-facing window, though, which made it lighter than most of the house. Through the window, Sostratos could look out at some of the olive trees on the farm. Indeed, narrow, silver-green leaves from one of the closest trees would probably blow into the room when the wind came from the south.

"Very nice, best one. Thank you." Again, Sostratos remembered he didn't want to quarrel with Damonax. He might have, if he didn't fear locking horns with him would cause trouble for his sister. Since he did, he tried to walk soft.

His brother-in-law also took a moment and visibly composed himself before saying, "If you like, you can rest here before supper, and I'll have a slave wake you if you're not up by then."

Now Sostratos' smile was broad and genuine. "By the dog, I'll take you up on that. One of the nuisances of life aboard ship is that you can never grab a nap in the afternoon. After a while, you get used to going without it, but I like one when I have the chance."

"I'll leave you to it, then." Damonax slipped out of the room, closing the door behind him. Sostratos used the chamber pot under the bed, then lay down. The mattress was thinner and lumpier than the one back home, but far softer than the *Aphrodite*'s planking. And travel had taught him to sleep nearly anywhere. He dozed off almost as soon as he closed his eyes.

Next thing he knew, someone was knocking on the door and saying, "Supper is ready, most noble one," in accented Greek.

The noise went on till Sostratos said, "I'm up. I'll be there in a moment." He rubbed sleep out of his eyes and ran his fingers through his hair and beard. He knew he wouldn't be so elegant as Damonax come what may. That being so, he didn't try too hard.

Because he was Erinna's brother, she and the baby dined with him and Damonax. "Good to see you, my dear," he told her. "And my goodness, but Polydoros is getting big." His nephew rewarded him with a smile wide enough to show top and bottom teeth.

"He's a good boy." Erinna smiled, too. She looked tired. Even though Damonax's slaves did a lot of the work of raising Polydoros, a mother had to do quite a bit, too, and it told on her.

"Here's the sitos," Damonax said as a slave carried in snowy-white barley rolls and olive oil in which to dip them. Proudly, he added, "All of it grown right here on the farm."

"That's good," Sostratos said. Then he tried one of the rolls, still warm from the oven. "Mm! That's very good."

"I'm *so* glad you like the oil." Damonax's voice had an edge to it.

"My dear, I never said I didn't like it. I merely said the *Aphrodite* wasn't the right ship to carry it, and Athens wasn't the right place to take it."

Erinna said, "Let's enjoy the supper, shall we, and not squabble over it?" Both her brother and her husband dipped their heads.

Cheese and olives appeared for opson. They too were products of the farm. Sostratos wondered if they would be all the opson there was. That would make a rustic supper, all right—more rustic than he really cared for. But then a slave brought in a ham on an earthenware platter;

the platter, ironically, was decorated with pictures of fish, a far more common fancy opson.

Damonax did the honors with a carving knife not much smaller than a hoplite's shortsword. He hacked off a generous chunk close to the shinbone that stuck out from the meat and gave it to Sostratos. "We raised the pig here, too," he declared, "and smoke the meat with our own wood."

"It's delicious," Sostratos said after he took a bite. "Do you eat meat here as often as you'd eat fish in town?"

"Not quite," Damonax answered, at the same time as Erinna said, "No." He sent her a hard look. She flushed and stared down at the ground. He'd wanted to give Sostratos the impression of greater abundance than he really had, and she'd spoiled it for him. *It's your fault, not hers,* Sostratos thought. *She just told the truth.*

The wine that went with dinner was severely ordinary. Sostratos praised it anyway, asking, "Is this also from the farm?"

"It certainly is," Damonax answered; as Sostratos had hoped, the question put him in a better humor. "As a matter of fact, I crushed some of the grapes myself."

Had Menedemos said something like that, Sostratos would have made a crack about being able to taste his feet. But his brother-in-law didn't take gibes like that in stride, and so he refrained. *No matter how angry I get at Menedemos, there's no denying he can laugh at himself. Damonax? No.*

"So you'll want to visit the Valley of the Butterflies tomorrow?" Damonax asked.

"If it's not inconvenient, yes," Sostratos answered. "I've heard of it since I was small, of course, but I've never had the chance to see it."

"We'll go, then," Damonax said. "It's not inconvenient. I told you I'd show it to you if you came out here. You're back from Athens a little sooner than I thought you would be, so I'm sure they'll still be there."

"Good." Sostratos manufactured a yawn to show he was tired and didn't much feel like talking. "I look forward to it."

Damonax dipped his head. Something in Erinna's eyes glinted. His sister knew him too well, and knew he wasn't so tired as all that. She didn't give him away, though. When Damonax went out of the room to tell a slave to bring in lamps, Sostratos grinned at her. Erinna smiled back.

"Is everything all right?" Sostratos asked her in a low voice.

"Everything is fine," she answered. "I've had a son, and I haven't caused any scandal. How could things be better?"

Did she sound bitter, or just matter-of-fact? Sostratos couldn't tell, and didn't dare ask. He'd never worried about how Hellenes treated women. He still didn't, not in any general way. But he worried a lot about how Damonax treated Erinna.

His brother-in-law came back. The slave followed a couple of minutes later. The lamps he set out fought the gloom without vanquishing it. As twilight deepened, their small yellow pools of radiance seemed weaker and more fragile by the moment. Sostratos yawned again, this time in earnest.

"You must be tired," his sister said—she could take a hint, even if Damonax seemed to have trouble.

"A bit," Sostratos admitted. "The nap helped less than I'd have liked." A slave with a lamp led him to his room. He hadn't intended to fall asleep right away, but there wasn't much else to do. He hadn't brought a book, and reading by lamplight was an unsatisfactory business anyhow. He stretched out on the bed and looked up at the beams of the ceiling. A little gecko with sticky feet scurried along upside down, on the prowl for moths and mosquitoes and spiders.

The next thing Sostratos knew, the room was dark except for a thin, pale strip of moonlight slanting in through the window. The smell of hot oil still lingering in the air said the lamp hadn't gone dry long before. Yawning, Sostratos reached under the bed and pulled out the pot. After easing himself, he lay down again. He watched the moonlight creep across the floor for a little while. Then sleep claimed him once more.

He woke with the morning sky going from deep blue toward predawn gray: early, but not impossibly so. Noises from the rest of the house said he wasn't the first one up. From the days when he was a boy and Erinna a baby, he remembered that infants woke up whenever they wanted to, not when anyone else wanted them to.

Sure enough, when he made his way to the dining room, he found a slave woman there feeding Polydoros bits of barley roll and heavily watered wine. A lot of the wine dribbled down the baby's chin. "Hail, sir," the woman said. "I hope he didn't bother you." If Polydoros had bothered Sostratos, she might get in trouble.

But he tossed his head. "No, I woke up on my own. Can you bring me some rolls and oil and wine for my breakfast, or tell me where to get them for myself?"

"I'll get them for you, sir," the slave said. "Will you make sure he doesn't wiggle off this chair while I'm gone?"

"Of course." Sostratos stuck out his tongue at his nephew. The baby's eyes widened. He gurgled laughter—and then he stuck out his tongue, too.

Sostratos was halfway through his breakfast when Damonax came in. "Hail," his brother-in-law said. "Ready for an early start, are you?"

"I'd rather travel in the morning than in the heat of the day," Sostratos answered. "Will we go by donkeyback or walk?"

"I was planning to walk." Damonax eyed Sostratos' feet. "Do you want to borrow a pair of shoes? Mine might fit you, or Anthebas' if they don't."

"Kind of you, best one, but don't put yourself to the trouble," Sostratos said. "I've spent too much time at sea, and fallen into the habit of staying barefoot wherever I go."

Damonax shrugged. "Suit yourself." He disappeared into the kitchen, returning with a breakfast much like Sostratos'. He ate quickly, so he finished not long after his guest. Rubbing crumbs off his hands, he said, "Shall we be off, then?"

"Lead the way. I'll stay with you."

When Sostratos went outside with Damonax, he saw the sun shining to the north. Damonax's farm remained shadowed a little while longer, for the mountain to the east shielded it from sunrise. Damonax set a brisk pace, heading up toward the peak. He seemed surprised when Sostratos had no trouble keeping up with him. "Your feet really *don't* trouble you," he blurted.

"No, not at all." Sostratos tried to hold amusement out of his voice. "I can't recall the last time I wore shoes, and my soles are hard as leather. I'd say we could race, but you know where you're going and I don't. Even if I knew, you'd probably win; I've never been a fast runner."

Damonax cocked his head to one side, plainly having trouble

believing that. "But didn't you fall just short of going to the Olympic Games a few years ago?"

"Me?" Sostratos laughed at the absurdity of the notion. Then he snapped his fingers. "I know why you think so. That wasn't me—that was Menedemos."

"So you say." Damonax kept waiting for him to start to sprint, or to offer a bet about which of them could run faster, or something of the sort. Only when Sostratos just kept placidly ambling along did it seem to occur to his brother-in-law that he might be telling the truth.

Several streams from the mountains ran down toward the sea. Most of them dried out in summer, leaving their beds nothing but rock-strewn gullies. One, though, kept a trickle of water even at the driest season of the year. A hare bounded away as Sostratos and Damonax came up.

Pointing upstream, Sostratos asked, "Does a spring feed this river?"

"That's right." Damonax dipped his head. "We follow it now, until we get to the Valley of the Butterflies."

They flushed another hare a few minutes later. Damonax sighed, perhaps wishing he had dogs along so he could hunt. A mouse skittered into the bushes. A hedgehog rolled itself into a ball. A lizard on a boulder by the stream stared at the Rhodians out of beady black eyes. It stuck out its tongue, as if in derision.

After a while, Damonax stooped and dipped some water from the stream with his hand. "Warm work," he remarked.

"Yes." Sostratos drank a little water, too, and splashed some on his face. It felt good.

They went on. The stream bent a little more toward the north. "There!" Damonax said. "You see those treetops? The trees themselves are growing down in the valley, or you'd be able to spy the rest of them. We're almost there."

The Valley of the Butterflies was long and narrow. Sostratos wondered how long the stream had taken to carve it from the hard gray stone. Branches from the trees on either side met above the gurgling stream, shading and cooling the valley. Sostratos sniffed. A faint, almost familiar spicy smell filled his nostrils. "What is that?" he asked, sniffing again.

"Styrax," Damonax answered. "They make incense from the gum. The butterflies seem to like the fragrance, too."

"The butterflies . . ." As Sostratos' eyes got used to the shade, he saw them, and let out a soft, marveling sigh. They were everywhere in the valley: on the rocks, and covering the trunks and branches of the trees. Their favorite spot seemed to be a big, mossy rock next to a little waterfall at the far end of the valley. Mist swirled around them; perhaps they especially liked the moisture there. "How marvelous!" Sostratos exclaimed. "Thank you so much for bringing me here!"

"My pleasure," Damonax said, as if he'd created the valley for Sostratos' benefit.

Sostratos reached out and delicately plucked an insect from a branch. Its body was about as long as the last joint of his thumb, though far thinner. Its upper wings were brown, almost black, and streaked with yellow. When it fluttered for a moment, lackadaisically trying to escape, it revealed lower wings of a rich crimson with a few dark spots. Then it seemed to resign itself to disaster and sat quiet in his hand.

After examining it a little longer, Sostratos turned to Damonax. "I'm sorry, best one, but this isn't a butterfly."

"No?" His brother-in-law raised both eyebrows. "What would you call it, then? A stingray? An olive, maybe?"

Though Sostratos smiled at the sarcasm, he answered, "A moth."

"By the dog, what's the difference?"

"Ah. Theophrastos must have skipped that lecture while you were at the Lykeion. Butterflies rest with their wings up over their backs, while moths let them lie flat—as this one does. And butterflies have slim, clublike antennae, while moths have thick, hairy ones—like these. If it has the characteristics of a moth, what else can it be?"

"Nothing else, I suppose," Damonax replied. "But would you have wanted to come here if I'd invited you to see the Valley of the Moths?"

"Me? Probably. I'm curious about such things. Most people would stay away, though, I admit." Sostratos put the moth back where he'd got it. It wriggled in among the others, then held still. He asked, "How is it that the birds don't come here and feed till they burst?"

"That I can tell you, for I've seen birds take these butterflies— moths, I mean." Damonax corrected himself before Sostratos could. "They take them, yes, but they don't swallow them. The . . . moths must taste nasty."

"How interesting!" Sostratos said. "And so they stay here undisturbed all through the summer?"

Damonax dipped his head. "That's right. When the rains come in the fall, they mate—some of them even fall in the stream while they're coupling—and then they fly away, so you might see them all over the island. But when things dry up in spring, here they are again."

"And why not?" Sostratos gazed around the valley in awe tempered by affection. "After all, they're Rhodians, too."

MENEDEMOS WATCHED HIS FATHER go over the accounts Sostratos had kept during their journey to Athens. "Almost a pity to take the rowers along," Philodemos remarked. "Their pay ate up a good chunk of profit. If you'd gone in a round ship instead—"

"We wouldn't have got there till later," Menedemos said. "As things were, we had the market in our goods to ourselves for quite a while. Who knows how it would have gone if we'd come in second? And we'd surely have had to carry Damonax's olive oil then."

"I suppose so." But Philodemos still sounded unhappy. He had other reasons to sound that way, too: "I wish your cousin would write larger. When you have to read at arm's length the way I do, these little squiggles drive you mad."

"Sorry, Father, but I can't do anything about that now," Menedemos said.

A slave came into the andron. "Excuse me, sir, but a man is here to see you. . . ." Philodemos started to get to his feet. The slave said, "No, sir. To see the young master."

"Me?" Menedemos said in surprise.

"Some husband catch you going after his wife?" his father asked. *I hope not,* Menedemos thought. Before he could say the words or so much as toss his head, Philodemos told the slave, "Bring this fellow here. I want to see this for myself." Menedemos couldn't even contradict the order. Miserably, he watched the slave hurry back to the entry hall.

When the caller appeared, though, his heart took wing with relief. "That's Admiral Eudemos!" he said, adding, "And in case you're wondering, I haven't had anything to do with his wife." His father only grunted.

Eudemos was in his mid- to late forties, burned walnut-brown by the sun, with a gray beard, a beaky nose, and hard eyes that seemed to see everything at once. "Hail, Philodemos," he said as he strode into the andron. "Need to talk to your son for a minute. Hope I'm not interrupting anything."

"Nothing that won't keep, most noble one." Philodemos *could* be polite; he just didn't bother while talking to Menedemos.

"Good." Eudemos turned to the younger man. "So you're back from Athens a little sooner than you thought you'd be."

"That's right, sir," Menedemos said, wondering why the admiral cared.

Eudemos was not the sort to keep a man hanging. With a brisk dip of the head, he said, "How would you like to take the *Dikaiosyne* out on a sweep after pirates? Seems a shame you weren't her first skipper, seeing as you were the one who came up with the idea for the class, but I know you've got to make a living. Still, anyone who can captain a merchant galley can captain a war galley, too, and anyone who can captain a merchant galley *should* captain a war galley, too. The more people who know how to do that, the better off the polis is. What do you say?"

"When does she sail?" Menedemos blurted. He wanted to burst with pride. He turned to see how his father responded: here was the Rhodian admiral acclaiming him not only as a seaman but also for inventing the trihemiolia. Philodemos, though, might have been carved from stone. Menedemos sighed quietly. He didn't suppose he should have expected anything different.

"Tomorrow at sunrise," Eudemos said. "You'll be there?"

"Yes, O best one. I'll be there," Menedemos said.

"Good. Farewell, then. Nice to see you, Philodemos." The admiral turned and left. Like any seafaring man, he went barefoot and wore only a chiton, though his was of very fine white wool.

"They want you to skipper one of those newfangled war galleys, do they?" Philodemos said.

"Yes, Father."

"Not bad." From the older man, that was the highest praise Menedemos got. "I was about your age when I first captained a trireme for the city. It's getting close to the end of the sailing season. I hope you have good luck catching pirates, and give them what they deserve." On that subject, Philodemos' views coincided perfectly with those of his son.

"I've fought them off in the akatos," Menedemos said. "Now *I'll* have the edge."

He woke while it was still dark. He'd been sure he would. The only question in his mind had been whether he would sleep at all, or whether excitement would keep him up all night. But excitement had faded after he lay in darkness for a while. Now he ran his fingers through his hair—no time to scrape whiskers from his chin—and hurried to the kitchen to snag a chunk of bread to eat on his way down to the naval harbor.

He was heading out to the front door when someone behind him called, "Farewell, Menedemos."

That voice stopped him in his tracks. "Thank you, Baukis. What are you doing up so early?"

"I wanted to say goodbye to you," Philodemos' wife answered. After a moment, she added, "Your father is very proud of you, you know."

"Is he?" Menedemos said tonelessly. To his way of thinking, a grudging *not bad* didn't translate into anything approaching great pride.

But Baukis dipped her head. "Yes," she said. "And so am I." She took a couple of steps toward him, then stopped nervously and looked around to make sure no slaves were awake to hear and see the two of them.

Menedemos understood those jitters. He had them himself. "I'd better go," he said, and did. But he might have been wing-footed Hermes as he made his way down through the night-silent streets of Rhodes toward the naval harbor. He didn't think his feet touched the hard-packed dirt at all. Baukis was proud of him! She'd said so! Each bite of rather stale bread suddenly seemed ambrosial. Yes, love was a disease, of course it was, but oh! what a sweet one!

Actually, the streets of Rhodes weren't so very silent after all. Though morning's gray light was just coming into the eastern sky, the sounds of drunken song floated up from the direction of the temple of Apollo in the southwest. Those were surely symposiasts reeling home after a night—a long night—of debauchery. Menedemos smiled and chuckled. He'd come home at this hour once or twice, and roused the whole household with his songs. He laughed again, remembering how splutteringly furious his father had been.

A night watchman with a torch patrolled the naval harbor. "Excuse me, O best one, but which shipshed houses the *Dikaiosyne?*" Menedemos asked.

"Who wants to know?" the watchman asked. Menedemos smelled

wine on his breath, too, though he hadn't passed the night in revelry.

"I'm Menedemos son of Philodemos, and I'm her captain this trip out." The pride he'd felt when Eudemos named him captain rang in his voice.

The night watchman pointed to one of the sheds on the western side of the harbor. Those were the narrow buildings that housed triremes and now trihemioliai as well. The shipsheds on the southern side of the harbor were broader, to accommodate fives and other bigger, beamier war galleys. A galley with dry timbers was lighter and therefore faster than a waterlogged ship, and so the naval vessels spent as much time as possible dragged up out of the sea and into the sheds.

Three or four men carrying oars and pillows made their way toward that shed without bothering to ask the watchman. Menedemos trotted after the rowers. He didn't have to be the first one there, but he wanted to get there ahead of most of the crew.

He got his wish. Only a couple of dozen men had boarded the *Dikaiosyne.* That would have been a big part of the *Aphrodite*'s complement, but was only a fraction of the trihemiolia's. Like a trireme, she carried 170 rowers plus a squad of marines, although her oarsmen in the rear part of the thalamite bank would join the marine contingent once their benches were stowed.

A burly man with a bald pate came up to Menedemos. "You're going to be the captain on this run?" he asked. When Menedemos dipped his head, the bald man went on, "Pleased to meet you. I'm Philokrates son of Timokrates, and I'm your keleustes. Is it true you were the one who had the idea for this class of ship?"

"Yes, that's right," Menedemos answered.

Philokrates stuck out his hand. Menedemos clasped it. The oarmaster said, "Some god must have put the notion into your head, for she's smooth and sweet as piggy." His grin showed a missing front tooth. Menedemos smiled back; Philokrates reminded him of Diokles. The older man asked, "You ever skipper anything this big before?"

"No. The past few years I've captained the *Aphrodite:* twenty oars on a side."

"Oh, sure. I know her." Philokrates banged himself on the side of the head with the heel of his hand, annoyed at forgetting. "Well, all right. Big difference between this ship and that one is that not everybody on the *Dikaiosyne* may hear you when you yell—she's too big, and a lot of her rowers are down below. We'll use pipes and drums to set the stroke, and you'll want to rely on your mates to pass orders. Remember 'em and count on 'em. They're both good men."

Menedemos met them moments later. Xenagoras was tall and thin, with a broken nose. Menedemos turned out to know the second mate, Nikandros, already: they'd run against each other, Menedemos usually having the better of it.

By then, the rowers crowded the shipshed and spilled out onto the walkway on either side. Real dawn had come. Before long, the rising sun would shine into the mouth of the shed. Philokrates said, "Looks like we're ready." Menedemos dipped his head. The oarmaster waited, then snapped his fingers. "That's right—you haven't done this before. The command you give is, 'Take her down!'"

"Take her down!" Menedemos shouted, and waited to see what happened next.

With a roar, the rowers and marines pushed the *Dikaiosyne* down the sloping ramp of the shipshed and into the water. The *Aphrodite*'s crew had trouble manhandling her. The swarm of sailors on the trihemiolia made it seem easy. Down the way she went, into the water of the naval harbor. They scrambled aboard her. The mates, the keleustes, and Menedemos were not behindhand.

The *Dikaiosyne* had a higher freeboard than the merchant galley. Standing at the stern, steering-oar tillers in hand, Menedemos felt able to see as far as a god. "You'll handle her yourself?" Philokrates asked.

"Yes, by the dog," Menedemos answered. "I want to find out how she feels. I'm not some gilded popinjay—I know how to steer."

"All right. Let's go, then." Philokrates beat out the stroke. The rowers began to pull. The *Dikaiosyne* glided across the harbor toward the outlet in the north.

A fresh breeze in his face, Menedemos grinned enormously. He felt like a man who'd been riding donkeys all his life and suddenly found himself on the back of a Nisaian charger. This ship *moved*. She was made for speed, and delivered it.

Once they cleared the mouth of the harbor, he swung the trihemiolia east, intending to cruise along the Karian coast looking for pirates—or for ships that could be pirates. "This is the first time I've skippered one of these patrols," he said to Philokrates. "What are the rules if we spy a pentekonter or a hemiolia going along minding her own business?"

"About what you'd expect," the oarmaster replied. "We go up to her, we question her crew, and we sink her if we don't like the answers we get. A captain or an owner who thinks we made a mistake can complain to the Rhodian government."

"If he hasn't drowned, of course," Menedemos said.

Philokrates dipped his head. "Well, yes. There is that."

Right away, Menedemos noticed one difference between the *Aphrodite* and the *Dikaiosyne.* Fishing boats and round ships fought shy of the akatos, fearing she might be a pirate ship. But sailors of all sorts waved toward the trihemiolia. A three-banked oar-powered ship had to be a war galley, a hound dedicated to hunting down the wolves of the sea.

"You don't want to get too close to land and let the wide-arsed catamites playing watchman for the pirate crews get a good look at you," Philokrates said.

"I understand," Menedemos answered. "You know what, O best one? It might be fun to send a round ship or a merchant galley close enough to the coast to be easy to spot, with the *Dikaiosyne* out far enough to see the decoy, but too far out to be seen from shore. Then, when the pirates come out for the nearer ship, this one could dash in and swoop down on them."

The oarmaster contemplated the scheme. A slow grin spread over his leathery features. "Fun, you say, do you? By Poseidon's trident, I like your notion of fun. You ought to talk with Admiral Eudemos when we get back to Rhodes. He's the one who'd have to give the orders to bring off something like that. Don't forget, now, because I think it could work."

"I won't forget," Menedemos said. "Even if I did, you could tell the admiral."

"You thought of it. You deserve the credit," Philokrates said, which went a long way toward making him a friend for life. He added, "You *are* a clever fellow, aren't you? First the notion for this class of ship, and now a pretty trap? Not bad. Not bad at all."

Menedemos was much more used to hearing Sostratos called clever than to having the word applied to him. He almost denied it—almost, but not quite. He *had* thought of trihemioliai, and he *had* come up with the decoying scheme. He would have praised anyone else who'd done such things. Didn't it follow that he deserved praise, too? He liked it as much as anybody else: more than some people he could think of. His father was sparing of praise, but that didn't mean other people had to be.

With its countless headlands and little bays and streams running down from the hills into the Aegean, the Karian coastline was a pirate's ream. It offered myriads of places to wait in ambush till a tempting target sailed by. A quick dash, and the victim was caught. It offered even more places to hide a pirate ship against the prying eyes of the Rhodians. Menedemos knew patrols like this didn't, couldn't, stop piracy altogether. But making it difficult, dangerous, and expensive was worth doing.

"Ship ho off the port bow!" the lookout bawled.

Menedemos swung the trihemiolia to the north. He told Philokrates, "Up the stroke, if you please. Let's see what she can do if the men put their backs into it."

The keleustes dipped his head. "Right you are, skipper." The tempo of the drumbeats he gave the rowers picked up. "Rhyppa*pai*! Rhyppa-*pai*!" he shouted, using his voice to emphasize the change. The piper matched his piercing note to the one Philokrates played on the drum.

And how the *Dikaiosyne* responded! The galley seemed to bound across the Aegean toward the other ship. And that other ship didn't hang around waiting to be questioned. She turned and fled toward the shore as fast as she could go. "Pentekonter!" the lookout said. "Probably full of cutthroats right to the gunwales."

"Not full enough, by the gods," Philokrates said. "No pentekonter ever made could outrun this ship. We outrun triremes. We run down hemioliai, by Zeus! A pentekonter? *This* for a stinking pentekonter!" He spat on the deck.

Sure enough, the *Dikaiosyne* ate up the distance between the two ships, plethron by plethron, stadion by stadion. But the Karian coast also drew closer with every surge from the oars. "Marine archers forward!" Menedemos shouted. When they didn't seem to hear him, he sent Xenagoras up to them, adding, "Tell 'em to shoot as fast as they can. The more rowers we hurt, the better our chance of catching them before they can beach."

Philokrates grinned. "You know your business. A lot of first-time skippers, you have to hold their hands and show 'em what to do. Not you."

"You and the mates know this ship better than I do," Menedemos answered. "But I've fought pirates before, too. Then they had more men and faster ships than I did. I've got the edge now, and it feels good—you'd best believe it does."

As the marine archers hurried forward, they put the trihemiolia down by the bow and slowed her just a touch. Menedemos ordered other men back toward the stern, restoring her trim. The archers began to shoot.

A couple of pirates went to the pentekonter's stern to shoot back, but her poop deck was even smaller and more crowded than, say, the *Aphrodite*'s; it would hold no more. One of the bowmen on the pirate ship reeled back, clutching at his chest, as a shaft from the *Dikaiosyne* went home. Another man took his place. Then a rower on the pentekonter took an arrow in the shoulder and fouled the man in front of him. Again, another pirate pulled him away, but the pentekonter needed some little while to straighten out her stroke.

Even so, the pirate ship made the beach. Menedemos had known she would. She rode half her length up onto the soft, golden sand. Rowers jumped off her and ran inland as fast as they could. "Do you want to go after them?" Nikandros asked. "We've got a lot more men. We could catch some of the rogues."

Menedemos had had time to think about that on the chase. Regretfully, he tossed his head and told the mate, "No. No telling how many pals the abandoned villains have back in the hills. We'll burn their ship. That'll put them out of business for a while."

Burn her they did. And the pentekonter made such a pyre, it was plain her timbers had been kept dry as carefully as a war galley's. Black smoke rose high into the sky. "Good riddance," Philokrates said. "Pity they weren't all in her."

"Oh, yes." Menedemos dipped his head. "But let's keep pushing east a little while longer now."

Before answering, the oarmaster glanced toward the sun. Menedemos did the same. It was somewhere right around noon. Philokrates said, "If we go much farther east, most noble one, we won't get back to Rhodes before sundown."

"I know that," Menedemos said. "But don't you think pirate crews know it, too? Wouldn't they be likely to base their ships out a little farther from Rhodes than our patrols usually go? They'd think they were likely to be safe. Maybe we can give them a surprise. And if we have to, we can find our way home by the stars or spend a night at sea. I've done it plenty of times in my akatos."

"An akatos isn't such a crowded ship as a trihemiolia," Philokrates pointed out. That was true. The war galley was bigger than the *Aphrodite,* but she wasn't four times as big, and she carried four times the crew—that was why she could go so fast. Menedemos wondered how real his command of the *Dikaiosyne* was: if he gave an order Philokrates didn't fancy, would the keleustes and the crew obey him or ignore him? He didn't find out here, for Philokrates grinned and said, "Let's try it. You make a good point, and we'd have a lot to be proud of if we came back to Rhodes after we'd skinned a pair of pirates."

The rowers dug in without a grumble. Catching and burning the pentekonter left them in a good mood. Catching pirates was why they went out on patrol in the first place, and Menedemos knew they didn't score even one triumph every time out. Far from it. The oars rose and fell, rose and fell, in smooth unison. If Rhodians weren't the best oarsmen around the Inner Sea, Menedemos had no idea who would be. So many of them made their living from the sea, they all had a good idea of what they were doing. From what Sostratos said, a hundred years before the same thing had been true in Athens. No more. If the Athenians ever built and tried to man the triremes for which Demetrios had said he would provide the timber, they'd have to pay foreigners to pull most of the oars. And a lot of the foreigners they paid would be Rhodians. Menedemos' countrymen also served in every Macedonian marshal's fleet.

By the time Menedemos ordered the *Dikaiosyne* to turn around, she was well into Lykian waters. He saw plenty of fishing boats and more than a few round ships, but none of the lean, vicious galleys he sought. He kicked at the timbers of the deck. He wanted that second pirate ship, wanted her bad enough to taste it. He wanted to show Admiral Eudemos and the rest of Rhodes' high naval officials that he could make something out of a command even if he wasn't rich enough to serve aboard a war galley all through a sailing season. And commanding a trihemiolia, a type that had sprung from his imagination as

Athena sprang from Zeus' forehead, made this patrol all the sweeter.

But the gods gave what they chose to give, not what any mortal wanted. As the sun sank in the west, the *Dikaiosyne* glided back toward Rhodes. Menedemos kept looking over his right shoulder toward the rugged coast, hoping to spy a hemiolia, perhaps painted sea-green or sky-blue to make her harder to spot while on the prowl. But all he saw were golden sands rising swiftly to rugged, forested hills: perfect places for pirates to take refuge.

And then, only a couple of hundred stadia from Rhodes, the lookout cried, "Ship ho!"

Menedemos lifted a hand off the steering-oar tiller to wave to Philokrates to increase the stroke. The oarmaster waved back. The drum beat faster. The piper matched the rhythm. The rowers responded magnificently. They'd been at the oars all day, to push the *Dikaiosyne* out as far from Rhodes as they could. Menedemos would never have worked the crew of a merchant galley so hard, not without a pirate on his heels. But they upped the stroke when Philokrates ordered it. Menedemos showed his teeth in a fierce grin. He didn't have a pirate on his heels this time. He was on the pirate's heels now, or hoped he was.

That other ship certainly behaved like a pirate. When the crew spotted the trihemiolia, they didn't stop and wait to be questioned. Instead, they sped north toward the Karian coast as fast as they could go. A long, creamy wake streamed out behind their ship—a hemiolia, for she had two banks of oars. She was fast—but the *Dikaiosyne* was faster.

Menedemos sneaked an anxious glance toward the sun. It was sinking fast, descending toward the sea that would quench its light. His gaze swung back to the scurrying, scuttling hemiolia. Would he have enough daylight left to finish the chase? He didn't know, but he intended to find out.

As before, he ordered marines to the bow to shoot at the fleeing ship. She wasn't in range yet, but he wanted to be ready ahead of time. Philokrates grinned and dipped his head to show he approved. "We're gaining on them!" the keleustes shouted for the benefit of the hardworking rowers, who were looking away from the chase. "Keep at it. We may catch 'em before they can beach."

If the *Dikaiosyne* could do that, if she could ram or come alongside, grapple, and board, the pirates wouldn't last long. Menedemos watched the hemiolia as the war galley came up on her. Her captain posted archers at the stern, too—posted them there and then started quarreling with them. Menedemos could guess why. A hemiolia was the fastest galley on the Inner Sea . . . except, now, a trihemiolia. The skipper and his crew couldn't have expected to get overhauled, and were probably blaming one another.

But the Karian coastline was coming closer with every stroke of the oars, and the *Dikaiosyne* wasn't *much* faster than her quarry. Getting within arrow range took longer than Menedemos had hoped it would. And then the pirates put on a mad spurt of rowing that would have burst their hearts if they kept it up for long. The oarsmen on the trihemiolia matched it, but the smaller ship slid up onto the beach. Men streamed from her, some naked but for weapons, others gaudy and glittering in finery and gold no doubt stolen. A few stayed close to the hemiolia to shoot at the *Dikaiosyne.* Most, though, ran for the nearest trees without looking back.

"Do we land and go after 'em, sir?" Philokrates asked.

Menedemos eyed the sun again. The flattened ruddy ball hung just above the horizon. Regretfully, he tossed his head. "No. No point to it, not when we'll be fumbling around in the dark. We'll burn the ship and go home."

No one argued with him. The hemiolia went up in flames, as the pentekonter had earlier in the day. "A pretty fair patrol," Philokrates said. "Yes, sir, pretty fair. Far as I'm concerned, O best one, you can take the *Dikaiosyne* out any time you please." Both mates grinned and dipped their heads.

"Thank you," Menedemos said. The words didn't come close to showing how delighted he was, but they were the best he had. He used them again: "Thank you, friends."

SOSTRATOS WENT TO THE GYMNASION more from a dogged sense that he really should than from any real enjoyment he got there. He wasn't ashamed to take off his clothes and exercise. He'd never had the kind of body a sculptor would choose as a model for Zeus or Ares, but he'd never let himself go soft or get fat, either. Looking down at his angular, knobby frame, he sometimes wondered if he *could* get fat, even with the most diligent effort. He didn't care to find out. Like most Hellenes, he believed no man had any business letting himself go to seed that way.

And so, dutifully, he exercised. He ran sprints, his bare feet kicking up the dust. Menedemos wasn't here; at least he didn't have to eat his cousin's dust along with his own. He threw javelins at canvas targets stretched across bales of hay. He shot arrows at the targets, too, grunting with effort because he'd chosen a bow he could barely draw. He was a tolerable—better than a tolerable—archer, which had helped more than once aboard the *Aphrodite*.

And he dusted his oiled body with sand and got into the wrestling pits to grapple with his fellow citizens. There he came close to having a good time, because he could hold his own with most of them. He didn't have the lizard-quick reactions that would have made him one of the very best wrestlers, but he used his long limbs to good advantage, he was stronger than he looked—because he was tall and lean, his muscles didn't bulge the way a squatter man's would have—and he was always one to come up with new holds and variations on old ones. He used his head when he wrestled, not just his arms and his back.

This morning, he cast down a fellow named Boulanax son of Damagoras, a man of about his own age. Boulanax spat dirt out of his mouth and said, "I didn't see that coming at all. Show me what you did."

"Certainly." Sostratos liked to teach. "When you came at me, I twisted and jerked and threw you over my hip. Do it again, slowly, and I'll show you just how I got the hold."

"All right." Boulanax did. Sostratos went through the throw at half speed this time. "I see." Boulanax dipped his head and smiled. *His* body could have been the model for a young Zeus. And he was handsome, too, handsome enough to have been almost as popular as Menedemos when they were youths. But he didn't seem offended to have lost, as some men did when Sostratos threw them. Instead, he said, "Well, I'll surprise the next fellow I take on, by the dog. Did you come up with that yourself?"

"As a matter of fact, I did." By Hellenic standards, Sostratos was modest, but not modest enough to keep from taking credit for what was really his.

"Good for you, then." Boulanax clapped his hands together in approval. "Why aren't you in the gymnasion more often?"

"I spent most of the spring and summer in Athens," Sostratos replied.

"That'll do it," the other Rhodian agreed. As Sostratos hoped he would, he took that to mean Sostratos had been studying there, not that he'd been engaging in commerce. Boulanax himself drew the sort of income from his lands that Damonax wished he did. He said, "So you were there when Antigonos' son drove out Demetrios of Phaleron?"

"Yes, I was," Sostratos said.

"What do you think of him?"

"He's formidable, no doubt about it," Sostratos answered. "Charming, too—I met him."

"Did you?" The other man's eyes widened, then narrowed. "Wait. Aren't you the son of Philodemos the merchant?"

Oh, well, Sostratos thought. *Now he won't believe I was studying in Athens.* But he answered with the truth: "Philodemos is my uncle. I'm the son of Lysistratos, his younger brother."

"That's right. It's Menedemos who's Philodemos' son." Boulanax's voice had a certain edge to it. Did he still think of Menedemos as a rival because they'd both been popular as youths? Maybe he did, for that edge remained when he asked, "And how is your cousin doing these days?"

"Very well, thanks," Sostratos said, pretending not to hear it. "He's just back from skippering the *Dikaiosyne* on a patrol against pirates. They burned two pirate ships when they were out there. Admiral Eudemos took him out drinking after he brought the trihemiolia back to Rhodes." He and Menedemos often chafed each other when they were together, but they presented a united front against the world.

"*Two* pirate ships?" Boulanax's eyes widened again. "*Euge!* That's fine work. Many goodbyes to them." No Rhodian would say a word against someone who hurt pirates, even if he didn't care for the man.

"Menedemos was the one who suggested building trihemioliai in the first place," Sostratos added, twisting the knife a little. "They're so fast, they've been giving pirates a hard time in these waters."

"Good." Boulanax hesitated, then went on, "I hope you'll excuse me, O best one, but I . . . just recalled I'm late for an appointment. Good day. Farewell." He hurried off.

Sostratos suspected that the appointment was mythical, that Boulanax had heard as much good news about Menedemos as he could stand. Selling truffles or wine or crimson dye in Athens wouldn't have impressed him; that was commerce, and commerce was vulgar. But thinking of a new type of war galley and burning pirate ships— things like those were a different story. They helped the polis, something every Rhodian citizen aspired to do. Boulanax couldn't look down his nose at Menedemos for them, no matter how much he might want to.

After glancing around in vain for another wrestling partner—the men he saw were too small to make a fair match—Sostratos went back to the javelin range and got in a few more throws. Then he rubbed himself down with fresh olive oil and scraped it from his sandy, sweaty skin with a curved bronze strigil. He put on his chiton and left the gymnasion.

The agora lay close by. It was smaller and less storied than Athens', but to Sostratos it was home. He'd come here with his father or with a pedagogue since he was a little boy. Here Rhodians gathered to spread and talk over the news of the day. And here Rhodians and all sorts of foreigners gathered to buy and sell and trade.

Even so late in the sailing season, Sostratos heard Hellenes speaking several different dialects: Dorians from Rhodes; Ionians with their dropped rough breathings; Athenians, who called the tongue *glotta* instead of *glossa* and the sea *thalatta* instead of *thalassa;* old-fashioned Cypriots; the buzzing, lisping sounds of those who used Aiolic; and Macedonians, whose native tongue was hardly Greek at all.

Phoenicians flavored Greek with their own harsh, guttural accent. Swaggering Keltic mercenaries turned it musical. Lykians spoke sneezingly. Karians and Lydians did their best to beat Hellenes at their own game. And—Sostratos eyed the fellow with interest—there was an Italian in a toga: a Samnite, or perhaps even a Roman from farther up the peninsula. Sostratos had no use for Romans. On the *Aphrodite's* last trip west, three years earlier, a Roman trireme had almost sunk her.

He strolled through the market square, mostly listening or watching, now and then pausing to examine merchandise or to gossip or to spend an obolos for a handful of chickpeas fried in olive oil. The name of Demetrios son of Antigonos was on a lot of men's lips. With his youth and energy—and with his spectacular swoop on Athens—he seemed to have eclipsed his father in many people's minds. "What will

Demetrios do next?" was a question Sostratos heard again and again.

He heard it so often, in fact, he finally lost patience and said, "Demetrios will do whatever Antigonos tells him to do, that's what. He's Antigonos' right arm and right hand, yes, with his brother Philippos the left, but Antigonos is the brain and the heart."

"And how do you know so much about it, O marvelous one?" sneered the last *What will Demetrios do next?*-sayer, a man who stood behind a table full of painted terra-cotta statuettes.

"Because I got back from Athens less than a month ago," Sostratos answered. "Because I heard Demetrios speak in the Assembly, and heard how he always gave credit to his father for everything he did. Because I had supper with him, when my cousin and I sold him truffles and wine. And because Antigonos has been an important marshal for more than thirty years now—since the days of Philip of Macedon— and he's not going to disappear like so much dandelion fluff."

The man with the table next to the statuette-seller's laughed. "Guess he told you, Lapheides."

Lapheides remained unquelled. "Huh!" he said. "Antigonos is as old as Zeus by now."

"He's almost as sly as Zeus, too," Sostratos said. "Forget Demetrios. Would you want Antigonos for an enemy? Would you want Rhodes to have Antigonos for an enemy? I know I wouldn't."

"I'd rather have him than Demetrios," Lapheides said stubbornly.

Sostratos wondered how some people could be so blind, and how Rhodes could hope to survive if they were. The only answer occurring to him was that other poleis also had their share of such fools, and so things evened out. That left him imperfectly reassured. "Don't you see?" he said, almost pleading. "You *can't* have Demetrios without Antigonos, because Demetrios doesn't do anything his father doesn't tell him to."

"He screws pretty women—lots of 'em, by what people say," Lapheides replied.

Was he changing the subject? Or did he honestly think that was a real comeback to what Sostratos had said? Sostratos wasn't sure, but suspected the worst. He said, "The best thing that could happen to Rhodes would be for both Antigonos and Demetrios"—he used the dual number to show the two of them made a natural pair—"to forget all about her."

Grammatical subtleties were lost on Lapheides. The statuette-seller stuck out his bristly chin and said, "I'm not afraid of 'em."

"You're surely swift-footed Akhilleus come again," Sostratos said. Taking the sarcasm for a compliment, Lapheides preened. Sostratos sighed. He'd feared the statuette-seller would.

12

BAUKIS TURNED A PIROUETTE IN THE COURTYARD. THE hem of her long chiton flew up for a moment, displaying a pair of shapely ankles. Menedemos watched appreciatively while doing his best not to be noticed at it: she was showing off for his father, not for him. Sounding anxious, she asked, "Do I look all right?"

Menedemos couldn't help dipping his head. Philodemos' eyes, fortunately, were on Baukis. The older man dipped his head, too. "You look fine, my dear," he said. There, for once, he and Menedemos agreed completely.

His wife clapped her hands together in excitement. Gold glittered on her fingers and on her wrists and in her ears. One of her rings held a big, deep-green emerald Philodemos had bought for himself—for her, in other words—after Menedemos got a good many of the precious stones from a merchant skipper from Alexandria.

"I get to go out in the city!" Baukis said—squeaked, really. She clapped her hands again. "I get to go out in the city without a veil! I even get to go out *of* the city without a veil!"

Philodemos muttered something, but had the sense not to make it any too clear. The parade to the temple of Hera eight or ten stadia south of the city wall—out beyond the graveyards—was a festival the women of Rhodes looked forward to every year. It gave them a momentary taste of the free and open life custom kept them from living most of the time.

Clouds drifted across the sky. The setting sun tinged them with pink. "I hope it doesn't rain," Baukis exclaimed. "That would be awful."

Philodemos and Menedemos shared an amused glance. Both of them were weatherwise. "I don't think you need to worry about that, my dear," Philodemos said, and Menedemos dipped his head. "No rain in those clouds. That shower we had day before yesterday was enough to lay the dust, but we shouldn't expect much more till later in the rainy season."

"Oh, good." Baukis' smile showed her projecting front teeth, but it also showed how very happy she was. "If you two sailors tell me it's so, then it must be." She pointed at Philodemos. "And if it does rain now, I'll blame you. You know that, don't you?"

"Of course. People always blame me for everything that goes wrong around here," Menedemos' father answered. "The rain's bound to be my fault, too." Baukis stuck out her tongue at him. He made as if to swat her on the backside. They both laughed. No Persian torturer could have devised anything more excruciating to Menedemos than the casual, happy byplay between them. Philodemos went on, "Make sure you stay with Lysistratos' wife and the other women of the neighborhood, mind you. You know how the young rowdies get when the women come out."

He lowered his brows a little as he looked toward Menedemos. Scandals on nights of religious processions and festivals *did* happen. Plenty of comedies revolved around who met whom or who ravished whom on such nights. And Menedemos *had* stolen a kiss or two, and once or twice more than a kiss or two, during festivals. But he just smiled back at his father. Philodemos might be fretting about him and some other woman, but wasn't worrying about him and Baukis.

"I'll be careful," Baukis promised. "And now I'd better go, or else I'll be late." She waved to Philodemos and then, plainly as an afterthought, to Menedemos, and hurried toward the door.

That left Menedemos and his father standing in the courtyard by themselves. They turned away from each other, both seeming nervous about being alone together. Menedemos cocked his head to one side and listened to Baukis and other women out and about calling greetings to one another. The same excitement rang in all their voices. They were out on a holiday, out doing something special, out doing something they thought was wonderful.

"And what will *you* do while the women are having their festival?" Philodemos asked suddenly, swinging back toward Menedemos. "Go out into the city and see if you can grab one and drag her off into the darkness somewhere while she's on her way home?"

"Did you ever do that, Father, when you were younger? Did you have a favorite spot near the route of the procession where you'd wait and hope for someone pretty to pass by?" Menedemos asked.

"Never mind me," his father said, a little too quickly. But then Philodemos rallied: "I never brought scandal to the family, and you'd better not, either. Now answer my question. What are you going to do tonight?"

"Me? I was going over to Uncle Lysistratos' house myself, to play Sostratos a game or two of diagrammismos. He just bought himself a new game board and pieces." Menedemos smiled. "Now we can play with dogs even if we don't go out hunting hares."

"Pah! You and your foolishness." But Philodemos dipped his head. "Well, go on, then. That's not a bad way to spend some time. And if you put a little money on who takes how many dogs, you won't want to get too drunk, for fear of playing like an idiot and costing yourself some silver."

"Sostratos never likes to drink much when he's playing games," Menedemos said, and then hurried out of the house before his father could start singing hymns of praise to his cousin. He'd heard too many of those, and didn't care to listen to another.

When he got to the door of his uncle's house, Sostratos opened it. "The slaves have gone to bed," he said. "I'll keep the lamps filled and the wine coming—not that we ought to drink a lot. The game deserves a clear head."

"Slaves are lazy creatures," Menedemos said, forgetting that they'd no doubt been working since the sun came up. He set a hand on his cousin's shoulder. "I told my father you'd want to go easy on the wine."

"You know me. We know each other. We'd better, by now, like it or not." By Sostratos' tone, he wasn't sure he did always like it. He stepped aside to let Menedemos in. "Come on. I've got the game board set up in the andron."

As Menedemos found when he went into the men's chamber, Sostratos had also arranged the lamps so they shone on the board to best advantage. A bowl of olives and another of figs sat on the little round table by it, so the cousins could snack as they played. Sostratos dipped up two cups of wine from the mixing bowl. When Menedemos sipped, he said, "What is this? One of wine to three of water?"

"Exactly," Sostratos said. "That's a little too weak for an ordinary drink, but it should be about right when we have to pay attention to what we're doing."

To Menedemos, it was too weak anyhow, but he let it pass. He sat down in front of the white pieces, Sostratos in front of the black. Diagrammismos was played on a twelve-by-twelve square board. Each player had thirty men, deployed at the start of the game on every other square of the first five rows. Playing the white pieces was supposed to give a slight advantage. Menedemos knew he would need all the help he could get, and probably more besides. He took hold of one of the bone dogs and shoved it forward one square.

Sostratos answered with a move on the far side of the board. The struggle developed rapidly. Whenever Menedemos moved his dogs so that a black piece was between two white ones, either vertically, horizontally, or diagonally, he captured the enemy dog. Whenever his cousin got a white between two blacks, Menedemos' dog was lost. A clever move could capture more than one piece at a time; a dog could also be sacrificed, losing itself to capture one or, with luck, more of his opponent's pieces. A piece could leap over an enemy to an open square just beyond, but did not necessarily capture by doing so. Sostratos massed his dogs into a formation experienced players called a polis. Menedemos tried to match him, but his mind wasn't altogether on the game. Before too long, he was down to one lonely dog, and Sostratos, with eight black pieces left, hunted him down and captured him.

"Got you!" he said, picking up the last white dog. "Try again?"

"Yes, let's," Menedemos answered. "You're a better player than I am, but I can put up more of a fight than that." They rearranged the dogs. Menedemos went first again. He did give Sostratos a tougher game the second time, but lost again.

Sostratos set up the dogs to show a crucial position late in the game. "If you'd gone here instead of *here,* you would have had me in trouble," he said, moving a piece different from the one Menedemos had chosen. "Do you see?"

"Afraid I do," Menedemos said ruefully. "And I see you're going to bring that polluted board along when we sail next season, aren't you, so you can thump me like a drum every night?"

"It won't be so bad," said Sostratos, who plainly intended to do just that. "You win some of the time when we play, and you get better when we play regularly. I've seen that. And watching is fun, too. It'll help keep the whole crew happy."

"Maybe." Menedemos sounded unconvinced. "I'll tell you, though, when somebody who's watching a game says, 'You thick-skinned idiot, you should have moved *there,*' I don't think it's fun. I want to clout the whipworthy villain."

"Mm, that's true. So do I," Sostratos said. "Most people know better, but one bigmouth is plenty to ruin things." He paused and muttered, then spoke aloud: "Teleutas would do something like that, and laugh afterwards."

"He probably would. But many goodbyes to him. He's sailed with us four years in a row, and this'll be the last," Menedemos said.

"About time." His cousin reached for the dogs, which sat on the table by the board. "One more game? After that, I think I'll turn in."

"All right. Why not?" Menedemos set up the pieces with him. He made the first move. Again, he gave Sostratos a hard fight. Again, Sostratos beat him. Sighing, Menedemos helped his cousin put the dogs back in the drawer built into the game board. "Almost," he said. "Almost, but not quite. Do you terrorize Uncle Lysistratos, too?"

"Father and I are pretty even, as a matter of fact," Sostratos replied. "I haven't played *your* father lately. From what I remember, though, and from what my father says, *he's* the dangerous one in the family."

"He would be," Menedemos said darkly. He hadn't played diagrammismos with his father since he was a youth. He'd lost then, but marked it down to youthful inexperience. He didn't want to try it again now. Knowing his father, he'd get trounced again, and would get sardonic lessons on the game along with the trouncing. That he could do without.

Sostratos ignored his comment, which was probably just as well. "Come on. I'll walk you to the door," he said. "Do you want a torchbearer to light your way back to your house? I can wake a slave."

"If I were going across town, I would," Menedemos answered. "Across the street? Not likely, my dear, though I thank you for the thought. Farewell." He went out through the door. Sostratos closed it after him.

Menedemos looked toward his own house. No lights showed at any of the windows he could see. His father's room faced toward Uncle Lysistratos' house. It was as dark as the rest, so presumably the older man had already gone to bed. Bare feet silent on the hard-packed dirt of the street, Menedemos went around till he could see all the windows. No, not a lamp lit anywhere.

The sky was dark, too. The moon wouldn't rise till midnight; the festival of Hera took place on the night of the third-quarter moon. Zeus' wandering star had blazed low in the west when the evening began, but it was setting now; buildings kept Menedemos from being sure whether it had already slipped below the horizon. Kronos' wandering star, dimmer and yellower, still glowed in the southwestern sky. It was the only wanderer Menedemos could see. Only starlight and a few lamps shining through shutter slats in other houses gave his eyes something to work with.

Someone hurried down the street not far away. Menedemos' hand fell to the knife he wore on his belt. *Maybe I should have had a torchbearer after all,* he thought. As in any Hellenic city, night was the time when the thieves and robbers came out. Rhodes had fewer than most, or so Menedemos had always thought. But meeting even one could prove disastrous.

This fellow, though, ignored Menedemos. He hurried south, toward the center of town. Menedemos brought a hand up to his mouth to muffle a chuckle. The other man was no thief, except perhaps of love. He was probably off to grab a woman—maybe one woman in particular, maybe any woman he could—when the celebrants came back from Hera's temple. Menedemos had done the same thing himself in years gone by. Sometimes he'd had good luck, sometimes none.

Another man, and then another, also slipped south. Menedemos stayed where he was. Only one woman mattered to him right now. He knew Baukis would be coming back to this part of town, to this very street. He didn't have to go looking for her. She would be here.

And then what? he asked himself. *She's still your father's wife. If you do anything like what you're thinking of doing . . .* He tossed his head. He hadn't *done* anything yet, or hadn't done anything much, anyhow. One kiss in three years—what was that? It couldn't be anything.

You shouldn't be out here. You should be in bed. You should be asleep. Relentless as the Furies, relentless as storm waves, his conscience battered him. At last, to his surprise, it beat him back inside the house. *Maybe I really will curl up and go to sleep. I'll feel good about it in the morning.* For him, feeling virtuous was a pleasant novelty.

He lay down, but sleep, no matter how coaxed, would not come. He stared up at the ceiling, his thoughts full of trouble. He knew what he should do, and he knew what he wanted to do, and the one had nothing to do with the other. Presently, the darkness in his room grew a little less absolute. A strip of moonlight came through the window. Menedemos muttered a curse.

Not too long after the moon came up, he heard in the distance hundreds—no, thousands—of women's voices raised in song. As they returned to the polis from the shrine, the women of Rhodes were praising the majesty of white-armed Hera. The chorus grew louder and sweeter as they drew nearer.

" 'Of Hera I sing, she of the golden throne, to whom Rheia gave birth,' " the women chanted.

" 'Queen of the immortals, who is outstanding for her beauty,
And the wife and sister of loud-thundering Zeus.
The glorious one, of whom all the blessed on lofty Olympos
Stand in awe and honor like Zeus who delights in thunder.' "

"Zeus!" Menedemos said. It wasn't a prayer. He sprang to his feet and threw on his chiton. When he left his room, he closed the door behind him. Anyone walking by would think he remained inside. Quiet as an owl gliding on soft-feathered wings, he went downstairs and left the house.

The women's song filled the city as one group after another left the main procession and went off toward their homes. Here and there, Menedemos also heard squeals and giggles and a couple of shrieks as Rhodian men paid calls of one sort or another on the returning women.

Voices raised in song came up the street toward Menedemos' house and the one where Sostratos lived. Menedemos ducked into a moon shadow blacker than the ink he and his cousin had sold in Athens. "Farewell!" he heard again and again, as women left the group, left the festival, and returned to their homes and their everyday lives.

And there came Baukis, arm in arm with Aunt Timokrate, both of them still hymning the praises of Zeus' consort. They stopped in front of Sostratos' mother's house. "Good night, dear," Timokrate said.

"Farewell," Baukis said. "Wasn't that wonderful?"

"It always is," the older woman answered. "To be one with the goddess . . ."

"To be out in the city," Baukis said. "To be out *of* the city!"

Timokrate laughed. "There is that," she agreed. Then she yawned, and laughed again. "To be out when I'm usually sleeping."

"I don't think I'll sleep all night." Baukis' voice thrummed with excitement like a plucked kithara string.

"All right, dear. I know *I* will." Aunt Timokrate sounded amused, and tolerant of her sister-in-law's youth. She opened the door, said, "Good night," one more time, and went inside.

Baukis sighed, then picked up the song of praise once more as she started to her own home. Menedemos hardly heard her above the hammering of his own heart. *You can let her go in ahead of you, then go in yourself and go back to bed. No one would be the wiser. You can.*

He stepped out of the shadow. Baukis' hymn to Hera suddenly stopped. She froze. "Who's there?"

"Only me." Menedemos' voice stumbled. His legs as light with fear as if he were going into a sea fight, he came toward her.

"Oh, Menedemos." Baukis' reply was only the tiniest thread of whisper. "What *are* you doing here?"

He almost laughed. But it wasn't funny, and he knew it wasn't, and she had to know as much, too. Without a word, without a sound, he reached out and brushed her cheek with the back of his hand.

It could have ended there. She might have flinched. She might have fled. She might have screamed. Instead, she sighed and shivered as if a winter downright Macedonian had all at once descended on this tiny corner of Rhodes. "Oh, Menedemos," she said again, this time in an altogether different tone of voice. She shivered again. "We shouldn't."

"I know," he answered. "But . . ." A shrug. "I've been trying to pretend this isn't here for three years now. Every spring, I've run away to sea so I wouldn't have to think about you. Every fall, when I come home . . ." He half turned away, but then swung back, drawn as irresistibly as iron by a lodestone. He stroked her cheek again. Just for the fragment of a heartbeat, her breath warmed his palm. But he was already on fire—or was that ice?

Baukis started to turn away, too, but found herself as unable as Menedemos. "We shouldn't," she said again. She looked up at the star-crowded sky. Menedemos stared, entranced, at the smooth line of her throat in moonlight. Maybe love *was* a disease. But how many other diseases did the physicians know where the sufferer wanted anything but to be cured?

Afterwards, he never knew which of them moved first. One instant, they stood close together, but not touching. The next, they were in each other's arms, each one trying to squeeze the breath from the other. The soft firmness of Baukis pressed against him drove Menedemos even further into that delicious madness everyone said he ought to fear.

And he *was* afraid, but not of that madness, only of what might come from it. His lips found hers. The kiss was deep and desperate: drowning-deep, and he never wanted to come up for air. At last, he had to. He trailed more kisses along the angle of her jaw, the side of her neck, the lobe of her ear, her fluttering eyelids. When his lips touched her cheek, he tasted tears, but she clung to him as if her ship had sunk and he were the only floating spar.

She still might have fled. When he cupped the round fullness of her breast through her tunic, he thought for a moment she would, even if her firm nipple thrust against the soft wool of the chiton. But then, with what might have been laugh or sob or both commingled, she clung to him more fiercely than ever. They kissed again. Baukis moaned, down deep in her throat.

Menedemos led her back to the shadowed wall where he'd waited. Some things, even the silent moon should not see. Baukis bent forward. "Oh," she said softly when he went into her. He set his hands on her hips, just where they swelled from her narrow waist. She looked back over her shoulder at him. "Hurry!"

Menedemos also knew he had to be quick, and did his best. But as much as he wanted to hurry, he wanted to please Baukis more. If he didn't, after waiting so long . . . The irony there was too cruel to contemplate. As his pleasure mounted and his breath came short, he listened anxiously to make sure hers did, too. Then a small mewling cry burst from her lips. She quivered, inside and out. Menedemos groaned as he spent himself.

Baukis pulled away from him and straightened. Her hiked-up chiton fell down around her ankles once more. "Darling," Menedemos said, quickly setting his own tunic to rights. He kissed her again. "I *do* love you."

"Yes." Baukis sounded as if she'd only half heard him. Her thoughts were elsewhere. "I'll go in first, and I won't bar the door. If you don't hear a commotion, you'll know your father—my husband—is still asleep." She gulped. He wondered if she would start to cry. Guilt filled some women after they were unfaithful; the innkeeper's wife Sostratos had known in Ioudaia was of that sort. But Baukis gathered herself, finishing, "And the slaves, too, of course."

"And the slaves," Menedemos echoed. "We'll have to act as though nothing's happened in the morning, you know."

She dipped her head. "Oh, yes. I'll remember. Don't *you* forget."

That was probably—no, certainly—good advice. Menedemos knew how much his father tried him. The temptation to fling this in Philodemos' face might grow overwhelming. He would have to hold it down. From the very first, he'd seen this could be death between them if it ever came to pass. Now it had, and now the secret had to stay a secret forever.

He kissed Baukis once more. She clung to him for a moment, then twisted free. "I'm going. If there's any trouble, I'll try to let you know. I—" She stopped. Had she been about to say, *I love you?* He never knew. She squared her shoulders and, almost as if marching into battle, went into the house.

Menedemos waited, there in the shadows. He cocked his head to one side, anxiously listening. All he heard were an owl and, off in the distance, a last hymn to Hera that suddenly stopped as the woman singing it found her way home. No sound of any sort came from inside the house.

He waited a little longer all the same. Then, as quietly as he could, he went to the door. He opened it, slid inside, and closed it behind him. When he reached for the bar, he made sure he took firm hold of it and didn't drop it as he set it in the brackets: the clatter would have roused the whole household. He breathed a silent sigh of relief after setting it in place.

At the edge of the courtyard, he paused again to listen. Everything was quiet but for a horrible rasping snore coming from Sikon's room. *Sleeping on his back,* Menedemos thought. Whenever the cook rolled over, he sounded like a sawmill.

Quickly, Menedemos crossed the courtyard, tiptoed upstairs, and ducked into his own room. He barred his door as carefully as he had the one to the house. Then he lay down, stared at the ceiling as he had earlier in the night, and let out a long sigh. "I did it," he murmured. "I really did it."

That wasn't pride talking. He didn't quite know what it was. Guilt? Shame? Some of those, more than he'd expected. Adultery for adultery's sake *was* losing its appeal. But what had passed between Baukis and him was more than adultery for adultery's sake, and what he felt had little to do with pride. Even though guilt and shame were mixed into it, they were only part—and a small part at that—of what crashed through him like storm waves. Up till now, he'd never made love with a woman with whom he was in love. All at once, he fully understood why the passion was so powerful, so dangerous. The only thing he could think of was making love to Baukis again.

I can't do that, he realized, and the knowledge burned like a viper's venom. The next time Baukis made love, she would lie in his father's arms. The mere idea filled Menedemos with fury. He'd long known that, if he was to lie with his father's wife, that could make Philodemos want to kill him. He'd never dreamt lying with Baukis might make him want to kill his father.

I can't do that, *either,* he thought. Part of him wished he'd stayed here alone in his room the whole night long. The rest, though . . . The rest wanted, yearned for, craved, more of Baukis than he could get from a quick coupling in darkest shadow. He wanted . . . He wanted to yawn, and did, enormously.

Next thing he knew, the morning sun was streaming through that east-facing window. He yawned once more, and stretched, and got out of bed. Had last night been real? Memory flooded back. It had! He put on his chiton and went out into the courtyard, intent on getting some breakfast.

His father was already there, talking with one of the house slaves. "Good day," the older man said when Menedemos emerged. "I wondered if you'd sleep the sun around and only come out at night, like an owl."

"Hail, Father," was all Menedemos said in reply. He glanced at the sun. It had risen almost three hours earlier, or he missed his guess.

Philodemos' eyes went the same way. "Don't tell me you were playing games with Sostratos all night long," Menedemos' father said. "*He's* not in the habit of staying up so late. You went prowling for women afterwards, didn't you? You must have found one, too, eh?"

A southbound crane flew by overhead. Menedemos watched it without saying anything. It was a straggler; most of its kind had gone south nearly a month before.

With an exasperated sigh, Philodemos asked, "Did you bring scandal down on our house? Will some angry husband lurk in the street outside, waiting for the chance to stick a knife in you?"

Still watching the crane, Menedemos tossed his head. "No, Father. You don't have to worry about that." *True. You wouldn't need to lurk in the street if you decided to knife me.*

"You must have found some slut, then, a wench who's as sunk in vice as you are," Philodemos growled.

Rage and horror filled Menedemos. *You fool! You're talking about your own wife!* One more thing he couldn't—mustn't—say. This felt like something out of a tragedy. And was Baukis listening, up there in the women's quarters? How could she be doing anything else? What sort of fight would she have to make now, just to hold her face straight?

"By the dog of Egypt, son, what am I going to do with you?" Philodemos said.

Menedemos only shrugged. "I don't know, Father. If you'll excuse me . . ." He hurried off to the kitchen, where he got a couple of barley rolls, some olive oil, and a cup of watered wine for breakfast. He watered it less than he might have; Sikon, who was kneading dough for the day's baking, leered at him. Menedemos ignored the cook. He made a point of ignoring him: made it so obviously, Sikon couldn't keep from laughing.

Philodemos came into the kitchen, too. Sikon immediately fell silent and started kneading as if his life depended on it. Menedemos would sooner have dealt with the cook than with his father. Philodemos wagged a finger under his nose. "When *are* you going to stop your nonsense and make a proper man of yourself?" he demanded.

"Admiral Eudemos thinks I make a proper man now," Menedemos answered.

"He worries about what you do at sea. *I* worry about what you do ashore. And what do you suppose he'd say to that if he knew about it?" his father snapped.

"From some of the stories he was telling when we celebrated after my patrol in the *Dikaiosyne,* he's chased a woman or two—dozen— himself," Menedemos said. Philodemos made a disgusted noise. Menedemos pointed at him. "And what about you, Father? I asked you before—when you were younger, didn't you ever try your luck when the women were coming home from a festival?" *As long as you think I had some other man's wife, this is another verse of the same old song. I hate it, but I can put up with it. But if you ever find out it was Baukis . . .* He shivered and raised the cup of wine to his lips.

Philodemos turned a dull red. "Never mind me. We're not talking about me. We're talking about you."

Menedemos could guess what that probably meant. He kept quiet, though. So could Sikon, and the cook knew no such restraint. He let out a loud, rude snort, then attacked the bread dough more fiercely than ever, as if trying to pretend he'd done no such thing.

From dull red, Philodemos went the color of iron in a smith's fire. His glare seared Sikon. "You mind your own business," he snarled.

"Yes, master," Sikon muttered: one of the few times Menedemos had ever heard him acknowledge he was a slave and not the lord of the household.

Philodemos also heard the submission, heard it and took it as no less than his due. His attention swung back to Menedemos. "We're talking about you," he repeated. "I want you to behave respectably from now on. Do you hear me?"

"Yes, Father." All Menedemos wanted was escape. He told the truth: he did hear his father. As for behaving respectably . . . after last night, too late for that. Or was it? What was respectability but not getting caught? No one knew what had passed but Baukis and him. As long as that stayed true, he could go on living under the same roof with his father. He said, "I'll do my best."

Gruffly, Philodemos said, "You'd better." But he sounded at least a little mollified. Maybe he hadn't expected even so much. He turned on his heel and left the kitchen.

After Menedemos finished breakfast, he went back out to the courtyard. He hadn't gone more than a couple of paces before stopping dead. Along with his father, Baukis stood there, looking at a plant in the garden. She went pale when she saw him. *Natural. You have to act natural,* he shouted to himself. "Good day," he said, and hoped his voice didn't shake too much.

"Hail," she managed, in something like her usual tones.

To Menedemos' vast relief, his father noticed nothing amiss. Philodemos said, "Now that we've had some rain, things are starting to sprout."

"They certainly are," Menedemos agreed. Baukis looked down at her feet. Menedemos remembered standing behind her and . . . He felt his face heating. Going on as if nothing had happened would be harder than he'd ever dreamt. If he didn't betray himself, his father's wife was liable to. *She's only seventeen,* he reminded himself. *She's a woman, yes, but barely.*

Perhaps fearing to give the game away, Baukis retreated to the house. Menedemos' father rounded on him. "Now that you've slept half the day away like a lazy hound, what will you do with the rest of it?"

"I don't know, Father. I was going to go out into the city," Menedemos answered.

"And go looking for the house of the woman you debauched last night?" Philodemos said. "Wasn't once enough to satisfy you? How much trouble will you find for yourself?"

Once wasn't anywhere close to enough, Menedemos thought. Aloud, he said, "I know where she lives, but I don't intend to go anywhere near there." That was a truth, but a deceptive truth. It made his father roll his eyes. Menedemos went on, "By Zeus of the aegis, Father, I don't." The oath made Philodemos take him a little more seriously. He added, "My life would get more complicated than it's worth if I did."

"Well, at least you realize that much," Philodemos said. "I thought you'd be blind to it, the way cockhounds usually are. Go on, then."

Menedemos left, doing his best to saunter and not flee. Once out in the street, he sighed loud and long. No, he hadn't begun to realize how hard this would be.

THERE HAD BEEN YEARS when seeing the *Aphrodite* drawn up out of the water at the Great Harbor in Rhodes left Sostratos sad. That seemed less true now than in times gone by. He had thought of the merchant galley as something almost magical: like Hermes' winged sandals, she could sweep him away to lands strange and mysterious, and what could be more marvelous than that? After going back to Athens, to the polis for which he'd pined like a man mourning a lost love, he thought he had an answer to that, which he hadn't before. What could be more marvelous than going off to lands strange and mysterious? Coming back to a home you loved.

Khremes the carpenter waved to Sostratos. "Hail, son of Lysistratos. How are you today?"

"Well, thanks," Sostratos answered. "And yourself?"

"Pretty well," Khremes said. "My son gave me a grandchild this summer, while you were at sea."

"Congratulations!" Sostratos said. "You're young to be a grandfather." That was no idle compliment; he doubted Khremes was much above fifty, and most men among the Hellenes didn't marry till they were thirty or so.

Sure enough, the carpenter chuckled in mingled embarrassment and pride. "I'll tell you what it is: we're a hot-pronged bunch, my family. I liked the thought of screwing without paying for it so well, I talked my father into letting me wed early. And Aristion, he's the same way. I had to marry him off. I was afraid he'd get some respectable girl in trouble."

"You don't want that," Sostratos agreed. "A feud between families doesn't do anybody any good."

They chatted a little while longer, then went their separate ways. Sostratos strolled south along the edge of the Great Harbor, eyeing the ships tied up at the quays or drawn up onto dry land. Most of them were as familiar to him as acquaintances he might meet in the agora. Every so often, he would note one that had had some major work done since the last time he saw her. He started with the same surprise he might have shown on seeing a bald man who came out sporting a wig.

He also saw a few ships that were new to him. One in particular gave him pause: a merchant galley bigger than the *Aphrodite,* and almost lean enough to make a pirate ship. Pointing to her, he asked a harborside lounger, "What ship is this, O best one?"

The man didn't answer. He might have been afflicted with deafness, or perhaps with idiocy. He might have been, but he wasn't. Sostratos knew exactly what his trouble was. An obolos effected a miraculous cure. Once the lounger had popped the little silver coin into his mouth, he said, "That's the *Thalia,* friend."

"*Abundance,* eh? A good name for a merchant ship," Sostratos said. "Who owns her?"

He wondered if the other Rhodian would have the hubris to try to squeeze a second obolos from him. The fellow started to, then visibly thought better of it. He said, "She belongs to Rhodokles son of Simos."

"*Does* she?" Sostratos said, and the lounger dipped his head. "He's come into some silver, then." Rhodokles was a competitor. Up till now, he'd never been a serious competitor. His ships had all been older and smaller than the *Aphrodite* and the other vessels Philodemos and Lysistratos owned. The *Thalia,* though, could go anywhere on the Inner Sea, and could get where she was going as fast as anything afloat.

Thoughtfully, Sostratos asked, "Has he got any others like her?"

This time, the other man did dummy up. Instead of paying him again, Sostratos turned his back. That earned him some of the hottest, earthiest curses he'd ever got. He ignored them and walked away. The lounger cursed louder, which won him no money.

Sostratos paused by a large, ramshackle warehouse only a long spit from the sea. No one stirred there till he stuck his head in the doorway and called, "Somebody's giving away decorated drinking cups in the agora."

He waited. He didn't have to wait long. A deep-voiced, gutturally accented rumble came from the bowels of the building: "Giving them away?" Out came Himilkon the Phoenician, swaddled in his long robe. A gold ring gleamed in one ear; more gold shone on several fingers. When he spotted Sostratos, suspicions spread across his narrow, hook-nosed face. "You liar, you cozener, you trickster!" he began, and went on from there. When he ran out of Greek, he switched to Aramaic.

Since he'd taught Sostratos that language, the Rhodian followed some of it. Even if he hadn't, the sounds would have been plenty to show Himilkon's displeasure. With its coughs and grunts and choking noises, Aramaic was a tongue made to show anger.

When Himilkon at last slowed down a little, Sostratos used a sentence of Aramaic of his own: "Peace be unto you, my friend."

"And to you also peace," Himilkon said grudgingly, "so long as you do not trick an honest man like that. What do you want? Besides trouble, I mean."

"Trouble? Me? No." Sostratos spoke in Aramaic, as the Phoenician merchant had. Having learned the language, he was glad to get a chance to use it, to keep it fresh. He did his best to look innocent. Instead of tossing his head to show that he hadn't meant to cause trouble, he shook it. He wanted to act as much like a native speaker as he could.

Himilkon noticed. Very little went on around Himilkon that he didn't notice. Still in his own language, he said, "Most Ionians"—in Aramaic, all Hellenes were Ionians, probably because Aramaic-speakers had met them first—"Most Ionians, I say, who took the trouble to learn my speech (and precious few care about any language but their own) would not bother with the gestures my folk use."

"If I do something, my master, I want to do it well. I want to do it as I should." In Greek, Sostratos would never have called any man his master. In Aramaic, though, it was only a polite phrase: another illustration of the difference between the two tongues, and of the differences in the thoughts of the men who spoke them. The Rhodian cast about for a word in Himilkon's language. Failing to find it, he dropped back into Greek: "When I do something, I want to do it *thoroughly.*"

"Your slave has known you for some years now, and has noticed this about you, yes." Even speaking Greek, Himilkon kept flowery Aramaic turns of phrase. Sostratos tried not to talk like a Hellene when using Aramaic; how well he succeeded might have been a different story.

Sostratos wondered how many people had noticed that about him. When men talked about him while he wasn't there, did they say things like, "Sostratos will drive you mad, trying to nail down every last little detail"? He hoped they did. A reputation for taking pains was far from the worst thing in the world.

Himilkon returned to Aramaic: "If you did not come here to wring my liver with your japes, my master, for what reason did you assail my peace?"

"To see what you got while Menedemos and I were in Athens," Sostratos replied. He had to pause for a heartbeat to come up with the second-person plural masculine verb form; Aramaic conjugations took gender into account, which Greek verb forms (except participles) didn't. "To learn if you have anything we might want for the next sailing season."

"When you bought papyrus from me last winter, you called me a thief," Himilkon said. "But now you want to do more business, eh?"

"I had to beat you down to a price where I could add in my profit and still sell in Athens at a level where other people could afford to buy," Sostratos said—in Greek, the idea being too complex for his rusty Aramaic. "I managed to do that. And besides, tell me you've never called me such names and I'll tell you you're a liar."

"I?" Himilkon was the picture of affronted dignity. He too went on in Greek: "I am calm. I am restrained. I am judicious." Sostratos laughed out loud. Himilkon glared. "I am going to bash you in the head with a board."

"A calm, restrained, judicious board, I have no doubt," Sostratos replied.

That made Himilkon laugh. "No one who grew up speaking Aramaic would ever think to call a board restrained or judicious. You Hellenes can do strange things with your language. That is probably why you are such a peculiar folk."

Now Sostratos, reminded he was a Hellene, tossed his head to show he disagreed. "We're not strange," he said. "It's all you folk who aren't Hellenes who are strange."

Himilkon laughed raucously. "No, O marvelous one, this time you are wrong. Everybody from Karia to Carthage, as the saying goes, thinks Hellenes are the ones who are peculiar. And if you go farther east, if you go among Phoenicians or Egyptians or Persians, well, they will all say the same thing. This proves my point; is it not so?"

Sostratos laughed once more to hear a barbarian use a stock tagline from any number of philosophical dialogues. The Rhodian also tossed his head again. "I'm sorry, my dear, but it proves nothing of the sort."

"What? Why not?" Himilkon's already swarthy features darkened with anger.

"Well, wouldn't everyone from Karia to Carthage say Egyptians are strange because of all the funny animal-headed gods they worship and the picture-writing they use?"

"Certainly. Egyptians *are* strange," Himilkon answered. "They do everything the opposite of the way most people do."

That made Sostratos laugh yet again, for Herodotos had written almost the same thing about the Egyptians. Sostratos went on, "And wouldn't everyone say the Ioudaioi are strange, with their god whom no one can see and who forbids them from doing so many perfectly ordinary things?"

"Oh, yes. The Ioudaioi are strange, too, no doubt about it. They are full of wicked customs." Himilkon spoke with the certainty and scorn only a neighbor could have.

"Some people," Sostratos remarked, "*some* people, mind you, might even say Phoenicians are strange."

"What?" Himilkon stared at him. "What a daft notion! Phoenicians strange? We are the salt of the earth, the most ordinary folk around. How could anyone, even an idiot"—he eyed Sostratos in a speculative way—"think Phoenicians are strange?"

"Well, for one thing, you burn your own children in times of trouble," Sostratos replied.

"That is not strangeness. That is piety, to show the gods we *are* their slaves and would give them anything and everything we have," Himilkon said, "It is only because other folk are not religious enough to do the same that it seems odd to them."

"There you are!" Sostratos pounced. "Whatever any one folk does will seem odd to other people. That doesn't prove the folk really *is* strange."

"Well . . . maybe," Himilkon said. Sostratos thought he'd vanquished the Phoenician, but Himilkon added, "Of course, you Hellenes do a great many odd things, which is why everyone else thinks you are peculiar."

"Oh, never mind," Sostratos said in some irritation. "We were going to go into your warehouse when all this came up."

"I suppose we were." Himilkon didn't seem angry about the argument. Belatedly, Sostratos realized he was lucky. Some people got offended when you presumed to disagree with them. He didn't want Himilkon offended, not when he did business with him. The Phoenician asked, "Where do you think you will go next spring? That will have something to do with what I show you."

"I'm not certain yet," Sostratos said. "Perhaps Alexandria. I've never been there, but a new, wide-open city like that gives a man plenty of chances for profit."

"Alexandria," Himilkon echoed. "Now there I have never been, either. In your grandfather's day, you know, or maybe your great-grandfather's, Rhodes was a new, wide-open city like that."

"Maybe." But Sostratos didn't sound convinced. "Rhodes never had all the wealth of Egypt to draw on, though."

"Not back then, she didn't," the Phoenician merchant said. "Now she does." With all the trade from Ptolemaios' realm that went through Rhodes these days, that held some truth: quite a bit, in fact. Himilkon ducked into the warehouse and gestured for Sostratos to follow. "Here, come along with me."

Sostratos was glad to obey. Himilkon's place of business fascinated him, for he could never be sure what would turn up there. He paused inside the doorway to let his eyes adapt to the gloom in the warehouse. He needed to see where he was going, for the passageways between cabinets and shelves were narrow. Things stuck out, ready either to trip him or to poke him in the eye. His nostrils twitched. Himilkon stocked frankincense, myrrh, cinnamon, and pepper, along with other spices and incenses the Rhodian had more trouble identifying.

"Here." Himilkon paused and took down a box of curious workmanship made from a pale wood Sostratos had never seen before. "Tell me what you think of . . . this." With a melodramatic flourish, Himilkon opened the box.

"Amber!" Sostratos exclaimed. The box was full of the precious, honey-colored stuff. It too had a faint, spicy odor, or maybe Sostratos was still smelling all the other things in the warehouse. He reached out and picked up a piece. Even unpolished like this, it was smooth against his palm. "Is that a fly trapped inside it?" he said, bringing it up close to his face for a better look.

"Let me see." Himilkon took it from him. "Some kind of bug, anyway. You find that fairly often in amber, you know. That piece you picked up isn't the only one in the box with something in it."

"I do know that about bugs," Sostratos said. "I just wonder how they could get into the stone in the first place. It's almost as if they got stuck in pine resin, and then the resin somehow petrified."

"I don't see how that could happen," Himilkon said.

"I don't, either," Sostratos admitted. "But it does look that way, doesn't it?"

"I suppose so," the Phoenician said. "But I didn't show you the amber on account of bugs. I showed it to you because it is something that comes down from the north. Alexandria has all manner of strange and wonderful things that come up the Nile. But does Alexandria have amber? I do not think so. Will the jewelers of Alexandria want amber? There, I think they will."

Sostratos thought they would, too. No matter what he thought, he didn't care to admit it to Himilkon. He said, "I don't even know yet if I want amber, O best one. That depends on how much I have to pay for it, and on what I can hope to get for it in Alexandria."

"Well, yes, of course," Himilkon said. "I am not in this for my health, either, you know. If I cannot make a profit, I will not sell you the lovely stuff at all."

"If I can't make a profit, I won't buy," Sostratos said. They glared at each other. Sostratos had looked for nothing else. In some exasperation, he asked, "How much do you want for all the amber you have in this box?"

"Three minai," Himilkon replied at once.

"Three minai?" Sostratos made as if he couldn't believe his ears. Actually, the price was more reasonable than he'd expected. But he couldn't let the Phoenician know that, or he'd lose the dicker before it even began. He threw his hands in the air to show the dismay he was supposed to be feeling. "That's ridiculous!" he said. "If I want my blood sucked, I'll go to an inn and let the bedbugs do it."

Himilkon made a face, as if he'd just taken a big swig of vinegar. "Funny man," he said. "You Hellenes write these comedies to go on the stage. This I know. Are you practicing to do one of them? I know you want to write things."

"Not comedies, by the dog of Egypt, and I wasn't joking," Sostratos answered. "You've given me a price you can't possibly expect me to pay." The more he pretended to be outraged, the more real outrage he felt. He knew that made no rational sense, but he'd had it happen before in other dickers.

Setting hands on hips, Himilkon haughtily demanded, "Well, O marvelous one, how much does your Majesty think the amber is worth?"

"Oh, a mina's probably a little high, but not too," Sostratos said.

"*One* mina? One?" Himilkon's eyes bulged. The veins in his neck swelled. So did the smaller ones on his forehead. He let loose with a torrent of Aramaic that should have burned down not only his warehouse but half the city. It amounted to "no," but he was a good deal more emphatic about it than that.

"Have a care, my dear, or you'll do yourself an injury," Sostratos said.

"Oh, no. *Oh,* no." Himilkon shook his head, too upset to impersonate the Hellenes. "I may do *you* an injury, but not myself. You are a brigand, a bandit, a pirate . . ." He ran out of Greek and went back to his own language again. This sounded even hotter than his first eruption.

"Gently. Gently." Now Sostratos held his hands out in front of him in a placating gesture. "Since you've let yourself get so overwrought, I suppose I could go up to a mina and twenty drakhmai." The Rhodian spoke with the air of a man making a great concession. And so, in a way, he was. He never liked being the first one to shift his price in a haggle. Now he had to see how much Himilkon would move—and whether Himilkon was inclined to move at all.

When the Phoenician kept on fuming in Aramaic, Sostratos feared he wouldn't move. Three minai wasn't a bad price, but it wasn't a great price, either. Sostratos hoped to drive him down further—and the Rhodian knew he could get a lot more in Alexandria, especially if he sold the amber chunk by chunk and not as a single lot.

At last, grudgingly, Himilkon said, "I don't suppose I would starve in the street—quite—if you paid me two minai, ninety drakhmai."

He hadn't moved much, but he had moved. He wasn't wedded to three drakhmai as his price. That was what Sostratos had needed to know. "You only came down half as much as I came up," he complained.

"By Ashtart's pink-tipped tits, you're lucky I came down at all," Himilkon growled.

So I am, Sostratos thought, but that agreement didn't show on his face. He said, "You'll have to come down some more, too, if we're going to make a deal."

Himilkon raised his eyes to the heavens, as if asking the gods why they'd given him such a cruel and unfeeling opponent in this dicker. "I try to keep myself from being robbed. I try to keep my family fed. And what does it get me? Nothing, that's what! Nothing, not a single, solitary thing! Here is amber, the frozen tears of the gods, brought down to the Inner Sea from beyond the lands of the Kelts, and—"

"Wait." He'd roused Sostratos' curiosity. "What do you know about the country from which amber comes? Herodotos says it's at the ends of the earth, but no more than that."

"All I know is, it's up in the north somewhere." Himilkon was plainly indifferent. "No: the other thing I know is, you won't see any of this amber ever again if you don't come closer to meeting my price. You may be dreaming of making a killing in Alexandria, but you can't make a killing if you haven't got the goods."

That, unfortunately, was true. Sostratos made the best comeback he could: "And you can't hope to make a profit on your amber if you ask an unreasonable price."

"Which I do not," Himilkon said indignantly.

That, unfortunately, was also true. Sostratos had no intention of admitting it. He did say, "Well, I suppose I could come up another twenty drakhmai." He sighed and spread his hands again, as if to show he was being magnanimous beyond the bounds of reason by doing so.

Himilkon came down another ten drakhmai. He grumbled and scowled and fumed, as if to show he was being put upon beyond the bounds of reason by doing so.

At length, they settled on two minai, forty-five drakhmai. Sostratos couldn't get the Phoenician to lower his price even another obolos. Part of him felt he'd made a pretty good deal: the part that had noted that even three minai wasn't a bad price. The other part mourned because he hadn't been able to get Himilkon down as far as he'd hoped. He shrugged. If he couldn't decide whether to be pleased, the Phoenician probably had just as many doubts, which meant they were within shouting distance of the right price.

"Do you have a scale?" Sostratos asked. "I want to weigh the amber."

"Why?" Himilkon was suspicion personified. "We already made the bargain."

"Yes, of course," Sostratos said impatiently. "I want to know just how much I have, though, so I can tell my father."

"Oh. All right." Himilkon grunted. "Come this way. I use it mostly to weigh spices." Sostratos followed him through the warren of the warehouse, reflecting that Theseus probably hadn't had a harder time finding his way through the Labyrinth. The Rhodian also had another reason for wanting the amber weighed: if he knew just how much he was getting, Himilkon couldn't make a chunk or two disappear before exchanging it for silver.

The amber turned out to weigh less than Sostratos had expected. That set him to worrying again. Was Himilkon laughing at him behind his curly beard? Sostratos said, "Let me take one piece to show my father."

"I would not do this for just anyone, mind you," Himilkon said. "For you, and especially for Lysistratos . . . very well. Take one piece, whichever you choose." Sostratos picked the one he'd eyed before, the one with the bug in it.

With it in his hand, he hurried up to his house. When he got there, Threissa was pouring water from an amphora onto the herb garden in the courtyard. His father sat on a bench in the courtyard, quietly but most attentively watching the snub-nosed, redheaded slave girl. As far as Sostratos knew, his father had never done anything more than watch Threissa; a husband who bedded a slave in his household was asking for trouble from his wife. Sostratos himself had lain with her several times. Sometimes his lust got the better of him, enough to overcome his disappointment at her lack of enthusiasm.

"Hail, Father," Sostratos said. "Come see what I've got."

"Oh, hail, Sostratos," Lysistratos said. Sostratos was convinced that, until he spoke, his father had had no idea he was there. Lysistratos reluctantly dragged his eyes away from the Thracian slave girl and got to his feet. "What is it?"

"Amber." Sostratos opened his hand to show the honey-colored jewel. "I've just bought quite a bit of it from Himilkon."

"You have? And this is a sample?" Lysistratos asked. Sostratos dipped his head. "Well, let me have a look," his father said. When Sostratos gave him the amber, he started to bring it up close to his face, then broke off the gesture with a frustrated grimace. "It gets all blurry when I try to look at it the way I used to," he grumbled. "Reading's a trial these days, too." He held the piece of amber out at arm's length. "That's better. . . . It does seem to be of good quality."

"I'm glad you think so. I did, too." Sostratos' grin held real relief. He and his father got on a lot better than Menedemos and Uncle Philodemos, for which he thanked the gods, but he still felt nervous when he made a large purchase in Rhodes on his own.

"This won't be the only chunk you bought, will it?" Lysistratos asked.

"Oh, no." Sostratos told exactly how much he'd bought, to the hemiobolos.

His father blinked, then smiled. "I might have known you'd be precise. And precisely how much did you pay? I'm assuming the rest was of the quality of this piece?"

Sostratos dipped his head again. "I thought it was," he answered. "I paid two minai, forty-five drakhmai for all of it. Himilkon started out wanting three minai, and he wouldn't come down much."

"Two minai, forty-five drakhmai." Lysistratos spoke in musing tones, almost tasting the words. He looked up into the sky, his lips moving silently, as he decided what he thought of that. He wasn't such a finicky calculator as Sostratos, but he had more experience and, perhaps, better instincts. After half a minute or so, he smiled again. "*Euge!* That's very well done, especially if you go to Alexandria next spring. You should get a fine price there."

"That's just what I had in mind when I made the deal." Sostratos beamed. "I'm glad you think I was right."

"Egypt is rich in gold. It has all manner of precious stones—I remember those fine emeralds your cousin got hold of a couple of years ago. But I've never heard of any amber there. The jewelers should slobber all over you, the way dogs will if you come out with a piece of meat."

"There's a pretty picture," Sostratos said, and Lysistratos laughed. Sostratos went on, "We'll get the rest when I bring Himilkon the silver. He talked about going to Alexandria with amber, too. I trust it more hearing it from you, I will say."

"I'm a little surprised he let you bring home any amber at all," his father said.

"He told me he wouldn't have for most people, but he was making an exception for me—and especially for you," Sostratos answered. "I took that for a typical piece of Phoenician flattery, but maybe I was wrong."

"Well, I am flattered that Himilkon would trust the two of us so far," Lysistratos said. "We've done business with him for a while now, and he knows we're reliable. He's pretty reliable, too, come to that, as long as you keep an eye on him."

"You'd better!" Sostratos exclaimed. "That little game he played just before we sailed, buying up all the papyrus in town and then gouging me when I bought it from him . . . It was cursed clever, and I wish I'd thought of it myself."

"He's sly, no doubt of that," Lysistratos said. "But if a Hellene can't stay up with a Phoenician when it comes to trade—well, he doesn't deserve to, that's all." He paused, then changed the subject: "Is your cousin well?"

"Menedemos? I think so, though I haven't seen much of him the past few days," Sostratos said. "Why?"

"Because I was talking with him this afternoon while you were down by the harbor, and he just didn't seem himself," Lysistratos said. "Half the time, when I asked him something, I'd have to ask him twice. It was as though he wasn't really paying attention to me, as though his mind were somewhere else. He looked worried, too, and that made me worry—about him."

"I wonder if he's had a love affair go wrong, or if some husband discovered he was sniffing around where he shouldn't," Sostratos said thoughtfully. "That's what your description sounds like, and I've seen him go through spells like that before. Sailing season before last, he seemed awfully glad to get out of Rhodes, and he needed weeks away to get back to his old self. I remember asking him about it, but he wouldn't say anything. That's strange all by itself, for he usually likes to brag. Whatever happened, it hit him hard. Maybe this is more of the same."

"Yes, it could be." His father also sounded thoughtful. "It certainly could. I'm glad you have better sense than to leap headlong into foolish love affairs, by the dog."

"Thank you," Sostratos said. Lysistratos set a hand on his shoulder. Sostratos laid his own hand on his father's. "And thank you for not jumping down my throat all the time, the way Uncle Philodemos does with Menedemos."

"Philodemos wants things just so. He always has." Lysistratos' face tightened for a moment. "Before he had a son, he used to jump on me instead. That's one reason I don't keep you on such a short leash as he does with Menedemos: he taught me not to. And I'm more naturally easygoing than he is. I know things *won't* always be just so, and I try not to fret about it the way Philodemos does. And you're steadier than your cousin, generally speaking, for which I praise the gods."

"*I* praise the gods that we do get along, whatever the reasons," Sostratos said. "Whenever I think of Menedemos and Uncle Philodemos, I know how lucky I am."

"How lucky *we* are," Lysistratos corrected. Sostratos grinned. He didn't mind that correction at all.

NOW I'VE HAD WHAT I WANTED *for so long,* Menedemos thought. *Why aren't I happier?* He had no trouble finding one of the reasons he wasn't happier: he hadn't been able to lie with Baukis since the night of the festival. He'd never found a time when either his father or some of the house slaves weren't around. He'd paid several visits to brothels since, but what he bought at a brothel made him feel good for a little while without solving his real problem, which was that making love with someone he loved had proved fundamentally different from taking pleasure with a whore.

His father noticed him moping, too, though Philodemos didn't know all of what he was noticing. He even offered what, from him, amounted to sympathy of sorts: "If her husband's home now, son, you have to make the best of things till he goes away again. No point to wandering around like a bitch who's just had her pups drowned."

Menedemos was eating olives in the andron when his father came out with that bit of advice. He'd been about to spit out a pit. Instead, he choked on it. His father pounded him on the back. The pit came loose. He spat it across the men's chamber, then wheezed, "Thank you, Father."

"Any time," Philodemos answered. "You can suffocate on one of those polluted things if you aren't careful and you aren't lucky. Or isn't that what you meant?"

"Well . . . some of both," Menedemos said.

With a sigh, Philodemos said, "Way you've been dragging around here, way you've been muttering snatches of poetry when you think nobody's listening, way you've . . . Well, a lot of things show you've gone and fallen in love with whoever your latest wife is. Adultery's bad enough, but love's worse, because it makes you stupider. I don't want you to do anything to get yourself in trouble, and I don't want you to do anything to get the family in trouble. If I talk to you now, maybe I can keep you from acting *too* foolish. Maybe. I hope so, anyway."

He does care about me, Menedemos realized with no small astonishment. *He mostly has no idea how to show it—it comes out as anger because I don't act the way he wants me to—but he does. And what am I supposed to do about that?*

It shamed him. The mere idea of wanting his father's wife had shamed him for years—but, finally, not enough to stop him. *He had it coming, on account of the way he treats me* had been in the back of his mind—sometimes in the front of his mind—ever since. If that wasn't true, if he couldn't even pretend it was . . .

He started to cry. It took him altogether by surprise. One moment he was fine, or thought he was, and the next tears were streaming down his cheeks.

"Here, now. Here, now," Philodemos said awkwardly, at least as startled as Menedemos was himself. "It can't be as bad as that."

"No—it's worse," Menedemos choked out. Once the tears started, they didn't want to stop. He saw his father as a series of shifting, blurry shapes, not as a man at all.

"You see? This is what love does to you." But Philodemos, for a wonder, didn't sound outraged or scornful. He put his arm around Menedemos: a rough caress, but a caress even so. "You think this never happened to me? You'd better think again."

Menedemos was sure *this* had never happened to his father, for his grandfather hadn't remarried after his grandmother died. Imagining his father in love with anyone took work. "Did it?" he asked in a small voice, trying to gulp his way out of weeping.

"Oh, yes. *Oh,* yes," Philodemos said. "She was a hetaira, not another man's wife—I'm not quite so foolish as you." Even in sympathy, even in consolation, he couldn't omit the gibe. He went on, "Her name was Arkhippe, and I thought the sun rose and set on her. This was before you were born, you understand, before I wed your mother." Now, as he looked back across the years, his voice softened. So did his features. As they did, Menedemos realized how much his father looked like Uncle Lysistratos. Most of the time, he had trouble seeing the resemblance, for Philodemos wore a severe expression that contrasted with his younger brother's cheerful air.

After some small silence, Menedemos asked, "What happened?"

His father's usual sour look returned. "I told you—she was a hetaira," he replied. "She was out for what she could get. When I gave her more than anyone else, she loved me—or she said she did. But when she took up with a gilded fop who owned a big farm on the east coast . . . well, after that she forgot she'd ever heard my name. She ended up betraying him, too. They're both dead now, and the fellow who beat me out had no sons. I go on, and so does my line." He spoke with a certain somber pride: about as much as he ever let himself show when the subject had anything to do with Menedemos.

"You've never talked much about this," Menedemos said. "Now I understand—a little—why you worry so about what I do with women."

"Of course I don't talk about it," Philodemos said impatiently. "A hurt like that isn't a battle scar you display to show how brave you were. You put it away and do your best to pretend it never happened. *I* do, anyway." His face defied Menedemos to challenge him on his choice. After another pause, he changed the subject: "High time we get you married off. Maybe then you won't play the cuckoo, leaving your eggs in other birds' nests. By the dog, you're old enough now."

Menedemos thought of Protomakhos and Xenokleia. His father,

fortunately, didn't know about that. He also thought about Baukis. Philodemos, even more fortunately, didn't know about that, either. Menedemos said, "I don't think I'm ready for a wife of my own." *Not when the one I wish I had is yours.*

But Philodemos, again fortunately, was unable to follow his thought, and replied, "It's time. Thirty is a good age to wed, and you're getting close. Finding the right family, finding the right girl, will take a while, and so will the dicker over her dowry. But you'll be glad when it's done. Having a woman to come home to every day will settle you down."

Not if she's someone I don't want, someone I don't care about. One more thing Menedemos found it best not to say. All he did say was, "Maybe."

His father took politeness for agreement. Philodemos was and always had been remarkably good at hearing what he wanted to hear, and hearing it the way he wanted to. He said, "I'll start asking around. I can think of three or four likely maidens about the right age just like *that.*" He snapped his fingers.

"There's no rush," Menedemos said. His father was also remarkably good at not hearing what he didn't want to hear. He hurried out of the house, as if he expected to come back with a match all sewn up by suppertime. Maybe he did. Menedemos started to call him back, but what was the use? He'd waste his breath, he might anger his father, and he wouldn't change a thing. Besides, *he* didn't think Philodemos would come back with a match. The older man had said it would take time, then ignored his own words.

As if to escape the mere possibility, Menedemos went to the stairway and started up to his own room. No sooner had he set foot on the lowest stair than he heard footsteps coming down. He climbed the stairs with a lightened heart after that, his feet hardly seeming to touch them—it was Baukis. Her pace sped up, too. As his eyes adjusted to the gloom of the stairwell, he saw the smile on her face. He knew his own wore the same kind of smile, too.

They both stopped halfway. Menedemos looked up past Baukis to the second story. She looked down past him to the doorway that led out to the courtyard. This was probably the only place in the house where they could meet without the fear that a slave was, or could be, spying on them.

"I love you," Menedemos said softly.

"I love you." Baukis' smile crumpled like the thin timbers of a fishing boat when a trihemiolia's ram slammed into them at full speed. "Oh, Menedemos, what are we going to do? We can't . . . I mean, we mustn't. . . ."

"I know." He reached out and took her hands in his. By the way she held on to him, she might have been pitched from the deck into a sea full of sharks. He leaned forward and brushed his lips against hers. He wanted to do so much more than that. He wanted to, but knew he couldn't. Even that little was too much, for it left him all on fire inside—on fire, and feeling as if a torturer were flaying him, one digit of hide at a time.

"After the festival, we never should have . . ." Baukis kept on leaving her sentences unfinished, but Menedemos kept on knowing how she would have ended them.

"I know," he said again. Regardless of what he said, though, he wouldn't have traded those few minutes for any in the rest of his life—or for all the rest of his life put together.

"I can't look at your father—at my husband—the same way any more," Baukis said miserably, but her hands kept clutching Menedemos'. He dipped his head. He couldn't look at his father the same way any more, either. Sudden alarm—no, sudden terror—in her voice, she asked, "Where *is* Philodemos?"

"He's not here. He decided I needed a wife, and he's gone off to start looking for a match." Menedemos spoke the truth without thinking.

Baukis gasped in dismay. "Oh, no! I couldn't stand it if—" She broke off again. Now she grabbed Menedemos' hands hard enough to hurt.

"Don't worry," he told her. "Nothing will come of it right away, if anything comes of it at all." He knew something *would* come of it in a couple of years, but that felt like forever to him.

"What will we do? What can we do?" Baukis moaned.

Before Menedemos could find any sort of answer, a noise in the courtyard sent the two of them flying apart. Baukis scurried down the stairs. Menedemos went up to the second story two steps at a time. That wasn't why his heart thuttered as he walked down the hall to his room, though.

What will we do? What can we do? He had no idea. He saw no good end ahead, either, no matter what happened. He couldn't even escape from Rhodes till spring, and spring seemed a hundred years away. And for Baukis there was no escape, no escape at all.

HISTORICAL NOTE

OWLS TO ATHENS is set in 307 B.C. Menedemos is a historical character, though little is known of him. The rest of his family is fictitious
in all respects. Other historical characters who appear in the novel
include Demetrios of Phaleron, Demetrios son of Antigonos, Dionysios the commander at Mounykhia, Dromokleides of Sphettos, Euxenides of Phaselis, Kratesipolis, Menandros the playwright,
Stratokles, and Theophrastos. The Macedonian marshals mentioned
from time to time—Antigonos (Demetrios' father), Lysimakhos,
Ptolemaios, and Seleukos—are also historical, as is Demetrios son of
Antigonos' brother, Philippos. Though Philip of Macedon died in
336 B.C. and his son, Alexander the Great, in 323 B.C., their shadows
dominate this period.

The decrees honoring Antigonos and his son Demetrios voted by
the Athenians after the ouster of Demetrios of Phaleron may seem
extravagant, but they are attested to by inscriptions, by the history of
Diodoros of Sicily, and by Plutarch's biography of Demetrios son of
Antigonos; the latter two are our principal literary sources for what
Antigonos and Demetrios called the restoration of Athenian democracy. Some scholars believe Dromokleides of Sphettos' decree came
later than those of Stratokles, during another conquest of Athens by
Demetrios. This is certainly possible, but Plutarch puts them all together under the events of 307 B.C., and a mere novelist may tread
where a historian fears to go.

It is not known in what year Menandros offered *The Flatterer,*
which survives in fragments. Other plays and poets said to be at the
Greater Dionysia are fictitious.

As usual in this series, all translations from the Greek are my own. I
claim no great poetic virtues for them, but do hope they accurately
present what their originals say. Most names of persons and places are
transliterated directly from Greek into English, with no detour

through Latin: Demetrios, not Demetrius; Euboia, not Euboea. Where names are very well known in a particular form—Alexander, Athens—I have for the most part preserved that form. Transliteration is always a compromise, and compromises rarely make anyone perfectly happy.